THE READER

453 -

James C. McDonald

University of Louisiana at Lafayette

Longman

New York   Boston   San Francisco
London   Toronto   Sydney   Tokyo   Singapore   Madrid
Mexico City   Munich   Paris   Cape Town   Hong Kong   Montreal

Acquisitions Editor: Lauren A. Finn
Director of Development: Mary Ellen Curley
Development Editor: Anne Brunell Ehrenworth
Senior Marketing Manager: Sandra McGuire
Senior Supplements Editor: Donna Campion
Production Manager: Denise Phillip
Project Coordination, Text Design, and Electronic Page Makeup: Nesbitt Graphics, Inc.
Senior Cover Design Manager/Designer: Nancy Danahy
Cover Image: ©Corbis, Inc.
Photo Researcher: Christine Pullo
Senior Manufacturing Buyer: Roy Pickering
Printer and Binder: Courier Corporation/Kendallville
Cover Printer: The Lehigh Press, Inc.

For permission to use copyrighted material, grateful acknowledgment is made to the copyright holders on pp. 464–465, which are hereby made part of this copyright page.

Library of Congress Cataloging-in-Publication Data

McDonald, James C., 1953-
  The reader / James C. McDonald.
      p. cm.
  Includes index.
  ISBN 978-0-321-35532-4
  1. College readers. 2. English language--Rhetoric. 3. Reading
comprehension. 4. Reading (Higher education) I. Title.
  PE1417.M246 2009
  808'.0427--dc22

                    2008047619

Longman
is an imprint of

www.pearsonhighered.com

ISBN 10: 0-321-35532-6
ISBN 13: 978-0-321-35532-4

3 4 5 6 7 8 9 10—CRK—12 11 10

To the Student

WRITING, READING, AND RESEARCHING are similar and intertwined processes of knowledge-making. The act of questioning is fundamental to all three processes and essential to your development as a critical thinker, as a reader, and as a writer.

I've been interested in how students and teachers bring reading and research into writing since I became a composition teacher and scholar. It fascinates me to see how students and other writers adjust their reading processes to understand an assignment, comment on a colleague's paper, imitate a model piece of writing, analyze a text, evaluate a possible source in their research, and revise, edit, and proofread their own writings; to observe how their reading processes influence how they write; and to understand what questions they ask themselves and what questions others ask them as they read and write. Every college student already possesses an incredible collection of writing, reading, and research strategies and abilities; you would not be in college without them. Yet even the most talented and experienced writers must work to improve and add to these abilities to meet the writing, reading, and research challenges of a complex and ever-changing world.

Composing *The Reader* has given me the chance to work out many of my ideas and research on writing, reading, and teaching; to figure out how I might help you tap into the writing, reading, and research abilities that you already possess; and to develop new strategies to prepare you for new demands on your abilities in your classes and careers. I want *The Reader* to help you develop the habits of asking new and more challenging questions as you read and write about your subject; respond inquisitively to the writing of your classmates; and reread, rethink, and revise your own writing—habits that will not only enrich your college experience but also your future career and your life as a citizen.

With this approach in mind, I've chosen readings that showcase the variety of genres we read, analyze, and produce every day both in and outside of college. Over one hundred essays, magazine and newspaper articles, speeches, radio commentaries, academic articles, literary works, Web pages, comics, advertisements, paintings and more explore enduring human questions and important contemporary issues. *The Reader*'s range of genres, topics, and perspectives helps ensure that you are always asking questions about a text's audience, purpose, context, structure, and strategies.

In fact, the entire publishing team that worked with me asked these same questions regarding the audience, context, structure, and strategies of *The Reader*. Our discussions of your desires and needs as our audience and your experiences and preferences as readers led us to abandon the look and design of a traditional textbook. You want course material that is visually appealing, well-designed, and looks more like what you read outside class. We know you want textbooks that weigh less and cost less. We hope that using our own questioning approach in creating *The Reader* has provided you with an engaging alternative to traditional textbooks.

How Does *The Reader* Help You Develop the Habits of Asking Challenging Questions?

While Chapter 1, "Writing," suggests an array of invention, drafting, revising, and editing strategies that you can use as you develop your own writing processes, it also emphasizes the social nature of writing and suggests practices that you can use when peer-reviewing your classmates' papers. The lengthy case study of a student's literacy narrative—with prewriting, rough drafts, comments by the student and her peers, and the final text—concludes with questions you can use for analyzing the student's writing.

Chapter 2, "Reading and Writing," encourages you to view reading as a dynamic process in which readers plan, draft, and revise their understanding and analysis of a text, just as they plan, draft, and revise any paper they are writing. In particular, you will see that reading for different purposes requires you to adapt the questions you ask about a text. "Writing-to-read" activities that include annotating and keeping a reading journal show how you can build on the invention activities in Chapter 1 to better understand and respond to another writer's text.

Chapter 3, "Researching and Writing," helps you apply the questions and strategies for critical reading to evaluating and selecting sources as well as incorporating them into your writing to develop and support your own arguments. And while Chapter 3 will help you write the college "research paper," it also helps you to see research as part of the process for most writing.

In addition, the introductory text in Chapters 4 through 12 features a list of questions to consider as you read the selections that follow in order to better understand how the readings work, what sources the authors consulted, and what you decide you want to say in response as your own contribution to the conversation.

What Range of Genres and Topics Will *The Reader* Help You Explore?

Over one hundred classic and contemporary essays, academic articles, newspaper and magazine articles, editorials, speeches, blogs, radio commentaries, advertisements, photographs, Web pages, literary selections, student papers, and comics are organized around nine important themes in academic and public discourse: identity; marriage and family; faith and religion; language; education; work; wealth and property; folk and popular culture; and war, terrorism, and protest.

The Reader often takes a broader view of these themes than other readers. For example, Chapter 4 on "Identity" includes selections on avatars, body image, corporate identities in advertising, advertisers' use of audience identification in persuasion, the effects of consumerism on individual identity, and student images of themselves as writers—in addition to more traditional fare about gender, race, sexual orientation, ethnicity, and disability. Chapter 10 on "Wealth and Property" includes texts that discuss intellectual property issues, especially those that impact your life as a college student such as file sharing and plagiarism, as well as more typical reader approaches to wealth and poverty. And Chapter 11 on "Folk and Popular Culture" includes selections about folk cultures—the art, traditions, beliefs, and celebrations of local cultures—as well as selections about television, film, popular music, and other art forms of mass media.

The Reader also includes three themes that run through every chapter. One such theme on student life, an innovation in composition readers that encourages you to reflect on, question, and write about the challenges of being a student, is expressed in readings that explore the high costs of going to college, credit card debt, and balancing coursework and paid employment. Often these selections showcase students as knowledge-makers because the authors build their arguments on student interviews, student responses to questionnaires, or students' academic writing.

The other two thematic threads running through the chapters are on issues of gender and technology because questions of gender and technology cannot be separated from subjects like identity, work, education, language, family, or war. Using these issues as lenses through which you can view, question, and explore all the other topics in *The Reader* may also suggest new topics for writing or research than those specifically suggested in the text.

Lastly, every chapter includes a selection written by a student: About one-half of these selections are documented research papers written for writing classes that also show you how to write and cite in MLA style. Other selections were written and published for audiences other than a classroom. A Youth Radio commentary that aired on National Public Radio, a guest editorial in *The Sporting News*, two pieces written for campus newspapers, and a Tutor's Column in the *Writing Lab Newsletter* show your peers engaging in public discourse, influencing and informing "real-world" audiences beyond the classroom.

What Kind of Thinking, Reading, Writing, and Researching Will You Be Doing?

How does the apparatus that introduces and follows readings in each chapter help you develop critical habits of questioning in your reading, writing, and research processes?

The core of each thematic chapter's introduction is a list of questions you can use as a heuristic for discussing the readings and writing on the theme. The introductory text also draws connections among the topic, its importance in our culture, and its relevance to your life. Each introduction concludes with Invitations for Journal Writing, prompts that ask you to explore what you already think and know about the chapter topic before you read in order to help you engage in active conversations with the authors.

Each reading is preceded by a headnote that describes the expertise and authority of the author, identifies the genre of the selection, and describes the original context and publication forum of the selection in order to help you survey and later analyze the text's genre, purposes, and audience.

Each selection is followed by two sets of questions: Journal and Discussion Questions and Topics for Writing. The Journal and Discussion Questions ask you to explore the content, organization, and language of each reading and then to analyze reasons behind the author's decisions and how the author's choices may affect readers' responses. They frequently ask you to identify the author's sources of research and to discuss how the author used these sources to develop and support his or her ideas. Topics for Writing offer several essay prompts that encourage you to respond to the reading with an analysis of the text or an argument about the selection's claims.

Several Connecting the Readings questions in each chapter point out the dialogic relationship between two selections and afford opportunities for you to analyze the relationships among the ideas in the two readings or to consider the opposing arguments in the texts.

Finally, each chapter concludes with a half dozen or more Suggestions for Essays that ask you to make connections among several of the readings and engage in conversations with the texts in the chapter, explaining, commenting on, synthesizing, and disagreeing with other writers.

Thanks to All Who Have Helped Along the Way

Any book is the product of the author's encounters with many people in his life, and a textbook in particular reflects my long history of lessons learned from my teachers, my students, and my colleagues as well as authors that have influenced my thoughts and practices about reading, writing, research, and teaching. And I have been privileged with many wonderful and intelligent students who have challenged me to become a better teacher and a more critical reader. I recognize in this book some of what I have learned as a student of Thomas Kass, Lucien Fournier, Walter Ong, Elias Chiasson, Gennifer Giannasi, Deborah Pickering, James Kinneavy, James Berlin, Jerome Bump, and John Ruszkiewicz, although I am sure this book reflects many other long forgotten but long internalized lessons from other teachers as well. I hope that all these teachers would be pleased with this book, even though they would certainly challenge a number of the decisions I made while composing it.

Similarly, many colleagues unwittingly helped me with this book by turning me on to an author or a publication or by telling me about how they used particular texts in their classes. But I need to recognize Lei Lani Michel for a presentation at a conference of the Louisiana Association for College Composition about having students at Nunez Community College analyze the captions of the two Hurricane Katrina photographs in Chapter 7. A number of friends, including Monica Busby, Mary Trachsel, Denise Rogers, Kathy Evertz, Richard Louth, and Connor Chauveaux, responded to my requests for student essays, and I regret that I could not include more of their students' writing here.

I could not have done this book without the valuable help that many people gave me as I was composing *The Reader*. I received detailed, invaluable criticism and encouragement from those who reviewed manuscript at various stages of composition that helped me shape and refine the book; I am also grateful to those who reviewed the text's design as it developed for their critique, suggestions, and support: Wanda G. Addison, National University; Peter Beurskens, Minnesota State College–Southeast Technical; Tina Boscha, University of Oregon; Sarah Brown, University of Mary Hardin-Baylor; Vincent Casaregola, Saint Louis University; Irene Clark, California State University–Northridge; Mary Clark-Upchurch, Ball State University; Huey Crisp, University of Arkansas at Little Rock; Sally Crisp, University of Arkansas at Little Rock; Beth Daniell, Kennesaw State University; Laura Dawkins, Murray State University; Carlton Downey, Houston Community College Southeast; Nicole P. Greene, Xavier University of Louisiana; Susan Hanson, Texas State University—San Marcos; Joe Hardin, University of Arkansas-Fort Mill; Christopher S. Harris, University of Louisiana at Monroe; Charles Harrison, San Jacinto College South; Karen Hattaway, San Jacinto College North; Reinhold Hill, Ferris State University; Sandi Hubnik, University of Texas—Arlington; Collin Hutchison, San Jacinto College South; Rebecca Jackson, Texas State University; Joseph Janangelo, Loyola University; T. R. Johnson, Tulane University; Audrey Kerr, Southern Connecticut State College; Jeffery Kosse, Iowa Western Community College; William B. Lalicker, West Chester University of Pennsylvania; Joseph McDade, Houston Community College Northeast; Kim C. McDonald, University of New Orleans; Ronda Mehrer, Black Hill State University; Irvin Peckham, Lousiana State University; Clancy Ratliff, University of Lousiana at Lafayette; James Reitter, University of Wisconsin—Sheboygan; Albert Rouzie, Ohio University; Dagmar Scharold, University of Houston, Downtown; Eileen Schell, Syracuse University; Robert A. Schwegler, University of Rhode Island; Allison Smith, Middle Tennessee State University; Amy E. Harris Tan, Houston Community College Southwest; William H. Thelin, University of Akron; Ruth Vise, El Paso Community College; Mary Ellen Weir, Belmont Abbey College; Tina Zigon, Texas State University—San Marcos.

But this book would not exist without a lot of work and direction from the people at Pearson Longman. Eben Ludlow first helped me sketch out what this project could be, and Joe Opiela helped me find my way in the early months of authoring, particularly after Hurricanes Katrina and Rita struck south Louisiana. But my greatest thanks go to Lauren Finn, who helped me develop my vision for the book and worked hard and imaginatively on the design, and Anne Brunell Ehrenworth, who kept me focused through the maze of details of creating a textbook. Both have been wonderful to work with.

James C. McDonald

v

Contents

* An asterisk denotes a reading on student life, gender, or technology.

07 Language 185

08 Education 256

* An asterisk denotes a reading on student life, gender, or technology.

09 Work 288

10 Wealth and Property 327

* An asterisk denotes a reading on student life, gender, or technology.

Rhetorical Contents

Process Analysis

Evaluation

Argument

Writing

WE HAVE ALL WATCHED A MOVIE or television show in which a character works hour after hour composing wedding vows or a closing argument for a murder trial. The character agonizes over the speech, rehearsing and revising, crumpling up one draft after another. But at the moment of truth, the character gazes at the audience, tosses the prepared text aside, and speaks from the heart; the audience responds with tears or applause. The message about writing is clear: Good writing comes spontaneously. Planning and revising drains writing of emotion, power, and truth. But the character's speech is almost never improvised. A team of screenwriters working with the director and actor have spent days writing and reworking the character's speech to make it sound powerful and spontaneous. Even the scene from the movie hints that the character needs to spend all those hours working on the bad speech in order to speak so eloquently when the time comes.

A similar scene happens at colleges every day. Believing that they write best under pressure, many students wait until near the deadline for a paper before starting to write, relying on panic and adrenaline to stimulate the inspiration to write. But relying on anxiety and inspiration in the last hours before a paper is due is a high-risk strategy. Although a looming deadline often energizes writers, anxiety can paralyze a writer. If inspiration doesn't come, a student faces the choice between missing the deadline (and taking a deduction in grade) or writing a paper of tired clichés and half-thought-out ideas just to turn in something. If a snag occurs while writing the paper—the first idea for a paper doesn't pan out or the power goes out in the dorm— there's no time to adjust.

Writing classes exist to help students recognize the habits that make writing a good paper more difficult. Students need to build a repertoire of useful composing strategies rather than get locked into one writing process. A resume, a poem, a research paper for a history class, and a lab report for a biology class typically require different composing processes. The time you have to write, the difficulty of your writing project, the expectations of your audience, and the mood you're in all affect how you should go about writing your text.

Components of a Writer's Composing Process

In general, a writer's composing process has several parts: planning and inventing, drafting, revising, consulting, and editing. In planning and inventing, you discover topics to write about; develop material for a piece; and analyze your assignment, audiences, and purposes in writing. Drafting involves judging, selecting, and organizing this material and beginning to form the piece itself. Revising involves reconsidering and making changes in your ideas, evidence and details, organization, tone, and style, sometimes even your purpose and intended audience for the paper. Consulting takes place whenever you discuss an assignment with a friend or roommate, a peer group in class, your teacher in class or in her office, or a tutor in the campus writing center. Editing focuses on sentence-level concerns and the presentation of the text on paper or online—assessing word choices, transitions, sentence structures, grammar, punctuation, mechanics, and documentation of sources and dealing with format and design concerns, such as fonts, page numbering, and margins. Although writers often focus on one component at a time, they usually engage in more than one part of their process at once or move back and forth among these activities.

Planning and Inventing

You should experiment with many invention activities to discover which ones work best for you and build a repertoire of strategies. You may use some strategies for almost every paper, but others may work only for certain kinds of writing. You might turn to some strategies only when your usual activities aren't working or you want to take your thinking in new directions.

KEEPING A JOURNAL OR BLOG. People write journals for many personal and professional purposes. Many people keep diaries to work out their thoughts and feelings about memories and experiences or leave a record of their lives for themselves or their children. But people often keep other kinds of journals with other purposes in mind, maybe only for a short time or for a specific project, such as a journal for a research paper or a memory log of a vacation trip. Professional writers usually keep journals to write down ideas, observations, and bits of conversation and writing they encounter that might be useful for their own essays, poems, and stories. Professional athletes sometimes write a daily journal during the season, then revise it into a book or use it to inform fans in a blog about everyday life as an athlete. Research scientists keep careful logs of their experiments, recording procedures, results, and possible implications of the results. Students in many courses are assigned to keep journals to help them comprehend the class material, consider the implications and applications of what they are learning, and identify questions to discuss in class.

> " A journal or blog for a writing class can take many different forms and include many different kinds of entries. "

Writing classes usually discuss journaling under invention, although a good journal may be just as useful in drafting and revising. The audience for most journals is the writer himself. Although a writer may decide to show his journal to someone close to him, he seldom worries about other readers when he writes in his journal. Whether teachers read and write responses to journal entries or just check to make sure students are writing in their journals regularly, they don't grade journals like essays written for outside audiences. In fact, they often tell students not to worry about spelling, punctuation, or grammar when writing in their journals so that students will put their energy into figuring out what they think, feel, and remember as they write. Once you get in the habit of keeping a journal, you may find that you enjoy journal writing for your own personal reasons and continue it after the class has ended.

Blogs are different from other journals because they *are* meant to be read by others online, and serious bloggers want others to respond to their entries or discuss their ideas in other blogs. Many people keep blogs to discuss a single subject like gardening or politics. A number of the writers in this book, in fact, keep blogs that invite readers like you to reply directly to the writer and her other readers. Your teacher may ask you to write a personal blog for your writing class or, more likely, to contribute to a class blog where you can read other class members' entries and engage in discussions with each other.

A journal or blog for a writing class can take many different forms and include many different kinds of entries, and you should experiment to discover what kinds of journal writing work best for you. You may have an entirely free hand in deciding what to write in your journal, at least some of the time, or your teacher may assign a topic of the day, such as those suggested throughout this book. You might use your journal to work on your papers: to do invention and revising activities such as those suggested in this book; to work on important passages of your papers; and to take notes about conferences you have with your teacher, classmates, and writing center tutors about your papers and discuss your thoughts and plans about these conferences. You might discuss readings and research for your class in your journal, try wordplay activities to develop and experiment with your style and voice, or even work on stubborn problems that you have with grammar, spelling, and punctuation. Or you might write mainly about what interests you. Many students find material for papers by taking this approach. Some writers include drawings and clippings in their journals.

You might keep your journal in a notebook or in a computer file. You might write in your journal at the same time every day, maybe at the end of the day or between classes. Or you might keep your journal handy for when an idea, a memory, or an observation strikes you. For a writing class, you should do more than simply record the daily events of your life: include your ideas, emotions, reactions, questions, and memories, as well as details about your experiences and readings. Write quickly about what comes to mind most of the time. And write in your journal often, but don't let journal writing become a chore. Its purpose is to make discovering and developing topics, ideas, and other material for your papers less of a chore.

FREEWRITING. Freewriting is a simple, flexible invention activity by itself or in combination with other exercises. The directions for freewriting are simple: write nonstop for a set period of time (five, ten, fifteen minutes). Write quickly, as fast as you can. Write whatever comes to your mind. Don't pause to think of the right word or to think of your next thought. If you get stuck, repeat a word or phrase over and over until something else pops into your head. Don't go back to correct or cross out anything you've written, and don't worry about spelling, punctuation, or grammar. You can freewrite with or without a topic in mind, but don't worry about getting off topic. Let your mind and hand go where they want.

Freewriting can be a cure for writer's block and the intimidation that most writers feel in front of a blank page or a blank computer screen because it's a quick and pressure-free way to get out words, ideas, and information that you can work with. Once your time period is up, read over what you've written to see what you've come up with. Some freewriting sessions may not be very productive, but usually you'll find at least a fragment that you can use, and often much more. You will get better at freewriting with experience.

Although freewriting is useful for getting started on a paper, you can use freewriting at any point in your composing process. You can freewrite for possible topics for an assignment; for ideas, questions, memories, and knowledge that you can use in a paper; for working out a specific idea or example in a part of your paper; or for thinking out the audience, purpose, and situation of your paper. You might freewrite in response to comments on a draft from your instructor or a classmate, to think through a paragraph that you aren't satisfied with as you are finishing up a paper, or to prepare for a conference with your teacher or peer review group.

LOOPING. Looping is a series of focused freewritings. After each freewriting, you write down a "center of gravity" sentence that identifies the most important idea, question, feeling, or piece of information from that freewriting. Use that sentence to start your next freewriting or "loop." You can generate several pages of material in an hour or so of looping. Some writers find looping a good way to discover a central idea for a paper, to generate ideas about that central idea for the different sections of their paper, or to come up with details to explain and support their ideas. If you have a lot of information or have done a lot of reading for a paper, as with a research paper, looping can help you discover your own ideas about all the information you've collected.

CUBING. Cubing is a focused series of six freewritings (corresponding to the six sides of a cube). Each freewriting responds to a different command about your topic.

1. Describe it. This freewriting can be a physical description; it can also provide definitions and history and origins.

2. Compare it. This freewriting can be one extended comparison and contrast or a series of brief comparisons.

3. Associate it. This step allows you to write about anything you associate or connect with the topic. Sometimes these are entirely personal associations from your experiences. Sometimes they are more public and general associations, drawing on classifications, divisions, causes, or effects.

4. Analyze it. Identify and describe the parts of the topic and how they relate to each other and to the whole. Or analyze the history of the topic and its causes and effects.

5. Apply it. Discuss the practicalities of the topic, how it is used or how it could be applied to a problem.

6. Argue for or against it. Identify an issue involving your topic, take a position, and defend that position.

Cubing might be most helpful when you have little time to write a paper because it can generate pages of material on a topic from different perspectives in an hour or two. Often you'll find yourself repeating some ideas for different sides of the cube, but the repetitions may help you to identify central ideas for a paper and begin to develop them. Although you must respond imaginatively to some commands for some topics, this can generate unexpected, creative ideas.

BRAINSTORMING, CLUSTERING, AND LISTING. In freewriting invention activities, writers typically write mainly in sentences. With brainstorming, listing, and clustering, you usually fill a page (or more) with words and phrases. These activities are most helpful for coming up with a topic or a main idea for an essay, but they can also be used to generate details and develop ideas or to analyze your assignment or your audience.

Brainstorming is the most freeform of these activities: Write down whatever comes to mind for a paper or a problem, no matter how silly it may seem—ideas, key words, questions, metaphors, and memories of events, experiences, and readings. Write quickly to fill up a sheet of paper or more with words and phrases. Brainstorming is not linear. Writers often scatter their words and phrases all over the page.

Clustering is similar to brainstorming, but here you circle each phrase and draw lines to connect phrases to each other, usually starting with a central word or phrase and branching several clusters of circles off of it. Some people draw empty circles and lines when nothing comes immediately to mind to keep their brain and hand going then fill them in later. Some clusters of ideas and material will probably be bigger and more detailed than others, indicating topics of interest to the writer or topics about which the writer has a lot to say. Used early for a paper, clustering can help you come up with topics or a central idea for a paper, and the clusters may suggest sections for organizing your draft.

With listing, you write down words and phrases in columns. Listing can help you focus on particular aspects of your paper: pros and cons; similarities and differences; sights, sounds, smells, tastes, and sensations; evidence; reasons; examples; key words; and metaphors. Often writers move from brainstorming and clustering to list making, using lists to organize and add to the material that they have produced in earlier invention activities.

HEURISTICS. The term *heuristics* is sometimes used to cover invention activities that are more formal and organized than activities like brainstorming, freewriting, and looping. Heuristics often take the form of a series of open-ended questions or specific writing activities about a subject that require the writer to think about a subject thoroughly from a number of different perspectives. Teachers often provide heuristics composed specially for an assignment. In this book, the questions in the introduction to each chapter and the questions and writing activities that follow each reading can be used as heuristics for writing an essay on the theme of the chapter or the subject of the selection.

But there are several general heuristics that can be used for any number of subjects. Most people have heard of the journalist's **who? what? when? where? why?** and **how?** heuristic, which works well for many informative writing projects. Two other popular heuristics are Kenneth Burke's *pentad* and *ratios* and the *topoi* from classical rhetoric. Each heuristic system provides a different way of thinking critically and thoroughly about a subject, and it's likely that you will find one heuristic that fits better with your ways of thinking than the others.

JOURNALIST'S QUESTIONS. Reporters often use "the five W's and an H" (who? what? when? where? why? and how?) in gathering information for and drafting a news story. A news story that provides clear and complete answers to these six questions about an event should be reasonably comprehensive and satisfy readers' major questions about the event. In college writing, these questions are most useful for informative writing, which is most concerned with providing readers with facts and information, especially in a narrative or a report. In persuasive, analytical, and reflective writing, the journalist's questions can be helpful for developing background information, composing an opening anecdote, or giving a detailed example about an incident or experience.

THE PENTAD. The pentad is similar to the journalist's questions because the five points of the pentad—**agent**, **act**, **scene**, **purpose**, and **agency**—correspond roughly to questions of who (agent), what happened (act), when and where (scene), why (purpose), and how (agency). But this heuristic asks writers not only to report on a subject but to analyze it. You can create as many as twenty "ratios," such as agent:scene, scene:agent, agency:act, and purpose:act to prompt you to think about how one part of the pentad affects the others. For example, how does writing on a computer rather than with a pen and paper affect what you write (agency:act)? How does writing in a college writing class affect your goals for writing compared to writing in another class (scene:purpose)? How should your purposes for writing an essay guide the impression that you create about yourself to your readers (purpose:agent)? It's possible to generate many questions with each ratio.

TOPOI. Aristotle lists almost 200 *topoi*, or lines of argument, in his *Rhetoric* and *Topics*, but modern composition textbooks usually limit themselves to his "formal topics," such as comparison and contrast, cause and effect, definition, classification and division, as lines of thought to consider with any subject. Jacqueline Berke's book *Twenty Questions for the Writer* converted Aristotle's formal topics into these questions for exploring a subject, figuring out a thesis statement, or planning a term paper:

1. What does X mean?
2. How can X be described?
3. What are the component parts of X?
4. How is X made or done?
5. How should X be made or done?
6. What is the essential function of X?
7. What are the causes of X?
8. What are the consequences of X?
9. What are the types of X?
10. How does X compare to Y?
11. What is the present status of X?
12. How should X be interpreted?
13. What are the facts about X?
14. How did X happen?
15. What kind of person is X?
16. What is my personal response to X?
17. What is my memory of X?
18. What is the value of X?
19. How can X be summarized?
20. What case can be made for or against X?

> **" Often the most productive invention activities involve talking about a topic with classmates, a writing center tutor, or a teacher. "**

The purpose of some heuristics is not to discover information and generate ideas for a paper but to analyze the assignment, audience, and situation for planning a paper. Such a heuristic can ask writers to think about what an assignment calls for; what its goals are; who the intended readers are; why they would read this paper; what knowledge, ideas, prejudices, and preconceptions they have; what purposes the writer may have for writing the paper; and what problems or challenges the assignment may present to the writer. In all cases, a heuristic provides a guide to thinking critically and creatively about a subject, an audience, or a writing assignment. While free-wheeling invention exercises like freewriting and brainstorming can lead to surprising associations and ideas that you might not discover with a heuristic, working through a good heuristic for a paper should also lead you to unexpected ideas and perspectives about a subject. Heuristics ask you to think about a subject in a thorough and comprehensive way, and for that reason, writers may use a heuristic after freewriting or brainstorming or may use freewriting or brainstorming to answer questions in a heuristic.

CONSULTING WITH OTHERS. Although finding a quiet place to think and write is important, it's a mistake to assume that invention should always be a solitary or silent activity. Often the most productive invention activities involve talking about a topic with classmates, a writing center tutor, or a teacher. Brainstorming often works better in a group, with everyone contributing ideas and someone keeping notes (or everyone taking turns as the group recorder). And a heuristic can be used as a source of questions for an invention conversation to discover a topic, decide on an idea for a paper, or develop ideas for an essay. Ideas will come to you listening to others talk about their ideas, and you'll get a sense of what ideas, memories, examples, and arguments others find most interesting and surprising. Often it makes sense to do some writing about your paper for a few minutes to prepare for a conference or group discussion, and you usually should do some writing immediately after the discussion while the ideas are still fresh in your mind.

Drafting Although it's convenient to discuss invention and drafting separately, they often work together. Some writers spend a lot of time conducting research and working through invention activities before they begin to select and organize material into a draft, using invention activities to reduce their fear of the blank computer screen and begin drafting with a wealth of ideas and information. Some writers use an invention activity or a journal entry as a rough draft. Others might write a quick draft and use invention activities to add to thin parts of the paper. In any event, invention doesn't end when you begin composing a draft—you often need to discover and develop ideas and material for your paper as you draft and revise.

Figuring out what you want and have to say is generally the main task in drafting. Some writers call the first draft of a paper their "discovery" draft because they don't really find out what they think until they have worked through their ideas and details in a rough draft. It's not unusual to begin a rough draft arguing one side of an issue only to find yourself arguing the opposite side at the end of the draft. So it's usually a bad idea to let concerns about your audience control and censor what you write while drafting. Unless you're writing under an imminent deadline (as with an in-class essay), you have time to change anything you write.

INTERPRETING THE ASSIGNMENT. Often the first matter to think about when drafting a paper is the assignment. What does it require you to do to fulfill the assignment? What options and freedom do you have in the assignment? What is the purpose of the paper (for example, to inform, to explore, to analyze, to argue)? Who is the audience for the paper? Some assignments give writers much freedom and responsibility to decide on the topic, content, organization, audience, and/or purpose of the paper. Other assignments lay out strict guidelines, and some assignments are strict about some matters and loose about others.

Misunderstanding the assignment is a major cause of poor grades. If the assignment is written out for you, you need to interpret it carefully, paying close attention to the verbs in the assignment: *argue, respond to, summarize, compare, analyze,* and *discuss* each calls for a different kind of writing (and the true meaning of *discuss* can be tricky). Take careful notes when the teacher discusses the assignment, and ask questions if you don't understand something. Still, you may realize that you are hazy about part of the assignment only when you begin drafting. Teachers usually give time at the beginning or end of class to answer questions and are available in their offices or by email at other times. If you schedule a conference in the writing center, the tutor will probably begin by asking you about the assignment and discussing what it seems to call for, helping you to develop your ability to interpret writing assignments. Class discussions and teacher comments about recent papers also provide information about what the teacher may be expecting in an assignment. For example, if the class has been discussing and analyzing introductions and the teacher has been commenting about a need for more examples in your papers, you should make introductions and examples a priority in your next assignment.

ORGANIZING A DRAFT. As you draft, you shape the material that you have collected into a text. As you support, explain, elaborate, and correct these ideas and information, you should continue invention to develop more material for your draft. We often use the metaphors of *content* and *form* to describe the relationship among the ideas, facts, and other material for a paper and the organization of that *material* (a metaphor similar to *content*). These are clumsy metaphors that imply that content and form are separate from each other, that writers first come up with ideas and facts and then mold them into shape or pour them into a container that gives them form. But form and content are intimately intertwined with each other. Deciding whether to write a poem instead of a love letter for Valentine's Day and whether that poem should be a limerick or a sonnet has everything to do with the ideas, experiences, and emotions that the writer is working out for himself. In beginning to work out the form of your paper, you are continuing to work out the meaning of your paper, for yourself and for your readers.

So in drafting a paper, you focus on the form of the paper—the genre, the organizational pattern, the paragraphing, and the sentences. Some genres give writers little choice of organizational pattern. Readers expect resumes, instructions, lab reports, grammar textbooks, sonnets and other genres of poetry, and romance novels to be organized in certain ways. The organization is determined by the uses that readers make of these genres. Form follows function. Other genres give writers great freedom to decide what organization works best considering what the writer wants to say and how she hopes to affect her readers.

COMPOSING AN INTRODUCTION. Writers are often advised not to spend much time on the introduction for a first draft. Write something just to get started that you can discard later when a better introduction comes to mind. Although some very good writers need to work out their introductions before they can proceed with the rest of the draft, getting started quickly on a draft is generally good advice— you can waste a lot of time agonizing over an introduction that would be better spent developing the ideas within your paper and then feel reluctant to revise a weak introduction because of all the work you invested at the beginning of the process.

Writing an introduction can be more difficult than any other part of the paper because its main purpose is to create expectations for the reader about the subject of the paper, the central idea or impression of that subject, the stance the writer is taking toward the subject, the intended audience, and the genre and the organization of the paper. From the title and introduction, readers decide whether they need or want to read the text, why they should read it, and what they hope to get out of the text. They begin to guess at what the text will say—an important part of the process of reading. Sometimes a writer will lay out very explicit expectations for readers, even announcing that "this paper will argue such-and-such a position and follow a specific organization . . ." (although an announcement like this usually also tells readers that the paper won't be fun to read). Professors often expect an introduction to an academic paper to state the central idea or thesis and set up quite specific expectations for the rest of the paper. But sometimes writers set up expectations in order to surprise readers. When a writer knows her position will be unpopular with readers, she may avoid stating her position too early, focusing early on points of agreement and revealing a thesis later. She may begin in a humorous way to gain readers' trust and interest and shift to a more serious or solemn tone later in the paper, or the paper may begin with a solemn tone to surprise readers with humor later. The selections in this book illustrate several different ways to introduce a text and set up different expectations about the rest of the paper for readers.

COMPOSING A CONCLUSION. When you draft a conclusion for a paper, keep your audience and purpose in mind. What is important for your readers to remember, believe, and feel after reading your paper? How do you hope to change your readers' beliefs and emotions with your paper? Why is it important for your readers to know about your subject and believe your claims?

The first requirement for a conclusion, obviously, is simply to give readers the sense that the text has come to an end and the author has finished what he wants to say. You don't want readers wondering whether you died before you finished writing. Sometimes a formal conclusion is unnecessary because the essay feels finished and leaves readers satisfied with the last paragraph of the body. Often, however, writers find it necessary to state or restate the thesis in the conclusion. If an essay is long, if the ideas are complicated, or if the paper implies the main idea without directly stating it until the conclusion, you especially need to make sure that your readers understand and remember the central idea or claim of the essay. But it's usually a bad idea to conclude a paper by just restating your thesis from the introduction. A two-to-five page paper takes only a few minutes to read, after all, so your readers won't have forgotten what they read in the introduction. Therefore, when you write a summary or restatement of your main idea for your conclusion, remember that your readers know more about this idea than they did when you introduced it and that they should feel differently about it now. As you consider your readers and purposes, you may decide to state your thesis in more detail or with different emphasis or with more emotionally persuasive language in your conclusion than you do in your introduction.

Conclusions often address the question: "So what?" Why should readers care about your idea? What should they do about it? That's why essays about a personal experience often conclude by discussing the meaning of the experience and why arguments frequently end by urging readers to take some action. Many conclusions try to convince readers that they should remember and care about what the writer has written by showing how the topic is connected to other issues and interests or by putting the topic in a larger historical, social, political, or moral context.

Like introductions, conclusions in student papers are often a single paragraph, but as you read the selections in this book, you will find conclusions as brief as one sentence and as long as several paragraphs. Notice the different kinds of conclusions that writers employ, what purposes each conclusion serves, and how each conclusion tries to influence readers' beliefs and emotions about the writer's subject. Often in your own drafts, you will need to experiment with two or three different kinds of conclusions before you can figure out the most effective way to conclude the paper.

Revising

Many people believe that only weak writers need to revise, that a good writer is able to produce a strong paper in a single sitting and that revising consists only of correcting errors in grammar and mechanics and improving word choices and transitions. But successful writers usually spend more time on revision than on any other part of the writing process. For them, the point of all the early planning, inventing, and drafting is to produce a rough draft that they can study, elaborate, rethink, and reshape. Revising is a "re-visioning" of the paper that can lead to new implications about what they have written, discoveries of gaps and weaknesses in their thinking and evidence, and sometimes entirely new ideas and radical changes in thought.

> **Successful writers usually spend more time on revision than on any other part of the writing process.**

Writers revise in different ways, often depending on what they are writing. Some writers plan and invent so extensively that they often don't need to revise extensively, especially on routine writing projects. Some writers revise extensively as they draft. Other writers work quickly to produce a draft and put most of their energy into revising. But the more difficult or important or unfamiliar a writing task is, the more revising you probably need to do. If you need to please a hostile audience or are writing something important to you, such as a personal statement for a law school application, you usually need to spend more time revising. If you've never written an exploratory essay or a environmental impact statement before, you should expect to spend more time revising. Many professors assign essays because they want students to get beyond the obvious and examine their research and ideas, and that usually means extensive revision.

KEEPING AUDIENCE IN MIND AND CONSULTING OTHERS FOR CRITICAL FEEDBACK. Audience is a central concern in revising. Writers try to predict how their audience will read their papers and often ask others for feedback. What parts of the draft are particularly clear, interesting, or persuasive? What passages are vague, boring, confusing, or unconvincing? What can the writer do to make the paper more persuasive? What might readers disagree with or object to? What changes can be made to reduce the problems and objections that readers might have with the paper and to take advantage of what they like and believe and know? Will they see the connections the writer intends between the different ideas in the paper and how the facts, examples, and research support the writer's claims? What will readers want to know more about? How might the writer encourage readers to be more interested in, open to, or sympathetic to what she has to say?

Critical reading and consulting are important tools for examining your ideas and reading from the perspective of your audience. Your composition class may require you to get comments on your drafts from your classmates and instructor, and your teacher may encourage you to bring a draft to her office for a conference or discuss it with a tutor in the writing center. You may be asked to comment on your classmates' papers in this class as well. Commenting on other writers' papers and hearing other people's responses to your papers should help you become a better reader and critic of your own writing.

There are many different approaches to commenting on other students' papers. Many comments are descriptive and not evaluative, explaining to the writer how you understand and react to what the paper says rather than judging the paper or making suggestions for improvements. Descriptive comments emphasize how the reader understood and responded to the draft—what they thought about and felt as they read or listened to the draft. A summary or outline of a classmate's paper, for example, can tell the writer what you understand (and don't understand) in a paper, what stands out and what's unclear, and how the focus, organization, and purpose of a paper appear to you. Sometimes very focused descriptive responses are helpful for working on a specific aspect of a paper. Marking or underlining examples or transitions can tell a writer whether he needs to include more evidence or transitions, for example. A detailed descriptive response can get into the feelings, reactions, and questions that occur to you as you read through a paper. One popular approach is to listen to the writer read the paper aloud and write notes as you listen, using a three-column format: a plus column for what you liked or what struck you as good or interesting, a minus column for what you didn't like or were confused about or found boring, and a question column for questions that occurred to you. The reader then gives a detailed spoken commentary about the paper using these notes. Of course, you may be asked to evaluate your classmates' drafts to identify main strengths and weaknesses and make suggestions for improvement. But even evaluative comments need descriptive details so that the writer knows why you consider something a strength or a weakness.

Teachers often provide students with questions and guidelines for responding to each other's papers. But there are a few rules of thumb for making useful comments.

1. Emphasize the positive at least as much as the negative. Writers need to know what works in their papers so they can build on what they are doing well, not just fix problems.

2. Be specific. Telling the writer that the organization is "good" or "bad" isn't very helpful. What did you find strong or weak about the organization?

3. Be tactful but don't be afraid to offer criticism. You aren't helping your classmates if you don't tell them the weaknesses that you see in their papers. Focus on the content of the paper rather than the writer in your comments, and emphasize your reactions rather than making judgmental comments ("I didn't understand the central claim in the third paragraph," rather than "You are vague and confusing in this part of the paper.").

4. Don't sweat the small stuff. Focus more on global matters than on grammar and mechanics, and focus on what's most important, especially with an early draft. What are the one or two biggest problems? What are the one or two greatest strengths? What one suggestion for improving the paper will help the paper the most? Writers should prioritize when revising, not come away with a list of a dozen or more things to do.

You are ultimately responsible for what you write. Even when you are revising considering your teacher's comments, you should remain in control of your paper. You still need to read your drafts critically and make your own decisions about revisions.

Editing and Proofreading

Editing focuses largely on sentence-level concerns: word choice, transitions, grammar, spelling, punctuation, and other mechanics such as capitalization. Proofreading is the last act before handing in a paper, looking for and correcting errors just before you turn in the finished copy. Writers often spend little time editing until near the end of the composing process because editing can disrupt their flow of thought. And why put time and energy into getting a sentence just right when you may decide to change the content of the sentence, move it to another part of the paper, or delete it entirely?

Focus on sentence-level matters once you've addressed the global concerns of your paper: the ideas and information of your paper, the organization, and how it works for your assignment, your intentions, and your audience. In editing you look mainly for problems to correct, such as sentences that are unclear or confusing, word choices that seem wrong in meaning or tone, weak transitions, missing definitions and examples, wordiness, choppy sentences, lack of variety in sentence beginnings and sentence lengths, sentences that may be grammatical but are difficult to comprehend, and errors in grammar, spelling, punctuation, and mechanics. Editing allows you to take care of problems and revise some of your sentences into something memorable and eloquent. Even in editing, you are working with the ideas, emotional tone, and audience of your paper, making sure that your statements say what you think and evoke the emotions and attitudes that you want your audience to feel. While editing, you may notice global improvements that you could make or think of new material for your paper and make global revisions, if there's time.

The proper presentation and format of your text is also a central concern in editing: The title (if you haven't come up with an interesting title yet), the design of the title page and the first page, page numbering, margins, fonts, line spacing, and especially the format for documentation and bibliography are all important. Editing is your last opportunity to make sure that there is no unintentional plagiarism, that you have used quotation marks when you have quoted even part of a sentence by another writer, and that you have credited your sources not only when you quote from a source but when you paraphrase and summarize ideas and information from another source.

Proofreading is the last stage of editing, something to do just before you hand in a paper. In proofreading, you focus almost entirely on finding and correcting typos and errors in mechanics and usage, such as fragments, misspellings, punctuation errors, subject–verb agreement errors, and missing words. Sometimes you'll notice a sentence that needs to be rewritten because it doesn't make sense. If you notice an error but don't have an opportunity to print out a corrected copy, you may make a neat correction on the page with a pen or pencil. Most teachers care more about correctness than neatness.

Editing and proofreading call for different kinds of reading than you practice while revising or while reading other writers' works. When we read for meaning, we usually take in several words at a time. For that reason, writers reading their own writing aloud sometimes read what they know *should be* in their papers rather than what is *actually on* the page, by supplying missing words and suffixes, for example. For editing you need to slow down your reading to notice each word, each letter, and each punctuation mark and what may be missing. Reading aloud or asking someone to read your paper aloud to you can be useful in editing. You can listen for sentences that are vague or don't sound right, sentences that cause the reader to stumble, and problems like choppiness and repetitiveness that may be easier to hear than see.

But mainly you need to read and reread your paper to focus on small details like spelling, punctuation, and word choice. In order to concentrate on these details, some writers read their papers backwards, starting with the last sentence, or they put a ruler underneath the line they are reading to force themselves to slow down and focus on the appearance of that line on the page. You might go through your paper at least once looking for stubborn or frequent problems in your writing: fragments and comma splices, perhaps, or shifts in verb tense and overuse of passive voice. The spell checker and grammar checker on your computer are useful tools, but they cannot edit or proofread your paper for you, for they miss some problems and mark other perfectly good words and sentences as incorrect. These tools can help you detect words and sentences that you need to inspect but can't help you if, for example, you often confuse the words *there* and *their* or *lose* and *loose*. Your teacher may allow you to work with a friend or classmate to edit or proofread your paper but you need to be clear on what kind of help is legal and what is considered cheating. Writing center staff do not proofread papers, but they often work with students on papers to help them improve their editing and proofreading skills.

One Student Composing an Essay

To illustrate one student's composing process for one writing assignment, take a look at some of Ashley Jankower's work on an essay for an advanced composition course for English education students at the University of Louisiana at Lafayette. Ashley's assignment was to write a literacy autobiography describing and examining her life as a reader and writer. Composition teachers often use this assignment to learn more about their students as writers and to encourage them to analyze their experiences and assumptions about writing. The instructor in this class, Monica Busby, also wanted the future English teachers in this course to examine how they learned and were taught to write.

Ashley began working on this assignment with an in-class "prewriting" on her view of herself as a writer and an ungraded essay on this topic that she handed in two days later. She wrote another extensive prewriting followed by three rough drafts before she turned in her final paper, almost a month after beginning her work on this assignment. Other students in her class read each draft and wrote questions and comments about her paper. Following you will find some of Ashley's prewriting, her first two drafts, her comments to herself and to her peer group about one draft, her group's responses to the draft, and Ashley's completed literacy autobiography.

Prewriting

ENG 355   8/22

I'm a detailed writer, yet I find difficulty in finding the right words to express the complex, analytical connections that are in my head. Sometimes this problem makes my writing somewhat incoherent. Not all the time, but sometimes I try to not use the same word to describe a similar idea that I'm discussing in my paper. So, I try to find synonyms for those words so that I can expand my vocabulary. You can never have an absolutely flawless paper. Sometimes you will make grammatical or contextual errors. It happens. Writing is a very advanced approach to effective communication. This separates us from beasts. There is no limit to writing. That's why I strive to improve my writing & ask others' opinions about my writing. I'm very good at developing analytical thoughts that some people don't see at first. I try to tackle ideas that are challenging—that's the only way I will grow as a writer. I just need to make conclusions more interesting than just restating the ideas I have already presented.

First Draft

Jankower 1

Learning Who I Am as a Writer

Perfection is never achievable in writing, and it irritates me so much. All my life I have strived for perfection in everything I do. Look at me now—I am trying to explain how I feel in proper, formal English. Sometimes I do not feel I have a strong voice. I see other people in my writing class have original ideas and creative ways of expressing them. I wish I could do that. For some reason, I am so focused on what other people think of my writing that I lose my voice in my writing. When people look at me, they see an overachiever that does everything perfectly. The truth is I am embarrassed when I hear that. It gives the impression that I have no soul—that I am on a different planet than everyone else. For some reason though, I can't stop striving for perfection.

To tell you the truth, I did not always have a love for English. I would hate reading and especially writing. I remember that I would always depend on my father to revise my papers before I turned them in to my teacher; of course, that meant that he would make them better. I could never trust myself to write a well developed essay. It was not until my junior year, when I was in Mrs. Guillory's Advanced Placement English class that I began to trust myself. On the first day of class when I heard Mrs. Guillory's eloquently articulated speech, I was awestruck. I did not realize how

Jankower 2

beautiful the English language could be. Her soothing tone made me so calm and at ease with myself. She challenged me to write timed essays almost every day. These essays weren't perfect, but they helped me to trust myself as a writer. I remember my father asking me one day if I needed his help with an essay and I told him no; he was amazed and looked at my paper anyway. He asked me if I wrote this myself, and I nodded my head sheepishly. He smiled and said, "That's better than I could have done." When he said this, I knew I could rely on myself as a writer.

My junior year in Mrs. Guillory's class was only the beginning. The next year, my senior year, I was in Mrs. Smith's class. She was a young, happy lady who had an ardent love for English. She showed us how awesome the English language was by teaching us Greek and Latin origins of words. It was tedious but so interesting. I diagrammed sentences for the first time in that class. I was always one to abhor grammar studies, but after learning how to diagram sentences, I realized how much fun it was. It was like solving a logic puzzle—figuring out where all the pieces go to make the big picture. Go figure—I liked diagramming! However, this was not what pushed me over the edge. Mrs. Smith kept explaining to my class the concept of how content and form must be analyzed back and forth when discussing connections in literary works. I remember racking my brains out to understand this concept. One night I was working on an essay about courtly love, using specific examples from Geoffrey Chaucer's *The Canterbury Tales*. All of a sudden, I noticed how the metaphors and descriptions of the characters expressed the overall theme of courtly love. It was like a lightning bolt. I finally understood what made the great literary works masterpieces and their authors geniuses. It was not the content that made them great—it was the careful work of the authors, placing every word and phrase into an artistic weave of metaphors and juxtapositions that brought the deepest internal themes of our very lives. It was amazing. I could not believe how exciting these masterpieces were. The next day, I let Mrs. Smith read my Chaucer essay. She smiled and told me that I now understood what made her excited to teach every day.

expand

I realize that I have a love hate relationship with writing. I love making connections with complex ideas, but I somehow never quite explain those connections in the way that I want them. Even though I now understand how to relate content with form, I still have some difficulty writing how I think. It was not until I had a group discussion in this class that I realized what was missing. It was my voice. That's what connects the writer to the reader. I realized that if I allowed my voice to dominate my writing, I would be able to connect my ideas to my readers. I just have one problem—what is my voice? What does

Jankower 3

it *sound* like? I feel that I am a generally formal writer that likes to explain ideas in detail. However, that is so boring. Why can I not be more daring in my writing? All this time, however, I have felt pretty confident in my writing. One day in a group discussion though, someone told me that I sounded timid as a writer. This shocked and confused me. This person then explained that I was confident, but I was scared when my writing was given up for review. I was amazed at this insight. This person was right—I am confident in my writing until I have to give it up to someone else to look at. This is because I want the approval from my peers, especially from my teacher. It was then that I realized why I lacked a strong voice. It was not because my writing was not clean or my ideas were bad. It was because of my need for the approval of my superiors that I hide my voice and use the voice that I know is acceptable.

I am an English Secondary Education major. Of course I want my writing to be exceptional. I want to be a good teacher. I want to set a good example for my students and have them hold high standards for themselves so that they can receive a good education. Every time I make a grammatical mistake when I am talking, my parents correct me and playfully tease me by saying, "And you want to be an English teacher." Please do not misunderstand me. My parents are extremely supportive of my aspirations to be a teacher and think that I will be a good teacher. However, they remind me that I am not perfect. Even though it irritates me so, I finally realize why my parents correct me when I make those kinds of mistakes. It is not because they want me to be perfect. It is to show me that I can learn from my mistakes. By realizing my own mistakes, possible to *it is* ⌃ have high standards for one's self, but impossible to achieve perfection. By realizing this, I can put myself in the position of my future students. My goal as a teacher is not to make my students into grammatically correct robots; rather, it is to show them their potential as writers and guide them on their paths of finding their true voice.

Conclusion focus on me as a writer instead of me as a teacher?

4–5 pages (OOPS!)

What should I expand on?

What should I add?

Is there anything that is not necessary?

— I think I need to change or limit my idiomatic expressions.

— This will not be 5¶ essay — I am making this longer

— I started making this an expository essay, but I think it ended up being a narrative. . .

Second Draft

My comments that I want you to look at are on the last page.   Jankower 1

Learning Who I Am as a Writer

Perfection is never achievable in writing, and it irritates me so much. All my life I have strived for perfection in everything I do. Look at me now—I am trying to explain how I feel in proper, formal English. Sometimes I do not feel I have a strong voice. I see other people in my writing class have original ideas and creative ways of expressing them. I wish I could do that. For some reason, I am so focused on what other people think of my writing that I lose my voice in my writing. When people look at me, they see an overachiever that does everything perfectly. The truth is I am embarrassed when I hear that. It gives the impression that I have no soul—that I am on a different planet than everyone else. For some reason though, I can't stop striving for perfection.

My parents influence me the most when it comes to my writing, particularly my father. I remember that I would always depend on my father to revise my papers before I turned them in to my teacher; of course, that meant that he would make them better. My father is a lawyer, so the revisions he made to my papers were very formal and detailed. After looking at those types of revisions many times, I started to imitate that *style of writing* I found that I had longwinded sentences with plenty of prepositional phrases. I made sure that every detail was mentioned, *just* to make sure I had everything written that needed to be said. My father's flawless writing somewhat intimidated me. I fully entrusted my work to his hands. I could never trust myself to write a well developed essay.

[*To tell you the truth,* I did not always have a love for English. I would hate reading and especially writing.] It was not until my junior year, when I was in Mrs. Guillory's Advanced Placement English class that I began to trust myself with my writing. On the first day of class when I heard Mrs. Guillory's eloquently articulated speech, I was awestruck. I did not realize how beautiful the English language could be. Her soothing tone made me so calm and at ease with myself. She challenged me to write timed essays almost every day. These essays *weren't* perfect, but they helped me to trust myself as a writer. I remember my father asking me one day if I needed his help with an essay and I told him no; he was amazed and looked at my paper anyway. He asked me if I wrote this myself, and I nodded my head sheepishly. He smiled and said, "That's better than I could have done." When he said this, I knew I could rely on myself as a writer.

My junior year in Mrs. Guillory's class was only the beginning of my journey towards loving English. The next year, my senior year, I was in Mrs. Smith's class.

writing style(?)
needed?

Is this sentence placed correctly?

were not

Jankower 2

She was a young, happy lady who had an ardent love for English. She showed us how awesome the English language was by teaching us Greek and Latin origins of words. [It was tedious but so interesting.] I diagrammed sentences for the first time in that class. I was always one to abhor grammar studies, but after learning how to diagram sentences, I realized how much fun it was. It was like solving a logic puzzle—figuring out where all the pieces go to make the big picture. Go figure—I liked diagramming! However, this was not what finally made me love English. Mrs. Smith kept explaining to my class the concept of how content and form must be analyzed back and forth when discussing connections in literary works. I remember trying so hard to understand this concept. One night I was working on an essay about courtly love, using specific examples from Geoffrey Chaucer's *The Canterbury Tales*. All of a sudden, I noticed how the metaphors and descriptions of the characters expressed the overall theme of courtly love. It was like a lightning bolt. I finally understood what made the great literary works masterpieces and their authors geniuses. It was not the content that made them great—it was the careful work of the authors, placing every word and phrase into an artistic weave of metaphors and juxtapositions that brought the deepest internal themes of our very lives. It was amazing. I could not believe how exciting these masterpieces were. The next day, I let Mrs. Smith read my Chaucer essay. She smiled and told me that I now understood what made her excited to teach every day.

I am an English Secondary Education major. Of course I want my writing to be exceptional. I want to be a good teacher. I want to set a good example for my students and have them hold high standards for themselves so that they can receive a good education. Every time I make a grammatical mistake when I am talking, my parents correct me and playfully tease me by saying, "And you want to be an English teacher?" Please do not misunderstand me. My parents are extremely supportive of my aspirations to be a teacher and think that I will be a good teacher. However, they remind me that I am not perfect. Even though it irritates me so, I finally realize why my parents correct me when I make those kinds of mistakes. It is not because they want me to be perfect. It is to show me that I can learn from my mistakes. By realizing my own mistakes, I can better understand myself as a writer and a speaker. I also realize that no one is perfect. It is possible to have high standards for one's self, but impossible to achieve perfection. By realizing this, I can put myself in the position of my future students. My goal as a teacher is not to make my students into grammatically correct robots; rather,

Margin annotations:

Is this okay? Don't think this is enough for a sentence.

This is the opposite of interesting

Love this, but it is not a finished sentence.

take out (?)

maybe worded another way

maybe make one sentence.

another wording (Now that I have realized)

it is to show them their potential as writers and guide them on their paths of finding their true voice.

I realize that I have a love/hate relationship with writing. Many times when I am given a writing assignment, I procrastinate until the night before the assignment is due before I write it. I keep pushing writing away, reluctant to look on the blank page and start writing. I hate those moments where I have difficulties thinking of *maybe use different wording* good ideas; my mind just stops. When those moments occur, I use that as an excuse to get something to eat or watch my favorite television program. When I have to return to my writing again after those "writer blocks," I start typing randomly on the keyboard out of frustration. Then, surprisingly, my ideas start coming back through those jumbled words. I remember how excited I get when a good idea comes to me. I love making connections with complex ideas. Sometimes, however, I have difficulties explaining those connections in the way that I want them. Even though I now understand how to relate content with form, I still have some difficulty writing how I think.

It was not until I had a group discussion in this class that I realized what was missing. It was my voice. That is what connects the writer to the reader. I realized that *in my writing* if I allowed my voice to dominate my writing, I would be able to connect my ideas to my readers. I just have one problem—what is my voice? What does it *sound* like? I feel that I am a generally formal writer that likes to explain ideas in detail. However, that is so boring. Why can I not be more daring in my writing? All this time, however, I have felt pretty confident in my writing. One day in a group discussion, ~~though~~, someone *however* told me that I sounded timid as a writer. This shocked and confused me. This person then explained that I was confident, but I was scared when my writing was given up for review. I was amazed at this insight. This person was right—I am confident in my writing until I have to give it up to someone else to look at. This is because I want the approval from my peers, especially from my teacher. It was then that I realized why I lacked a strong voice. It was not because my writing was not clean or my ideas were bad. It was because of my need for the approval of my superiors that I hide my voice and use the voice that I know is acceptable.

I realize now that one person can have many voices depending on the presence, or lack of presence, of an audience. My voice can be direct, meek, strong, soothing, energetic, polite, or polished. Many factors contribute to my voice: my family, my

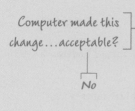

Computer made this
change...acceptable?

No

OK...

teachers, my friends, and I. No matter what my voice is at the moment, my voice does not define me. My writing does not define me. It is a way for people to connect to me.

Notes to Self: (& Peer)
— I think I need to make my transitions between paragraphs smoother. Any suggestions?
— Get rid of contractions — too casual
— Are ¶'s in a coherent order?
— Do I need a more definite conclusion?
— Anything I need to expand on? Leave out? Missing?

— Good paper, try to 're-word' a couple of sentences. Good ideas in paper. Try to restructure a couple of sentences along with the 'rewording'. Good job.

Final Draft

Jankower 1

Ashley Jankower

Ms. Busby

ENG 355.002

21 September 2006

Learning Who I Am as a Writer

Perfection is never achievable in writing, and it irritates me so much. All my life I have strived for perfection in everything I do. Look at me now—I am trying to explain how I feel in proper, formal English. Sometimes I do not feel as though I have a strong voice. I see other people in my writing class have original ideas and creative ways of expressing them. I wish I could do that. For some reason, I am so focused on what other people think of my writing that I lose my voice in my writing. When people look at me, they see an overachiever who does everything perfectly. The truth is I am embarrassed when I hear that. It gives the impression that

I have no soul—that I am different from everyone else. For some reason, I cannot stop striving for perfection.

My parents influenced me the most when it comes to my writing, particularly my father. I remember that I would always depend on my father to revise my papers before I turned them in to my teacher; of course, that meant that he would make them better. My father is a lawyer, so the revisions he made to my papers were very formal and detailed. After looking at those types of revisions many times, I started to imitate that style of writing. I found that I had longwinded sentences with plenty of prepositional phrases. I made sure that every detail was mentioned, just to make sure I had everything written that needed to be said. My father's flawless writing somewhat intimidated me. I fully entrusted my work in his hands. I could never trust myself to write a well developed essay.

To be honest, I did not always have a love for English. I hated reading and especially writing. It was not until my junior year, when I was in Mrs. Guillory's Advanced Placement English class that I began to trust myself with my writing. On the first day of class when I heard Mrs. Guillory's eloquently articulated speech, I was awestruck. I never realized how beautiful the English language could be. Her soothing tone made me so calm and at ease with myself. She challenged me to write timed essays almost every day. These essays were not perfect, but they helped me to trust myself as a writer. I remember my father asking me one day if I needed his help with an essay and I told him no; he was amazed and looked at my paper anyway. He asked me if I had written this myself, and I nodded my head sheepishly. He smiled and said, "That's better than I could have done." When he said this, I knew I could rely on myself as a writer.

My junior year in Mrs. Guillory's class was only the beginning of my journey towards loving English. The next year, my senior year, I was in Mrs. Smith's class. She was a young, happy lady who had an ardent love for English. She showed us how awesome the English language was by teaching us Greek and Latin origins of words. It was tedious but so interesting. I diagrammed sentences for the first time in that class. I was always one to abhor grammar studies, but after learning how to diagram sentences, I realized how much fun it was. It was like solving a logic puzzle—figuring out where all the pieces go to make the big picture. Go figure— I liked diagramming! However, this was not what finally made me love English.

Mrs. Smith kept explaining to my class the concept of how content and form must be analyzed back and forth when discussing connections in literary works. I remember trying so hard to understand this concept. One night I was working on an essay about courtly love, using specific examples from Geoffrey Chaucer's *The Canterbury Tales*. All of a sudden, I noticed how the metaphors and descriptions of the characters expressed the overall theme of courtly love. It was like a lightning bolt. I finally understood what made the great literary works masterpieces and their authors geniuses. It was not the content that made them great—it was the careful work of the authors, placing every word and phrase into an artistic weave of metaphors and juxtapositions that brought out the deepest internal themes of our very lives. It was amazing. I could not believe how exciting these masterpieces were. The next day, I allowed Mrs. Smith to read my Chaucer essay. She smiled and said to me, "Now you understand what makes me excited to teach every day."

I am an English Secondary Education major. Of course I want my writing to be exceptional. I want to be a good teacher. I want to set a good example for my students and have them hold high standards for themselves so that they can receive a good education. Every time I make a grammatical mistake when I am talking, my parents correct me and playfully tease me by saying, "And you want to be an English teacher?" Please do not misunderstand me. My parents are extremely supportive of my aspirations to be a teacher and think that I will be a good teacher. However, they remind me that I am not perfect. Even though it irritates me so, I finally realize why my parents correct me when I make those kinds of errors. It is not because they want me to be flawless when I speak or write; rather, it is to show me that I can learn from my mistakes. By realizing my imperfections, I can better understand myself as a writer and a speaker. I now understand that no one is perfect. It is possible to have high standards for one's self, but impossible to achieve perfection. Finally, I can put myself in the position of my future students; I understand the struggle and frustration that my future students will have. My goal as a teacher is not to make my students into grammatically correct robots; rather, it is to show them their potential as writers and guide them on their paths of finding their true voices.

I realize that I have a love/hate relationship with writing. Many times when I am given a writing assignment, I procrastinate until the night before the assignment is due before I write it. I keep pushing writing away, reluctant to look on the blank page and start writing. I hate those moments where I have difficulty thinking of good ideas; my mind just stops. When those moments occur, I use that as an excuse to get something to eat or watch my favorite television program. When I have to return to my writing again after those "writer's blocks," I start typing randomly on the keyboard out of frustration. Then, surprisingly, my ideas start coming back through those jumbled words. I remember how excited I get when a good idea comes to me. I love making connections with complex ideas. Sometimes, however, I have difficulty explaining those connections in the way that I want them. Even though I now understand how to relate content with form, I still have some difficulty in writing how I think.

It was not until I had a group discussion in this class that I realized what was missing in my writing. It was my voice. That is what connects the writer to the reader. I realized that if I allowed my voice to dominate my writing, I would be able to connect my ideas to my readers. I just have one problem—what is my voice? What does it *sound* like? I feel that I am a generally formal writer who likes to explain ideas in detail. However, that is so boring. Why can I not be more daring in my writing? All this time, however, I have felt pretty confident in my writing. One day in a group discussion, however, someone told me that I sounded timid as a writer. This shocked and confused me. This person then explained that I was confident, but I was scared when my writing was given up for review. I was amazed at this insight. This person was right—I am confident in my writing until I have to give it to someone else to review because I want the approval from my peers, especially from my teacher. It was then that I realized why I lack a strong voice. Even though my writing and ideas are clean and coherent, those are not important. My voice is weak because my need for my peers' approval hides the strength in my voice. I only use the voice that I know is acceptable.

I realize now that one person can have many voices depending on the presence, or lack of presence, of an audience. My voice mainly adapts to how I feel at the time of writing. It can be direct, meek, strong, soothing, energetic, polite, or harsh. No matter how hard I try, I will never be able to create the perfect voice because there is no such thing. Overall, my voice is unique to me. Many factors contribute to my voice: my family, my teachers, my friends, and my personality. In the end, I must depend on myself to develop my true voice. My voice represents who I am as a writer. The voice I give to my writing creates an image of me that my readers can see and hear. By allowing my voice to be free in my writing, I am finally able to make a bridge that connects my readers to me.

Questions for Discussing Ashley's Composing Process

1. Compare Ashley's first prewriting to her first draft. What ideas, information, and language from her prewriting appear in her draft? To what extent did her prewriting influence the organization, tone, and voice of her draft? How did her ideas change as she worked through her essay?

2. How did Ashley's thinking develop between her prewriting and her first draft?

3. Compare Ashley's second draft to her first draft and her prewriting. How has she revised her essay? What changes did she make in the content, organization, and language in revising her first draft? What did she keep from her first draft? How do you think she decided what to keep and what to change?

4. What do Ashley's questions and comments to her peer group about her second draft reveal about her own criticisms of her essay so far? How would you answer her questions? What other questions might she have asked her peer group?

5. How did Ashley change her essay between her second and final drafts? Have these changes improved her essay? Why or why not?

6. Describe Ashley's composing process as a whole. What did her planning and invention contribute to her paper? What decisions did she make in organizing and developing her thoughts and knowledge from draft to draft? What was Ashley trying to accomplish in her revisions? What are the strengths and weaknesses of her composing process for this essay?

7. Compare your usual composing process for writing a paper to Ashley's. What similarities and differences do you see between your approach to writing and Ashley's? What advantages does her process have over yours? What are the strengths of your process over Ashley's?

02 Reading and Writing

YOU READ A LOT IN A WRITING class. You make sense of your course syllabus and assignments, use your teacher's comments on a paper in revising that paper and composing your next paper, and respond to your classmates' papers. You analyze published texts (like those in this book). You refer to a grammar handbook, a dictionary, or a thesaurus to answer questions about sentence construction, word choice, spelling, punctuation, bibliography format, or page design. You read textbook chapters for ideas and strategies that you can use in your writing and to do well in quizzes and class discussions. Most importantly, you read your own writing, looking through your journal or blog and invention activities for material for an essay; analyzing a draft to see how you can make the paper more interesting, informative, and persuasive; and editing and proofreading your papers to improve the smaller details of writing, such as word choices, spelling, word endings, pronoun usage, and punctuation.

Reading as a Process

Like writing, reading is a process, and, like writing processes, your reading process changes with each situation, depending on what you are reading and why. People don't read textbooks, business contracts, detective novels, religious scripture, text messages from friends, love letters, or celebrity magazine articles in the same way or at the same speed. How you read a text is affected by your purposes for reading, by your interest in and familiarity with the subject and writer, and by the text's reading level. A marketing major reads an advertisement for a new computer differently than someone thinking about buying a computer or someone who works for a rival computer company or for a consumer protection association. A new or difficult reading assignment challenges you to make adjustments in your usual approaches to reading just as a difficult or unfamiliar writing assignment can challenge your usual process of writing.

Effective reading processes resemble effective writing processes. Both involve planning, drafting, revising, and consulting. We set goals for each reading of a text. We decide how we will read the text, what we want to get out of the reading, how the reading is related to what we know and have experienced, and what use we'll make of what we read. As we read, we compose a draft about the text in our minds, making predictions and decisions about its meaning, its point of view, its tone, the scope and importance of its ideas and information, and our opinions about the text. This draft gives a sense of the whole of what we are reading, and as we read each part of the text, we figure out how it is connected to the rest of the text. As we read we respond to the text. Are we enjoying it? How much do we agree with the writer? How does the text's meaning fit in with our knowledge, beliefs, and feelings? We continually make predictions about what we're reading (what it's about, what it will say, why it was written, and how we'll respond to it). We evaluate these predictions and the goals, plans, and expectations that we've formed as we read and make revisions in them, sometimes drastic revisions. We ask questions as we read, make more predictions, and elaborate on the draft in our heads, or sometimes abandon the draft if the text turns out to be very different from what we anticipated.

Revision continues as we think about what we have read, discuss the text with others, and question, strengthen, and change our impressions and thoughts about the text. The revision process sometimes requires us to reread all or part of the text, sometimes during our first reading of the text, sometimes afterward, as we try to determine the meaning of passages, how a passage relates to the rest of the text, and how the text relates to other works we have read and to our knowledge, experiences, beliefs, and worldviews. We also reread to notice aspects of the text that we couldn't see before; to savor passages we particularly enjoy; to think about surprising, troubling, or intriguing ideas in the paper; to memorize something we want to remember; to come up with counterarguments to claims we disagree with; to pick out what we might want to borrow from a text for a paper or presentation. Often the whole process of reading a text takes place quickly. But often we need to read a text intensively, analyze it, appreciate it, memorize from it, or write about it. In revising our writing, we need the same intensity. We need to read our own words critically. We engage in intensive reading when we are not satisfied with our first drafts and our first impressions of a text.

Consultation, talking to others about what we've read and listening to their responses about a text, is also important in intensive reading. We test each others' drafts of the reading as we test and revise our own drafts, sometimes strengthening our ideas and responses as we agree and disagree with other readings, sometimes making small or large changes in our reading. Think about discussing a movie with friends when the group disagrees about whether they liked the movie or about what happened in the movie. Don't you sometimes change your mind about the movie because of the discussion or get a better grasp of what you liked or disliked about the film?

EFFECTIVE NOTE-TAKING. Another connection between reading and writing is that reading often works best with a pencil in your hand. You can use writing to figure out the meaning of an elusive text and to begin to work out your ideas and feelings about the text. The most common kind of "writing to read" is annotating. Write in the margins and between the lines of the text, highlighting key words and passages; noting your opinions, reactions, and questions about something you read; and jotting down ideas, implications, applications, arguments, and connections to other ideas as you read.

Following is an example of annotations of a passage from Neil Postman's *Technopoly: The Surrender of Culture to Technology.* This passage is taken from "Invisible Technologies," a chapter that describes language, statistics, IQ tests, and opinion polls as invisible technologies that shape our perceptions of the world.

There are several kinds of annotations shown here. Some point out rhetorical features of the passage, such as the introduction, the language, its central question and thesis, and the conclusion. Some notes focus on the meanings of the passage—its main idea, the meaning of key words and phrases, and terms that are puzzling or that the reader needs to define. Other annotations are personal or emotional responses and questions that connect passages to the reader's life. Some notes question or challenge the claims in the passage or mention concerns that Neil Postman has not discussed. Finally, some notes take a writer's perspective, pointing out issues that the reader might want to write about. Several of these notations are reminders to do more thinking or research about issues raised in the passage.

And there is another point, which in fact is the core of this chapter. Some technologies come in disguise. Rudyard Kipling called them "technologies in repose." They do not look like technologies, and because of that they do their work, for good or ill, without much criticism or even awareness. This applies not only to IQ tests and to polls and to all systems of ranking and grading but to credit cards, accounting procedures, and achievement tests. It applies in the educational world to what are called "academic courses," as well. A course is a technology for learning. I have "taught" about two hundred of them and do not know why each one lasts exactly fifteen weeks, or why each meeting lasts exactly one hour and fifty minutes. If the answer is that this is done for administrative convenience, then a course is a fraudulent technology. It is put forward as a desirable structure for learning when in fact it is only a structure for allocating space, for convenient record-keeping, and for control of faculty time. The point is that the origin of and raison d'être for a course are concealed from us. We come to believe it exists for one reason when it exists for quite another. One characteristic of those who live in a Technopoly is that they are largely unaware of both the origins and the effects of their technologies.[7]

Margin annotations:

- Introduces concept of tech in disguise
- What does "repose" metaphor add to "disguise"?
- Main idea
- Stops short of arguing the claim but clearly believes it
- Certainly convenient for me in many ways, and for students? What alternatives?
- Harsh!
- How can you decide which structure is desirable? Possible paper topic
- Back to disguise and what it hides
- Conclusion—how disguised technologies affect us
- Endnote on SAT exam as disguised tech—another paper topic

USING A READING JOURNAL. A reading journal is another common "writing-to-read" tool, giving you a place to summarize and quote from what you read and to record the reactions, questions, memories, and ideas that come to you in your reading. Most of the invention activities in Chapter 1, in fact, can be used as writing-to-read activities. You can use freewriting, looping, brainstorming, clustering, and heuristics to work out the meaning of a difficult passage, to express your thoughts and feelings about the text, and to find and begin to develop ideas from your reading for a paper, a presentation, or an up-coming test. Outlining a text can help you isolate and clarify the main ideas of a work, to see the structure of the text, and to work out how the ideas are connected. Finally writing to read makes it easy to remember what you read (and how you responded to the text) and provides a handy reference for reviewing your readings.

Here is an example of a reading journal entry on Nisha Ramachandran's article, "Working Life," in Chapter 9:

> "Working Life" tries to juggle two opposite ideas about college jobs. For most of the article, Nisha R. talks about jobs as something students do because they can't afford not to and as educational if you can get into an internship. Then at the end, she talks about jobs causing low grades and dropping classes. So what kind of advice is Nisha giving? Find a job that pays three times minimum wage, that's related to your career, and only involves a few hours a week? Yeah, right. What kinds of jobs like these are out there for freshmen still deciding on a major? How realistic is this essay?

This journal entry not only briefly summarizes "Working Life" and offers a brief critical analysis of Ramachandran's article; it also holds the seeds of several possible papers: an analysis of "Working Life," an analytical or argumentative essay about the problem of balancing work and school, or a research paper about the availability of student internships.

Using the SQ3R Approach

At some point in your education, you were probably taught the SQ3R approach to reading—survey, question, read, recite, and review (maybe with *relate* added as a fourth *R;* let's call it *SQ3R+R*). SQ3R is similar to the writing process described in the previous chapter. Surveying and questioning are like planning and invention in writing, reading is similar to drafting, and reciting, reviewing, and relating parallel revising in writing. SQ3R takes an active, process approach to reading and usually encourages students to write as they read, especially if you use SQ3R as a recursive process and not a rigid, step-by-step process. Because it takes a process approach that emphasizes questioning in reading, you can make SQ3R+R into a flexible framework not only for reading for comprehension but for different kinds of critical reading. You can adapt the SQ3R+R frame to fit your purposes by asking different questions and altering the ways in which you survey, read, review, recite, and relate to a text.

SURVEY. In surveying or previewing a text, you usually begin by reading the text's title and headings; scanning the introduction, conclusions, and illustrations; and going over any headnotes, questions, and other material about the text that appear before and after it. You may also analyze where the text was published—a magazine cover and table of contents, for example, can reveal much about the interests, purposes, and intended audiences of the publication. If there are no headings, skim the first sentences of the text's paragraphs. Determine the genre or kind of text you are reading (e.g., textbook, news article, fictional story, autobiographical essay, editorial, speech, academic article, how-to article). From your survey you should form rough hypotheses about the text. What is the subject? What position or central idea does the piece take on that subject? What is the author's purpose and intended audience? How is the text organized? What tone and point-of-view does it take?

For a good close reading, however, you should also survey the knowledge, beliefs, and interests that you bring to the subject of the text you are reading. For example, think about what you know about the subject and the author and what experiences you have had that may be relevant to this reading, then predict how this text might affect what you know and believe. Consider your reasons for reading this text and how they will affect what you should be looking for and recalling in your survey. It usually takes only a few minutes to survey a text, but those few minutes can make the rest of your reading easier and more productive. If you need to do a particularly intensive or critical reading or if you will be writing about a text, you can incorporate freewriting, brainstorming, or other invention activities into your survey of your knowledge and ideas.

QUESTION. Questioning should occur throughout your reading process. What you ask as you read should be guided by your goals for reading the text. As part of your survey of the text, you can begin asking questions about the text and jotting down questions to ask as you read. As you read, more questions should occur to you. Often you should form a central question to guide your reading and use your survey of the features of the text to generate specific questions. The answers to these early questions should prompt new questions. The title, the introduction, the conclusion, and each heading, illustration, and key term can suggest separate questions that you expect the text to answer. These questions will reflect the expectations that you have formed about the text. Such questions are important for understanding the meaning of a text—its main claims, ideas, arguments, and evidence. But as a critical reader, you should also question why the subject and claims of the text are important, how the text relates to your life and interests, how the text connects to other works you have read, and how you might connect it to what you are writing about. Your questions will depend on your purposes as a reader. If you are reading a text as a model or example to help you write a similar paper, reading a classmate's draft, or reading a rough draft that you have written, your questions will focus more on the organization, style, tone, diction, audience, and purposes of the work than if you are reading a work that you will be analyzing for an essay you are writing or if the work is a potential source for a paper.

In addition to the questions that you make up yourself, you may also use heuristics to guide your questioning of a text. Each heuristic described in Chapter 1 can be used in your reading process. For example, with Burke's pentad, you can ask what is the central act or action the text discusses or describes, who or what are the major and minor agents propelling the action, how can the scene (time and place) be described, what are the causes or reasons behind the actions, and how the actions are accomplished. Using the ratios as a heuristic, you can ask how the purposes determine the action and agencies (or vice versa, how the purposes are shaped by the action and agencies), how the setting affects the agents, and so on. Frequently you can get more out of a heuristic like Burke's pentad and ratios in discussions. You can also use other invention activities such as freewriting, clustering, listing, and journaling to think of questions, respond to questions, and respond to your reading in less structured ways. Your teacher may supply questions to ask when you read a text, and this textbook provides questions and activities for reading each selection.

READ. Reading actively, the third element of SQ3R+R, usually is more effective with a pencil in your hand. Active reading calls for you to annotate your text, to underline and highlight passages, and write notes and questions in the margins. Underline or highlight key terms and passages, but don't overdo this part of your annotation. You won't be able to quickly find an important passage that you want to mention in class or quote or paraphrase in a paper if a third of your text is in yellow. Note passages that you find confusing, troubling, or surprising, maybe with a question mark ("?") or exclamation point ("!"), to mark for rereading and for discussing with others. Use your own words to answer the questions that you have formed and write down new questions as they occur, especially when you encounter a difficult or troubling passage, or to form new hypotheses about the text, especially if your early expectations about the text were mistaken. Some questions should challenge the author and the text. How well does the text explain and back up its claims and assumptions? Has the author forgotten, ignored, or left out any important arguments or facts?

What might an opponent say in response to some of the writer's arguments and claims? Can you think of additional reasons and evidence that support the text's claims? Can you apply the ideas in the text to other situations, other problems?

Writing on the text itself isn't always possible, however, if you're reading from a book or magazine borrowed from a friend or the library, for example, or if you're reading from a rented textbook or a computer screen. If that's the case, get out a notebook or open a computer file and take notes. In fact, you may want to keep a reading journal to go beyond what you can write in annotations. Here you can address questions, explore associations and connections with other readings and knowledge, recount memories inspired by the reading, and argue against or in support of the text at length. A double-entry or dialogue journal is especially useful for reading. You create a double entry journal by creating two columns on a page or in a computer file or writing on facing pages in a notebook. On one side you write down important words, phrases, and sentences and paraphrase or summarize important or interesting ideas and details from your reading. "Notice what you notice," suggests Ann Berthoff, who invented the double-entry journal. On the other side you write down your questions, responses, memories, associations, and agreements and disagreements with what you have written on the first side. Often readers write on the first side as they read and come back to write their responses a little later, giving their ideas about the text time to percolate.

RECITE. Reciting in SQ3R+R involves remembering and summarizing a text in your own words and then checking your summary against the text for accuracy. This part of the process is particularly important when you need to understand and memorize textbook material. SQ3R discussions generally recommend that students recite as they read, taking a section of a text at a time, dividing the text into sections that are easier to memorize from. Although memory is important for your performance in class discussions, reading quizzes, and oral presentations, reading to memorize is less important in a writing class than in most other classes, so formal reciting of what you read isn't usually necessary with most of your readings. But the summarizing at the heart of reciting is still important in your reading in a writing class, especially texts that you will be writing about or discussing in class. In summarizing a text, you recognize the main ideas of what you have read, connect the ideas to each other, and put them in an intelligent order. Rephrasing those ideas into words of your own forces you to understand the text more fully than word-for-word memorization. You can't rephrase another text without connecting what you have read to your own ways of thinking. So most critical readings of a text begin by summarizing what the text means

> **" In summarizing a text, you recognize the main ideas of what you have read, connect the ideas to each other, and put them in an intelligent order. "**

and checking that summary against the text. Class discussions of readings usually begin with students' summaries (sometimes in answer to a reading quiz) and move on to other questions about the text, and most essay assignments about other texts or research involve some summarizing. When you are responding to a classmate's draft, your summary of the paper can tell the writer if the paper is expressing her ideas clearly and often help the writer get a clearer sense of the points she is making.

REVIEW. Reviewing your reading not only helps you recall the text more accurately and fully but also gives you an opportunity to test, develop, and revise your understanding, criticisms, and insights about what you have read. You may see whether your initial interpretation and first impressions of the text hold up to closer inspection, ask new questions about the text, and probe more deeply into the questions you have asked. Intensive, critical reading almost always involves rereading at least the critical passages of the text and often the entire work. It's a mistake to assume that only weak readers need to reread texts or that good writers always read quickly and are able to understand and recall what they have read after one reading. Just as writers spend more time revising works that they find challenging or important to them, readers spend more time reviewing difficult texts and works that are interesting and important to them. When a scientist finds an article important to her research, for example, she rereads it many times, examining the article's results and conclusions, studying the research methods, and thinking out the implications the article has for her own research. Similarly, when a text is important for one of your writing projects, you shouldn't be satisfied with your first impressions about the text. Review is usually your best opportunity to play the doubting and believing games with a text, looking for weaknesses and imagining what a hostile reader would see in it but also working out the implications, applications, and possibilities that a text offers from a sympathetic perspective.

Consultation and discussion can be as important in a review as rereading. Two or more readers, working together, can get much more out of a text than they can separately. Even talking about a text with someone who hasn't read it can help you gain insight about the text that you might not discover alone, especially if you are speaking to someone good at asking questions, such as your teacher or a tutor in the writing center.

Writing also is important in review. In your journal or in invention activities such as free-writing, you can reflect about your readings, test and rethink your early interpretations and opinions about a text or develop those ideas in more depth and detail, and think out the implications of the text for your writings and other readings. Returning to the text itself and to what you wrote as you surveyed and read the text after a time and writing some more often leads to new questions and new insights about the text, a re-visioning of the work and your response to it.

RELATE. The extra R in the SQ3R+R model, *relate*, asks you to make connections between what you read and your knowledge, experiences, and interests; other texts that you have read; and your writing. You may begin making these connections when you preview the text and continue to make and strengthen them as you read and review the text. Or you may make many connections only upon later reflection, after coming to an understanding of a text's meaning and dedicating much of your review to relating what you have written beyond the text. Relating what you have read to your life and knowledge is important for you to enjoy, appreciate, and remember what you have read, and making such connections helps you develop personal insights into the text and a more individual reading. When you relate the text to other texts that you have read, you apply your reading to a world of ideas and experiences and bring the writer and yourself into conversation with other writers, raising and answering questions with each other, agreeing, differing, and revising. Often the connections that you make between two or more writers will lead you to new ideas, to make your own contributions to the conversation among these writers. Sometimes, what seems like a minor statement in the text you are reading will become important because of the implications that that statement has for your life or for your readings of other texts.

Finally, you need to relate what you read to your writing. What does the text say, suggest, and imply about the questions that you have for a writing assignment? What do you have to say in response to what the text says or implies on this matter? How might you make use of the text in your writing? Again invention activities such as journaling, freewriting, looping, brainstorming, and heuristics, sometimes in consultation with others, are important in exploring and developing possible connections of a text to your life, other works, and your papers.

Little has been said here about reading for pleasure, but when you enjoy what you are reading, understanding and critical reading come more easily. You should enjoy reading some of the texts in this book with little trouble because you relate to the experiences in a story or essay or are interested in the topics and issues that the writer is discussing. But you should look for ways to take pleasure in other texts that don't seem interesting to you at first. Many of the reading strategies described here can help you enjoy what you are reading. Relating what you read to your life, your interests, your knowledge, and your beliefs; talking about what you have read with others; and using critical reading strategies to help you discover what is interesting about a text can make it enjoyable. Reading and writing always involve work, but finding ways to enjoy what you are reading and writing is one of the keys to success in college.

Practicing SQ3R+R: A Reading and Writing Activity

Practice SQ3R+R with Judith Ortiz Cofer's "The Myth of the Latin Woman: I Just Met a Girl Named Maria" in Chapter 4. This activity is just one way of applying the elements of SQ3R+R to a critical reading of a text, but by the end of this activity, you will have formed a thorough interpretation of and response to Cofer's essay and have a sense of how you can adapt this approach to other readings for this class.

Spend about fifteen or twenty minutes surveying Cofer's essay and your own knowledge and beliefs about Cofer's subject. In surveying Cofer's essay, start with the title. What predictions can you make about the subject of Cofer's essay and her attitude toward this subject from the title? What does the word *myth* suggest about the essay? How about the quotation from a song from *West Side Story* as a subtitle? What does the fact that the essay is included in a chapter on identity suggest about the ideas in "The Myth of the Latin Woman"?

Read the headnote and the questions that follow Cofer's essay. What predictions about the content of "The Myth of the Latin Woman" can you make from these texts? Now read the opening and concluding paragraphs. Cofer starts her essay with a personal anecdote and ends by quoting one of her own poems but does not state an explicit thesis. Considering the essay's title and introduction, predict the most likely thesis that Cofer may be arguing. What predictions can you

make about how Cofer develops and organizes her argument after reading her conclusion? Now take a minute or two to scan the essay, focusing especially on the first sentences of her paragraphs. What claims and facts do you notice? What words and phrases stand out? How do these words affect your predictions about Cofer's essay? After completing this survey, what questions do you expect Cofer's essay to answer?

Next, do a five- or ten-minute freewriting about what you know, feel, and believe about the subjects of "The Myth of the Latin Woman." Consider how you think Cofer's essay will connect with what you know. What do you expect to learn from her essay? Do you expect her essay to fit comfortably with your beliefs? Do you think Cofer will challenge or reinforce some of your beliefs?

Next, look over the questions you've formed in your survey as well as the questions at the end of "The Myth of the Latin Woman." Read and annotate Cofer's essay with these questions in mind. Don't write or underline too much; one or two notes on each paragraph may be enough. Your annotations should focus on the questions that you bring to the text and new questions that arise as you read, but if you read something particularly interesting, unexpected, or confusing, make a note of it.

When you finish reading "The Myth of the Latin Woman" for the first time, without looking at the essay, write a four- or five-sentence paragraph or sentence outline summarizing Cofer's essay, in your own words. Then, spend another minute or two writing about your reaction and opinions to the essay. What predictions from your survey held up? What surprised you as you read?

For your review of "The Myth of the Latin Woman," discuss your ideas about Cofer's essay and share what you have written with two or three classmates. Select someone to take notes for the group as you talk. Discuss the similarities and differences in your summaries and responses and try to clarify each other's confusing passages, referring back to Cofer's essay. Spend part of your discussion relating Cofer's essay to your own writing. What did you notice in her essay that you might be able to use in your own writing? Then, as a group, write a brief report about your discussion. Summarize Cofer's main ideas, your group's responses to her essay (including important disagreements about her essay), and suggest a couple of writing techniques from Cofer's essay that you might use in your own writing.

If your teacher makes this exercise an in-class activity, he or she may ask each group to give an oral report of their reading of "The Myth of the Latin Woman" and continue the discussion and review of Cofer's essay with the entire class. Take a couple of minutes at the end of this activity to write how your discussions have revised your first reading or draft of Cofer's essay.

Research and Writing

IT'S A MISTAKE TO ASSUME THAT the only writing project that requires research is a research paper. Most writing—even fiction, poetry, and autobiography—involves research. Although few selections in this book are research articles, most include quotations, paraphrases, and data from books, articles, interviews, and the Internet. Sometimes research is woven throughout a selection. Sometimes a writer only occasionally quotes an authority, cites a statistic, or provides an example from outside reading to connect her thoughts and experiences to an outside world of ideas and information. As part of your invention process, consider whether research would improve your paper. Even a personal essay can benefit from looking at photographs and diaries, visiting a place from your past, talking to people who knew you when, or reading sources that discuss the time and place of your experiences.

When extensive research is required for a documented paper, some students treat writing like sewing a quilt. They select and stitch together material from several sources, threading their quotations and paraphrases with an introduction, conclusion, and transitions. Instead, imagine the research writer as a bee that flies from flower to flower taking in nectar and transforming it into honey. The bee selects its flowers, drinks in their nectars, combines them with its own chemicals, and creates something new. Similarly, experienced writers take in information and insights from many sources, question and analyze their sources, and combine their own knowledge and ideas with their research. Their writing, as a result, reflects the individuality of their research *and* their own thinking.

Your opinion is important in research writing. Perhaps a teacher in the past has warned you not to include your own opinions in a research paper. That restriction often makes sense for inexperienced writers just learning how to research. But in academic, professional, and other situations, you frequently need to do more than just report your research. You often need to critique that research and apply it to new situations to make informed decisions and compose persuasive, insightful arguments.

Applying Reading and Writing Processes to Research Writing

Research writing requires effective critical reading and writing processes. You should survey, question, read, summarize, review, and relate as you select and read your sources and plan, draft, revise, consult, and edit as you write. Adjust your writing process to relate the voices and knowledge of your sources to your own voice, thoughts, and knowledge. You still need invention activities such as freewriting and heuristics to decide on your topic, explore your thoughts about this subject as you learn more about it, and decide on the central claim that you will argue. Think about your purpose and audience as you draft and revise to arrive at a clear, intelligent, persuasive vision of how everything that you have read is connected. Your editing must include decisions on proper and effective quotation, paraphrasing, and documentation of sources and avoidance of plagiarism.

Finding a Topic and Creating a Research Question

Before you do much research, you need to decide on a topic and a research question about that topic for your paper. Your research question will guide your critical reading process for selecting and reading sources as well as your writing process. Without this question, you'll waste a lot of time on sources that do not tell you what you need to know or fit with what you want to say.

A good research question will reflect curiosity to know more about your topic with readers' interest in an important moral, political, social, or academic issue. Good questions are often "why" or "how" questions about causes and effects or about problems and possible solutions. For "College and Allowance" in Chapter 8, for example, Lauren Silverman asked a problem/solution question: What problems might the cost of attending college cause for students, and how can students cope with these problems? This question is personally important to Silverman as she prepares for college and relates to readers' interest in the expense of higher education. Lisa Nakamura's "Head Hunting in Cyberspace" in Chapter 4 is driven by her curiosity about how race affects people's online behavior. Kalyn Guidry's "The French Language: The Heart of Louisiana" in Chapter 7 asks why French is important to Cajun culture in Louisiana. Each question is shaped by the writer's interests and sense of what readers will find interesting and important. Invention activities, such as listing possible topics and questions, freewriting, and brainstorming with others, can help you find a good topic, find interesting questions, and discover what people argue about when this topic comes up.

Once you settle on a research question, you can develop a research plan. To find answers to her question, Silverman interviewed college students about their financial situations. Nakamura investigated an important chat space run by African Americans and read articles about race in cyberspace. Guidry found sources on Cajun culture and the influence of languages on other cultures. The answer to your central question will become the thesis that you will explain and argue in your paper, so the question needs to push you to form an opinion and take a position that some people may disagree with. Be flexible with your question. You often need to revise your central question as you read and write, and sometimes your reading and thinking will lead you to another more important or interesting question. Deciding on a topic and a question may require some preliminary research. Browsing reference books, Web sites, news sources, and databases like *LexisNexis* or *JSTOR* can acquaint you with key information about your topic and with important questions and issues on your subject. Talking about your interest in a topic with classmates, your teacher, a writing center tutor, or someone with expertise about your subject can reveal issues that will engage you and others.

Initially, you may choose a question that is too big, a question that might take a book to answer. Perhaps Guidry began with a question about the uniqueness of Cajun culture in general, a huge question. But for this essay, she focused on the question of the influence of the French language on the culture and character of Cajuns in Louisiana. Her more focused question addresses the broader question, but focusing on one important feature of Cajun culture kept Guidry's research project to a manageable size so that she could discuss her question in some depth, with interesting details for her readers. Similarly, because Nakamura focused on one Web site instead of trying to cover all of cyberspace, her discussion of the effects of racial attitudes is more detailed, more personal, more probing, and more interesting.

Choosing and Evaluating Print and Online Sources

Once you know your research question, you can begin finding and evaluating possible sources. Using a search engine to find Web sites on your topic should be part of your search, but, as vast as the World Wide Web is, you cripple your research if you rely on it alone. For many topics, the best sources are books, journals, and magazines that are unavailable online, and some of the most valuable online sources are not available on the Internet. Remember, one of the reasons that first-year composition courses assign research papers is to familiarize you with the resources, reference materials, government documents, and online databases available in your library that you will need for future research projects. Composition handbooks often describe dozens of print and online reference works that you can find in most libraries. And reference librarians in your library should be eager to point you toward the best reference materials for your topic.

One of the best ways to find good sources is to consult someone knowledgeable about your subject and ask for recommendations of what to read. If you are interviewing someone as part of your research, ask her to recommend readings. Textbooks, encyclopedia articles, magazine articles, and books on a subject often include a list of recommended readings. You can also often find recommendations on the Internet: try typing the name of your topic with the word *bibliography* or *syllabus* in a search engine (to see what sources professors teaching classes related to your topic are assigning and suggesting). When you read one source, notice what sources the writer cites and what she says about them to decide whether you should look at some of her sources yourself.

SELECTING USEFUL AND CREDIBLE SOURCES. As you find sources, begin to evaluate and select the most useful and credible sources for your research question. Rather than pick the first sources that you find on your subject, decide which sources are worth your and your readers' time. How relevant are these sources to your research question? Should you rely on the information, generalities, and judgments of these authorities in forming your opinions? Will readers believe that your sources are credible and trustworthy and see you as a reliable and knowledgeable researcher? You might consult others for opinions about an authority's trustworthiness and the effect it could have on your credibility with readers. A quick preliminary survey and questioning of a source can help you decide whether to examine that source more closely or put it aside, although you'll need to do more critical reading to decide how it helps you answer your research question and how you might use the source in your paper.

CHECKING THE INTEGRITY AND CREDIBILITY OF A SOURCE.
Consider your subject, purpose, and audience as you survey possible sources to determine whether they will help you answer your research question and if they will be credible to your audience. This analysis can help you make quick decisions to look more closely at some sources and ignore others. Although there is no one-size-fits-all formula that you can apply to all sources on all topics, a brief survey of a source's date of publication, its place of publication, and the credentials of the author will often tell you whether a source might be useful. Because library catalogs and most bibliographies provide a source's date and place of publication and because you can find information and opinions about authors and sources on the Internet, in online databases, and reference books in the library, you can conduct much of your selection process quickly, without even putting your hands on many sources. The library catalog page about the book *The Center Will Hold: Critical Perspectives on Writing Center Scholarship* pictured here provides all the information you need for the works cited page in a paper: title, editors (Michael A. Pemberton and Joyce Kinkead), city of publication (Logan, Utah), publisher (Utah State University Press), and date of publication (2003). In addition, the catalog page shown here gives the table of contents for this collection, listing the titles and authors of all the chapters in this book. Library databases like *Lexis-Nexis* and *JSTOR* also provide all the bibliographic information you need for the works cited page and often other information that you can use to evaluate a potential source. *JSTOR's* listing of Nancy Maloney Grimm's article "Rearticulating the Work of the Writing Center" has links to a description of the article and a listing of other articles by Grimm.

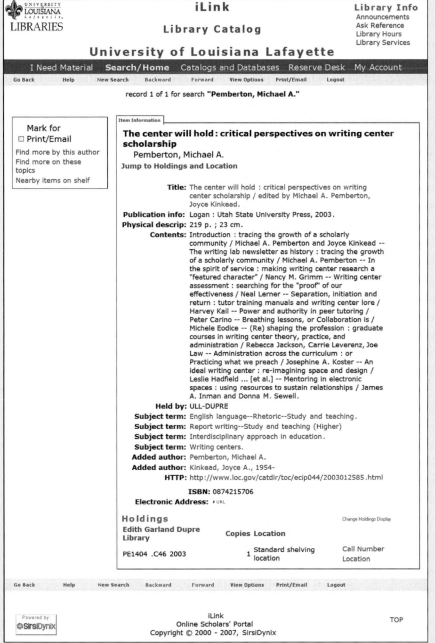

CHECKING THE DATE OF A SOURCE.
In most research, it is important to use recent sources—especially when you are searching for facts. You wouldn't, for example, rely on maps and statistics from 1960 in a paper about parking problems on your campus today (although old maps might give you a historical perspective about your campus' parking situation). But there is no magic date for eliminating sources. A 1990 article on computers or global warming

would be considered old for most research questions, but a 1990 article on Shakespeare or the Civil War is fairly recent. Also, a research paper about a historical topic, such as the arguments Americans made for and against slavery in the nineteenth century, is enhanced by sources from the time, such as newspaper articles, editorial cartoons, and political pamphlets, that you might find in the library or in an online archive.

If you are interested in a source for its expert opinions and analyses about your topic, the date may be less crucial than it is if you are using a source for claims of fact. The arguments of past writers, even from centuries ago, may have important insights and be persuasive authorities on many subjects in literary studies, history, religion, and other areas. Writers today still quote John Milton's seventeenth-century essay "Areopagetica" in essays about censorship and the ancient Greek philosophers Plato and Aristotle in discussions about ethics, rhetoric, and even politics when their statements are relevant to a writer's issue. Recent arguments, however, have the advantages of access to more information, discussion, and arguments about the topic and awareness of questions of interest to readers today. For these reasons, the terrorist attacks of September 11, 2001, instantly outdated many (though not all) books and articles on terrorism, government spending, international relations, Middle Eastern politics, and other subjects.

CHECKING AN AUTHOR'S KNOWLEDGE AND EXPERTISE. Whether a writer has knowledge and expertise in a subject should be one of your main concerns when you examine an author's credentials. Readers usually give greater authority to scholars and journalists who specialize on a topic, although experts have less credibility when they write outside their areas of expertise. For example, because he has no special expertise in health, Linus Pauling has been criticized for using his authority as a Nobel Prize-winning physicist to advocate megadoses of vitamin C as a cold remedy. Errol Morris' documentary *Mr. Death: The Rise and Fall of Fred A. Leuchter, Jr.* critiques the expertise of an authority often cited in Holocaust denial arguments. Leuchter uses his expertise as an engineer of prison electric chairs and gas chambers to try to persuade audiences that Nazi Germany could not have murdered six million Jews. Morris, however, shows that Leuchter's ignorance of forensic research methods, Nazi records, Nazi technology, and the German language led him to tragically wrong conclusions.

In judging the expertise and reliability of your writers and interview subjects, you should ask yourself how you can tell whether the person knows what she is talking about. A quick background check of the author and publisher or Web site of your source may eliminate some sources immediately and point to promising sources. Books and journals often provide information about their authors, and Web sites sometimes provide links to information about their writers and sponsors. Still, sometimes it isn't wise to rely entirely on the source itself for this information. Using a search engine, you can conduct a quick Internet search for information about the writer and opinions about his work. The library has reference books, such as the *Book Review Index* and various *Who's Who* books and online databases, with biographical information on authors and reviews of books that you are considering. A composition handbook or a reference librarian can suggest references to check the background of your sources.

The place of publication is another clue about the credibility of a source. A book published by a university press or an article in an academic journal is more credible than an article in a popular magazine or a book from a popular press because university presses and academic journals usually ask experts on a subject to read submissions, suggest revisions, and recommend what deserves to be published. But for some subjects, texts for wider audiences are more accessible, readable, and up-to-date than those written for specialists. It would be difficult to write a research paper about recent issues and events such as the War in Iraq or Hurricane Katrina without heavy reliance on journalists for sources. Major newspapers, magazines, and commercial book publishers have staffs of editors and fact-checkers who try to ensure that articles are accurate and their sources of information are reliable. You can investigate the reputation of a newspaper, magazine, or popular press on the Internet and by consulting others such as your teacher.

Print sources and sources in library databases are usually easier to evaluate than Web sites because a network of editors, reviewers, fact-checkers, and librarians decides what to publish and what to purchase for a library. The material published on most Web sites is seldom given such scrutiny, although there are many exceptions. The Internet is an important distributor of both useful information and arguments and of misinformation and deliberate distortion. Even the founder of the online encyclopedia *Wikipedia* warns students not to use *Wikipedia* as a source for research papers because of inaccuracies in some of its articles. Although many Web sites are honest and informative about their agendas and biases, some Web sites misleadingly present themselves as neutral, objective, or scientific to gain readers' trust. So before you decide to cite a Web

> **&& Although many Web sites are honest and informative about their agendas and biases, some Web sites misleadingly present themselves as neutral, objective, or scientific to gain readers' trust. &&**

site as an authority on your subject, get information about the site and see what others have to say about it.

CONSIDERING THE FAIRNESS AND BIASES OF A SOURCE. Obviously, you need to be aware of the biases and fairness of your sources. Bias and fairness are separate but related issues in evaluating a source. A writer's views about subjects from politics, religion, economics, and sexuality to animal rights, smoking, fashion, and child rearing cannot help but influence how he sees an issue; what questions he asks (and fails to ask); what evidence, arguments, and sources he takes seriously; and what he ignores. Sometimes a writer's biases can lead him to write unfair, distorted, and manipulative reports and arguments.

But writers with strong biases and commitments often write honestly, fairly, and carefully on their issues. It's not necessarily wise or practical to limit your research to unbiased sources. For example, if you are writing about women's rights, does it make sense to ignore sources that support equality for women? For a paper on government policy, does it make sense to ignore writers who are deeply committed to democratic values in favor of writers uncommitted to democracy? Rather than quickly dismissing a source because it has a bias, try to judge a source to see whether it presents fair and open-minded arguments and reporting, whatever the interests and commitments of the writer. But when a source's biases lead her to employ questionable logic and evidence, distort opponents' arguments, ignore evidence and arguments that challenge her positions, attack the character of those who disagree with her, and appeal to her readers' prejudices, you should look for other sources. Fair writers try to avoid distorting and ignoring facts and ideas that disagree with their opinions. Open-minded writers reexamine their knowledge, assumptions, and beliefs and are willing to change their minds, and, as a result, they command more respect.

It is wise to select sources that reflect a range of perspectives rather than sources that represent a single ideology or way of thinking. When your argu-

ment relies heavily on expert opinion, consider how your readers may evaluate the knowledge, fairness, and good will of your authorities. Conservative radio commentator Rush Limbaugh, for example, has great credibility with conservative audiences, but his statements usually anger liberals. Independents are unlikely to accept the authority of Limbaugh or liberal Maureen Dowd without question. So if you are writing on a political issue, you should cite authorities with a range of political perspectives and usually avoid obvious political partisans for more open-minded writers. With a little background research about a journal, Web site, or book publisher, you can discover its ideological perspective and intended audience: For example, *The National Review* and the Cato Institute Web site are conservative publications; *Ms.* and *Sign* are feminist publications; and *Commonweal* is a liberal Catholic magazine.

One advantage of the Internet, however, is that nonmainstream perspectives are more available than they are in print. Many groups and individuals use the Internet to publish information and arguments that are ignored or undercovered by mainstream media, and your paper may be better informed and more interesting with their perspectives. But you need to recognize sources that are not mainstream and decide whether they actually do have something to contribute to your research. These sources may lack credibility with audiences of mainstream sources for good reason, so scrutinize their evidence and arguments closely. If you use a nonmainstream source in your research, give your readers information about the source and the perspective it represents.

You cannot know for certain whether you should use a source without looking at it to evaluate the quality of its research and reasoning and to see how well it addresses your research questions. A brief overview of the title, headings, table of contents, bibliography, index, tables, and illustrations, and a quick skimming of the text can answer questions about a document's readability, intelligence, fairness, credibility, and relevance to your research question. A critical survey usually indicates in a few minutes how useful a source will be, although you may not know the value of a source until you examine its assumptions, logic, evidence, language, and emotional appeals more closely.

INFORMING YOUR READERS ABOUT YOUR SOURCES. The information that you learn about your sources is research that you may include in your papers. Writers often include information about the background, expertise, and biases of their sources. "David Boaz of the conservative Cato Institute explains some of the most important reasons behind President Bush's Social Security reform plan." *The New York Times*, in a report based on anonymous White House sources, ..." "In the National Marriage Project's annual report, Professor Barbara Dafoe Whitehead of Rutgers University argues . . . ." Including this information can have several benefits. If you have strong sources, sharing information about your sources' credentials should make your arguments more convincing and help persuade readers that you are a knowledgeable and trustworthy writer on your topic. Information about your sources also helps readers evaluate your research and decide what to believe considering the biases of your sources. You may have been careful to include conservative and liberal or mainstream and nonmainstream or U.S. and foreign sources in your research, and you should want your readers to realize how broad your research is. And if your paper on logging policies in national forests compares the arguments of environmentalists and the logging industry, you want readers to realize which statements come from environmentalists and which from loggers.

Choosing What to Include in Your Research Writing

You should read each source that you use critically to decide what you should cite, how the source relates to what other sources say and to what you know and think about your subject, how the material you use from the source will work in your arguments, and what you might write in response to that material. When you use a source only for limited information such as a definition, a statistic, or an example, you should read a little before and after the passage that you are citing to make sure that you are not misinterpreting your source by taking a passage out of context. You should also determine how your source learned

about the statistic or story that you want to use. In 2005 and 2006, many articles repeated a statistic that universities in China were graduating 600,000 engineers a year, until some Duke University students asked where that statistic came from and conducted a study that showed that the number was a huge exaggeration.

It's especially important to use critical reading strategies with sources that you cite for their expert opinions. The critical reading strategies in Chapter 2 will help you develop your own responses to your sources and your own ideas about your topic. Don't be satisfied with your first reading of a source. Ask questions about your readings. Play the doubting and believing games with your sources to explore their weaknesses and discover their implications. Schedule a conference with your instructor or with a tutor in the writing center to discuss your readings.

Reading-to-write strategies are especially valuable in your research process. If you photocopy pages from a source or copy or print an online source, annotate the pages that you find most interesting or important. Take notes not only about what the source says but about your thoughts and questions about what the source says. If you are keeping a journal for your class, you may want to keep these notes in that journal. If you are not keeping a journal as part of your class, consider starting a research journal where you can record what is important or interesting from your readings and interviews and also explore your own thoughts, questions, and responses to those readings and other ideas and questions about your subject that occur to you as you read. The double-entry journal described in Chapter 2 works especially well for research writing if you use one column for writing quotations, paraphrases, and summaries of facts and ideas from your sources and the second column for your responses, questions, and comments about this material.

Invention strategies are as useful in research writing as they are for other writing projects. Once you have read through a number of sources, freewriting and looping may help you push past your source material into your own thoughts because you cannot check your sources during a freewriting. The center-of-gravity sentences in your loopings may reveal important opinions to argue in your essay. Brainstorming, listing, and clustering can help you organize your thoughts and your research, and a heuristic such as a set of questions developed from the pentad or Aristotle's topics help you systematically examine your ideas about a source.

Avoiding Plagiarism

Plagiarism is copying or paraphrasing a text without giving credit to the source for that language, ideas, and information. Failing to mention a source that you quote, paraphrase, or summarize; failing to put quotation marks around language that you copy from a source; and handing in a paper that was written or largely written by someone else[1] constitute plagiarism. Deliberate plagiarism is academic dishonesty and carries severe penalties. But even unintentional plagiarism is such a serious error that most teachers fail papers that are partly plagiarized.

> ❝
> **Deliberate plagiarism is academic dishonesty and carries severe penalties. But even unintentional plagiarism is such a serious error that most teachers fail papers that are partly plagiarized.**
> ❞

Plagiarism is a serious problem in higher education, and people who publish plagiarized material in print or on the Internet or record plagiarized music are subject to lawsuits, firing, and public humiliation. (Chapter 10 discusses the issue of plagiarism and pirating in education, publishing, film, and music.) For most teachers, the minimum penalty for a plagiarized paper is an F on the paper, and often the minimum penalty is a failing grade for the course. Colleges and universities regard deliberate plagiarism as a form of theft and lying. A student who deliberately plagiarizes a paper or helps another student plagiarize may be charged with academic dishonesty and suspended or expelled from school. But even a teacher who recognizes that a student did not intend to cheat by copying large parts of another text in a paper or a take-home exam

is likely to fail the paper because it does not demonstrate the student's knowledge and ability to write, reason, analyze, and argue.

Inexperienced writers sometimes set themselves up for plagiarism when taking notes from their sources. One form of plagiarism is "patch writing" or "mosaic plagiarism," when a writer combines the sentences and phrases of sources with his own words and phrases without putting quotation marks around the sentences or parts of sentences that were taken from the source. Another frequent error that students make is documenting direct quotations from sources but neglecting to document paraphrases and summaries, when a student restates an idea or fact from the source in her own words. These problems sometimes occur when writers cannot tell what phrases and sentences in their notes were taken directly from their sources, what were paraphrased, and what represents their own thoughts. When you take notes on your sources, use quotation marks or another notation to identify sentences or even parts of a sentence that you copy directly from a source, and jot down the source and page numbers of the passages that you may quote or rephrase. If you take careful notes, you can avoid accidental plagiarism and avoid having to recheck where your material came from as you draft your paper.

As you read the selections in this book, notice the different citation practices that appear in different kinds of writing. Personal essays and articles in popular magazines and newspapers usually credit sources in the text without a bibliography and seldom cite the sources of statistics. Books for general audiences typically document sources in notes at the back of the book to avoid distracting readers who are not interested in the writer's sources. But academic writing, including most of the writing that you will do in college, requires writers to precisely document all their research so that readers can find each passage that a writer has quoted and paraphrased. You must follow academic practices of documentation carefully to avoid charges of plagiarism in college.

---

[1] It is possible to plagiarize yourself by turning in a paper in one class that you wrote for another class. Some teachers call this "auto-plagiarism" or "self-plagiarism." If you want to use a paper that you wrote for another class, even if you plan to revise that paper, check with your teacher to make sure your plans do not violate class policies on cheating and academic dishonesty.

04 | Identity

ENTERING COLLEGE BEGINS AN important time of self-discovery. It is a unique time when you may confront who you are and who you will become. The reputation that you have had in your family, neighborhood, school, and jobs is largely unknown and may not matter much to the people around you in college. You take on a new identity—college student. Your choice of a major and a profession depends a great deal on who you are and who you want to become in the world (one reason why many people change their majors and career plans several times in college). Choosing to join a fraternity or sorority or another campus organization also depends on and can change who you are. In class and in making new friends you are confronted with new ideas and questions that sometimes challenge your beliefs and values and may lead you to a better understanding of those values and beliefs. Even in writing a paper, you are presenting an image of yourself to an audience, and how readers respond to what you say depends—to an extent—on their impression of you. All of these matters are issues of identity.

But identity isn't all about you. Our images of others affect how we treat them, speak to them, and speak about them, just as their images of us affect how we are treated and represented. Everyone's process to discover who they are and determine who they will become is affected by other people's images of them. Some people recognize things about us that we cannot see about ourselves; everyone has to deal with stereotypes and other assumptions that can limit their identities. For example, women who want to be strong leaders in government or business still deal with the stereotypes that women are soft and weak and that strong women aren't feminine. People make decisions about other people based on their accents, their clothing, their age, their gender, their skin color, their religion, and a host of other traits. As a college student, you encounter people of complex and different beliefs, personalities, ambitions, backgrounds, ethnicities, and cultures, not only the students, faculty, and others that you meet on campus, but also the writers whose texts you read and the people that they write about. College courses and social encounters often ask you to think about your images and feelings about people who may be quite different than you are. How accurate and fair are these images and feelings? How should you speak and act toward others? How should you write about them?

Identity is not an issue confined to individuals. People frequently get into arguments about what it means to be an American or Irish or African American or a Southerner. They disagree about what values and positions a true conservative or liberal or feminist should hold. They debate what a Baptist or a Lutheran or a Moslem or a Jew should believe and how they should act. Universities and businesses, charitable organizations, political parties, and, for that matter, sororities and fraternities are often concerned about their images in the world, who they are and what their mission is, and whether actions that they take are consistent with their mission and character. And when we consider whether or not to join or align ourselves with a group or an institution, we usually think about how this will affect who we are and who we want to become, and we often become involved in discussions about the identity of the group or organization.

Here are some important questions about identity addressed in this chapter and that you might consider in your writings and class discussions.

- To what extent is one's identity something that we control? To what extent is it something determined by biology and genetics, by cultural forces and influences, by one's upbringing, and by one's education?

- How is one's sense of identity shaped by, even determined by, one's family?

- How is one's sense of identity shaped and determined by gender?

- How is one's sense of identity shaped and determined by race and ethnicity?

- How is it shaped and determined by social class?

- How is it shaped and determined by one's nationality, by the region of the country one comes from, by a life lived in different regions?

- How does one's job (or unemployment) affect one's sense of oneself? How does one's job affect people's perceptions of one's identity?

- How does a person's schooling affect his or her sense of self and image in the world?

- How does a person's sexual orientation affect their self-image and their image in society? How does being gay or lesbian affect who one is? How should it affect one's identity?

- How does a physical disability affect a person's identity?

- What other factors might affect a person's self-image? What other factors can influence other people's perceptions about a person?

- What stereotypes exist about people of different genders, races, ethnicities, sexual orientation, social class, education, and jobs? Why does stereotyping and racial profiling exist? What harm does each stereotype (or racial profiling) do? How does the media promote stereotypes? How does the media discourage stereotyping? What can be done to resist and discourage stereotyping?

- How do advertisers and others appeal to people's identities to persuade them? How do companies and other groups represent themselves in public? What purposes do corporate images serve? How do advertisers and others try to persuade audiences to identify with them and their interests?

Invitations for Journal Writing

1 How would you describe yourself? To what extent does who you are depend on your situation or company at the time?

2 How do race, ethnicity, gender, religion, age, occupation, social class, physical appearance and disabilities, and other characteristics affect how you perceive and describe other people? How do you think these qualities affect other people's conceptions of people's identities? Why?

3 How does the mass media, including television, movies, popular music, computer games, commercials, and national news coverage, generally portray different people of different races and ethnicities? How do they tend to portray people in blue-collar jobs, people in white-collar jobs, the rich, and the poor? How do they represent people of various religious faiths? How does age affect how individuals are portrayed? Is the media sometimes guilty of stereotyping? If yes, give an example.

ON SELF-RESPECT

BY JOAN DIDION

Joan Didion is a novelist (*Play It as It Lays*, *A Book of Common Prayer*, *The Last Thing He Wanted*) and one of the most important essayists in modern American literature. She wrote for *Vogue* magazine for seven years before she published her first novel, *Red River*, in 1963. Didion has published essays in magazines and books, such as *The White Album*, on a wide range of subjects, including war, politics, and literature, often taking an ironic or satiric stance in her criticism of American culture. "On Self-Respect" is a reflective essay from Didion's 1968 collection of essays, *Slouching Toward Bethlehem*. Like many essays, "On Self-Respect" takes a question and works toward an answer rather than arguing a position stated at the outset. Although Didion (1934–) refers to a personal experience, "On Self-Respect" is not a personal essay—Didion draws on a lifetime of reading and observation as well as her experiences to work out her thoughts about the meaning and importance of self-respect.

ONCE, IN A DRY SEASON, I WROTE IN large letters across two pages of a notebook that innocence ends when one is stripped of the delusion that one likes oneself. Although now, some years later, I marvel that a mind on the outs with itself should have nonetheless made painstaking record of its every tremor, I recall with embarrassing clarity the flavor of those particular ashes. It was a matter of misplaced self-respect.

I had not been elected to Phi Beta Kappa. This failure could scarcely have been more predictable or less ambiguous (I simply did not have the grades), but I was unnerved by it; I had somehow thought myself a kind of academic Raskolnikov, curiously exempt from the cause-effect relationships which hampered others. Although even the humorless nineteen-year-old that I was must have recognized that the situation lacked real tragic stature, the day that I did not make Phi Beta Kappa nonetheless marked the end of something, and innocence may well be the word for it. I lost the conviction that lights would always turn green for me, the pleasant certainty that those rather passive virtues which had won me approval as a child automatically guaranteed me not only Phi Beta Kappa keys but happiness, honor, and the love of a good man; lost a certain touching faith in the totem power of good manners, clean hair, and proven competence on the Stanford-Binet scale. To such doubtful amulets had my self-respect been pinned, and I faced myself that day with the nonplused apprehension of someone who has come across a vampire and has no crucifix at hand.

Although to be driven back upon oneself is an uneasy affair at best, rather like trying to cross a border with borrowed credentials, it seems to me now the one condition necessary to the beginnings of real self-respect. Most of our platitudes notwithstanding, self-deception remains the most difficult deception. The tricks that work on others count for nothing in that very well-lit back alley where one keeps assignations with oneself: no winning smiles will do here, no prettily drawn lists of good intentions. One shuffles flashily but in vain through one's marked cards—the kindness done for the wrong reason, the apparent triumph which involved no real effort, the seemingly heroic act into which one had been shamed. The dismal fact is that self-respect has nothing to do with the approval of others—who are, after all, deceived easily enough; has nothing to do with reputation, which, as Rhett Butler told Scarlett O'Hara, is something people with courage can do without.

To do without self-respect, on the other hand, is to be an unwilling audience of one to an interminable documentary that details one's failings, both real and imagined, with fresh footage spliced in for every screening. *There's the glass you broke in anger, there's the hurt on X's face; watch now, this next scene, the night Y came back from Houston, see how you muff this one.* To live without self-respect is to lie awake some night, beyond the reach of warm milk, phenobarbital, and the sleeping hand on the coverlet, counting up the sins of commission and omission, the trusts betrayed, the promises subtly broken, the gifts irrevocably wasted through sloth or cowardice or carelessness. However long we postpone it, we eventually lie down alone in that notoriously uncomfortable bed, the one we make ourselves. Whether or not we sleep in it depends, of course, on whether or not we respect ourselves.

To protest that some fairly improbable people, some people who *could not possibly respect themselves* seem to sleep easily enough is to miss the point entirely, as surely as those people miss it who think that self-respect has necessarily to do with not having safety pins in one's underwear. There is a common superstition that "self-respect" is a kind of charm against snakes, something that keeps those who have it locked in some unblighted Eden, out of strange beds, ambivalent conversations, and trouble in general. It does not at all. It has nothing to do with the face of things, but concerns instead a separate peace, a private reconciliation. Although the careless, suicidal Julian English in *Appointment in Samarra* and the careless, incurably dishonest Jordan Baker in *The Great Gatsby* seem equally improbable candidates for self-respect, Jordan Baker had it, Julian English did not. With that genius for accommodation more often seen in women than in men, Jordan took her own measure, made her own peace, avoided threats to that peace: "I hate careless people." she told Nick Carraway. "It takes two to make an accident."

Like Jordan Baker, people with self-respect have the courage of their mistakes. They know the price of things. If they choose to commit adultery, they do not then go running, in an access of bad conscience, to receive absolution from the wronged parties; nor do they complain unduly of the unfairness, the undeserved embarrassment, of being named corespondent. In brief, people with self-respect exhibit a certain toughness, a kind of moral nerve; they display what was once called *character*, a quality which, although approved in the abstract, sometimes loses ground to other, more instantly negotiable virtues. The measure of its slipping prestige is that one tends to think of it only in connection with homely children and United States senators who have been defeated, preferably in the primary, for reelection. Nonetheless, character—the willingness to accept responsibility for one's own life—is the source from which self-respect springs.

Self-respect is something that our grandparents, whether or not they had it, knew all about. They had instilled in them, young, a certain discipline, the sense that one lives by doing things one does not particularly want to do, by putting fears and doubts to one side, by weighing immediate comforts against the possibility of larger, even intangible, comforts. It seemed to the nineteenth century admirable, but not remarkable, that Chinese Gordon put on a clean white suit and held Khartoum against the Mahdi; it did not seem unjust that the way to free land in California involved death and difficulty and dirt. In a diary kept during the winter of 1846, an emigrating twelve-year-old named Narcissa Cornwall noted coolly: "Father was busy reading and did not notice that the house was being filled with strange Indians until Mother spoke about it." Even lacking any clue as to what Mother said, one can scarcely fail to be impressed by the entire incident: the father reading, the Indians filing in, the mother choosing the words that would not alarm, the child duly recording the event and noting further that those particular Indians were not, "fortunately for us," hostile. Indians were simply part of the *donnée*.

> "
> ## Self-respect is something that our grandparents, whether or not they had it, knew all about.
> "

In one guise or another, Indians always are. Again, it is a question of recognizing that anything worth having has its price. People who respect themselves are willing to accept the risk that the Indians will be hostile, that the venture will go bankrupt, that the liaison may not turn out to be one in which *every day is a holiday because you're married to me*. They are willing to invest something of themselves; they may not play at all, but when they do play, they know the odds.

That kind of self-respect is a discipline, a habit of mind that can never be faked but can be developed, trained, coaxed forth. It was once suggested to me that, as an antidote to crying, I put my head in a paper bag. As it happens, there is a sound physiological reason, something to do with oxygen, for doing exactly that, but the psychological effect alone is incalculable: it is difficult in the extreme to continue fancying oneself Cathy in *Wuthering Heights* with one's head in a Food Fair bag. There is a similar case for all the small disciplines, unimportant in themselves; imagine maintaining any kind of swoon, commiserative or carnal, in a cold shower.

But those small disciplines are valuable only insofar as they represent larger ones. To say that Waterloo was won on the playing fields of Eton is not to say that Napoleon might have been saved by a crash program in cricket; to give formal dinners in the rain forest would be pointless did not the candlelight flickering on the liana call forth deeper, stronger disciplines, values instilled long before. It is a kind of ritual, helping us to remember who and what we are. In order to remember it, one must have known it.

To have that sense of one's intrinsic worth which constitutes self-respect is potentially to have everything: the ability to discriminate, to love and to remain indifferent. To lack it is to be locked within oneself, paradoxically incapable of either love or indifference. If we do not respect ourselves, we are on the one hand forced to despise those who have so few resources as to consort with us, so little perception as to remain blind to our fatal weaknesses. On the other, we are peculiarly in thrall to everyone we see, curiously determined to live out—since our self-image is untenable—their false notions of us. We flatter ourselves by thinking this compulsion to please others an attractive trait: a gist for imaginative empathy, evidence of our willingness to give. *Of course* I will play Francesca to your Paolo, Helen Keller to anyone's Annie Sullivan: no expectation is too misplaced, no role too ludicrous. At the mercy of those we cannot but hold in contempt, we play roles doomed to failure before they are begun, each defeat generating fresh despair at the urgency of divining and meeting the next demand made upon us.

It is the phenomenon sometimes called "alienation from self." In its advanced stages, we no longer answer the telephone, because someone might want something; that we could say *no* without drowning in self-reproach is an idea alien to this game. Every encounter demands too much, tears the nerves, drains the will, and the specter of something as small as an unanswered letter arouses such disproportionate guilt that answering it becomes out of the question. To assign unanswered letters their proper weight, to free us from the expectations of others, to give us back to ourselves—there lies the great, the singular power of self-respect. Without it, one eventually discovers the final turn of the screw: one runs away to find oneself, and finds no one at home.

Journal and Discussion Questions

1 Reflective essays often are organized to suggest the train of thought that the writer pursued to work out her thoughts. Outline "On Self-Respect." What does the organization suggest about how Didion approached the question of self-respect and thought through her ideas? Why does Didion use white space to separate paragraphs on page 37?

2 In what ways, according to Didion, is a person with self-respect different from a person without self-respect? Do you agree with Didion? Why or why not?

3 Why were character and self-respect more important to the generation of Didion's grandparents than they were when Didion wrote this essay in the late 1960s? How important are these concepts today? Why?

4 Why do you think Didion introduces her exploration of the meaning and importance of self-respect with a personal anecdote about not being elected to the Phi Beta Kappa honor society as a college student? Compare and contrast her present perspective about that experience with her feelings as a nineteen-year-old student. What do these two perspectives reveal about Didion's own self-respect?

5 Why does Didion choose shallow and superficial characters like Scarlett O'Hara in *Gone with the Wind* and Jordan Baker in *The Great Gatsby* as examples of people with self-respect? Considering that Jordan Baker was the hit-and-run driver in a fatal car accident in *The Great Gatsby*, why do you think Didion writes about her, "Like Jordan Baker, people with self-respect have the courage of their mistakes"?

6 Identify the different sources that Didion cites in "On Self-Respect." How does Didion make use of each source to develop and support her ideas? Why are so many of her sources novels? Would "On Self-Respect" be more persuasive or true if Didion took more of her examples from nonfiction? Why or why not?

7 Why does Didion conclude her essay with a description of "alienation from self"? How does this discussion contribute to her definition of self-respect?

Topics for Writing

1 Analyze "On Self-Respect," focusing on one of the important ideas in Didion's essay.

2 Choose two people from literature, history, or popular culture—one who you believe has self-respect and one who you believe doesn't. Compare and contrast these two persons' "character," as Didion uses the term.

3 Research several arguments about the importance of personal responsibility in American society, taking notes about the different positions that writers take, their definitions of "responsibility," and why they believe responsibility is important. Write a research paper arguing how important self-respect and personal responsibility should be.

THE MYTH OF THE LATIN WOMAN: I Just Met a Girl Named Maria

BY JUDITH ORTIZ COFER

Judith Ortiz Cofer (1952–) is the author of the autobiographical books *Silent Dancing: A Partial Remembrance of a Puerto Rican Childhood* (1990) and *Woman in Front of the Sun: Becoming a Writer* (2000), as well as books of poetry such as *Reaching for the Mainland* (1996) and a novel, *The Line of the Sun,* which was nominated for a 1989 Pulitzer Prize. Cofer was born in a small Puerto Rican community in New Jersey and grew up in Paterson, New Jersey. She teaches creative writing at the University of Georgia. In "The Myth of the Latin Woman: I Just Met a Girl Named Maria," an essay from her 1993 book, *The Latin Deli: Prose and Poetry,* Cofer discusses Latina stereotypes and how they affect her sense of identity.

ON A BUS TRIP TO LONDON FROM Oxford University where I was earning some graduate credits one summer, a young man, obviously fresh from a pub, spotted me and as if struck by inspiration went down on his knees in the aisle. With both hands over his heart he broke into an Irish tenor's rendition of "María" from *West Side Story*. My politely amused fellow passengers gave his lovely voice the round of gentle applause it deserved. Though I was not quite as amused, I managed my version of an English smile: no show of teeth, no extreme contortions of the facial muscles—I was at this time of my life practicing reserve and cool. Oh, that British control, how I coveted it. But María had followed me to London, reminding me of a prime fact of my life: you can leave the Island, master the English language, and travel as far as you can, but if you are a Latina, especially one like me who so obviously belongs to Rita Moreno's gene pool, the Island travels with you.

This is sometimes a very good thing—it may win you that extra minute of someone's attention. But with some people, the same things can make *you* an island—not so much a tropical paradise as an Alcatraz, a place nobody wants to visit. As a Puerto Rican girl growing up in the United States and wanting like most children to "belong," I resented the stereotype that my Hispanic appearance called forth from many people I met.

Our family lived in a large urban center in New Jersey during the sixties, where life was designed as a microcosm of my parents' casas on the island. We spoke in Spanish, we ate Puerto Rican food bought at the bodega, and we practiced strict Catholicism complete with Saturday confession and Sunday mass at a church where our parents were accommodated into a one-hour Spanish mass slot, performed by a Chinese priest trained as a missionary for Latin America.

As a girl I was kept under strict surveillance, since virtue and modesty were, by cultural equation, the same as family honor. As a teenager I was instructed on how to behave as a proper señorita. But it was a conflicting message girls got, since the Puerto Rican mothers also encouraged their daughters to look and act like women and to dress in clothes our Anglo friends and their mothers found too "mature" for our age. It was, and is, cultural, yet I often felt humiliated when I appeared at an American friend's party wearing a dress more suitable to a semiformal than to a playroom birthday celebration. At Puerto Rican festivities, neither the music nor the colors we wore could be too loud. I still experience a vague sense of letdown when I'm invited to a "party" and it turns out to be a marathon conversation in hushed tones rather than a fiesta with salsa, laughter, and dancing—the kind of celebration I remember from my childhood.

I remember Career Day in our high school, when teachers told us to come dressed as if for a job interview. It quickly became obvious that to the barrio girls, "dressing up" sometimes meant wearing ornate jewelry and clothing that would be more appropriate (by mainstream standards) for the company Christmas party than as daily office attire. That morning I had agonized in front of my closet, trying to figure out what a "career girl" would wear because, essentially, except for Marlo Thomas on TV, I had no models on which to base my decision. I knew how to dress for school: at the Catholic school I attended we all wore uniforms; I knew how to dress for Sunday mass, and I knew what dresses to wear for parties at my relatives' homes. Though I do not recall the precise details of my Career Day outfit, it must have been a composite of the above choices. But I remember a comment my friend (an Italian-American) made in later years that coalesced my impressions of that day. She said that at the business school she was attending the Puerto Rican girls always stood out for wearing "everything at once." She meant, of course, too much jewelry, too many accessories. On that day at school, we were simply made the negative models by the nuns who were themselves not credible fashion experts to any of us. But it was painfully obvious to me that to the others, in their tailored skirts and silk blouses, we must have seemed "hopeless" and "vulgar." Though I now know that most adolescents feel out of step much of the time, I also know that for the Puerto Rican girls of my generation that sense was intensified. The way our teachers and classmates looked at us that day in school was just a taste of the culture clash that awaited us in the real world, where prospective employers and men on the street would often misinterpret our tight skirts and jingling bracelets as a come-on.

Mixed cultural signals have perpetuated certain stereotypes—for example, that of the Hispanic woman as the "Hot Tamale" or sexual firebrand. It is a one-dimensional view that the media have found easy to promote. In their special vocabulary, advertisers have designated "sizzling" and "smoldering" as the adjectives of choice for describing not only the foods but also the women of Latin America. From conversations in my house I recall hearing about the harassment that Puerto Rican women endured in factories where the "boss men" talked to them as if sexual innuendo was all they understood and, worse, often gave them the choice of submitting to advances or being fired.

It is custom, however, not chromosomes, that leads us to choose scarlet over pale pink. As young girls, we were influenced in our decisions about clothes and colors by the women—older sisters and mothers who had grown up on a tropical island where the natural environment was a riot of primary colors, where showing your skin was one way to keep cool as well as to look sexy. Most important of all, on the island, women perhaps felt freer to dress and move more provocatively, since, in most cases, they were protected by the traditions, mores, and laws of a Spanish/Catholic system of morality and machismo whose main rule was: *You may look at my sister, but if you touch her I will kill you.* The extended family and church structure could provide a young woman with a circle of safety in her small pueblo on the island; if a man "wronged" a girl, everyone would close in to save her family honor.

This is what I have gleaned from my discussions as an adult with older Puerto Rican women. They have told me about dressing in their best party clothes on Saturday nights and going to the town's plaza to promenade with their girlfriends in front of the boys they liked. The males were thus given an opportunity to admire the women and to express their admiration in the form of *piropos:* erotically charged street poems they composed on the spot. I have been subjected to a few piropos while visiting the Island, and they can be outrageous, although custom dictates that they must never cross into obscenity. This ritual, as I understand it, also entails a show of studied indifference on the woman's part; if she is "decent," she must not acknowledge the man's impassioned words. So I do understand how things can be lost in translation. When a Puerto Rican girl dressed in her idea of what is attractive meets a man from the mainstream culture who has been trained to react to certain types of clothing as a sexual signal, a clash is likely to take place. The line I first heard based on this aspect of the myth happened when the boy who took me to my first formal dance leaned over to plant a sloppy overeager kiss painfully on my mouth, and when I didn't respond with sufficient passion said in a resentful tone: "I thought you Latin girls were supposed to mature early"—my first instance of being thought of as a fruit or vegetable—I was supposed to *ripen*, not just grow into womanhood like other girls.

It is surprising to some of my professional friends that some people, including those who should know better, still put others "in their place." Though rarer, these incidents are still commonplace in my life. It happened to me most recently during a stay at a very classy metropolitan hotel favored by young professional couples for their weddings. Late one evening after the theater, as I walked toward my room with my new colleague (a woman with whom I was coordinating an arts program), a middle-aged man in a tuxedo, a young girl in satin and lace on his arm, stepped directly into our path. With his champagne glass extended toward me, he exclaimed, "Evita!"

Our way blocked, my companion and I listened as the man half-recited, half-bellowed "Don't Cry for Me, Argentina." When he finished, the young girl said: "How about a round of applause for my daddy?" We complied, hoping this would bring the silly spectacle to a close. I

> **" She ordered a cup of coffee from me, assuming that I was the waitress. Easy enough to mistake my poems for menus, I suppose. "**

was becoming aware that our little group was attracting the attention of the other guests. "Daddy" must have perceived this too, and he once more barred the way as we tried to walk past him. He began to shout-sing a ditty to the tune of "La Bamba"—except the lyrics were about a girl named María whose exploits all rhymed with her name and gonorrhea. The girl kept saying "Oh, Daddy" and looking at me with pleading eyes. She wanted me to laugh along with the others. My companion and I stood silently waiting for the man to end his offensive song. When he finished, I looked not at him but at his daughter. I advised her calmly never to ask her father what he had done in the army. Then I walked between them and to my room. My friend complimented me on my cool handling of the situation. I confessed to her that I really had wanted to push the jerk into the swimming pool. I knew that this same man—probably a corporate executive, well educated, even worldly by most standards—would not have been likely to regale a white woman with a dirty song in public. He would perhaps have checked his impulse by assuming that she could be somebody's wife or mother, or at least *somebody* who might take offense. But to him, I was just an Evita or a María: merely a character in his cartoon-populated universe.

Because of my education and my proficiency with the English language, I have acquired many mechanisms for dealing with the anger I experience. This was not true for my parents, nor is it true for the many Latin women working at menial jobs who must put up with stereotypes about our ethnic group such as: "They make good domestics." This is another facet of the myth of the Latin woman in the United States. Its origin is simple to deduce. Work as domestics, waitressing, and factory jobs are all that's available to women with little English and few skills. The myth of the Hispanic menial has been sustained by the same media phenomenon that made "Mammy" from *Gone with the Wind* America's idea of the black woman for generations; María, the housemaid or counter girl, is now indelibly etched into the national psyche. The big and the little screens have presented us with the picture of the funny Hispanic maid, mispronouncing words and cooking up a spicy storm in a shiny California kitchen.

This media-engendered image of the Latina in the United States has been documented by feminist Hispanic scholars, who claim that such portrayals are partially responsible for the denial of opportunities for

upward mobility among Latinas in the professions. I have a Chicana friend working on a Ph.D. in philosophy at a major university. She says her doctor still shakes his head in puzzled amazement at all the "big words" she uses. Since I do not wear my diplomas around my neck for all to see, I too have on occasion been sent to that "kitchen," where some think I obviously belong.

One such incident that has stayed with me, though I recognize it as a minor offense, happened on the day of my first public poetry reading. It took place in Miami in a boat-restaurant where we were having lunch before the event. I was nervous and excited as I walked in with my notebook in my hand. An older woman motioned me to her table. Thinking (foolish me) that she wanted me to autograph a copy of my brand new slender volume of verse, I went over. She ordered a cup of coffee from me, assuming that I was the waitress. Easy enough to mistake my poems for menus, I suppose. I know that it wasn't an intentional act of cruelty, yet of all the good things that happened that day, I remember that scene most clearly, because it reminded me of what I had to overcome before anyone would take me seriously. In retrospect I understand that my anger gave my reading fire, that I have almost always taken doubts in my abilities as a challenge—and that the result is, most times, a feeling of satisfaction at having won a convert when I see the cold, appraising eyes warm to my words, the body language change, the smile that indicates that I have opened some avenue for communication. That day I read to that woman and her lowered eyes told me that she was embarrassed at her little faux pas, and when I willed her to look up at me, it was my victory, and she graciously allowed me to punish her with my full attention. We shook hands at the end of the reading, and I never saw her again. She has probably forgotten the whole thing but maybe not.

Yet I am one of the lucky ones. My parents made it possible for me to acquire a stronger footing in the mainstream culture by giving me the chance at an education. And books and art have saved me from the harsher forms of ethnic and racial prejudice that many of my Hispanic *compañeras* have had to endure. I travel a lot around the United States, reading from my books of poetry and my novel, and the reception I most often receive is one of positive interest by people who want to know more about my culture. There are, however, thousands of Latinas without the privilege of an education or the entrée into society that I have. For them life is a struggle against the misconceptions perpetuated by the myth of the Latina as whore, domestic or criminal. We cannot change this by legislating the way people look at us. The transformation, as I see it, has to occur at a much more individual level. My personal goal in my public life is to try to replace the old pervasive stereotypes and myths about Latinas with a much more interesting set of realities. Every time I give a reading, I hope the stories I tell, the dreams and fears I examine in my work, can achieve some universal truth which will get my audience past the particulars of my skin color, my accent, or my clothes.

I once wrote a poem in which I called us Latinas "God's brown daughters." This poem is really a prayer of sorts, offered upward, but also, through the human-to-human channel of art, outward. It is a prayer for communication, and for respect. In it, Latin women pray "in Spanish to an Anglo God/with a Jewish heritage," and they are "fervently hoping/that if not omnipotent,/at least He be bilingual."

Journal and Discussion Questions

1 What points does Cofer make in her opening anecdote about a bus trip in England? Is this an effective introduction?

2 Cofer's essay is organized around three stories at the beginning, the middle, and the end of "The Myth of the Latin Woman." Outline this essay. How is each story connected to the claims and ideas that Cofer is making in each part of her essay?

3 "The Myth of the Latin Woman" is both an autobiographical essay and an essay about a public issue, the nature of the Latina stereotypes and the effects of this stereotype on Latinas. How would you describe Cofer as a person from this essay? How do her descriptions and reflections about her experiences develop her argument about the general problem of Latina stereotypes? How does Cofer try to avoid overgeneralizing from her life?

4 Cofer's essay draws from a number of sources in addition to her memories of personal experiences, such as remembered family conversations that she overheard as a girl; recent conversations that she has had with Latin women about stereotyping; musicals, books, movies, and advertising from popular culture; and academic writings by feminist Hispanic scholars. What information and ideas does she take from each of these sources? What do these sources add to Cofer's essay that she could not provide from her personal experiences alone?

5 What differences does Cofer describe between how Puerto Rican women of her generation interpret women's clothing and accessories and how Anglo men interpret women's appearances? What do the fashion choices of these Puerto Rican women have to do with "the Spanish/Catholic system of morality and machismo"? How do Anglo assumptions about women's appearance and Anglo misreadings of women's clothing and accessories contribute to Latina stereotypes?

6 "The Myth of the Latin Woman" makes a number of comparisons: between the "sexual firebrand" and domestic menial stereotypes of Latin women, between the Latina stereotypes and the lives of Cofer and other Hispanic women, between stereotypes of black and Hispanic women, between Cofer and other Latinas, and between Latinas of different generations. What points is Cofer making with each comparison?

7 If you read "The Myth of the Latin Woman" as a problem-solution essay, what is the problem that it describes, and what is the solution that Cofer proposes? How effective do you think this solution will be in solving this problem? Why?

Topics for Writing

1 Analyze "The Myth of the Latin Woman: I Just Met a Girl Named Maria" focusing on one of the essay's arguments about identity and stereotyping.

2 Write a research paper about images of Latin women in popular culture (movies, television, music, news stories, etc.), arguing whether popular culture continues to stereotype Hispanic women and, if so, whether the stereotypes have changed since Cofer wrote "The Myth of the Latin Woman."

3 Drawing on "The Myth of the Latin Woman," your own experiences and observations, and perhaps other sources, explain how cultural misunderstandings can lead to stereotyping and propose a solution to this problem.

A VERY BIG ORDER:
Reconstructing Identity

BY ERNEST J. GAINES

Ernest J. Gaines (1933–) is a writer of novels, short stories, and autobiographical essays like "A Very Big Order: Reconstructing Identity." All of his published fiction, including *The Autobiography of Miss Jane Pittman, A Gathering of Old Men*, and *A Lesson Before Dying,* is set in the former slave quarters of a plantation near the small town of Bayonne, Louisiana, a fictionalized version of the sharecropper quarters where Gaines was raised by his aunt and grandmother outside New Roads, Louisiana. At the age of 15, Gaines left Louisiana to rejoin his mother and her husband near San Francisco. "A Very Big Order: Reconstructing Identity" reflects upon his move from rural Louisiana to California and how that move and his attempts to understand his past in his writing have shaped his identity—and continue to shape it. "A Very Big Order" originally appeared in 1990 in the *Southern Review,* an important literary journal that publishes short stories, poetry, and essays by Southern writers. The essay can also be found in Gaines' 2005 collection of essays and short stories, *Mozart and Leadbelly.*

A FIFTEEN-YEAR-OLD BOY IS standing on a riverbank in South Louisiana with a worn-out leather suitcase at his feet and a white pocket handkerchief in his hand. There is no way he can possibly imagine what he will be forty-one years and four months later, in December of 1989.

He is tall, thin; he is worried and frightened. But he continues to stand there as steadily as his legs will allow, because he knows he must go. He must go not only for himself, but for the others as well, because he will be the first male in the history of the family to go away and finish school. It had been planned by the others—if not planned, dreamed—long, long before he was aware of it and definitely long before he was aware of who he was.

There are others about him, his brothers and friends. They are not leaving home, so they are much more relaxed: they can play, chasing one another alongside the highway and up and down the riverbank.

Where the boy stands, he can see the road from which he has just left—the quarter. He cannot see his own home—it is too far down into the quarter—so he cannot see the old people who must still be sitting out on the porch with his aunt.

An hour ago he was packing his suitcase to leave. The few pieces of clothes—two shirts or so, but no more than three; two extra pairs of pants, underclothes, and an extra pair of shoes. Then there was the food that the old people had brought him, fried chicken, bread, tea cakes, pralines, probably oranges, and some unpeeled pecans. After he had finished packing, he tied up the suitcase and looked around the room. His ancestors, who had once been slaves, lived, if not in this house, then in one just like this one in the quarter. (He would be told that much later by a man who had spent all of his life here.)

The bus came around the bend of the road and he waved his handkerchief, and when the bus stopped he climbed on with the suitcase, and after paying his fare, he went all the way to the back of the bus where he was supposed to go, passing under the little signs hanging over the aisle that read "White" and "Colored." He must have found a seat because he cannot remember standing all the way to New Orleans, where he would take a train to California. But he can remember that until he got to Southern California he saw no other white person in his car except the conductor. When he changed trains in Los Angeles, he noticed the different races together.

His mother and stepfather now lived in government-subsidized projects in Vallejo, California. In the projects were blacks, whites, Asians, Latinos—all the groups, races, who were Californians at that time. He got along with the blacks immediately, but it took him a while to get up enough courage to approach the others. He watched them play basketball, football, tennis. He had never done any of this, so he watched them. Eventually he would be a member, but now he stood back and watched everything that was going on around him.

> ## But he can remember that until he got to Southern California he saw no other white person in his car except the conductor.

One day while he and one of the Asians stood on the sidelines watching a football game, the Asian said to him (and he still cannot recall what brought it about) that he, the Asian, was not as good as white people are, but better than blacks, because blacks had not contributed anything to civilization. They, he and the Asian, were watching a football game, and from what he could see of the game, the black kids were holding their place as well as or better than any of the other group. So what was this little fellow talking about?

He had never thought himself less than anyone else, nor better. He had come from a world where the two races, white and black, were separated, but he had never thought he was less than anyone else. He had always carried his share of the load. He had gone into the fields at eight years old, and he could do as much work as any other eight-year-old could do. He had gone into the swamps at eleven or twelve, and he could pull the saw as well as anyone of that age could. So he had never thought less of himself than he did of any other. There were those who were stronger than he, those who were better ballplayers and marble shooters than he, but he was better in other things than they were—reading, for example; writing letters, for example. So he had never thought himself less. So what was this little fellow talking about?

Once upon a time there was a tall, slim, frightened black boy who sat in the back row of all of his classes in California. Once he was called on to explain what he knew about the American Civil War. None of his teachers in the South had ever mentioned the Civil War to him that he could remember, and he thought his instructor had asked him what he knew about the silver war. He did not know anything about a silver war either, but he talked about a minute through the laughter of his classmates—until the instructor told him to sit back down.

This same boy was also told by other recent black migrants to California that you were never supposed to tell people you came from the country. Best to say you don't know a thing about picking cotton, or chitlins, beef tripe, watermelons—and all the rest of that country stuff like pig feet, pig lips, pig ears, pig tails. And you came from New Orleans—and never say N'awlens. It's New Or-lea-ans. Which he tried to do for several months—until someone asked him about Bourbon Street. He knew nothing about Bourbon Street, and he realized that to go on lying to others meant lying to himself. Not only was he lying to himself, but he was also denying knowing the others, the ones he had left, and wasn't that the same as denying who he was?

But it seems that we've skipped too far ahead. A while ago we were concerned with a young man who was searching for that elusive "I." Part of it he found by reading American, Russian, and French literature. Now he had to sit and think: how could he relate this to the lives of his ancestors and to the people whom he had grown up around; how to articulate their, his own people's, experience; how to articulate thoughts that they had been denied to articulate for over three hundred years? There were those recent migrants to the West who told him that digging into the past would be embarrassing, too painful; forget the past. But he wanted to become "I." And to do that meant to confront the past.

An interviewer from one of the more popular magazines would ask him one day, "What book of all those you read helped you to become the person you are today?" After thinking awhile, he shook his head; he didn't know. "Maybe it was the one that was not there," the interviewer said, "and you felt that you had to put it there."

His first effort as a writer was a love story between light-skinned and darker-skinned blacks, whose religions were Catholic and Protestant. He knew something about each because he had both in his own family. After five years of wrestling with the idea—articulating it was the problem for him, so as not to embarrass anyone—the book, or one little chapter, as he would call it, was finally accepted for publication. In the book he would have the main character say, "I feel like a dry leaf, broken away from the tree and now drifting with the least bit of wind toward no true destination."

In each of the following books he found that he was moving farther and farther back into the past until he realized that to find the tree from which the leaf had been broken was to go back to those who sat out on the porch the day he left. What were they talking about that day while he was inside packing? What did they talk about the day before, the year before, years and years and years before? Because his aunt was crippled and could not go to them, they came to her, summer and winter, day and night, weekdays as well as weekends, and talked. Sometimes in English, sometimes in Creole; sometimes their voices would hush when he came into the room. What was so secret, so painful that they did not want him to know? Why did they say it was none of his business when he asked the question?

His aunt as well as many of the others were dead by now—twenty years later. He went to the younger ones, their children, their nieces, nephews, and asked could they recall a phrase the old ones liked using or a song they liked singing. Was there a Bible they liked holding even though they did not know the words, or a hymnal they had saved even though they could not read a verse?

Recently, at a high school in Lafayette, the writer was asked by a white student what was an American. The writer told the student that he had been searching for that answer for nearly forty years now. The student asked, "Do you think you will ever find out?" The writer said he did not know, but he could not think of anything else more important in his life to do. The student said, "Well, I sure got a lot out of Miss Jane Pittman." The writer asked him what did he get. The student said, "Well, er, I, er, er—well, she made you think." Good, the writer said. That's good.

Journal and Discussion Questions

1 What is the meaning of the title, "A Very Big Order: Reconstructing Identity"? Why do you think Gaines uses the verb *reconstructing* instead of *finding* or *discovering*?

2 What do you think Gaines has figured out about himself by writing about his past? How have his family, his race, and his life in both Louisiana and California contributed to who he is?

3 Gaines does not tell his story in strict chronological order. Trace the timeline of the events in the essay. How does Gaines help readers keep track of the timeline of the events that he discusses? Why does he tell the story of his life in this order? How would the essay be different if Gaines told the story in strict chronological order?

4 Gaines describes himself and his trip to California in some detail. Which details are particularly significant to his essay? Why? How does this description and narration prepare readers for the rest of the essay?

5 Why isn't Gaines able to answer the interviewer's question "What book of all those you read helped you to become the person you are today?" How does this question set up his discussion of the books Gaines has written?

6 What does Gaines mean when he writes, "But he wanted to become 'I'"? Why do you think Gaines refers to himself in the third person throughout this essay? How would using first person change the essay?

7 Why does Gaines raise the question "what is an American?" as he concludes his essay? How does his story address this question? How is the reconstruction of his own identity related to this question? Why does Gaines point out that a *white* high school student asked him this question?

Topics for Writing

1 Analyze the concept of *reconstructing identity* in "A Very Big Order."

2 Explain how Gaines' "A Very Big Order" answers the question what it means to be an American.

3 Describe and analyze an important move in your life, such as a move to a different home, school, or job and how that move has affected who you are or who you are becoming.

4 Write an essay describing the influence of your reading or writing on your life.

NO NAME WOMAN

BY MAXINE HONG KINGSTON

Maxine Hong Kingston (1940–) is a professor *emeritus* at the University of California at Berkeley. She is an essayist and novelist known best for her creative nonfiction, including the books *China Men, Hawaii One Summer, To Be the Poet,* and *The Fifth Book of Peace.* "No Name Woman" is an autobiographical essay about Kingston, her mother, and her aunt that explores changing Chinese and Chinese-American attitudes about individuality, identity, family, and gender. It first appeared in the January 1975 issue of *Viva: The International Magazine for Women,* an erotic magazine for women in the 1970s that published interviews, fiction, and reviews and articles about the arts, sexuality, beauty, and fashion. The version here is a slight revision published as the first chapter of Kingston's 1976 book, *The Woman Warrior: Memoirs of a Girlhood Among Ghosts.*

'YOU MUST NOT TELL ANYONE,' MY mother said, 'what I am about to tell you. In China your father had a sister who killed herself. She jumped into the family well. We say that your father has all brothers because it is as if she had never been born.

'In 1924 just a few days after our village celebrated seventeen hurry-up weddings—to make sure that every young man who went "out on the road" would responsibly come home—your father and his brothers and your grandfather and his brothers and your aunt's new husband sailed for America, the Gold Mountain. It was your grandfather's last trip. Those lucky enough to get contracts waved good-bye from the decks. They fed and guarded the stowaways and helped them off in Cuba, New York, Bali, Hawaii. "We'll meet in California next year," they said. All of them sent money home.

'I remember looking at your aunt one day when she and I were dressing; I had not noticed before that she had such a protruding melon of a stomach. But I did not think, "She's pregnant," until she began to look like other pregnant women, her shirt pulling and the white tops of her black pants showing. She could not have been pregnant, you see, because her husband had been gone for years. No one said anything. We did not discuss it. In early summer she was ready to have the child, long after the time when it could have been possible.

'The village had also been counting. On the night the baby was to be born the villagers raided our house. Some were crying. Like a great saw, teeth strung with lights, files of people walked zigzag across our land, tearing the rice. Their lanterns doubled in the disturbed black water, which drained away through the broken bunds. As the villagers closed in, we could see that some of them, probably men and women we knew well, wore white masks. The people with long hair hung it over their faces. Women with short hair made it stand up on end. Some had tied white bands around their foreheads, arms, and legs.

'At first they threw mud and rocks at the house. Then they threw eggs and began slaughtering our stock. We could hear the animals scream their deaths—the roosters, the pigs, a last great roar from the ox. Familiar wild heads flared in our night windows; the villagers encircled us. Some of the faces stopped to peer at us, their eyes rushing like searchlights. The hands flattened against the panes, framed heads, and left red prints.

'The villagers broke in the front and the back doors at the same time, even though we had not locked the doors against them. Their knives dripped with the blood of our animals. They smeared blood on the doors and walls. One woman swung a chicken, whose throat she had slit, splattering blood in red arcs about her. We stood together in the middle of our house, in the family hall with the pictures and tables of the ancestors around us, and looked straight ahead.

'At that time the house had only two wings. When the men came back, we would build two more to enclose our courtyard and a third one to begin a second courtyard. The villagers pushed through both wings, even your grandparents' rooms, to find your aunt's, which was also mine until the men returned. From this room a new wing for one of the younger families would grow. They ripped up her clothes and shoes and broke her combs, grinding them underfoot. They tore her work from the loom. They scattered the cooking fire and rolled the new weaving in it. We could hear them in the kitchen breaking our bowls and banging the pots. They overturned the great waist-high earthenware jugs; duck eggs, pickled fruits, vegetables burst out and mixed in acrid torrents. The old woman from the next field swept a broom through the air and loosed the spirits-of-the-broom over our heads. "Pig." "Ghost." "Pig," they sobbed and scolded while they ruined our house.

'When they left, they took sugar and oranges to bless themselves. They cut pieces from the dead animals. Some of them took bowls that were not broken and clothes that were not torn. Afterwards we swept up the rice and sewed it back up into sacks. But the smells from the spilled preserves lasted. Your aunt gave birth in the pigsty that night. The next morning when I went for the water, I found her and the baby plugging up the family well.

'Don't let your father know that I told you. He denies her. Now that you have started to menstruate, what happened to her could happen to you. Don't humiliate us. You wouldn't like to be forgotten as if you had never been born. The villagers are watchful.'

Whenever she had to warn us about life, my mother told stories that ran like this one, a story to grow up on. She tested our strength to establish realities. Those in the emigrant generations who could not reassert brute survival died young and far from home. Those of us in the first American generations have had to figure out how the invisible world the emigrants built around our childhoods fits in solid America.

The emigrants confused the gods by diverting their curses, misleading them with crooked streets and false names. They must try to confuse their offspring as well, who, I suppose, threaten them in similar ways—always trying to get things straight, always trying to name the unspeakable. The Chinese I know hide their names; sojourners take new names when their lives change and guard their real names with silence.

Chinese-Americans, when you try to understand what things in you are Chinese, how do you separate what is peculiar to childhood, to poverty, insanities, one family, your mother who marked your growing with stories, from what is Chinese? What is Chinese tradition and what is the movies?

If I want to learn what clothes my aunt wore, whether flashy or ordinary, I would have to begin, 'Remember Father's drowned-in-the-well sister?' I cannot ask that. My mother has told me once and for all the useful parts. She will add nothing unless powered by Necessity, a riverbank that guides her life. She plants vegetable gardens rather than lawns; she carries the odd-shaped tomatoes home from the fields and eats food left for the gods.

Whenever we did frivolous things, we used up energy; we flew high kites. We children came up off the ground over the melting cones our parents brought home from work and the American movie on New Year's Day—*Oh, You Beautiful Doll* with Betty Grable one year, and *She Wore a Yellow Ribbon* with John Wayne another year. After the one carnival ride each, we paid in guilt: our tired father counted his change on the dark walk home.

> ## My aunt could not have been the lone romantic who gave up everything for sex.

Adultery is extravagance. Could people who hatch their own chicks and eat the embryos and the heads for delicacies and boil the feet in vinegar for party food, leaving only the gravel, eating even the gizzard lining—could such people engender a prodigal aunt? To be a woman, to have a daughter in starvation time was a waste enough. My aunt could not have been the lone romantic who gave up everything for sex. Women in the old China did not choose. Some man had commanded her to lie with him and be his secret evil. I wonder whether he masked himself when he joined the raid on her family.

Perhaps she had encountered him in the fields or on the mountain where the daughters-in-law collected fuel. Or perhaps he first noticed her in the marketplace. He was not a stranger because the village housed no strangers. She had to have dealings with him other than sex. Perhaps he worked an adjoining field, or he sold her the cloth for the dress she sewed and wore. His demand must have surprised, then terrified her. She obeyed him; she always did as she was told.

When the family found a young man in the next village to be her husband, she had stood tractably beside the best rooster, his proxy, and promised before they met that she would be his for ever. She was lucky that he was her age and she would be the first wife, an advantage secure now. The night she first saw him, he had sex with her. Then he left for America. She had almost forgotten what he looked like. When she tried to envision him, she only saw the black and white face in the group photograph the men had had taken before leaving.

The other man was not, after all, much different from her husband. They both gave orders: she followed. 'If you tell your family, I'll beat you. I'll kill you. Be here again next week.' No one talked sex, ever. And she might have separated the rapes from the rest of living if only she did not have to buy her oil from him or gather wood in the same forest. I want her fear to have lasted just as long as rape lasted so that the fear could have been contained. No drawn-out fear. But women at sex haz-arded birth and hence lifetimes. The fear did not stop but permeated everywhere. She told the man. 'I think I'm pregnant.' He organized the raid against her.

On nights when my mother and father talked about their life back home, sometimes they mentioned an 'out-cast table' whose business they still seemed to be set-tling, their voices tight. In a commensal tradition, where food is precious, the powerful older people made wrong-doers eat alone. Instead of letting them start separate new lives like the Japanese, who could become samurais and geishas, the Chinese family, faces averted but eyes glowering sideways, hung on to the offenders and fed them leftovers. My aunt must have lived in the same house as my parents and eaten at an outcast table. My mother spoke about the raid as if she had seen it, when she and my aunt, a daughter-in-law to a different house-hold, should not have been living together at all. Daugh-ters-in-law lived with their husbands' parents, not their own; a synonym for marriage in Chinese is 'taking a daughter-in-law'. Her husband's parents could have sold her, mortgaged her, stoned her. But they had sent her back to her own mother and father, a mysterious act hinting at disgraces not told me. Perhaps they had thrown her out to deflect the avengers.

She was the only daughter; her four brothers went with her father, husband, and uncles 'out on the road' and for some years became western men. When the goods were divided among the family, three of the broth-ers took land, and the youngest, my father, chose an edu-cation. After my grandparents gave their daughter away to her husband's family, they had dispensed all the adventure and all the property. They expected her alone to keep the traditional ways, which her brothers, now among the barbarians, could fumble without detection. The heavy, deep-rooted women were to maintain the past against the flood, safe for returning. But the rare urge west had fixed upon our family, and so my aunt crossed boundaries not delineated in space.

The work of preservation demands that the feelings playing about in one's guts not be turned into action. Just watch their passing like cherry blossoms. But per-haps my aunt, my forerunner, caught in a slow life, let dreams grow and fade and after some months or years went towards what persisted. Fear at the enormities of the forbidden kept her desires delicate, wire and bone. She looked at a man because she liked the way the hair was tucked behind his ears, or she liked the question-mark line of a long torso curving at the shoulder and straight at the hip. For warm eyes or a soft voice or a slow walk—that's all—a few hairs, a line, a brightness, a sound, a pace, she gave up family. She offered us up for a charm that vanished with tiredness, a pigtail that didn't toss when the wind died. Why, the wrong lighting could erase the dearest thing about him.

It could very well have been, however, that my aunt did not take subtle enjoyment of her friend, but, a wild woman, kept rollicking company. Imagining her free with sex doesn't fit, though. I don't know any women like that, or men either. Unless I see her life branching into mine, she gives me no ancestral help.

To sustain her being in love, she often worked at herself in the mirror, guessing at the colours and shapes that would interest him, changing them fre-quently in order to hit on the right combination. She wanted him to look back.

On a farm near the sea, a woman who tended her appearance reaped a reputation for eccentricity. All the married women blunt-cut their hair in flaps about their ears or pulled it back in tight buns. No nonsense. Neither style blew easily into heart-catching tangles. And at their weddings they displayed themselves in their long hair for the last time. 'It brushed the backs of my knees,' my mother tells me. 'It was braided, and even so, it brushed the backs of my knees.'

At the mirror my aunt combed individuality into her bob. A bun could have been contrived to escape into black streamers blowing in the wind or in quiet wisps about her face, but only the older women in our picture album wear buns. She brushed her hair back from her forehead, tucking the flaps behind her ears. She looped a piece of thread, knotted into a circle between her index fingers and thumbs, and ran the double strand across her forehead. When she closed her fingers as if she were making a pair of shadow geese bite, the string twisted together catching the little hairs. Then she pulled the thread away from her skin, ripping the hairs out neatly, her eyes watering from the needles of pain. Opening her fingers, she cleaned the thread, then rolled it along her hairline and the tops of her eyebrows. My mother did the same to me and my sisters and herself. I used to believe that the expression 'caught by the short hairs' meant a captive held with a depilatory string. It espe-cially hurt at the temples, but my mother said we were lucky we didn't have to have our feet bound when we were seven. Sisters used to sit on their beds and cry together, she said, as their mothers or their slaves removed the bandages for a few minutes each night and let the blood gush back into their veins. I hope that the man my aunt loved appreciated a smooth brow, that he wasn't just a tits-and-ass man.

Once my aunt found a freckle on her chin, at a spot that the almanac said predestined her for unhap-piness. She dug it out with a hot needle and washed the wound with peroxide.

More attention to her looks than these pullings of hairs and pickings at spots would have caused gossip among the villagers. They owned work clothes and good clothes, and they wore good clothes for feasting the new seasons. But since a woman combing her hair hexes

> **She kept the man's name to herself throughout her labour and dying; she did not accuse him that he be punished with her. To save her inseminator's name she gave silent birth.**

beginnings, my aunt rarely found an occasion to look her best. Women looked like great sea snails—the corded wood, babies, and laundry they carried were the whorls on their backs. The Chinese did not admire a bent back; goddesses and warriors stood straight. Still there must have been a marvellous freeing of beauty when a worker laid down her burden and stretched and arched.

Such commonplace loveliness, however, was not enough for my aunt. She dreamed of a lover for the fifteen days of New Year's, the time for families to exchange visits, money, and food. She plied her secret comb. And sure enough she cursed the year, the family, the village, and herself.

Even as her hair lured her imminent lover, many other men looked at her. Uncles, cousins, nephews, brothers would have looked, too, had they been home between journeys. Perhaps they had already been restraining their curiosity, and they left, fearful that their glances, like a field of nesting birds, might be startled and caught. Poverty hurt, and that was their first reason for leaving. But another, final reason for leaving the crowded house was the never-said.

She may have been unusually beloved, the precious only daughter, spoiled and mirror gazing because of the affection the family lavished on her. When her husband left, they welcomed the chance to take her back from the in-laws; she could live like the little daughter for just a while longer. There are stories that my grandfather was different from other people, 'crazy ever since the little Jap bayoneted him in the head'. He used to put his naked penis on the dinner table, laughing. And one day he brought home a baby girl, wrapped up inside his brown western-style greatcoat. He had traded one of his sons, probably my father, the youngest, for her. My grandmother made him trade back. When he finally got a daughter of his own, he doted on her. They must have all loved her, except perhaps my father, the only brother who never went back to China having once been traded for a girl.

Brothers and sisters, newly men and women, had to efface their sexual colour and present plain miens. Disturbing hair and eyes, a smile like no other threatened the ideal of five generations living under one roof. To focus blurs, people shouted face to face and yelled from room to room. The immigrants I know have loud voices, unmodulated to American tones even after years away

from the village where they called their friendships out across the fields. I have not been able to stop my mother's screams in public libraries or over telephones. Walking erect (knees straight, toes pointed forward, not pigeon-toed, which is Chinese-feminine) and speaking in an inaudible voice, I have tried to turn myself American-feminine. Chinese communication was loud, public. Only sick people had to whisper. But at the dinner table, where the family members came nearest one another, no one could talk, not the outcasts nor any eaters. Every word that falls from the mouth is a coin lost. Silently they gave and accepted food with both hands. A preoccupied child who took his bowl with one hand got a sideways glare. A complete moment of total attention is due everyone alike. Children and lovers have no singularity here, but my aunt used a secret voice, a separate attentiveness.

She kept the man's name to herself throughout her labour and dying; she did not accuse him that he be punished with her. To save her inseminator's name she gave silent birth.

He may have been somebody in her own household, but intercourse with a man outside the family would have been no less abhorrent. All the village were kinsmen, and the titles shouted in loud country voices never let kinship be forgotten. Any man within visiting distance would have been neutralized as a lover— 'brother', 'younger brother', 'older brother'—one hundred and fifteen relationship titles. Parents researched birth charts probably not so much to assure good fortune as to circumvent incest in a population that has but one hundred surnames. Everybody has eight million relatives. How useless then sexual mannerisms, how dangerous.

As if it came from an atavism deeper than fear, I used to add 'brother' silently to boys' names. It hexed the boys, who would or would not ask me to dance, and made them less scary and as familiar and deserving of benevolence as girls.

But, of course, I hexed myself also—no dates. I should have stood up, both arms waving, and shouted out across libraries, 'Hey, you! Love me back.' I had no idea, though, how to make attraction selective, how to control its direction and magnitude. If I made myself American-pretty so that the five or six Chinese boys in the class fell in love with me, everyone else—the Caucasian, Negro, and Japanese boys—would too. Sisterliness, dignified and honourable, made much more sense.

Attraction eludes control so stubbornly that whole societies designed to organize relationships among people cannot keep order, not even when they bind people to one another from childhood and raise them together. Among the very poor and the wealthy, brothers married their adopted sisters, like doves. Our family allowed some romance, paying adult brides' prices and providing dowries so that their sons and daughters could marry strangers. Marriage promises to turn strangers into friendly relatives—a nation of siblings.

In the village structure, spirits shimmered among the live creatures, balanced and held in equilibrium by time and land. But one human being flaring up into violence could open up a black hole, a maelstrom that pulled in the sky. The frightened villagers, who depended on one another to maintain the real, went to my aunt to show her a personal, physical representation of the break she had made in the 'roundness'. Misallying couples snapped off the future, which was to be embodied in true offspring. The villagers punished her for acting as if she could have a private life, secret and apart from them.

If my aunt had betrayed the family at a time of large grain yields and peace, when many boys were born, and wings were being built on many houses, perhaps she might have escaped such severe punishment. But the men—hungry, greedy, tired of planting in dry soil—had been forced to leave the village in order to send food-money home. There were ghost plagues, bandit plagues, wars with the Japanese, floods. My Chinese brother and sister had died of an unknown sickness. Adultery, perhaps only a mistake during good times, became a crime when the village needed food.

The round moon cakes and round doorways, the round tables of graduated sizes that fit one roundness inside another, round windows and rice bowls—these talismans had lost their power to warn this family of the law: a family must be whole, faithfully keeping the descent line by having sons to feed the old and the dead, who in turn look after the family. The villagers came to show my aunt and her lover-in-hiding a broken house. The villagers were speeding up the circling of events because she was too shortsighted to see that her infidelity had already harmed the village, that waves of consequences would return unpredictably, sometimes in disguise, as now, to hurt her. This roundness had to be made coin-sized so that she would see its circumference: punish her at the birth of her baby. Awaken her to the inexorable. People who refused fatalism because they could invent small resources insisted on culpability. Deny accidents and wrest fault from the stars.

After the villagers left, their lanterns now scattering in various directions towards home, the family broke their silence and cursed her. 'Aiaa, we're going to die. Death is coming. Death is coming. Look what you've done. You've killed us. Ghost! Dead ghost! Ghost! You've

never been born.' She ran out into the fields, far enough from the house so that she could no longer hear their voices, and pressed herself against the earth, her own land no more. When she felt the birth coming, she thought that she had been hurt. Her body seized together. 'They've hurt me too much,' she thought. 'This is gall, and it will kill me.' Her forehead and knees against the earth, her body convulsed and then released her on to her back. The black well of sky and stars went out and out and out for ever; her body and her complexity seemed to disappear. She was one of the stars, a bright dot in blackness, without home, without a companion, in eternal cold and silence. An agoraphobia rose in her, speeding higher and higher, bigger and bigger; she would not be able to contain it; there would be no end to fear.

Flayed, unprotected against space, she felt pain return, focusing her body. This pain chilled her—a cold, steady kind of surface pain. Inside, spasmodically, the other pain, the pain of the child, heated her. For hours she lay on the ground, alternately body and space. Sometimes a vision of normal comfort obliterated reality: she saw the family in the evening gambling at the dinner table, the young people massaging their elders' backs. She saw them congratulating one another, high joy on the mornings the rice shoots came up. When these pictures burst, the stars drew yet further apart. Black space opened.

She got to her feet to fight better and remembered that old-fashioned women gave birth in their pigsties to fool the jealous, pain-dealing gods, who do not snatch piglets. Before the next spasms could stop her, she ran to the pigsty, each step a rushing out into emptiness. She climbed over the fence and knelt in the dirt. It was good to have a fence enclosing her, a tribal person alone.

Labouring, this woman who had carried her child as a foreign growth that sickened her every day, expelled it at last. She reached down to touch the hot, wet, moving mass, surely smaller than anything human, and could feel that it was human after all—fingers, toes, nails, nose. She pulled it up on to her belly, and it lay curled there, butt in the air, feet precisely tucked one under the other. She opened her loose shirt and buttoned the child inside. After resting, it squirmed and thrashed and she pushed it up to her breast. It turned its head this way and that until it found her nipple. There, it made little snuffling noises. She clenched her teeth at its preciousness, lovely as a young calf, a piglet, a little dog.

She may have gone to the pigsty as a last act of responsibility: she would protect this child as she had protected its father. It would look after her soul, leaving supplies on her grave. But how would this tiny child without family find her grave when there would be no marker for her anywhere, neither in the earth nor the family hall? No one would give her a family hall name. She had taken the child with her into the wastes. At its birth the two of them had felt the same raw pain of separation, a wound that only the family pressing tight could close. A child with no descent line would not soften her life but only trail after her, ghostlike, begging her to give it purpose. At dawn the villagers on their way to the fields would stand around the fence and look.

Full of milk, the little ghost slept. When it awoke, she hardened her breasts against the milk that crying loosens. Towards morning she picked up the baby and walked to the well.

Carrying the baby to the well shows loving. Otherwise abandon it. Turn its face into the mud. Mothers who love their children take them along. It was probably a girl; there is some hope of forgiveness for boys.

'Don't tell anyone you had an aunt. Your father does not want to hear her name. She has never been born.' I have believed that sex was unspeakable and words so strong and fathers so frail that 'aunt' would do my father mysterious harm. I have thought that my family, having settled among immigrants who had also been their neighbours in the ancestral land, needed to clean their name, and a wrong word would incite the kinspeople even here. But there is more to this silence: they want me to participate in her punishment. And I have.

In the twenty years since I heard this story I have not asked for details nor said my aunt's name; I do not know it. People who can comfort the dead can also chase after them to hurt them further—a reverse ancestor worship. The real punishment was not the raid swiftly inflicted by the villagers, but the family's deliberately forgetting her. Her betrayal so maddened them, they saw to it that she would suffer for ever, even after death. Always hungry, always needing, she would have to beg food from other ghosts, snatch and steal it from those whose living descendants give them gifts. She would have to fight the ghosts massed at crossroads for the buns a few thoughtful citizens leave to decoy her away from village and home so that the ancestral spirits could feast unharassed. At peace, they could act like gods, not ghosts, their descent lines providing them with paper suits and dresses, spirit money, paper houses, paper automobiles, chicken, meat, and rice into eternity—essences delivered up in smoke and flames, steam and incense rising from each rice bowl. In an attempt to make the Chinese care for people outside the family, Chairman Mao encourages us now to give our paper replicas to the spirits of outstanding soldiers and workers, no matter whose ancestors they may be. My aunt remains forever hungry. Goods are not distributed evenly among the dead.

My aunt haunts me—her ghost drawn to me because now, after fifty years of neglect, I alone devote pages of paper to her, though not origamied into houses and clothes. I do not think she always means me well. I am telling on her, and she was a spite suicide, drowning herself in the drinking water. The Chinese are always very frightened of the drowned one, whose weeping ghost, wet hair hanging and skin bloated, waits silently by the water to pull down a substitute.

> **Her betrayal so maddened them, they saw to it that she would suffer for ever, even after death.**

Journal and Discussion Questions

1 Compare Kingston's account of her aunt's story to her mother's account. Why is Kingston's account so different from her mother's account? Why did her mother tell her this story at the start of Kingston's puberty? What lesson does Kingston take from this story as a middle-aged woman?

2 Why is the story of her aunt important to Kingston as a first-generation Chinese-American woman? How does Kingston see herself connected to her aunt and her aunt's experiences? How is Kingston different from her aunt—or trying to be different from her aunt? What does "No Name Woman" reveal about what it means to be Chinese or, as in Kingston's case, the daughter of Chinese immigrants?

3 Why do you think Kingston chose the title "No Name Woman" for this essay? Why is the name of her aunt and the fact that she doesn't know her name important? Why didn't Kingston use standard English in her title (such as "The Woman with No Name")?

4 How important is individuality to the various people in "No Name Woman"—Kingston's aunt, her mother, her father, the villagers, and Kingston herself? How do their attitudes about individuality seem to reflect cultural attitudes of Chinese, Chinese immigrants in the U.S., and first-generation Americans of Chinese descent? What does Kingston seem to be saying about the relationship between individuality and being a woman?

5 How are the ideas and practices about courtship and marriage in her aunt's village different from most Americans'? What do Kingston's discussions about these practices reveal about the village's assumptions about family, gender, and freedom? What does a comparison of these practices to American courtship and marriage practices reveal about American assumptions?

6 Why is it important that Kingston's grandfather tried to trade one of his sons to obtain a daughter? Why is it important that the son was probably Kingston's father?

Topics for Writing

1 Analyze one of the themes of "No Name Woman," such as identity, individuality, gender, freedom, marriage, family, the effect of starvation on a society's moral behavior, marriage, sex, freedom, immigrant experience, generational differences, Chinese vs. American values, or another topic.

2 Compare what the two versions of the story of Kingston's aunt reveal about the values and concerns of the two women telling the story, Kingston and her aunt.

3 Write a research paper about one of the Chinese or Chinese-American culture topics discussed in "No Name Woman," for example, women, courtship, marriage, family, children born out of wedlock, individuality, personal freedom, or another facet of Chinese or Chinese-American culture.

Connecting the Readings

Compare how ethnic or racial identities affect people's identity as Americans in Ernest J. Gaines' "A Very Big Order: Reconstructing Identity" and Maxine Hong Kingston's "No Name Woman."

PROMOTING ETHNIC IDENTITIES ON THE WEB

People with a common heritage or common interests often form associations. These associations encourage a sense of group identity for their members and often promote positive images of the group and combat stereotyping by outsiders. Many of these associations, especially those with a national or international membership, have Web sites that publicize the group and its activities, recruit new members, provide news of interest to members, and perform other functions, such as political lobbying and collecting dues. The American-Arab Anti-Discrimination Committee (ADC) and the National Congress of Vietnamese Americans (NCVA) represent ethnic groups of American citizens who immigrated to the United States or are the descendants of immigrants. These pages from the Web sites of the ADC (www.adc.org) and the NCVA (www.ncvaonline.org) describe the organizations.

The Web site of the American-Arab Anti-Discrimination Committee

ADC

Click here to Help ADC During this Time of Crisis

Join ADC's Email List   American-Arab Anti Discrimination Committee   Join or Donate to ADC

Navigation menu:
- Home
- About ADC
- 2008 ADC Board Resolutions
- Board of Directors
- Fast Facts
- Mission Statement
- Chapters
- Contact Us
- Join or Donate
- ADC Email Updates
  - President's Corner
  - Media Desk
  - Publications
  - Legal Section
  - Education
  - Events
  - Feedback
  - Government Affairs
  - Community Profiles
  - Search

Donations

ADC

Membership

Intern Program

ADC

2006

DONATE
Your generosity will
make a big difference.
Go >

ACTION ALERT

What is ADC?
ADC is a grassroots civil rights organization which welcomes people of all backgrounds, faiths and ethnicities as members. Go >

Fast Facts >>

Board of Directors

Did you know?
Over 3 million Americans can trace their roots back to an Arab country.

ADC is committed to:
1. Empowering Arab Americans;
2. Defending the civil rights of all people of Arab heritage in the United States;
3. Promoting civic participation;
4. Encouraging a balanced U.S. foreign policy in the Middle East and;
5. Supporting freedom and development in the Arab World.
Now more than ever, the Arab-American community needs a powerful, effective national and local organization to defend its interests. ADC is that organization. ADC was founded in 1980 by former U.S. Senator James Abourezk. Learn more >>

"ADC: Protecting civil rights and advocating a balanced Mideast policy"

How can you help?
- ✓ By joining ADC you make it a stronger organization.
- ✓ By becoming an active member of your local chapter you can participate in media, education, political, legal and other activities.
- ✓ By registering to vote and encouraging others to vote.
- ✓ By helping to bring other members into ADC and helping to support ADC as an independent, self-sustaining national institution for Arab Americans, you take the most effective steps to make the Arab-American voice part of the national political conversation.
- ✓ By writing to Congress and expressing your views.
- ✓ By getting involved in the civic and political life of your community, whether through school boards, town councils, state legislatures or the federal government, you help make Arab Americans a force in decision making at all levels.
- ✓ By writing a "Letter to the Editor" to your local paper as well as to national news organizations.

What ADC Does:

1. Whenever Arab Americans face discrimination, ADC's Legal Department is there to provide advice and referrals. ADC has a cadre of full time staff attorneys ready to help defend the interests of the community, one person at a time. Our staff attorneys have helped hundreds of people defend themselves against a wide variety of abuses, and been instrumental in many important legal victories in the fight for civil rights and

WHAT'S NEW

▸ **ADC Events**

▸ ADC Letter in Argus Leader
June 29

▸ ADC Letter in NYTimes
June 27

▸ ADC Submits Comment to DHS Regarding the Proposed US-VISIT Exit Program
June 25

▸ ADC, ATFP, AAI Continue to Raise Entry Denial Concerns with State Department
June 24

▸ ADC Column in Arab American News
June 23

▸ ADC Thanks Sen. Obama for Taking Leadership and Personally Speaking with Muslim Supporters
June 20

▸ Oppose Congress' Compromise on our Constitution!
June 19

▸ ADC Calls on Sen. Obama to Personally Address Hijab Removal

The Web site of the National Congress of Vietnamese Americans

National Congress of Vietnamese Americans
Nghi Hội Toàn Quốc Người Việt Tại Hoa Kỳ

E PLURIBUS UNUM - OUT OF MANY, ONE

go Google™

○ Search NCVA   ○ Search www

| HOME | eREPORTER | PROGRAMS | RESOURCES | EVENTS | MEDIA CENTER | MEMBERS | ABOUT NCVA |

Executive Committee

Buy a Book

Focus Areas
Domestic Violence
Economic Development
Internships
Health
Housing
Human Rights
Hurricane Relief Efforts
Immigration
Legislation
Policy Analysis
Voter Education
Youth Leadership
Other Issues

Resources
Census Data
Census - Vietnamese
Americans
Community
Organizations
Database of Capacity-
Building Programs
Grant Writing
Southeast Asian
American Directory
Translator - English to
Vietnamese

Join Mailing List

Make a Donation

About NCVA

Founded in 1986, the
National Congress of
Vietnamese Americans
is a 501(c)(3) nonprofit
community advocacy
organization working to
advance the cause of
Vietnamese Americans

ABOUT NCVA

- History
- Events
- Board of Directors
- Advisory Board
- Consultants

Mission Statement

Founded in 1986, the **National Congress of Vietnamese Americans** is a 501(c)(3) nonprofit community advocacy organization working to advance the cause of Vietnamese Americans in a plural but united America – e *pluribus unum* – by participating actively and fully as civic minded citizens engaged in the areas of education, culture and civil liberties.

NCVA's motto is "e *pluribus unum*" - "*from many, one.*" Organizational colors is light blue with a flowing field of red with three yellow horizontal bars moving from flushed left to focal point on a map of the United States of America. The yellow represents the color of golden rice grains, and the three red bands represent the three north, central and south regions of Vietnam. Red symbolizes success.

The **National Congress of Vietnamese Americans / Nghi Hội Toàn Quốc Người Việt Tại Hoa Kỳ (NCVA)** aims to:

- Promote active participation of Vietnamese and Asian Pacific Americans in both civic and national matters and in community engagements;
- Defend human and civil rights secured by law for Vietnamese and Asian Pacific Americans;
- Seek to eliminate prejudices, stereotypes and ignorance against Vietnamese and Asian Pacific Americans;
- Promote economic development and self sufficiency for Vietnamese and Asian Pacific Americans;
- Foster youth leadership;
- Promote the cultural heritage of Vietnamese and Asian Pacific Americans.

NCVA has grown to become the major deliberative forum of the Vietnamese American community, a federation of organizations and concerned individuals across the 50 states. It is estimated that over the years, some 200 Vietnamese American organizations have been at one point or another affiliated with NCVA. There are others who chose to stay outside of the organizational structure of NCVA, but who still cooperate with it on issues of common concern.

Regular, Open and Public Meetings

NCVA organizes every year a national convention, usually in late summer, alternating between the East and the West Coasts for purposes of balanced attendance. Besides, the Board of Directors meets once or twice a year to review the work of the Executive Board which meets monthly (2nd Saturday of the month) to assess recent developments in the community, both domestically and abroad, designing timely

Nguyen Quoc Hung - President/CEO

Hoang Quoc Tuan - VP External Affairs

Huynh Si Nghi - VP Economic Development

Tran Truong Van-Lan - VP Membership

Lu Anh Thu - Secretary General

Nguyen Dinh Ky - Treasurer

Nguyen Ngoc Bich -

Journal and Discussion Questions

1 Compare the texts and images of the ADC and NCVA Web sites. What is the mission of each association? Who belongs to the associations? What ideas and impressions about the two associations are created by the words and images?

2 What image or images of Arab-Americans and of Vietnamese Americans are promoted by the ADC and NCVA Web sites? What stereotypes are they challenging?

3 The main text of the ADC is divided into three sections—"What is ADC?" "How can you help?" and "What ADC Does"—with the answer to each question in the form of a list. Is this an effective organization for a Web site describing the organization? Why or why not? Would the text be more effective if the "How can you help?" section followed the "What ADC Does" section? Why or why not? How do you think the ADC decided on the order of the items on each list?

4 The central text of the NCVA Web site is organized under three headings: "Mission Statement," "Regular, Open and Public Meetings," and "A Forum and a Network" (which is not shown on p. 54). What does each section discuss? Is this central text effectively organized? Why or why not?

5 The first and second sections of the ADC's main text are separated by a slogan, "ADC: Protecting civil rights and advocating a balanced Mideast policy." The NCVA uses the Latin phrase *e pluribus unum* as its slogan. What do these two slogans suggest about the associations and the ethnic groups they represent? How do the slogans try to attract readers to listen to or to join the ADC and NCVA?

6 Describe the similarities and differences between the two Web sites. Which Web site is better written and designed? Why?

Topics for Writing

1 Write an essay comparing the ethnic associations of the American-Arab Anti-Discrimination Committee and the National Congress of Vietnamese Americas, based on their Web sites. Include a discussion of what the associations try to contribute to their members' sense of identity and to the images that others have of these ethnic groups.

2 Write an essay comparing and evaluating the two Web sites. How well does each Web site describe the association and promote its agenda?

3 Write an essay analyzing a Web site of another group of people brought together by a common heritage or common interests. Discuss how the association and its Web site create a sense of identity among its members and promote an image of its members to outsiders.

ON BEING A CRIPPLE

BY NANCY MAIRS

A poet and essayist, Nancy Mairs (1943–) has a Ph.D. in English from the University of Arizona, where she directed the women's studies program for several years. "On Being a Cripple" first appeared in *Plaintext,* Nancy Mairs' 1986 collection of autobiographical essays. In it, Mairs discusses the complicated relationship between her identity, her multiple sclerosis, and society's stereotypes about cripples. Mairs' other books include the essay collections *Carnal Acts, Voice Lessons: On Becoming a (Woman) Writer,* and *Waist-High in the World: Living Among the Nondisabled;* the poetry collection *Instead It Is Winter;* a memoir, *Remembering the Bone House;* and a spiritual autobiography, *Ordinary Time: Cycles in Marriage, Faith, and Renewal.* Her Web site can be found at www.maskink.com/mairs/.

To escape is nothing. Not to escape is nothing.
—LOUISE BOGAN

THE OTHER DAY I WAS THINKING OF writing an essay on being a cripple. I was thinking hard in one of the stalls of the women's room in my office building, as I was shoving my shirt into my jeans and tugging up my zipper. Preoccupied, I flushed, picked up my book bag, took my cane down from the hook, and unlatched the door. So many movements unbalanced me, and as I pulled the door open I fell over backward, landing fully clothed on the toilet seat with my legs splayed in front of me: the old beetle-on-its-back routine. Saturday afternoon, the building deserted, I was free to laugh aloud as I wriggled back to my feet, my voice bouncing off the yellowish tiles from all directions. Had anyone been there with me, I'd have been still and faint and hot with chagrin. I decided that it was high time to write the essay.

First, the matter of semantics. I am a cripple. I choose this word to name me. I choose from among several possibilities, the most common of which are "handicapped" and "disabled." I made the choice a number of years ago, without thinking, unaware of my motives for doing so. Even now, I'm not sure what those motives are, but I recognize that they are complex and not entirely flattering. People—crippled or not—wince at the word "cripple," as they do not at "handicapped" or "disabled." Perhaps I want them to wince. I want them to see me as a tough customer, one to whom the fates/gods/viruses have not been kind, but who can face the brutal truth of her existence squarely. As a cripple, I swagger.

But, to be fair to myself, a certain amount of honesty underlies my choice. "Cripple" seems to me a clean word, straightforward and precise. It has an honorable history, having made its first appearance in the Lindisfarne Gospel in the tenth century. As a lover of words, I like the accuracy with which it describes my condition: I have lost the full use of my limbs. "Disabled," by contrast, suggests any incapacity, physical or mental. And I certainly don't like "handicapped," which implies that I have deliberately been put at a disadvantage, by whom I can't imagine (my God is not a Handicapper General), in order to equalize chances in the great race of life. These words seem to me to be moving away from my condition, to be widening the gap between word and reality. Most remote is the recently coined euphemism "differently abled," which partakes of the same semantic hopefulness that transformed countries from "undeveloped" to "underdeveloped," then to

> **"People—crippled or not—wince at the word 'cripple,' as they do not at 'handicapped' or 'disabled.'"**

"less developed," and finally to "developing" nations. People have continued to starve in those countries during the shift. Some realities do not obey the dictates of language.

Mine is one of them. Whatever you call me, I remain crippled. But I don't care what you call me, so long as it isn't "differently abled," which strikes me as pure verbal garbage designed, by its ability to describe anyone, to describe no one. I subscribe to George Orwell's thesis that "the slovenliness of our language makes it easier for us to have foolish thoughts." And I refuse to participate in the degeneration of the language to the extent that I deny that I have lost anything in the course of this calamitous disease; I refuse to pretend that the only differences between you and me are the various ordinary ones that distinguish any one person from another. But call me "disabled" or "handicapped" if you like. I have long since grown accustomed to them; and if they are vague, at least they hint at the truth. Moreover, I use them myself. Society is no readier to accept crippledness than to accept death, war, sex, sweat, or wrinkles. I would never refer to another person as a cripple. It is the word I use to name only myself.

I haven't always been crippled, a fact for which I am soundly grateful. To be whole of limb is, I know from experience, infinitely more pleasant and useful than to be crippled; and if that knowledge leaves one open to bitterness at my loss, the physical soundness I once enjoyed (though I did not enjoy it half enough) is well worth the occasional stab of regret. Though never any good at sports, I was a normally active child and young adult. I climbed trees, played hopscotch, jumped rope, skated, swam, rode my bicycle, sailed. I despised team sports, spending some of the wretchedest afternoons of my life, sweaty and humiliated, behind a field-hockey stick and under a basketball hoop. I tramped alone for miles along the bridle paths that webbed the woods behind the house I grew up in. I swayed through countless dim hours in the arms of one man or another under the scattered shot of light from mirrored balls, and gyrated through countless more as Tab Hunter and Johnny Mathis gave way to the Rolling Stones, Creedence Clearwater Revival, Cream. I walked down the aisle. I pushed baby carriages, changed tires in the rain, marched for peace.

When I was twenty-eight I started to trip and drop things. What at first seemed my natural clumsiness soon became too pronounced to shrug off. I consulted a neurologist, who told me that I had a brain tumor. A battery of tests, increasingly disagreeable, revealed no tumor. About a year and a half later I developed a blurred spot in one eye. I had, at last, the episodes "disseminated in space and time" requisite for a diagnosis: multiple sclerosis. I have never been sorry for the doctor's initial misdiagnosis, however. For almost a week, until the negative results of the tests were in, I thought that I was going to die right away. Every day for the past nearly ten years, then, has been a kind of gift. I accept all gifts.

Multiple sclerosis is a chronic degenerative disease of the central nervous system, in which the myelin that sheathes the nerves is somehow eaten away and scar tissue forms in its place, interrupting the nerves' signals. During its course, which is unpredictable and uncontrollable, one may lose vision, hearing, speech, the ability to walk, control of bladder and/or bowels, strength in any or all extremities, sensitivity to touch, vibration, and/or pain, potency, coordination of movements—the list of possibilities is lengthy and, yes, horrifying. One may also lose one's sense of humor. That's the easiest to lose and the hardest to survive without.

In the past ten years, I have sustained some of these losses. Characteristic of MS are sudden attacks, called exacerbations, followed by remissions, and these I have not had. Instead, my disease has been slowly progressive. My left leg is now so weak that I walk with the aid of a brace and a cane: and for distances I use an Amigo, a variation on the electric wheelchair that looks rather like an electrified kiddie car. I no longer have much use of my left hand. Now my right side is weakening as well. I still have the blurred spot in my right eye. Overall, though, I've been lucky so far. My world has, of necessity, been circumscribed by my losses, but the terrain left me has been ample enough for me to continue many of the activities that absorb me: writing, teaching, raising children and cats and plants and snakes, reading, speaking publicly about MS and depression, even playing bridge with people patient and honorable enough to let me scatter cards every which way without sneaking a peek.

Lest I begin to sound like Pollyanna, however, let me say that I don't like having MS. I hate it. My life holds realities—harsh ones, some of them—that no right-minded human being ought to accept without grumbling. One of them is fatigue. I know of no one with MS who does not complain of bone-weariness; in a disease that presents an astonishing variety of symptoms, fatigue seems to be a common factor. I wake up in the morning feeling the way most people do at the end of a bad day, and I take it from there. As a result, I spend a lot of time *in extremis* and, impatient with limitation, I tend to ignore my fatigue until my body breaks down in some way and forces rest. Then I miss picnics, dinner parties, poetry readings, the brief visits of old friends from out of town. The offspring of a puritanical tradition of exceptional venerability, I cannot view these lapses without shame. My life often seems a series of small failures to do as I ought.

I lead, on the whole, an ordinary life, probably rather like the one I would have led had I not had MS. I am lucky that my predilections were already solitary, sedentary, and bookish—unlike the world-famous French cellist I have read about, or the young woman I talked with one long afternoon who wanted only to be a jockey. I had just begun graduate school when I found out something was wrong with me, and I have remained, interminably, a graduate student. Perhaps I would not have if I'd thought I had the stamina to return to a full-time job as a technical editor; but I've enjoyed my studies.

In addition to studying, I teach writing courses. I also teach medical students how to give neurological examinations. I pick up freelance editing jobs here and there. I have raised a foster son and sent him into the world, where he has made me two grandbabies, and I am still escorting my daughter and son through adolescence. I go to Mass every Saturday. I am a superb, if messy, cook. I am also an enthusiastic laundress, capable of sorting a hamper full of clothes into five subtly differentiated piles, but a terrible housekeeper. I can do italic writing and, in an emergency, bathe an oil-soaked cat. I play a fiendish game of Scrabble. When I have the time and the money, I like to sit on my front steps with my husband, drinking Amaretto and smoking a cigar, as we imagine our counterparts in Leningrad and make sure that the sun gets down once more behind the sharp childish scrawl of the Tucson Mountains.

This lively plenty has its bleak complement, of course, in all the things I can no longer do. I will never run again, except in dreams, and one day I may have to write that I will never walk again. I like to go camping, but I can't follow George and the children along the trails that wander out of a campsite through the desert or into the mountains. In fact, even on the level I've learned never to check the weather or try to hold a coherent conversation: I need all my attention for my wayward feet. Of late, I have begun to catch myself wondering how people can propel themselves without canes. With only one usable hand, I have to select my clothing with care not so much for style as for ease of ingress and egress, and even so, dressing can be laborious. I can no longer do fine stitchery, pick up babies, play the piano, braid my hair. I am immobilized by acute attacks of depression, which may or may not be physiologically related to MS but are certainly its logical concomitant.

These two elements, the plenty and the privation, are never pure, nor are the delight and wretchedness that accompany them. Almost every pickle that I get into as a result of my weakness and clumsiness—and I get into plenty—is funny as well as maddening and sometimes painful. I recall one May afternoon when a friend and I were going out for a drink after finishing up at school. As we were climbing into opposite sides of my car, chatting, I tripped and fell, flat and hard, onto the asphalt parking lot, my abrupt departure interrupting him in mid-sentence. "Where'd you go?" he called as he came around the back of the car to find me hauling myself up by the door frame. "Are you all right?" Yes, I told him, I was fine, just a bit rattly, and we drove off to find a shady patio and some beer. When I got home an hour or so later, my daughter greeted me with "What have you done to yourself?" I looked down. One elbow of my white turtleneck with the green froggies, one knee of my white trousers, one white kneesock were bloodsoaked. We peeled off the clothes and inspected the damage, which was nasty enough but not alarming. That part wasn't funny: The abrasions took a long time to heal, and one got a little infected. Even so, when I think of my friend talking earnestly, suddenly, to the hot thin air while I dropped from his view as though through a trap door, I find the image as silly as something from a Marx Brothers movie.

I may find it easier than other cripples to amuse myself because I live propped by the acceptance and the assistance and, sometimes, the amusement of those around me. Grocery clerks tear my checks out of my checkbook for me, and sales clerks find chairs to put into dressing rooms when I want to try on clothes. The people I work with make sure I teach at times when I am least likely to be fatigued, in places I can get to, with the materials I need. My students, with one anonymous exception (in an end-of-the-semester evaluation), have been unperturbed by my disability. Some even like it. One was immensely cheered by the information that I paint my own fingernails; she decided, she told me, that if I could go to such trouble over fine details, she could keep on writing essays. I suppose I became some sort of bright-fingered muse. She wrote good essays, too.

The most important struts in the framework of my existence, of course, are my husband and children. Dismayingly few marriages survive the MS test, and why should they? Most twenty-two- and nineteen-year-olds, like George and me, can vow in clear conscience, after a childhood of chicken pox and summer colds, to keep one another in sickness and in health so long as they both shall live. Not many are equipped for catastrophe: the dismay, the depression, the extra work, the boredom that a degenerative disease can insinuate into a relationship. And our society, with its emphasis on fun and its association of fun with physical performance, offers little encouragement for a whole spouse to stay with a crippled partner. Children experience similar stresses when faced with a crippled parent, and they are more helpless, since parents and children can't usually get divorced. They hate, of course, to be different from their peers, and the child whose mother is tacking down the aisle of a school auditorium packed with proud parents like a Cape Cod dinghy in a stiff breeze jolly well stands out in a crowd. Deprived of legal divorce, the child can at least deny the mother's disability, even her existence, forgetting to tell her about recitals and PTA meetings, refusing to accompany her to stores or church or the movies, never inviting friends to the house. Many do.

But I've been limping along for ten years now, and so far George and the children are still at my left elbow, holding tight. Anne and Matthew vacuum floors and dust furniture and haul trash and rake up clog droppings and button my cuffs and bake lasagna and Toll House cookies with just enough grumbling so I know that they don't have brain fever. And far from hiding me, they're forever dragging me by racks of fancy clothes or through teeming school corridors, or welcoming gaggles of friends while I'm wandering through the house in Anne's filmy pink babydoll pajamas. George generally calls before he brings someone home, but he does just as many dumb thankless chores as the children. And they all yell at me, laugh at some of my jokes, write me funny letters when we're apart—in short, treat me as an ordinary human being for whom they have some use. I think they like me. Unless they're faking. . . .

Faking. There's the rub. Tugging at the fringes of my consciousness always is the terror that people are kind to me only because I'm a cripple. My mother almost shattered me once, with that instinct mothers have—blind, I think, in this case, but unerring nonetheless—for striking blows along the fault-lines of their children's hearts, by telling me, in an attack on my selfishness. "We all have to make allowances for you, of course, because of the way you are." From the distance of a couple of years, I have to admit that I haven't any idea just what she meant, and I'm not sure that she knew either. She was awfully angry. But at the time, as the words thudded home, I felt my worst fear, suddenly realized. I could bear being called selfish: I am. But I couldn't bear the corroboration that those around me were doing in fact what I'd always suspected them of doing, professing fondness while silently putting up with me because of the way I am. A cripple. I've been a little cracked ever since.

Along with this fear that people are secretly accepting shoddy goods comes a relentless pressure to please—to prove myself worth the burdens I impose, I guess, or to build a substantial account of goodwill against which I may write drafts in times of need. Part of the pressure arises from social expectations. In our society, anyone who deviates from the norm had better find some way to compensate. Like fat people, who are expected to be jolly, cripples must bear their lot meekly and cheerfully. A grumpy cripple isn't playing by the rules. And much of pressure is self-generated. Early on I vowed that, if I had to have MS, by God I was going to do it well. This is a class act, ladies and gentlemen. No tears, no recriminations, no faint-heartedness.

One way and another, then, I wind up feeling like Tiny Tim, peering over the edge of the table at the Christmas goose, waving my crutch, piping down God's blessing on us all. Only sometimes I don't want to play Tiny Tim. I'd rather be Caliban, a most scurvy monster. Fortunately, at home no one much cares whether I'm a good cripple or a bad cripple as long as I make vichyssoise with fair regularity. One evening several years ago, Anne was reading at the dining-room table while I cooked dinner. As I opened a can of tomatoes, the can slipped in my left hand and juice spattered me and the counter with bloody spots. Fatigued and infuriated, I bellowed, "I'm so sick of being crippled!" Anne glanced at me over the top of her book. "There now," she said, "do you feel better?" "Yes," I said, "yes, I do." She went back to her reading. I felt better. That's about all the attention my scurviness ever gets.

> ## In our society, anyone who deviates from the norm had better find some way to compensate.

Because I hate being crippled, I sometimes hate myself for being a cripple. Over the years I have come to expect—even accept—attacks of violent self-loathing. Luckily, in general our society no longer connects deformity and disease directly with evil (though a charismatic once told me that I have MS because a devil is in me) and so I'm allowed to move largely at will, even among small children. But I'm not sure that this revision of attitude has been particularly helpful. Physical imperfection, even freed of moral disapprobation, still defies and violates the ideal, especially for women, whose confinement in their bodies as objects of desire is far from over. Each age, of course, has its ideal, and I doubt that ours is any better or worse than any other. Today's ideal woman, who lives on the glossy pages of dozens of magazines, seems to be between the ages of eighteen and twenty-five; her hair has body, her teeth flash white, her breath smells minty, her underarms are dry; she has a career but is still a fabulous cook, especially of meals that take less than twenty minutes to prepare; she does not ordinarily appear to have a husband or children; she is trim and deeply tanned; she jogs, swims, plays tennis, rides a bicycle, sails, but does not bowl; she travels widely, even to out-of-the-way places like Finland and Samoa, always in the company of the ideal man, who possesses a nearly identical set of characteristics. There are a few exceptions. Though usually white and often blonde, she may be black, Hispanic, Asian, or Native American, so long as she is unusually sleek. She may be old, provided she is selling a laxative or is Lauren Bacall. If she is selling a detergent, she may be married and have a flock of strikingly messy children. But she is never a cripple.

Like many women I know, I have always had an uneasy relationship with my body. I was not a popular child, largely, I think now, because I was peculiar: intelligent, intense, moody, shy, given to unexpected actions and inexplicable notions and emotions. But as I entered adolescence, I believed myself unpopular because I was homely: my breasts too flat, my mouth too wide, my hips too narrow, my clothing never quite right in fit or style. I was not, in fact, particularly ugly, old photographs inform me, though I was well off the ideal; but I carried this sense of self-alienation with me into adulthood, where it regenerated in response to the depredations of MS. Even with my brace I walk with a limp so pronounced that, seeing myself on the videotape of a television program on the disabled, I couldn't believe that anything but an inch-worm could make progress humping along like that. My shoulders droop and my pelvis thrusts forward as I try to balance myself upright, throwing my frame into a bony S. As a result of contractures, one shoulder is higher than the other and I carry one arm bent in front of me, the fingers curled into a claw. My left arm and leg have wasted into pipestems, and I try always to keep them covered. When I think about how my body must look to others, especially to men, to whom I have been trained to display myself, I feel ludicrous, even loathsome.

At my age, however, I don't spend much time thinking about my appearance. The burning egocentricity of adolescence, which assures one that all the world is looking all the time, has passed, thank God, and I'm generally too caught up in what I'm doing to step back, as I used to, and watch myself as though upon a stage. I'm also too old to believe in the accuracy of self-image. I know that I'm not a hideous crone, that in fact, when I'm rested, well dressed, and well made up, I look fine. The self-loathing I feel is neither physically nor intellectually substantial. What I hate is not me but a disease.

I am not a disease.

And a disease is not—at least not singlehandedly—going to determine who I am, though at first it seemed to be going to. Adjusting to a chronic incurable illness, I have moved through a process similar to that outlined by Elisabeth Kübler-Ross in *On Death and Dying*. The major difference—and it is far more significant than most people recognize—is that I can't be sure of the outcome, as the terminally ill cancer

> ❝ Each night I'd get into bed wondering whether I'd get out again the next morning, whether I'd be able to see, to speak, to hold a pen between my fingers. ❞

patient can. Research studies indicate that, with proper medical care, I may achieve a "normal" life span. And in our society, with its vision of death as the ultimate evil, worse even than decrepitude, the response to such news is, "Oh well, at least you're not going to *die*." Are there worse things than dying? I think that there may be.

I think of two women I know, both with MS, both enough older than I to have served me as models. One took to her bed several years ago and has been there ever since. Although she can sit in a high-backed wheelchair, because she is incontinent she refuses to go out at all, even though incontinence pants, which are readily available at any pharmacy, could protect her from embarrassment. Instead, she stays at home and insists that her husband, a small quiet man, a retired civil servant, stay there with her except for a quick weekly foray to the supermarket. The other woman, whose illness was diagnosed when she was eighteen, a nursing student engaged to a young doctor, finished her training, married her doctor, accompanied him to Germany when he was in the service, bore three sons and a daughter, now grown and gone. When she can, she travels with her husband; she plays bridge, embroiders, swims regularly; she works, like me, as a symptomatic-patient instructor of medical students in neurology. Guess which woman I hope to be.

At the beginning, I thought about having MS almost incessantly. And because of the unpredictable course of the disease, my thoughts were always terrified. Each night I'd get into bed wondering whether I'd get out again the next morning, whether I'd be able to see, to speak, to hold a pen between my fingers. Knowing that the day might come when I'd be physically incapable of killing myself, I thought perhaps I ought to do so right away, while I still had the strength. Gradually I came to understand that the Nancy who might one day lie inert under a bedsheet, arms and legs paralyzed, unable to feed or bathe herself, unable to reach out for a gun, a bottle of pills, was not the Nancy I was at present, and that I could not presume to make decisions for that future Nancy, who might well not want in the least to die. Now the only provision I've made for

the future Nancy is that when the time comes—and it is likely to come in the form of pneumonia, friend to the weak and the old—I am not to be treated with machines and medications. If she is unable to communicate by then, I hope she will be satisfied with these terms.

Thinking all the time about having MS grew tiresome and intrusive, especially in the large and tragic mode in which I was accustomed to considering my plight. Months and even years went by without catastrophe (at least without one related to MS), and really I was awfully busy, what with George and children and snakes and students and poems, and I hadn't the time, let alone the inclination, to devote myself to being a disease. Too, the richer my life became, the funnier it seemed, as though there were some connection between largesse and laughter, and so my tragic stance began to waver until, even with the aid of a brace and a cane, I couldn't hold it for very long at a time.

After several years I was satisfied with my adjustment. I had suffered my grief and fury and terror, I thought, but now I was at ease with my lot. Then one summer day I set out with George and the children across the desert for a vacation in California. Part way to Yuma I became aware that my right leg felt funny. "I think I've had an exacerbation," I told George. "What shall we do?" he asked. "I think we'd better get the hell to California," I said, "because I don't know whether I'll ever make it again." So we went on to San Diego and then to Orange, up the Pacific Coast Highway to Santa Cruz, across to Yosemite, down to Sequoia and Joshua Tree, and so back over the desert to home. It was a fine two-week trip, filled with friends and fair weather, and I wouldn't have missed it for the world, though I did in fact make it back to California two years later. Nor would there have been any point in missing it, since in MS, once the symptoms have appeared, the neurological damage has been done, and there's no way to predict or prevent that damage.

The incident spoiled my self-satisfaction, however. It renewed my grief and fury and terror, and I learned that one never finishes adjusting to MS. I don't know now why I thought one would. One does not, after all, finish adjusting to life, and MS is simply a fact of my life—not my favorite fact, of course—but as ordinary as my nose and my tropical fish and my yellow Mazda station wagon. It may at any time get worse, but no amount of worry, or anticipation can prepare me for a new loss. My life is a lesson in losses. I learn one at a time.

And I had best be patient in the learning, since I'll have to do it like it or not. As any rock fan knows, you can't always get what you want. Particularly when you have MS. You can't, for example, get cured. In recent years researchers and the organizations that fund research have started to pay MS some attention even though it isn't fatal; perhaps they have begun to see that life is something other than a quantitative phenomenon, that one may be very much alive for a very long time in a life that isn't worth living. The researchers have made some progress toward understanding the mechanism of the disease: It may well be an autoimmune reaction triggered by a slow-acting virus. But they are nowhere near its prevention, control, or cure. And most of us want to be cured. Some, unable to accept incurability, grasp at one treatment after another, no matter how bizarre: megavitamin therapy, gluten-free diet, injections of cobra venom, hypothermal suits, lymphocyto-pharesis, hyperbaric chambers. Many treatments are probably harmless enough, but none are curative.

The absence of a cure often makes MS patients bitter toward their doctors. Doctors are, after all, the priests of modern society, the new shamans, whose business is to heal, and many an MS patient roves from one to another, searching for the "good" doctor who will make him well. Doctors too think of themselves as healers, and for this reason many have trouble dealing with MS patients, whose disease in its intransigence defeats their aims and mocks their skills. Too few doctors, it is true, treat their patients as whole human beings, but the reverse is also true. I have always tried to be gentle with my doctors, who often have more at stake in terms of ego than I do. I may be frustrated, maddened, depressed by the incurability of my disease, but I am not diminished by it, and they are. When I push myself up from my seat in the waiting room and stumble toward them, I incarnate the limitation of their powers. The least I can do is refuse to press on their tenderest spots.

This gentleness is part of the reason that I'm not sorry to be a cripple. I didn't have it before. Perhaps I'd have developed it anyway—how could I know such a thing?—and I wish I had more of it, but I'm glad of what I have. It has opened and enriched my life enormously, this sense that my frailty and need must be mirrored in others, that in searching for and shaping a stable core in a life wrenched by change and loss, change and loss, I must recognize the same process, under individual conditions, in the lives around me. I do not deprecate such knowledge, however I've come by it.

All the same, if a cure were found, would I take it? In a minute. I may be a cripple, but I'm only occasionally a loony and never a saint. Anyway, in my brand of theology God doesn't give bonus points for a limp. I'd take a cure; I just don't need one. A friend who also has MS startled me once by asking, "Do you ever say to yourself, 'Why me, Lord?'" "No, Michael, I don't." I told him, "because whenever I try, the only response I can think of is 'Why not?'" If I could make a cosmic deal, who would I put in my place? What in my life would I give up in exchange for sound limbs and a thrilling rush of energy? No one. Nothing. I might as well do the job myself. Now that I'm getting the hang of it.

Journal and Discussion Questions

1 How does Mairs connect the specific physical symptoms of multiple sclerosis to the social and emotional effects that the disease has on her and the people in her life?

2 Why does Mairs entitle her essay "On Being a Cripple"? Why does she usually refer to herself as a "cripple" rather than as "disabled" or "handicapped"? Why doesn't she usually use the word *cripple* to refer to other people? Why does she strongly reject the phrase "differently abled"? Why does she compare this naming problem to the labels Americans use to refer to nations that suffer widespread poverty and starvation?

3 According to Mairs, how typical is her experience compared to the experiences of other people with disabilities? What generalities about disabled people should readers make from her essay? What generalities should readers avoid making from Mairs' essay? Why?

4 What does Mairs mean when she writes, "I am not a disease"? What stereotypes about the disabled does "On Being a Cripple" oppose? How does Mairs argue against these stereotypes?

5   Why does Mairs begin her essay with the story of her accident in a restroom stall? Why did this incident convince her "that it was high time to write the essay" on being a cripple? Is this an effective introduction? Why or why not?

6   Although most of "On Being a Cripple" is based on Mairs' personal experience, she also brings in knowledge that she obtained from reading and conversations. Where does Mairs refer to this knowledge? How does she use this outside knowledge with her personal experience to develop and support her ideas?

7   Mairs does a great deal of listing in her essay. Find the different listings in "On Being a Cripple." How does each of these passages contribute to the ideas and impressions that Mairs is developing? Why do you think Mairs does so much listing in this essay?

Topics for Writing

1   Write an analysis of "On Being a Cripple," focusing on Mairs' discussion of how her disease has and has not shaped her identity.

2   Write a research paper about living with a specific disease or disability such as multiple sclerosis or blindness. Find several different perspectives about this situation—those with the disease or disability, their family members, doctors, nurses, therapists, support groups, employers, fellow workers, teachers, and government officials.

3   Research arguments about laws or college policies regarding the disabled, for example, about making buildings accessible to the handicapped or giving the disabled equal access to education and jobs. Select one of these issues and write a research paper that argues your position on that issue.

IS THIS WHAT YOU REALLY WANT?

BY LAUREN MOAK

Lauren Moak (1988–) is a student at the University of Louisiana at Lafayette. She wrote "Is This What You Really Want?" in a first-year composition course in spring 2007. Her essay is a critique of how physical appearance and media portrayals of beauty shape the identities and self-esteem of teenage girls and a process or how-to essay describing how girls can resist media definitions of beauty to develop positive, constructive images of themselves. In a letter about this assignment to her teacher, Monica Busby, Moak writes that her "chosen audience was teenage girls fifteen and sixteen" who read magazines like *Seventeen* and *Teen Magazine*. Earlier she had written an academic research paper about this issue, but Moak writes that for this essay, "I liked not having to write in such a formal tone, and being able to turn the paper into a heart-to-heart discussion. [. . .] I love assignments that allow me to reach out and make a difference in other people's lives."

Lauren Moak

Ms. Busby

English–102, Section 56

1 May 2007

Is This What You Really Want?

What exactly is the message the media is sending out to you girls? Well, that is simple. The media sends the same message on every commercial, billboard, and television show out there. If you do not have the perfect shape, clear complexion, bleached white teeth, and tanned skin, well, you're not "beautiful." You know it's true. You feel the media's pressure and hear its lies everyday. But even though you know that this message isn't true and is pretty much an impossible task, why do you strive so hard anyway? Why do you still feel that you must look this way to succeed in life?

"Who?" you ask? YOU! Fifteen- and sixteen-year-old teenage girls all struggling with the same problem; the media. We all watch the same television, read the same magazines, and listen to the same message sent across the United States. Teenage girls are reached by the media throughout the entire United States from coast to coast. It doesn't matter if you live in the country or the inner-city. Wherever you are, that is where the media will be. But why is this image being so strongly pressed upon you? That is what I will be helping you to understand and overcome.

The reason you are constantly at war with yourself over looking attractive has a lot to do with growing up. The time of puberty for girls carries a great amount of both physical and emotional changes. Physically, you face rapid hormonal and bodily changes; psychologically you are very concerned with your body image (Gerrish). You have no control over puberty and the way your body will react to the new hormones rushing around. However, the way you view yourself can be turned into a healthier self-image. This is a time of weakness, and the media jumps at the opportunity.

How exactly does the media get their message out, and how does it affect you? First we will start out with how the media gets the message across the United States. This unreal body image is sent out every way possible. Models are plastered on newspapers, magazines, Internet pages, television shows, and billboards; you name it, they are there. Airbrushed and cropped pictures are rapidly produced and slapped on anything producers can get their hands on in order to sell, well, everything! This image is being promoted as being the only way to look if you want to be beautiful. The women are extremely tall, thin, and have often had several cosmetic surgeries to become this way.

When girls look at this unobtainable body image, and when you come into contact with this message several times a day every day, it's no wonder why plastic surgery is on the rise and so many are suffering from depression and eating disorders. Girls your age are trying so hard to fit in and look acceptable that approximately 306,000 adolescent girls undergo plastic surgery each year. This is 33,000 more girls than in 2000 (*TeensHealth*)! Something must be done. Not only is plastic surgery being sought out by teenage girls like yourself, but also their self-image is declining and thus resulting in eating disorders such as anorexia (self-starvation), and bulimia (binging and purging).

A positive self-image is very important. The media's influence on females during adolescent development has been linked to lowered self-esteem, negative body image concept, and eating dysfunctions (Cusumano and Thompson). If you do not want to let the media have an effect on you, work on your self-esteem and self- image. If the difference between self-esteem and body image is unclear to you, let me clear it up. Self-esteem is all about how much you value yourself; body image is how you feel about your own physical appear-ance (*TeensHealth*). Having a negative self-image leads to lowered self-esteem, which in turn leads to eating disorders. Add in the media's influence on top of all of this, and you have yourself a big problem (Gerrish).

How does the media leave you experimenting with eating disorders? Again, at this point in your life everything seems to be going crazy. The media feeds you fake pictures of beautiful women. Many are airbrushed, two women cropped together, or tremendously edited by computer or plastic surgery; it is not natural to look this way, especially at fifteen and sixteen. You may feel as if you do not have control over much of anything anymore. Controlling their own body through deciding what they eat or do not eat makes many teens feel as if this is helping them to gain control again (Gerrish). Anorexia and bulimia are definitely not the way to go, but when your role model is a 90-pound woman, it sure seems like a great idea. The media says that if we fail at achieving this "ideal" body image, we must try harder no matter what the costs ("Body Image").

The media also causes us to categorize beauty and place people into specific groups. For example, many individuals describe attractiveness in types such as beauty queens, jocks, studs, jerks, and fashion goddesses of the world (Weiss 1–5). How ads sell this fantasy image is not hard to see, but hearing people talk about it is hard to ignore.

This section is all about how you can overcome the media's false portrayal of beauty. The following will help you develop a greater self-esteem, better self-image, and make you happy to be unique and beautiful for who you are, not for who you are trying to pretend to be.

Self-Image: There are several ways you can work on your self-image. One thing you can try, is not to compare. It is a bad idea to compare yourself with celebrities and models. In reality, most people do not look like the limited body types expressed in the media. Most of the time, models do not even look like that either. Many of those "perfect" bodies appear that way because of photo editing, not nature (*TeensHealth*). Another way is simply knowing that you are beautiful the way you are no matter what anyone says. That is always a great way to build a positive self-image.

Sometimes, we need to realize that our body is not in our control; the size and shape of our bodies are as genetically determined as skin and eye color ("Body Image"). This is why it is so important to overcome the pressures of the media, and be happy with who you are. When you have a positive self-image, you value and respect your body; you are also more likely to feel good about living a healthy lifestyle (Tackett).

Self-Esteem: Self-esteem is made stronger by having a positive self-image. When the two are put together, you are happier and all around healthier. A positive, optimistic attitude can help people develop a strong self-esteem.

For example, saying, "Hey, I'm human," instead of "Wow, I'm such a loser," when you have made a mistake, or not blaming others when things do not go as expected is a good way to start. A positive attitude and a healthy lifestyle are a great combination for building good self-esteem (*TeensHealth*). A healthy self-esteem is very attractive and makes others love to be around you.

Develop Your Own Opinion: Beauty is not something that can be manufactured. It is personal, and thus needs to be something you see as attractive, not what others try to impress upon you as what is beautiful to them. It has been found that beauty seems to have deep biological roots. Beautiful faces, like addictive substances, excite specific reward centers in the brain. Being beautiful and looking at beautiful people make us happy.

Attractiveness is an opinion made by an individual and should not be confined to what the media insists is attractive (Diller). Mere physical attractiveness exerts a generally positive influence on the attitudes and behavior of observers, an effect known as the Attractiveness Halo ("Physical Attractiveness"). Research definitely suggests that being attractive is connected to being content with our life.

Teenage girls need to realize that their view of beauty should not be formed by the media, but through personal reflection and confidence in themselves. The attractive part of a soul mate complements and completes another individual, taking the hidden best part and burnishes it until it glows (Hales 102).

Less Television: Television is a huge part of how the media reaches out to young girls. By watching less television, you will come into contact with these images at a lower rate, and ultimately struggle less with the message being sent out to you. Now, I am not saying cut television out of your life. We all love television, and it is not a horrible thing.

Unfortunately, television is the main highway for the false images pressuring us every day. The average time adolescents spend in front of a television is increasing and is currently at approximately 22–28 hours per week. This has given the media an even more powerful position in the lives of young adults (Santrock 176).

Beauty Is Not Everything: Girls, you also need to realize that being beautiful is not everything. You could be the prettiest girl is the world, but with an unattractive personality, no one would want to be around you. In a study done by Casey Gonzales on eighty-nine students from Loyola University in New Orleans,

Louisiana, it was proved that ultimately personality rather than physical attractiveness was the most important factor to both men and women when pursuing a dating relationship or friendship. This proves that although the media says we must look a certain way, it is not as important as having an attractive personality.

Always Remember: Be confident in yourself, stand proud, keep your personality attractive, and remember that no matter what anyone says, you are beautiful.

[NEW PAGE]

Works Cited

"Body Image and 'Eating Disorders'." *Barnard/Columbia Women's Handbook 1992*. Feminism and
    Women's Studies, 18 Jan. 2005. Web. 9 Mar. 2007.

Cusumano, Dale L., and J. Kevin Thompson. "Body Image and Body Shape Ideals in Magazines:
    Exposure, Awareness, and Internalization." *Sex Roles: A Journal of Research* 37.9 (1997): n.pag.
    Web. 9 Mar. 2007.

Diller, Vivian, and Hara Estroff Marano. "Physical Attractiveness Survey." *Psychology Today* Sept./
    Oct. 1997: n.pag. Web. 9 Mar. 2007.

Gerrish, Christa. "Sociocultural Models of Media Effects." 1998. U of Maine-Machias.
    Web. 9 Mar. 2007.

Hales, Dianne. *How Gender Science Is Redefining What Makes Us Female*. New York: Bantam Books,
    1999. Print.

"Physical Attractiveness of the Face and the Attractiveness Halo." *DataFace*. N.d. Web. 9 Mar. 2007.

Santrock, John W. *Adolescence*. 7th ed. New York: McGraw-Hill, 1998. Print.

Tackett, Chad. "Accept Your Body and Learn to Have a Positive Self Image." *Health Discovery*. Health
    Discovery Network, 2003. Web. 9 Mar. 2007.

TeensHealth. Nemours Foundation, 2006. Web. 9 Mar. 2007.

Weiss, Stefanie Iris. *The Beauty Myth*. New York: Rosen Group, 2003. Print.

Journal and Discussion Questions

1 According to "Is This What You Really Want?" how does the media influence self-image of teenage girls? Why does Lauren Moak believe that adolescent girls are particularly vulnerable to media messages about beauty and body image? What evidence does Moak cite to support her arguments?

2 Is the title "Is This What You Really Want?" effective in encouraging Moak's intended readers to read the essay with an open mind about her position? Why or why not?

3 What advice does Moak offer in her concluding section? How do these solutions address the causes of the problems Moak describes in the rest of her essay? Which of these tips seem most valuable to you? Why?

4 Describe the tone of "Is This What You Really Want?" How are the tone and document design used to persuade Moak's audience of teenage girls?

5 How does Moak use her sources to develop and support her argument? Are her sources credible authorities?

6 Is Moak's essay persuasive? Why or why not? What other arguments and evidence could be added to her essay?

Topics for Writing

1 Write an essay analyzing the relationships between body image, identity, and gender (whether, for example, girls are more likely than boys to tie their self-image or their opinions of others to physical appearance).

2 Write a research paper about other ways, positive or negative, that television, movies, magazines, or other media affect people's sense of identity or self-esteem.

Connecting the Readings

Discuss the relationship between individuals' self-image and society's images of physical normality and beauty in Nancy Mair's "On Being a Cripple" and Lauren Moak's "Is This What You Really Want?"

IDENTITY AND IDENTIFICATION IN MAGAZINE ADVERTISEMENTS

Advertisements often persuade by "identification," inviting the reader or viewer to connect and identify with someone associated with the product or service of the advertisement. That person is often a consumer who uses the product, sometimes a worker who helps make the product or provide the service, and occasionally the owner or chief executive officer of the company that produces the product. The advertisement creates an impression of a person and a strong association of the person with the product, hoping that readers will see themselves—or a person they would like to become—in that individual. Identification not only sells the product but also tries to persuade readers about an image of the self and a set of values associated with that sense of self. Because of the importance of identification in persuasion, magazine advertisements are often composed with the audience of the magazine specifically in mind.

THE ADVERTISEMENT FOR THE DOVE Self-Esteem Fund appeared in many magazines in 2008 and on the Dove Web site. Dove markets face, hair, and skin care products for women. The MyRichUncle Education Finance advertisement appeared in the annual *U.S. News & World Report* issue on "America's Best Colleges" on August 29, 2005.

Magazine and newspaper advertisements are often designed to encourage readers to follow a "Z" design when they look at the ad. Typically, something in the upper left corner will catch the reader's eye and lead him or her into the ad. The lines, text, colors, and images usually lead readers to move their eyes across to the right side of the page, then down the page toward the lower lefthand corner, and finally across to the lower righthand corner. The advertisement's design will try to draw readers' attention to the most important words and images on the page (and away from any health warnings in a cigarette and drug advertisement). You may notice how each of these advertisements works with a "Z" design to direct your attention.

thinks she's fat

So many little girls want to change everything about themselves. All we want to change is their minds.
The Dove Self-Esteem Fund supports uniquely ME!, a partnership program with Girl Scouts of the USA
that fosters self-esteem for girls ages 8 to 17 through educational resources and hands-on activities.
We can help every little girl see how beautiful she really is. **Get involved at** campaignforrealbeauty.com

**the dove
self-esteem
fund**

The Dove Self-Esteem Fund does not accept donations.

BANKS LEND 17 TIMES MORE MONEY FOR CARS THAN STUDENTS.

I AM NOT A CAR.

MyRichUncle™
EDUCATION FINANCE

Funding Students - That's All We Do.

You don't have to wear a license plate to get our attention.
Learn more at: www.myrichuncle.com | 1-888-MyRichUncle.   Faster Approvals. Better Rates.

In 2003, the most recent published data, banks funded $186 Billion in auto loans and $10.6 Billion in private student loans.
Banks also funded $1.28 Trillion in mortgages in the same time span, but students had trouble impersonating houses.

Journal and Discussion Questions

1 What is the central message of each advertisement? How is each ad designed to communicate and develop that message?

2 Analyze the design of each advertisement, describing how it builds its argument. What does the advertiser want readers to read or notice first? Next? After that? Why is the argument organized in this way?

3 Describe the people pictured in each advertisement. What image of women is promoted in the Dove ad? What image of college students is suggested by the MyRichUncle ad? How do these images appeal to the readers (and their self-images) of each magazine?

4 What image does each advertisement create about the company it is promoting? What image does each advertisement create about the people who use the products advertised? How does each ad expect readers to identify with the company and/or its customers?

5 What facts or information does the MyRichUncle ad provide about the company and its products? How does this information help persuade readers? Why doesn't the Dove ad give any information about its soap and beauty products?

6 How does the MyRichUncle ad use statistics and other information to persuade readers? Why is there such a difference between the amount of private loans for going to college compared to the amount of private loans for buying a car and buying a house? Is this a fair comparison? Why or why not?

7 How does the MyRichUncle Education Finance advertisement appeal to people reading the college issue of *U.S. News & World Report*? What kinds of magazines are most appropriate for the Dove ad and why? Considering their appeals to their audiences, which advertisement is more persuasive? Why?

Topics for Writing

1 Write an essay analyzing one of the two advertisements here. Focus on the ways that the advertisement uses identification to persuade readers. Analyze the images and values that the advertisement creates of the sponsors of the advertisement and of readers who might be persuaded by the ad.

2 Write an essay analyzing what the two advertisements imply about readers' images of gender, race, and ethnicity and how the advertisements make use of these implications in their appeals.

3 Write a paper analyzing how advertisements represent members of a specific group of people (e.g., women, Asian-Americans, college students, senior citizens, office workers, or sports fans). Your paper should examine at least eight advertisements from different sources (broadcast and cable television; radio; various magazines, newspapers, and Web sites). You may want to focus on a particular kind of product (e.g., sports fans in beer advertisements or children in toy advertisements).

Connecting the Readings

Discuss the Dove Self-Esteem Fund advertisement as a response to media criticism like Lauren Moak's "Is This What You Really Want?".

THE UNKNOWN CITIZEN

BY W. H. AUDEN

A poet and essayist, W. H. Auden (1907–1973) was one of the century's most important literary figures in the English-speaking world. "The Unknown Citizen" was published in 1939, the year that World War II began and Auden emigrated from his native England to the United States. Auden would later become a U.S. citizen. Perhaps his most famous poem, "The Unknown Citizen" takes a satirical look at the problem of establishing personal identity and individuality in a modern technological and bureaucratic society. Auden's books of poetry include *New Year Letter*; *Nones*; *Homage to Clio*; *Thank You, Fog*; and *Age of Anxiety*, which not only won the 1947 Pulitzer Prize but also named the period following World War II.

To JS/07/M/378
This Marble Monument Is Erected by the State

He was found by the Bureau of Statistics to be
One against whom there was no official complaint,
And all the reports on his conduct agree
That, in the modern sense of an old-fashioned word, he was a
    saint,
For in everything he did he served the Greater Community.
Except for the War till the day he retired
He worked in a factory and never got fired,
But satisfied his employers, Fudge Motors Inc.
Yet he wasn't a scab or odd in his views,
For his Union reports that he paid his dues,
(Our report on his Union shows it was sound)
And our Social Psychology workers found
That he was popular with his mates and liked a drink.
The Press are convinced that he bought a paper every day
And that his reactions to advertisements were normal in every
    way.
Policies taken out in his name prove that he was fully insured,
And his Health-card shows he was once in hospital but left it cured.
Both Producers Research and High-Grade Living declare
He was fully sensible to the advantages of the Installment Plan
And had everything necessary to the Modern Man,
A phonograph, a radio, a car and a frigidaire.
Our researchers into Public Opinion are content
That he held the proper opinions for the time of year;
When there was peace, he was for peace; when there was war,
    he went.

He was married and added five children to the population,
Which our Eugenist says was the right number for a parent of
      his generation,
And our teachers report that he never interfered with their
      education.
Was he free? Was he happy? The question is absurd:
Had anything been wrong, we should certainly have heard.

Journal and Discussion Questions

1 The title "The Unknown Citizen" alludes to tombs of the Unknown Soldier in many countries that honor unidentified soldiers killed in war. Considering this information, what is the meaning of the title? Why does Auden follow the title with the inscription, "To JS/07/M/378 / This Marble Monument Is Erected by the State."

2 What is known about the unknown citizen? Considering all this information about him, why is the poem entitled "The Unknown Citizen"? What is unknown about him?

3 What are the speaker's sources of information about the unknown citizen? Why do all these institutions have information about the unknown citizen? What may Auden be saying about privacy in a bureaucratic society? What sources of information about the unknown citizen are missing from the poem? Why?

4 What does the line "And our teachers report that he never interfered with their education" mean?

5 "The Unknown Citizen" ends with two questions that the poem immediately answers: "Was he free? Was he happy? The question is absurd: / Had anything been wrong, we should certainly have heard." What is ironic about the answer? What does the answer reveal about the speaker or persona of the poem? How would you answer the two questions?

6 What might "The Unknown Citizen" be saying about individuals' identities in a modern bureaucratic, consumerist, democratic society? How can you arrive at this conclusion from the details of the poem? If you were to update "The Unknown Citizen" for the present day, what details would you change? Why?

Topics for Writing

1 Write an analysis of "The Unknown Citizen," focusing on what the poem may be saying about one's identity in modern society.

2 Write an analysis evaluating the benefits and harm caused by governments' and businesses' (and often others') access to so much information about individuals.

3 Write a research paper that takes a position about how state and corporate bureaucracy, the media, or commercialism and consumerism affects individuals' individuality and sense of identity.

HEAD HUNTING IN CYBERSPACE

BY LISA NAKAMURA

Lisa Nakamura is an associate professor of speech communication and Asian and American studies at the University of Illinois at Urbana-Champaign and a specialist in ethnic studies and cyberculture studies. She has a Ph.D. in English from the City University of New York and taught in English and speech-communications departments at Vista Community College, Sonoma State University, and the University of Wisconsin before moving to Illinois. She is the author of two books, *Digitizing Race: Visual Cultures of the Internet* and *Cybertypes: Race, Ethnicity, and Identity on the Internet*, and co-editor of the book *Race in Cyberspace*. "Head Hunting in Cyberspace" was published in the academic journal *Women's Review of Books*, in a 2001 special issue on "New Technologies, New Women." The journal was published by Wellesley University from 1983 through 2004, describing itself as "a unique forum for serious, informal discussion of new writing by and about women." Interestingly, Nakamura's article focuses on race rather than gender in her study of how race figures into the identities that people create for themselves with avatars in the chatspace Club Connect.

AS THE WELL-KNOWN QUOTE GOES, "on the Internet, nobody knows you're a dog." Is it accurate also to say that on the Internet, nobody can tell what race you are? For the large (and increasing) number of people who use the Internet as a social space via chatrooms and other forms of online interaction, this seemingly philosophical question has acquired increasing urgency. Despite claims by digital utopians that the Internet is an ideally democratic, discrimination-free space, a space without gender, race, age, disability and so on, a quick visit to both textual and graphical chatspaces such as LambdaMOO and Club Connect will reveal that these identity positions are still very much in evidence. Though it is true that users' physical bodies are hidden from other users, race has a way of asserting its presence in the language users employ, in the kinds of identities they construct, and in the ways they depict themselves online, both through language and through pictures. These depictions of the self, or online identities, have been termed "avatars." How are avatars raced?

On the Internet, it can be said that everyone is passing. The Internet is a theatre of sorts, a theatre of performed identities. Passing is a cultural phenomenon which has the ability to call stable identities into question, and in that sense can be a progressive thing, but the fact remains that passing is often driven by structural cultural inequities, a sense that it really *would* be safer, more powerful and better to be a different race, gender, age. Millions of computer users "pass" every day, and much scholarly work has been devoted to examining how and why, and what it means that this happens in relation to gender. Piles of articles have been written about cross-gender passing, or computer cross-dressing, but very little has been done on the topic of cross-racial passing, despite the fact that it may be as common, or even more so. I read this notable lack of research on race in cyberspace as springing from the "digital divide," that is, the relative lack of computer and network access minorities enjoy in comparison to whites.

I wish to question the celebration of the Internet as a democratic, "race-less" place, both to interrogate the assumption that race is something that ought to be left behind in the best of all possible cyber-worlds, and to examine the prevalence of racial representation in this supposedly un-raced form of social and cultural interaction.

If race is indeed a cultural construct rather than a biological fact (as Anthony Appiah and others have asserted), then cyberspace is a particularly telling kind of example when we look at the vexed and contested position of race in the digital age. The Internet is literally a "construct"; like race itself, it is a product of culture and its attendant power dynamics rather than a thing or a place which existed somehow prior to linguistic and cultural definition. Race and cyberspace seem to go together like—spam and rice? Cyberspace is a place of wish-fulfillments and myriad gratifications, material and otherwise, and nowhere is this more true than in chatspaces. Both textual and graphical chatspaces encourage users to build different identities, to take on new nicknames and to describe themselves in any way they wish to appear. Digital avatars, or renditions of self, provide a pipeline into the phantasmic world of identities, those conscious or not-so-conscious racial desires and narratives which users construct and inhabit during their interactions in cyberspace.

When I first started researching the topic of race and cyberspace in 1993, the Web was still text-only. Early chatroom participants had recourse only to text when they constructed their avatars. Nicknames like Asian_Geisha, Big10inch, and GeekKing were accompanied by often floridly-written self-descriptions which advertised not who users "really" were, but rather what they wanted to be (which in some sense may boil down to the same thing). These textual descriptions had to do the work of physical description. Race was invisible unless a player chose to inscribe it or include it in their textual character description, and since many did not, a kind of default whiteness reigned.

However, the Web's dominance of the Internet has transformed cyberspace into a world of visual images, a world in which text has taken a back seat. Graphical avatars are visible, and thus race, which was invisible in textual avatars unless specifically put there, became visible as well. Websites like Time Warner's "The Palace" and Avaterra's "Worlds Away Club Connect" allow users to create images of themselves which they can move through space and customize. In this way, graphical chat resembles a video game more than it does live action email, in the sense that other users can see you and interact with you as an image.

I chose to focus on NetNoir's chatspace Club Connect, which is run by Avaterra, a company specializing in web-based meeting spaces, primarily for business. NetNoir is probably the oldest and certainly one of the best-known examples of an ethnic-identity website, which makes it a rare and important example of a minority presence on the Web and the Internet in general. NetNoir started out as a bulletin board addressing African American concerns, and though it is less

than ten years old, it is still about as venerable as a website can be. (It is well known that Internet years are like dog years: one of them equals seven in "normal" time.) I wanted to experience graphical chat through a minority-run website to see if this factor might prove an exception to the overwhelming whiteness I had seen on the Internet in general. I wish I could say that it did, but unfortunately it didn't, or rather only in fairly limited ways. As Thomas Foster writes, "Virtual reality privileges vision as a mode of information processing, and visual perception remains inextricably linked to a history of racial stereotyping."

> "
>
> However, the Web's dominance of the Internet has transformed cyberspace into a world of visual images, a world in which text has taken a back seat.
>
> "

My initial experiences with Club Connect did prove to inject race into graphical chat in ways that I had not seen before. The architects' dream of a multi-cultural virtual world is visible from the start. The log-on screen, the first thing that you see when you enter the site, features a little cartoon icon of a person's head which greets you and asks you if you're having a problem with your password. Since it is practically guaranteed that most new users, especially ones who aren't computer-savvy, will have trouble with this step, viewers are given a great deal of exposure to this virtual greeter. The greeter is an icon of a fairly dark male with dreadlocks and African American features. Though it is generally a shaky move to make claims about which visual images look black, Asian, or otherwise "ethnic," since these judgments are always subjective and can tend to reduplicate the language of essentialism and racialism, if not racism, this figure struck me as undeniably African American.

The figure's position on this screen figures him as "tech support"—both a servant of sorts and a technological expert—paradoxically merging images of domestic laborers, like butlers and house-boys, long associated with both blacks and Asians, and the computer geek figure, an image reserved for young white males. The figure looks young and "hip," as signified by the dreadlocks. These dreadlocks also gesture towards an ethnicity which is up front and center rather than elided or hidden—a real departure from the norm and a genuine innovation. I can count the number of black icons I've seen on the Internet on no fingers. This is a hopeful sign, particularly if one subscribes to the notion popular in media studies that models with color, images that "look like me," contribute to the inclusion of minorities off-screen as well.

Examining icons and avatars provides a wonderful occasion for an analysis of the principles of cybernetic iconography, a field that has yet to be born in relation to ethnic studies. (Jeff Ow's article on yellow-face imagery in video games, "The Revenge of the Yellow-faced Cyborg: The Rape of Digital Geishas and the Colonization of Cyber-Coolies in 3D Realms' Shadow Warrior," published in *Race in Cyberspace*, is an exception to this rule.) Analyzing icons and avatars allows us to lay bare the principles of ethnic image-building on the Net that may seem transparent and "natural" to computer users, who are surrounded by icons every day.

Once you've gotten past the password screen, Club Connect's software invites you to choose your gender, and then assigns you a "starter" or default body which you can customize after getting acquainted with the site. The first time I logged on, I chose the gender "female" and was given the body and face of a young black woman, with fairly dark skin, African American features and short dark hair. I chose a name for my avatar, and began to explore the site.

The first thing I noticed is that I was the only avatar among hundreds who was noticeably dark. Many players chose light-skinned black female characters, Latino-presenting male characters, or Asian-presenting female characters, but there were relatively few black-presenting males. And while I saw many "Asian-presenting" female avatars, I saw no Asian-presenting male ones. This disparity can be accounted for, I am sure, by the fact that it isn't really a disparity; images of Asians in popular culture and the media do tend to be dominated by females (as in newscasting), though this is slowly changing. On the other hand, I didn't see many strictly Anglo-presenting avatars, either.

I found other players extremely helpful and friendly. Perhaps this was because they could tell that I was a new player, but on a site this busy and populated, I suspect that their perceptions of me as "new" were conditioned by another factor: I was the only truly dark character I could see anywhere. A friendly blonde female, named "mspiggy," offered to show me around, and when I expressed interest in exploring the ways I could customize my avatar, actually gave me a new head as a gift! This head, named "Rebecca," was one of dozens of models available for sale in virtual vending machines. Significantly, "Rebecca" was blonde and white-skinned; in fact she greatly resembled my new friend.

While a great deal could be read into this psychologically if one were so inclined, it seems to me indicative of the ways that beauty and race interact together in graphical chatspaces. Her assumption that I would want a head that looked less "ethnic" seemed to project a particular image of beauty that was less—well,

dark. Mspiggy showed me how to detach my old head, which I tucked under my arm, and helped me insert the new one. She then pointed out that my skin color and head color didn't match, saying "lol you look like you have a tan only on your arms!" and offered to help me to acquire some "body spray" so that I could change it. All this time, no mention of race was made.

Mspiggy led me to a vending machine, where I viewed the multitude of different heads available to me. In an unconscious parody of cosmetic surgery and other technological image "enhancements," these were priced across a wide range. None of them were as dark as my old one had been. This commodification of identity is reflected in the chatroom's help screens on the topic of "changing and customizing your avatar's head." I quote: "Each head comes with its own default hair and face colors, which you may be able to customize. If custom face and hair colors are available, look for vending machines that sell or dispense head spray. If your head is sprayable, the popup menus of your avatar and the spray can will give you the necessary options for using the spray. Go ahead and experiment; you'll be able to change and adjust the colors again and again until you find the combination you like."

As hilarious as this description is, it seems to be doing more than simply pointing out the extent to which race has become elective in cyberspace; indeed, the passage omits any mention of race altogether. Instead of inviting you to give your avatar a race, just as you had given it a gender, the passage invites you to "experiment." Here, race is constructed as a matter of aesthetics, or finding the color that you "like," rather than as a matter of ethnic identity or shared cultural referents. This fantasy of "color" divorced from politics, oppression, or racism seems also to celebrate color as infinitely changeable and customizable, as entirely elective as well as non-political.

Clearly, we must look to the subtextual, to the omitted and repressed, to find the place of race in graphical chat. The marketplace and traffic in heads and body spray work in a traditional capitalistic system of supply and demand: the types of heads for sale are available because there is demand for them. Avatars are market-driven. If more players wanted to buy, say, extremely dark or Asian-looking male heads, undoubtedly they would have been on display, but they were not. The prevalent type seemed to be ethnically hybrid along particular lines: Asian-white female, light-skinned black female, etc. There were many male-presenting avatars with animal heads—tigers, cats, etc.—a fact in which a more inquiring mind than mine could undoubtedly find much meaning. Perhaps players choosing this option wished to defer the question of race permanently.

I did not try to ascertain the "real" racial identity of the other players on the site. The veracity of this information would always be in doubt, and it hardly seemed to matter, in a way. This conundrum, and condundrum it is, reminded me of a similar one from literary studies: does race reside in the author or in the text? It seems silly to say that a text like *The Woman Warrior* should be discussed without any reference to the author's ethnicity and race. On the other hand, would that text not be just as "Asian" if we did not know the race and ethnicity of the author? (I'm still working on that one.) I knew that many of the players had come from NetNoir's website, which was a good indication that many of them were African American, but since there are other ways to gain access to the site I knew that many were not. The more interesting aspect of this whole thing seems to be: when users are allowed to choose their races in graphical chatspaces, what do they choose? What do their choices say about the place of race in cyberspace? Why do they create the personae that they do? Where does race go when Asian American and African American users log on? Does it disappear?

As in text-only chat, the identities users choose say more about what they want than who they are, or rather, since these are eminently social spaces, what they think others want. In some sense, Club Connect is a racially diverse space, since players are choosing Asian and African-American presenting avatars, but since it is impossible to tell the race and ethnicity of these avatars off-line, one must ask what kind of authenticity, integrity, or political efficacy these communities can have. Club Connect displays a plethora of raced and gendered bodies, Asian and otherwise, which

gesture towards a complex, multi-faceted and sometimes conflicted awareness of racial diversity. The notion that race can be customized, changed, and taken on or off as easily as one pops the head off a Barbie doll invokes the idea of a fluid identity, a kind of identity tourism. The metaphor of head-hunting in cyberspace is a powerful one, since it also locates identity tourism in a matrix of colonial trophy-getting—a way of eating the Other, to use bell hooks' phrase. Taming and framing the Other by buying its signs and signifiers with virtual tokens seems indeed to be a form of virtual tourism, a kind of souvenir acquisition. The tyranny of visibility, of cybernetic "ways of seeing" in regards to race, has yet to be challenged in spaces like these.

REFERENCES

Appiah, Anthony. "The Uncompleted Argument: Du Bois and the Illusion of Race." *"Race," Writing, and Difference*, ed. Henry Louis Gates, Jr. Chicago: University of Chicago, 1996.

Foster, Thomas. "'The Souls of Cyberfolk'": Performativity, Virtual Embodiment, and Racial Histories." *Cyberspace Textualities: Computer Technology and Literary Theory*, ed. Marie-Laure Ryan. Bloomington and Indianapolis: Indiana University Press, 1999.

Kolko, Beth, Lisa Nakamura, and Gil Rodman, eds, *Race in Cyberspace*. New York: Routledge, 2000.

Nakamura, Lisa. "Race In/For Cyberspace: Identity Tourism and Racial Passing on the Internet." *Cyber-Reader*, 2nd edition, ed. Victor Vitanza. Boston: Allyn and Bacon, 1999.

Journal and Discussion Questions

1 What is the central idea of Lisa Nakamura's "Head Hunting in Cyberspace"? How does the title relate to the purpose and main idea of Nakamura's article?

2 Outline "Head Hunting in Cyberspace." How does Nakamura use white space to divide her article into three sections? What is the central question or idea of each section? How does each section support and develop the central idea of her article?

3 Why did Nakamura choose to study Club Connect? What are the most important details of the story of her experience in Club Connect? Why? What does this story suggest about how people represent themselves with avatars online and why?

4 What does Nakamura mean when she calls race "a cultural construct rather than a biological fact" on page 74? Why does she question the idea that the Internet is "a democratic, 'race-less' place"? How does her analysis of avatars in Club Connect develop this idea? How persuasive is this analysis?

5 Why does Nakamura ask a series of questions in the next-to-last paragraph of "Head Hunting in Cyberspace" instead of drawing conclusions? How do you think she would answer these questions? Why?

6 Name the sources cited in "Head Hunting in Cyberspace." What does each source contribute to Nakamura's argument? How would her article be different if Nakamura relied entirely on her personal experiences with and observations of chatrooms without mentioning other sources?

7 What is positive or encouraging about Nakamura's findings about the identities that people create for themselves online? What is negative or disturbing about her findings? Explain.

Topics for Writing

1 Drawing on Lisa Nakamura's "Head Hunting in Cyberspace" and your own observations and experiences in electronic environments, such as chatrooms, discuss to what extent the Internet approaches a utopian democratic world that avoids or overcomes the racism, sexism, and other prejudices of the "real" world and to what extent it reflects and reproduces those problems.

2 Compare Nakamura's description of Club Connect to the treatment of race and identity in a chatspace that you are familiar with.

3 Write a research paper analyzing people's identities online, focusing on a particular aspect of identity, such as race, gender, ethnicity, age, or behavior, or on a particular electronic environment.

Connecting the Readings

Compare the ideas about the effects of modern technological society on individuals' sense of identity in W. H. Auden's "The Unknown Citizen" and Lisa Nakamura's "Head Hunting in Cyberspace."

CALVIN AND HOBBES

BY BILL WATTERSON

Bill Watterson (1958–) was part of a new wave of comic strip artists that appeared in the 1980s. They argued that comic strips should be respected as art and often created Sunday comic strips that violated the strict panel format of conventional comics. The comic strip *Calvin and Hobbes* ran in hundreds of daily newspapers from 1985 through 1995 and was one of the most popular comics at the time. Anthologies of *Calvin and Hobbes* strips continue to sell well, and many of these strips can be found on www.gocomics.com/calvinandhobbes. *Calvin and Hobbes* explores the imaginative powers of young children while often providing social commentary in the conversations between Calvin, a highly imaginative and bratty seven-year-old boy, and his stuffed tiger, Hobbes, who engages Calvin in conversations when no one else is around. In this strip Watterson comments on consumerism's importance to Americans' sense of individuality.

Journal and Discussion Questions

1 What is Calvin's idea of individuality? What is ironic and humorous about his ideas and the way he expresses them?

2 How does Hobbes respond to Calvin's ideas? How does Watterson use Hobbes to comment on Calvin's ideas, without having Hobbes say many words?

3 What argument is Bill Watterson making about the relationship among individual identity and corporate advertising and consumerism? How does Watterson develop his argument—and the humor—of the strip from panel to panel?

4 Do you agree with Calvin that clothing that displays a logo are often somehow better than clothing that doesn't? Why or why not?

5 Do you agree with Watterson about why people wear clothing that displays commercial logos? Do you wear clothing that displays commercial logos? Why? Why do you think other people wear clothing with commercial logos?

6 What examples of clothing with logos do you think Watterson has in mind? Do you think T-shirts, sweatshirts, and hats with logos of sports teams, bands, or colleges are included in Watterson's criticisms? Why or why not? How about logos for charities or blood drives?

Topics for Writing

1 Write an essay that explains the argument in this *Calvin and Hobbes* comic strip and argues for or against Bill Watterson's position.

2 Analyze the ways in which people's identities—either how they see themselves or how others see them—are shaped by what they own (and do not own), such as clothing, cars, and homes.

STUDENT METAPHORS OF THEMSELVES AS WRITERS

BY JAMES C. McDONALD

James C. McDonald (1954–) is the author of this textbook and a professor of English at the University of Louisiana at Lafayette who writes about teaching college composition. "Student Metaphors of Themselves as Writers," an academic article published in *English Journal* in 1992, examines the issue of identity in students' views and opinions of themselves as writers and college students. *English Journal* is a monthly periodical for high school and college English teachers that features articles on teaching composition and literature, often articles that analyze and discuss student writing.

EARLY IN THE SEMESTER OF MY WRITING classes I have asked students to use their journals to compose several metaphors that describe their images of themselves as writers. Students take several days to think of two or three metaphors (an animal, an occupation, and perhaps an open topic) and compose a brief explanation. I offer a couple of deliberately bland and unimaginative metaphors as models (which most students easily surpass), and, later, I share and explain a couple of metaphors describing myself as a writer, nothing very dazzling. On the day the metaphors are due, I ask all students to share, explain, and discuss their best or favorite metaphor with the class.

Although I doubt that this simple assignment is original, I have found it to be an assignment with transformative possibilities, one that can encourage students to rethink their assumptions about writing and about themselves as writers. I originally developed this exercise for the basic writing course at the University of Southwestern Louisiana, as one exercise that helped me learn quickly some of the background of my students and, more important, some of their attitudes about writing and being in a remedial course so that we could confront resentments and insecurities immediately and discuss, write about, and begin to critique students' feelings and experiences as writers. I sometimes ask students to use the metaphor exercise as a heuristic for a larger writing assignment about their images of themselves as writers.

The success of this assignment has encouraged me to use it in most of my writing courses, including honors and advanced writing classes. The prose in the journals for these classes is more sophisticated and less error-ridden, yet the metaphors of the students in basic writing seem just as imaginative and revealing and are often more poignant, for these students often reflect about failures and frustrations with writing as well as successes and comment on fears as well as hopes about the future. Most students are able to use their metaphors to express a wealth of information about themselves as writers in a few words.

METAPHORS OF PROCESS AND SPEED.

Student metaphors often describe their writing processes and rituals, sometimes contrasting them with the process that they believe "good writers" follow. One woman, for example, compared herself to her pet cat Kitty Wells (because she writes most comfortably in a special chair and place in her home), her profession as a dental assistant (because she has "to have all my tools around [her] in a special order [including her] Dr. Pepper, cigarettes, astrary [ashtray], & food"), and her car "on a cold winter morning" (because she finds it hard to get started, but works quickly once she is warmed up). Some students have compared themselves to chemists or chefs, trying to blend all the "elements" or "ingredients" of good writing (usually with a large amount of grammar and punctuation) to create something. Others are more concrete, focusing on what kind of manuscript they produce: "I think I somehow write like an elephant, because I write very wide and I get very sloppy." Another student wrote that her writing is "small and messy" like a mouse and that she resembles a doctor because

> Doctors write so you can not read or understand what they wrote. And my writing is like

that because it is messay and I can not understand sometimes what I meant to say in a sentence.

Often students use sports and race metaphors to describe a goal-oriented, often competitive process. Two students who selected race-car driver metaphors described themselves as starting slowly, picking up speed, and eventually crossing the finish line in triumph.

Students often select metaphors to describe their writing process as slow or chaotic, prone to failure and requiring hard, pain-staking work. As with the student who compared herself to a car on a cold morning, slowness is a sign of poor writing.

> Well to start off with, I figure I write like a turtle. It takes me awhile to get started with ideas of what to put in my paper. Sometimes I can come up with great ideas, but I don't quite know how to put them together. Often my paper sounds quite confusing to me after I finish. Sometimes after I get started, if it is a good subject, my ideas flow rather easily. . . . I think I write like the subject chemistry. Very confusing and sometimes hard to understand. I also feel thogh if I work at it long enough I can come up with something quite good.

Another who chose a turtle metaphor wrote,

> I work so slow to try to avoid problems. However by me working so slow and intense my ideas seem to be blocked. It's so hard for me to cross the finish line once I get started. Writing is like for me is like a turtle trying to win a race against a rabbit. Writing is basically just a hard finish for me.

Slowness is a major concern of students who use metaphors of trying to start and drive an old automobile. One student wrote,

> I write like an old car. It takes time to get started. Once it get started and gas keep flowing into the engine the car keeps on moving. Once it stop it takes a long time to get it started again. As long as the car is not cold it keep going. Just don't put to much on the engine at one time because it will stop and we do not want that to happen: Right now I am writing like an old car because I been off for a while. Once the car get use to the highway a gain it would be as good as new.

Equating writing slowly with writing ineffectively may reflect the fact that many English classes and the writing portions of standardized examinations expect students to compose an essay in an hour or less. Only occasionally do students hint that taking time to prepare to write or writing slowly might be necessary because of the difficulty of their writing task or that proceeding carefully might be wise when considering complex issues or assessing the challenges of a writing situation.

The sports and race metaphors are often more complicated, suggesting ambivalent attitudes about writing. Most students writing these metaphors portray themselves as winners or heroes (if not now at least some day in the future), but typically these students raise the possibility of losing and failing, as in the simile of the turtle racing the rabbit, or they intensify the adversity of the situation to create a more dramatic metaphor. The race-car driver metaphor is particularly interesting because in a typical auto race only a few cars cross the finish line as most cars crash or break down well before the end of the race. It is all or nothing for the writers. They triumph or fail. There is no middle ground. In another sports metaphor, one freshman compared himself to a field-goal kicker whose kick "hits the upright and goes through the goal"; only an inch or two separated being a hero from being a goat. The same student offered a metaphor of himself as an eagle.

> I am the Eagle who flys the lake stocking [stalking] a trout. Constanly looking for the shine of his scales reflecting off the water. From one shore to the next only to stop at a tree for a rest. Then only two take off again serching for the matter to fill the empty void I have deep in my stomack. There off the point where the willo hangs in the water is that sparkle I was looking for. Turning slowly and gaining altitude so I can get a good perspective of the area. There it is again. My eyes follow the sparkle as it moves towads the shore. Down I plunge my speed is up to Mack I not lossing sight of my prey. Now with in claw distance. I throw my wings back and use the air to stop my decent. Now directly over the prey I extend my claws and grab the delecious treat from the water. Not as big as I thought but it will do. Now up to the my nest and reap over my rewards, All of a sudden a sharp pain comming from the toe of my right claw. The prey seems to stop me in mid air. As I try to to stop from tubling to the water. I then see my mistake as the fisherman on the bank stares in his amazement at what he has caught with the artificial bait.

He did everything right but still ended up hurt and embarrassed. The student told the class that grammar, spelling, and punctuation normally were the things that stopped him in mid-flight.

METAPHORS OF FEAR AND COURAGE. Not surprisingly, many metaphors show writing as a dangerous or fearful activity that the student must negotiate with courage and trepidation. "Bravery is a number one priority," wrote one student who compared himself to a matador. One student pictured herself as a successful shoplifter who grabs ideas wherever she can; a shopping metaphor could have suggested grabbing ideas just as well—but it would have lacked the sense of risk and daring. Another woman compared herself to a person beginning a new or difficult job.

> I get nerves when I have to write a paper because I feel like I am going to fail because I am not good at it. I want to be able to write good, but when it comes time to write something it comes out terrible. I say it is like a new job because a person is always nerves at their new or first job. And they do not want to fail. If the job is difficult they may get scared because they fear they might fail. I do not know how to begin a paper or write a godd sentence. Just like anything if you work at it, it will become easier.

Another woman, a one-time basic English student, wrote,

> In writing, I would describe myself as a cat crossing a busy highway. The cat takes a long time to even take that 1st step in crossing the street. But once the cat get that little stretch to make it to the other side, he goes for it and won't stop. At least that's what going throug the cat's mind. Unfortunatly, the cat get stuck in the middle of the high way and can't get that little boost to go futher cause the cars are coming too fast. The cat sits patiently. Finally there's a split second for the cat to get to the other side and he makes it.
>
> I compare myself in that way cause it takes me a long time to to get started on writing my paper and I have to put alot of thought into what I'm writing. When I get started there's no stopping me until I get stuck in the middle and have nothing else to say. I keep concentrating until something comes up & I go for it. When I've finished the paper & if I make a good grade then I feel that I've accomplished something. Even if I don't make an good grade but put forth

> **"Writers confident of their abilities see themselves facing a flood of ideas, knowledge, and possibilities pouring forth from their own minds."**

all my effort into that paper then it's still an accomplishment for me.

In their journals and class discussions, students reveal that the dangers that they most fear are receiving low grades, reading hurtful comments by teachers, and seeing their paper filled with red marks about errors. Students with successful writing experiences in high school, however, express a sense of risk and fear much less often, and typically their fears are different. An honors student wrote that she would like to compare herself to a lion, "brave, strong & sure. However, I am more a literary fawn. I am unsure of my ability & more than a little afraid to step out in the open." But her explanation revealed a fear of what people will think of her ideas, not of being caught making an error.

> I'm sometimes afraid others will think I'm strange if I reveal my real thoughts. . . . I remember what happened to someone else who always questioned everything. Others made him drink hemlock.

Honors students, in fact, sometimes represent themselves as predators, a kind of metaphor I have yet to see in a weaker writer. One honors student wrote,

> I am like a cobra in the sense of both being short but lethal. . . . The cobra is an animal who slithers through the underbrush, until he has sighted some pray. I am a writer who goes quietly through life, until I reach something that interests me. I am like a cobra in the sense that our prey is not left unscathed.

Another in the same class compared herself to a panther and an industrialist.

> Like a panther, I hide behind a pair of cold, glaring eyes. I hunt for my food for thought just as a panther searches for his prey. I am quick to pounce upon an idea and delve further into its meaning looking for a purpose within it. The panther silently kills his prey in order to satisfy himself. I must search for ideas and thoughts which I can feed upon until I have exhausted the its purpose.
>
> An industrialist thrives on his greed and selfishness much as I thrive on my emotions. I capitalize off of my ability to think. I am also

quite selfish in the sense of my writings. I use them as weapons against the world.

METAPHORS OF CONTROL. Related to these metaphors are metaphors that picture the student taking "control" of a chaotic or dangerous situation. The eagle/field-goal kicker compared himself to "the helicopter before the rotary was involved. The flight would happen but there was no direction or control." Another student used the metaphor of a business executive running a large corporation and

> telling all of my employees to do this and do this. I see myself making tremendous amounts of money and buyin everything I want. As a writer sitting in a class room having control of everything I write down is quite the same as telling people what to do. Making good grades is similiar to making large amounts of money.

Honors students also use metaphors about control:

> Other times I am an electrician, trying to ground the live wires in my mind. All those ideas, phrases & thoughts that seem to come from nowhere must be sorted out. Some I throw away, others I write down to think out later.

"I think of myself as a traffic director," wrote another honors student.

> I have to keep my ideas for my paper flowing so I won't get stuck on what to write. This is like a traffic director trying to keep traffic flowing smoothly so there will not be a trafficjam. When I lose my train of thought and I stop thinking of ideas, everything gets confusing & I don't know what to write. When a traffic director stops directing traffic all the vehicles are in confusion.

I sense a difference between the metaphors of control used by confident and unconfident writers. Writers confident of their abilities see themselves facing a flood of ideas, knowledge, and possibilities pouring forth from their own minds. Control metaphors imply that the challenge of writing is to direct this flow, to select, focus, and organize data and opinions without being overwhelmed by all the possibilities. Less confident writers tend to see language and writing as difficult to control: they often see writing, especially in school, as a multitude of rules and as an alien exercise where their language often becomes incommunicative and inadequate, where errors seem to be just waiting to happen. Students who have problems filling out a five-hundred-word assignment are worried, not about choosing from a flood of ideas, but about being washed away in a flood of red ink.

The metaphors of weak writers frequently describe their struggles with their errors and inadequacies. One student, for example, comparing herself to a doctor, wrote,

> My writing would naturally be the patient. We would start with an enema to rid the system of all the impurities—lack of direction, long fragmented sentences, and lack of detail—in the patient. After the system is cleared the nurse will begin bandaging, splinting and appling salve until the patient is healed. With all of the tender loving care and attention the patient will be on the road to recovery. As I hope that my writing will progress an recover from all of the ailments it suffers from.

Although optimistic, this student is concerned about surviving, not triumphing. For many students, survival is the most they think they can hope for.

> I think that I am a cat in water. Fighting to get out of it. The cat runs away from the water. It tries to find away around the water. The cat just can't stand water. Cats and water just don't mix. You don't even attempt to put a cat into water. Before you can do it the cat claws his way lose and escapes. If you do manage to get the cat into the water, the cat doesn't stay in the water long. The cat in water is like me being a writer. I try to stay away of writing.

METAPHORS OF SILENCE.

I find that many of the most powerful and moving metaphors are the metaphors of silence and failure that students, especially basic writers, use to describe themselves. One student compared herself to an alligator because "it opens its mouth but nothing comes out." Another saw herself as a mockingbird who can only repeat the songs of others and never sing a song of its own. What was interesting in class was that these two students were excited and eager to share their metaphors with others and were obviously proud of what they had written. These students realized that they could not have composed such metaphors if their metaphors about their inabilities were completely true. Metaphors of silence and failure belie themselves, for through the metaphor the alligator spoke her silence, and the mockingbird finally sang a mournful song of her own.

CONCLUSION: METAPHORS AS INVITATIONS.

Poststructuralists, of course, often argue that all metaphors belie themselves. Having students compose these metaphors, often as an invention strategy, resists the tendency of most composition textbooks to treat metaphors and other figures as "adventitious adornment," to use J. Hillis Miller's phrase, and to assume that writers "write a literal version first and perhaps add metaphors later" (1983, "Composition and Decomposition: Deconstruction and the Teaching of Writing," *Composition and Literature: Bridging the Gap*, ed. Winifred Bryan Horner, Chicago: U of Chicago P, 55). Andrew P. Debicki, in his essay "New Criticism and Deconstruction: Two Attitudes in Teaching Poetry," argues that teachers should bring into the classroom a poststructuralist view of metaphor as something that

> breaks the rules of literal reality in order to engender perspective play, to open up a process of reading and misreading without seeking the closure that is engendered by the production of . . . definitive meaning,

a view of metaphor as "an invitation to explore diverse implications that were engendered by it" (1985, *Reading and Writing Differently: Deconstruction and the Teaching of Composition and Literature*, Ed. G. Douglas Atkins and Michael L. Johnson, Lawrence: U of Kansas P, 175). Student metaphors about themselves as writers are rich in implications and assumptions about writing, about themselves, and about teachers and schools (typically the source of danger in the metaphors). I am uncomfortably aware that my commentary and classifications are inadequate, that the metaphors suggest much more about the writers' concepts and attitudes about language, writing, creativity, and teaching and about who they are and who they are becoming than I could explore in a much longer article. I have begun encouraging students to view their metaphors as invitations, to explore the meanings of their own words, to play with unexpected implications and ambiguities in their metaphors. We try to identify the sources and nature of the dangers that appear in their metaphors, and to discuss their metaphors' limitations—to what extent the students are not like mockingbirds and turtles, and writing is not like chemistry and auto racing. It is valuable for teachers as well as students to discuss and examine such metaphors to encourage students to begin to see themselves, not as drowning cats and muted alligators, but as writers, and to encourage all of us to reflect about what we mean when we call ourselves writers.

Journal and Discussion Questions

1   Outline "Student Metaphors of Themselves as Writers." How is the article organized? What is the central claim of each section of the article? How does each section contribute to the overall thesis of this article?

2   How does James C. McDonald introduce "Student Metaphors of Themselves as Writers"? How does this introduction try to interest *English Journal* readers? If this article were revised for a magazine for teenagers or for college students, what would you suggest for an introduction?

3   McDonald organizes his students' metaphors into four categories: of process and speed, of fear and courage, of control, and of silence. How does he use these categories to analyze the possible meanings of the students' metaphors? What other categories could be used to group the metaphors in this article?

4   Compare McDonald's commentaries about his students' metaphors to the students' own explanations of their metaphors. What was McDonald looking for as he analyzed his students' metaphors? How does his analysis build on the students' explanations? How is McDonald's perspective about his students as writers different from their perspectives?

5   What definitions of "writer" or "good writer" are implied by the student metaphors? How do you think McDonald would define a good writer? Do you agree with these definitions? Why or why not? What metaphors particularly stood out when you read "Student Metaphors of Themselves as Writers"? Why did these stand out from the other metaphors for you?

6   Which ideas and conclusions offered by McDonald about his students seem strongest to you? Why? Which seem most questionable? Why?

Topics for Writing

1   Using "Student Metaphors of Themselves as Writers" as a source, as well as your own experiences and observations about writers, write an essay discussing how students' images of themselves can affect their writing in college or their performance in other classes and what students and teachers can do to encourage or change students' images of themselves in helpful ways.

2   Complete the journal assignment in the article. Think of three metaphors that describe you as a writer; an animal, an occupation, and a topic of your choosing. Then explain what each metaphor says about you and your writing.

3   If the class shares its best metaphors with each other, use these metaphors to write an essay analyzing the class' metaphors of themselves as writers.

Suggestions for Essays on IDENTITY

1   Apply Joan Didion's idea of self-respect to an analysis of Cofer, Mairs, Nakamura, McDonald, Moak, or the Dove Self-Esteem Fund advertisement.

2   Drawing on Gaines and Kingston, discuss what it means to be an American.

3   Discuss how gender, race, and/or ethnicity are involved in individuals' sense of identity drawing from at least two of the following as sources—Cofer, Gaines, Kingston, Nakamura, Moak, and the Web sites of the American-Arab Anti-Discrimination Committee and the National Congress of Vietnamese Americans.

4   Analyze the problems of stereotyping and discrimination using at least two of the following authors as sources—Cofer, Mairs, Nakamura, and the Web site of the American-Arab Anti-Discrimination Committee.

5   Discuss the relationship between advertising and commercialism and identity, drawing on your analysis of Auden, Nakamura, the two advertisements in the chapter, and the *Calvin and Hobbes* comic strip. How does commercialism and advertising affect people's sense of self and how others view people different from themselves. How do commercialism and advertising take advantage of people's sense of self and their ideas and stereotypes they hold about other people?

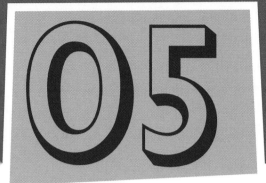

05 Marriage and Family

THE WORD *FAMILY* BRINGS UP MOSTLY warm and positive feelings and associations for most people. For years, sports teams made an anthem of the late '70s song "We Are Family" to celebrate their camaraderie and friendships. Employers like to tell others, "We're like a family here," to describe a close community of employees. You may think of people in your life as family even if they are not related to you. (Whether a network or community of close friends, teammates, or co-workers should be defined as a *family* is an issue you may want to write about.) Yet when people speak and write seriously about family, they describe relationships of conflict, resentment, abuse, and betrayal as much as they describe relationships of love, warmth, loyalty, and support. Many of our greatest and most popular stories, going back to the Bible and Greek mythology, are stories of family conflict, both tragic (e.g., Cain and Abel, *Oedipus Rex*, *The Death of a Salesman*, and *The Godfather*) and comic (e.g., Chaucer's story about the Wife of Bath, *The Taming of the Shrew*, *Everybody Loves Raymond*, and *Little Miss Sunshine*). Often these stories explore the differences between our romantic images and expectations about happy families and the complicated, messy reality of actual family life.

The word *marriage* evokes a greater mix of feelings and associations. We expect almost everyone to get married. Most Americans believe people need to marry to enjoy a complete and happy life, and almost everyone in a successful marriage feels their marriage is the source of their greatest happiness. A woman's wedding day is supposed to be the happiest day of her life (why we don't typically say this about a man's wedding day is also something you might want to write about). And people spend a fortune to fulfill these wedding dreams. Yet half of all marriages end in divorce, and we know that marriage is all too often a scene of argument, boredom, neglect, infidelity, and abuse. Because of our society's mixed experiences and feelings about marriage, many couples are deciding not to get married even as gays and lesbians are fighting for the right to marry.

As a result, marriage and family is a rich topic for essays and arguments. People like to talk about their families and marriages. When we meet someone new, the conversation often drifts to family, partly because family is an inexhaustible topic of discussion and partly because we can share and learn a great deal about ourselves when we talk about family. And friends know their relationship is moving to a new level when they share important stories and feelings about their family lives. But it's not that all conversations about family are harmonious. If someone brings up the topics of same-sex marriage, disciplining children, the effects of divorce on children, or mothers who work outside the home, almost everyone will have an opinion—usually a strong one. We all feel something important is at stake with issues of marriage and family. Our views of the world, our relationships with others and our images and feelings about ourselves are strongly shaped by our family experiences and our judgments about those experiences. So issues about marriage and family are often tied to our most deeply held beliefs about ourselves and our lives.

Because we all have a rich store of experiences, observations, knowledge, beliefs, and emotions to draw from when we write about family, writing about family and marriage can be especially satisfying and worthwhile, both personally and for your readers. Your detailed, unique knowledge about your family and the thoughts and feelings you have about them can be a source of powerful, insightful writing, whether you are writing a personal essay about your family relationships and memories, analyzing an autobiography or work of literature about family, or writing an argument about a social or political issue that affects family life. Still, writing about your family experiences can be tricky. Your most important thoughts and experiences about your family may be too personal or painful to share with others, especially in a college class. If you are writing about complicated and emotionally charged memories, opinions, and beliefs about family, you may find it difficult to analyze and discuss them with the clarity and distance that an assignment may call for. You may also find it hard to listen to questions and criticism about an essay that discusses family experiences and beliefs that are very personal to you. Sometimes you can work out a solution to a problem posed by an emotionally charged subject with the help of a teacher, a classmate, or a writing center tutor. But sometimes the best thing to do is to choose another subject or to write about a different experience.

Finding interesting and important topics about marriage and family that you are able to write about shouldn't be difficult, however, because the range of family issues is vast. Here are a few questions that you can use to guide you in choosing and developing marriage and family topics to write about.

- How do you define marriage? How is your definition different from other people's?

- How do you define family? What are other important definitions of family?

- Why do people marry? How have people's reasons for marrying changed over time?

- Why do couples divorce? Why has the divorce rate in the U.S. and western culture exploded in the last century?

- What is meant by traditional families and by "family values"? What are the strengths and weaknesses of the "traditional" image of the family?

- What alternative images of the family exist? Where do these images come from? How have these families affected American ideas of family values? What are the strengths and weaknesses of these images?

- How should children be raised? What kinds of families are healthiest for children?

- What role should a father have in a family? Why? What are his duties and responsibilities toward his wife, toward his children, and toward himself?

- What role should a mother have in a family? Why? What are her duties and responsibilities toward her husband, toward her children, and toward herself?

- How are families affected by wealth, poverty, and social class? How does family life affect people's standard of living and quality of life?

- How do race, ethnicity, and regionality affect family life and beliefs about family?

- How do television, movies, music, literature, advertising, and other forms of popular culture depict marriage and family? How do these depictions of families affect people's concepts and opinions about marriage and family?

- How do people's family experiences affect their views of the world, their relationships with others, and their political, social, and religious beliefs? Why?

- How do parents' jobs affect their families? What, if anything, should employers do to promote healthy and happy family lives for their employees?

- How do laws governing marriage, divorce, adoption, education, welfare, health care, child care, and sex education affect families? What other government laws and policies affect families? How?

- What role should government take in promoting marriage and family life? What should—and shouldn't—government do to support and guide families? Why?

COMING HOME AGAIN

BY CHANG-RAE LEE

Chang-Rae Lee (1965–) was born in Seoul, South Korea, and emigrated with his family to the United States at age three. He has an M.F.A. from the University of Oregon and has taught creative writing at Hunter College of the City University of New York and Princeton University. His novels, such as *Native Speaker* and *A Gesture Life*, often portray Korean-Americans dealing with issues of identity and acculturation. "Coming Home Again," which first appeared in the *New Yorker* in 1994, is an autobiographical essay that explores Lee's relationship to his mother, the importance of food in family relationships, and the dynamics of American schooling and socialization on an immigrant family.

WHEN MY MOTHER BEGAN USING the electronic pump that fed her liquids and medication, we moved her to the family room. The bedroom she shared with my father was upstairs, and it was impossible to carry the machine up and down all day and night. The pump itself was attached to a metal stand on casters, and she pulled it along wherever she went. From anywhere in the house, you could hear the sound of the wheels clicking out a steady time over the grout lines of the slate-tiled foyer, her main thoroughfare to the bathroom and the kitchen. Sometimes you would hear her halt after only a few steps, to catch her breath or steady her balance, and whatever you were doing was instantly suspended by a pall of silence.

I was usually in the kitchen, preparing lunch or dinner, poised over the butcher block with her favorite chef's knife in my hand and her old yellow apron slung around my neck. I'd be breathless in the sudden quiet, and, having ceased my mincing and chopping, would stare blankly at the brushed sheen of the blade. Eventually, she would clear her throat or call out to say she was fine, then begin to move again, starting her rhythmic *ka-jug*; and only then could I go on with my cooking, the world of our house turning once more, wheeling through the black.

I wasn't cooking for my mother but for the rest of us. When she first moved downstairs she was still eating, though scantily, more just to taste what we were having than from any genuine desire for food. The point was simply to sit together at the kitchen table and array ourselves like a family again. My mother would gently set herself down in her customary chair near the stove. I sat across from her, my father and sister to my left and right, and crammed in the center was all the food I had made—a spicy codfish stew, say, or a casserole of gingery beef, dishes that in my youth she had prepared for us a hundred times.

It had been ten years since we'd all lived together in the house, which at fifteen I had left to attend boarding school in New Hampshire. My mother would sometimes point this out, by speaking of our present time as being "just like before Exeter," which surprised me, given how proud she always was that I was a graduate of the school.

My going to such a place was part of my mother's not so secret plan to change my character, which she worried was becoming too much like hers. I was clever and able enough, but without outside pressure I was readily given to sloth and vanity. The famous school—which none of us knew the first thing about— would prove my mettle. She was right, of course, and while I was there I would falter more than a few times, academically and otherwise. But I never thought that my leaving home then would ever be a problem for her, a private quarrel she would have even as her life waned.

Now her house was full again. My sister had just resigned from her job in New York City, and my father, who typically saw his psychiatric patients until eight or nine in the evening, was appearing in the driveway at four-thirty. I had been living at home for nearly a year and was in the final push of work on what would prove a dismal failure of a novel. When I wasn't struggling over my prose, I kept occupied with the things she usually did—the daily errands, the grocery shopping, the vacuuming and the cleaning, and, of course, all the cooking.

When I was six or seven years old, I used to watch my mother as she prepared our favorite meals. It was one of my daily pleasures. She shooed me away in the beginning, telling me that the kitchen wasn't my place, and adding, in her half-proud, half-deprecating way, that her kind of work would only serve to weaken me. "Go out and play with your friends," she'd snap in Korean, "or better yet, do your reading and homework." She knew that I had already done both, and that as the evening approached there was no place to go save her small and tidy kitchen, from which the clatter of her mixing bowls and pans would ring through the house.

I would enter the kitchen quietly and stand beside her, my chin lodging upon the point of her hip. Peering through the crook of her arm, I beheld the movements of her hands. For *kalbi*, she would take up a butchered short rib in her narrow hand, the flinty bone shaped like a section of an airplane wing and deeply embedded in gristle and flesh, and with the point of her knife cut so that the bone fell away, though not completely, leaving it connected to the meat by the barest opaque layer of tendon. Then she methodically butterflied the flesh, cutting and unfolding, repeating the action until the meat lay out on her board, glistening and ready for seasoning. She

scored it diagonally, then sifted sugar into the crevices with her pinched fingers, gently rubbing in the crystals. The sugar would tenderize as well as sweeten the meat. She did this with each rib, and then set them all aside in a large shallow bowl. She minced a half-dozen cloves of garlic, a stub of ginger-root, sliced up a few scallions, and spread it all over the meat. She wiped her hands and took out a bottle of sesame oil, and, after pausing for a moment, streamed the dark oil in two swift circles around the bowl. After adding a few splashes of soy sauce, she thrust her hands in and kneaded the flesh, careful not to dislodge the bones. I asked her why it mattered that they remain connected. "The meat needs the bone nearby," she said, "to borrow its richness." She wiped her hands clean of the marinade, except for her little finger, which she would flick with her tongue from time to time, because she knew that the flavor of a good dish developed not at once but in stages.

Whenever I cook, I find myself working just as she would, readying the ingredients—a mash of garlic, a julienne of red peppers, fantails of shrimp—and piling them in little mounds about the cutting surface. My mother never left me any recipes, but this is how I learned to make her food, each dish coming not from a list or a card but from the aromatic spread of a board.

I've always thought it was particularly cruel that the cancer was in her stomach, and that for a long time at the end she couldn't eat. The last meal I made for her was on New Year's Eve, 1990. My sister suggested that instead of a rib roast or a bird, or the usual overflow of Korean food, we make all sorts of finger dishes that our mother might fancy and pick at.

We set the meal out on the glass coffee table in the family room. I prepared a tray of smoked-salmon canapés, fried some Korean bean cakes, and made a few other dishes I thought she might enjoy. My sister supervised me, arranging the platters, and then with some pomp carried each dish in to our parents. Finally, I brought out a bottle of champagne in a bucket of ice. My mother had moved to the sofa and was sitting up, surveying the low table. "It looks pretty nice," she said. "I think I'm feeling hungry."

This made us all feel good, especially me, for I couldn't remember the last time she had felt any hunger or had eaten something I cooked. We began to eat. My mother picked up a piece of salmon toast and took a tiny corner in her mouth. She rolled it around for a moment and then pushed it out with the tip of her tongue, letting it fall back onto her plate. She swallowed hard, as if to quell a gag, then glanced up to see if we had noticed. Of course we all had. She attempted a bean cake, some cheese, and then a slice of fruit, but nothing was any use.

She nodded at me anyway, and said, "Oh, it's very good." But I was already feeling lost and I put down my plate abruptly, nearly shattering it on the thick glass. There was an ugly pause before my father asked me in a weary, gentle voice if anything was wrong, and I answered that it was nothing, it was the last night of a long year, and we were together, and I was simply relieved. At midnight, I poured out glasses of champagne, even one for my mother, who took a deep sip. Her manner grew playful and light, and I helped her shuffle to her mattress, and she lay down in the place where in a brief week she was dead.

> ## My mother could whip up most anything, but during our first years of living in this country we ate only Korean foods.

My mother could whip up most anything, but during our first years of living in this country we ate only Korean foods. At my harangue-like behest, my mother set herself to learning how to cook exotic American dishes. Luckily, a kind neighbor, Mrs. Churchill, a tall, florid young woman with flaxen hair, taught my mother her most trusted recipes. Mrs. Churchill's two young sons, palish, weepy boys with identical crew cuts, always accompanied her, and though I liked them well enough, I would slip away from them after a few minutes, for I knew that the real action would be in the kitchen, where their mother was playing guide. Mrs. Churchill hailed from the state of Maine, where the finest Swedish meatballs and tuna casserole and angel food cake in America are made. She readily demonstrated certain techniques—how to layer wet sheets of pasta for a lasagna or whisk up a simple roux, for example. She often brought gift shoeboxes containing curious ingredients like dried oregano, instant yeast, and cream of mushroom soup. The two women, though at ease and jolly with each other, had difficulty communicating, and this was made worse by the often confusing terminology of Western cuisine ("corned beef," "deviled eggs"). Although I was just learning the language myself, I'd gladly play the interlocutor, jumping back and forth between their places at the counter, dipping my fingers into whatever sauce lay about.

I was an insistent child, and, being my mother's firstborn, much too prized. My mother could say no to me, and did often enough, but anyone who knew us—particularly my father and sister—could tell how much the denying pained her. And if I was overconscious of her indulgence even then, and suffered the rushing pangs of guilt that she could inflict upon me with the slightest wounded turn of her lip, I was too happily ob-

tuse and venal to let her cease. She reminded me daily that I was her sole son, her reason for living, and that if she were to lose me, in either body or spirit, she wished that God would mercifully smite her, strike her down like a weak branch.

In the traditional fashion, she was the house accountant, the maid, the launderer, the disciplinarian, the driver, the secretary, and, of course, the cook. She was also my first basketball coach. In South Korea, where girls' high school basketball is a popular spectator sport, she had been a star, the point guard for the national high school team that once won the all-Asia championships. I learned this one Saturday during the summer, when I asked my father if he would go down to the schoolyard and shoot some baskets with me. I had just finished the fifth grade, and wanted desperately to make the middle school team the coming fall. He called for my mother and sister to come along. When we arrived, my sister immediately ran off to the swings, and I recall being annoyed that my mother wasn't following her. I dribbled clumsily around the key, on the verge of losing control of the ball, and flung a flat shot that caromed wildly off the rim. The ball bounced to my father, who took a few not so graceful dribbles and made an easy layup. He dribbled out and then drove to the hoop for a layup on the other side. He rebounded his shot and passed the ball to my mother, who had been watching us from the foul line. She turned from the basket and began heading the other way.

"*Um-mah*," I cried at her, my exasperation already bubbling over, "the basket's over *here!*"

After a few steps she turned around, and from where the professional three-point line must be now, she effortlessly flipped the ball up in a two-handed set shot, its flight truer and higher than I'd witnessed from any boy or man. The ball arced cleanly into the hoop, stiffly popping the chain-link net. All afternoon, she rained in shot after shot, as my father and I scrambled after her.

When we got home from the playground, my mother showed me the photograph album of her team's championship run. For years I kept it in my room, on the same shelf that housed the scrapbooks I made of basketball stars, with magazine clippings of slick players like Bubbles Hawkins and Pistol Pete and George (the Iceman) Gervin.

It puzzled me how much she considered her own history to be immaterial, and if she never patently diminished herself, she was able to finesse a kind of self-removal by speaking of my father whenever she could. She zealously recounted his excellence as a student in medical school and reminded me, each night before I

> **❝ Her face blanched, and her neck suddenly became rigid, as if I were throttling her. ❞**

started my homework, of how hard he drove himself in his work to make a life for us. She said that because of his Asian face and imperfect English, he was "working two times the American doctors." I knew that she was building him up, buttressing him with both genuine admiration and her own brand of anxious braggadocio, and that her overarching concern was that I might fail to see him as she wished me to—in the most dawning light, his pose steadfast and solitary.

In the year before I left for Exeter, I became weary of her oft-repeated accounts of my father's success. I was a teenager, and so ever inclined to be dismissive and bitter toward anything that had to do with family and home. Often enough, my mother was the object of my derision. Suddenly, her life seemed so small to me. She was there, and sometimes, I thought, *always* there, as if she were confined to the four walls of our house. I would even complain about her cooking. Mostly, though, I was getting more and more impatient with the difficulty she encountered in doing everyday things. I was afraid for her. One day, we got into a terrible argument when she asked me to call the bank, to question a discrepancy she had discovered in the monthly statement. I asked her why she couldn't call herself. I was stupid and brutal, and I knew exactly how to wound her.

"Whom do I talk to?" she said. She would mostly speak to me in Korean, and I would answer in English.

"The bank manager, who else?"

"What do I say?"

"Whatever you want to say."

"Don't speak to me like that!" she cried.

"It's just that you should be able to do it yourself," I said.

"You know how I feel about this!"

"Well, maybe then you should consider it *practice*," I answered lightly, using the Korean word to make sure she understood.

Her face blanched, and her neck suddenly became rigid, as if I were throttling her. She nearly struck me right then, but instead she bit her lip and ran upstairs. I followed her, pleading for forgiveness at her door. But it was the one time in our life that I couldn't convince her, melt her resolve with the blandishments of a spoiled son.

When my mother was feeling strong enough, or was in particularly good spirits, she would roll her machine into the kitchen and sit at the table and watch me work. She wore pajamas day and night, mostly old pairs of mine.

She said, "I can't tell, what are you making?"

"*Mahn-doo* filling."

"You didn't salt the cabbage and squash."

"Was I supposed to?"

"Of course. Look, it's too wet. Now the skins will get soggy before you can fry them."

"What should I do?"

"It's too late. Maybe it'll be OK if you work quickly. Why didn't you ask me?"

"You were finally sleeping."

"You should have woken me."

"No way."

She sighed, as deeply as her weary lungs would allow.

"I don't know how you were going to make it without me."

"I don't know, either. I'll remember the salt next time."

"You better. And not too much."

We often talked like this, our tone decidedly matter-of-fact, chin up, just this side of being able to bear it. Once, while inspecting a potato fritter batter I was making, she asked me if she had ever done anything that I wished she hadn't done. I thought for a moment, and told her no. In the next breath, she wondered aloud if it was right of her to have let me go to Exeter, to live away from the house while I was so young. She tested the batter's thickness with her finger and called for more flour. Then she asked if, given a choice, I would go to Exeter again.

I wasn't sure what she was getting at, and I told her that I couldn't be certain, but probably yes, I would. She snorted at this and said it was my leaving home that had once so troubled our relationship. "Remember how I had so much difficulty talking to you? Remember?"

She believed back then that I had found her more and more ignorant each time I came home. She said she never blamed me, for this was the way she knew it would be with my wonderful new education. Nothing I could say seemed to quell the notion. But I knew that the problem wasn't simply the *education*; the first time I saw her again after starting school, barely six weeks later, when she and my father visited me on Parents Day, she had already grown nervous and distant. After the usual campus events, we had gone to the motel where they were staying in a nearby town and sat on the beds in our room. She seemed to sneak looks at me, as though I might discover a horrible new truth if our eyes should meet.

My own secret feeling was that I had missed my parents greatly, my mother especially, and much more than I had anticipated. I couldn't tell them that these first weeks were a mere blur to me, that I felt completely overwhelmed by all the studies and my much brighter friends and the thousand irritating details of living alone, and that I had really learned nothing, save perhaps how to put on a necktie while sprinting to class. I felt as if I had plunged too deep into the world, which, to my great horror, was much larger than I had ever imagined.

I welcomed the lull of the motel room. My father and I had nearly dozed off when my mother jumped up excitedly, murmured how stupid she was, and hurried to the closet by the door. She pulled out our old metal cooler and dragged it between the beds. She lifted the top and began unpacking plastic containers, and I thought she would never stop. One after the other they came out, each with a dish that traveled well—a salted stewed meat, rolls of Korean-style sushi. I opened a container of radish kimchi and suddenly the room bloomed with its odor, and I reveled in the very peculiar sensation (which perhaps only true kimchi lovers know) of simultaneously drooling and gagging as I breathed it all in. For the next few minutes, they watched me eat. I'm not certain that I was even hungry. But after weeks of pork parmigiana and chicken patties and wax beans, I suddenly realized that I had lost all the savor in my life. And it seemed I couldn't get enough of it back. I ate and I ate, so much and so fast that I actually went to the bathroom and vomited. I came out dizzy and sated with the phantom warmth of my binge.

And beneath the face of her worry, I thought, my mother was smiling.

From that day, my mother prepared a certain meal to welcome me home. It was always the same. Even as I rode the school's shuttle bus from Exeter to Logan airport, I could already see the exact arrangement of my mother's table.

I knew that we would eat in the kitchen, the table brimming with plates. There was the *kalbi* of course, broiled or grilled depending on the season. Leaf lettuce, to wrap the meat with. Bowls of garlicky clam broth with miso and tofu and fresh spinach. Shavings of cod dusted in flour and then dipped in egg wash and fried. Glass noodles with onions and shiitake. Scallion-and-hot-pepper pancakes. Chilled steamed shrimp.

Seasoned salads of bean sprouts, spinach, and white radish. Crispy squares of seaweed. Steamed rice with barley and red beans. Homemade kimchi. It was all there—the old flavors I knew, the beautiful salt, the sweet, the excellent taste.

After the meal, my father and I talked about school, but I could never say enough for it to make any sense. My father would often recall his high school principal, who had gone to England to study the methods and traditions of the public schools, and regaled students with stories of the great Eton man. My mother sat with us, paring fruit, not saying a word but taking everything in. When it was time to go to bed, my father said good night first. I usually watched television until the early morning. My mother would sit with me for an hour or two, perhaps until she was accustomed to me again, and only then would she kiss me and head upstairs to sleep.

During the following days, it was always the cooking that started our conversations. She'd hold an inquest over the cold leftovers we ate at lunch, discussing each dish in terms of its balance of flavors or what might have been prepared differently. But mostly I begged her to leave the dishes alone. I wish I had paid more attention. After her death, when my father and I were the only ones left in the house, drifting through the rooms like ghosts, I sometimes tried to make that meal for him. Though it was too much for two, I made each dish anyway, taking as much care as I could. But nothing turned out quite right—not the color, not the smell. At the table, neither of us said much of anything. And we had to eat the food for days.

I remember washing rice in the kitchen one day and my mother's saying in English, from her usual seat, "I made a big mistake."

"About Exeter?"

"Yes. I made a big mistake. You should be with us for that time. I should never let you go there."

"So why did you?" I said.

"Because I didn't know I was going to die."

I let her words pass. For the first time in her life, she was letting herself speak her full mind, so what else could I do?

"But you know what?" she spoke up. "It was better for you. If you stayed home, you would not like me so much now."

I suggested that maybe I would like her even more.

She shook her head. "Impossible."

Sometimes I still think about what she said, about having made a mistake. I would have left home for college, that was never in doubt, but those years I was away at boarding school grew more precious to her as her illness progressed. After many months of exhaustion and pain and the haze of the drugs, I thought that her mind was beginning to fade, for more and more it seemed that she was seeing me again as her fifteen-year-old boy, the one she had dropped off in New Hampshire on a cloudy September afternoon.

I remember the first person I met, another new student, named Zack, who walked to the welcome picnic with me. I had planned to eat with my parents—my mother had brought a coolerful of food even that first day—but I learned of the cookout and told her that I should probably go. I wanted to go, of course. I was excited, and no doubt fearful and nervous, and I must have thought I was only thinking ahead. She agreed wholeheartedly, saying I certainly should. I walked them to the car, and perhaps I hugged them, before saying goodbye. One day, after she died, my father told me what happened on the long drive home to Syracuse.

He was driving the car, looking straight ahead. Traffic was light on the Massachusetts Turnpike, and the sky was nearly dark. They had driven for more than two hours and had not yet spoken a word. He then heard a strange sound from her, a kind of muffled chewing noise, as if something inside her were grinding its way out.

"So, what's the matter?" he said, trying to keep an edge to his voice.

She looked at him with her ashen face and she burst into tears. He began to cry himself, and pulled the car over onto the narrow shoulder of the turnpike, where they stayed for the next half hour or so, the blank-faced cars droning by them in the cold, on-rushing night.

Every once in a while, when I think of her, I'm driving alone somewhere on the highway. In the twilight, I see their car off to the side, a blue Olds coupe with a landau top, and as I pass them by I look back in the mirror and I see them again, the two figures huddling together in the front seat. Are they sleeping? Or kissing? Are they all right?

Journal and Discussion Questions

1 Outline "Coming Home Again." Why does Chang-Rae Lee use white space on pages 89 and 90 to divide his essay into three large sections? How does Lee move back and forth between the story of his mother's death, the story of his going to boarding school, and earlier memories of his life as a child? Why doesn't Lee organize his essay into a straightforward narrative that begins with the earliest incident and ends with the latest?

2 Why does Lee introduce "Coming Home Again" with a description of the pump that fed and medicated his mother? Is this a good introduction? Why or why not?

3 What does Lee mean when he writes, "My going to such a place was part of my mother's not so secret plan to change my character, which she worried was becoming too much like hers"? How did her status as a South Korean immigrant in the United States affect how she raised Lee and why she sent him to boarding school?

4 Why is eating and preparing food so important to Lee's memories of his mother and family? What does "Coming Home Again" reveal about the roles that meals and cooking have for families?

5 How did Lee's leaving home to attend Exeter for high school affect his relationship with his family and affect the person that he became? How did this experience benefit him and his family, and how did it hurt them? How is Lee's experience similar to and different from the experience of leaving home to attend college? Why does Lee conclude "Coming Home Again" with the story of his parents' drive home after bringing him to boarding school?

6 Why is the title of Lee's essay "Coming Home Again"? How is his experience and appreciation of "home" different after years of living at Exeter and college? What does "Coming Home Again" reveal about how education can change a person's relationship to home and family?

7 To what extent is "Coming Home Again" an essay about an American *immigrant* family and to what extent is it an essay about an American family? Why?

Topics for Writing

1 Analyze Chang-Rae Lee's "Coming Home Again," focusing on issues such as immigrant family life in the U.S., Lee's image of an Asian-American family, the importance of food and meals in family life, the influence of schooling on family, or mother–son relationships.

2 Write a research paper about immigrant families. Possible topics include the relationships between immigrant parents and their children, the socialization of immigrant families into American life, and comparisons between immigrant families from different cultures or different generations.

ONCE MORE TO THE LAKE

BY E. B. WHITE

E. B. White (1899–1985) was a satirist, a poet, a writer of children's literature (e.g., *Stuart Little* and *Charlotte's Web*), and perhaps the most renowned essayist in modern American literature. *Is Sex Necessary?*, a satirical book he co-authored with James Thurber, was a best-seller, and *The Elements of Style*, with co-author William Strunk, Jr., is the most famous book on writing of the twentieth century. White was a regular columnist for *Harper's Magazine* from 1938 to 1943 and collected those essays into his book *One Man's Meat*. But he wrote most of his essays for his Notes and Comments column for the *New Yorker*, where he worked from 1927 until his retirement. "Once More to the Lake," originally published in White's Talk of the Town column in the *New Yorker*, is White's most famous essay, and it touches many of the themes that White is known for—respect for nature (despite White's love of New York City and urban life), the pleasures of a simple life, and skepticism about the value of modern technologies—while also contemplating the complexities of memory and relationships between fathers and sons.

ONE SUMMER, ALONG ABOUT 1904, my father rented a camp on a lake in Maine and took us all there for the month of August. We all got ringworm from some kittens and had to rub Pond's Extract on our arms and legs night and morning, and my father rolled over in a canoe with all his clothes on; but outside of that the vacation was a success and from then on none of us ever thought there was any place in the world like that lake in Maine. We returned summer after summer—always on August 1 for one month. I have since become a salt-water man, but sometimes in summer there are days when the restlessness of the tides and the fearful cold of the sea water and the incessant wind that blows across the afternoon and into the evening make me wish for the placidity of a lake in the woods. A few weeks ago this feeling got so strong I bought myself a couple of bass hooks and a spinner and returned to the lake where we used to go, for a week's fishing and to revisit old haunts.

I took along my son, who had never had any fresh water up his nose and who had seen lily pads only from train windows. On the journey over to the lake I began to wonder what it would be like. I wondered how time would have marred this unique, this holy spot—the coves and streams, the hills that the sun set behind, the camps and the paths behind the camps. I was sure that the tarred road would have found it out, and I wondered in what other ways it would be desolated. It is strange how much you can remember about places like that once you allow your mind to return into the grooves that lead back. You remember one thing, and that suddenly reminds you of another thing. I guess I remembered clearest of all the early mornings, when the lake was cool and motionless, remembered how the bedroom smelled of the lumber it was made of and of the wet woods whose scent entered through the screen. The partitions in the camp were thin and did not extend clear to the top of the rooms, and as I was always the first up I would dress softly so as not to wake the others, and sneak out into the sweet outdoors and start out in the canoe, keeping close along the shore in the long shadows of the pines. I remembered being very careful never to rub my paddle against the gunwale for fear of disturbing the stillness of the cathedral.

The lake had never been what you would call a wild lake. There were cottages sprinkled around the shores, and it was in farming country although the shores of the lake were quite heavily wooded. Some of the cottages were owned by nearby farmers, and you would live at the shore and eat your meals at the farmhouse. That's what our family did. But although it wasn't wild, it was a fairly large and undisturbed lake and there were places in it that, to a child at least, seemed infinitely remote and primeval.

I was right about the tar; it led to within half a mile of the shore. But when I got back there, with my boy, and we settled into a camp near a farmhouse and into the kind of summertime I had known, I could tell that it was going to be pretty much the same as it had been before—I knew it, lying in bed the first morning, smelling the bedroom and hearing the boy sneak quietly out and go off along the shore in a boat. I began to sustain the illusion that he was I, and therefore, by simple transposition, that I was my father. This sensation persisted, kept cropping up all the time we were there. It was not an entirely new feeling, but in this setting it grew much stronger. I seemed to be living a dual existence. I would be in the middle of some simple act, I would be picking up a bait box or laying down a table fork, or I would be saying something, and suddenly it would be not I but my father who was saying the words or making the gesture. It gave me a creepy sensation.

We went fishing the next morning. I felt the same damp moss covering the worms in the bait can, and saw the dragonfly alight on the tip of my rod as it hovered a few inches from the surface of the water. It was the arrival of this fly that convinced me beyond any doubt that everything was as it always had been, that the years were a mirage and that there had been no years. The small waves were the same, chucking the rowboat under the chin as we fished at anchor, and the boat was the same boat, the same color green and the ribs broken in the same places, and under the floorboards the same fresh-water leavings and débris—the dead helgramite, the wisps of moss, the rusty discarded fishhook, the dried blood from yesterday's catch. We stared silently at the tips of our rods, at the dragonflies that came and went. I lowered the tip of mine into the water, tentatively, pensively dislodging the fly, which darted two feet away, poised, darted two feet back, and came to rest again a little farther up the rod. There had been no years between the ducking of this dragonfly and the other one—the one that was part of memory. I looked at the boy, who was silently watching his fly, and it was my hands that held his rod, my eyes watching. I felt dizzy and didn't know which rod I was at the end of.

We caught two bass, hauling them in briskly as though they were mackerel, pulling them over the side of the boat in a businesslike manner without any landing net, and stunning them with a blow on the back of the head. When we got back for a swim before lunch, the lake was exactly where we had left it, the same number of inches from the dock, and there was only the merest suggestion of a breeze. This seemed an utterly enchanted sea, this lake you could leave to its own devices for a few hours and come back to, and find that it had not stirred, this constant and trustworthy body of water. In the shallows, the dark, water-soaked sticks and twigs, smooth and old, were undulating in clusters

> **❝ I looked at the boy, who was silently watching his fly, and it was my hands that held his rod, my eyes watching. ❞**

on the bottom against the clean ribbed sand, and the track of the mussel was plain. A school of minnows swam by, each minnow with its small individual shadow, doubling the attendance, so clear and sharp in the sunlight. Some of the other campers were in swimming, along the shore, one of them with a cake of soap, and the water felt thin and clear and unsubstantial. Over the years there had been this person with the cake of soap, this cultist, and here he was. There had been no years.

Up to the farmhouse to dinner through the teeming, dusty field, the road under our sneakers was only a two-track road. The middle track was missing, the one with the marks of the hooves and the splotches of dried, flaky manure. There had always been three tracks to choose from in choosing which track to walk in; now the choice was narrowed down to two. For a moment I missed terribly the middle alternative. But the way led past the tennis court, and something about the way it lay there in the sun reassured me; the tape had loosened along the backline, the alleys were green with plantains and other weeds, and the net (installed in June and removed in September) sagged in the dry noon, and the whole place steamed with midday heat and hunger and emptiness. There was a choice of pie for dessert, and one was blueberry and one was apple, and the waitresses were the same country girls, there having been no passage of time, only the illusion of it as in a dropped curtain—the waitresses were still fifteen; their hair had been washed, that was the only difference—they had been to the movies and seen the pretty girls with the clean hair.

Summertime, oh, summertime, pattern of life indelible, the fade-proof lake, the woods unshatterable, the pasture with the sweetfern and the juniper forever and ever, summer without end; this was the background, and the life along the shore was the design, the cottagers with their innocent and tranquil design, their tiny docks with the flagpole and the American flag floating against the white clouds in the blue sky, the little paths over the roots of the trees leading from camp to camp and the paths leading back to the outhouses and the can of lime for sprinkling, and at the souvenir counters at the store the miniature birchbark canoes and the postcards that showed things looking a little better than they looked. This was the American family at play, escaping the city heat, wondering whether the newcomers in the camp at the head of the cove were "common" or "nice," wondering whether it was true that the people who drove up for Sunday dinner at the farmhouse were turned away because there wasn't enough chicken.

It seemed to me, as I kept remembering all this, that those times and those summers had been infinitely precious and worth saving. There had been jollity and peace and goodness. The arriving (at the beginning of August) had been so big a business in itself, at the railway station the farm wagon drawn up, the first smell of the pine-laden air, the first glimpse of the smiling farmer, and the great importance of the trunks and your father's enormous authority in such matters, and the feel of the wagon under you for the long ten-mile haul, and at the top of the last long hill catching the first view of the lake after eleven months of not seeing this cherished body of water. The shouts and cries of the other campers when they saw you, and the trunks to be unpacked, to give up their rich burden. (Arriving was less exciting nowadays, when you sneaked up in your car and parked it under a tree near the camp and took out the bags and in five minutes it was all over, no fuss, no loud wonderful fuss about trunks.)

Peace and goodness and jollity. The only thing that was wrong now, really, was the sound of the place, an unfamiliar nervous sound of the outboard motors. This was the note that jarred, the one thing that would sometimes break the illusion and set the years moving. In those other summertimes all motors were inboard; and when they were at a little distance, the noise they made was a sedative, an ingredient of summer sleep. They were one-cylinder and two-cylinder engines, and some were make-and-break and some were jump-spark, but they all made a sleepy sound across the lake. The one-lungers throbbed and fluttered, and the twin-cylinder ones purred and purred, and that was a quiet sound, too. But now the campers all had outboards. In the daytime, in the hot mornings, these motors made a petulant, irritable sound; at night, in the still evening when the afterglow lit the water, they whined about one's ears like mosquitoes. My boy loved our rented outboard, and his great desire was to achieve single-handed mastery over it, and authority, and he soon learned the trick of choking it a little (but not too much), and the adjustment of the needle valve. Watching him I would remember the things you could do with the old one-cylinder engine with the heavy flywheel, how you could have it eating out of your hand if you got really close to it spiritually. Motorboats in those days didn't have clutches, and you would make a landing by shutting off the motor at the proper time and coasting in with a dead rudder. But there was a way of reversing them, if you learned the trick, by cutting the switch and putting it on again exactly on the final dying revolution of the flywheel, so that it would kick back against compression and begin reversing. Approaching a dock in a strong following breeze, it was difficult to slow up sufficiently by the ordinary coasting method, and if a boy felt he had complete mastery over his motor, he was tempted to keep it running beyond its time and then reverse it a few feet from the dock. It took a cool nerve, because if you threw the switch a twentieth of a second too soon you would catch the flywheel when it still had speed enough to go up past center, and the boat would leap ahead, charging bull-fashion at the dock.

We had a good week at the camp. The bass were biting well and the sun shone endlessly, day after day. We would be tired at night and lie down in the accumulated heat of the little bedrooms after the long hot day and the breeze would stir almost imperceptibly outside and the smell of the swamp drift in through the rusty screens. Sleep would come easily and in the morning the red squirrel would be on the roof, tapping out his gay routine. I kept remembering everything, lying in bed in the mornings—the small steamboat that had a long rounded stern like the lip of a Ubangi, and how quietly she ran on the moonlight sails, when the older boys played their mandolins and the girls sang and we ate doughnuts dipped in sugar, and how sweet the music was on the water in the shining night, and what it had felt like to think about girls then. After breakfast we would go up to the store and the things were in the same place—the minnows in a bottle, the plugs and spinners disarranged and pawed over by the youngsters from the boys' camp, the Fig Newtons and the Beeman's gum. Outside, the road was tarred and cars stood in front of the store. Inside, all was just as it had always been, except there was more Coca-Cola and not so much Moxie and root beer and birch beer and sarsaparilla. We would walk out with the bottle of pop apiece and sometimes the pop would backfire up our noses and hurt. We explored the streams, quietly, where the turtles slid off the sunny logs and dug their way into the soft bottom; and we lay on the town wharf and fed worms to the tame bass. Everywhere we went I had trouble making out which was I, the one walking at my side, the one walking in my pants.

One afternoon while we were there at that lake a thunderstorm came up. It was like the revival of an old melodrama that I had seen long ago with childish awe. The second-act climax of the drama of the electrical disturbance over a lake in America had not changed in any important respect. This was the big scene, still the big scene. The whole thing was so familiar, the first feeling of oppression and heat and a general air around camp of not wanting to go very far away. In midafternoon (it was all the same) a curious darkening of the sky, and a lull in everything that had made life tick; and then the way the boats suddenly swung the other way at their moorings with the coming of a breeze out of the new quarter, and the premonitory rumble. Then the kettle drum, then the snare, then the bass drum and cymbals, then crackling light against the dark, and the gods grinning and licking their chops in the hills. Afterward the calm, the rain steadily rustling in the calm lake, the return of light and hope and spirits, and the campers running out in joy and relief to go swimming in the rain, their bright cries perpetuating the deathless joke about how they were getting simply drenched, and the children screaming with delight at the new sensation of bathing in the rain, and the joke about getting drenched linking the generations in a strong indestructible chain. And the comedian who waded in carrying an umbrella.

When the others went swimming, my son said he was going in, too. He pulled his dripping trunks from the line where they had hung all through the shower and wrung them out. Languidly, and with no thought of going in, I watched him, his hard little body, skinny and bare, saw him wince slightly as he pulled up around his vitals the small, soggy, icy garment. As he buckled the swollen belt, suddenly my groin felt the chill of death.

Journal and Discussion Questions

1 How does the introductory paragraph prepare readers for the ideas and emotions that E. B. White will discuss later? Considering White's pleasant and nostalgic feelings about the lake, why does he introduce "Once More to the Lake" by mentioning getting ringworm and his father accidentally falling into the lake?

2 Why does White associate summer vacations on this lake with his relationships with his father and his son? Why doesn't White mention his mother in "Once More to the Lake," except for a few vague references to "us all" and "our family"? Why do you think White took only his son with him (and no other family member) when he returned to the lake?

3 Describe the "dual existence" in paragraph four that White lived during his visit to the lake with his son. How does White's sense of a dual existence affect how he observes the lake and his son on his present vacation? How does this dual existence affect how he remembers the lake and how he remembers his father? What ideas about how memory works, especially for family memories, are suggested by White's discussion of his dual existence?

4 Why is White concerned about how the lake has changed since his childhood as he and his son drive to the lake? In what ways has the lake remained the same? What changes does White notice? How does he feel about the similarities and differences that he has noticed? Why?

5 Why do you think White saves the description of the thunderstorm for the last paragraph of the body of "Once More to the Lake"? How is this description connected to the main ideas of White's essay?

6 How does the conclusion continue to develop the themes of White's essay? How is it different in tone, emotion, and ideas from the rest of the essay? Why does White conclude "Once More to the Lake" with a scene that brings on a sudden feeling of "the chill of death"?

7 What conclusions about father–son relationships can you draw from "Once More to the Lake"? Why?

Topics for Writing

1 Analyze E. B. White's "Once More to the Lake," focusing on the workings of memory and White's sense of "dual existence" as he compares his childhood vacations with his father to his current vacation with his son and what the essay suggests about father–son relationships.

2 Write a research paper about family vacations. Possible topics include the importance of family vacations in American life, the reasons why families go on vacations (often on vacations in the country or in nature), or changes in family vacations over the decades.

Connecting the Readings

Compare what the writers learn about themselves and their families by returning as adults to a place important in their childhoods in Chang-Rae Lee's "Coming Home Again" and E. B. White's "Once More to the Lake."

MY PAPA'S WALTZ

BY THEODORE ROETHKE

Theodore Roethke (1908–1963) is one of the most respected American poets of the twentieth century. He was a professor of English and creative writing teacher at several universities, including Lafayette College, Penn State University, and the University of Washington. His books include *The Waking: Poems, 1933–1953*, which won the Pulitzer Prize for Poetry; the children's book *Party at the Zoo*; and *The Collected Poems of Theodore Roethke*. "My Papa's Waltz," published in 1948 and probably his most famous poem, recalls a scene from Roethke's childhood that reveals the complexities of the relationships between his father, his mother, and himself.

The whiskey on your breath
Could make a small boy dizzy;
But I hung on like death:
Such waltzing was not easy.

We romped until the pans
Slid from the kitchen shelf;
My mother's countenance
Could not unfrown itself.

The hand that held my wrist
Was battered on one knuckle;
At every step you missed
My right ear scraped a buckle.

You beat time on my head
With a palm caked hard by dirt,
Then waltzed me off to bed
Still clinging to your shirt.

Journal and Discussion Questions

1 What kind of man is the poet's father? What did the boy feel toward his father at the moment described in this poem? How does the adult poet's perspective, looking back on the moment, differ from the boy's perspective? Which perspective is reflected in the line "Such waltzing was not easy"? Why?

2 Why is the mother frowning in the poem? Why do you think Theodore Roethke described her with such unusual words: "My mother's countenance / Could not unfrown itself"? What does "My Papa's Waltz" suggest about her relationship to the poet's father?

3 How do the first two lines, "The whiskey on your breath / Could make a small boy dizzy," affect your perceptions and emotions of the rest of the scene described in "My Papa's Waltz"? Why?

4 Why does the poet address his father directly, as "you," in his memory? What difference would it make if the poet were talking about his father rather than to his father?

5 Critics disagree about whether "My Papa's Waltz" describes a son's warm memory of a moment with his father or suggests a family in trouble because of the father's drinking problem. What do you think? What generalizations about families are suggested in "My Papa's Waltz"?

Topics for Writing

1 Analyze Theodore Roethke's "My Papa's Waltz" and what it reveals about the relationship between the boy and his parents.

2 Research some of the criticism about "My Papa's Waltz," focusing on critics who disagree about how fondly or portentously Roethke is describing this memory. Write a research paper explaining what critics think about Roethke's poem.

EASTER MORNING

BY NORMAN ROCKWELL

From 1916 to 1963, Norman Rockwell (1894–1978) created 321 covers for the *Saturday Evening Post*, one of the most popular magazines in the U.S. So popular were his covers that copies of the *Post* with a Rockwell cover sold 50,000 to 75,000 more copies than other issues. American families were often the subject of Rockwell's paintings as well as the intended audience of his paintings, and these paintings helped shape our images of American families and sense of family values. Rockwell painted *Easter Morning* for the cover of the May 16, 1959, issue of the *Saturday Evening Post*. The scene outside the window is the view from Rockwell's studio in Stockbridge, Massachusetts, with his daughter-in-law posing as the young mother. The father is trying to read the sports page as his wife and children, dressed up for Easter morning, head off to church. Rockwell wrote an autobiography entitled *My Adventures as an Illustrator* with his son Thomas. More information about Rockwell, and reproductions of many of his pictures can be found on his official Web site at www.normanrockwell.com.

Journal and Discussion Questions

1 What story is being told in *Easter Morning*? What may have happened before the moment captured by Norman Rockwell? What details in the picture suggest the story?

2 What thoughts and emotions are communicated by the facial expressions and body language of each person in *Easter Morning*?

3 What kind of family is pictured in *Easter Morning*? What does Rockwell indicate about the social class, values, tastes, and happiness of this family? How? What does Rockwell suggest about the relationship between the husband and wife?

4 What does *Easter Morning* suggest about the place of religion in American families? Why doesn't Rockwell picture the father leading the family to church and the mother staying at home?

5 Do you think Rockwell intended to depict a "typical" family in *Easter Morning*? Why or why not? Would *Easter Morning* be substantially different if Rockwell had portrayed a poorer or a richer family? What if the family were black or Hispanic or Jewish?

6 Aside from the clothing and furniture, could *Easter Morning* be a picture of an American family today, or should this picture be seen more as a depiction of an American family in the 1950s? Why?

Topics for Writing

1 Analyze Norman Rockwell's *Easter Morning*, focusing on what the painting implies about the roles of religion, gender roles, and suburban life in family life.

2 Find other paintings and drawings by Norman Rockwell of American families. Research cultural criticism on his work. Write a research paper about Rockwell's vision of the American family.

THE MOMENT OF LIFE

BY BRIAN LANKER

Brian Lanker (1947–) took this photograph of Lynda Coburn giving birth to her daughter Jacki Lynn with the support of her husband Jerry on January 27, 1972. It was published as part of a photo essay "The Moment of Life" in the *Topeka Capital-Journal* that tells the story of Jacki Lynn's natural childbirth. The photograph won the Pulitzer Prize for feature photography the following year. Although images of natural childbirth are common today, in the early 1970s, the Lamaze method of natural childbirth was new, unfamiliar, and, for many people, possibly dangerous. For decades, mothers had been giving birth under anesthesia as their husbands worried in a hospital waiting room. Newspaper readers of the time might have viewed Lanker's photograph not only as an image of a new trend in medicine but also as vi-sual argument encouraging expectant parents to take Lamaze lessons and choose natural childbirth. Lanker worked as director of photography for the *Eugene (Oregon) Register-Guard* from 1975–1982 and has been taking photographs for advertisers and for *Life* and *Sports Illustrated* since 1982. He has published a book of photographs entitled *I Dream a World: Portraits of Black Women Who Changed America* and directed the documentary film *They Drew Fire: Combat Artists of WWII*. More of Lanker's photographs and other information can be found at www.brianlanker.com, and an interview with Lanker about "The Moment of Life" can be found at www.newsmuseum.org. Lanker eventually married Lynda Coburn after she and Jerry Coburn divorced several years after this photograph was taken.

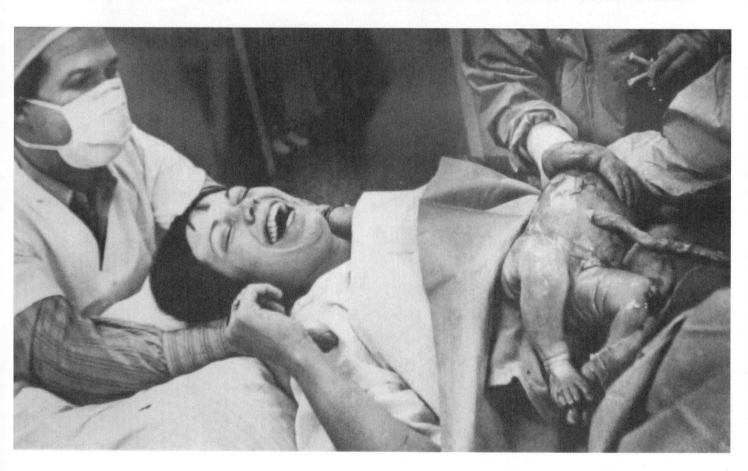

Journal and Discussion Questions

1 Imagine the story behind "The Moment of Life." What was happening the moment the photo was taken? What occurred before this moment? What may have happened afterward?

2 Briefly describe each person in Lanker's photograph: the mother, Lynda Coburn; her husband, Jerry; the doctor; the baby daughter, Jacki Lynn; and the two people in the doorway. Which person in the photograph draws your attention most? Why? How does this focus emphasize the central impression, emotions, and message of Lanker's photograph?

3 What do you notice about the two men in the photograph? What does the photograph suggest about the roles of men in natural childbirth? Does it matter that we cannot see the doctor's face and that the husband's face is largely covered by a surgical mask? Is the gender of the doctor important to this photograph? Why or why not?

4 If you read Lanker's photograph as an argument about natural childbirth, what is it saying? Does the photograph deal with any fears and problems concerning natural childbirth?

5 Does the fact that the Coburns divorced several years after this photograph and that Lynda married the photographer affect the meaning of Lanker's photograph? Why or why not?

6 What general changes in American families and child rearing are suggested by the change to natural childbirth? Why?

Topics for Writing

1 Analyze Brian Lanker's photograph of Lynda and Jerry Coburn. Discuss what the photograph might mean to people today about childbirth and parenting and what it might have meant to people in 1973 at the beginning of the women's liberation movement and the natural childbirth movement.

2 Write a research paper about changes in childbirth throughout history and how these approaches are related to the culture's assumptions about parenting, children, and gender roles as well as medical developments. You may narrow your subject to a particular period or method of childbirth, such as the natural childbirth movement, the movement to give birth in hospitals rather than at home, or the recent return to home birthing as a choice.

POVERTY AND THE FATHER FACTOR

BY WILLIAM RASPBERRY

From 1966 until his retirement in 2005, William Raspberry (1935–) wrote a column on urban affairs for the *Washington Post* that was syndicated in over 200 newspapers. Winner of a Pulitzer Prize in 1994, Raspberry usually writes about race, education, crime and justice, drug abuse, and housing. An African American, Raspberry was born in Okolona, a small town in Mississippi, and graduated from the University of Indianapolis in 1958 with a B.S. in history. He now teaches at Duke University's Sanford Institute of Public Policy as Knight Professor of the Practice of Communications and Journalism. Some of his columns are collected in his book *Looking Backward at Us*. "Poverty and the Father Factor" is an editorial column that first appeared in the *Washington Post* on August 1, 2005, in which Raspberry argues about the importance of fathers in African American families and the connections between poverty and fatherless families.

I FIRST HEARD THE NUMBERS FROM sociologist Andrew Billingsley:

In 1890, 80 percent of black American households were headed by husbands and wives. That's just 25 years after the end of the Civil War.

In 1900, the percentage was mostly unchanged, and so it remained—between the high 70s and the low 80s—for 1910, 1920, 1930, for every decennial census report until 1970, when it was down to 64.

For the 2000 Census, the percentage of black families headed by married couples was 38. The only good news is that it was also 38 percent in 1990, suggesting that the trend may have stopped getting worse.

Now consider this: Fatherless families are America's single largest source of poverty. The Annie E. Casey Foundation's "Kids Count" once reported that Americans who failed to complete high school, to get married and to reach age 20 before having their first child were nearly 10 times as likely to live in poverty as those who did these three things.

Poverty, it goes without saying, is associated with poorer academic outcomes, which, in turn, are associated with poorer job prospects. That means, among other things, reduced ability to choose neighborhoods to bring children up in safety. Non-marriage has consequences.

Two things need to be said: The phenomenon obviously does not apply to all black families, nor is it *restricted* to black families. An impressive number of African Americans are succeeding beyond what earlier generations could even imagine (though I suspect that a disproportionate percentage of those outstanding successes are from two-parent families).

There's nothing inherently racial about the trend, of course. The 2000 Census showed that only 69 percent of all American children were born into two-parent households—65 percent for Hispanics and 77 percent for whites.

Further, fatherlessness does not affect all people equally. Whenever I address the topic, I am certain to hear from some people who want me to know that they were raised by a single mother and managed to turn out quite well, thank you. That doesn't surprise me, of course. There are children who are, for unexplained reasons, unusually resilient and self-motivated, and there are single mothers whose skill and discipline are so heroic that their children are virtually driven to succeed.

But acknowledging that "Peg Leg" Bates was a helluva tap dancer shouldn't obscure the fact that dancers are generally better off with the full complement of nether limbs.

So am I urging all single mothers to grab the nearest adult male and haul him off to the altar?

Of course not. As Mary Frances Berry, then chair of the U.S. Commission on Civil Rights, once told me: "If all the single mothers in poor communities married single men in those same communities, and the men all moved in, the only effect would be to increase by one the number of disabled people in each household."

She was right, of course. But while marriage may not be a cure for poverty, it does turn out to be a fairly reliable *preventative* . Isn't it worthwhile to spend more time and resources helping young people to understand the economic implications of single parenthood *before* they become single parents? Wouldn't it make sense to rethink our relatively recent easy acceptance of out-of-wedlock parenting?

And might it not be a good idea to work at restoring the influence of the community institutions, religious and civic, that used to help strengthen families? The trends Billingsley talked about were a long time developing, and they won't be reversed in a day or two.

As he told me, "You can't have strong families unless you have strong communities, and you can't have strong communities unless you have strong institutions."

Phillip Jackson, executive director of Chicago's Black Star Project and promoter of the Million Father March, cites the oft-repeated proverb that it "takes a village to raise a child."

In too many parts of the black community, he said, "the proverb has little relevance. There is no village to raise the children . . . no collective community effort to ensure that most black children will grow up capable of succeeding in the 21st century.

"Unfortunately, African proverbs don't raise children. People do."

Journal and Discussion Questions

1 What is the thesis of William Raspberry's "Poverty and the Father Factor"? What arguments does he make to persuade readers to accept this claim? Are you persuaded by these arguments? Why or why not?

2 Why, according to Raspberry, are fatherless families more likely to be poor than other families? How might Raspberry have developed this part of his argument in a longer column?

3 Why does Raspberry begin his argument with a statistical history of the percentage of black American families headed by both a husband and wife? Why does he mention the source of his data before the statistics themselves? Is this an effective introduction? Why or why not?

4 What research does Raspberry use in his argument? How does he use his sources to support his argument?

5 What are Raspberry's thoughts about the African proverb it "takes a village to raise a child"? Why does he conclude his argument with a discussion of this proverb?

6 What proposals does Raspberry suggest might improve the situation that he describes and why? What other policy changes could be proposed based on his analysis of the problem?

7 If Hispanic and white single-parent households are prone to poverty, as Raspberry argues, why does he focus on black households in "Poverty and the Father Factor"?

Topics for Writing

1 Write an argumentative essay that refutes the arguments made by William Raspberry in "Poverty and the Father Factor."

2 Argue in favor of one of the solutions that Raspberry proposes in "Poverty and the Father Factor" or propose a different solution to the problem Raspberry describes.

3 Write a research paper investigating the effects of being raised by a single parent on children.

HAIRCUT

BY GELEVE GRICE

After serving in the U.S. Navy during World War II, Geleve Grice (1922–2004) earned a bachelor's degree in psychology at Arkansas Agricultural, Mechanical, and Normal College, a historically black college now named the University of Arkansas at Pine Bluff. Grice took thousands of photographs in over sixty years as a commercial photographer and news photographer in Pine Bluff. Although Grice took many photographs of celebrities and political figures and photographed events of the civil rights movement in Arkansas, he also took thousands of photographs, like "Haircut," of everyday African American life in Arkansas. He took these for himself in order to "do something constructive for humanity and myself." He kept most of these photographs in his archive until two exhibitions of his work in Pine Bluff and Little Rock and the 2003 publication of *A Photographer of Note: Arkansas Artist Geleve Grice*, a collection of his photographs edited by Robert Cochran. Grice's caption for this photograph reads, "Haircut, near Pine Bluff [Arkansas], 1950s". The photograph presents a scene of African American family life in poverty-stricken rural Arkansas in the early years of the civil rights movement, despite the fact that Grice does not identify the people in the photograph or even whether the people in the photograph are all members of the same family. The photograph appears in *A Photographer of Note*.

Journal and Discussion Questions

1 Describe Geleve Grice's "Haircut" photograph. What does Grice's photograph suggest about the mood, personality, and character of each person? What can you surmise about the relationships of the people in this photograph? What does the setting—the buildings, furniture, tools, and other objects in the picture—suggest about the life of the people in "Haircut"?

2 What story does "Haircut" tell? What do you imagine occurred before and after the photograph was taken?

3 Why do you think that Grice took this photograph? Why do you think he and Robert Cochran decided to include it in a collection of Grice's important photographs?

4 What does Grice's photograph reveal about family life for African Americans in rural Arkansas in the 1950s? Is it important to know that the photograph was taken in the early years of the civil rights movement, when many blacks were living under Jim Crow laws? Why or why not?

5 Compare "Haircut" to media images of poor families, black families, and rural Southern families. Does Grice's photograph support any stereotypes about these families, or does it challenge or correct any stereotypes (or some of both)?

6 Compare this photograph of family life to images of middle-class family life in photographs, movies, and television. What does this photograph have in common with those images? How is it different? What does the photograph suggest about the effects of poverty on family life?

Topics for Writing

1 Analyze the portrayals of family, race, and poverty in Geleve Grice's photograph "Haircut."

2 Write a research paper about family life for African Americans in the era of Jim Crow laws. Your essay may discuss middle-class black families as well as poor families.

PLAYING THE PRINCESS

BY MOLLY KLANE

Molly Klane (1985–) graduated from Carleton College in Minnesota with a B.A. in American Studies and a concentration in Educational Studies. She earned a license to teach social studies at the secondary level. She wrote "Playing the Princess" in fall 2004 as her final research project for a course taught by Pamela Feldsman-Savelsberg, The Anthropology of Gender. In her research paper, Klane interprets the meanings behind the typical American wedding ceremony, how these meanings have changed with the changes of men's and women's roles in society, and how the wedding functions as a transition from single life to married life, especially for the bride. In an email about her paper, Klane writes, "Although weddings, marriage, and gender have not been my primary areas of focus during my undergraduate education, I consider myself a student of culture. I saw weddings as a window into our cultural values and gendered imagery. While I have not spent extensive time considering my own wedding, I found that many children—girls especially—seem to have longstanding beliefs and ideas about how their weddings will look and, more subtly, what roles they will take on as women choosing to wed."

Molly Klane

Dr. Feldsman-Savelsberg

Anthropology of Gender

16 November 2004

Playing the Princess

With white-tiered dresses matching four-tiered vanilla cakes, the imagery of an American wedding distinctly resonates in societal consciousness. The perfection entailed by these wedding details separates the wedding from routine life, uniquely allowing participants transformation in their routine life roles. Marking the distinct point of identity and kinship transformation, weddings serve a ritualized function. By adding symbolic meaning and cultural imaginings, weddings additionally reveal societal ideologies and gender cosmologies. Contemporary American weddings integrate the symbolism of Christianity, patriarchy, and consumerism and correspondingly endow them with notions of fantasy and romance. The trend toward fancifully symbolic, elaborate weddings occurs in parallel to the expansion of women's opportunities and achievement. Even as the message girls collectively receive allows them greater access to resources and power, another facet of that message enforces the importance of feminine gender performance and perfection that will necessarily manifest itself in the wedding ritual. Consequently, the bride plays the role of princess for her unique wedding day. She is wrapped up in symbolic images and values, which encompass a tradition of girlhood imaginings, societal projections, and predetermined feminine roles.

In understanding the heavy weight weddings carry in describing societal ideologies and gender cosmologies, it becomes necessary to place weddings in the context of American society. From the 1830s when a majority of weddings were simple home-based affairs, the overwhelming trend has brought wedding ceremonies into traditional churches (Freeman 25; Currie 405). As weddings moved from private to public affairs, they adopted values characteristic of the dominant male societal structure. Money, individualization, and distinctivism achieved an added importance in the wedding performance. Despite the traditional masculinity of these characteristics, they have increasingly influenced women through media and consumer networks. From soap operas and sitcoms to films and magazines, the presence and pervasiveness of weddings in the fabric of American culture is expanding.[1] Clearly, people perceive that weddings are important, with 750 million viewers watching Prince Charles marry Lady Diana Spencer in 1981 and as many as 400,000 people visiting *Weddingchannel.com* (Otnes and Pleck 3). Understanding the women who tune in and the cultural messages they glean becomes centrally important to interpreting the place of weddings in American society.

The obvious cultural message arising from weddings is the importance of marriage and dyadic partnerships. Weddings emblematize romanticism and "the ability to find perfection only in heterosexual partnership" (Geller 261). This achieves heightened importance especially with challenges to gender norms from women's permeation into the workplace, the gay and lesbian rights movement and individualism's centrality. Surrounded by societal uncertainty, the wedding can represent a performance of social norms and a public display of commitment (Kalmijn 592). By cementing notions of the couple and of their union, weddings become rituals of performance.

In their role as rituals, weddings serve a societal function. Rituals, according to sociologist Diana Leonard, are "largely expressive, symbolic, formalized acts [through which] we can get profound insights into [the] values and institutions" of cultures (Otnes and Pleck 4). Although weddings do carry great meaning for the individual couple, they are also placed in a line of generational tradition. Engaging in the largely unchanged formality of a church wedding, families connect between disparate kinship lines and, perhaps equally importantly, across generations. In this way weddings create culture by the continuation of traditions centered around a symbolic exchange of women which encourages fertility and species propagation (Bell 470–76). Beyond the wedding's intracultural connective power, its ritualization deeply and centrally affects the wedding couple, especially the bride. Inherent in the wedding symbolism and language is a sense that the couple is embarking on a new journey, characterized by a newfound independence from parents and a dependence on each other (Geller 307–10). Supporting this idea, weddings are generally quieter affairs if the couple already lives together and has already transitioned from parental dependence (Kalmijn 593). The ritual act transforms girls into women and individuals into couples, borrowing on symbolic cultural traditions to do so.

Symbolism borrowed from Christianity, antiquity, and ancestry heightens the cultural meanings of the wedding ritual. The white wedding dress perhaps fulfills the most central role in wedding symbolism. It is necessarily dazzling, simultaneously conjuring images of princesses and purity. Costuming in weddings allows participants to perform symbolic roles, temporarily imposing Mary's virginal purity, Victorian England's royal chivalry, Greek and Roman mythic romanticism, and Grandmother's legacy on the glowing bride (Frese; Wolf 38). The ability to connect religion, history, and poetry to the woman in her bridal gown extends over a century of wedding tradition, yet the more important facet is the feelings brides ascribe to their dress and appearance during the wedding ritual. Wanting the white dress connects virtually all brides in American weddings, regardless of class or generation. One bride—representing the general tone—asserted, "I felt pretty strongly that I wanted a dress that was beautiful and I wanted a dress that I felt like a princess in" (Schuster 94). Behind this desire for princess white dresses, wedding symbolism speaks to the underlying values and performance of gender that American brides hope to attain in their wedding ritual.

An unconscious function of the wedding attire enforces Sheri Ortner's gender dichotomy linking women to nature and men to culture. Perfect white wedding dresses and the attention they demand associate the American bride with nature, purity, and motherhood. Names such as "pearl" and "milk white" to describe the color of bridal gowns subconsciously suggest the natural phenomenon of oysters ("pearl") and of lactation ("milk"). To underscore this, pearls, crystals, flower blossoms, and lace often adorn the wedding dress, drawing attention back to natural creations (Frese 102–05). The flower motif linking nature and feminine sexuality carries throughout the wedding, further suggesting an association of women with nature since traditionally the bride and bridesmaids carry bouquets (Wolf 36). Whereas the bride's dress, veil, and flowers link her with nature and the changing seasons reminiscent of her changing roles, the groom remains stoic and static. The bride captures the room's attention as she cascades down the aisle and climactically unveils herself; the groom remains rooted. His dark rented suit will likely return to the store without his mark on it or its mark on him, for the wedding ceremony does not function to change the male role. Instead, this contrast provides the bride with transformation from girl to woman through the act of gender performance (Frese 105–06).

The symbolism in wedding costumes contributes to the liminality of the wedding ritual. Wedding fantasies function outside the constraints of society. They create an idealized female bride and male groom that do, however, bind participants to real societal gender roles (Frese 104–05). The bride especially exists in an other-worldly state. She is between daughter and wife, reality and fantasy (Freeman 31). Her perfectly glowing dress, her veil reminiscent of a halo, and her ability to grab attention places her outside of any traditional state (Frese 104–05; Freeman 31). Weddings exist independent of marriage and reality; "brideland [is] eternally transient: you enter, you are transformed completely, and then, presumably, you depart" (Wolf 36). Through the bride's transformation in this state, she associates with nature and societal suppositions of femininity, yet she also attains great power in her unique qualities and magical status.

The pervasiveness of wedding symbolism linking the bride to regality and transformation highlights an important function of weddings as markers of social status for women specifically. For one day, the woman believes herself to truly command the spotlight (Schuster 88–89). Consequently she must perfectly orchestrate the display of her image and values. Not only does the white wedding gown present bridal purity and femininity, it follows the tradition of Queen Victoria, layering regal meaning onto the white dress (Otnes and Pleck 171). Playing the princess takes on an almost literal meaning, supported by symbolic bridesmaid attendants, Victorian images of romanticism, regality, and purity, and even a tiara atop her head to complete the suggestion of bridal aristocracy (Wolf 39; Otnes and Pleck 190). Naomi Wolf suggests that women need this temporary moment of status, saying, "There is a terrible spiritual and emotional longing among [women] for social behavior or ritual that respects, even worships, female sexuality and reproductive potential" (Wolf 39). For Victorian women, weddings celebrated the bride's sustained feminine virginity and also thanked her for essentially agreeing to marry into a chained life of domestic servitude (Otnes and Pleck 191). In the context of American feminism, the patriarchy, liminality, and romanticism of weddings offer the only opportunity to celebrate women as delicate princesses in new American egalitarian constructs of gender.

Celebrating the woman in the wedding's temporary fantasyland extends to give her and her groom enhanced social status. Because the bride places importance on her dazzling visual appearance, often the entire event can center on the appearance of beauty and perfection in the name of the couple.[2] The wedding serves a performative function, where the spotlight casts its eye upon the bride and groom, encouraging them not only to display idealized gender roles but also their status achievements (Geller 4–5). Weddings allow—even encourage—couples to spend beyond their means and to display status (Otnes and Pleck 30–31).[3] Middle and working class couples stretch their financial means by consistently choosing big white weddings over the equivalent money for house down payments (Schuster 95–97). This supports the claim that visibility and status drive lavish weddings, as couples choose a performed, visible status action over a popular status symbol and long-term financial security. For affluent couples, weddings can also be key events to shed a traditional guard about conspicuous consumption and to fully exhibit taste and status in a formal context (Otnes and Pleck 186). Across socioeconomic class lines, weddings allow ritualized performance of one's actual or desired social status.

As the vast majority of couples choose expensive and visible weddings, the ability to individualize social status and clearly demonstrate prestige has become more difficult. Consequently the focus of status performance centers both on the size and scope of the wedding and also the quality and taste demonstrated. Consumption—measured in both quantity and type—becomes essential to wedding culture. As recent bride Rachael realized when she bought her first two bridal magazines, media culture encourages consumption as an integral part of weddings (Currie 412). Throughout the last century, the trend has been toward an increase in the marketing of bridal and wedding culture (Freeman 25–32).[4] Advertisements do not sell wedding gowns; they sell transformation. Between 1955 and 1992, more than one-third of the ads in bridal magazines promised users transformation through the magic of the featured product or service (Otnes and Pleck 32). This directly supports the claim that weddings provide women with a stage for feminine performance and transformation, existing outside their place in society, without limits of gender, class, or achievement.

Consumption as an integral part of wedding culture does, however, both reflect and create specific gender roles and expectations for women. Often wedding guides—notably bridal magazines—enforce the notion that women are the central focus and responsible for the wedding celebration. *Today's Bride* featured checklists for brides and grooms to plan their wedding: the groom's list contained 20 to-do items, while the bride's had 42, including choosing the groom's attire, sending invitations, meeting with the caterer, and establishing hair and beauty appointments (Currie 417). As part of the necessary wedding plan, women are expected to take the central role in consumption choices. In advertising and selling the perfect wedding with specific interest in the feminine bride, stores can establish a relationship with the woman who likely will become the household's primary shopper (Otnes and Pleck 18–19). Specifically for middle and working class women, the wedding provides the first opportunity to make large-scale financial and purchasing decisions, which adds to the liminal power and transformation she receives from her wedding.[5] This power from consumption has evolved in the past fifty years as women have gained status and achievement from their increasing presence in the workplace and public sphere.

Consumption trends can also reflect the societal move toward egalitarian gender roles and the climate that necessitates feminine gender performance through weddings. The growing tradition to exchange rings not only reflects greater levels of consumption, it also equalizes the bride and groom. By the 1940s and 50s, middle-class Americans had predominantly adopted the double ring tradition and allowed the groom's band to symbolize his "masculine domesticity" (Howard 850). Resulting from migration to suburbia, men increased their domestic responsibilities and identities, adding rings to their fingers and child and lawn care to their repertoire of duties. The manifestation of this changed expectation did not occur organically: Marketers heavily pushed for the double band ceremony (Howard 851). In doing so they expanded consumption and visual display, two central aspects to the modern American wedding.

Although contemporary American weddings do demonstrate changing gender relations and some egalitarian ideologies, many elements remain that connect weddings to women. Weddings are expectedly and unquestionably the bride's day. Perfectly hosting and performing in a large, glamorous wedding is like an initiation test for a woman, inherently measuring her ability to manage many tasks and care about small domestic details (Frese 101). While the wedding measures the woman's accomplishment, the man is seen as incapable in this feminized sphere. One recent groom lamented that when planning his wedding his mind would go completely blank, that he "couldn't figure it out to save my life" because "it's not in men's genes" (Currie 414). His wife replied, "He just has better and more pressing things to think about" (Currie 415). Although the wife values her wedding and its status, she demonstrates that the value of her husband's activities supersedes the wedding. Yet for her and many other brides, nothing trumps the importance of the wedding day. It is distinctly her stage and her domain, on which she may artfully transform from whimsical girl to competent woman.

The power of the white wedding ritual is specifically and purposefully rooted in the imaginations of American girls. Early on girls receive messages on the power of romance and the importance of consumption, the very foundations upon which American weddings are now based. If fairy tales speak to the collective consciousness, Cinderella creates a desire in girls specifically for the fantasy and luxury that a white wedding provides (Kolbenschlag 71–75). She represents the ideals that rags can change to riches, romantic love can lead to marriage, and magic can sustain happiness (Otnes and Pleck 28). Seeking these virtues, girls habitually play the princess, first by dressing up with pillowcase veils and then by projecting those desires into a fantasy wedding with a gorgeous gown.[6] Marketers enthusiastically support this notion of playing the princess with sets such as Sears's "Radiant Bride" costume and Barbie's "Wedding Day Set," which quickly became the best selling Barbie outfit (Otnes and Pleck 47). From an early age, the American girl's fantastic wishes are expected to focus on a future ideal of femininity:

> While little boys are dreaming heroic dreams of conquering worlds, little girls are yearning for
> transformation—becoming beautiful, becoming a woman, becoming a mommy. As marriage is
> the single event, which will presumably guarantee that metamorphosis, it is, naturally, the day
> which her entire life has been in preparation. (Seligson 9–10)

Although it is unlikely that all girls fantasize about their wedding days, the expectation that a girl should imagine her wedding and its transformative role in her life speaks to an underlying societal belief about gender and its specific place in wedding rituals.

Weddings as holistic events are distinctly gendered and feminized. Combining the symbolic imagery of patriarchy, purity, and nature with the authority and status afforded to women, society provides the bride a central role. Ultimately she removes herself from the societal structure of achievement and equality to receive heightened status as a woman transforming. Across socioeconomic, racial, and generational lines, "there is a democratization of status and appearance in the bridal role because regardless of social class brides are similarly attired, and all are considered beautiful" (Schuster 92). The white dress and the perceived perfection are constants in contemporary American weddings that support notions of femininity within wedding rituals. In the context of American society, the gender egalitarian ideal and a history of gendered hierarchies necessitate a wedding performance of femininity. Weddings thus reflect the underlying gender ideology in contemporary America and create a separate space for feminine gender performance and transformation.

Notes

1. Weddings are increasingly central themes in popular culture entertainment. From 1890 to 1999 sociologist Chrys Ingraham counted more than 350 films titled with the words "wedding" or "bride" (Ingraham 177–83). Additionally the energy and enthusiasm for shows such as *Who Wants to Marry a Millionaire* and *A Wedding Story* illustrate a societal involvement with the meanings and images of weddings (Otnes and Pleck 10).

2. This was very much the sentiment expressed by Helen, a bride in Dawn Currie's study. Helen said, "I had an image in my mind, like a pretty wedding, so I wanted to have a nice dress. Then it seemed to me that there was a lot of things that went along with having a nice dress—If you're spending a lot of money on your dress then you've got to invite people to come and see it. So, we started getting relatives coming. Then you've got to have some place for them to go after the wedding, for food and stuff like that. As it turned out, we had a reception, which we weren't planning on" (Currie 410). Hence Helen's desire to wear a gorgeous dress motivated a grand event of social status performance for her friends and relatives to observe.

3. The concept of conspicuous consumption applies nicely to wedding values of consumption. Christopher J. Berry coined the term to describe the action of consuming for the sake of consumption itself and for the reaction of an audience (Otnes and Pleck 10).

4. Starting in the late 1800s department stores encouraged bridal consumption with special rooms for consulting on wedding dresses; since then the advertising and encouragement of consumption has overwhelmingly increased (Freeman 28).

5. Personal consumption choices—or at least the illusion that she creates and controls financial power—have a profound influence on the woman: "Once she has obtained the promise of commitment from a man, the modern woman's concern with jewelry, costumes, announcements, save-the-date cards, bridesmaids, invitations, registration, showers, floral arrangements, music, cuisine, and photographs, constitutes a different kind of romantic vortex in which she can easily lose herself. This fetishistic obsessiveness, ironically, effaces her lover and exists independently of him" (Geller 275).

6. In her sociological study of recent brides, Sherril Horowitz Schuster found that almost half of the women had played "wedding" as a child or fantasized about their wedding details as a teenager. Nearly three-quarters of the brides believed the wedding was specifically "the bride's special day" (Schuster 183).

Works Cited

Bell, Vikki. "Taking Her Hand: Becoming, Time and the Cultural Politics of the White Wedding." *Cultural Values* 2 (1998): 463–85. Print.

Currie, Dawn H. "Here Comes the Bride." *Journal of Comparative Family Studies* 24 (1993): 404–21. Print.

Freeman, Elizabeth. *The Wedding Complex*. Durham: Duke UP, 2002. Print.

Frese, Pamela R. "The Union of Nature and Culture: Gender Symbolism in American Wedding Rituals." *Transcending Boundaries: Multidisciplinary Approaches to the Study of Gender*. Ed. Pamela R. Frese and John M. Coggeshall. New York: Bergin & Garvey, 1991. 97–112. Print.

Geller, Jaclyn. *Here Comes the Bride*. New York: Four Walls Eight Windows, 2001. Print.

Howard, Vicki. "'A Real Man's Ring': Gender and the Invention of Tradition." *Journal of Social History* 36 (2003): 837–56. Print.

Ingraham, Chrys. *White Weddings: Romancing Heterosexuality in Popular Culture*. London: Routledge, 1999. Print.

Kalmijn, Matthijs. "Marriage Rituals as Reinforcers of Role Transitions: An Analysis of Weddings in The Netherlands." *The Journal of Marriage and Family* 66 (2004): 582–94. Print.

Kolbenschlag, Madonna. *Kiss Sleeping Beauty Good-Bye*. San Francisco: HarperCollins, 1988. Print.

Otnes, Cele C., and Elizabeth Pleck. *Cinderella Dreams*. Berkeley: U of CA P, 2003. Print.

Schuster, Sherril Horowitz. *Princess for a Day: Perpetuating the White Wedding as a Traditional Ritual*. Diss. Rutgers U, 2002. Print.

Seligson, Marcia. *The Eternal Bliss Machine: America's Way of Wedding*. New York: William Morrow, 1973. Print.

Wolf, Naomi. "Brideland." *Be Real: Telling the Truth and Changing the Face of American Feminism*. Ed. Rebecca Walker. New York: Anchor, 1995. 35–40. Print.

Journal and Discussion Questions

1 What is Molly Klane's thesis in "Playing the Princess"? How is the title related to her thesis?

2 Outline "Playing the Princess." What aspects of wedding ceremonies does Klane discuss? How does her discussion of each aspect contribute to her central claim about weddings?

3 According to Klane, American weddings combine symbols and values from several sources. What are these sources, and what has each source contributed to American wedding traditions and values?

4 How does the wedding help men and women make the transition from single to married life, according to Klane? Why is the wedding more important for the bride than for the groom?

5 Why, according to Klane, have American wedding ceremonies changed little during the feminist movement, with the great increase in the number of women in the workforce and with changes in the institution of marriage?

6 Except for the introduction and conclusion, almost every sentence in "Playing the Princess" is documented. What kinds of sources does Klane use from her research? What information and ideas does she take from her sources? Where do you see Klane's mind at work in her paper?

7 What criticisms does Klane have for the contemporary American wedding? What benefits does she see in the American wedding? Do you agree with her assessment of the American wedding? Why or why not?

Topics for Writing

1 Analyze other aspects of the contemporary American wedding ceremony or other parts of the wedding tradition, such as bridal showers and bachelor parties, that Klane does not discuss. Do these aspects reinforce the symbolism and values that Klane describes, or do they introduce other symbols and values?

2 Analyze another ritual or tradition connected to family or marriage (for example, marriage proposals, family reunions, baby showers, wedding anniversaries, or a child's first birthday party) for their symbolic meaning and values.

FOR BETTER, FOR WORSE: Marriage Means Something Different Now

BY STEPHANIE COONTZ

Stephanie Coontz (1944–) is Director of Research and Public Education for the Council on Contemporary Families and has taught history and family studies at Evergreen State College in Olympia, Washington, since 1975. She is the author of five books about American families, including *The Way We Never Were: American Families and the Nostalgia Trap* and *Marriage, a History: From Obedience to Intimacy, or How Love Conquered Marriage*, and editor of *American Families: A Multicultural Reader*. "For Better, for Worse: Marriage Means Something Different Now" first appeared as a guest editorial in the *Washington Post* on May 1, 2005. In this argument, as in other of her writings, Coontz takes issue with "traditional" ideas and images of marriage and family.

THIRTEEN YEARS AGO, VICE President Dan Quayle attacked the producers of TV sitcom's *Murphy Brown* for letting her character bear a child out of wedlock, claiming that the show's failure to defend traditional family values was encouraging America's youth to abandon marriage. His speech kicked off more than a decade of outcries against the "collapse of the family." Today, such attacks have given way to a kinder, gentler campaign to promote marriage, with billboards declaring that "Marriage Works" and books making "the case for marriage." What these campaigns have in common is the idea that people are willfully refusing to recognize the value of traditional families and that their behavior will change if we can just enlighten them.

But recent changes in marriage are part of a worldwide upheaval in family life that has transformed the way people conduct their personal lives as thoroughly and permanently as the Industrial Revolution transformed their working lives 200 years ago. Marriage is no longer the main way in which societies regulate sexuality and parenting or organize the division of labor between men and women. And although some people hope to turn back the tide by promoting traditional values, making divorce harder or outlawing gay marriage, they are having to confront a startling irony: The very factors that have made marriage more satisfying in modern times have also made it more optional.

The origins of modern marital instability lie largely in the triumph of what many people believe to be marriage's traditional role—providing love, intimacy, fidelity and mutual fulfillment. The truth is that for centuries, marriage was stable precisely because it was *not* expected to provide such benefits. As soon as love became the driving force behind marriage, people began to demand the right to remain single if they had not found love or to divorce if they fell out of love.

Such demands were raised as early as the 1790s, which prompted conservatives to predict that love would be the death of marriage. For the next 150 years, the inherently destabilizing effects of the love revolution were held in check by women's economic dependence on men, the unreliability of birth control and the harsh legal treatment of children born out of wedlock, as well as the social ostracism of their mothers. As late as the 1960s, two-thirds of college women in the United States said they would marry a man they didn't love if he met all their other, often economic, criteria. Men also felt compelled to marry if they hoped for promotions at work or for political credibility.

All these restraints on individual choice collapsed between 1960 and 1980. Divorce rates had long been rising in Western Europe and the United States, and although they had leveled off following World War II, they climbed at an unprecedented rate in the 1970s, leading some to believe that the introduction of no-fault divorce laws, which meant married couples could divorce if they simply fell out of love, had caused the erosion of marriage.

The so-called divorce revolution, however, is just one aspect of the worldwide transformation of marriage. In places where divorce and unwed motherhood are severely stigmatized, the retreat from marriage simply takes another form. In Japan and Italy, for example, women are far more likely to remain single than in the United States. In Thailand, unmarried women now compete for the title of "Miss Spinster Thailand." Singapore's strait-laced government has resorted to sponsoring singles nights in an attempt to raise marriage rates and reverse the birth strike by women.

> ## In Japan and Italy, for example, women are far more likely to remain single than in the United States. In Thailand, unmarried women now compete for the title of 'Miss Spinster Thailand.'

In the United States and Britain, divorce rates fell slightly during the 1990s, but the incidence of cohabitation and unmarried child-raising continues to rise, as does the percentage of singles in the population.

Both trends reduce the social significance of marriage in the economy and culture. The norms and laws that traditionally penalized unwed mothers and their children have weakened or been overturned, ending centuries of injustice but further reducing marriage's role in determining the course of people's lives. Today, 40 percent of cohabiting couples in the United States have children in the household, almost as high a proportion as the 45 percent of married couples who have kids, according to the 2000 Census. We don't have a TV show about that yet, but it's just a matter of time.

The entry of women into the workforce in the last third of the 20th century was not only a U.S. phenomenon. By the 1970s, women in America and most of Europe could support themselves if they needed to. The 1980s saw an international increase in unmarried women having babies (paving the way for Murphy Brown), as more people gained the ability to say no to shotgun marriages, and humanitarian reforms

> ❝ **Almost half of all kids spend part of their childhood in a household that does not include their two married biological parents.** ❞

lowered the penalties for out-of-wedlock births. That decade also saw a big increase in couples living together before marriage.

Almost everywhere, women's greater participation in education has raised the marriage age and the incidence of non-marriage. Even in places where women's lives are still largely organized through marriage, fertility rates have been cut in half and more wives and mothers work outside the home.

From Turkey to South Africa to Brazil, countries are having to codify the legal rights and obligations of single individuals and unmarried couples raising children, including same-sex couples. Canada and the Netherlands have joined Scandinavia in legalizing same-sex marriage, and such bastions of tradition as Taiwan and Spain are considering following suit.

None of this means that marriage is dead. Indeed, most people have a higher regard for the marital relationship today than when marriage was practically mandatory. Marriage as a private relationship between two individuals is taken more seriously and comes with higher emotional expectations than ever before in history.

But marriage as a public institution exerts less power over people's lives now that the majority of Americans spend half their adult lives outside marriage and almost half of all kids spend part of their childhood in a household that does not include their two married biological parents. And unlike in the past, marriage or lack of marriage does not determine people's political and economic rights.

Under these conditions, it is hard to believe that we could revive the primacy of marriage by promoting traditional values. People may revere the value of universal marriage in the abstract, but most have adjusted to a different reality. The late Pope John Paul II was enormously respected for his teaching about sex and marriage. Yet during his tenure, premarital sex, contraception use and divorce continued to rise in almost all countries. In the United States, the Bible Belt has the highest divorce rate in the nation. And although many American teens pledged abstinence during the 1990s, 88 percent

ended up breaking that pledge, according to the National Longitudinal Study of Adolescent Youth that was released in March.

Although many Americans bemoan the easy accessibility of divorce, few are willing to waive their personal rights. In American states where "covenant" marriage laws allow people to sign away their right to a no-fault divorce, fewer than 3 percent of couples choose that option. Divorce rates climbed by the same percentage in states that did not allow no-fault divorce as in states that did. By 2000, Belgium, which had not yet adopted no-fault divorce, had the highest divorce rates in Europe outside of Finland and Sweden.

Nor does a solution lie in preaching the benefits of marriage to impoverished couples or outlawing unconventional partnerships. A poor single mother often has good reason not to marry her child's father, and poor couples who do wed have more than twice the divorce risk of more affluent partners in the United States. Banning same-sex marriage would not undo the existence of alternatives to traditional marriage. Five million children are being raised by gay and lesbian couples in this country. Judges everywhere are being forced to apply many principles of marriage law to those families, if only to regulate child custody should the couple part ways.

We may personally like or dislike these changes. We may wish to keep some and get rid of others. But there is a certain inevitability to almost all of them.

Marriage is no longer the institution where people are initiated into sex. It no longer determines the work men and women do on the job or at home, regulates who has children and who doesn't, or coordinates care-giving for the ill or the aged. For better or worse, marriage has been displaced from its pivotal position in personal and social life, and will not regain it short of a Taliban-like counterrevolution.

Forget the fantasy of solving the challenges of modern personal life by re-institutionalizing marriage. In today's climate of choice, many people's choices do not involve marriage. We must recognize that there are healthy as well as unhealthy ways to be single or to be divorced, just as there are healthy and unhealthy ways to be married. We cannot afford to construct our social policies, our advice to our own children and even our own emotional expectations around the illusion that all commitments, sexual activities and care-giving will take place in a traditional marriage. That series has been canceled.

Journal and Discussion Questions

1 How has marriage changed, in Stephanie Coontz's argument? What are the causes of these changes?

2 What reasons and evidence does Coontz give to support her claim that basing marriage on love has destabilized marriage? Why does she disagree with those who argue that no-fault divorce laws are the main cause for the increase in divorce rates and "the erosion of marriage"? How does she support her claim and refute her opponents' arguments? How persuasive is her argument? Why?

3 Why does Coontz begin her analysis with references to the '90s television comedy *Murphy Brown* and to books and billboards that promote marriage today? Is this an effective introduction? Why or why not?

4 Why does Coontz bring up marriage and divorce trends in other countries besides the U.S.? Why are Pope John Paul II's teachings about sex and marriage, the divorce rate in the Bible Belt, and the success of teens' abstinence pledges important to Coontz's argument? How might someone arguing against Coontz respond to her use of this information?

5 What does Coontz recommend to those who are troubled by the marriage trends of today? Why? What, if any, social policies regarding marriage does Coontz seem to support, based on her argument? Why?

6 Why doesn't Coontz clearly state what changes in marriage she approves of and what changes she disapproves of? What changes does she seem to approve of or disapprove of? How do you know?

7 What does Coontz mean by "a Taliban-like counterrevolution"? Why does she allude to the Taliban as she begins to conclude her argument?

Topics for Writing

1 Argue in response to Stephanie Coontz's "For Better, for Worse," agreeing or disagreeing with her assessment of the condition of marriage in the U.S. today and the causes for its condition.

2 Write an editorial supporting or opposing a current law or proposal, such as no-fault divorce, covenant marriages, or tougher divorce laws, that might affect the stability of marriage. Or write an editorial in support of a proposal of your own.

3 Write a research paper describing and evaluating how marriage has changed in recent decades and arguing what has caused these changes. Your paper may build on Coontz's analysis, disagree with some or all of her claims, and/or explore other ideas not mentioned by Coontz.

GAY MARRIAGE

BY ANDREW SULLIVAN AND DAVID FRUM

Andrew Sullivan (1963–) is a political conservative, a practicing Roman Catholic, and a leading advocate of same-sex marriage in books such as *Virtually Normal: An Argument About Homosexuality*, *Same Sex Marriage: Pro and Con*, and *Love Undetectable: Notes on Friendship, Sex and Survival*. Sullivan has a Ph.D. in Public Administration from Harvard's John F. Kennedy School of Government and writes about a range of political, social, and religious issues in magazines and newspapers. A Canadian citizen and one of the leading conservative voices in the U.S. and Canada, David Frum (1960–) is a fellow of the conservative think tank American Enterprise Institute, a former fellow of the Manhattan Institute for Policy Research, and a one-time speechwriter and special assistant for President George W. Bush. He is the author of five books, including *What's Right: The New Conservative Majority and the Remaking of America*, *How We Got Here: The '70s—The Decade That Brought You Modern Life—for Better or Worse*, and (with Richard Perle) *An End to Evil: How to Win the War on Terror*, as well as numerous editorials and radio and television commentaries. Other writings by Frum, including a daily blog that he writes for the conservative journal *National Review Online*, can be located through his Web site, www.davidfrum.com. Sullivan keeps a blog called *The Daily Dish* on the *Time* magazine Web site at time.blogs.com/daily_dish/.

In March and April 1997, Frum and Sullivan debated whether same-sex marriage should be legalized for the online newsmagazine *Slate*. Under the title "Gay Marriage" the two conservatives exchanged eight memos, and in the course of this dialogue, they argue about the definition and purposes of marriage, how marriage has changed, and the present condition of marriage. Here are the first two memos of their exchange.

From: David Frum
To: Andrew Sullivan
Posted Tuesday, March 11, 1997, at 3:30 AM ET

Dear Andrew,

After two decades of denial, Americans are at last coming to accept that the erosion of marriage indeed represents the country's gravest social problem. Fewer than half the American children born this year will live to the age of 18 with both their father and mother present. The unlucky half will be dramatically more likely to suffer child abuse, to be poor, to drop out of school, to go to jail, to become pregnant as teen-agers.

Faced with a social disaster of this magnitude, we are entitled to ask someone who proposes to reinvent marriage: Will your ideas help or hurt? Will they tend to stabilize marriage, to discourage divorce and illegitimacy? Or will they destabilize it, and condemn millions of more young Americans to life in a broken or never-formed family, with all the accompanying dangers?

It's a credit to your honesty, Andrew, that you frankly admit that gay marriage will tend to make the institution of marriage even wobblier. You even tell us why. The debate over gay marriage, as you say in the introduction to your new reader, helps us to "realize that marriage itself has changed. From being an institution governed by men, it has been placed on a radically more egalitarian footing. From being a contract for life, it has developed into a bond that is celebrated twice in many an American's lifetime. From being a means to bringing up children, it has become primarily a way in which two adults affirm their emotional commitment to one another. From being an institution that buttresses certain bonds—family, race, religion, class—it has become, for many, a deep expression of the modern individual's ability to transcend all of those ties in an exercise of radical autonomy."

I'd prefer to phrase that thought a little less polemically, but otherwise it seems to me exactly right—and exactly the problem. If we still thought about marriage the way we did 35 years ago, gay marriage would seem to us just as impossible as it seemed then. If we can give serious consideration to gay marriage today, it is only because we have lived through an intellectual revolution that has eroded society's understanding of the difference between a marriage and a love affair. And since two men or two women can fall in love as well as a man and woman can, we find it harder and harder to explain why they shouldn't be issued a wedding license if they want it.

After all, a modern wedding license is such a valuable and yet simultaneously unburdensome thing! It can get you health insurance and Social Security survivors' benefits and American citizenship. In return, you are committed to really very little. The Unitarian wedding service states matters candidly. It asks the marrying couple: "Do you promise to love, honor, and cherish each other as long as love shall last?" That's all that modern American law asks anyone, Unitarian or otherwise, to promise.

But imagine something else. Suppose we took marriage as seriously as Americans did when a divorce cost Nelson Rockefeller the presidency. Suppose we made it difficult for all but the most unhappy marriages to dissolve, and then expected the richer partner to pay alimony to the poorer partner for life. Suppose we were prepared to talk frankly about the differences between the sexes: about how men need children (and must surrender their sexual liberty to get them) and how women need security (and must limit their personal independence in order to achieve it). Suppose we frankly acknowledged that marriage is not a very feminist institution: that it does not bring together two interchangeable "partners," but assigns different roles and responsibilities to husbands and wives, arising out of the different natures of the sexes. Suppose everybody—the priest, one's relatives, the teachers at your children's school, the grocer, the cleaning lady—expected all but the unhappiest married couples to tough it out, to stay together despite their disagreements, and that they felt free to look down their noses at husbands or wives who failed to meet this expectation.

If all of this were still true, would homosexuals still be bringing lawsuits asking for the right to marry?

And would non-homosexuals still find it so difficult to explain why this request isn't just misplaced, but is actually logically impossible?

The value of marriage to society—and the joy it can bring people—arises entirely from the fact that, as an institution, it rejects "the radical autonomy" that you seem to endorse. Marriage submerges our autonomy in a new commitment to our spouse, our children, our in-laws, and on and on in an ever-widening circle. Individuals unwilling to let their autonomy go are unlikely to discover much happiness in marriage. Radical autonomists make lousy husbands—and worse parents.

Advocates of gay marriage talk as if they were proposing to integrate a country club. The truth is, they are proposing to bulldoze the club and build a subdivision in its place. They aren't talking about extending the much maligned *Leave It to Beaver* marriage to gays. They are talking about completing the replacement of the *Leave It to Beaver* marriage with a new form of legal union that shares nothing with the marriages of 35 years ago but the name. This new union, available equally to gays and straights, is focused on the happiness of adults, not the needs of children. It presupposes a rigid economic equality between the partners, and cheerfully permits the stronger partner to impose disadvantageous prenuptial agreements on the weaker. It insists that marriage brings together unisex "partners" rather than reconciling the very different needs and duties of men and women. And, finally, this new form of union that is replacing traditional marriage can be canceled at any time, by either party, for any reason, regardless of the wishes of the other. We already see that this new sort of union is proving a flimsy thing. "The only difference between a caprice and a life-long passion," quipped Oscar Wilde, "is that a caprice lasts a little longer." But feminists and gay-rights advocates insist that it doesn't matter that the new union that is replacing marriage is flimsy, so long as it seems egalitarian.

Which takes us, as I think you understand, to the heart of the issue. The fight over gay marriage is only secondarily a fight about gays. Only 5 percent of the population, or less, is homosexual, but—as you point out—33 percent of Americans favor gay marriage. These people, I believe, favor gay marriage because they favor the revolution in family life of the past three decades, and understand that gay marriage is the logical culmination of this revolution.

If you believe it's fine for millions of kids to be raised by mom and a succession of stepdads, then you probably won't be greatly shocked by the thought of thousands of

> **Individuals unwilling to let their autonomy go are unlikely to discover much happiness in marriage.**

kids being reared by mom and a stepmom. If you mistrust organized religion, then you won't be shocked by weddings that defy religious teachings. If you want to banish traditional sex roles entirely from family life, then what better marriage could there be than one between two people of the same sex?

But those of us who oppose gay marriage, and we remain the majority at least for now, believe that these new values are not changing the family—they are destroying it, and harming those within it. As such beliefs become more widespread, so do divorce and illegitimacy. The proponents of gay marriage can only get what they want by weakening Americans' attachment to the traditional family even more than it has already been weakened. And as such, these proponents are hastening a process of social dissolution that has already brought misery to untold millions of people, with children suffering most grievously of all.

From: Andrew Sullivan
To: David Frum
Posted Friday, March 14, 1997, at 3:30 AM ET

It's a credit to your honesty that you admit that your opposition to marriage rights for gay and lesbian Americans is inextricable from your opposition to most of the other changes in marriage for the last 35 years. But I am a little taken aback by the extent of your hostility, as I'm sure other readers will be. Do you really think that working women should return to the kitchens of the 1950s or that domesticated men are a grave threat to the social fabric? Are you saying that the end of rigid sex roles in many heterosexual marriages is a reason for rising levels of divorce and illegitimacy? Or that love should not be a primary part of the motivation to marry? I can see why you might want to define marriage back to an institution that put procreation ahead of love, that encompassed rigid notions of a wife's role and a husband's duty, and that eschewed the companionship of equals—because it's the only way you can redefine marriage to exclude homosexuals. But this is surely a somewhat eccentric view, even among conservatives. Indeed, it's only by thinking through the radicalism of your assault on the state of sex relations in America that I have begun to understand better why the Republican right has come to seem so marginal to the country's real debates these days.

But much as it might be interesting to debate you on the alleged failures of heterosexual America (I think it's doing a better job balancing freedom and responsibility than you do, as recently improving statistics on divorce suggest), our conversation here is about something a little more specific: whether we should allow homosexual citizens the same right to marry as their heterosexual peers. I begin with a simple observation. This is 1997, not 1962. Barring an unprecedented and sudden groundswell back to '50s-style sexual inequality, what we are addressing as a practical matter today is whether homosexuals should be excluded from marriage as it exists now. If, as you concede, modern marriage is not very gender-specific, if it does not demand the production of children or rigid sex roles, if it is not the model of 1962, then why should homosexuals be excluded from it?

So far as I can tell, your only argument is that same-sex marriage is the straw that will break the camel's back, and that homosexuals should be excluded from marriage because heterosexuals have already made such a mess of it. Homosexuals, in other words, should be excluded from marriage because they would make explicit the very lack of strict gender roles that heterosexuals have already embraced. I wonder whether you have pondered for very long what this argument implies. Are you saying that a group of people, who have played no part in the alleged decline of this institution, who have petitioned for 30 years to be a part of it, should now bear the burden of rescuing it from collapse? And they should bear that burden by willingly accepting their exclusion from one of the most basic civil rights our society provides? Maybe you are numb to the crass unfairness of this, or you have become so used to thinking of homosexuals as objects manipulable for larger social purposes that it doesn't even occur to you that there's something wrong here. Be that as it may. Let me propose a deal: I will join you in a campaign to restigmatize adultery and tighten no-fault divorce, if you will join with me in fighting for the right of lesbian and gay citizens to marry on just those terms. That way we can both do our bit to rescue marriage, and homosexuals can stop being the scapegoats for any other social decline you wish to mention. What could be fairer than that?

In any case, your premise about the social agenda of most gay men and women who want the right to marry is completely misplaced. Most of us have no intention of transforming the existing institution into a responsibility-free zone. We don't want to "bulldoze the [country] club and build a subdivision in its place." We want the opposite. We are seeking the responsibilities that marriage both recognizes and encourages. Many of us would gladly join you in helping to shore up the institution, if you would only let us in. Most of us were born into families we love and cherish and want to sustain. Most of us do not mistrust organized religion; we practice it. Most of us do not want to make life worse for children; we want to protect our own and others in our families and give hope to a generation of gay children who are told from an early age that their lives will never fully appear in their family albums. Your distortion of my phrase "radical autonomy" typifies your blindness on this point. I'm clearly referring there not to the responsibilities of marriage itself, but to the radical ability to choose a partner with whom to live the rest of one's life. This radical autonomy is not a social given. Thirty-five years ago, remember, in the age you eulogize so lovingly, African-Americans were not allowed to marry whites in many states—and social constraints forbade mixed marriages of many kinds. No doubt you're glad that that convention has changed, although it was approved of at the time by "everybody—the priest, one's relatives, the teachers at your children's school, the grocer, the cleaning lady." So let me reiterate what I think is the lesson of that reform and the reform now before us: Everyone should be radically free to choose the person he or she marries. But the marriage itself should carry with it all the responsibilities and obligations it traditionally has. Why do you—as a conservative who allegedly upholds equal opportunity for all Americans—have a problem with that?

Sincerely,
Andrew

Journal and Discussion Questions

1 Summarize the main reasons why David Frum opposes legalizing gay marriage and the main reasons that Andrew Sullivan advocates the legalization of same-sex marriage. Outline each memo. How do Frum and Sullivan organize their essays to build their arguments and win over their readers?

2 Frum and Sullivan disagree about how the issue of gay marriage is and is not wrapped up in the issue of whether the institution of marriage is in trouble. How are these two issues connected for Frum? For Sullivan? On what points about the condition of marriage in general do they agree? On what points do they disagree?

3 According to Frum, how has marriage changed since the early 1960s and why? How does Sullivan describe the history and purposes of marriage? How do Frum and Sullivan use these histories to justify their positions about the legalization of same-sex marriage?

4 What positions do Frum and Sullivan take on the question of the effects that legalizing gay marriage will have on children? Whose argument is more persuasive? Why?

5 According to Frum, what are the weaknesses in Sullivan's arguments? What weaknesses does Sullivan claim to find in Frum's arguments? How persuasive are each of their rebuttals? How do they use each other's words to refute each other's arguments? Why do they sometimes disagree about what each other has said?

6 Frum uses several sources in his memo, including Sullivan's book *Virtually Normal: An Argument About Homosexuality*, an influential argument in favor of legalizing same-sex marriage. What other sources does he cite? How does he use his sources to support his arguments?

7 Who do you think "won" the first round of their debate? Why? How do you think Frum responded to Sullivan in his second memo? Why?

Topics for Writing

1 Analyze the arguments made by David Frum and Andrew Sullivan in "Gay Marriage." Your analysis may explain why Frum or Sullivan "won" the first round of their debate. However, especially if you believe that their debate was inconclusive or too close to call, your analysis may assess the strengths and weaknesses of Frum's and Sullivan's arguments without declaring a winner. You may decide to narrow your analysis to a single question or claim that they argued or to focus on how they represented and refuted each other's arguments. Or your analysis may focus on why Frum and Sullivan disagree, such as the differences in their assumptions about marriage, homosexuality, and society.

2 Read and analyze the entire dialogue between Frum and Sullivan published in the online journal *Slate*.

3 Write your own argument on the issue of same-sex marriage.

4 Write a research paper analyzing how the public argument about same-sex marriage has developed since Frum and Sullivan's dialogue, considering new laws, proposed laws and constitutional amendments, and political debates since 1997. Your research paper might focus on why same-sex marriage has become a more important and divisive political issue since 1997 or discuss how the pro and con arguments mapped out by Frum and Sullivan have developed and changed.

WHAT'S IN A WORD?

BY GEORGE LAKOFF

George Lakoff (1941–) is Richard and Rhoda Goldman Professor of Cognitive Science and Linguistics at the University of California, Berkeley, and author of books on language for both academic audiences (*Metaphors We Live By*, co-authored with Mark Johnson) and general audiences (*Moral Politics: How Liberals and Conservatives Think* and *Don't Think of an Elephant! Know Your Values and Frame the Debate: The Essential Guide for Progressives*). "What's in a Word?," like many of Lakoff's writings, applies linguistic analysis to examine political language and metaphors. "What's in a Word?" first appeared in the liberal online magazine *AlterNet* on February 18, 2004, during the 2004 U.S. presidential campaign and was included as a chapter in his *Don't Think of an Elephant* later that year. *AlterNet*, as the name implies, publishes liberal, sometimes partisan articles on subjects that might not be represented in mainstream media. In "What's in a Word?" Lakoff attempted to influence the ways that the press and liberal candidates discussed marriage issues in the campaign, especially gay marriage. His essay examines the language used in liberal and conservative arguments about marriage and then makes recommendations about the arguments liberals should use to discuss the gay marriage issue based on his analysis and the questions that reporters should ask political candidates.

WHAT'S IN A WORD? PLENTY, IF the word is "marriage."

Marriage is central to our culture. Marriage legally confers over 600 benefits, but that is only its material aspect. Marriage is an institution, the public expression of lifelong commitment based on love. It is the culmination of a period of seeking a mate, and, for many, the realization of a major goal, often with a build-up of dreams, dates, gossip, anxiety, engagement, shower, wedding plans, rituals, invitations, bridal gown, bridesmaids, families coming together, vows, and a honeymoon. Marriage is the beginning of family life, commonly with the expectation of children and grandchildren, family gatherings, in-laws, little league games, graduations, and all the rest.

Marriage is also understood in terms of dozens of deep and abiding metaphors: a journey through life together, a partnership, a union, a bond, a single object of complementary parts, a haven, a means for growth, a sacrament, a home. Marriage confers a social status—a married couple with new social roles. And for a great many people, marriage legitimizes sex. In short, marriage is a big deal.

Like most important concepts, marriage comes with a variety of prototypical cases: The ideal marriage is happy, lasting, prosperous, with children, a nice home, and friendships with other married couples. The typical marriage has its ups and downs, its joys and difficulties, typical problems with children and in-laws. The nightmare marriage ends in divorce, due perhaps to incompatibility, abuse, or betrayal. It is a rich concept with a cultural stereotype: it is between a man and a woman.

Because marriage is central to family life, it has a political dimension. As I discuss in my book *Moral Politics*, conservative and progressive politics are organized around two very different models of married life: a strict father family and a nurturing parent family.

The strict father is moral authority and master of the household, dominating both the mother and children and imposing needed discipline. Contemporary conservative politics turns these family values into political values: hierarchical authority, individual discipline, military might. Marriage in the strict father family *must* be heterosexual marriage: the father is manly, strong, decisive, dominating—a role model for sons and a model for daughters of a man to look up to.

The nurturing parent model has two equal parents, whose job is to nurture their children and teach their children to nurture others. Nurturance has two dimensions: empathy and responsibility, for oneself and others. Responsibility requires strength and competence. The strong nurturing parent is protective and caring, builds trust and connection, promotes family happiness and fulfillment, fairness, freedom, openness, cooperation, community development. These are the values of a strong progressive politics. Though the stereotype again is heterosexual, there is nothing in the nurturing family model to rule out same-sex marriage.

In a society divided down the middle by these two family models and their politics, we can see why the issue of same-sex marriage is so volatile. What is at stake is more than the material benefits of marriage and the use of the word. At stake is one's identity and most central values. This is not just about same-sex couples. It is about which values will dominate in our society.

When conservatives speak of the "defense of marriage," liberals are baffled. After all, no individual's marriage is being threatened. It's just that more marriages are being allowed. But conservatives see the strict father family, and with it, their political values as under attack. They are right. This is a serious matter for their politics and moral values as a whole. Even civil unions are threatening, since they create families that cannot be traditional strict father families.

Progressives are of two minds. Pragmatic liberals see the issue as one of benefits—inheritance, health care, adoption, etc. If that's all that is involved, civil unions should be sufficient—and they certainly are an advance. Civil unions would provide equal *material* protection under the law. Why not leave civil unions to the state and marriage to the churches, as in Vermont?

Idealistic progressives see beyond the material benefits, important as they are. Most gay activists want more than civil unions. They want full-blown marriage, with all its cultural meanings—a public commitment based on love, all the metaphors, all the rituals, joys, heartaches, family experiences—and a sense of normality, on a par with all other people. The issue is one of personal freedom: the state should not dictate who should marry whom. It is also a matter of fairness and human dignity. Equality under the law includes social and cultural, as well as material benefits. The slogan here is "freedom to marry."

Language is important. The radical right uses "gay marriage." Polls show most Americans overwhelmingly against anti-gay discrimination, but equally against "gay marriage." One reason, I believe, is that "marriage" evokes the idea of sex and most Americans do not favor gay sex. Another is that the stereotype of marriage is heterosexual. "Gay" for the right connotes a wild, deviant, sexually irresponsible lifestyle. That's why the right prefers "gay marriage" to "same-sex marriage."

But "gay marriage" is a double-edged sword. President Bush chose not to use the words "gay marriage" in his State of the Union Address. I suspect that the omission occurred for a good reason. His position is that "marriage" is defined as between a man and a woman, and so the term "gay marriage" should be an oxymoron, as meaningless as "gay apple" or "gay telephone." The

more "gay marriage" is used, the more normal the idea of same-sex marriage becomes, and the clearer it becomes that "marriage" is not defined to exclude the very possibility. This is exactly why some gay activists want to use "same-sex marriage" or even "gay marriage."

The Democratic presidential nominees are trying to sidestep the issue. Kerry and Dean claim marriage is a matter for the church, while the proper role for the state is civil unions and a guarantee of material benefits. This argument makes little sense to me. The ability of ministers, priests, and rabbis to perform marriage ceremonies is granted by governments, not by religions. And civil marriage is normal and widespread. Besides, it will only satisfy the pragmatic liberals. Idealistic conservatives will see civil unions as tantamount to marriage, and idealistic progressives will see them as falling far short of equal protection. It may work in Vermont and perhaps in Massachusetts, but it remains to be seen whether such an attempt to get around the issue will play in most of the country.

And what of the constitutional amendment to define marriage legally as between a man and a woman? Conservatives will be for it, and many others with a heterosexual stereotype of marriage may support it. But it's unlikely to get enough progressive support to pass. The real question is, will the very proposal of such an amendment help George Bush keep the White House?

It's hard to tell right now.

But the progressives who are *not* running for office can do a lot. Progressives need to reclaim the moral high ground—of the grand American tradition of freedom, fairness, human dignity, and full equality under the law. If they are pragmatic liberals, they can talk this way about the civil unions and material benefits. If they are idealistic progressives, they can use the same language to talk about the social and cultural, as well as the material benefits of marriage. Either way, our job as ordinary citizens is to reframe the debate, in everything we say and write, in terms of our moral principles.

The rest of us have to put our ideas out there so that candidates can readily refer to them. For example, when there is a discussion in your office, church, or other group, there is a simple response to someone who says, "I don't think gays should be able to marry, do you?" The response is, "I believe in equal rights, period. I don't think the state should be in the business of telling people who they can or can't marry." The media does not have to accept the right wing's frames. What can a reporter ask besides "Do you support gay marriage?" Try this: "In San Francisco, there has been a lot of discussion of the freedom to marry, as a matter of equal rights under the law. How do you feel about this?"

Reframing is everybody's job.

Journal and Discussion Questions

1 Outline "What's in a Word?" What is George Lakoff's thesis? What are the main parts of his argument? How is this essay organized to persuade Lakoff's audience?

2 Lakoff's ideas are organized as a binary or contrast between the values and assumptions of the left and the right. Make two columns labeled "liberal" and "conservative" and make a list of liberal and conservative beliefs, according to Lakoff, placing opposing ideas next to each other. Do you agree with this explanation of liberal and conservative beliefs? Why or why not?

3 Why does Lakoff prefer the term "same-sex marriage" instead of "gay marriage"? Why, according to Lakoff, do opponents of same-sex or gay marriage prefer the term "gay marriage" or prefer to avoid either term? Why are liberals "baffled" by the phrase "defense of marriage"? What do these examples suggest about Lakoff's concept about how language "frames" political issues and the relationship between one's language and one's perspectives and beliefs about the world? How does Lakoff's idea lead him to the conclusion that "reframing is everybody's job"?

4 Summarize Lakoff's argument that a person's political ideology is often a result of the person's ideas about family life. Do you agree with Lakoff's claims here? Should people's model for the family determine their political beliefs? Why or why not?

5 Lakoff mentions just two specific sources in his article: George W. Bush's 2004 State of the Union address and Lakoff's own book *Moral Politics*. However, he brings up other sources in his article: "anthropological studies of American marriage," opinion polls, and remarks by John Kerry and Howard Dean in the presidential campaign, and he makes general statements about what liberal and conservative commentators have written and said about the same-sex marriage issue. Why did he select these sources? How does he use each source to support or develop his argument?

6 Lakoff writes, "What is at stake [in the debate about same-sex marriage] is more than the material benefits of marriage and the use of the word. At stake are one's identity and most central values. This is not just about same-sex couples. It is about which values will dominate in our society." What does Lakoff mean in this passage? What does this debate imply about "one's identity and most central values"? Do you agree with Lakoff?

7 How would this article be different if it were written for an academic journal? As a student research paper? What would an editorial for a newspaper say if it followed Lakoff's suggestions? What might be a conservative response to this argument? Sketch outlines of these arguments.

Topics for Writing

1 Argue for or against the legalization of same-sex marriage or of same-sex civil unions for a general audience with mixed political beliefs.

2 Select another political issue and analyze a few of the key terms used in political debates about the issue, consulting editorials and columns and political Web sites for your research. Write an essay like Lakoff's in which you analyze the language and make recommendations about how liberals or conservatives can make their arguments more persuasive to audiences that do not already agree with them.

3 Lakoff writes that same-sex marriage is a volatile issue because it has wider implications about identity and the central values that should dominate society. Analyze the arguments on two sides of another volatile issue and discuss what general values each side is appealing to. Although you may make clear what your position is in this debate, avoid vilifying the opposing side. Try to describe each side's values in terms that both sides can agree are accurate and fair.

Connecting the Readings

Compare and evaluate the arguments for and against the legalization of gay or same-sex marriage made by Andrew Sullivan and David Frum in "Gay Marriage" and by George Lakoff in "What's in a Word?"

THE FINE ART OF LETTING GO

BY BARBARA KANTROWITZ AND PEG TYRE
WITH JOAN RAYMOND, PAT WINGERT, AND MARC BAIN

"The Fine Art of Letting Go" is an article that first appeared in the May 22, 2006, issue of the newsmagazine *Newsweek*, in a section called "The Boomer Files: Parenting." Although the authors focus on the problems and responsibilities that parents deal with when their children go to college, Barbara Kantrowitz and Peg Tyre also discuss how wealth and technology have affected and complicated parent–child relationships today, when the "child" moves out of the house and begins adulthood. Now a contributing editor at *Newsweek*, Kantrowitz was a senior editor in the newsmagazine's Society section, responsible for many cover stories on education, religion, health, and women's issues when she co-wrote this article. She joined *Newsweek* in 1985 after working at the *Philadelphia Inquirer*, *People*, *Newsday*, the *New York Times*, and the *Hartford Courant*. A fiction writer as well as a journalist, Kantrowitz is co-author of Newsweek.com's "Her Body" column on women's health and of the book *Is It Hot in Here? Or Is It Me? The Complete Guide to Menopause*. Tyre is a general editor and senior writer for *Newsweek* who writes about education and social trends. Before joining *Newsweek*, she worked as an on-air correspondent at CNN and a reporter at *Newsday*. She has also authored three mystery novels and co-authored the book *Two Seconds Under the World: Terror Comes to America—The Conspiracy Behind the World Trade Center Bombing*.

IMAGINE TEARS, LOTS OF TEARS. IMAGINE a trail of tears trickling across upstate New York. Judie Comerford and her husband, Michael, are in their minivan on a highway somewhere between Potsdam and their home in Buffalo. They've just bid farewell to their oldest child, Meghan, who's starting college. "I cried, and then I cried some more, and then I cried again," Judie recalls. "I didn't think it was possible for someone to cry for going on five hours." The Comerfords were so distraught that they failed to notice the speedometer hitting 92 miles an hour. "The next thing I knew, there were these flashing red lights," Judie says. They pulled over to the side, but the tears kept coming. The trooper asked, "Is there a problem here?"

Judie couldn't speak. Michael was no help; he was bawling, too. Finally, Judie blurted out, "We just took my daughter to college. My life is over. She's my little girl."

The cop got it. "I have a little girl," he said. (Perhaps that's why the Comerfords escaped with only a $15 ticket.) Since that difficult day in 1993, Judie and Michael have said goodbye to three other kids—all now out of school and living successfully on their own. And each time, Judie, a 52-year-old medical receptionist, was inconsolable. With all the birds out of the nest, Judie can joke about her overly emotional goodbyes—and about

the solace she still gets from talking to her kids on the phone "oh, about 40 times a week." She laughs. "And then there's text messaging, too."

Letting go. Are there two more painful words in the boomer-parent lexicon? One minute, there's an adorable, helpless bundle in your arms. Then, 18 years go by in a flash, filled with Mommy and Me classes, Gymboree, Little League, ballet, drama club, summer camp, traveling soccer teams, piano lessons, science competitions, SAT prep classes and college visits. The next thing you know, it's graduation. Most boomers don't want to be "helicopter parents," hovering so long that their offspring never get a chance to grow up. Well versed in the psychological literature, they know that letting go is a gradual process that should begin when toddlers take their first steps without a parental hand to steady them. And hovering is certainly not a new phenomenon; both Gen. Douglas MacArthur and President Franklin Delano Roosevelt had mothers who moved to be near them when they went to college. But with cell phones and e-mail available 24/7, the temptation to check in is huge. Some boomer parents hang on, propelled by love (of course) and insecurity about how the world will treat their children. After years of supervising homework, they think nothing of editing the papers

> **❝ More students than ever are entering college, and rates of teen pregnancy, crime and drug abuse are all down. ❞**

their college students have e-mailed them. A few even buy textbooks and follow the course syllabi. Later they're polishing student resumes and calling in favors to get summer internships. Alarmed by these intrusions into what should be a period of increasing independence, colleges around the country have set up parent-liaison offices to limit angry phone calls to professors and deans. Parent orientations, usually held alongside the student sessions, teach how to step aside.

Letting go is the final frontier for boomer parents, who've made child rearing a major focus of their adult lives. The 76,957,164 Americans born between 1946 and 1964 are the wealthiest and best-educated generation of parents in human history, and they've had unparalleled resources to aid them as they've raised an estimated 80 million children. Although there have been some economic ups and downs, unemployment has been generally low, and the rise of two-career families has meant more for all. While their incomes grew, boomers kept family sizes small, thanks to the availability of birth control and abortion. "In the old days, parents thought of kids like waffles," says William Damon, director of the Stanford University Center on Adolescence. "The first couple might not turn out just right, but you could always make more. Now many families have only one or two kids to work with, so they focus all their attention and energy on one or two and want them to do well." An explosion of child-development research stressing the importance of the early years reinforces boomers' determination to give their kids the best. They've carefully followed expert advice on everything from music that nurtures the developing brain in utero to gaming the college-admissions process.

By many standards, all that effort has paid off. More students than ever are entering college, and rates of teen pregnancy, crime and drug abuse are all down. And the recipients of that guidance certainly appear to be grateful. "Their connection to their parents is deep and strong," says Barbara Hofer, an associate professor of psychology at Middlebury College who studies the transition to college. "They say, 'My parents are my best friends.' People would have seen that as aberrant a generation ago, as pathological." Hofer and her student Elena Kennedy recently surveyed Middlebury freshmen and found that students and parents reported an average of 10.41 communications per week over cell phone, e-mail, Instant Messenger, dorm phone, text

messaging and postal mail. Parents initiate most of this contact, Hofer found, but their children don't seem to mind; most students said they were satisfied with the amount of communication they had with their parents and 28 percent wanted even more with their fathers.

But that closeness is a double-edged sword. When admissions directors get together, sharing horror stories of overinvolved parents is one of their favorite pastimes. "There are cases where the parent tells the adviser that their son wants to be a doctor," says one Midwestern dean, "and these are the classes he wants to take, and then, when the parent leaves the room, the students say, 'I'm not sure I want to be a doctor at all. English and art are more interesting to me'."

Parents who hover risk crippling their children's fledgling sense of self-sufficiency. Missa Murry Eaton, an assistant professor at Penn State University Shenango who studies parent-child relationships, says she's seen a number of parents who think it's OK to call their freshman sons or daughters early in the morning to make sure they wake up or check in late at night to see if they're studying. "They don't allow their children to deal with the consequences of their decisions," says Eaton. "So when a decision goes badly, they just fix it." Children and young adults build up confidence by tackling things that are hard, says Damon. "When they do succeed, they earn real self-esteem."

In fact, it's not the number of e-mails or phone calls that really matter, but the content of the connection. Here, boomers run into trouble. Chatting about the weather or politics is one thing; micromanaging decisions about courses or majors is quite another. But many parents think that economic pressures compel them to intervene. Sending a child to college these days is a huge financial commitment, more than $40,000 a year at elite private schools. For a lot of parents, that means substantial sacrifices like taking out a second mortgage or cutting into retirement savings. "Parents feel this is an economic investment, and they want that investment to pay off," says Hofer.

What's helpful and what's hovering? At Washington University in St. Louis, Karen Coburn, the assistant vice chancellor for students, says helping parents understand the challenges their students will face is a major part of her job. One important lesson: "No one was ever happy all the time between 18 and 22, and your kids aren't going to be, either." She tells parents to take tearful calls in stride. Walking across campus, she often hears students on the phone with a parent, complaining about a cold or a bad grade. "Then I see them click off the phone and go running over to a friend and say, 'Hi, how are you? Things are great!' And I think of those poor parents, sitting in their offices."

As graduation approaches, there's even more pressure on college career offices and prospective employers. "We have parents calling us to ask why little Johnny wasn't accepted to interview at Goldman," says Jennifer Floren, CEO of experience.com, a Web site that connects 3,800 universities with employers. "They're demanding passwords so they can get into the student's account. It's just bizarre." In an experience.com survey of career-center offices, respondents said parents were substantially more involved than even five years ago and that this trend cut across all regions of the country and all incomes.

Parents worry that their kids will never get jobs and end up home after graduation, living in the basement. It's not an unreasonable fear. Many kids graduate with debt from student loans, which makes it difficult to find affordable housing even if they do find work. According to the 2000 Census, 10.5 percent of Americans 25 to 34 were living in their parents' houses, compared with 8 percent in 1970, the low point for young adults moving home.

It takes will power to hold back. Rosalie Fuller knew what she had to do when her oldest son, Brinson, 20, left for Appalachian State University. "I'm trying very hard to force them to leave the nest," she says. Fuller, 48, who lives in New Bern, N.C., and her husband, Walt, 53, a timber buyer for Weyerhaeuser, have agreed to pay for Brinson's tuition, room and board, but he is supposed to pay for fraternity dues, car insurance and general expenses. In the middle of sophomore year, Brinson ran out of cash and the Fullers decided to take over his car-insurance payments but nothing else. Then his grades took a plunge—all C's and D's. The reason: too much partying and not enough studying. In an e-mail, Rosalie told him how many hours a week she spent working for a company that sells aviation fuel in order for him to go to college. "I told him that I would never again pay for a semester like this." Brinson got the message. He wrote her back a three-page mission statement laying out his plan of action to get better grades. "First and foremost," he wrote, "I will attend every class." Brinson followed up on his promise—his grades are up—and he's leaning toward an accounting major.

Closeness to their kids doesn't mean boomers are lenient. Sheila Walker, 51, a grocery clerk from Cleveland, doesn't think there's anything wrong with being in the face of her son, Ronald, 17. "He's a good boy, but I'm the mom," she says. "Part of our responsibility as parents is to know who your kids are with. Technology, like cell phones, makes it easier for us to monitor our kids." This fall, Ronald heads off to college. "Sure, I'm going to miss him," she says, "but I want him to be a man."

Many parents say letting go is hard because the stakes seem so much higher than when they were starting out. At every stage of their parenting careers, they've felt the pressure of competition—whether it's getting their kids into a good preschool, summer camp or college. Boomers might have spent their young-adult years shuffling from major to major or job to job, but many say they'd never condone that behavior in their kids. In fact, experimentation can be critical to real accomplishment, while following lockstep in a pre-ordained path is often deadening. "The idea of taking good risks and doing your best and then learning from whatever happens is a necessary part of becoming a successful person," says Dave Verhaagen, a child and adolescent psychologist in North Carolina and author of "Parenting the Millennial Generation."

Barrie Smith, 45, of Old Westbury, N.Y., concedes that her son, Chase Steinlauf, about to turn 18, who just finished his freshman year at Duke University, has been at the center of her life. "Raising him was my career," she says proudly. She scheduled her days chauffeuring him to tennis, chess and math team. Things really ramped up when the college-admissions race started. She admits she pushed him to apply to the best schools. "You want that Harvard sticker on your car," she says. "They make a lot of connections at these schools."

Chase was a National Merit Scholar and graduated at the top of his class. Still, says Smith, "there was a lot of stress and fighting." She wanted Harvard. "I could see myself there," she says. Chase liked Yale. "He was trying to assert his independence," she says. He didn't succeed. Smith made him apply early to Harvard and he was deferred. He was rejected by Yale and got into Duke. "It was my mistake," Smith says. "I should have let him apply to the college of his choice."

She channeled her anxiety about his leaving into preparing his dorm room. Smith bought Ralph Lauren sheets, a cashmere throw, leather slippers, a sisal rug. "He lives like that at home," she explains. "I wanted to make it homey." Chase says he stuffed the decorative pillows, comforter and cashmere throw into his suitcase. "She likes things formal in a way that I find cluttered," he says diplomatically. Smith nearly passed out from anxiety about Chase's well-being after she dropped him off, but soon afterward, she started a Web site for equally worried moms of freshmen called mofchat.com. "It became a kind of catharsis," she says. When Chase talks about the Web site, he sounds more like the proud parent. "It was a lot more professional than I had anticipated," he says. "It's good to have a place where [parents] can talk to each other."

During college and the first years after gradua- tion, young adults should be learning to make deci- sions for themselves and dealing with the conse- quences. Parents can help or hinder that process. "You have to go from manager to consultant, from on- site supervisor to mentor," says Helen Johnson, coau- thor of "Don't Tell Me What to Do, Just Send Money." "You have to let them fail and face those tough situa- tions. It's not easy to do. But if you don't, think about the message you are conveying to your son or daugh- ter—that they're not able to handle their own life."

> **During college and the first years after graduation, young adults should be learning to make decisions for themselves and dealing with the consequences.**

That means a period of adjustment for both parent and child. Tom and Pam Burkardt, who live in subur- ban Boston, are getting ready for the day their youngest child, Colin, 17, goes to college. "We just told Colin the other day to 'Pick any college and we'll follow you,'" says Pam, 52. "We were joking . . . sort of." Their older sons—Michael, 22, and Sean, 20—are both in col- lege, but Tom, 47, says he talks to them "all the time," via cell phone, e-mail and instant messaging. When Colin leaves, Tom anticipates "a tough, tough time." But he knows that encouraging his sons' independence is the only way to help them lead happy and productive adult lives. All his sons worked during high school and summers between college semesters even though the family's bank account expanded considerably after Tom sold his telecommunications business. "Just be- cause we have money doesn't mean we're going to spoil them," Tom says. "You have to learn the value of a dol- lar." Tom's personal measure of success? "Man, it warms my heart when one calls and says, 'Hey Dad, want to play some golf?'"

In the early years of the 20th century, parents hung on to their kids for as long as possible because children, who often started working at a young age, were an important source of income. "The kid would finally have to break away if they wanted to keep any of their own money," says Stephanie Coontz, a family historian at the Evergreen State College in Olympia, Wash. By the time the oldest baby boomers were born, parents expected their kids to grow up and move out— period. Half of all women were married by the age of 20, a move parents generally supported because they thought marriage promoted maturity.

As the older boomers were coming of age in the 1960s and '70s, ideas about leaving home shifted again. Young adults thought they had to rebel against their parents in order to achieve independence, Coontz says. Younger boomers were more likely to suffer from the sharp rise in divorce rates beginning in the late 1960s, which meant that sometimes parents left home before the kids. So both older and younger boomers entered parenthood with strong reasons to find a bet- ter way to raise their own children.

Jim Tully, 44, a sales manager for a beef company, was the youngest of six kids. His mother died when he was 9 and his father was working all the time. "There was no helicopter in my house when I was growing up," says Jim, who lives in Brock- ton, Mass. His wife, Sharon, 43, was the youngest of seven. "Everything is completely differ- ent from the way that I grew up," says Jim. "My wife and I dedicate our lives to our chil- dren." The four Tully children are now ages 21 to 8. "We talk about the sex, the drugs, the rock and roll," says Jim. In many ways, he says he feels close to his kids be- cause he shares some of their interests and tastes. "I still love Jimi Hendrix and Aerosmith," says Jim. His daugh- ter Jill, 18, who's going off to college in the fall, says the open relationship she has with her parents keeps her out of trouble. "Because my parents listen to me," she says, "I don't have any secrets from them. We can talk." They have, for example, talked about parties where there might be some drinking. Jill knows that if she did decide to drink, all she would have to do is call home and some- one would come and get her. "Because we talk about things so much, I don't even want to drink," she says. "It's the kids whose parents don't talk to them who sneak around and do dumb things." Her parents are her role models. "That's the kind of relationship I want to have with my children in the future," she says.

But to get to that place of mutual trust and re- spect, parents do have to let go a little. "It is good and healthy for parents to want their kids to be success- ful, but there are many ways to get there," says Lau- rence Steinberg, a Temple University psychology pro- fessor and the author of "The Ten Basic Principles of Good Parenting." "Part of good parenting is facilitat- ing your child's personal development, not just their accomplishments." Julia Cruz, 58, and her husband, Allen Russell Chauvenet, are both doctors who live in Winston-Salem, N.C. They chose their house because it is just a mile from the hospital where they work and they could be home for dinner with their kids, Nicholas, now 21, and Christina, 19.

As their kids grew older, Julia and Allen worked hard to encourage their independence, but the final goodbyes were wrenching. Julia will never forget the day she dropped Nicholas off at the University of North Carolina at Chapel Hill. As she helped him set up his room, she was crying. Before she left to go home, she told her son she was going off to the other end of campus to get a copy of the parent handbook. Nicholas said he was going to visit a friend. As they walked outside together in the sunny, late August weather, Julia tried to gather her composure. Nicholas said, "Are you going to be all right?" Julia said, "Yes, and you're going to be all right, too." They tearfully embraced. He started walking away. Julia didn't move. She just watched him—her baby—and then watched the girls watching him and suddenly saw him for who he had become, a handsome young man firmly in adulthood. She wanted to cry out a warning: be careful, wear clean clothes, don't fall in love with someone who will break your heart. But she remained silent.

And then her son turned and headed back to his dorm. She stood rooted to the spot while he walked past without seeing her. He was in his new world now.

Journal and Discussion Questions

1 Outline "The Fine Art of Letting Go." What is its central idea? How do Barbara Kantrowitz and Peg Tyre develop this argument and deal with opposing ideas?

2 On page 126, Kantrowitz and Tyre ask, "What's helpful and what's hovering?" as they discuss how parents intervene in their sons' and daughters' lives in college. How does "The Fine Art of Letting Go" answer this question? Do you agree with the article's definition of "helpful" and "hovering" parenting? Why or why not?

3 Kantrowitz and Tyre introduce and conclude "The Fine Art of Letting Go" with two stories about parents bringing their son to college for the first time. What is the point of each story? How effective are the introduction and the conclusion?

4 To persuade people to read "The Fine Art of Letting Go," *Newsweek* included this teaser under the title: "As parents, boomers face their final frontier: how to stand aside as their children become independent adults. Where's the line between caring and coddling?" How do Kantrowitz and Tyre answer these two questions? Do you agree with them? Why or why not?

5 According to Kantrowitz and Tyre, how have cell phones, text-messaging, email, and the Internet changed the relationship between college students and their parents? What is beneficial about these changes? What problems are caused or exacerbated by these new technologies? What other technologies and technological developments do Kantrowitz and Tyre mention in their discussion of American families?

6 What sources do Kantrowitz and Tyre cite in "The Fine Art of Letting Go"? What does each source contribute to their portrait of the American family and of college students and their parents? What information do they provide about the parents and experts that they interviewed? Why do they include this information?

7 Does "The Fine Art of Letting Go" describe situations similar to your own experiences as a college student? Why or why not? What kinds of students and families do Kantrowitz and Tyre focus on? What kinds of students and families do they ignore in their article?

Topics for Writing

1 Analyze Barbara Kantrowitz and Peg Tyre's "The Fine Art of Letting Go." Your analysis might focus on how Kantrowitz and Tyre develop and support their thesis, what their article reveals about the effects of wealth and technology on American family life, or how their portrait of American families is shaped by the kinds of families they interviewed and the kinds of families they ignored.

2 Drawing on "The Fine Art of Letting Go" and your own observations and experiences, write an essay for a magazine marketed mainly to college students about how families (not necessarily just parents) affect the lives of college students. Discuss how students should best deal with their families.

3 Using interviews or questionnaires, conduct research on your campus about the relationships of students to their parents, how parents affect students' behavior and academic performance, and what programs and policies your campus has for students' parents. Use the library and the Internet to research how other colleges and universities deal with the needs and demands of parents. Write a research paper evaluating the role of parents in college students' lives on your campus and how well your school is dealing with the needs and demands of parents.

IMAGES OF FAMILY IN ADVERTISING

The advertisement "Parents. The Anti-Drug" ran in the December 2006/January 2007 issue of the magazine *Working Mother* (and probably a number of other popular magazines as well). The advertisement publicizes a Web site, www.theantidrug.com, established by the National Youth Anti-Drug Media Campaign and an anti-drug campaign created by the White House Office of National Drug Control Policy in 1998. The campaign's purpose is to help parents and other adults caring for children to discourage drug use among children and adolescents. Working with many national, community, and church organizations and employing advertisements like this as well as commercials, after-school activities, and the AntiDrug Web site, the campaign strives to educate people about the seriousness of drug use by minors, to provide parents with information on drugs and drug prevention, and to help parents find and develop support communities. The advertising campaign often appeals to Americans' anxieties about raising children while promoting greater parental involvement in adolescents' lives.

Journal and Discussion Questions

1 What is the central message or thesis of the "Parents. The Anti-Drug" advertisement? How does the advertisement get its message across to readers? How does the ad appeal to the interests and concerns of the readers of *Working Mother*?

2 Magazine and newspaper advertisements are often organized in a "Z" pattern, with images and print designed to draw readers first to the upper left section of the advertisement, then across the page, then down the page, and finally coming to a rest in the lower right section. Does the Anti-Drug advertisement follow this design? What words and images are emphasized by the ad's design? Why? What parts of the advertisement are deemphasized? Why?

3 Summarize the text or copy of the "Parents. The Anti-Drug" advertisement. What thesis does the ad argue? Why does the Anti-Drug ad begin with the lead "It's a fine line between respecting your teen's privacy and doing your job as a parent" and follow immediately with the question, "How far should you go?" How do these two sentences set up the rest of the advertisement's argument?

4 Describe the teenager pictured in the Parents advertisement. How are teens described in the text of the advertisement? How does her picture support and contribute to the message and emotions of the Anti-Drug advertisement? Is it important that the teenager is a white female? Why or why not?

5 What problems or anxieties about the American family are expressed in the advertisement? How does the ad attempt to allay our concerns about the family? Do you agree with the advertisement's implied argument about the condition of the American family? Why or why not?

Topics for Writing

1 Analyze the image of family in the "Parents. The Anti-Drug" advertisement.

2 Research the needs and problems of working parents and the ways that companies do (and do not) try to accommodate these needs. Write a research paper about whether companies should accommodate the needs of parents who work for them, and, if so, how.

3 Write a research paper about the National Youth Anti-Drug Media Campaign and the Parents. The Anti-Drug Web site and advertising campaign or about another organization to help parents. Your research paper should describe, analyze, and evaluate the goals and methods of the organization and consider what critics say about the organization.

It's a fine line between respecting your teen's privacy and doing your job as a parent.

How far should you go? As far as you have to. Because teenagers today have a minefield of risky behaviors to navigate—

drugs, drinking, tobacco, sex

—with powerful influences like peer pressure and mixed messages from pop culture, and new technologies such as the internet.

Fortunately, there's one influence in your teenager's life that trumps them all. You. So take action.

Let them know just where you stand on risk-taking and its consequences. And spell things out, because it's the contract both you and your teen will be living by. Set clear rules with your teen for safety and guidance. That's right, getting them to agree to the rules and understand the consequences gives them more responsibility and every teen wants that.

And yes, do keep close tabs on your teens. Know where they are and who they're with. Cell phones make it easier than ever to just "check in." It's not saying you don't trust your teen, it's saying you care. Get on the internet, too. Familiarize yourself with the kind of content they might be exposed to.

Above all else, one of the most powerful things you can do for your teenager is to set a good example when it comes to drug, tobacco and alcohol use. Respect them, be honest with them, be clear with them and they'll do the same. Everyone wins.

Signed,
American Academy of Child and Adolescent Psychiatry, American Academy of Family Physicians, American Academy of Pediatrics, American Legacy Foundation, American Lung Association, CTIA–The Wireless Association®, Cox Communications, Leadership to Keep Children Alcohol Free, National African American Tobacco Prevention Network, National Asian Pacific American Families Against Substance Abuse, National Cable and Telecommunications Association, National Campaign to Prevent Teen Pregnancy, National Families in Action, National Latino Children's Institute, Qwest Communications, and The Partnership for a Drug-Free America.

PARENTS.
THE ANTI-DRUG.

Office of National Drug Control Policy   For more tips and support on parenting your teen, call 1-800-788-2800 or visit www.theantidrug.com

Connecting the Readings

Compare and contrast the ideas about what constitutes proper or healthy parenting in twenty-first century American society in Barbara Kantrowitz and Peg Tyre's "The Fine Art of Letting Go" with those in the advertisement for "Parents. The Anti-Drug."

Suggestions for Essays on MARRIAGE AND FAMILY

1 Write an essay comparing the images of family in at least two of the following: Lee, White, Rockwell's *Easter Morning*, and Lanker's photograph. Discuss and compare the generalities about family that are suggested by these portraits of individual families.

2 Compare the views of parenting in Lakoff, Kantrowitz and Tyre, and the Parents. The Anti-Drug advertisement. You might address whether these texts discuss similar concerns and anxieties about parenting today or the same ideas about how parents should raise children. Your essay might evaluate and take a position about the views about parenting discussed in each text. Or your essay might explain the reasons behind the disagreements about parenting in these texts.

3 Discuss how politicians, businesses, and advertisers use people's ideas about family to sell their ideas and politics drawing on Lakoff, Klane, and the "Parents. The Anti-Drug" advertisement. Or write an essay drawing on these texts arguing how politics and business influence the public's ideas about family.

4 Considering several arguments about the changes in American families by Raspberry, Sullivan and Frum, Klane, Coontz, and Kantrowitz and Tyre, describe how the American family has changed and how these changes are benefitting and/or harming American society.

5 Drawing on arguments made by Sullivan and Frum, Lakoff, and Coontz, discuss how the issue of same-sex marriage is connected to other changes in the institution of marriage.

6 Analyze how gender affects the roles of family members using at least three of the following as sources: Lee, White, Raspberry, Roethke, Rockwell, Lanker, and Klane.

7 Analyze how wealth, poverty, and social class affect families using Raspberry, Coontz, Kantrowitz and Tyre, Rockwell's *Easter Morning*, and Grice's "Haircut" as sources.

06 Faith and Religion

YOU'VE PROBABLY BEEN ADVISED TO avoid the topics of politics and religion in friendly conversation (undoubtedly wise advice when meeting the parents of a boyfriend or girlfriend). Americans often have trouble discussing politics or religion without bruising feelings and straining friendships. Politics is a frequent subject of college classes, partly because one of the missions of higher education is to prepare students to participate in a democracy, to argue with each other productively, and to respectfully disagree with each other. Outside courses in religious studies and the Bible as literature, religion and belief systems are often taboo subjects for class discussions, even though students' beliefs are frequently challenged and reexamined in college. But, as Thomas Bartlett discusses in his article "Most Freshmen Say Religion Guides Them," this situation is changing. Religious beliefs and affiliations, as well as secularism, agnosticism, and atheism, are too important to people's understanding of themselves, to their relations with other people and to culture, and, increasingly, in national and international politics to ignore as just a personal matter. The U.S. has the most church-going population of any western industrialized nation, along with strong traditions of secularism, religious pluralism, and separation of church and state. So, more and more, Americans are talking with each other about God, sin and evil, morality, and the roles that religion should and should not have in political debate and policy decisions. And we are trying to figure out how agnostics, atheists, Baptists, Buddhists, Catholics, Episcopalians, Jews, Lutherans, Methodists, Mormons, Muslims, Presbyterians, Quakers, Seventh-Day Adventists, and Unitarians, among others, can discuss these issues productively and respectfully.

Some of the issues being debated today are centuries old, while other debates have bubbled up out of the cauldron of present-day culture and social circumstances. Here are some of the questions that are addressed by the writers in this chapter, questions that you might address in your writings and discussions for this class.

- Why do people believe what they believe? What is the basis for an individual's or a community's faith or skepticism?

- What is faith? Does faith mean the same thing as religion?

- Why and how do people's faiths or belief systems change? What causes individuals to gain, change, or reject a religious faith?

- What is the nature of evil? Why does evil exist?

- How should one's beliefs affect how one lives?

- What is the purpose of organized religion? Why do people form churches and communities to worship their god(s)?

- How do religions affect the cultures around them? How are these religions influenced by the cultures around them?

- What role, if any, should religious beliefs and organized religion have in government policies? Why?

- What place, if any, should prayer, religious expression, and religious discussions have in public education and government?

- Why have religious differences been a source of violent conflict in the world? How can such conflicts be resolved or avoided?

- Should a teacher bring his or her religious and moral beliefs, including agnostic and atheist positions, into the classroom? Should students? Can this be done without imposing one's beliefs on others in the class or threatening their religious freedom?

- How do one's religious beliefs and practices help determine—and sometimes fail to influence—people's actions and positions on topics such as war and peace, marriage and family, sexuality, and education?

- How can one argue questions of morality to audiences of mixed faiths?

Invitations for Journal Writing

1 How would you describe your religious faith or belief system? What are your beliefs about God, and how do your beliefs affect your view of yourself, of humanity in general, and of the universe? How did you acquire your belief system? How would you and your life be different with another faith or set of beliefs?

2 What experience in your life has had the biggest influence on your religious faith (strengthening, challenging, or shaking your belief system)?

3 What place should religion have in education, public policy, and business? Why?

MOST FRESHMEN SAY RELIGION GUIDES THEM

BY THOMAS BARTLETT

Thomas Bartlett is a reporter for *The Chronicle of Higher Education*, a weekly newspaper on higher education read by college and university faculty and administrators. "Most Freshmen Say Religion Guides Them" was the *Chronicle*'s cover article on April 22, 2005, and reports on and summarizes a large national survey about college students' religious beliefs. Bartlett's article has many familiar features of a newspaper article: short paragraphs, a strong lead sentence, a brief summary of the study with charts, and comments on the study from interviews.

MOST FRESHMEN SAY RELIGION GUIDES

them but almost half describe their views as conflicted, a first-of-its-kind study finds. Most college freshmen believe in God, but fewer than half follow religious teachings in their daily lives. A majority of first-year students (69 percent) say their beliefs provide guidance, but many (48 percent) describe themselves as "doubting," "seeking," or "conflicted."

Those are some of the results of a national study released last week that is believed to be the first broad, in-depth look at the religious and spiritual views of college students. The study, "Spirituality in Higher Education: A National Study of College Students' Search for Meaning and Purpose," was conducted by the Higher Education Research Institute at the University of California at Los Angeles (http://www.gseis.ucla.edu/heri/heri.html). Last fall 112,232 freshmen were asked how often they attended religious services, whether they prayed, and if their religious beliefs affected their actions.

Among the findings was a strong correlation between students' religious beliefs and their views on hot-button political issues. For instance, students who considered themselves religious were more likely to oppose same-sex marriage. Religious students were also less likely to believe that abortion should be legal.

On other questions, however, there was little difference between religious and nonreligious students. For instance, a majority of both groups believed that the federal government should do more to control the sale of handguns and that colleges should ban racist and sexist speech on campus.

The survey also found that while first-year students were not always sure what they believed, most of them were interested in grappling with big questions like the meaning of life.

What that suggests, according to Alexander W. Astin, director of the research center at UCLA, is that colleges should be searching for ways to incorporate spiritual and religious questions into the curriculum—even if doing so makes some professors uncomfortable.

"There's an unwritten assumption that we just don't talk about these issues," says Mr. Astin. "I don't think we're taking advantage of the opportunity to help students explore those questions with each other and in their course work."

That is because higher education is "a little more repressed" when the conversation turns to spiritual matters, according to Claire L. Gaudiani, a former president of Connecticut College who helped oversee the study. "For a lot of intellectuals, religion and spirituality are seen as a danger to intellectual inquiry," says Ms. Gaudiani.

She argues, however, that dealing with questions about meaning and purpose "doesn't have to mean indoctrination." She compares what she calls "educating the spirit" to teaching good nutrition or physical fitness. "Right now students get the sense that we don't do spirituality," she says.

"BURNING QUESTIONS." If most professors do not "do spirituality," then Mark Wallace is an exception. The associate professor of religion at Swarthmore College teaches a first-year seminar called "Religion and the Meaning of Life." He agrees that many professors are reluctant to engage in what he calls "meaning teaching." Which is a shame, he says, because meaning is exactly what students are looking for. "They hunger and crave that sort of conversation in a college environment," says Mr. Wallace.

He also agrees with Ms. Gaudiani that it is possible to deal with religious questions without promoting a particular ideology. What his students seem to want is an "open, safe place" for the discussion of universal issues where they won't be "censored or yelled at or ignored." As proof, he cites the fact that he usually has three times as many students sign up for his seminar as he can accept. "They have burning questions about life issues," he says. "And they feel those kinds of issues get ignored in the classroom."

Not in David K. Glidden's classroom: The professor of philosophy at the University of California at Riverside teaches "The Care of the Soul," a course that focuses on how to live a purposeful life. While Mr. Glidden is not sure that students will complete his class knowing how to care for their souls, he thinks such courses are a good start and should be a part of a college's curriculum. "My sense is that the students I've taught are a lot like what T. S. Eliot called 'hollow men.' They are living in a world and they don't know what they're here for—they don't know how to live their lives."

And they want to know how to live their lives, says Richard F. Galvin, a professor of philosophy at Texas Christian University. He is part of a team-taught, freshman-level course called "The Meaning of Life." The course has two sections of 50 students and the seats are always filled. "I can tell by talking to them in office hours, looking at their faces in class, and reading their work that it affects them," Mr. Galvin says. "They want to talk about these issues. What I like to tell them is that there is plenty of time to be worried about their careers but this might be the last time they get to talk about big questions."

Readings for the course include Plato's dialogues and works by Friedrich Nietzsche and John Stuart Mill.

Jeffrey Sebo took Mr. Galvin's class when he was a freshman. The senior philosophy major was intrigued by the title of the course and became fascinated by the discussions—so much so that he has returned to the class twice as a teaching assistant. "It was the big questions that got me hooked," he says.

The results of the UCLA study were heartening to Carol Geary Schneider, president of the Association of American Colleges and Universities, which has long advocated a more holistic and less career-centered approach to higher education. "Students are more idealistic than we thought," she says. "But what this data shows us is that we have a long way to go. Students have idealism that can be tapped but we're not doing all we can to help them connect that idealism to important challenges in the world around us."

Figuring out how to do that is not simple, but colleges need to start trying, according to Mr. Astin. "If you want to take seriously the claims we make about liberal learning, this is what you have to do," he says. "There are large numbers of students who are involved in spiritual and religious issues and who are trying to figure out what life is all about and what matters to them. We need to be much more creative in finding ways to encourage that exploration."

Freshmen's Views on Religion and Spirituality. Last fall the Higher Education Research Institute at the University of California at Los Angeles asked 112,232 college freshmen about their views on religion and spirituality. Here are some of the findings:

Students' religious preferences

Roman Catholic	28%
None	17%
Baptist	13%
Other Christian	11%
Methodist	6%
Lutheran	5%
Presbyterian	4%
Church of Christ	3%
Other religion	3%
Episcopalian	2%
Jewish	2%
Buddhist	1%
Eastern Orthodox	1%
Hindu	1%
Islamic	1%
United Church of Christ	1%
Latter-day Saints (Mormon)	0.4%
Unitarian	0.4%
Quaker	0.2%

Current views about spiritual/religious matters

Secure	42%
Seeking	23%
Conflicted	15%
Not interested	15%
Doubting	10%

Note: Figures add up to more than 100 percent because students could choose more than one option.

Indicators of students' religiousness

Believe in God	79%
Pray	69%
Attend religious services (*)	81%
Discussed religion/spirituality with friends (*)	80%
Discussed religion/spirituality with family (*)	76%
Religious beliefs provide strength, support, and guidance (†)	69%
Follow religious teachings in everyday life (‡)	40%

(*) Occasionally or frequently
(†) Agree strongly or somewhat
(‡) Consider it essential or very important

Indicators of students' spirituality

Believe in the sacredness of life (*)	83%
Have an interest in spirituality (*)	80%
Search for meaning/purpose in life (*)	76%
Have discussions about the meaning of life with friends (*)	74%
My spirituality is a source of joy (†)	64%
Seek out opportunities to help me grow spiritually (‡)	47%

(*) Describes students to some or a great extent
(†) Agree strongly or somewhat
(‡) Consider it essential or very important
Source: Higher Education Research Institute

Journal and Discussion Questions

1 Although Thomas Bartlett is reporting on a study, "Most Freshmen Say Religion Guides Them" makes an argument. What is the thesis of this argument? What reasons does the story provide to support this thesis? What other reasons could be added to these ideas?

2 News articles are often organized from most important or surprising information to least important or surprising. Outline "Most Freshmen Say Religion Guides Them." Does Bartlett's article follow this order? How do you think Bartlett determined the importance of each piece of information?

3 What do the charts reveal about what the survey found? What do you find significant about this information? Why?

4 What do you think are some of "the big questions" that the students in the survey "were interested in grappling with"? What do you think Mark Wallace means by "meaning"? How often have these questions been addressed in your schooling?

5 Why, according to Bartlett's story, are some professors "uncomfortable" addressing religious and spiritual matters in class? Why do some professors believe addressing religion and spirituality risks "indoctrination"?

6 How does Bartlett describe and present the results of the study "Spirituality in Higher Education: A National Study of College Students' Search for Meaning and Purpose" to enhance the study's credibility with readers? What are the strengths and limitations of a statistical survey in trying to understand students' religious and spiritual beliefs?

7 Why do you think that there was a strong correlation between students' religious beliefs and their positions on "hot-button issues" like same-sex marriage? Why do you think there was no strong correlation between their religious beliefs and their opinions on issues such as the sale of handguns?

Topics for Writing

1 Look up "Spirituality in Higher Education: A National Study of College Students' Search for Meaning and Purpose," the study conducted by the Higher Education Research Institute at UCLA, at www.gseis.ucla.edu/heri. Analyze Thomas Bartlett's report of this study, considering what Bartlett included, and what he left out, and how accurately and fairly he represented the study's findings.

2 Write an editorial for the student newspaper arguing for or against providing more attention to spiritual and religious questions in your college curriculum.

3 Investigate the religious beliefs of freshmen on your campus by conducting a survey or interviews. Write an essay comparing your findings to the findings in "Spirituality in Higher Education."

COHABITATION: Today's New Lifestyle—or Not

BY SHANNON GAVIN

Shannon Gavin is a nursing student at the University of Iowa. She wrote the research paper "Cohabitation: Today's New Lifestyle—or Not" for a first-year rhetoric course taught by Mary Trachsel in the spring 2007 semester. In "Cohabitation," Gavin examines sociologist Jean M. Twenge's claim that couples who wait until they marry to live together make up a minority of her generation and how this fact is related to the importance her generation places on religion. As she discusses in her paper, her decision to write on this subject was prompted by her surprise about Twenge's finding and her own religion's opposition to premarital sex. The personal importance of her subject leads her to question Twenge's conclusion, to examine her own beliefs, and to explore the relationship between her generation's religious commitment and their ideas about marriage and cohabitation.

Gavin 1

Shannon Gavin

Dr. Trachsel–Rhetoric II

Final Rhetoric Paper

1 May 2007

Cohabitation: Today's New Lifestyle—or Not

In my second semester at The University of Iowa, I was required to take the class Rhetoric II. In this course, my class and I read and discussed sociologist Jean M. Twenge's book *Generation Me*, which provided studies on my generation's defining characteristics. As I read through the book, I was intrigued by Twenge's reports on today's sexual revolution, pregnancy rates and premarital habits in Chapter Six, "Sex: Generation Prude Meets Generation Crude." In particular, I was interested in the part of the chapter that discussed cohabiting, or couples living together prior to marriage. Twenge claims that "Couples who wait to live together until after the wedding are not the minority, and this trend is likely to continue" (177). As I read this line in the book, I was shocked! What Twenge was presenting to her readers was the opposite of everything my parents have taught me since I was a young girl. I had always been taught that marriage comes before sex and that living with members outside of my own gender is not "appropriate." So, as Twenge continued to write about the "eleven million unmarried people" who cohabit because "living together is a normal step in a relationship," I began to wonder (177).

As I referenced Twenge's book for more information about divorce rates and religious commitment, the topics caught my attention. I was alarmed once again when I read Twenge's declaration that "almost half of GenMe has seen their parents divorce" (111) and "Divorce after only a few years of marriage has become so common that [. . .]" (112). I have always viewed divorce as an undesirable situation, despite the fact that I have many friends who come from split families. I partially think this way because I come from a happy home with two parents. My Catholic religion also does not look favorably upon those who choose to divorce. I am aware of this because I attend church every Sunday and read the Bible. But in this, too, I apparently am in the minority. According to Twenge, "church attendance across all faiths has declined 30% since the 1950s and about half of that decline occurred since the 1980s. [. . .] GenMe is not very religious" (34). Therefore many people may not have been taught the same beliefs as I was. Being a Catholic has played a large role in my life because up until my confirmation I went to Sunday school, I have always attended church every Sunday, and I constantly engage in daily prayers; however, until I read Twenge's book I did not know that I am among the minority of my generation. This new knowledge about cohabitation, divorce, and religion made me realize that what I have learned over the years does not correspond with the beliefs and behaviors of the majority of members in Generation Me. Because I am a part of GenMe, I began to question how valid my values actually were, and why I thought and acted so differently from other members of my generation. I began to think about my upbringing,

Twenge's claims, and the world around me in hopes of finding connections. How do other sources examine cohabitation and why has it become so popular? Can a connection be made between cohabitation and religious views? Are increasing divorce rates in any way correlated with an increase in premarital cohabitation?

I began to advance my research in hopes of finding an answer to each of my questions; however, I found numerous answers. Twenge supports her argument that cohabitation has increased by citing a poll taken in 2001, in which the majority of respondents claimed "living together is the best way to predict if the relationship will last" (176). She also discusses financial and tax laws that make cohabitation economically beneficial either to individuals or to couples. In addition to Twenge, I found three journal articles, two personal interviews, two letters responding to an editor, two sections in a textbook, and one website that have a variety of added views on the increasing popularity of premarital living. While all agree that cohabitation is on the rise, they differ in the reasons why. For example, some individuals, including Twenge, choose to live together before marriage for no other reason than personal desire; others follow the Bible and Christian or Jewish religious teachings when deciding their view on cohabitation outside of marriage, and still others feel more secure in a cohabiting relationship because they are aware of the high percentage of marriages that end in divorce today, a destiny they hope to avoid.

As Papalia, Old, and Feldman write in their *Human Development* textbook, "cohabitation" describes the "status of an unmarried couple who live together and maintain a sexual relationship" (526). Like Twenge, the textbook authors describe this new lifestyle as "increasingly common" (526). Currently, cohabitation is more widespread among young adults than those in mid or later life. Papalia, Old, and Feldman estimate that "25 percent of unmarried women ages 25 to 39 are currently cohabiting (528)." Because this way of life is adopted much more frequently than in the past, acceptance of cohabitation is also on the rise. Strong social judgment against premarital living is decreasing, so there is "[. . .] less social pressure to marry," which means that "cohabitation becomes a lifestyle in itself rather than a transition to marriage" (527–528). This alternative to marriage is supported on the website *Civitas*: The Institute for the Study of Civil Society. CIVITAS is located in London and it is a registered charity that provides current, but liberal, viewpoints on today's news and current events. In one of their many "fact sheets," the website insists that marriage is not an automatic outcome of cohabitation. In fact the article states that an extramarital living situation is "less likely than marriage to lead to a long-term stable commitment [. . .]. [T]hey are always more likely to break up than marriages entered into at the same time, regardless of age or income." The CIVITAS website emphasizes that although living with someone may seem like a long-term action, the guarantee is much less stable than the promise made through marriage. For example, "less than four percent of cohabitations last for ten years or more" (CIVITAS). This statistic stresses the fragility of cohabitating lifestyles.

The essence of Twenge's argument is that living with your partner before marriage is more casually accepted than it used to be in past decades. She illustrates this when she openly tells the many readers of her book that she lived with Craig, her future husband, for a year and a half before they said their vows. Twenge reports that when she was making the decision to cohabit, her peers advised that sexual compatibility is important when finding someone to marry. Twenge quotes "Emily" comparing cohabitation to a test drive; "'You wouldn't buy a car you haven't test driven, would you?'" (163). This analogy represents how Generation Me members are thinking through their choices nowadays in order to make a final decision.

The search for the right partner is explained through new research by an individual named R. L. Oberst and by Melissa Bradley, a psychotherapist, both of whom wrote letters to a news editor regarding previous news articles titled "Cohabitation Is Replacing Dating" and "Divorce Is Declining, but So Is Marriage." Each of their letters tells readers that those who participate in cohabiting relationships are fulfilling their desires for freedom. The letters claim that pleasure, rejection of traditional marriage roles, and selfish desires for minimal responsibility sum up the true reasons for cohabitation over marriage. Oberst asserts that cohabitation is almost promised to cause unhappiness when the relationship ends more quickly than the couple assumed. However, he believes that cohabiters of today's generation are too self-focused to consider this message. In support of both Oberst and Bradley's positions, Jay Tolson, a journalist and the author of "No Wedding? No Ring? No Problem," suggests the reason for cohabitation is the appeal of a socially acceptable alternative to marriage which still allows for children and a higher level of sexual activity among unmarried couples. Such selfish actions prove to be untraditional, since children born out of wedlock and the act of premarital sex were less accepted in the past.

In my search to know how religion intersects with cohabitation, I found myself talking to and interviewing my mom, Denise Gavin. Her opinion was as strong and negative as I figured it would be when I first brought up the topic. Gavin is a happily married woman of the baby boomer generation who devotes much of her life to God. She reads and refers to the Bible for guidance in life decisions, and this is where she has learned to regard premarital sex as a sin. Premarital sex typically relates hand-in-hand with cohabitation; therefore, Gavin argues that both are wrong. She does not understand the position taken by Generation Me over the question of cohabitation. Instead she defends her own position by pointing out that if a child is born outside the legal bonds of marriage, either parent is able to walk away from this child with minimal legal consequences in the future. She has reinforced her Catholic beliefs to me throughout the years. As a result, I have come to think that my parents' relationship will forever outlast those who cohabited and then married.

Many Judeo-Christian religions disapprove of cohabitation and extramarital sex. In the article "Should Clergy Endorse 'Living in Sin'?" Gerald L. Zelizer, a rabbi, claims to speak for members of most religious clergy when he, like Gavin, predicts that premarital living may cause an unsteady marriage rate in years to come. However, Zelizer informs his readers that attitudes about cohabiting have changed throughout the different generations. He may not approve of premarital living, but he accepts it as a fact and encourages "those who choose cohabitation to restrict their relationship to someone they intend to marry" (13a). In this way Zelizer gives a small measure of acceptance or support for today's living arrangements, while still stressing the importance of eventually marrying the one you live with.

Not only is cohabitation much more common today than it has been in the past; but the same can be said about divorce. Papalia, Old, and Feldman, the authors of the *Human Development* textbook, inform readers that the United States divorce rate is "about 18 divorces per 1,000 married women ages 15 and older" (538); in other words, "1 out of 5 U.S. adults have been divorced" (538). I do not fully understand how these statistics can be associated with each other considering their numbers do not correlate to accurately represent our population. But still, the reasons for this pattern of increased divorce rates are endless, ranging from the increased liberality of divorce laws, "the decline in the perception of marriage as a sacred union," the fact that women are working and getting paid, and most importantly "free choice" (Papalia, Old, and Feldman 538). This free choice movement may be fueled by the scary divorce rates throughout America's population. For example, David Lipke, writing in *American Demographics*, claims that marriage is declining or at least being put off until a later age, and he believes that is partially due to today's increased divorce rates. He provides statistics to show that among today's young adult generation, "couples have a 40 percent to 50 percent chance of divorce" (14). He also offers readers the statistic of a one thousand percent increase in cohabitation rates from 1960 to 1998. These statistics are interesting; however, they conflict with the ones mentioned previously from the book titled *Human Development*. After rereading the statistics several times, I do not know what to make of any of these numbers. None of them agrees with the others. The only conclusion that I can draw from the numbers is that divorce rates are on the rise.

Divorce is not the only measure of marital instability. Tolson specifically explains in his article that unstable marriages and divorce rates tend to increase as a result of the widespread occurrences in cohabitation. In relation to Tolson's argument, Victoria Mueller, a freshman at the University of Iowa, explained to me in an interview that her parents had lived together before marriage for two and a half years, but after 27 months of marriage they ended their relationship in a divorce. After hearing my research on the possible connection between premarital living arrangements and divorce, Victoria feels that if her parents would have refrained from cohabiting, then maybe they would have stayed married or at least have been married for a longer period of time. She believes that if her parents would have remained together her family relationship would have more love, happiness, and cohesion; but instead, they have endured frustration and many struggles over the years.

According to research and my personal observation, cohabitation is on the rise, and the correlation between decreased religious values and increased divorce rates seems to point out the reasons why. However, the exact nature of the connection is unclear. Twenge's information on cohabitation sheds light on

Gavin 5

the importance of today's decline in church attendance and high divorce rates. Although I agree with Twenge and my other sources that cohabitation has increased over the years, I cannot, like Twenge, view cohabitation as a "normal" style of living or just another step in the relationship. I have a strong personal belief in the tenets of the Catholic religion and I plan to continue practicing this faith for the rest of my life. According to my religious authorities, premarital living is a cardinal sin, so I would never feel comfortable taking part. However, if I did, I know that I would have a conscience full of guilt that would never go away.

Also, since I have gone away to college, I have noticed more than ever what family means to me. Being hours away from home, I have regretted the fights I created with my parents in high school, the time I used selfishly for myself instead of spending it with my parents and siblings, and I have realized just how much I miss seeing them in person every day. My parents, whom I greatly look up to, would lose the pride they have for me if I were to ever cohabitate. Moreover, I do not think that I would ever feel complete happiness in my life if I did not have approval from my family, especially my parents.

Not only does the family that raised me matter, but also the family that is my future. I am already envisioning my wedding day, the relationship I hope to embrace with my husband, and the four cute children I plan to give birth to. Although I am just daydreaming of my future's details right now, I am positive that I want a functional family that will stay together as one unit as long as I live. I feel this way more than ever since coming to college. The stories I have heard from friends, in particular Mueller, are heartbreaking and lonely. What she shared with me makes me realize that I never want to go through a divorce or put my children through such an experience. My friends who have lived through their parents' divorce are normal people, who have told me sad stories and have gone through troubled times. Some have had to choose between Mom or Dad, mediate their parent's fights, or struggle with everyday life because money had suddenly become short after the divorce. Yes, every family has a different situation, and of course families with married parents can go through similar life problems; but still my goal is to never get a divorce. But my goal is to avoid these problems so that I won't ever want to divorce. Not cohabitating, my research on the connection between premarital living and increased divorce rates suggests, eliminates at least one possible path to divorce. It is not just the published research I have found that makes me trust this correlation, but also through my life experiences with authority figures and through hearing my friends' sad stories, I have learned that cohabitation does not guarantee (or promote) long-term or happy relationships.

In addition, I understand many cohabiters desire to express their freedom through premarital living. I, however, consider myself a traditional young Catholic woman, and I look forward to having a traditional wedding in the future. Thus, cohabitation just does not fit my values, nor does it go along with my visions for the future. All in all, I see and accept the increasing trend of cohabitation among my peers, but I cannot choose to cohabitate myself. I know that in my future, my lifestyle will not strengthen the statistics on premarital living.

Gavin 6

In this paper, my research opened my eyes to new and interesting points of view. I have always been brought up to follow one way of life, but through all my research, I have been challenged and tempted by different lifestyles. In the end, I still hope to grow up the way I have been taught and only live with my boyfriend once he becomes my husband. But I enjoyed learning about other options and how the majority of people today are choosing to live their lives. Because I do not approve of today's cohabitation trend, I hope that those who share similar values with me know that they are not alone. If young voices like mine are heard in the conversation of Generation Me'ers in the 21st century, we might be able to effect changes among our peers, leading to increased church attendance, spiritual growth, and a decline in divorce rates.

[NEW PAGE]

Gavin 7

Works Cited

Bradley, Melissa. Letter. "Stability of Marriage Is Needed to Foster Strong Families." *USA Today* 27 July 2005: 14A. Print.

Civitas. N.p., n.d. Web. 15 Apr. 2008.

Gavin, Denise. Personal interview. 6 Apr. 2007. Print.

Lipke, David J. "The State of Matrimony." *American Demographics* 22 (2000): 14–16. Print.

Mueller, Victoria. Personal interview. 7 Apr. 2007. Print.

Oberst, R. L. Letter. "Stability of Marriage Is Needed to Foster Strong Families." *USA Today* 27 July 2005: 14A. Print.

Papalia, Diane E., Sally Wendkos Olds, and Ruth Duskin Feldman. *Human Development*. 9th ed. New York: McGraw-Hill, 2004. Print.

Tolson, Jay. "No Wedding? No Ring? No Problem: An Ethical Essay Concerning Unmarried Cohabitation." *U.S. News & World Report* 13 Mar. 2000: 48. Print.

Twenge, Jean M. *Generation Me: Why Today's Young Americans Are More Confident, Assertive, Entitled—and More Miserable Than Ever*. New York: Free Press, 2006. Print.

Zelizer, Gerald L. "Should Clergy Endorse 'Living in Sin'?" *USA Today* 23 July 2003: 13A. Print.

Journal and Discussion Questions

1   What connections does Shannon Gavin see between the religious commitments of Generation Me (GenMe) and their sexual behavior? Do you agree with the connections Gavin makes? Why or why not?

2   What generalities about the present generation of young adults made by Jean M. Twenge in the book *Generation Me* bother Gavin? Why? How does she examine Twenge's conclusions?

3   What does Gavin conclude in her study of GenMe's ideas about marriage, sex, and religion? How does she arrive at these conclusions? Which conclusions does Gavin argue and support most persuasively? Why? Which conclusions seem weaker or less convincing to you? Why?

4   What sources and interview subjects does Gavin consult in "Cohabitation: Today's New Lifestyle—or Not" besides *Generation Me*? What do Gavin's sources and interview subjects contribute to her ideas about GenMe's beliefs about sex, marriage, and religion?

5   According to Gavin and her research, what does her parents' generation think about premarital sex and the cohabitation of unmarried couples? What do the baby boomers' religious beliefs have to do with these opinions? Why does Gavin discuss baby boomers' beliefs in a paper about GenMe?

6   Why does Gavin include details about her own life and religious and moral upbringing? Considering that some teachers discourage students from including personal experience in research papers, do you think Gavin should have included biographical information in her paper? Why or why not?

7   How, in the end, does Gavin compare herself to her generation and their religious, sexual, and marital beliefs? What does Gavin's study of the differences between her and the majority of her generation lead her to conclude about herself? What does she conclude about people who hold religious and moral positions opposed to hers?

Topics for Writing

1   Defend or challenge the morality of premarital sex and cohabitation, with references to Shannon Gavin's "Cohabitation: Today's New Lifestyle—or Not."

2   Considering Gavin's "Cohabitation," discuss how an individual's beliefs and moral behavior can be or should be influenced and complicated by the beliefs and actions of others. Keep in mind that Gavin discusses three groups of people in "Cohabitation": Generation Me, the Catholic Church, and her family.

3   Conduct further research about the beliefs and actions of the generation that you belong to, focusing on a specific set of issues, as Gavin has. Analyze and evaluate the generation's popular beliefs and behavior, using "Cohabitation" as a model.

Connecting the Readings

Compare and evaluate the two descriptions of the religious and moral beliefs of the present generation of college students in Thomas Bartlett's "Most Freshmen Say Religion Guides Them" and Shannon Gavin's "Cohabitation: Today's New Lifestyle—or Not." Your essay should discuss similarities in the two selections and try to account for differences between the two descriptions. Like Gavin, you may discuss differences between your impressions about the religious beliefs of college students today and the surveys discussed by Bartlett and Gavin.

A SIMPLE INVITATION

BY SONDRA PERL

Sondra Perl is a scholar in composition studies and the author of numerous books and articles about student writing and composition instruction. "A Simple Invitation" is the first chapter of her 2005 book *On Austrian Soil: Teaching Those I Was Taught to Hate*, a kind of spiritual autobiography, a genre that explores spiritual and ethical questions as it tells stories about the writer's life. In "A Simple Invitation," Perl describes and analyzes her experience teaching a class of English teachers in Austria that led her to confront her identity as a Jew, her attitudes and memories about the Holocaust, and her prejudices about the German and Austrian people. Much of her narration describes her doubts, reasons, and emotions as she makes moral decisions about what she should share with her class and invites readers to think through her moral dilemmas with her and evaluate her decisions.

WHEN THE PHONE RINGS ONE January morning in 1996, I have no inkling that the invitation I am about to accept will be the beginning of an odyssey. I hear only a voice at the other end of the line proposing a compelling piece of work.

Dr. Susan Weil, who coordinates a cross-cultural literacy program at The City College of The City University of New York, is inviting me to spend a few weeks in the summer teaching in Austria. There are eleven students, Susan tells me, two Americans and nine Austrians. All but one are practicing teachers of English. All are enrolled in a master's degree program in language and literacy at City College. But while the teachers receive their degrees from The City College of The City University of New York, they never actually attend classes in the States. The two- to three-week intensive courses are taught in Austria—in this case, Innsbruck—by City University faculty.

Quickly I take stock of my life. I am an English professor whose specialty is the teaching of writing. I've led teacher training institutes for over twenty years. Before I had children, I traveled every summer. But for the past twelve years, since the birth of my daughter, Sara, and twin sons, Josh and Sam, I've stayed close to home. The trip I make most frequently is to the pediatrician's office.

I'm tempted to accept. I have always dreamed of combining teaching with traveling. Working with teachers for whom English is a second language intrigues me. I am certain my husband will understand, and we have a babysitter we trust. I say yes on the spot.

It is only after I put down the phone that doubts begin to creep in. What have I done? It's not the teaching that troubles me; it's the place. For as much as I yearn to travel, Germany is the last place on Earth I want to go. Austria is a close second.

On June 28, I am sitting in the plane, imagining two and a half weeks without kids, dogs, phone calls, or car pools. Amazing—I have the next nine hours to myself, to read, review my plans for the course, or just sit there and not do a thing.

As I settle back in my seat, my attention is drawn to the large screen at the front of the cabin where every few minutes a map charting our progress appears. The major cities are labeled first in German, then in English.

Without warning, I hear the voice of my mother: *We're Jews. If we had been born there instead of here, we would have been herded into cattle cars and sent to the camps.*

Images of the Holocaust come unbidden: photographs of emaciated prisoners in striped pajamas, their agonies clearly visible in their hollow eyes and haggard faces; film clips of Hitler, right arm raised in the *Sieg Heil*; the worn pages of a novel I cherished, Meyer Levin's *Eva*, the story of a Jewish girl who tried to survive by "passing," living in Nazi-occupied Austria under an assumed name, pretending to be Christian. At thirteen, I was gripped by her courage and imagined myself in her place, spending hours in my bedroom practicing the sign of the cross, genuflecting, yearning to be safe—and Gentile, like the popular girls in my junior high school. A question that haunted me then: If I had been born there, would I have survived? A question that haunts me still.

Suddenly, my face feels hot; sweat breaks out on my forehead, gathers in my armpits. I am an adolescent awash in fear, assaulted by language and all it calls up in me. The Holocaust. The gas chambers. Auschwitz. Treblinka. Tears sting my eyes, slide down my cheeks. I don't want to be hated or hunted. I don't want to be counted among the dead or despised. I hate Hitler with all the fury a thirteen-year-old can muster. I hate the Germans. I hate the entire world for allowing this to happen. I want to scream, to stamp my feet in protest, to turn my back on all of it: atrocity, history, Judaism.

Taking long, slow breaths, I tell myself to calm down. Reaching for my bag, I find a tissue, wipe my eyes, and put on my sunglasses. I glance sideways, hoping no one has noticed. Why have I agreed to teach in Austria?

The answers come quickly: I've been hired to do a job I love. The Holocaust ended over fifty years ago. I'm an adult, not a thirteen-year-old. I miss traveling. Why should I refuse? After all, Austrian teachers shouldn't be different from other teachers.

But then, once again, I hear my mother's voice. *No matter what they say or do, no matter how stunning their accomplishments in art, music, and philosophy, within every German, every Austrian, lies a Nazi in disguise.*

On June 29, I arrive at the airport in Innsbruck and am greeted by Tanja Westfall, the coordinator of the Innsbruck courses and one of the two American participants in the course. A bubbly, vivacious woman in her late twenties, with thick, brown hair and a big smile, Tanja has invited me to stay with her in the tiny village of Hatting, a short train ride from the city and the University of Innsbruck, where the courses are to be held.

As I deplane, all I can do is stare, eyes wide open, mouth agape. The snowcapped mountains that rise so steeply seem to protect the order and calm of all that lies below: the churches with their steeples rising above the towns; the towns, almost toy-like in their precision, surrounded by fields in nuanced shades of green, sloping ever higher; on each slope, sturdy wooden houses in brown and ocher; on each house, window boxes overflowing with geraniums. I had no idea Innsbruck was so beautiful. Only later do I realize that for a moment I have forgotten this exquisite land once harbored unspeakable horrors.

After we collect my luggage, Tanja drives us to her flat. While she is making lunch, I unpack and settle in. Joining her in the kitchen, I glance out the window. I

notice her neighbor, an old man, working in the garden next door. He is wearing blue overalls and a cap, using a scythe to cut the grass. Raising both arms up above his head, he brings them down swiftly, neatly cutting through the dry yellow weeds; then piling them to one side, he takes a step and begins again. I imagine such a scene has repeated itself for centuries: peasants in the fields, cutting hay, storing it for winter as feed for the animals. A simple world, bucolic, peaceful, timeless.

Only later do I realize that for a moment I have forgotten this exquisite land once harbored unspeakable horrors.

But suddenly I wonder if he was a Nazi. Maybe he still is. What would he say if he knew a Jew was sleeping in the next house? And then, just as suddenly, I turn from the window.

On July 1, the first day of class, Tanja and I arrive early. The room is airy with large windows facing the Inn River. The mountains and their snow peaks rise in the distance. The tables and chairs are arranged in rows with a lectern at the front. I ask Tanja to help me move the furniture. This is not the way I want to begin. We push the lectern into a corner and rearrange the tables into one large square. Then we place twelve chairs around the perimeter. This will be a collaborative endeavor; we will be speaking to and with one another. I will lead the conversation, but I won't dominate it.

Soon the teachers, my students, arrive. We begin formally, with handshakes and introductions. Thomas, the other American student, has a round face, kind eyes, and an arresting dark beard. Hans, fair-haired and portly, is the only other man; his wife, Martina, trim and businesslike, is also in the course. Both appear to be in their forties. Andrea, with curly red hair and bright green eyes, is in her twenties. The youngest member of the group, she has brought some bread and cheese for our first day. The eldest, Hilde, a large, soft-spoken woman in her fifties, has brought bottles of apple juice and club soda to mix the popular *Apfelsaft gespritzt*.

Tanja introduces me to several women with blond hair: Margret, big-boned with a strong, purposeful handshake; Ursula, willowy and graceful, with a shy smile; and Christa whose face causes me to gasp inwardly. With hair the color of straw, clear blue eyes, a perfectly straight nose, and prominent cheekbones, Christa looks to me like a member of Hitler's master race, an Aryan beauty.

The last two to arrive are Astrid, an attractive woman whose long white hair is pulled back in a bun, and Ingrid, thin and birdlike, with sharp eyes behind wire-rimmed glasses. Astrid, in her late forties, has a daughter who plays cello with the Vienna Philharmonic; Ingrid, turning thirty, has two young children at home.

Margret and Andrea, I soon discover, have each already obtained one master's degree and teach in prestigious *Gymnasien*, Austrian high schools for college-bound students. Christa teaches at a private Catholic school for girls. Tanja and Hans both teach at the university. Thomas works in a language immersion program for adults. The others all work in the *Hauptschule* system, roughly equivalent to the vocational tracks in American schools.

I am to teach two graduate courses—one on the teaching of writing, the other on the teaching of literature. Rather than lecture, I invite my students to join me in a range of activities and then to reflect with me on what they are learning. When it comes to reading and writing, I know of no other approach that makes as much sense.

We begin that first night, simply enough, by writing about our experiences with writing. I write along with the group, then invite people to read aloud all or a part of what they have written. I respond to each person's draft by carefully rephrasing what I hear, focusing on the theme of each story. As we go around the room, we hear a range of increasingly sad tales.

Hans, brash and bold, vividly recounts the harsh criticism he received. "I stopped writing," he reveals, smiling ruefully, a shock of blond hair falling over his eyes, "I was so ashamed of my errors."

Margret recalls that at the university "writing was not about our ideas." Her chin juts out as she speaks with some anger: "Your writing had to be perfect, or you felt you were stupid."

Most of these teachers admit that they dislike writing, don't do it very often, and associate it with struggle and pain. The most common denominator: feeling judged and falling short.

"Isn't there another way?" Thomas implores, his dark eyes serious and brooding.

"There is," I promise. "There are ways to make writing come alive so that each person's voice counts. So that teaching is about much more than what students do wrong. We will explore this way of teaching together over the next few weeks. Tonight was just a start, but can you already begin to see what's different here?"

The teachers spontaneously rap their knuckles on the tabletop. I flinch. "Did I say something wrong?"

Hans quickly explains, smiling broadly, "That's our way of saying thanks. It was a great beginning."

On the drive home, Tanja tells me this is high praise.

At our second meeting on July 2, everyone is a bit more familiar. Smiles are wider, handshakes and hellos more heartfelt. Christa places a vase of homegrown flowers on the snack table. Andrea, chatty and effervescent, adds a platter of *Speck mit Brot*, explaining to me that thin slices of ham and hardy bread are an Austrian staple; Margret brings a bowl of strawberries. Hilde, once again, mixes *Apfelsaft gespritzt*.

I begin a discussion of one of the texts I had assigned, *A Letter to Teachers* by Vito Perrone, an educator who invites teachers to consider the meaning and purpose of their work. "What do we most want our students to come to understand as a result of their schooling?" Perrone asks.[1] He then articulates a clear and hopeful vision of what is possible in classrooms:

> If we saw the development of active inquirers as a major goal, much that now exists—workbooks and textbooks, predetermined curriculum, reductionism, teaching to tests—would, I believe, begin to fade. Teachers would be free to address the world, to make living in the world a larger part of the curriculum.[2]

It was statements like these that I expected to discuss with the Austrian teachers.

But they are struck by something else Perrone has written, something so obvious to me I have never before stopped to examine it: "Education at its best is first and foremost a moral and intellectual endeavor."[3]

Andrea, her green eyes clouded, is bewildered. "What does this mean?" she asks. "Do you honestly think education is connected to morality?"

I do, I think to myself. But I want to move slowly here. I want to understand why Andrea is asking this question and to discover if her bewilderment is shared by others.

"Do most of you have this question?" I ask, looking around the room, examining their faces. Several people nod.

I suggest that they break into small groups to talk about their responses. But as I move from group to group, I hear: "We all follow the same procedures"; "Teachers here are taught not to speak about what they believe"; "We can't deal with morality in the classroom."

"This is not our way," says Hans, with quiet certainty, crossing his arms on his chest and nodding his head.

"That's right," echoes his wife, Martina. "We have been trained to keep ourselves and our values outside of the curriculum. In the classroom, we must be morally neutral."

The other text I have assigned also challenges the views of these teachers. In *Literature as Exploration*, Louise Rosenblatt claims that teaching involves taking an ethical stance. She writes:

> The teaching of literature inevitably involves the . . . reinforcement of ethical attitudes. It is practically impossible to treat . . . any literary work . . . in a vital manner without confronting some problem of ethics and without speaking out of the context of some social philosophy. A framework of values is essential to any discussion of human life.[4]

Andrea finds the whole issue curious. She is perplexed by Rosenblatt's insistence that a teacher should not "try to pose as a completely objective person" and that "a much more wholesome educational situation is created when the teacher is a really live person" who, when appropriate, can state his or her "attitudes and assumptions . . . frankly and honestly."[5]

"How can one be a whole human being in the classroom?" she wonders aloud, her red curls framing her face. But most of the others seem not to share her curiosity.

I am taken aback that this group of Austrian teachers, at least those who have spoken so far, seem to find a focus on ethics troubling. But only a few have spoken. Most have remained silent.

What did you expect? You are working with the children or grandchildren of Nazis, says my mother's voice. *Have you told them you are Jewish? If they knew, would they still rap their knuckles with such enthusiasm?*

This is not an issue, I respond. *Almost everyone in the room looks younger than I, and I was born after the war. These teachers in front of me are not responsible for what happened.*

Well, their parents were alive then, she replies. *Your father was a staff sergeant in the U.S. Army. Their parents could easily be my age. What did their parents or even their grandparents do?*

But Mother, I answer, *I have not come here to accuse them. I have come to teach them.*

But then, I ask myself, isn't this precisely the issue? What am I teaching here? Do the moral questions that concern me have a place in this classroom?

At break time, as the teachers snack on cheese and chat in German, I stand back and observe. As a group they appear kind, caring, bright. They have come with the desire to understand new theories and progressive practices in the teaching of writing and literature. This much I can impart to them. And yet there is so much I already feel I can't impart,

can't say, can't admit, don't want to face, here or ever. Slowly, I let out a sigh.

On July 4, I am sitting in Tanja's garden at a wooden table under an apple tree. The homework assignment is to compose a piece of writing that matters; the topic and form are open. I have come outside to work on mine.

The sun feels warm on my back; flies buzz around my head. Annoyed, I swat them away. Once again, I am haunted by thoughts of the Holocaust, of what happened literally on the ground on which I am now walking, living, breathing. I picture the SS, marching through the streets of Innsbruck, hounding the Jews, pulling them from their homes, rounding them up and packing them off in cattle cars. I see blood staining the streets, the blood of those who were too slow or too old, those who tried to hide or dared to resist. I hear the screams of mothers as children are pulled from their arms, the burst of machine gunfire. Tears spring to my eyes as I write:

> What am I doing here
> in the homeland of Hitler's birth?
>
> Why have I come
> across an ocean
> to a land and a language
> I've never wanted to know?
>
> Never would I come here
> to the land where Nazis reigned,
> to the place where your people
> turned my people
> into objects of derision and hate.
>
> Like the numbers
> etched into their forearms
> images are seared in my brain
> of bodies, piled high
> in ditches, of hair
> and teeth, piled high
> in corners.
> I see the laboratories
> the wombs of young women
> filled with concrete
> the bodies of babies
> flung aside
>
> And the Mengele selection
> the preference for twins
>
> Oh
> my twins

> **" I cannot go on. I want to go home, to get out of this place, this country. Back to my own people. "**

This thought blots out all others. I am wordless. I cannot go on. I want to go home, to get out of this place, this country. Back to my own people. I'm startled at this. I'm not religious. For most of my life, I have been ambivalent about Judaism, more interested in blending into a Christian world than standing out as a Jew. And yet, here, the Jews have become my people.

On July 5, the fourth class meeting, there is turmoil in the classroom. The teachers are finding it excruciatingly difficult to write. No matter how many different methods I show them, when they have to sit down and face the blank page, they freeze.

Ingrid, one of the young teachers from the *Hauptschule* system, precise and pointed in both looks and style, challenges me openly with her frustration. "I just can't do this. Why should I even try? If I want to say something to someone, I can call them up and talk."

Hans, who teaches business courses at the university, concurs, tossing that unruly shock of blond hair out of his eyes. "What is the point of writing if the teacher does not give you a topic? I do not mean to be rude, but to me this activity is a waste of time."

I recognize this phenomenon. American teachers who have written only academic papers often resist invitations to write more creatively. But never before have I seen such deep distress in a group.

We are sitting around our classroom table. "Why do you think this is so hard?" I ask.

Ingrid responds promptly: "Our professors never asked us to be so creative. When we are asked to write in school, we expect to be given assignments with specific requirements."

I am aware that how I respond is crucial. Eleven teachers are watching me.

I say, "It sounds as if many of you are blocked." I can see their bodies relax. "In fact, it sounds to me as if you are describing a kind of paralysis."

I can almost hear the sighs of relief. I have adequately named their dilemma. But while I am speaking, I realize that I am also speaking about myself; they are mirroring my own paralysis.

"Look," I say. "I can answer the question, 'Why write?' But for now, I think it's important to let the question sit. Why don't we break into small groups and see what others have to say. You can either share the

work you have brought or talk about why writing was hard for you. You know," I add, "you can be fairly certain that if you are experiencing a problem here, at some point, your students may too."

I have placed myself in a group with three Austrian women: Margret, whose comments in class have impressed me; Christa, whose quiet presence intrigues me; and Martina, who other than supporting Hans, has been reserved. We move our chairs into a corner of the classroom. As they pass out copies of their work, Christa and Margret each comment that neither of them experienced any trouble finding a topic.

Christa agrees to read first. In a quiet voice, she reads aloud the story of her mother's struggle with cancer and her quiet death at home; by the time she finishes, we are there with her, standing around her mother's bed, praying for her release. We all have tears in our eyes.

Margret volunteers to read next. Her piece is not as straightforward, her voice less certain. It takes me a moment to realize that she is using a child's point of view to convey utter helplessness in the face of an abusive father.

Christa comments on the power of Margret's last line—"How can you cross the chasm if the bridge is not there?"

"I feel, what is the word . . . ?" Christa asks pausing, "stranded?"

"Yes," I say, jumping in. "That's exactly the word. I also feel how stranded and lost that child is."

Margret's face, closed until now, relaxes. I see the hint of a smile.

We turn to Martina who has remained remarkably quiet. "I have not been able to write a thing," she admits, the lines around her thin mouth tightening. "I've tried, really, but I am just so tired, and for me the school year is still not yet over. I still have meetings and paperwork to complete. It is not possible for me to do this right now . . ." Her voice trails off.

We listen sympathetically and suggest that she find some way to make her exhaustion the subject of her writing.

"Well, that could work," she says, smiling ruefully, "maybe . . ."

Now it is my turn. I inhale deeply, still not sure what to say. "I have been keeping a journal about my experiences in Austria," I begin, "but I doubt whether I can tell you what I am writing about."

They look at me with surprise. They have no idea, I think, and I have no idea what to say next.

I look at Christa's face, still tear-stained. Then I imagine the stranded child Margret just described. "It's a lot like Margret's chasm," I say. "I don't know if there is a bridge here."

They sit quietly, waiting for me to go on. I know I have to continue, to make some explanation. But what? We are just beginning to build some trust in the group. Will I shatter it if I mention the Holocaust? Do I dare? And yet, if I don't, how can I possibly explain what is happening to me?

I look at each one, and in a halting voice, I finally say, "O.K., I'll tell you what's going on. The more I walk on this land, the more my mind fills with images of the Holocaust. I see it everywhere I turn, every time I see an old person, every time I try to write. But how can I talk about this? I . . . well . . . I don't think I should. This is not why I am here."

Margret straightens her back and looks at me hard, her eyes narrowing. With undisguised vehemence, she exclaims, "How can you *not* talk about this? We never discuss our past, but we must! Of course, you should continue to write, and you must let us hear it."

"You are encouraging me?" I ask, startled.

She nods.

I am speechless. I can barely face what I am feeling. Each time it surfaces I want to push it away. Now this Austrian woman is urging me to make my fears public in a roomful of Austrians?

"I don't know," I respond hesitantly. "I'll try to keep writing. Maybe I'll be able to read some of my work to the three of you, but I'm not sure I can share this with the large group."

"You must try," urges Margret.

"You all agree?" I ask.

"Yes," says Christa.

"Yes," says Martina.

"There is nothing more important you can do here," adds Margret.

For the rest of the evening, I am in turmoil. I suspect it might be useful for the teachers to learn that I, too, am having a writing block. But I am petrified to raise the issue of the Holocaust with them, scared that they will reject me and my questions, even more scared to face these questions myself.

Several hours later, when the entire group reassembles to reflect together on the night's work, I have made up my mind to speak. It's a risk, I know. But how better to emerge from behind the mask of professor than to reveal what moves inside me? How

better to answer Andrea's question about how to be a whole human being in the classroom?

The twelve of us are seated around our large table. My heart pounds as I begin to talk: "Before we write reflections tonight, I want to say something about the paralysis that Ingrid and Hans mentioned earlier today. I, too, have been experiencing it. Every time I try to write, I silence myself."

Not a sound in the room. I have caught their attention.

"I came here to teach," I continue, "but I now realize I also came with questions about what happened here, in Austria, over fifty years ago. I don't expect you to explain the war to me. But I am curious about all of you. How do you cope with the knowledge of what happened here?"

It is so quiet I can hear the clock on the wall ticking.

"For the past few days, I have been plagued by questions about your history. I have felt I cannot ask them, that I cannot write about them, that it is not my place. But I also realize that I am not morally neutral and if I pretend I am—if I act as if these questions are not important to me—then I am contradicting myself, denying theories I have asked you to consider, subverting my own values."

I take a breath. I am greeted by blank stares. I assume that references to war and moral neutrality are sufficient to explain what I am referring to. I cannot bring myself to utter the words "Holocaust" or "Jew."

"You don't need to speak right now," I say. "But if you have a response, I'd like to hear it. I am mentioning this tonight because I want you to see that even a writing teacher can, at times, be blocked. And that one way out of this block is to begin to speak about it. So why don't we all write some reflections, now, on whatever comes to mind about tonight's work."

People pick up their pens. The concentrated quiet in the room tells me that everyone is writing.

I ask for volunteers to read. It is as if no one has heard a word I've said. Astrid, strands of white hair escaping from her bun, excitedly describes what is happening in her writing group. It is so valuable, she says, to see what her peers are writing. Ursula demurely expresses interest in changing topics. Hilde sees a new way to begin.

Margret reads last:

How can we not address Sondra's questions? How can we avoid talking about the fascism in our land, our country, our blood? How can we not teach our children who they are and be willing to take the beating of the world? We are the generation that must respond. Our parents can't and won't. We must own our dark side.

As Margret looks up, our eyes meet. This night as we leave, there is no knuckle-rapping. Only silence.

For July 6, the fifth session, we have an eight-hour class with time to work in both small and large groups. Following this session, we have a four-day break. It would be so much safer to move on, to act as if I hadn't raised anything unusual the night before. But my instincts tell me it would be wrong. I want to name what occurred, to mark it in some way. I also want to see if anyone is feeling unsettled by the personal turn of events I have initiated.

As we gather around the table to go over the day's schedule, I ask for everyone's attention: "I want to begin today by returning to some of the issues we raised last night. I want to take a few minutes to retrace the steps we took." There is no fidgeting, no looking out of the window.

I summarize the events—beginning with Ingrid's and Hans's questions about the purpose of writing and ending with my revelation about my own writer's block. Then I say, "I can't help thinking that we have an unusual opportunity here. We can act as if nothing momentous happened last night, or we can approach the questions I raised with care and respect and see what occurs. We have a chance, I think, to speak across cultures."

As I conclude my talk, people get up and begin the day's work. I do not know whether I

> **"Do they understand I am suggesting that Austria is not the only country where a violent, eliminationist racism took hold?"**

have reached them; do not know if they are aware that when I refer to "my questions" I am referring to the Holocaust, to their parents, to their own knowledge and responses. I am still speaking obliquely, wanting to open a dialogue, not shut it down. And I still cannot say the word "Jew" in front of them.

For the literature course, we have been meeting in reading groups, discussing our responses to Toni Morrison's *Sula*, a poignant and powerful novel. Almost everyone seems to be pleased with the experience of keeping a "reading log" or a "response journal." Ingrid comments that this approach encourages students to respond honestly. Hilde, whose vision of classrooms has not dimmed with increasing age, plans to use this approach with her weakest students. With these teachers, I have discovered, it is easy to talk about pedagogy.

But the conversation stalls when I move us into the larger implications of the novel. "It's hard to be

born in America," I say slowly, looking at the group, "without absorbing prejudice."

They look at me without commenting. I continue, "The question for many American teachers is what to do about racism. We often use Toni Morrison's work because it helps us address a range of racial issues. But many teachers I know well, particularly white teachers in urban classrooms, also wrestle with their own prejudices, knowing that the roots of racism are deep, that they may have to acknowledge and combat racism in themselves before they can really reach their students."

Do they see the connection? I wonder. Do they understand I am suggesting that Austria is not the only country where a violent, eliminationist racism took hold? I don't know. The teachers nod, smile, even take notes, but they do not respond.

The pace picks up again several hours later when writing groups meet. Now it is obvious that everyone is actively engaged. The talk is lively, even boisterous. One writing group does not return for a scheduled activity. They report later, shocked by their own behavior, that they were so involved with one another's work, they just couldn't stop. I am delighted by their disobedience.

Sitting at our small table, Martina, Margret, and Christa encourage me to read the poem I have been working on. I consent, but I lower my eyes as I recite the lines about Nazis, about "your people" and "my people." My voice quivers as I read.

When I finish, I look up. I see tears in their eyes. "Thank you," says Margret quietly.

One hurdle overcome, I think to myself. I've admitted that I am Jewish. They could not know how hard this was for me. But I notice that I also feel relieved. For now I assume the group will understand why I am asking about the past. After today, I assume, the classroom grapevine will transmit the news: Sondra is a Jew.

Several hours later, I am sitting on a stool in a local bar with Tanja, Thomas, Andrea, Martina, and Hans. Drinking beer, enveloped in cigarette smoke, we tell stories of family life. Andrea, a mother of three, asks me about child rearing in New York. "Can you leave your baby in the car while you run into a shop?" she asks, alluding to a common practice in Innsbruck.

"Are you kidding?" I exclaim. I describe my fear of having my kids out of my sight for even a minute when we are in a supermarket or at a playground. "New York is a wonderful, exciting place," I continue, "but as a parent, it is hard not to worry or to imagine threats even when there aren't any."

Then she asks, "Is it safe to visit Chinatown and Harlem and the Jewish quarter?"

I can only smile. "Being aware of personal safety is important in every neighborhood," I respond first. "Chinatown is relatively safe; so is Harlem these days. But in New York, Andrea, there is no Jewish quarter. In New York, being Jewish is so common, it's like, well . . ." I burst out laughing, recalling a quip a British colleague once made, "it's as if everyone is Jewish."

I doubt that the group has any notion of what I am referring to, but everyone joins in laughing. Suddenly, I notice, I feel a greater sense of ease among them. Not bad, I think, making a Jewish joke at the half-way mark.

NOTES
[1]Perrone, Vito. *A Letter to Teachers: Reflections on Schooling and the Art of Teaching.* San Francisco: Jossey-Bass, 1991, 4.
[2]*Ibid.,* 9.
[3]*Ibid.,* 1.
[4]Rosenblatt, Louise. *Literature as Exploration.* New York: Modern Language Association, 1938/1995, 16.
[5]*Ibid.,* 124.

Journal and Discussion Questions

1 "A Simple Invitation" is organized chronologically around a series of decisions that Sondra Perl makes in the course of teaching a class for Austrian students, beginning with her decision to accept an invitation to travel to Austria to teach. Outline this essay, highlighting the decisions Perl makes. What reasons does she give for each decision? What doubts does she express about what she should do?

2 How do Perl's and her students' writings help her make her decisions?

3 What impressions do you have of each student in Perl's class? What does Perl do to create individual impressions of each student and to make each student a distinct character in her story? Does your impression of some of the students develop or change as the essay continues? How?

4 Although "A Simple Invitation" is a personal essay, Perl cites and quotes several books and supplies endnotes when quoting from a book. What is the function of these citations and quotations in the midst of an essay about a personal experience? What do the quotations add to the story and the moral questioning in the essay?

5 An important quotation in Perl's essay is "Education at its best is first and foremost a moral and intellectual endeavor," from Vito Perrone's *A Letter to Teachers.* Perl believes this statement, but most of her students at first disagree. What arguments about this issue, pro and con, are raised in "A Simple Invitation?" How does Perl's belief in the moral nature of education affect what she says and does not say to her class? Do you agree with her decisions? Why or why not?

6 Why does Perl mention that she was not very religious and was more concerned about fitting into a predominantly Christian society than about Jewish beliefs? If this is true, why can she joke that in New York "it's as if everyone is Jewish"?

7 Later in the essay, Perl discusses Louise Rosenblatt's insistence "that 'a much more wholesome educational situation is created when the teacher is a really live person' who, when appropriate, can state his or her 'attitudes and assumptions [. . .] frankly and honestly'." How does Rosenblatt decide when and how it is appropriate for her to tell students that she is Jewish and struggling with her feelings about Austria's part in the Holocaust? Do you think her admission makes for a "much more wholesome educational situation" in the class?

Topics for Writing

1 Argue whether or not teachers should disclose their moral beliefs and positions to their students.

2 Perl compares Americans' problems coming to terms with racism to Austrians' difficulties in confronting their Nazi past. Write an essay discussing that comparison.

SIN AND GUILT

BY W. ROSS WINTEROWD

W. Ross Winterowd is Bruce McElderry Professor of English Emeritus at the University of Southern California, founder of one of the nation's first graduate programs in rhetoric at USC, and author of many books and articles on rhetoric and the teaching of writing. "Sin and Guilt" is a chapter from his 2004 book *Searching for Faith: A Skeptic's Journey*, a spiritual autobiography in which Winterowd reflects on his own acts of evil, the writings of several important philosophers, and accounts of Nazis and serial killers in an attempt to understand the problem of everyday evil, sin, and guilt in his life and the lives of others. Although he has read widely in philosophy and theology as part of his exploration of his own faith, Winterowd does not write as an expert in philosophy or religious studies. And though the strong Mormon faith of his wife and her family encouraged him to examine matters of faith and morality, he conducts his spiritual exploration as a "skeptic" rather than as a member of a particular church. "Sin and Guilt," in fact, is both a personal and an exploratory essay because the writer is trying to figure out the answers to his problem instead of trying to persuade readers to believe a thesis. Winterowd considers a number of possible answers to his question and forms his own answer gradually and perhaps only partially as the essay develops.

. . . what in me is dark
Illumine, what is low raise and support;
That, to the height of this great argument,
I may assert Eternal Providence,
And justify the ways of God to men.

—Milton, *Paradise Lost*

Know then thyself, presume not God to scan;
The proper study of Mankind is Man.

—Pope, *Essay on Man*

HE WAS THE MOST INEPT OF students—a young man who was completely out of place in a freshman English class in a large state university. In a paper about wolverines, he wrote, "The wolverian is a corss bitwin a beer and a snuck," which, translated, means, "The wolverine is a cross between a bear and a skunk," the intention of which was to say that the wolverine *looks like* a cross between a bear and a skunk. At the very beginning of my career, this unfortunate young man was my student, I a teaching assistant working on a doctorate. For the faculty in the English department, both graduate teaching assistants and regular professors, this sentence became the sign and evidence of the decline

of literacy in the population and of the decline of standards in the university. Though mercifully he was unaware of it, the student became an object of guffaws and scorn, a symbol of the stupidity and cultural barbarism of the unanointed.

In my relationships with this student, I was never bluntly brutal, but he must have sensed my scorn, and I made no attempt to help him survive the trauma of being on an alien planet surrounded by robotic creatures of whom he would ultimately be the victim. I was in my red-pencil phase, splattering my students' papers with the scarlet letters (Frag, CF, Par, Sp) branding the students' illiteracy. I have no exact memory of what I said about "A wolverian is a corss bitwin a beer and a snuck," but I'm certain the comment was biting and witty. I'm equally certain that my comment and my whole attitude toward this student must either have devastated him or have contributed to his growing anger and frustration.

It was years until this episode in my long career brought the onus of guilt and remorse to me. Far too late, I have come deeply to regret what I did to this student. Far too late, I have come deeply to regret the evils that I caused those who associated with me and those I loved.

Not that I am an extraordinarily sinful person. I represent the everyday, ordinary sinner. In the sum total of things—in a universe that contained the Holocaust—

my sins are small potatoes, but my view is not universal, my focus being sharply on my own past, both remote and recent. Many of the acts that tradition would call sinful bother me not in the least: lechery here and mendacity there, periods of sloth, episodes of gluttony, and perpetual green-eyed envy soured into personal enmity expressed by semi-conscious mutterings. I use myself for a case study in the nature of quotidian sinfulness.

The wages of sin is guilt. My sense of guilt causes me to suffer, but this spiritual discomfort, becoming, at times, almost an agony, is, paradoxically, a blessing, allowing me to sense a cleansing of my soul, giving me penance for my sins.

I ask myself, "Am I entitled to such a facile easing of my conscience?" Of late, I am much given to requiems, those of Brahms, Fauré, Mozart, and Verdi and to the eerie insistence of Philip Glass and the mysticism of Hovhaness. As I listen, I mull over the injustices I have done my wife, the traumas I have caused students, my intolerance of my disturbed and disturbing mother. But the catalogue of my sins is really beside the point. What interests me is the relationship between the evil I have done and my sense of guilt for that evil. What interests me is what I take to be the universal phenomenon of evil and guilt.

An acquaintance told me the other day that at the end of the services each Sunday, the priest implores the congregants to pray for forgiveness of their sins. "But," says my Christian friend blandly, "I can't think of anything to ask forgiveness for." Which of us is pathological, my sinless friend or guilt-ridden I? What credit can I take for the esthetically satisfying expiation of my own guilt? What I do know is that I have deep regrets. Perhaps that is enough to humanize me.

The greatest problem of theology must be to develop the perfect theodicy—in other words to reconcile God's benevolence and omnipotence with the problem of evil.

1. Evil exists.

2. God is benevolent.

3. God is omnipotent.

To eliminate the first premise is to deny that evil exists. To eliminate the second premise is to deny God's benevolence. To eliminate the third premise is to deny God's omnipotence.

The easiest solution to the problem is that of Leibniz, who argued that ultimately a transcendent "calculus" would enable us to understand God's universe and the reason for evil in it, for this is, after all, the best of all possible worlds; though we humans are benighted, ultimately the light will dawn.

At the other extreme, in the darkness where I find myself, is Nietzsche, who tells us that the reality which Is

and the Ought which is the ideal cannot be reconciled. One always condemns the other. But perversely, in the attempt to reconcile Is and Ought, we invent God and torture ourselves with the chimera of what-might-be: if only we had the prescience, all of life's tragedy would make sense, as if anyone could translate the meaninglessness of life into a meaningful narrative or a coherent statement.

In the prelapsarian world, there were no earthquakes, tornadoes, plagues, or erupting volcanoes; these evils, traditional theology tells us, resulted from Adam's fault and fall. Until the Enlightenment, the clergy and laity took natural disasters to be evils inflicted on humankind by an omnipotent deity. As John Donne said, "Moving of the earth brings harms and fears. Men reckon what it did and meant." With Rousseau, according to Susan Neiman, the idea that natural disasters were God's punishment for sinfulness was supplanted by a "modern" vision of nature's forces at work having nothing to do with human sinfulness. "Natural disaster" replaced "Natural Evil."

I, however, adapt the concept of Natural Evil for my own purposes. There are the monsters who by *nature* commit evil acts. I knew such a person, a hydrocephalic, mentally defective child who bashed puppies to death and who attempted to smother his baby sister. This child, of course, was incapable of feeling guilt and hence was not guilty. If a person is *naturally* incapable of *feeling* guilt, can he or she sin? Is a mass murderer such as William Bonin or Jeffrey Dahmer a sinner if that person has no sense of guilt—that is, in common parlance, has no conscience? Of course, both Bonin and Dahmer were unquestionably guilty in the legal sense as defined by the McNaghten rule: both knew the "nature and quality" of their actions and that what they did was wrong (according to law and community standards). Bonin, "the Freeway Killer," had murdered and sexually mutilated twenty-one boys and men, yet he expressed no remorse and uncannily seemed detached from his own fate as he awaited execution by lethal injection. The *Los Angeles Times* of February 24, 1966, describes his last hours thus:

> Bonin, who spent his final hours watching the television show "Jeopardy," eating pizza and ice cream and chatting with a Catholic prison chaplain, was moved from his death-watch cell just before midnight. He did not struggle, walking himself to the table where he would die. Technicians had trouble finding a good vein, and accidentally punctured a usable vein in his left arm and had to start over, said prison spokesman Vernell Crittendon.

From all indications, there was a void in Bonin's personality, a blank spot in his mind and soul, a miswiring in his brain, a genetic defect—something uncanny and beyond the realm in which "conscience" is operative, in which the sense of guilt is activated. Bonin apparently could not feel sorry even for himself.

As *reasonable* men, Bonin and Dahmer knew what they did was wrong, but as *natural* men, they were clearly members of that class termed "psychopath" by some and "sociopath" by others, deviance that Robert D. Hare characterizes in *Without Conscience*. They were glib and superficial, egocentric and grandiose; they lacked remorse or a sense of guilt and empathy; they were deceitful and manipulative and shallow emotionally. They were impulsive, could not control their behavior, needed excitement, lacked responsibility, had behavior problems early in life, and were antisocial (Hare 34).

Neiman (90–91) cites an anecdote from Kant's *Critique of Practical Reason* that is salient here. A man must enter and patronize whenever he passes a brothel. His desire seems uncontrollable. But if this sex fiend were to be shown a gallows on which he would be hanged immediately after he had satisfied his desire, he would, according to Kant, be quite able to resist his urges. To Kant's argument, one codicil must be added: *if the patron of whores were naturally evil, the gallows would be no deterrent*. Or we can go to de Sade's *argumentum ad absurdum*. Since all crimes are natural, there can be no such thing as a crime against nature. In *Dialogue between a Priest and a Dying Man*, the priest asks the dying man to repent. But, says the dying man, I have repented according to my own interpretation of what repentance means.

> By Nature created, created with very keen tastes, with very strong passions; placed on this earth for the sole purpose of yielding to them and satisfying them, and these effects of my creation being naught but necessities directly relating to Nature's fundamental designs, or, if you prefer, naught but essential derivatives proceeding from her intentions in my regard, all in accordance with her laws, I repent not having acknowledged her omnipotence as fully as I might have done, I am only sorry for the modest use I made of the faculties (criminal in your view, perfectly ordinary in mine) she gave me to serve her; I did sometimes resist her, I repent it. (165–66)

It greatly interests me that in my own acts I have had much in common with Bonin and the hydrocephalic idiot. On occasion, evil has been as natural to me as breathing. In my deplorable reaction to the student who wrote about "wolverians," and in my relationship with him, I was simply doing what came naturally in my role as an acolyte intellectual, human-

ist, and scholar. My goal in life was to join that rarefied priesthood of those who professed literature and thus, presumably, dispensed sweetness and light, but whose culture valued cleverness and cynicism. In my actions, I was doing what comes naturally in a corrupt culture.

However, there is more to the story than that. In my actions and in my values, I was not atypical of the witty, cynical aspiring neophyte scholars and well ensconced professors surrounding me. Yet now I realize that there was something more: a kind of sociopathic lack of empathy that kept me from identifying with the agonies of others, that insulated me from emotional reactions to tragedies large and small. At the time, my wife, my dear wife, was suffering hellishly with clinical depression, and this in the age before Prozak, Zoloft, and Celexa. All this courageous woman could hope for was alleviation of her misery through "the talking cure" and the *empathetic* sympathy of a loving family. As I look back, I realize that Norma's suffering fazed me very little, engaged as I was in defense of my own ego and in the struggle to become a member of the intellectual elite who dispense sweetness and light in the academy. I was too shallow emotionally to identify with and understand either my wife or my student. I was, I think, incapable of love.

> **" On occasion, evil has been as natural to me as breathing. "**

The blessing that maturity and old age have conferred on me is the ability to be empathetic, to identify, and to love. And to regret my past.

I suppose there is a touch of natural evil in all of us, but my concern is not with the Bonins or the Dahmers. I am interested in what I might call "everyday evil," perpetrated by you and me and everyone else—except Christ and, apparently, my church-going, Christian friend.

What I call "routine evil" comes about from those who are simply doing their jobs within institutions. A good example is Albert Speer, who was the epitome of routine evil, Hitler having promoted him from official architect of the Third Reich to armaments minister in charge of providing materiel for war. Speer functioned with admirable skill; he was the ideal administrator, perfectly satisfied as long as he was doing his job—and I think that "job," not "duty," is the right term here, for Speer was singularly without convictions. In fact, Speer shielded himself from direct knowledge of or involvement in the Final Solution. On one occasion Nazi party functionary Karl Hanke mentioned a camp in Upper Silesia, which must have been Auschwitz. In his book *The Third Reich*, Speer said, "I did not want to know what was happening there [. . .] for fear of discovering something that would make me turn from my course" (qtd. in Fest 189).

The perfect example of a routinely evil person is Adolf Eichmann, the subject of Hannah Arendt's classic study.

He was a creature of the quotidian, an everyday family man, and in terms of the Third Reich, he was perfectly normal, a law-abiding citizen. In a study that, because of the horrors it documents, is difficult to read, Daniel Jonah Goldhagen portrays such Third Reich monsters as Karl Wagner of the SS unit in charge of a "work camp" at Majdanek, who forced female prisoners to undress before he beat them to death with a whip (Goldhagen 307). Even as you and I, Wagner would have disgusted Eichmann. When forced directly to observe a mass killing, Eichmann was nauseated and horrified. "I hardly looked; I could not; I could not; I had had enough" (qtd. in Arendt 87). He was a man of conscience, who, he said, lived by the ethic of Kant's categorical imperative, "Act only according to that maxim by which you can at the same time will that it should become a universal law," which, in the Third Reich, had, as Arendt (136) points out, been transformed into "Act in such a way that the Führer, if he knew your action, would approve it." And Eichmann could find no one who disapproved of the Final Solution (Arendt 116). Why should he hold himself accountable for acts that were universally approved? It is a stunning irony that Eichmann considered himself a Pontius Pilate. Reflecting back on the Wannsee Conference, when the Nazi hierarchy actually began to map out the Final Solution, Eichmann said, "At that moment, I sensed a kind of Pontius Pilate feeling, for I felt free of all guilt." What had he to feel guilty about when "the most important people had spoken, the Popes of the Third Reich"? (qtd. in Arendt 114). The Pharisees had ordered the mass crucifixion, enabling Eichmann, like Pilate, to wash his hands of the whole affair and let matters take their course.

So this everyday man of conscience went about his duties methodically and assiduously. He kept track of the capacities at the various camps and arranged transport to the camps from the sites where Jews had been assembled by the SS and other units of the Nazi terror. Eichmann was routinely—and *greatly*—evil.

In what sense was the evil I perpetrated in the case of the "Wolverian" student simply routine? Was I an Albert Speer, merely doing my job? The complete answers to these questions would take us on a multi-page aside, the gist of which can be stated thus: during the first years of my career, the academy made no provision for students who needed special help or who should have been counseled out of higher education and into more suitable paths toward their futures. The practice, if not the stated philosophy, was Darwinian, survival of the fittest, and the fittest were, by and large, the economically and socially privileged. Like Speer, I was doing my job in a corrupt system. My evil was routine.

Beyond routine, there is an evil that I call "diabolical." The diabolically evil person creates the situation or system in which routine evil can flourish.

The prime example of *diabolical* evil is Hitler, yet somehow Himmler is more sinister. Hitler's diabolism was eerily disinterested. There are no records of Hitler's having visited the death camps to watch the agonies of the dying; one envisions him above it all, in his alpine Eagle's Nest, boring guests with his interminable monologues and then bursting into one of his rants against the Jew conspiracy to humble the Vaterland. As Ian Kershaw convincingly argues in his massive biography of Hitler, der Führer ranted out his ideology, but remained aloof from its implementation. As Kershaw says, Hitler was "at one and the same time the absolutely indispensable fulcrum of the entire regime, and yet largely detached from any formal machinery of government" (*Hitler: 1889–1936 Hubris* 532). In following Hitler's will, not his direct orders, Nazi functionaries set up the machinery of the Holocaust. Hitler was Milton's Satan.

On the other hand, Himmler was a sadist, delighting in Schadenfreude. He was not the disinterested, dispassionate bureaucrat carrying out the orders of his Fuehrer. On the contrary, he was the architect of the Final Solution, and he morbidly viewed the horrors of the death camps..

Visiting Minsk in 1941, Himmler told the commander of the Einsatzgruppe, Arthur Nebe, that he wanted to view an execution. Nebe rounded up two hundred or so alleged partisans and marched them outside the city to the area of a deep trench. Group after group, the victims were ordered to lie face down in the trench, and the policemen under Nebe's command shot them. After one group had been executed, the bodies were covered with a shallow layer of earth, and another group, forced to lie atop the bodies of their fellow victims, were shot.

Quite understandably, the executioners became more and more disquieted, but Himmler assured them that they were simply doing their duty and that the responsibility was his, not theirs (Breitman 195–96).

Himmler took more than an administrative and bureaucratic interest in the extermination camps. In 1941, he visited the deadly Mauthausen camp and viewed abuse of prisoners so brutal that many committed suicide (Breitman 161).

The aloof, disinterested diabolism of Hitler. The sadistic diabolism of Himmler. The diabolical Winterowd?

Insofar as I was architect of the class (a sub-system of a sub-system) in which the *naturally* and *routinely* evil act of my relationship with the Wolverian student was the norm and not a one-time anomaly, then I was diabolically evil, for I created and perpetuated the system whereby a group of beings suffered. (In my own defense, I must say that throughout my career, I have had largely favorable evaluations by my students, and even the least favorable did not compare my classes to Auschwitz or me to Commandant Höss.)

On the basis of my argument, I make what is perhaps a grandiose claim. I believe that my rubric of evil—natural, routine, and diabolical—enables one to gain insight into evils committed against one, around one, and by one.

But my rubric is incomplete, for I do not include *sins of the body*. As long as a pure soul is trapped in a corrupt body, sin and hence guilt are inevitable. After he found faith, the dilemma of a sinful body clothing a pure soul troubled Augustine constantly and deeply.

BIBLIOGRAPHY. Arendt, Hannah. *Eichmann in Jerusalem: A Report on the Banality of Evil*. New York: Penguin, 1994.

Breitman, Richard. *The Architect of Genocide: Himmler and the Final Solution*. London: Bodley Head, 1991.

Fest, Joachim. *Speer: The Final Verdict*. Trans. Ewald Osers and Alexandra Dring. New York: Harcourt, 2001.

Goldhagen, Daniel Jonah. *Hitler's Willing Executioners*. New York: Vintage, 1997.

Hare, Robert D. *Without Conscience: The Disturbing World of the Psychopaths Among Us*. New York: Guilford, 1993.

Kershaw, Ian. *Hitler: 1889–1936 Hubris*. New York: Norton, 1998.

Neiman, Susan. *Evil in Modern Thought: An Alternative History of Philosophy*. Princeton: Princeton UP, 2002.

Nietzsche, Friedrich. *Beyond Good and Evil. Basic Writings of Nietzsche*. Trans. Walter Kaufmann. New York: Modern Library, 1992, 179–435.

Sade, Marquis de. "Dialogue Between a Priest and a Dying Man." *The Marquis de Sade: The Complete Justine, Philosophy in the Bedroom, and Other Writings*. Trans. Richard Seaver and Austin Wainhouse. New York: Grove, 1965. 163–75.

Journal and Discussion Questions

1 Why did W. Ross Winterowd begin "Sin and Guilt" with the story of "the Wolverian student"? What was evil about his treatment of "the Wolverian student"? How and why did Winterowd compare how he acted and felt to the evils committed by the Nazis? Do you agree with his comparison?

2 Outline "Sin and Guilt." How does Winterowd make the transition from a discussion of the wrongs he has done to a discussion of "the greatest problem of theology," "to reconcile God's benevolence and omnipotence with the problem of evil"?

3 How does Winterowd interpret "the problem of evil"? What solutions to this problem have philosophers like Liebniz and Nietzsche offered?

4 What kinds of sources, in addition to the writings of philosophers, does Winterowd use? How does he use these sources to figure out his own answer to his question rather than just repeat a source's ideas and agree with them? How can you tell when Winterowd agrees with a source, when he disagrees, and when he is holding off from forming an opinion?

5 What kinds of evil does Winterowd identify? How does he define each type of evil? How do his classifications help him understand and answer the nature of everyday evil? Compare his definitions of evil to your own definitions.

6 Compare the feelings of guilt and conscience felt by serial killers, by Winterowd about actions with his student, and by Nazis Albert Speer, Adolf Eichmann, Hitler, and Himmler. How is the nature of the evil of one's actions connected to the guilt one feels? Which kind of evil is worse in Winterowd's thinking and why?

7 Winterowd uses the terms and methods of formal logic (*premise, calculus*) to explain the problem of evil. How does formal logic work to clarify this problem? Why doesn't Winterowd use formal logic in other parts of the essay?

Topics for Writing

1 Take an incident like Winterowd's treatment of "the Wolverian student," an incident of everyday evil that you have experienced or observed, and analyze it using Winterowd's categories of evil.

2 Describe a problem that you consider evil but that seems to be considered "routine" by the people responsible for the problem. Try to persuade these people that the problem is wrong and serious and that they are at least partly responsible for solving the problem.

SACRAMENTS

BY ANDRE DUBUS

Andre Dubus (1936–1999) was a short story writer, essayist, and college teacher at Bradford College, the University of Alabama, and Boston University, with two collections of essays, *Broken Vessels* and *Meditations from a Movable Chair*, and several collections of short stories. Many of his essays discuss his life as a paraplegic after he had one leg amputated and lost the use of the other after being hit by a car while trying to help two stranded motorists in 1986. A practicing Roman Catholic and a former Marine, Dubus frequently discusses moral and spiritual matters in essays like "Sacraments." "Sacraments" was first published in *Portland Magazine* and later included in *Meditations from a Movable Chair* (1999). In this personal essay, Dubus uses several of his life experiences to define his idea of *sacrament*, a definition that builds on but goes well beyond the concept of sacrament that he learned in the Catholic Church.

A SACRAMENT IS PHYSICAL, AND WITHIN it is God's love; as a sandwich is physical, and nutritious and pleasurable, and within it is love, if someone makes it for you and gives it to you with love; even harried or tired or impatient love, but with love's direction and concern, love's again and again wavering and distorted focus on goodness; then God's love too is in the sandwich. A sacrament is an outward sign of God's love, they taught me when I was a boy, and in the Catholic church there are seven. But, no, I say, for the church is catholic, the world is catholic, and there are seven times seventy sacraments, to infinity. Today I sit at my desk in June in Massachusetts; a breeze from the southeast comes through the window behind me, touches me, and goes through the open glass door in front of me. The sky is blue, and cumulus clouds are motionless above green trees lit brightly by the sun shining in dry air. In humid air, the leaves would be darker, but now they are bright, and you can see lighted space between them, so that each leaf is distinct; and each leaf is receiving sacraments of light and air and water and earth. So am I, in the breeze on my skin, the air I breathe, the sky and earth and trees I look at.

Sacraments are myriad. It is good to be baptized, to confess and be reconciled, to receive Communion, to be confirmed, to be ordained a priest, to marry, or to be anointed with the sacrament of healing. But it is limiting to believe that sacraments occur only in churches, or when someone comes to us in a hospital or at home and anoints our brows and eyes and ears, our noses and lips, hearts and hands and feet. I try to receive Communion daily, and I never go to Mass day after day after day, because I cannot sleep when I want to, I take pills, and if the pills allow me to sleep before midnight, I usually can wake up at seven-thirty and do what I must to get to Mass. But I know that when I do not go to Mass, I am still receiving Communion, because I desire it; and because God is in me, as He is in the light, the earth, the leaf. I only have to lie on my bed, waking after Mass has already ended, and I am receiving sacraments with each breath, as I did while I slept; with each movement of my body as I exercise my lower abdomen to ease the pain in my back caused by sitting for fifteen hours: in my wheelchair, my car, and on my couch, before going to bed for the night; receiving sacraments as I perform crunches and leg lifts, then dress and make the bed while sitting on it. Being at Mass and receiving Communion give me joy and strength. Receiving Communion of desire on my bed does not, for I cannot feel joy with my brain alone. I need sacraments I can receive through my senses. I need God manifested as Christ, who ate and drank and shat and suffered, and laughed. So I can dance with Him as the leaf dances in the breeze under the sun.

Not remembering that we are always receiving sacraments is an isolation the leaves do not have to endure: they receive and give, and they are green. Not remembering this is an isolation only the human soul has to endure. But the isolation of a human soul may be the cause of not remembering this. Between isolation and harmony, there is not always a vast distance. Sometimes it is a distance that can be traversed in a moment, by choosing to focus on the essence of what is occurring, rather than on its exterior: its difficulty or beauty, its demands or joy, peace or grief, passion or humor. This is not a matter of courage or discipline or will; it is a receptive condition.

" I need sacraments I can receive through my senses. "

Because I am divorced, on Tuesdays I drive to my daughters' school, where they are in the seventh and second grades. I have them with me on other days, and some nights, but Tuesday is the school day. They do not like the food at their school, and the school does not allow them to bring food, so after classes they are hungry, and I bring them sandwiches, potato chips, Cokes, Reese's peanut butter cups. My kitchen is very small; if one person is standing in it, I cannot make a three-hundred-and-sixty-degree turn. When I roll into the kitchen to make the girls' sandwiches, if I remember to stop at the first set of drawers on my right, just inside the door, and get plastic bags and write *Cadence* on one and *Madeleine* on the other, then stop at the second set of drawers and get three knives for spreading mayonnaise and mustard and cutting the sandwiches in half, then turn sharply left and reach over the sink for the cutting board leaning upright behind the faucet, then put all these things on the counter to my right, beside the refrigerator, and bend forward and reach into the refrigerator for the meat and cheese and mustard and mayonnaise, and reach up into the freezer for bread, I can do all of this with one turn of the chair. This is a First World problem; I ought to be only grateful. Sometimes I remember this, and then I believe that most biped fathers in the world would exchange their legs for my wheelchair and house and food, medical insurance and my daughters' school.

Making sandwiches while sitting in a wheelchair is not physically difficult. But it can be a spiritual trial; the chair always makes me remember my legs, and how I lived with them. I am beginning my ninth year as a cripple, and have learned to try to move slowly, with concentration, with precision, with peace. Forgetting plastic bags in the first set of drawers and having to turn the chair around to get them is nothing. The memory of having legs that held me upright at this counter and the image of simply turning from the counter and stepping to the drawer are the demons I must keep at bay, or I will rage and grieve because of space, and time, and this wheeled thing that has replaced my legs. So I must try to know the spiritual essence of what I am doing.

On Tuesdays when I make lunches for my girls, I focus on this: the sandwiches are sacraments. Not the miracle of transubstantiation, but certainly parallel with it, moving in the same direction. If I could give my children my body to eat, again and again without losing it, my body like the loaves and fishes going end-lessly into mouths and stomachs, I would do it. And each motion is a sacrament, this holding of plastic bags, of knives, of bread, of cutting board, this pushing of the chair, this spreading of mustard on bread, this trimming of liverwurst, of ham. All sacraments, as putting the lunches into a zippered book bag is, and going down my six ramps to my car is. I drive on the highway, to the girls' town, to their school, and this is not simply a transition; it is my love moving by car from a place where my girls are not to a place where they are; even if I do not feel or acknowledge it, this is a sacrament. If I remember it, then I feel it too. Feeling it does not always mean that I am a happy man driving in traffic; it simply means that I know what I am doing in the presence of God.

If I were much wiser, and much more patient, and had much greater concentration, I could sit in silence in my chair, look out my windows at a green tree and the blue sky, and know that breathing is a gift; that a breath is sufficient for the moment; and that breathing air is breathing God.

You can receive and give sacraments with a telephone. In a very lonely time, two years after my crippling, I met a woman with dark skin and black hair and wit and verbal grace. We were together for an autumn afternoon, and I liked her, and that evening I sat on my couch with her, and held and kissed her. Then she drove three and a half hours north to her home in Vermont. I had a car then, with hand controls, but I had not learned to drive it; my soul was not ready for the tension and fear. I did not see the woman until five weeks later. I courted her by telephone, daily or nightly or both. She agreed to visit me and my family at Thanksgiving. On Halloween, I had a heart attack, and courted her with the bedside telephone in the hospital. Once after midnight, while I was talking to her, a nurse came into the room, smiled at me, and took the clipboard from the foot of the bed and wrote what she saw. Next morning, in my wheelchair, I read: *Twelve-fifteen. Patient alert and cheerful, talking on the phone.*

In the five weeks since that sunlit October day when I first saw her, I knew this woman through her voice. Then on Thanksgiving, she drove to a motel in the town where I live, and in early afternoon came to my house for dinner with my family: my first wife and our four grown children, and one daughter's boyfriend and one son's girlfriend, and my two young daughters. That night, when the family left, she stayed and made love to my crippled body, which did not feel crippled with her, save for some pain in my leg. Making love can be a sacrament, if our souls are as naked as our bodies, if our souls are in harmony with our bodies, and through our bodies are embracing each other in love and fear and trembling, knowing that this act could be the beginning of a third human being, if we are a man and a woman; knowing that the roots and trunk of death are within each of us, and that one of its branches may block or rupture an artery as we kiss. Surely this is a sacrament, as it may not be if we are with someone whose arms we would not want holding us as, suddenly, in passion, we died; someone whose death in our arms would pierce us not with grief but regret, fear, shame; someone who would not want to give life to that third person who is always present in lovemaking between fertile men and women. On the day after Thanksgiving, she checked out of the motel and stayed with me until Monday, and I loved her; then she went home.

With the telephone, she gave me sacraments I needed during that fall and winter when my body seemed to be my enemy.

She came to me on other weekends, four to six weeks apart, and we loved each other daily by telephone. That winter, she moved to New York City. I still did not drive, and her apartment was not a place I could enter and be in with my wheelchair; it was very small, and so was the shared bathroom down the hall. I could not fly to her, because my right knee does not bend, so I have to sit on the first seat of an airplane, and that means a first-class ticket. Trains are inaccessible horrors for someone in a wheelchair: the aisles are too narrow. A weekend in New York, if I flew there and stayed in a hotel, would have cost over a thousand dollars, before we bought a drink or a meal. So she flew to Boston or rode on the train, and a friend drove me to meet her. I was a virtual shut-in who was in love. One day a week, my oldest son drove me to horseback-riding lessons; in the barn, he pushed me up a ramp to a platform level with the horse's back, and I mounted and rode, guarded from falling by my son and volunteer women who walked and jogged beside me. A driver of a wheelchair van came for me two mornings a week and took me to Mass and left, then came back and took me to physi-

cal therapy, then came back and took me home, where I lay on my bed and held the telephone and talked to the woman, sometimes more than once a day. With the telephone, she gave me sacraments I needed during that fall and winter when my body seemed to be my enemy. We were lovers for a year, and then we were not, and now our love remains and sharing our flesh is no longer essential.

On Christmas Eve, in that year when we were lovers, I was very sad and I called her. The Christmas tree was in the living room, tall and full, and from the kitchen doorway, where I held the telephone, I could see in the front windows the reflection of the tree and its ornaments and lights. My young daughters' stockings were hanging at the windows, but my girls were at their mother's house, and would wake there Christmas morning, and would come to me in the afternoon. I was a crippled father in an empty house. In my life, I have been too much a father in an empty house; and since the vocation of fatherhood includes living with the mother, this is the deepest shame of my life, and its abiding regret. I sat in my chair and spoke into the phone of the pain in my soul, and she listened, and talked to me, and finally said: "You're supposed to be happy. It's your hero's birthday."

I laughed with my whole heart at the humor of it, at the truth of it, and now my pain was bearable, my sorrow not a well, but drops of water drying in the winter room.

In March, I decided one day that I must stop talking to her on the telephone because, while I did, I was amused, interested, passionate, joyful; then I said good-bye and I was a cripple who had been sitting in his wheelchair or lying on his bed, holding plastic to his ear. I told her that if I were whole, and could hang up the telephone and walk out of the house, I would not stop calling her; but I knew that living this way, receiving her by telephone, was not a good crippled way to live; and I knew there was a better crippled way to live, but I did not know yet what it was. She understood; she always does, whether or not she agrees.

I did not call her for days, and on the first day of April, I woke crying, and on the second; and on the third, I could not stop, and I phoned my doctor's receptionist and, still crying, I told her to tell him to give me a shot or put me away someplace, because I could not bear it anymore. At noon, he brought me spinach pie and chili dogs, and I said: "That's cholesterol."

"Depression will kill you sooner," he said, and I ate with him and still did not understand that the food and his presence at my table were sacraments. He made an appointment for me with a psychologist, and two days later my youngest son drove me to the office of this paternal and compassionate man, who said: "This is not depression; it's sorrow, and it'll always be with you, because you can't replace your legs."

As my son drove me home, I told him that I wanted a swimming pool, but I did not want to be a man who needed a swimming pool to be happy. He said: "You're not asking the world for a swimming pool. You're asking it for motion."

At home, I called a paraplegic friend and asked him to teach me to drive my car, and two days later he did. I phoned a swimming pool contractor, a durably merry and kind man, and his cost for building me a forty-by-fifteen-by-three-foot lap pool was so generous that I attribute it to gimpathy. Sacraments abounded. I paid for some, and the money itself was sacramental: my being alive to receive it and give it for good work. On that first day, after calling the paraplegic and the contractor, I called the woman, and I continued to call her, and to receive that grace.

On the last day of my father's life, he was thirsty and he asked me to crush some ice and feed it to me. I was a Marine captain, stationed at Whidbey Island, Washington, and I had flown home to Lake Charles, Louisiana, to be with my father before he died, and when he died, and to bury him. I did not know then that the night flight from Seattle was more than a movement in air from my wife and four young children to my dying father, that every moment of it, even as I slept, was a sacrament I gave my father; and they were sacraments he gave me, his siring and his love drawing me to him through the night; and sacraments between my mother and two sisters and me, and all the relatives and friends I was flying home to; and my wife and children and me, for their love was with me on the plane and I loved them and I would return to them after burying my father; and from Time itself, God's mystery we often do not clearly see; there was time now to be with my father. Sacraments came from those who flew the plane and worked aboard it and maintained it and controlled its comings and goings; and from the major who gave me emergency leave, and the gunnery sergeant who did my work while I was gone. I did not know any of this. I thought I was a son flying alone.

My father's cancer had begun in his colon, and on the Saturday before the early Sunday morning when he died, it was consuming him, and he was thin and weak on his bed, and he asked for ice. In the kitchen, I emptied a tray of ice cubes onto a dish towel and held its four corners and twisted it, then held it on the counter and with a rolling pin pounded the ice till it was crushed. This is how my father crushed ice, and how my sisters and I, when we were children, crushed it and put it in a glass and spooned sugar on it, to eat on a hot summer day. I put my father's ice into a tall glass and brought it with an iced-tea spoon to the bedroom and fed him the ice, one small piece at a time, until his mouth and throat were no longer dry.

As a boy, I was shy with my father. Perhaps he was shy with me too. When we were alone in a car, we were mostly silent. On some nights, when a championship boxing match was broadcast on the radio, we listened to it in the living room. He took me to wrestling matches because I wanted to go, and he told me they were fake, and I refused to believe it. He took me to minor-league baseball games. While we listened to boxing matches and watched wrestling and baseball, we talked about what we were hearing and seeing. He took me fishing and dove hunting with his friends, before I was old enough to shoot; but I could fish from the bank of a bayou, and he taught me to shoot my air rifle; taught me so well that, years later, my instructors in the Marine Corps simply polished his work. When I was still too young to use a shotgun, he learned to play golf and stopped fishing and hunting, and on Saturdays and Sundays he brought me to the golf course as his caddy. I did not want to caddy, but I had no choice, and I earned a dollar and a quarter; all my adult life, I have been grateful that I watched him and listened to him with his friends, and talked with him about his game. My shyness with him was a burden I did not like carrying, and I could not put down. Then I was twenty-one and a husband and a Marine, and on the morning my pregnant wife and I left home, to drive to the Officers' Basic School in Quantico, Virginia, my father and I tightly embraced, then looked at each other's damp eyes. I wanted to say *I love you*, but I could not.

I wanted to say it to him before he died. On the afternoon of his last day, he wanted bourbon and water. A lot of ice, he told me, and a lot of water. I made drinks for my sister and me too, and brought his in a tall glass I did not hold for him. I do not remember whether he lifted it to his mouth or rested it on his chest and drank from an angled hospital straw. My sister and I sat in chairs at the foot of the bed, my mother talked with relatives and friends in the living room and brought them in to speak to my father, and I told him stories of my year of sea duty on an aircraft carrier, of my work at Whidbey Island. Once he asked me to light him a cigarette. I went to his bedside table, put one of his cigarettes between my lips, lit his Zippo, then looked beyond the cigarette and flame at my father's eyes: they were watching me. All my life at home before I left for the Marine Corps, I had felt him watching me, a glance during a meal or in the living room or on the lawn, had felt he was trying to see my soul, to see if I was strong and honorable, to see if I could go out into the world, and live in it without him. His eyes watching me light his cigarette were tender, and they were saying good-bye.

That night, my father's sisters slept in the beds that had been mine and my sister's, and she and I went to the house of a neighbor across the street. We did not sleep. We sat in the kitchen and drank and cried, and I told her that tomorrow I would tell my father I loved him. Before dawn he died, and for years I regretted not saying the words. But I did not understand love then, and the sacraments that make it tactile. I had not lived enough and lost enough to enable me to know the holiness of working with meat and mustard and bread; of moving on wheels or wings or by foot from one place to another; of holding a telephone and speaking into it and listening to a voice; of pounding ice with wood and spooning the shards onto a dry tongue; of lighting a cigarette and placing it between the fingers of a man trying to enjoy tobacco and bourbon and his family as he dies.

Journal and Discussion Questions

1 "Sacraments" begins with a short explanation of Dubus' meaning of sacrament. What are the qualities of a sacrament for Dubus? Compare his definition of sacrament to the definition that he learned as a boy in the Catholic Church. Considering the differences between the official Catholic definition of sacrament and his own, why do you think Dubus uses the term "sacrament" instead of finding or inventing another word?

2 Dubus develops his definition of sacrament with a series of examples from his life. Outline "Sacraments," and then explain how each example adds to or clarifies his definition. How does your understanding of Dubus' idea of sacrament by the end of the essay change from the original definition that Dubus gives?

3 Dubus' essay can be read as an argument that one's spiritual life is closely intertwined with one's physical life, even in the most routine of activities. How would you describe Dubus' idea of the relationship between the spiritual and physical?

4 At a couple of moments in the essay, Dubus slows the pace of his essay to describe a process in detail, how he prepares sandwiches for his children and how he prepared crushed ice for his father. What do these descriptions contribute to his discussion of the nature of sacrament?

5 Dubus describes some of the physical and emotional hardships he endures as a paraplegic and ends the essay with a description of his relationship with his father at the end of his father's life. Summarize the hardships that he and his father suffered. Why does Dubus focus on stories of dealing with one's own suffering and the suffering of others with this topic?

6 Although Christian churches teach that sex outside marriage is a sin, Dubus claims that his love-making with a friend after his accident was a sacrament. What reasons does he suggest for this controversial position? Under what conditions, according to Dubus, is love-making a sacrament? Why does he set these conditions? What reasons might be given against Dubus' claim?

7 Why does Dubus write an essay on the meaning of *sacrament*? What larger idea about life is he arguing by focusing on this definition?

Topics for Writing

1 "Sacraments" takes a word that has a specialized meaning for a group of people, Roman Catholics, and expands that definition, making it relevant to everyday life. Take a specialized term from a class, a religion, or other area of life, or a slang phrase used by a small group of people, and write an essay expanding the meaning of the term, building on its usual meaning but showing how useful the word can be in understanding other parts of life.

2 Write an essay that shows the emotional or spiritual effects of a physical activity, such as preparing a meal or conducting an exercise routine.

3 Drawing on Dubus' essay, write an essay about how a person can try to deal with suffering and/or loss.

SINGING WITH THE FUNDAMENTALISTS

BY ANNIE DILLARD

Annie Dillard (1945–) is a poet, a creative writing teacher, and a nature writer who is best known for her literary nonfiction, including her Pulitzer Prize-winning *Pilgrim at Tinker Creek*; her essay collection, *Teaching a Stone to Talk*; and her memoir, *An American Childhood*. "Singing with the Fundamentalists," first published in the *Yale Review* in 1984, is a personal narrative that explores how people express their worship of God and challenges the attitudes and stereotypes about fundamentalist Christians held by many people on college campuses, including herself.

T IS EARLY SPRING. I HAVE A temporary office at a state university on the West Coast. The office is on the third floor. It looks down on the Square, the enormous open courtyard at the center of the campus. From my desk I see hundreds of people moving between classes. There is a large circular fountain in the Square's center.

Early one morning, on the first day of spring quarter, I hear singing. A pack of students has gathered at the fountain. They are singing something which, at this distance, and through the heavy window, sounds good.

I know who these singing students are: they are the Fundamentalists. This campus has a lot of them. Mornings they sing on the Square; it is their only perceptible activity. What are they singing? Whatever it is, I want to join them, for I like to sing; whatever it is, I want to take my stand with them, for I am drawn to their very absurdity, their innocent indifference to what people think. My colleagues and students here, and my friends everywhere, dislike and fear Christian fundamentalists. You may never have met such people, but you've heard what they do: they pile up money, vote in blocs, and elect right-wing crazies; they censor books; they carry handguns; they fight fluoride in the drinking water and evolution in the schools; probably they would lynch people if they could get away with it. I'm not sure my friends are correct. I close my pen and join the singers on the Square.

There is a clapping song in progress. I have to concentrate to follow it:

Come on, rejoice,
And let your heart sing,
Come on rejoice,

Give praise to the king.
Singing alleluia—
He is the king of kings;
Singing alleluia—
He is the king of kings.

Two song leaders are standing on the broad rim of the fountain; the water is splashing just behind them. The boy is short, hardfaced, with a moustache. He bangs his guitar with the backs of his fingers. The blonde girl, who leads the clapping, is bouncy; she wears a bit of makeup. Both are wearing blue jeans.

The students beside me are wearing blue jeans too—and athletic jerseys, parkas, football jackets, turtlenecks, and hiking shoes or jogging shoes. They all have canvas or nylon book bags. They look like any random batch of seventy or eighty students at this university. They are grubby or scrubbed, mostly scrubbed; they are tall, fair, or red-headed in large proportions. Their parents are white-collar workers, blue-collar workers, farmers, loggers, orchardists, merchants, fishermen; their names are, I'll bet, Olsen, Jensen, Seversen, Hansen, Klokker, Sigurdsen.

Despite the vigor of the clapping song, no one seems to be giving it much effort. And no one looks at anyone else; there are no sentimental glances and smiles, no glances even of recognition. These kids don't seem to know each other. We stand at the fountain's side, out on the broad, bricked Square in front of the science building, and sing the clapping song through three times.

It is quarter to nine in the morning. Hundreds of people are crossing the Square. These passersby—faculty, staff, students—pay very little attention to us; this morning singing has gone on for years. Most of them look at us directly, then ignore us, for there is nothing to see; no animal sacrifices, no lynchings, no collection plate for Jesse Helms, no seizures, snake handling, healing, or glossolalia. There is barely anything to hear. I suspect the people glance at us to learn if we are really singing: How could so many people make so little sound? My fellow singers, who ignore each other, certainly ignore passersby as well. Within a week, most of them will have their eyes closed anyway.

We move directly to another song, a slower one.

He is my peace
Who has broken down every wall;
He is my peace,
He is my peace.

Cast all your cares on him,
For he careth for you—oo—oo
He is my peace,
He is my peace.

I am paying strict attention to the song leaders, for I am singing at the top of my lungs and I've never heard any of these songs before. They are not the old American low-church Protestant hymns; they are not the old European high-church Protestant hymns. These hymns seem to have been written just yesterday, apparently by the same people who put out lyrical Christian greeting cards and bookmarks.

"Where do these songs come from?" I ask a girl standing next to me. She seems appalled to be addressed at all, and startled by the question. "They're from the praise albums!" she explains, and moves away.

The songs' melodies run dominant, subdominant, dominant, tonic, dominant. The pace is slow, about the pace of "Tell Laura I Love Her," and with that song's quavering, long notes. The lyrics are simple and repetitive; there are very few of them to which a devout Jew or Mohammedan could not give wholehearted assent. These songs are similar to the things Catholics sing in church these days. I don't know if any studies have been done to correlate the introduction of contemporary songs into Catholic churches with those churches' decline in membership, or with the phenomenon of Catholic converts' applying to enter cloistered monasteries directly, without passing through parish churches.

I'm set free to worship,
I'm set free to praise him,
I'm set free to dance before the Lord . . .

At nine o'clock sharp we quit and scatter. I hear a few quiet "see you"s. Mostly the students leave quickly, as if they didn't want to be seen. The Square empties.

The next day we show up again, at twenty to nine. The same two leaders stand on the fountain's rim; the fountain is pouring down behind them.

After the first song, the boy with the moustache hollers, "Move on up! Some of you guys aren't paying attention back there! You're talking to each other. I want you to concentrate!" The students laugh, embarrassed for him. He sounds like a teacher. No one moves. The girl breaks into the next song, which we join at once:

In my life, Lord,
Be glorified, be glorified, be glorified;
In my life, Lord.
Be glorified, be glorified, today.

At the end of this singularly monotonous verse, which is straining my tolerance for singing virtually anything, the boy with the moustache startles me by shouting, "Classes!"

Each has a private relationship with 'the Lord' and will put up with a lot of junk for it.

At once, without skipping a beat, we sing, "In my classes, Lord, be glorified, be glorified . . ." I give fleet thought to the class I'm teaching this afternoon. We're reading a little "Talk of the Town" piece called "Eggbag," about a cat in a magic store on Eighth Avenue. "Relationships!" the boy calls. The students seem to sing "In my relationships, Lord," more easily than they sang "classes." They seemed embarrassed by "classes." In fact, to my fascination, they seemed embarrassed by almost everything. Why are they here? I will sing with the Fundamentalists every weekday morning all spring; I will decide, tentatively, that they come pretty much for the same reasons I do: Each has a private relationship with "the Lord" and will put up with a lot of junk for it.

I have taught some Fundamentalist students here, and know a bit of what they think. They are college students above all, worried about their love lives, their grades, and finding jobs. Some support moderate Democrats; some support moderate Republicans. Like their classmates, most support nuclear freeze, ERA, and an end to the draft. I believe they are divided on abortion and busing. They are not particularly political. They read *Christianity Today* and *Campus Life* and *Eternity*—moderate, sensible magazines, I think; they read a lot of C. S. Lewis. (One such student, who seemed perfectly tolerant of me and my shoddy Christianity, introduced me to C. S. Lewis's critical book on Charles Williams.) They read the Bible. I think they all "believe in" organic evolution. The main thing about them is this: There isn't any "them." Their views vary. They don't know each other.

Their common Christianity puts them, if anywhere, to the left of their classmates. I believe they also tend to be more able than their classmates to think well in the abstract, and also to recognize the complexity of moral issues. But I may be wrong.

In 1980, the media were certainly wrong about television evangelists. Printed estimates of Jerry Falwell's television audience ranged from 18 million to 30 million people. In fact, according to Arbitron's actual counts, fewer than 1.5 million people were watching Falwell. And, according to an Emory University study, those who did watch television evangelists didn't necessarily vote with them. Emory University sociologist G. Melton Mobley reports, "When that message turns political, they cut it off." Analysis of the 1982 off-year election turned up no Fundamentalist bloc voting. The media were wrong, but no one printed retractions.

The media were wrong, too, in a tendency to identify all fundamentalist Christians with Falwell and his ilk, and to attribute to them, across the board, conservative views.

Someone has sent me two recent issues of *Eternity: The Evangelical Monthly*. One lead article criticizes a television preacher for saying that the United States had never used military might to take land from another nation. The same article censures Newspeak, saying that government rhetoric would have us believe in a "clean bomb," would have us believe that we "defend" America by invading foreign soil, and would have us believe that the dictatorships we support are "democracies." "When the President of the United States says that one reason to support defense spending is because it creates jobs," this lead article says, "a little bit of *1984* begins to surface." Another article criticizes a "heavy-handed" opinion of Jerry Falwell Ministries—in this case a broadside attack on artificial insemination, surrogate motherhood, and lesbian motherhood. Browsing through *Eternity*, I find a double crosstic. I find an intelligent, analytical, and enthusiastic review of the new London Philhar-

monic recording of Mahler's second symphony—a review which stresses the "glorious truth" of the Jewish composer's magnificent work, and cites its recent performance in Jerusalem to celebrate the recapture of the Western Wall following the Six Day War. Surely, the evangelical Christians who read this magazine are not bookburners. If by chance they vote with the magazine's editors, then it looks to me as if they vote with the American Civil Liberties Union and Americans for Democratic Action.

Every few years some bold and sincere Christian student at this university disagrees with a professor in class—usually about the professor's out-of-hand dismissal of Christianity. Members of the faculty, outraged, repeat the stories of these rare and uneven encounters for years on end, as if to prove that the crazies are everywhere, and gaining ground. The notion is, apparently, that these kids can't think for themselves. Or they wouldn't disagree.

Now again the moustached leader asks us to move up. There is no harangue, so we move up. (This will be a theme all spring. The leaders want us closer together. Our instinct is to stand alone.) From behind the tall fountain comes a wind; on several gusts we get sprayed. No one seems to notice.

We have time for one more song. The leader, perhaps sensing that no one likes him, blunders on, "I want you to pray this one through," he says. "We have a lot of people here from a lot of different fellowships, but we're all one body. Amen?" They don't like it. He gets a few polite Amens. We sing:

Bind us together, Lord,
With a bond that can't be broken;
Bind us together, Lord,
With love.

Everyone seems to be in a remarkably foul mood today. We don't like this song. There is no one here under seventeen, and, I think, no one here who believes that love is a bond that can't be broken. We sing the song through three times; then it is time to go.

The leader calls after our retreating backs, "Hey, have a good day! Praise Him all day!" The kids around me roll up their eyes privately. Some groan; all flee.

The next morning is very cold. I am here early. Two girls are talking on the fountain's rim; one is part Italian. She says, "I've got the Old Testament, but I can't get the New. I screw up the New." She takes a breath and rattles off a long list, ending with "Jonah, Micah, Nahum, Habakkuk, Zephaniah, Haggai, Zechariah, Malachi." The other girl produces a slow, sarcastic applause. I ask one of the girls to help me with the words to a song. She is agreeable, but says, "I'm sorry, I can't. I just became a Christian this year, so I don't know all the words yet."

The others are coming; we stand and separate. The boy with the moustache is gone, replaced by a big, serious fellow in a green down jacket. The bouncy girl is back with her guitar; she's wearing a skirt and wool knee socks. We begin without any preamble, by singing a song that has so few words that we actually stretch one syllable over eleven separate notes. Then we sing a song in which the men sing one phrase and the women echo it. Everyone seems to know just what to do. In the context of our vapid songs, the lyrics of this one are extraordinary:

> I was nothing before you found me.
> Heartache! Broken people! Ruined lives
> Is why you died on Calvary.

The last line rises in a regular series of half-notes. Now at last some people are actually singing; they throw some breath into the business. There is a seriousness and urgency to it: "Heartache! Broken people! Ruined lives . . . I was nothing."

We don't look like nothing. We look like a bunch of students of every stripe, ill-shaven or well-shaven, dressed up or down, but dressed warmly against the cold: jeans and parkas, jeans and heavy sweaters, jeans and scarves and blow-dried hair. We look ordinary. But I think, quite on my own, that we are here because we know this business of nothingness, brokenness, and ruination. We sing this song over and over.

Something catches my eye. Behind us, up in the science building, professors are standing alone at opened windows.

The long brick science building has three upper floors of faculty offices, thirty-two windows. At one window stands a bearded man, about forty; his opening his window is what caught my eye. He stands full in the open window, his hands on his hips, his head cocked down toward the fountain. He is drawn to look, as I was drawn to come. Up on the building's top floor, at the far right window, there is another: An Asian-American professor, wearing a white shirt, is sitting with one hip on his desk, looking out and down. In the middle of the row of windows, another one, an old professor in a checked shirt, stands sideways to the open window, stands stock-still, his long, old ear to the air. Now another window cranks open, another professor—or maybe a graduate student—leans out, his hands on the sill.

We are all singing, and I am watching these five still men, my colleagues, whose office doors are surely shut—for that is the custom here: five of them alone in their office in the science building who have opened their windows on this very cold morning, who motionless hear the Fundamentalists sing, utterly unknown to each other.

We sing another four songs, including the clapping song, and one which repeats, "This is the day which the Lord hath made; rejoice and be glad in it." All the professors but one stay by their opened windows, figures in a frieze. When after ten minutes we break off and scatter, each cranks his window shut. Maybe they have nine o'clock classes too.

I miss a few sessions. One morning of the following week, I rejoin the Fundamentalists on the Square. The wind is blowing from the north; it is sunny and cold. There are several new developments.

Someone has blown up rubber gloves and floated them in the fountain. I saw them yesterday afternoon from my high office window, and couldn't quite make them out: I seemed to see hands in the fountain waving from side to side, like those hands wagging on springs which people stick in the back windows of their cars. I saw these many years ago in Quito and Guayaquil, where they were a great fad long before they showed up here. The cardboard hands said, on their palms, HOLA GENTE, hello people. Some of them just said HOLA, hello, with a little wave to the universe at large, in case anybody happened to be looking. It is like sending radio signals to planets in other galaxies: HOLA, if anyone is listening. Jolly folk, these Ecuadorians, I thought.

Now, waiting by the fountain for the singing, I see that these particular hands are long surgical gloves, yellow and white, ten of them tied off at the cuff. They float upright and they wave, *hola, hola, hola*; they mill around like a crowd, bobbing under the fountain's spray and back again to the pool's rim, *hola*. It is a good prank. It is far too cold for the university's maintenance crew to retrieve them without turning off the fountain and putting on rubber boots.

From all around the Square, people are gathering for the singing. There is no way I can guess which kids, from among the masses crossing the Square, will veer off to the fountain. When they get here, I never recognize anybody except the leaders.

The singing begins without ado as usual, but there is something different about it. The students are growing prayerful, and they show it this morning with a pe-

> " I look around and see that almost everyone in this crowd of eighty or so has his eyes shut and is apparently praying the words of this song or praying some other prayer. "

culiar gesture. I'm glad they weren't like this when I first joined them, or I never would have stayed.

Last night there was an educational television special, part of "Middletown." It was a segment called "Community of Praise," and I watched it because it was about Fundamentalists. It showed a Jesus-loving family in the Midwest; the treatment was good and complex. This family attended the prayer meetings, healing sessions, and church services of an unnamed sect—a very low-church sect, whose doctrine and culture were much more low-church than those of the kids I sing with. When the members of this sect prayed, they held their arms over their heads and raised their palms, as if to feel or receive a blessing or energy from above.

Now today on the Square there is a new serious mood. The leaders are singing with their eyes shut. I am impressed that they can bang their guitars, keep their balance, and not fall into the pool. It is the same bouncy girl and earnest boy. Their eyeballs are rolled back a bit. I look around and see that almost everyone in this crowd of eighty or so has his eyes shut and is apparently praying the words of this song or praying some other prayer.

Now as the chorus rises, as it gets louder and higher and simpler in melody—

I exalt thee,
I exalt thee,
I exalt thee,
Thou art the Lord—

then, at this moment, hands start rising. All around me, hands are going up—that tall girl, that blond boy with his head back, the red-headed boy up front, the girl with the MacDonald's jacket. Their arms rise as if pulled on strings. Some few of them have raised their arms very high over their heads and are tilting back their palms. Many, many more of them, as inconspicuously as possible, have raised their hands to the level of their chins.

What is going on? Why are these students today raising their palms in this gesture, when nobody did it last week? Is it because the leaders have set a prayerful tone this morning? Is it because this gesture always ac-

companies this song, just as clapping accompanies other songs? Or is it, as I suspect, that these kids watched the widely publicized documentary last night just as I did, and are adopting, or trying out, the gesture?

It is a sunny morning, and the sun is rising behind the leaders and the fountain, so those students have their heads tilted, eyes closed, and palms upraised toward the sun. I glance up at the science building and think my own prayer: Thank God no one is watching this.

The leaders cannot move around much on the fountain's rim. The girl has her eyes shut; the boy opens his eyes from time to time, glances at the neck of his guitar, and closes his eyes again.

When the song is over, the hands go down, and there is some desultory chatting in the crowd, as usual: Can I borrow your library card? And, as usual nobody looks at anybody.

All our songs today are serious. There is a feudal theme to them, or a feudal analogue:

I will eat from abundance of your household.
I will dream beside your streams of righteousness.
You are my king.
Enter his gates
with thanksgiving in your heart;
come before his courts with praise.
He is the king of kings.

Thou art the Lord.

All around me, eyes are closed and hands are raised. There is no social pressure to do this, or anything else. I've never known any group to be less cohesive, imposing fewer controls. Since no one looks at anyone, and since passersby no longer look, everyone out here is inconspicuous and free. Perhaps the palm-raising has begun because the kids realize by now that they are not on display; they're praying in their closets, right out here on the Square. Over the course of the next weeks, I will learn that the palm-raising is here to stay.

The sun is rising higher. We are singing our last song. We are praying. We are alone together.

He is my peace
Who has broken down every wall . . .

When the song is over, the hands go down. The heads lower, the eyes open and blink. We stay still a second before we break up. We have been standing in a broad current; now we have stepped aside. We have dismantled the radar cups; we have closed the telescope's vault. Students gather their book bags and go. The two leaders step down from the fountain's rim and pack away their guitars. Everyone scatters. I am in no hurry, so I stay after everyone is gone. It is after nine o'clock, and the Square is deserted. The fountain is playing to an empty house. In the pool the cheerful hands are waving over the water, bobbing under the fountain's veil and out again in the current, *hola*.

Journal and Discussion Questions

1 Compare Annie Dillard's descriptions of stereotypes of Fundamentalist students with her descriptions of the students singing and her research on Fundamentalists. What do you know about Fundamentalists from Dillard's essay? What don't you know about them?

2 Why does Dillard join the singers? Why does she write that she would not have stayed with the singers if they had been using the raised-hand gesture from the first? Why does she continue to stay?

3 How would you describe the group dynamics of the Fundamentalist students? What does this dynamic imply about the relationship of community and individualism in worshiping God?

4 Dillard calls the lyrics of the hymns that the Fundamentalists sing "vapid," comparing them to poems on greeting cards and bookmarks, yet she frequently quotes the hymns. Why? Why are the lyrics of the hymns important in the essay?

5 Where in the essay does Dillard go beyond personal experience to discuss her knowledge and research? What sources does she use? How does her research support her ideas?

6 Dillard uses white space to divide her essay into blocks. Outline "Singing with the Fundamentalists." What is the logic behind her divisions? Where does the essay digress from the story of Dillard and the Fundamentalist singers? What does this digression contribute to the essay?

7 What do you learn about Dillard's religious and spiritual beliefs? What details suggest these beliefs?

Topics for Writing

1 Analyze Annie Dillard's "Singing with the Fundamentalists," discussing what her essay may be saying about people's expressions of worship, religious stereotyping, or fundamentalist Christianity.

2 Analyze the lyrics and music of a hymn. What do the lyrics reveal about the beliefs of the writer?

ISLAM: A Broad Perspective on Other Faiths

BY KABIR HELMINSKI

Shaykh Kabir Helminski (1947–) is head of the Mevlevi Order of Muslims and co-director of the Threshold Society, a nonprofit educational foundation that promotes Sufism, a mystic and ascetic movement of Islam that is particularly influential among American Muslims. Helminski writes Sufi poetry, has translated several volumes of Sufi writings, and has authored two books on Sufism, *Living Presence* and *The Knowing Heart*. "Islam: A Broad Perspective on Other Faiths" was first published in the 2002 book *Taking Back Islam: American Muslims Reclaim Their Faith*, edited by Michael Wolfe and Beliefnet, a firm that promotes multifaith understanding, as a response to many Americans' hostility towards Muslims after the terrorist attacks of September 11, 2001. In this essay, Helminski interprets passages of the Qur'an to argue that religious tolerance and pluralism are central elements of Islam.

MY FIRST ENCOUNTER WITH ISLAM was not in a mosque or through a book, but by meeting a Muslim. I don't mean a normal Muslim, but someone who was actually in the "state" of *Islam*, which literally means the peace that comes from submission to God's will. I definitely was not looking for a "religion," but I was looking for what I imagined to be Truth or Reality, and I felt that Reality in the presence of this person. In a sense, you could say that Islam is not a formulation, an ethical system, a practice, or even a revelation as much as it is a relationship to the divine.

The five pillars of Islam—bearing witness that there is one Absolute Being, worship, fasting, charity, pilgrimage—are a means to establish that relationship and are common to all sacred traditions. But that essential, conscious relationship with a spiritual dimension is the heart of the matter.

So orient yourself to the primordial religion, the innate nature upon which Allah has created humanity, without altering Allah's creation. That is the authentic religion, but the great majority do not comprehend.

Turn in repentance to Him and remain conscious of Him: be constant in prayer and do not be among those who worship other than God, those who split apart the Religion and create sects—each group separately rejoicing in what it has! (Qur'an 30:30–32)

This verse suggests a broad perspective, as it refers to the timeless monotheism associated with the Prophet Abraham. This primordial religion corresponds to the human nature instilled by God. The purpose of religion, therefore, is to safeguard the human soul from "altering God's creation," from being less than human. It is possible, then, to make a distinction between that primordial religion or essential Islam, the authentic core of all revealed traditions, and the Islam practiced by the community of Muhammad, which is just one possible manifestation of humanity's primordial religion.

It is from the perspective of this primordial religion that pluralism must be accepted. Muslims may believe that their faith corresponds most truly to that "first" religion, but this is not sufficient reason to deny that other religions offer an approach to God. *For each one of you (several communities) We have appointed a Law and a Way of Life. If God had so willed, He would have made all of you one community, but He has not done so that He may test you in what He has given you; so compete in goodness. To God shall you all return and He will tell you (the Truth) about what you have been disputing.* (5:48)

This suggests that God has not granted a spiritual monopoly to any one religion. Competition in virtue reduces the chances that we will become complacent and lazy; competition in goodness increases the likelihood of humility and cooperation. *To every people have We appointed ways of worship which they observe.*

Therefore let them not dispute with thee, but bid them to thy Sustainer for thou art on the right way. (22:67–69)

These ways of worship have been established by God Himself. Muhammad is not asked to convert people, but to establish a harmonious relationship with them by acknowledging one Sustainer. This verse in particular seems to guide the Prophet Muhammad to a cooperative relationship with other faiths. The Islamic worldview accepts other faiths, guaranteeing the right of other religious communities to follow their own revealed tradition. As the Qur'an says, "There shall be no coercion in religion."

RIGHTING THE MISUSE OF THE QUR'AN.

Now let us turn to some verses of the Qur'an that have been misused by those who try to turn Islam into a narrow, exclusive belief system.

Indeed, with God the essential religion is submission, And it was only because of envy that the People of the Book developed other views, and only after knowledge had come to them, but whoever denies the signs of God, with God the reckoning is swift. (3:19)

Here we have one of the most important passages in the Qur'an, one that deserves careful reflection. Its context is a discussion of the essential elements of faith. The passage begins with a confirmation of the authenticity of books revealed to Moses and Jesus, referring specifically to the Torah and the Gospel. Within the context of this acknowledgment of religious pluralism, humankind is given a clear warning: "Those who reject the signs of God will suffer the severest penalty" (3:4). What does it mean to reject the signs of God? It is said that various things distract us from recognizing the signs of God: women and sons, heaps of gold and silver, fine horses (or nowadays cars), and real estate. Our *exclusive* preoccupation with the things of the world blinds us to the signs.

Submission, here, should therefore be understood as "islam" with a small "i"—a state of being, a kind of relationship with God—rather than the specific forms of religion we understand as "Islam" with a capital "I."

A friend of mine was visiting a Sufi lodge or *tekkye*, in Bosnia. It was an enchanting location under an immense rock near a beautiful river. My friend asked a young man there how old the center was. "Two thousand years old," was the reply. "How could that be?" my friend asked. "We here in Bosnia have been practicing Islam even before the coming of the Prophet Muhammad," the boy replied.

Therefore, a verse like—*And whoso seeks a religion other than islam, it will not be accepted from him, and he will be at a loss in the Hereafter.* (3:85)—needs to be understood in light of others such as the following: *We bestowed from on high the Torah, in which there is guidance and light. . . . If any fail to judge by what Allah has revealed, they are unbelievers* (kufâr). (5:44) In other words, Jews who follow the Torah are believers.

Finally, we have what may be considered a definitive statement on the subject in this verse: *Those who believe (Muslims), the Jews, the Christians, and the Sabaeans—whosoever believe in God and the Last Day and do good deeds, they shall have their reward from their Lord, shall have nothing to fear, nor shall they grieve.* (2:62)

Of course there are those who claim that this verse has been "abrogated" by verses like the previous one:

> **The Islamic worldview accepts other faiths, guaranteeing the right of other religious communities to follow their own revealed tradition.**

And whoso seeks a religion other than islam . . . Nevertheless, Islamic commentators say that a verse can't be abrogated if it applies to a promise. Abrogation is permissible only with legal judgments, which may be altered because of changing times.

What principles of conduct and communication are proposed by the Qur'an in relation to people of other faiths? Without a doubt, it is an approach based on courtesy and gentleness: *And do not argue with the followers of earlier revelation otherwise than in a most kindly manner* (29:46; cf. 17:53; 16:125–28).

Even in the most extreme cases, where it is believed that people are following beliefs that are out of accord with reality: *But do not revile those whom they invoke instead of God, lest they revile God out of spite, and in ignorance: for We have made the deeds of every people seem fair to them. In time, they must return to their Lord, and then He will make them understand what they have done.* (6:108)

When the great Sufi Jalaluddin Rumi heard of two people arguing about religion, he said, "These people are involved in a very trivial affair. Instead of arguing which of their religions is best, they could be considering how far each of them are from the teachings of their own prophets."

It should be clear that Islam is in a unique position to act as a reconciling force among different faiths because Islam has built into its very nature the tolerance and respect for all religious communities and sacred traditions.

Furthermore, we are in a position to help realign these other communities with the original spirit of revelation. I can say that from my own experience, although I was raised as a Catholic, my affection for and understanding of Jesus only deepened through my Islamic perspective; I have heard others say the same. Islam can help them to understand the extent to which man-made beliefs have led to irrational theologies and self-serving institu-

tions. We must safeguard our own religion from the same corruption. Anyone who thinks that these reflections contribute to a weakening of faith is, in my opinion, missing the point. It is precisely because of this perspective that I can call myself a Muslim. What is faith (or *iman*) if not the widest possible perspective on our lives, and what is disbelief or denial (*kufr*) if not a constriction upon our own narrow, egoistic concerns? It is because of this sweeping panorama of faith that I can take the Divine Revelation given to Muhammad into my heart and try to walk in his footsteps.

Journal and Discussion Questions

1 What is the thesis of "Islam: A Broad Perspective on Other Faiths"? How does Shaykh Kabir Helminski develop his thesis about Islam?

2 What common perceptions or misperceptions about Islam does Helminski attempt to correct? How does he refute these ideas about Islam? Has Helminski ignored any important hostile ideas and images about Islam?

3 Helminski examines eight verses from the Qur'an to support his argument. Why did he select these particular passages? How do his comments on each passage support and develop his central claim about Islam? How does Helminski refute opposing interpretations of controversial passages?

4 What religious terms and details about Islam does Helminksi introduce to his readers in "Islam: A Broad Perspective on Other Faiths"? What does this information contribute to his argument? How does Helminski define and explain unfamiliar terms and concepts about Islam and still keep his readers focused on the thesis he is arguing?

5 Why does Helminski at times include biographical information in his essay, about his first encounter with Islam and eventual conversion and about a friend's conversation at a Sufi lodge in Bosnia? What do these details about the lives of Muslims contribute to his depiction of Islam?

6 Is Helminski's background—as a former Catholic who converted to Islam and as a Sufi scholar, poet, translator, and religious leader—important to "Islam: A Broad Perspective on Other Faiths"? How might this essay be different if it were written by an expert on Islam who was not a Muslim?

7 Besides the Qur'an, Helminski cites only one source by name: Jalaluddin Rumi, the founder of the Sufi movement, on page 170. How does the quotation by Rumi support and clarify Helminski's argument? Where else does Helminski refer to other people's interpretations of the Qur'an and for what reasons? Why doesn't he name any of these commentators?

Topics for Writing

1 Identify and argue against popular misconceptions about the Muslim religion, using Helminski's "Islam: A Broad Perspective on Other Faiths" as a source. You might expand this argument into a research paper by consulting other sources.

2 Analyze "Islam: A Broad Perspective on Other Faiths" as a response to changes in the world since September 11, 2001, considering how Helminski addresses westerners' fears of Muslims and radical Islamists' claims about Islam.

THE GREAT MYSTERY

BY CHARLES A. EASTMAN (OHIYESA)

Charles A. Eastman (1858–1939) was one of the most famous Native Americans of the late nineteenth and early twentieth centuries. A mixed-blood Sioux, Eastman was educated in Indian ways under the guidance of his grandmother, taking the Sioux name of Ohiyesa, but he started attending white schools at age fifteen. He earned a medical degree from Boston University in 1890 and was the only physician at the Wounded Knee massacre, traditionally considered the end of the Indian Wars. Dr. Eastman believed his education put him in a unique position to understand Native American culture and work for understanding between whites and Native Americans. With the encouragement of another well-known Native American writer, Zitkala-Sa, Eastman wrote eleven books, several co-authored with his wife, Elaine Goodale Eastman. Eastman's story is told in the book and film *Bury My Heart at Wounded Knee*.

"The Great Mystery" is the first chapter of *The Soul of the Indian: An Interpretation* (1911). Eastman wrote that this book was his attempt "to paint the religious life of the typical American Indian as it was before he knew the white man. [. . .] My little book does not pretend to be a scientific treatise. It is as true as I can make it to my childhood teaching and ancestral ideals, but from the human, not the ethnological standpoint. I have not cared to pile up more dry bones, but to clothe them with flesh and blood. So much that has been written by strangers of our ancient faith and worship treats it chiefly as matters of curiosity. I should like to emphasize its universal quality, its personal appeal!"

THE ORIGINAL ATTITUDE OF THE American Indian toward the Eternal, the "Great Mystery" that surrounds and embraces us, was as simple as it was exalted. To him it was the supreme conception, bringing with it the fullest measure of joy and satisfaction possible in this life.

The worship of the " Great Mystery" was silent, solitary, free from all self-seeking. It was silent, because all speech is of necessity feeble and imperfect; therefore the souls of my ancestors ascended to God in wordless adoration. It was solitary, because they believed that He is nearer to us in solitude, and there were no priests authorized to come between a man and his Maker. None might exhort or confess or in any way meddle with the religious experience of another. Among us all men were created sons of God and stood erect, as conscious of their divinity. Our faith might not be formulated in creeds, nor forced upon any who were unwilling to receive it; hence there was no preaching, proselyting, nor persecution, neither were there any scoffers or atheists.

There were no temples or shrines among us save those of nature. Being a natural man, the Indian was intensely poetical. He would deem it sacrilege to build a house for Him who may be met face to face in the mysterious, shadowy aisles of the primeval forest, or on the sunlit bosom of virgin prairies, upon dizzy spires and pinnacles of naked rock, and yonder in the jeweled vault of the night sky! He who enrobes Himself in filmy veils of cloud, there on the rim of the visible world where our Great-Grandfather Sun kindles his evening campfire, He who rides upon the rigorous wind of the north, or breathes forth His spirit upon aromatic southern airs, whose war-canoe is launched upon majestic rivers and inland seas—He needs no lesser cathedral!

That solitary communion with the Unseen which was the highest expression of our religious life is partly described in the word *hambeday*, literally "mysterious feeling," which has been variously translated "fasting" and "dreaming." It may better be interpreted as "consciousness of the divine."

The first *hambeday*, or religious retreat, marked an epoch in the life of the youth, which may be compared to that of confirmation or conversion in Christian experience. Having first prepared himself by means of the purifying vapor-bath, and cast off as far as possible all human or fleshly influences, the young man sought out the noblest height, the most commanding summit in all the surrounding region. Knowing that God sets no value upon material things, he took with him no offerings or sacrifices other than symbolic objects, such as paints and tobacco. Wishing to appear before Him in all humility, he wore no clothing save his moccasins and breech-clout. At the solemn hour of sunrise or sunset he took up his position, overlooking the glories of earth and facing the "Great Mystery," and there he remained, naked, erect, silent, and motionless, exposed to the elements and forces of His arming, for a night and a day to two days and nights, but rarely longer. Sometimes he would chant a hymn without words, or offer the ceremonial "filled pipe." In this holy trance or ecstasy the Indian mystic found his highest happiness and the motive power of his existence.

When he returned to the camp, he must remain at a distance until he had again entered the vapor-bath and prepared himself for intercourse with his fellows. Of the vision or sign vouchsafed to him he did not speak, unless it had included some commission which must be publicly fulfilled. Sometimes an old man, standing upon the brink of eternity, might reveal to a chosen few the oracle of his long-past youth.

The native American has been generally despised by his white conquerors for his poverty and simplicity. They forget, perhaps, that his religion forbade the accumulation of wealth and the enjoyment of luxury. To him, as to other single-minded men in every age and race, from Diogenes to the brothers of Saint Francis, from the Montanists to the Shakers, the love of possessions has appeared a snare, and the burdens of a complex society a source of needless peril and temptation. Furthermore, it was the rule of his life to share the fruits of his skill and success with his less fortunate brothers. Thus he kept his spirit free from the clog of pride, cupidity, or envy, and carried out, as he believed, the divine decree—a matter profoundly important to him.

It was not, then, wholly from ignorance or improvidence that he failed to establish permanent towns and to develop a material civilization. To the untutored sage, the concentration of population was the prolific mother of all evils, moral no less than physical. He argued that food is good, while surfeit kills; that love is good, but lust destroys; and not less dreaded than the pestilence following upon crowded and unsanitary dwellings was the loss of spiritual power inseparable from too close contact with one's fellow-men. All who have lived much out of doors know that there is a magnetic and nervous force that accumulates in solitude and that is quickly dissipated by life in a crowd; and even his enemies have recognized the fact that for a certain innate power and self-poise, wholly independent of circumstances, the American Indian is unsurpassed among men.

The red man divided mind into two parts,—the spiritual mind and the physical mind. The first is pure spirit, concerned only with the essence of things, and it was this he sought to strengthen by spiritual prayer, during which the body is subdued by fasting and hardship. In this type of prayer there was no beseeching of favor or help. All matters of personal or selfish concern, as success in hunting or warfare, relief from sickness, or the sparing of a beloved life, were definitely relegated to the plane of the lower or material mind, and all ceremonies, charms, or incantations designed to secure a benefit or to avert a danger, were recognized as emanating from the physical self.

The rites of this physical worship, again, were wholly symbolic, and the Indian no more worshiped the Sun than the Christian adores the Cross. The Sun and the Earth, by an obvious parable, holding scarcely more of poetic metaphor than of scientific truth, were in his view the parents of all organic life. From the Sun, as the universal father, proceeds the quickening principle in nature, and in the patient and fruitful womb of our mother, the Earth, are hidden embryos of plants and men. Therefore our reverence and love for them was really an imaginative extension of our love for our immediate parents, and with this sentiment of filial piety was joined a willingness to appeal to them, as to a father, for such good gifts as we may desire. This is the material or physical prayer.

The elements and majestic forces in nature, Lightning, Wind, Water, Fire, and Frost, were regarded with awe as spiritual powers, but always secondary and intermediate in character. We believed that the spirit pervades all creation and that every creature possesses a soul in some degree, though not necessarily a soul conscious of itself. The tree, the waterfall, the grizzly bear, each is an embodied Force, and as such an object of reverence.

The Indian loved to come into sympathy and spiritual communion with his brothers of the animal kingdom, whose inarticulate souls had for him something of the sinless purity that we attribute to the innocent and irresponsible child. He had faith in their instincts, as in a mysterious wisdom given from above; and while he humbly accepted the supposedly voluntary sacrifice of their bodies to preserve his

> **" We believed that the spirit pervades all creation and that every creature possesses a soul in some degree, though not necessarily a soul conscious of itself. "**

own, he paid homage to their spirits in prescribed prayers and offerings.

In every religion there is an element of the supernatural, varying with the influence of pure reason over its devotees. The Indian was a logical and clear thinker upon matters within the scope of his understanding, but he had not yet charted the vast field of nature or expressed her wonders in terms of science. With his limited knowledge of cause and effect, he saw miracles on every hand,—the miracle of life in seed and egg, the miracle of death in lightning flash and in the swelling deep! Nothing of the marvelous could astonish him; as that a beast should speak, or the sun stand still. The virgin birth would appear scarcely more miraculous than is the birth of every child that comes into the world, or the miracle of the loaves and fishes excite more wonder than the harvest that springs from a single ear of corn.

Who may condemn his superstition? Surely not the devout Catholic, or even Protestant missionary, who teaches Bible miracles as literal fact! The logical man must either deny all miracles or none, and our American Indian myths and hero stories are perhaps, in themselves, quite as credible as those of the Hebrews of old. If we are of the modern type of mind, that sees in natural law a majesty and grandeur far more impressive than any solitary infraction of it could possibly be, let us not forget that, after all, science has not explained everything. We have still to face the ultimate miracle,—the origin and principle of life! Here is the supreme mystery that is the essence of worship, without which there can be no religion, and in the presence of this mystery our attitude cannot be very unlike that of the natural philosopher, who beholds with awe the Divine in all creation.

It is simple truth that the Indian did not, so long as his native philosophy held sway over his mind, either envy or desire to imitate the splendid achievements of the white man. In his own thought he rose superior to them! He scorned them, even as a lofty spirit absorbed in its stern task rejects the soft beds, the luxurious food, the pleasure-worshiping dalliance of a rich neighbor. It was clear to him that virtue and happiness are independent of these things, if not incompatible with them.

There was undoubtedly much in primitive Christianity to appeal to this man, and Jesus' hard sayings to the rich and about the rich would have been entirely comprehensible to him. Yet the religion that is preached in our churches and practiced by our congregations, with its element of display and self-aggrandizement, its active proselytism, and its open contempt of all religions but its own, was for a long time extremely repellent. To his simple mind, the professionalism of the pulpit, the paid exhorter, the moneyed church, was an unspiritual and unedifying thing, and it was not until his spirit was broken and his moral and physical constitution undermined by trade, conquest, and strong drink, that Christian missionaries obtained any real hold upon him. Strange as it may seem, it is true that the proud pagan in his secret soul despised the good men who came to convert and to enlighten him!

Nor were its publicity and its Phariseeism the only element in the alien religion that offended the red man. To him, it appeared shocking and almost incredible that there were among this people who claimed superiority many irreligious, who did not even pretend to profess the national faith. Not only did they not profess it, but they stooped so low as to insult their God with profane and sacrilegious speech! In our own tongue His name was not spoken aloud, even with utmost reverence much less lightly or irreverently.

More than this, even in those white men who professed religion we found much inconsistency of conduct. They spoke much of spiritual things, while seeking only the material. They bought and sold everything: time, labor, personal independence, the love of woman, and even the ministrations of their holy faith! The lust for money, power, and conquest so characteristic of the Anglo-Saxon race did not escape moral condemnation at the hands of his untutored judge, nor did he fail to contrast this conspicuous trait of the dominant race with the spirit of the meek and lowly Jesus.

He might in time come to recognize that the drunkards and licentious among white men, with whom he too frequently came in contact, were condemned by the white man's religion as well, and must not be held to discredit it. But it was not so easy to overlook or to excuse national bad faith.

When distinguished emissaries from the Father at Washington, some of them ministers of the gospel and even bishops, came to the Indian nations, and pledged to them in solemn treaty the national honor, with prayer and mention of their God; and when such treaties so made, were promptly and shamelessly broken, is it strange that the action should arouse not only anger but contempt? The historians of the white race admit that the Indian was never the first to repudiate his oath.

It is my personal belief, after thirty-five years' experience of it, that there is no such thing as "Christian civilization." I believe that Christianity and modern civilization are opposed and irreconcilable, and that the spirit of Christianity and of our ancient religion is essentially the same.

Journal and Discussion Questions

1 What is the thesis of "The Great Mystery"? Outline the essay. How does the organization serve the purpose and thesis of the essay?

2 According to Charles A. Eastman, how is Indian religion similar to Christianity? How is it different? What are his purposes in comparing the two religions? What critique does "The Great Mystery" offer of white Christian society?

3 Eastman sometimes expresses concerns about white people's ignorance about Native Americans. Where does he address particular prejudices and mistaken beliefs that white readers may hold?

4 According to Eastman, how did religion influence Indian society?

5 Eastman writes that his book is based on his schooling in the traditions of his Sioux ancestors and his experiences growing up in his religion, rather than an ethnological or sociological study of Indian religious beliefs and practices. How does the source of his knowledge lend authority and insight to his explanations? How might his reliance on his schooling and experiences weaken his essay?

6 Eastman makes no mention of different Native American tribes in his essay or the differences in their religious beliefs and rites, and he does not discuss women in Indian religion. How do these omissions affect Eastman's portrait of Indian religion? How might "The Great Mystery" be different if Eastman considered tribal differences and women in his explanations?

7 What does Eastman believe is universal about the beliefs of Indian religion? How does he support his claim of universality? Are you persuaded by Eastman? Why or why not?

Topics for Writing

1 Conduct research on the religious beliefs and practices of a specific tribe of Native Americans. Evaluate "The Great Mystery," comparing your findings to Eastman's explanations and descriptions.

2 Write a research paper on how Native American religions have changed since Eastman's time.

3 Write an essay like Eastman's explaining your own religion or belief system for an audience not familiar with these beliefs.

Connecting the Readings

Compare the purposes and audiences for Kabir Helminski's "Islam: A Broad Perspective on Other Faiths" and Charles A. Eastman's "The Great Mystery" and how the writers address their readers' misconceptions about and prejudice against their religions.

AND THESE THINGS GIVE BIRTH TO EACH OTHER

BY TONY HOAGLAND
PAIGE DESHONG, PHOTOGRAPH

Tony Hoagland (1953–) is a poet and a professor of English at the University of Houston. He has published three books of poetry, including *Donkey Gospel* and *What Narcissism Means to Me*, as well as *Real Sofistikashun: Essays on Poetry and Craft*. Paige DeShong is a poet and a member of the English faculty at Austin Community College. "And These Things Give Birth to Each Other" was published in a 1998 collection of poetry entitled *Keeping Death: A Collaborative Exhibit of Poetry and Photography*, edited by DeShong and Gilberto Lucero. In parts of rural Mexico and the U.S., people put up small roadside shrines, typically crosses, to mark the places where loved ones died, usually in a car accident. DeShong took photographs of many roadside shrines on a trip to Mexico and asked each contributor to *Keeping Death* to write a poem or short prose piece that makes reference to one of the photographs. Hoagland's poem, inspired by DeShong's picture of a shrine marking the death of four people on a Mexican road, considers the difficulties of believing and disbelieving in a spiritual realm in the face of death.

It is hard to look at the world of matter
There are afternoons when the light is such
A wind blows through the graves
The priest says, here is a word
Inside the word is a world.
You think, I have a hat. I have a car. I have a wife.
This place is a terrible place.
It eats what lives on it
It was never innocent
And the mouth is full of dirt.
We ask, how can I live with death?
When we should be asking, How
can I kill my disbelief?

Journal and Discussion Questions

1 What does the title "And These Things Give Birth to Each Other" mean? What things is Tony Hoagland referring to? How do they "give birth to each other"?

2 Why, according to Hoagland, is it "hard to look at the world of matter"? How does this line set up the rest of the poem? Why do the graves prompt the poet to contemplate the world of matter? What is the poet's attitude toward death?

3 Describe Paige DeShong's photograph of the roadside shrine. How does Hoagland make use of the photograph in his poem? What does the photo contribute to the poem?

4 Explain the lines "the priest says, here is a word / Inside the word is a world." What is this world, and how is it from "the world of matter"?

5 Why does Hoagland believe that "How / can I kill my disbelief?" is a more important question than "How can I live with death?" How are these two questions related to the rest of the poem? Why is it difficult to kill disbelief?

6 What is "And These Things Give Birth to Each Other" saying about the reasons why humans want to believe in a spiritual world yet often find it difficult to believe in one?

Topics for Writing

1 Analyze Tony Hoagland's "And These Things Give Birth to Each Other" with Paige DeShong's photograph, considering the relationship between the poet's reaction to the graves that he sees and his faith and disbelief in God or an afterlife.

2 Write a research paper about one or more of the ways that cultures deal with death and remember the dead, analyzing what these ceremonies and memorials suggest about the culture's attitudes toward and beliefs about death and an afterlife.

AN IDEAL OF SERVICE TO OUR FELLOW MAN

BY ALBERT EINSTEIN

Albert Einstein (1879–1955) was *Time*'s "Person of the Twentieth Century" because his theory of relativity and other scientific work revolutionized physics and paved the way for many of the technological developments that shaped the century. The most celebrated scientist of his time, Einstein took advantage of his status to speak out about political and moral issues, such as nuclear war, Zionism, and the role of science in society, as in his books *Ideas and Opinions*, *About Zionism*, and *The World As I See It*. Einstein wrote "An Ideal of Service to Our Fellow Man" in 1954 for *This I Believe*, a CBS Radio series in which people wrote and recited three-minute essays that expressed their personal philosophies. These essays expressed a core belief held by the writer, usually in simple, personal language, but the originator and host of the series, Edward R. Murrow, did not want essays that offered "a pat answer for the problems of life." When he read this essay on CBS radio (written in German and translated by David Domine into English), Einstein was a professor at Princeton University, a vocal opponent of the nuclear weapons that his scientific theories and research had helped to develop, and a strong advocate for peace. Here Einstein discusses the relationship between science and religion and the importance of living a life in service to others. Archives of essays written for *This I Believe* in the 1950s and since the revival of the series in 2005 can be found at www.thislbelieve.org and npr.org/thisibelieve.

THE MOST BEAUTIFUL THING WE can experience is the Mysterious—the knowledge of the existence of something unfathomable to us, the manifestation of the most profound reason coupled with the most brilliant beauty. I cannot imagine a God who rewards and punishes the objects of his creation, or who has a will of the kind we experience in ourselves. I am satisfied with the mystery of life's eternity and with the awareness of—and glimpse into—the marvelous construction of the existing world together with the steadfast determination to comprehend a portion, be it ever so tiny, of the reason that manifests itself in nature. This is the basis of cosmic religiosity, and it appears to me that the most important function of art and science is to awaken this feeling among the receptive and keep it alive.

I sense that it is not the State that has intrinsic value in the machinery of humankind, but rather the creative, feeling individual, the personality alone that creates the noble and sublime.

Man's ethical behavior should be effectively grounded on compassion, nurture and social bonds.

What is moral is not the divine, but rather a purely human matter, albeit the most important of all human matters. In the course of history, the ideals pertaining to human beings' behavior towards each other and pertaining to the preferred organization of their communities have been espoused and taught by enlightened individuals. These ideals and convictions—results of historical experience, empathy and the need for beauty and harmony—have usually been willingly recognized by human beings, at least in theory.

The highest principles for our aspirations and judgments are given to us westerners in the Jewish-Christian religious tradition. It is a very high goal: free and responsible development of the individual, so that he may place his powers freely and gladly in the service of all mankind.

The pursuit of recognition for their own sake, an almost fanatical love of justice and the quest for personal independence form the traditional themes of the Jewish people, of which I am a member.

But if one holds these high principles clearly before one's eyes and compares them with the life and spirit of our times, then it is glaringly apparent that mankind finds itself at present in grave danger. I see the nature of the current crises in the juxtaposition of the individual to society. The individual feels more than ever dependent on society, but he feels this dependence not in the positive sense—cradled, connected as part of an organic whole. He sees it as a threat to his natural rights and even his economic existence. His position in society, then, is such that that which drives his ego is encouraged and developed, and that which would drive him toward other men (a weak impulse to begin with) is left to atrophy.

It is my belief that there is only one way to eliminate these evils, namely, the establishment of a planned economy coupled with an education geared towards social goals. Alongside the development of individual abilities, the education of the individual aspires to revive an ideal that is geared towards the service of our fellow man, and that needs to take the place of the glorification of power and outer success.

Journal and Discussion Questions

1 What would you identify as Albert Einstein's "core belief" in "An Ideal of Service to Our Fellow Man"? What principles does Einstein believe are most important, not only for his life, but for western culture? Why?

2 Einstein expresses some of his beliefs in this essay as his individual beliefs and some as beliefs that he holds in common with others. How does he signal which beliefs are unique to him and which beliefs come out of experiences or religious traditions shared by many people? Why is it important to make these distinctions?

3 Einstein uses several comparisons and contrasts to develop the ideas of this essay (art and science, the individual and society or the State, feeling and reason, convictions and behavior). Why are these comparisons important in his essay?

4 How does science contribute to Einstein's experience and understanding of God and "the Mysterious"? What is the relationship between religion and science for Einstein?

5 Halfway through the essay, Einstein identifies himself as a Jew. Why does he wait to do this? Which of his beliefs come from his Jewish heritage? Which beliefs are in conflict with Jewish teachings?

6 What kind of relationship between the individual and society does Einstein advocate? How does his concept of individual aspiration fit in with the importance of serving mankind?

7 Einstein ends his essay with a critique of his society in the penultimate paragraph and a call for action and reform in the last paragraph. What is wrong with society in Einstein's view, and how does his discussion of the Mysterious, the individual, and conviction lead up to this critique? How will his proposals address the "crises" he describes?

Topics for Writing

1 Write a *This I Believe* essay of between 350 and 500 words expressing one of your core beliefs. When National Public Radio (NPR) revived the *This I Believe* series in 2005, it provided instructions to listeners who wanted to submit an essay for this series. NPR suggested that writers be able to name their beliefs in a sentence or two and that they use a story from their lives to "[t]ake your belief out of the ether and ground it in the events of your life." NPR further suggested that writers should focus on what they believe rather than what they do not believe, avoid editorializing, use "I" and avoid "we," and use language that they would be comfortable speaking aloud on the radio.

2 Discuss whether the study of science can or should contribute to an appreciation and feeling of the unfathomable and the spiritual.

3 Einstein's essay follows a simple structure. He begins with a discussion of specific ethical principles that he argues should affect people's behavior, then claims that society is harmed because people are not following these principles, and concludes with an argument to take specific action to improve society based on these principles. Choose an important principle that you believe would improve society if more people's behavior was guided by this principle and write an argument to persuade people to act according to this ideal.

ORGANIZING BELIEVERS ON THE WEB

The B'nai B'rith International, Christian Coalition of America, and the National Council of Churches are three of the most influential religious organizations in the United States. Although influencing political policies is not their only mission, lobbyists for these associations, influence all levels of government to affect their political and social policies. Their Web sites seek to introduce outsiders to their organizations, recruit new members and contributions, inform readers about their activities and accomplishments, keep readers abreast of news that is important to their missions, and persuade readers on various religious and social positions—often to act on these positions. B'nai B'rith International is an important organization that supports Jewish causes and organizations and fights anti-Semitism. The Christian Coalition of America is a conservative political association of Christians. The National Council of Churches is an association of 36 Christian churches or denominations that usually supports liberal political positions. The Web sites here are the home page of the B'nai B'rith International Web site and the mission statements from the Web sites of the Christian Coalition of America and the National Council of Churches.

The Web site of B'nai B'rith International

The Web site of the Christian Coalition of America

Navigation:
- HOME
- ABOUT US
- MEMBERS/LOG IN
- ISSUES
- GET INVOLVED
- VOTER EDUCATION
- ACTION ALERTS
- NEWS
- COMMENTARY
- PHOTO ARCHIVES
- NEWSLETTER
- PRESS ROOM
- ONLINE STORE

Search: [ ] Go

See what's happening in the U.S. Congress — SENATE HOUSE

About Us

Thank you for visiting the Christian Coalition of America's website. You have come to the home of the largest and most active conservative grassroots political organization in America. The Christian Coalition of America offers people of faith the vehicle to be actively involved in shaping their government - from the County Courthouse to the halls of Congress.

Today, Americans are bombarded with countless political messages from across the ideological spectrum. Because of this, it is becoming increasingly difficult to separate truth from fiction and right from wrong. The Christian Coalition of America is committed to representing the pro-family agenda and educating America on the critical issues facing our society. Whether it is the fight to end Partial Birth Abortion or efforts to improve education or lower the family's tax burden, the Christian Coalition stands ready and able to work for you.

Our hallmark work lies in voter education. Prior to the November election the Christian Coalition of America distributed a record 70 million voter guides throughout all 50 states. These non-partisan guides gave voters a clear understanding of where various candidates stood on the issues important to them. With this knowledge, millions of voters went to polls ready to make their voices heard.

Our efforts, however, do not stop with voter guides. We actively lobby Congress and the White House on numerous issues, hold grassroots training schools around the country, host events all around the country and in Washington that draw thousands of pro-family supporters from around the nation and organize community activists regarding issues facing their local government.

If you are interested in having a positive pro-family impact on your government, the Christian Coalition of America is your organization.

Please take some time to investigate the numerous resources this web site offers. Your involvement is paramount to our efforts. After deciding how you want to be involved, please contact us by letter, phone or email so we can send you the information you need to be successful.

In politics, every voice counts.

The Christian Coalition was founded in 1989 as a means towards helping to give Christians a voice in their government again. We represent a growing group of over 2 million people of faith all across America.

Sign up for our E-mail Newsletters!
[ ] Action Alerts and weekly newsletter
[ ] Daily news summary
Your Email: [ ] Subscribe

"Freedom is never more than one generation away from extinction." - Ronald Reagan

A Letter from Roberta Combs

Thank you for visiting the Christian Coalition web-site. Our organization is dedicated to defending America's Godly heritage by getting Christians involved in their government again.

Take time and visit all the areas of our site. You will find many useful tools that will help you to educate and activate Christians for effective political action at the local, state and national levels.

May God richly bless you and your family!

Roberta Combs, President

The Holyland Collection — Everything Christian — Home Decor Gam

The Web site of the National Council of Churches

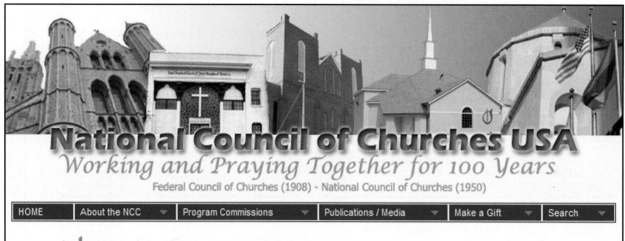

National Council of Churches USA
Working and Praying Together for 100 Years
Federal Council of Churches (1908) - National Council of Churches (1950)

HOME	About the NCC ▼	Program Commissions ▼	Publications / Media ▼	Make a Gift ▼	Search ▼

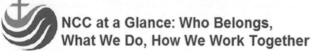

NCC at a Glance: Who Belongs, What We Do, How We Work Together

Since its founding in 1950, the National Council of the Churches of Christ in the USA has been the leading force for ecumenical cooperation among Christians in the United States. The NCC's member faith groups — from a wide spectrum of Protestant, Anglican, Orthodox, Evangelical, historic African American and Living Peace churches — include 45 million persons in more than 100,000 local congregations in communities across the nation. Click a topic below or scroll down to find details.

- Statement of Faith
- Member Communions
- General Assembly and Governing Board
- Program Commissions

- Scholarship and Publication
- Humanitarian and Public Policy Initiatives
- A Partnership Among People of Faith
- Other Information about the Council

Statement of Faith

"The National Council of Churches is a community of Christian communions, which, in response to the gospel as revealed in the Scriptures, confess Jesus Christ, the incarnate Word of God, as Savior and Lord. These communions covenant with one another to manifest ever more fully the unity of the Church.

Relying upon the transforming power of the Holy Spirit, the communions come together as the Council in common mission, serving in all creation to the glory of God."

--from the Preamble to the NCC Constitution.

This general statement is accepted by all of the NCC's member communions (also called churches, conventions and denominations), which as Christian bodies hold these and many other beliefs in common. Each of the member communions also has a unique heritage, including teachings and practices that differ from those of other members.

As they gather in the Council, the member communions **grow** in understanding of each other's traditions. They work to identify and fully **claim** those areas of belief they hold in

Journal and Discussion Questions

1 What do you learn about each organization from these Web sites? What is the purpose of each organization? Who probably belongs to these associations? What does each association stand for? What do the three associations have in common? How are they different?

2 Identify the key words or "buzz words" in each Web site, both "god terms," such as "pro-family," "diversity," and "human rights," and "devil terms," such as "anti-Christian bigotry" and "anti-Semitism." Compare the terms that you select from each Web site. What do these terms mean? What makes them powerful words for these organizations?

3 How do the photographs, other visual images, and the visual design of each Web site contribute to each organization's message?

4 Describe how each Web site is organized. What are the different parts of the Web site? What are the different sections of the written texts? What do you immediately see and read? Why do you think each association chose this organization for the Web site?

5 Compare how each webpage presents its organization and tries to persuade readers to join the organization and support its positions. What kinds of arguments, evidence, and logical and emotional appeals appear in the Web site? How does the organization establish its credibility and construct its image? Which Web site is designed and written the most effectively of the three? Which is the least effective?

6 What roles do religion and religious faith have in deciding social and political debates, as indicated by these three organizations? What kinds of issues do the organizations address? What kinds of issues do they seem to ignore? How do you account for the different political beliefs of the two Christian organizations here, the Christian Coalition of America and the National Council of Churches?

7 What do the Web sites suggest about the role of the Internet in spreading religious and political messages and in increasing and organizing the membership of religious organizations? Compare the strengths and weaknesses of religion's use of the Internet compared to other ways of spreading the word, for example, church activities, sermons, print media, television, radio, and home visits.

Topics for Writing

1 Read more of the Web sites of B'nai B'rith International, the Christian Coalition of America, and the National Council of Churches, and compare and contrast how the organizations try to influence social and political policies in the U.S.

2 Conduct research about one of these organizations or another religious group that engages in political lobbying, including outside analysis and criticism of the organization. Write an essay evaluating the mission of the organization and its methods of achieving its goals.

3 Write a research paper analyzing the functions of various technologies and modern media for churches and other religious or spiritual movements and organizations.

4 Write a research paper analyzing the role that organized religion has had or is having on a particular political issue. Argue what influence on government policy religious organizations should or should not have.

Suggestions for Essays on FAITH AND RELIGION

1 Compare the different ways that a religion or belief system guides people's lives in at least two of the following selections: Bartlett, Gavin, Perl, Winterowd, Dubus, Helminski, Eastman, and Einstein.

2 Compare how Perl, Winterowd, and Dubus work out for themselves what they believe spiritually and how they should act morally.

3 Analyze the conflicts caused by religious differences and the ability of people to overcome these differences in at least two of the following selections: Gavin, Perl, Dillard, Helminski, Eastman, and the three Web sites in this chapter.

4 Discuss how religion influences and is influenced by the culture around it in at least two of the following selections: Bartlett, Gavin, Perl, and Eastman.

5 Argue what place, if any, religious expression might have in public educational programs, considering at least two of the following selections: Bartlett, Gavin, Perl, and Dillard.

6 Argue what role religious faith should have in determining public policies considering Eastman, Einstein, and the three Web sites in this chapter. For this argument, you may focus on a specific policy issue.

07 Language

A NUMBER OF YEARS AGO, ONE OF the television networks aired—and quickly cancelled—a situation comedy about a married couple who switched bodies because of a magic spell. Forced to disguise what had happened, they had to live each other's lives and take on each other's jobs as a sportswriter and an executive in a cosmetics company. Both were lost at first. To the sportswriter, all lipsticks were red, while to the cosmetics company executive, football teams moved downfield in chaotic, mysterious ways. The sportswriter didn't begin to see different shades of red until he began to learn the nuanced language of color in cosmetics, while the cosmetics executive could not really see what was happening in a football game until she started to learn the names of plays and positions. Their new languages enabled them to see what they had not seen and to understand, analyze, and critique what they saw. In addition, the cursed couple quickly realized that they needed to learn the languages of their workplaces not only to do their jobs but to also fit in with others where they worked—to become part of the group.

College students experience the problems of learning new ways of speaking, writing, and thinking in every class they take. Introductory courses in every field begin by teaching students the basic terms and definitions of the discipline, because we can't separate learning how to think and see the world as a historian or a biologist from learning how to talk and write as a historian or a biologist. As you take more advanced courses, especially in your major, you learn more and more how to "talk the talk" of the field. Something similar usually occurs in the social lives of college students because each group of friends that you join or help to form develops its own special language, with its own perspectives about people and the world.

Partly because language is the stuff that writers work with, they often write about language issues. A writer interested in language might try to describe the language of an ethnic group, a profession, or another group by identifying their dialects, slang, and specialized phrases and vocabularies and how they use their language to create identities, strengthen relationships, express emotions, and get things done. Another writer may be interested in how language changes in response to changes in the culture, for example, how text messaging on cell phones is changing how people write or how past British colonization of India and recent immigration of Indians to the United Kingdom have given rise to a blending of the languages of English and Hindi (called "Hinglish"). While some writers are interested in describing and understanding the language, images, and body language that different people use to communicate in different situations, other writers are more interested in figuring out ways to improve how people make use of their language to communicate, persuade, entertain, and get things done in the world. Other writers want to explore how language is intertwined with people's values, beliefs, self-images, and prejudices and how people's language can bring people together or keep them apart (and often both at the same time).

And, of course, people argue about language. People are often critical of the ways that other people use language. They argue for and against changes in people's use of language, in their attitudes toward people who speak and write differently than they do, and in all kinds of policies that involve language. Should English be declared the official language of the United States? Should schools offer bilingual education programs for students who do not speak English? Should governments offer election ballots in Spanish for Spanish-speaking voters? Should college campuses have rules against hate speech? Should college students have to take foreign language courses as a graduation requirement? Should schools do more to promote the knowledge of American Sign Language for the general population? Are words like *chairman* and *fireman* sexist? Should publications use gender-neutral terms, such as *chairperson* and *firefighter* instead? Should laws and contracts be written in plain language that is more accessible to the general public? Should television and radio stations be heavily fined if they broadcast offensive words? Do current regulations of the language in commercials and advertising do enough to discourage false and misleading claims? People even argue about George W. Bush's pronunciation of *Iraq* and *nuclear* and whether it indicates anything about his knowledge and intelligence and whether his pronunciation helped him appeal to specific segments of the population.

Here are a few general questions to consider as you read the selections about language in this chapter and use your language knowledge to discuss and write about language issues.

- How does one's language affect how a person sees the world and how he or she thinks and feels?

- Why do groups (families, people in the same profession, computer "geeks," youth groups, sports fans, college writing teachers, etc.) tend to develop their own languages, including slang, shorthand expressions, and acronyms, nicknames, and specialized jargon? What purposes do their particular ways of speaking serve?

- Do men and women use language differently? If so, how and why?

- How does language figure in political debates about specific issues (e.g., abortion, taxes, same-sex marriage)? How does the language of people on one side of the issue differ from the language of their opponents? What causes these differences?

- How do people tailor their languages for different audiences, especially when they are trying to persuade people? How should you decide whether the language that they are using is fair or unethical, accurate or misleading?

- Is censorship justified with some words that people find offensive? Why or why not?

Invitations for Journal Writing

1 How do you adjust how you talk with different people in different situations? Why do you make these adjustments?

2 Compare the way people write and talk (including body language) in two different groups that you have associated with (e.g., family, school, church, workplace, a club, or sports team).

INVISIBLE TECHNOLOGIES

BY NEIL POSTMAN

Neil Postman (1931–2003) was a critic of media and culture and a scholar and teacher of communications at New York University for more than forty years. His writings often take controversial stands and make dire predictions about communication technology and education in books addressed to general audiences, such as *Amusing Ourselves to Death*, *Teaching as a Subversive Activity*, and *The Disappearance of Childhood*, and essays in magazines such as *Atlantic*, *Harper's*, *Time*, and *The New York Times Magazine*. "Invisible Technologies" is a selection from his 1993 book *Technopoly: The Surrender of Culture to Technology*. Postman defines "technopoly" as a state of both mind and culture that is changing the social order; subverting democracy, religion, privacy, and other human rights; and undermining traditional beliefs by creating a "culture that seeks its authorization in technology, finds its satisfactions in technology, and takes its orders from technology." In "Invisible Technologies," Postman argues that language is a technology and an ideology that guides how we think—and what we don't think about. Several of Postman's essays and interviews can be found at www.bigbrother.net/~mugwump/Postman/.

I F WE DEFINE IDEOLOGY AS A SET OF assumptions of which we are barely conscious but which nonetheless directs our efforts to give shape and coherence to the world, then our most powerful ideological instrument is the technology of language itself. Language is pure ideology. It instructs us not only in the names of things but, more important, in what things can be named. It divides the world into subjects and objects. It denotes what events shall be regarded as processes, and what events, things. It instructs us about time, space, and number, and forms our ideas of how we stand in relation to nature and to each other. In English grammar, for example, there are always subjects who act, and verbs which are their actions, and objects which are acted upon. It is a rather aggressive grammar, which makes it difficult for those of us who must use it to think of the world as benign. We are obliged to know the world as made up of things pushing against, and often attacking, one another.

Of course, most of us, most of the time, are unaware of how language does its work. We live deep within the boundaries of our linguistic assumptions and have little sense of how the world looks to those who speak a vastly different tongue. We tend to assume that everyone sees the world in the same way, irrespective of differences in language. Only occasionally is this illusion challenged, as when the differences between linguistic ideologies become noticeable by one who has command over two languages that differ greatly in their structure and history. For example, several years ago, Susumu Tonegawa, winner of the 1987 Nobel Prize in Medicine, was quoted in the newspaper *Yomiuri* as saying that the Japanese language does not foster clarity or effective understanding in scientific research. Addressing his countrymen from his post as a professor at MIT in Cambridge, Massachusetts, he said, "We should consider changing our thinking process in the field of science by trying to reason in English." It should be noted that he was not saying that English is better than Japanese; only that English is better than Japanese for the purposes of scientific research, which is a way of saying that English (and other Western languages) have a particular ideological bias that Japanese does not. We call that ideological bias "the scientific outlook." If the scientific outlook seems natural to you, as it does to me, it is because our language makes it appear so. What we think of as reasoning is determined by the character of our language. To reason in Japanese is apparently not the same thing as to reason in English or Italian or German.

To put it simply, like any important piece of machinery—television or the computer, for example—language has an ideological agenda that is apt to be hidden from view. In the case of language, that agenda is so deeply integrated into our personalities and world-view that a special effort and, often, special training are required to detect its presence. Unlike television or the computer, language appears to be not an extension of our powers but simply a natural expression of who and what we are. This is the great secret of language: Because it comes from inside us, we believe it to be a direct, unedited, unbiased, apolitical expression of how the world really is. A machine, on the other hand, is outside of us, clearly created by us, modifiable by us, even discardable by us; it is easier to see how a machine re-creates the world in its own image. But in many respects, a sentence functions very much like a machine, and this is nowhere more obvious than in the sentences we call questions.

> ## "
> To put it simply, like any important piece of machinery—television or the computer, for example—language has an ideological agenda that is apt to be hidden from view.
> ""

As an example of what I mean, let us take a "fill-in" question, which I shall require you to answer exactly if you wish full credit:

Thomas Jefferson died in the year _____.

Suppose we now rephrase the question in multiple-choice form:

Thomas Jefferson died in the year (a) 1788 (b) 1826 (c) 1926 (d) 1809

Which of these two questions is easier to answer? I assume you will agree with me that the second question is easier unless you happen to know precisely the year of Jefferson's death, in which case neither question is difficult. However, for most of us who know only roughly when Jefferson lived, Question Two has arranged matters so that our chances of "knowing" the answer are greatly increased. Students will always be "smarter" when answering a multiple-choice test than when answering a "fill-in" test, even when the subject matter is the same. A question, even of the simplest kind, is not and can never be unbiased. I am not, in this context, referring to the common accusation that a particular test is "culturally biased." Of course questions can be culturally biased. (Why, for example, should anyone be asked about Thomas Jefferson at all, let alone when he died?) My purpose is to say that the structure of any question is as devoid of neutrality as is its content. The form of a question may ease our

way or pose obstacles. Or, when even slightly altered, it may generate antithetical answers, as in the case of the two priests who, being unsure if it was permissible to smoke and pray at the same time, wrote to the Pope for a definitive answer. One priest phrased the question "Is it permissible to smoke while praying?" and was told it is not, since prayer should be the focus of one's whole attention; the other priest asked if it is permissible to pray while smoking and was told that it is, since it is always appropriate to pray. The form of a question may even block us from seeing solutions to problems that become visible through a different question. Consider the following story, whose authenticity is questionable but not, I think, its point:

Once upon a time, in a village in what is now Lithuania, there arose an unusual problem. A curious disease afflicted many of the townspeople. It was mostly fatal (though not always), and its onset was signaled by the victim's lapsing into a deathlike coma. Medical science not being quite so advanced as it is now, there was no definite way of knowing if the victim was actually dead when burial appeared seemly. As a result, the townspeople feared that several of their relatives had already been buried alive and that a similar fate might await them. How to overcome this uncertainty was their dilemma.

One group of people suggested that the coffins be well stocked with water and food and that a small air vent be drilled into them, just in case one of the "dead" happened to be alive. This was expensive to do but seemed more than worth the trouble. A second group, however, came up with a less expensive and more efficient idea. Each coffin would have a twelve-inch stake affixed to the inside of the coffin lid, exactly at the level of the heart. Then, when the coffin was closed, all uncertainty would cease.

The story does not indicate which solution was chosen, but for my purposes the choice is irrelevant. What is important to note is that different solutions were generated by different questions. The first solution was an answer to the question, How can we make sure that we do not bury people who are still alive? The second was an answer to the question, How can we make sure that everyone we bury is dead?

Questions, then, are like computers or television or stethoscopes or lie detectors, in that they are mechanisms that give direction to our thoughts, generate new ideas, venerate old ones, expose facts, or hide them.

Journal and Discussion Questions

1 What is the thesis of "Invisible Technologies"? How does Neil Postman explain and support his thesis?

2 What is the meaning of the title, "Invisible Technologies"? How does Postman define *ideology* and *technology*? What does he mean when he says that language is an "ideology" and a "technology"? What reasons and evidence support this claim?

3 Outline "Invisible Technologies." How does the organization of the essay support Postman's argument? Will it persuade readers who might find it hard to think of language as a technology?

4 Where does Postman discuss opposing ideas about language? Summarize these opposing ideas. How does Postman respond to these objections?

5 By defining language as a technology and an ideology, Postman is also arguing that all technologies are ideologies. No technology is neutral. All technologies shape and reflect how we view the world and ourselves. Why does Postman believe this about technology? What reasons support the idea that technologies are neutral? How does technology affect how we think and live? Why?

6 What benefits and problems does Postman see in the power that language has over our thoughts and actions? Why is it important for us to recognize that language is a technology?

7 Why does Postman conclude his discussion of language by focusing on the biases of questions? What does Postman's discussion of questions imply about school exams, opinion polls, and the role of questioning in people's reading and writing processes?

Topics for Writing

1 Examine other ways in which language shapes the ways that we think and believe. You may want to focus on a specific issue or subject area, such as how language determines how we think and what we know and believe about education, business, sports, or another subject. You may want to look at several articles or editorials that take opposing views on your subject.

2 Because of the influence of language on people's thoughts and attitudes, individuals and organizations often call for language reforms, for example, to reduce or eliminate sexism or to fight government and advertising propaganda and "doublespeak." The term *political correctness* was coined by opponents of some of these reforms, who are often disturbed by the thinking and attitudes behind the "reformed" language that others promote. Research both sides of one of these arguments about language, such as sexist language, and write a research paper arguing your position on the issue.

3 In *Technopoly*, Postman argues that the number zero, business management, IQ exams, high school and college courses, and political polls are all "invisible technologies." Write a research paper that explains and evaluates the effects that one of these invisible technologies has on society or that makes an argument that something else is an invisible technology.

IF IT'S ORWELLIAN,
IT'S PROBABLY NOT

BY GEOFFREY NUNBERG

Geoffrey Nunberg (1945–) is a linguistics scholar at the University of California at Berkeley's School of Information and at Stanford University's Center for the Study of Language and Information, and he chairs the Usage Panel of the *American Heritage Dictionary*. Nunberg writes frequent informal essays about the English language for general audiences for the National Public Radio show *Fresh Air* and for newspapers such as the *New York Times*, the *Los Angeles Times*, the *San Francisco Chronicle*, and the *San Jose Mercury News*. "If It's Orwellian, It's Probably Not," was first published in the *New York Times* on June 22, 2003, and was reprinted in Nunberg's 2004 collection of essays *Going Nucular: Language, Politics, and Culture in Confrontational Times*. In this essay, Nunberg explores what people today mean by the word *Orwellian* and why. As he does so, he comments on George Orwell's "Politics and the English Language" and his concept of Newspeak and disagrees with some of Orwell's ideas about language. More information about Nunberg can be found at his Web site, www.ischool.berkeley.edu/~nunberg/.

ON GEORGE ORWELL'S CENTENARY— he was born on June 25, 1903—the most telling sign of his influence is the words he left us with: not just *thought police, doublethink,* and *unperson,* but also *Orwellian* itself, the most widely used adjective derived from the name of a modern writer. In the press and on the Internet, it's more common than *Kafkaesque, Hemingwayesque,* and *Dickensian* put together. It even noses out the rival political reproach *Machiavellian,* which had a 500-year head start.

Eponyms are always the narrowest sort of tribute, though. *Orwellian* doesn't have anything to do with Orwell as a socialist thinker, or for that matter, as a human being. People are always talking about Orwell's decency, but "Orwellian decency" would be an odd phrase indeed. And *Orwellian* commemorates Orwell the writer only for three of his best known works: the novels *Animal Farm* and *1984* and the essay "Politics and the English Language." The adjective reduces Orwell's palette to a single shade of noir. It brings to mind only sordid regimes of surveillance and thought control and the distortions of language that make them possible.

Orwell's views on language will probably outlive his political ideas. At least they seem to require no updating or apology, whereas his partisans feel the need to justify the continuing relevance of his politics. Yet Orwell was scarcely the first writer to protest against political euphemism. More than 150 years earlier, Edmund Burke sounded a very Orwellian note in his attacks on the apologists for the French Revolution who tried to extenuate the September Massacres of 1792: "The whole compass of the language is tried to find sinonimies and circumlocutions for massacre and murder. Things are never called by their common names. Massacre is sometimes *agitation,* sometimes *effervescence,* sometimes *excess;* sometimes too continued an exercise of *a revolutionary power.*"

But it was Orwell who popularized the modern picture of language as the active accomplice of power, whether by concealing its abuses or, as with Newspeak, by making dissent literally unthinkable. In "Politics and the English Language," he wrote that "Political language . . . is designed to make lies sound truthful and murder respectable," and spoke of "words that fall upon the facts like soft snow, blurring the outlines and covering up all the details."

That was an appealing notion to an age that had learned to be suspicious of ideologies, and critics on all sides have found it useful to cite "Politics and the English Language" in condemning the equivocations of their opponents. Critics on the left hear Orwellian resonances in phrases like "weapons of mass protection," or in names like the Patriot Act or the Homeland Security Department's Operation Liberty Shield, which authorizes indefinite detention of asylum-seekers from certain nations. Critics on the right hear them in phrases like "reproductive health services," "Office of Equality Assurance," and "English Plus," for bilingual education. And just about everyone discerned an Orwellian note in the name of the Pentagon's Total Information Awareness project, which was aimed at mining a vast centralized database of personal information for patterns that might reveal terrorist activities. (The name was finally changed to the Terrorist Information Awareness program, in an effort to reassure Americans who have nothing to hide.)

> " Political language is still something to be wary of, but it doesn't work as Orwell feared. "

Of course, where one side sees deceptive packaging, the other is likely to see only effective branding. But there's something troubling in the easy use of the label *Orwellian*, as if these phrases committed the same sorts of linguistic abuses that led to the gulags and the death camps. In fact the specters that *Orwellian* conjures aren't really the ones we have to worry about. Newspeak may have been a plausible invention in 1948, when totalitarian thought control still seemed an imminent possibility. But the collapse of Communism revealed the bankruptcy not just of the Stalinist social experiment, but of its linguistic experiments as well. After seventy-five years of incessant propaganda, "socialist man" turned out to be a cynic who didn't even believe the train schedules.

Political language is still something to be wary of, but it doesn't work as Orwell feared. In fact the modern language of control is more effective than Soviet Newspeak precisely because it's less bleak and intimidating. Think of the way business has been re-engineering the language of ordinary interaction in the interest of creating "high-performance corporate cultures." To a reanimated Winston Smith, there would be something wholly familiar in being told that he had to file an annual "vision statement" or that he should henceforth eliminate "problems" from his vocabulary in favor of "issues." But the hero of *1984* would find the whole exercise much more convivial than the Two-Minute Hate at the Ministry of Truth. And he'd be astonished to see management condoning its employees' playing buzzword bingo and posting Dilbert strips on the walls of their cubicles.

For Orwell, the success of political jargon and euphemism required an uncritical or even unthinking audience: A "reduced state of consciousness," as he put it, was "favorable to political conformity." As things turned out, though, the political manipulation of language seems to thrive on the critical skepticism that Orwell encouraged. In fact, there has never been an age that was so well-schooled in the perils of deceptive language or in decoding political and commercial messages, as witness the official canonization of Orwell himself. Thanks to the schools, *1984* is probably the best-selling political novel of modern times (current Amazon sales rank: No. 93), and "Politics and the English Language" is the most widely read essay about the English language—and very likely in it as well.

But as advertisers have known for a long time, no audience is easier to beguile than one that is smugly confident of its own sophistication. The word *Orwellian* contributes to that impression. Like *propaganda*, it implies an aesthetic judgment more than a moral one. Calling an expression Orwellian means not that it's deceptive but that it's crudely deceptive.

Today, the real damage isn't done by the euphemisms and circumlocutions that we're likely to describe as Orwellian. *Ethnic cleansing, revenue enhancement, voluntary regulation, tree-density reduction, faith-based initiatives, extra affirmative action*—those terms may be oblique, but at least they wear their obliquity on their sleeves.

Rather, the words that do the most political work are simple ones—*jobs and growth, family values*, and *color-blind*, not to mention *life* and *choice*. Concrete words like these are the hardest ones to see through—they're opaque when you hold them up to the light. Orwell knew that, of course. "To see what is in front of one's nose needs a constant struggle." It's not what you'd call an Orwellian sentiment, but it's very like the man.

Journal and Discussion Questions

1 What is the thesis of "If It's Orwellian, It's Probably Not"? How does the title relate to this thesis?

2 What is an *eponym*? What is wrong with the way people use the eponym *Orwellian*, according to Nunberg? What does Nunberg mean when he writes, "Like *propaganda*, it [the word *Orwellian*] implies an aesthetic judgment more than a moral one. Calling an expression Orwellian means not that it's deceptive but that it's crudely deceptive"? How do the problems with the word *Orwellian* illustrate Nunberg's problem with eponyms in general?

3 Outline "If It's Orwellian, It's Probably Not." How is Nunberg's discussion of the eponym *Orwellian* in the first part of his essay related to his critique of Orwell's ideas about language and politics?

4 What is Nunberg's disagreement with "Politics and the English Language"? Why does he believe Orwell's ideas about language are less relevant for understanding the language of politics and advertising than they were in the 1940s? What is Nunberg's overall evaluation of the relevance of Orwell for people like him who want to understand how language influences and is used by politics and culture?

5 Why does Nunberg write, "But as advertisers have known for a long time, no audience is easier to beguile than one that is smugly confident of its own sophistication"? What examples and other evidence can you think of that might support this claim? What evidence can you think of that might dispute Nunberg's idea? Do you think Nunberg is right about this? Why or why not?

6 Nunberg's two-paragraph conclusion contrasts "Orwellian" words like "ethnic cleansing" and "tree-density reduction" to simple words like "color-blind" and "family values" that Nunberg says "do most of the political work" in today's society. What is Orwellian about the first list of words? What "political work" does the second list of words do? How are these two sets of words different? Why does Nunberg believe words like those in his second set are more important politically and "the hardest ones to see through"? Do you agree with Nunberg? Why or why not?

7 What sources did Nunberg use in his essay and why? Where do you think he came up with the words that he used as examples?

Topics for Writing

1 Analyze an important "simple" and "opaque" word or phrase as it is used in political discussions, like "jobs and growth," "life," or "choice."

2 Research less famous works written by George Orwell as well as biographies and criticism of Orwell's writings, and write a research paper that gives a more accurate picture of Orwell and his beliefs than the popular image of Orwell that Nunberg describes.

3 Explain the meaning of another eponym, such as *Darwinian, Homeric,* or *Lincolnesque.* You should find examples of sentences that include the word on the Internet or in electronic databases and analyze what the eponym means in those sentences as well as conduct research about the life and work of the person named by the eponym. Part of your essay should decide whether the meaning of the eponym oversimplifies or distorts people's image of the person.

4 Create an eponym from your last name (using a suffix, such as *-ian, -esque,* or *-ic*. Considering your personal qualities and reputation with friends and family, compose a definition for your eponym and explain how you determined its meaning.

THE GETTYSBURG POWERPOINT PRESENTATION

BY PETER NORVIG

Peter Norvig is the Director of Research at Google Inc., co-author of the textbook *Artificial Intelligence: A Modern Approach*, and a one-time head of the Computational Sciences Division at NASA. He has a Ph.D. in computer science from the University of California, Berkeley, and he was a professor of computer science there and at the University of Southern California. "The Gettysburg PowerPoint Presentation" is a parody of Abraham Lincoln's Gettysburg Address, re-imagining Lincoln delivering the Gettysburg Address with slides prepared in PowerPoint. Like many critics today, Norvig believes that PowerPoint is responsible for a decline in public speaking. People often use PowerPoint slides to outline their lectures, but their lectures often consist mainly of reading the words on the slides (and then giving the audience photocopies of the slides to take home). Norvig uses satire to make his argument about the harm PowerPoint has had on public speaking and business presentations. More information about Norvig can be found at his Web site, norvig.com, including a link to the world's longest palindromic sentence, which he created with a computer program that he wrote.

The Gettysburg Powerpoint Presentation

11/19/1863

And now please welcome President Abraham Lincoln.

Good morning. Just a second while I get this connection to work. Do I press this button here? Function-F7? No, that's not right. Hmmm. Maybe I'll have to reboot. Hold on a minute. Um, my name is Abe Lincoln and I'm your president. While we're waiting, I want to thank Judge David Wills, chairman of the committee supervising the dedication of the Gettysburg cemetery. It's great to be here, Dave, and you and the committee are doing a great job. Gee, sometimes this new **technology** does have glitches, but **we couldn't live without it, could we?** Oh - is it ready? OK, here we go:

Click here to start

Table of Contents

Gettysburg Cemetery Dedication

Agenda

Not on Agenda!

Review of Key Objectives & Critical Success Factors

Organizational Overview

Summary

Speaker Notes

Author: Abraham Lincoln

Email: president@whitehouse.gov

Home Page: http://www.whitehouse.gov

Download presentation: Gettysburg.ppt

This presentation prepared with the help of Microsoft Powerpoint Autocontent Wizard. Where could we go without it?

Peter Norvig -- See **the making of** the presentation and a related essay. -- Permission is granted to use this presentation in any course or educational presentation.

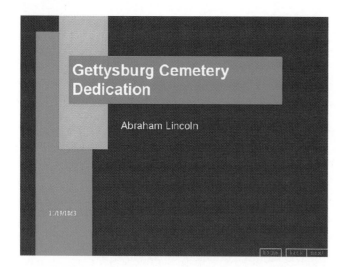

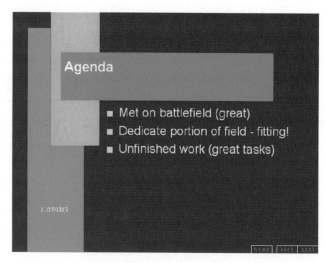

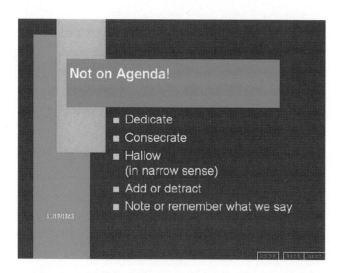

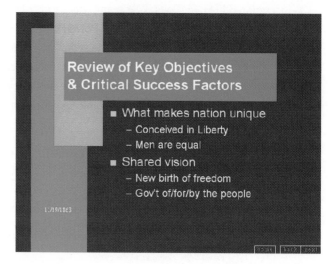

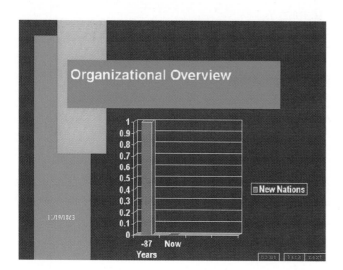

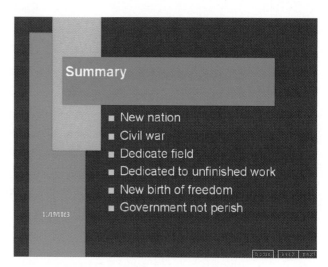

SPEAKER NOTES

[Transcribed from voice recording by A. Lincoln, 11/18/1863]

These are some notes on the Gettysburg meeting. I'll whip them into better shape when I can get on to my computer.

Four score and seven years ago our fathers brought forth on this continent a new nation, conceived in liberty and dedicated to the proposition that all men are created equal. Now we are engaged in a great civil war, testing whether that nation or any nation so conceived and so dedicated can long endure. We are met on a great battlefield of that war. We have come to dedicate a portion of that field as a final resting-place for those who here gave their lives that that nation might live. It is altogether fitting and proper that we should do this. But in a larger sense, we cannot dedicate, we cannot consecrate, we cannot hallow this ground. The brave men, living and dead who struggled here have consecrated it far above our poor power to add or detract. The world will little note nor long remember what we say here, but it can never forget what they did here. It is for us the living rather to be dedicated here to the unfinished work which they who fought here have thus far so nobly advanced. It is rather for us to be here dedicated to the great task remaining before us—that from these honored dead we take increased devotion to that cause for which they gave the last full measure of devotion—that we here highly resolve that these dead shall not have died in vain, that this nation under God shall have a new birth of freedom, and that government of the people, by the people, for the people shall not perish from the earth.

Journal and Discussion Questions

1 Why do you think Peter Norvig chose the Gettysburg Address for his PowerPoint parody?

2 How well does the PowerPoint presentation summarize the Gettysburg Address, which appears as "Speaker Notes" at the end of Norvig's parody? What is accurate about the presentation? What from the original address gets left out of the presentation? What does the PowerPoint presentation get wrong in trying to summarize the Gettysburg Address? What ideas are changed or distorted?

3 Compare the diction, tone, and emotional power of the language in the Gettysburg Address with that of the Gettysburg PowerPoint Presentation. What is wrong with the diction of the PowerPoint presentation?

4 What criticisms about PowerPoint presentations are implied in some of the details of the Gettysburg PowerPoint Presentation, such as Lincoln's remarks after his introduction, the table of contents on the first screen, and the Organizational Overview bar graph in slide 5?

5 What image do you have of the Abraham Lincoln who gives the PowerPoint presentation? How would you compare the character of the speaker of the Gettysburg Address with the character of the presenter of the Gettysburg PowerPoint Presentation?

6 What point is Norvig making when he writes, "This presentation prepared with the help of Microsoft PowerPoint Autocontent Wizard. Where could we go without it?" Summarize the criticisms about PowerPoint presentations and business jargon implied in the Gettysburg PowerPoint Presentation. Do you think his criticisms are fair? Why or why not?

Topics for Writing

1 Analyze Peter Norvig's "The Gettysburg PowerPoint Presentation," comparing it with the Gettysburg Address and discussing what criticisms Norvig is making about public speaking today with his parody.

2 Attack or defend the use of PowerPoint in public speaking, or write an argument that advises readers about what they should or should not do if they are giving a public presentation using PowerPoint.

3 Choose another selection in this book and design your own humorous PowerPoint version of the selection.

NON SEQUITUR

BY WILEY MILLER

Non Sequitur is an award-winning daily comic strip by Wiley Miller (1951–) that is syndicated in more than 700 newspapers. Miller's strip and his award-winning editorial cartoons are characterized by Miller's close observations and appreciation of the absurdities of everyday life in modern culture. The name *Non Sequitur* is taken from a Latin term for a logical fallacy, meaning "it does not follow." This strip was originally published July 18, 2006. In it Wiley has fun with the language of text messaging while commenting on how electronic communication may be affecting face-to-face conversation.

Journal and Discussion Questions

1 What observations is Wiley Miller making in his strip about the effects of cell phone text messaging on society and family life? How does Miller use drawings and words to make these observations?

2 How is text messaging affecting how people carry on conversations, according to *Non Sequitur*? Why do the daughters disagree with their father's claim, "Text messaging isn't a real conversation"? What is a "real conversation" for the father? For the daughters?

3 Why are there no dialogue bubbles in the middle two panels of this strip? Why does Miller fill the air in the second panel with versions of the word *click* and show the father and daughters staring at each other in the third panel?

4 What side of this disagreement does Miller appear to sympathize with more? Why?

5 Compare the daughters' language (tone, pace, vocabulary, etc.) in the last panel with the father's language in the first panel. What effect is text messaging having on language, as implied in this strip? Does Miller appear to be critical of these language changes? Why or why not?

6 Is this strip funny? Why or why not?

Topics for Writing

1 Analyze the ideas about language and conversation in this *Non Sequitur* strip.

2 Compare text messaging conversations with face-to-face conversations. What is gained and lost by conversing with text messages?

3 Write a research paper on the language of text messaging on cell phones, considering questions such as how words and phrases are abbreviated, what text messaging is used for, and what benefits and problems are associated with this new technology.

4 According to a number of cultural critics, technology like televisions and computers brings people together in some ways while isolating them in other. Pick a single technology, such as cell phones, and write a research paper about the effect that this technology is having on communication and community.

A HOMEMADE EDUCATION

BY MALCOLM X

Malcolm X (1925–1965) changed his name from Malcolm Little when he converted to Islam and became a follower of Elijah Muhammed while serving a prison sentence as a young man. After his release, he became a minister of the Nation of Islam under Muhammed. A powerful, inspiring public speaker and writer, Malcolm X soon became one of the most influential and controversial national and international leaders of the civil rights movement. "A Homemade Education" is taken from *The Autobiography of Malcolm X* (1965), which Malcolm X wrote with Alex Haley and completed shortly before he was assassinated. Malcolm X intended his *Autobiography* to be more than a record of his life but to promote the political, religious, and educational purposes of his life as a minister and civil rights leader. In "A Homemade Education," he describes how he educated himself in prison and the political purposes and discoveries of his language education.

IT WAS BECAUSE OF MY LETTERS that I happened to stumble upon starting to acquire some kind of a homemade education.

I became increasingly frustrated at not being able to express what I wanted to convey in letters that I wrote, especially those to Mr. Elijah Muhammad. In the street, I had been the most articulate hustler out there—I had commanded attention when I said something. But now, trying to write simple English, I not only wasn't articulate, I wasn't even functional. How would I sound writing in slang, the way I would say it, something such as, "Look, daddy, let me pull your coat about a cat, Elijah Muhammad—"

Many who today hear me somewhere in person, or on television, or those who read something I've said, will think I went to school far beyond the eighth grade. This impression is due entirely to my prison studies.

It had really begun back in the Charlestown Prison, when Bimbi first made me feel envy of his stock of knowledge. Bimbi had always taken charge of any conversations he was in, and I had tried to emulate him. But every book I picked up had few sentences which didn't contain anywhere from one to nearly all of the words that might as well have been in Chinese. When I just skipped those words, of course, I really ended up with little idea of what the book said. So I had come to the Norfolk Prison Colony still going through only book-reading motions. Pretty soon, I would have quit even these motions, unless I had received the motivation that I did.

I saw that the best thing I could do was get hold of a dictionary—to study, to learn some words. I was lucky enough to reason also that I should try to improve my penmanship. It was sad. I couldn't even write in a straight line. It was both ideas together that moved me to request a dictionary along with some tablets and pencils from the Norfolk Prison Colony school.

I spent two days just riffling uncertainly through the dictionary's pages. I'd never realized so many words existed! I didn't know which words I needed to learn. Finally, just to start some kind of action, I began copying.

In my slow, painstaking, ragged handwriting, I copied into my tablet everything printed on that first page, down to the punctuation marks.

I believe it took me a day. Then, aloud, I read back, to myself, everything I'd written on the tablet. Over and over, aloud, to myself, I read my own handwriting.

I woke up the next morning, thinking about those words—immensely proud to realize that not only had I written so much at one time, but I'd written words that I never knew were in the world. Moreover, with a little effort, I also could remember what many of these words meant. I reviewed the words whose meanings I didn't remember. Funny thing, from the dictionary first page right now, that "aardvark" springs to my mind. The dictionary had a picture of it, a long-tailed, long-eared, burrowing African mammal, which lives off termites caught by sticking out its tongue as an anteater does for ants.

I was so fascinated that I went on—I copied the dictionary's next page. And the same experience came when I studied that. With every succeeding page, I also learned of people and places and events from history. Actually the dictionary is like a miniature encyclopedia. Finally the dictionary's A section had filled a whole tablet—and I went on into the B's. That was the way I started copying what eventually became the entire dictionary. It went a lot faster after so much practice helped me to pick up handwriting speed. Between what I wrote in my tablet, and writing letters, during the rest of my time in prison I would guess I wrote a million words.

I suppose it was inevitable that as my word-base broadened, I could for the first time pick up a book and read and now begin to understand what the book was saying. Anyone who has read a great deal can imagine the new world that opened. Let me tell you something: from then until I left that prison, in every free moment I had, if I was not reading in the library, I was reading on my bunk. You couldn't have gotten me out of books with a wedge. Between Mr. Muhammad's teachings, my correspondence, my visitors—usually Ella and Reginald—and my reading of books, months passed without my even thinking about being imprisoned. In fact, up to then, I never had been so truly free in my life.

The Norfolk Prison Colony's library was in the school building. A variety of classes was taught there by instructors who came from such places as Harvard and Boston universities. The weekly debates between inmate teams were also held in the school building.

You would be astonished to know how worked up convict debaters and audiences would get over subjects like "Should Babies Be Fed Milk?"

Available on the prison library's shelves were books on just about every general subject. Much of the big private collection that Parkhurst had willed to the prison was still in crates and boxes in the back of the library—thousands of old books. Some of them looked ancient: covers faded; old-time parchment-looking binding, Parkhurst, I've mentioned, seemed to have been principally interested in history and religion. He had the money and the special interest to have a lot of books that you wouldn't have in general circulation. Any college library would have been lucky to get that collection.

As you can imagine, especially in a prison where there was heavy emphasis on rehabilitation, an inmate was smiled upon if he demonstrated an unusually intense interest in books. There was a sizable number of well-read inmates, especially the popular debaters. Some were said by many to be practically walking encyclopedias. They were almost celebrities. No university would ask any student to devour literature as I did when this new world opened to me, of being able to read and understand.

I read more in my room than in the library itself. An inmate who was known to read a lot could check out more than the permitted maximum number of books. I preferred reading in the total isolation of my own room.

When I had progressed to really serious reading, every night at about ten P.M. I would be outraged with the "lights out." It always seemed to catch me right in the middle of something engrossing.

Fortunately, right outside my door was a corridor light that cast a glow into my room. The glow was enough to read by, once my eyes adjusted to it. So when "lights out" came, I would sit on the floor where I could continue reading in that glow.

At one-hour intervals the night guards paced past every room. Each time I heard the approaching footsteps, I jumped into bed and feigned sleep. And as soon as the guard passed, I got back out of bed onto the floor area of that light-glow, where I would read for another fifty-eight minutes—until the guard approached again. That went on until three or four every morning. Three or four hours of sleep a night was enough for me. Often in the years in the streets I had slept less than that.

The teachings of Mr. Muhammad stressed how history had been "whitened"—when white men had written history books, the black man simply had been

> ❝ No university would ask any student to devour literature as I did when this new world opened to me, of being able to read and understand. ❞

left out. Mr. Muhammad couldn't have said anything that would have struck me much harder. I had never forgotten how when my class, me and all of those whites, had studied seventh-grade United States history back in Mason, the history of the Negro had been covered in one paragraph, and the teacher had gotten a big laugh with his joke, "Negroes' feet are so big that when they walk, they leave a hole in the ground."

This is one reason why Mr. Muhammad's teachings spread so swiftly all over the United States, among *all* Negroes, whether or not they became followers of Mr. Muhammad. The teachings ring true—to every Negro. You can hardly show me a black adult in America—or a white one, for that matter—who knows from the history books anything like the truth about the black man's role. In my own case, once I heard of the "glorious history of the black man," I took special pains to hunt in the library for books that would inform me on details about black history.

I can remember accurately the very first set of books that really impressed me. I have since bought that set of books and I have it at home for my children to read as they grow up. It's called *Wonders of the World*. It's full of pictures of archaeological finds, statues that depict, usually, non-European people.

I found books like Will Durant's *Story of Civilization*. I read H. G. Wells' *Outline of History*. *Souls of Black Folk* by W. E. B. Du Bois gave me a glimpse into the black people's history before they came to this country. Carter G. Woodson's *Negro History* opened my eyes about black empires before the black slave was brought to the United States, and the early Negro struggles for freedom.

J. A. Rogers' three volumes *of Sex and Race* told about race-mixing before Christ's time; about Aesop being a black man who told fables; about Egypt's Pharaohs; about the great Coptic Christian Empires; about Ethiopia, the earth's oldest continuous black civilization, as China is the oldest continuous civilization.

Mr. Muhammad's teaching about how the white man had been created led me to *Findings in Genetics* by Gregor Mendel. (The dictionary's G section was where I had learned what "genetics" meant.) I really

studied this book by the Austrian monk. Reading it over and over, especially certain sections, helped me to understand that if you started with a black man, a white man could be produced; but starting with a white man, you never could produce a black man—because the white gene is recessive. And since no one disputes that there was but one Original Man, the conclusion is clear.

During the last year or so, in the *New York Times*, Arnold Toynbee used the word "bleached" in describing the white man. (His words were: "White [i.e., bleached] human beings of North European origin. . . .") Toynbee also referred to the European geographic area as only a peninsula of Asia. He said there is no such thing as Europe. And if you look at the globe, you will see for yourself that America is only an extension of Asia. (But at the same time Toynbee is among those who have helped to bleach history. He won't write that again. Every day now, the truth is coming to light.)

I never will forget how shocked I was when I began reading about slavery's total horror. It made such an impact upon me that it later became one of my favorite subjects when I became a minister of Mr. Muhammad's. The world's most monstrous crime, the sin and the blood on the white man's hands, are almost impossible to believe. Books like the one by Frederick Olmstead opened my eyes to the horrors suffered when the slave was landed in the United States. The European woman, Fannie Kimball, who had married a Southern white slaveowner, described how human beings were degraded. Of course I read *Uncle Tom's Cabin*. In fact, I believe that's the only novel I have ever read since I started serious reading.

Parkhurst's collection also contained some bound pamphlets of the Abolitionist Anti-Slavery Society of New England. I read descriptions of atrocities, saw those illustrations of black slave women tied up and flogged with whips; of black mothers watching their babies being dragged off, never to be seen by their mothers again; of dogs after slaves, and of the fugitive slave catchers, evil white men with whips and clubs and chains and guns. I read about the slave preacher Nat Turner, who put the fear of God into the white slavemaster. Nat Turner wasn't going around preaching pie-in-the-sky and "nonviolent" freedom for the black man. There in Virginia one night in 1831, Nat and seven other slaves started out at his master's home and through the night they went from one plantation "big house" to the next, killing, until by the next morning fifty-seven white people were dead and Nat had about seventy slaves following him. White people, terrified for their lives, fled from their homes, locked themselves up in public buildings, hid in the woods, and some even left the state. A small army of soldiers took two months to catch and hang Nat Turner. Somewhere I have read where Nat Turner's example is said to have inspired John Brown to invade Virginia and attack Harper's Ferry nearly thirty years later, with thirteen white men and five Negroes.

I read Herodotus, "the father of History," or, rather, I read about him. And I read the histories of various nations, which opened my eyes gradually, then wider and wider, to how the whole world's white men had indeed acted like devils, pillaging and raping and bleeding and draining the whole world's non-white people. I remember, for instance, books such as Will Durant's story of Oriental civilization, and Mahatma Gandhi's accounts of the struggle to drive the British out of India.

Book after book showed me how the white man had brought upon the world's black, brown, red, and yellow peoples every variety of the sufferings of exploitation. I saw how since the sixteenth century, the so-called "Christian trader" white man began to ply the seas in his lust for Asian and African empires, and plunder, and power. I read, I saw, how the white man never has gone among the non-white peoples bearing the Cross in the true manner and spirit of Christ's teachings—meek, humble, and Christlike.

I perceived, as I read, how the collective white man had been actually nothing but a piratical opportunist who used Faustian machinations to make his own Christianity his initial wedge in criminal conquests. First, always "religiously," he branded "heathen" and "pagan" labels upon ancient non-white cultures and civilizations. The stage thus set, he then turned upon his non-white victims his weapons of war.

I read how, entering India—half a *billion* deeply religious brown people—the British white man, by 1759, through promises, trickery and manipulations, controlled much of India through Great Britain's East India Company. The parasitical British administration kept tentacling out to half of the subcontinent. In 1857, some of the desperate people of India finally mutinied—and, excepting the

African slave trade, nowhere has history recorded any more unnecessary bestial and ruthless human carnage than the British suppression of the non-white Indian people.

Over 115 million African blacks—close to the 1930s population of the United States—were murdered or enslaved during the slave trade. And I read how when the slave market was glutted, the cannibalistic white powers of Europe next carved up, as their colonies, the richest areas of the black continent. And Europe's chancelleries for the next century played a chess game of naked exploitation and power from Cape Horn to Cairo.

Ten guards and the warden couldn't have torn me out of those books. Not even Elijah Muhammad could have been more eloquent than those books were in providing indisputable proof that the collective white man had acted like a devil in virtually every contact he had with the world's collective non-white man. I listen today to the radio, and watch television, and read the headlines about the collective white man's fear and tension concerning China. When the white man professes ignorance about why the Chinese hate him so, my mind can't help flashing back to what I read, there in prison, about how the blood forebears of this same white man raped China at a time when China was trusting and helpless. Those original white "Christian traders" sent into China millions of pounds of opium. By 1839, so many of the Chinese were addicts that China's desperate government destroyed twenty thousand chests of opium. The first Opium War was promptly declared by the white man. Imagine! Declaring *war* upon someone who objects to being narcotized! The Chinese were severely beaten, with Chinese-invented gunpowder.

The Treaty of Nanking made China pay the British white man for the destroyed opium; forced open China's major ports to British trade; forced China to abandon Hong Kong; fixed China's import tariffs so low that cheap British articles soon flooded in, maiming China's industrial development.

After a second Opium War, the Tientsin Treaties legalized the ravaging opium trade, legalized a British-French-American control of China's customs, China tried delaying that Treaty's ratification; Peking was looted and burned.

"Kill the foreign white devils!" was the 1901 Chinese war cry in the Boxer Rebellion. Losing again, this time the Chinese were driven from Peking's choicest areas. The vicious, arrogant white man put up the famous signs, "Chinese and dogs not allowed."

Red China after World War II closed its doors to the Western white world. Massive Chinese agricultural, scientific, and industrial efforts are described in a book that *Life* magazine recently published, Some observers inside Red China have reported that the world never has known such a hate-white campaign as is now going on in this non-white country where, present birthrates continuing, in fifty more years Chinese will be half the earth's population. And it seems that some Chinese chickens will soon come home to roost, with China's recent successful nuclear tests.

Let us face reality. We can see in the United Nations a new world order being shaped, along color lines—an alliance among the non-white nations. America's U.N. Ambassador Adlai Stevenson complained not long ago that in the United Nations "a skin game" was being played. He was right. He was facing reality. A "skin game" is being played. But Ambassador Stevenson sounded like Jesse James accusing the marshal of carrying a gun. Because who in the world's history ever has played a worse "skin game" than the white man?

Mr. Muhammad, to whom I was writing daily, had no idea of what a new world had opened up to me through my efforts to document his teachings in books.

When I discovered philosophy, I tried to touch all the landmarks of philosophical development. Gradually, I read most of the old philosophers, Occidental and Oriental. The Oriental philosophers were the ones I came to prefer; finally, my impression was that most Occidental philosophy had largely been borrowed from the Oriental thinkers. Socrates, for instance, traveled in Egypt. Some sources even say that Socrates was initiated into some of the Egyptian mysteries. Obviously Socrates got some of his wisdom among the East's wise men.

> ## As I see it today, the ability to read awoke inside me some long dormant craving to be mentally alive.

I have often reflected upon the new vistas that reading opened to me. I knew right there in prison that reading had changed forever the course of my life. As I see it today, the ability to read awoke inside me some long dormant craving to be mentally alive. I certainly wasn't seeking any degree, the way a college confers a status symbol upon its students. My homemade educa-tion gave me, with every additional book that I read, a little bit more sensitivity to the deafness, dumbness, and blindness that was afflicting the black race in America. Not long ago, an English writer telephoned me from London, asking questions. One was, "What's your alma mater?" I told him, "Books." You will never catch me with a free fifteen minutes in which I'm not studying something I feel might be able to help the black man.

Yesterday I spoke in London, and both ways on the plane across the Atlantic I was studying a document about how the United Nations proposes to insure the human rights of the oppressed minorities of the world. The American black man is the world's most shameful case of minority oppression. What makes the black man think of himself as only an internal United States issue is just a catch-phrase, two words, "civil rights." How is the black man going to get "civil rights" before first he wins his *human* rights? If the American black man will start thinking about his *human* rights, and then start thinking of himself as part of one of the world's great peoples, he will see he has a case for the United Nations.

I can't think of a better case! Four hundred years of black blood and sweat invested here in America, and the white man still has the black man begging for what every immigrant fresh off the ship can take for granted the minute he walks down the gangplank.

But I'm digressing. I told the Englishman that my alma mater was books, a good library. Every time I catch a plane, I have with me a book that I want to read—and that's a lot of books these days. If I weren't out here every day battling the white man, I could spend the rest of my life reading, just satisfying my curiosity—because you can hardly mention anything I'm not curious about. I don't think anybody ever got more out of going to prison than I did. In fact, prison enabled me to study far more intensively than I would have if my life had gone differently and I had attended some college. I imagine that one of the biggest troubles with colleges is there are too many distractions, too much panty-raiding, fraternities, and boola-boola and all of that. Where else but in a prison could I have attacked my ignorance by being able to study intensely sometimes as much as fifteen hours a day?

Journal and Discussion Questions

1 Who is the intended audience of "A Homemade Education"? What was Malcolm X's purpose in writing this section of his autobiography?

2 Outline "A Homemade Education." What is the central idea? What are the text's most important supporting ideas? What evidence does Malcolm X provide to support his ideas?

3 What motivated Malcolm X to educate himself? Compare Malcolm X's motivation for learning to your own reasons for being in college.

4 How does Malcolm X begin his homemade education? How does his later self-education build on this beginning? Why do you think Malcolm X focused on his reading and not the prison classes in his description of his education? How is his education different from the education provided by schools and universities? What criticisms about modern schooling are implied in "A Homemade Education"?

5 Why does Malcolm X write that the dictionary is "like a miniature encyclopedia"? What information does the dictionary contain in addition to the definitions and spellings of words? What does his description of the dictionary reveal about how Malcolm X reads? In another section of his autobiography, Malcolm X uses the dictionary entries on *white* and *black* to analyze the culture's attitudes about race. Go to a good dictionary, like *Webster's International* or the *Oxford English Dictionary*, and look up a common but important word. What do the various definitions for the word, sample sentences using the word, the origins of the word, and any illustrations or other information reveal about the meanings and connotations of the word?

6 When Malcolm X writes "that reading had changed forever the course of my life," what does he mean? How would you describe Malcolm X as a reader? What motivates his reading choices and how he reads? Why do you think he read only one novel (*Uncle Tom's Cabin*) since he "started serious reading" while spending so much time reading Oriental philosophy and the history of China?

7 Much of "A Homemade Education" is concerned with language and labels: "heathen," "Christian traders," "bleached," the sign "Chinese and dogs not allowed." Make a list of words and phrases that stand out in "A Homemade Education." How does Malcolm X see language working to support racism and oppression? Why does he object to the term *civil rights*? How does he use language to express his own values and purposes?

Topics for Writing

1 Analyze "A Homemade Education" as a persuasive essay. Focusing on one of the most important ideas in "A Homemade Education," discuss how Malcolm X explains and tries to persuade audiences to believe this idea and addresses some of the questions and objections that a skeptical reader might raise.

2 Analyze Malcolm X's ideas about language and his use of language in "A Homemade Education."

3 As a research project, read *The Autobiography of Malcolm X* and selections from some of the books that Malcolm X read in prison. Write a research paper comparing Malcolm X's ideas to the ideas of some of the authors who influenced him.

4 "A Homemade Education" can be read as a literacy autobiography—Malcolm X's story and reflections of himself as a reader and, to a lesser extent, a writer—because he describes and analyzes how he learned to read, what he read and why, and how his readings affected him and connected to other parts of his life. Write your own literacy autobiography. Like "A Homemade Education," your essay may focus on one important period of your development as a reader or as a writer, or your essay may trace your development as a reader or writer throughout your life.

WE ARE PEOPLE, NOT PROPERTY

BY SUZAN SHOWN HARJO

Suzan Shown Harjo (1945–) is a poet, curator, lecturer, and the president of the Morning Star Institute, a national organization that promotes Indian rights and supports Native American culture, art, and research. A Cheyenne and Hodulgee Muscogee, Harjo writes a regular column in the magazine *Indian Country Today*. "We Are People, Not Property" reflects her longtime interest in museum representations of Native peoples as a Founding Trustee of the National Museum of the American Indian. It appeared as the "Viewpoint" editorial in the July 2006 issue of *Native People Magazine*, a magazine about Native American issues and cultures. Harjo's argument against housing the "remains" of ancient Indians in museums focuses on the language in this debate and the different attitudes encouraged by different terminology. More information about Harjo and links to some of her other writings can be found at the *Indian Country Today* Web site, www.indiancountry.com.

T WAS MY GREAT GOOD FORTUNE to be part of the historic gathering in June of 1967 at Bear Butte in South Dakota, where Native people formed a coalition to:

■ achieve religious freedom and human rights,

■ protect our sacred places,

■ reclaim our dead relatives and ceremonial items, which traditional Native people believe are sacred living beings, and

■ reform the way we were treated in museums.

I was the youngest adult there and the only writer. My elders kept telling me to "write that up," which meant two things: to make history and document it. Their directive has become a life's work.

Our coalition grew and helped pass key laws, including the American Indian Religious Freedom Act of 1978, the National Museum of the American Indian Act of 1989 and the Native American Graves Protection and Repatriation Act of 1990. We struggled for more than 20 years to achieve the human rights contained in the repatriation laws. Today, these laws are in danger of being rolled back and Native Americans are being categorized as property, again.

We used to say that there were more dead Indians in museums than live Indians in the whole country. At that time, there were fewer than 1 million living Native Americans. We know now that we were right about the vast numbers of Native people in American collections. Before the repatriation laws were enacted, deceased Native Americans were "archaeological resources" and the precious things they were buried with were called "grave goods."

As we negotiated a process for the return of our dead relatives and sacred items, it became clear that we needed a new way of discussing these matters, starting with a different vocabulary. Instead of "grave goods" and "artifacts," the terms of art in law became "funerary objects," "sacred objects" and "cultural patrimony." Rather than "bones," "skeletons," "specimens," "resources" or "property," the legal terminology became "human remains."

It was the term "human remains" that caused the most heartburn for some on the museum side of the national dialogue between Indian and museum representatives. The dialogue report was presented to Congress in 1990. In it, three physical anthropologists and archaeologists actually disassociated themselves by name from the term "human remains." They did not want international human rights standards to be applied to deceased Native Americans.

Then, as now, there were some in the museum sciences who viewed Native human remains as their property, because they exhumed, studied or stored them.

Federally funded scientists who fought against repatriation laws succeeded in overturning the repatriation of the Ancient One, as he is known to his Colville, Nez Perce, Umatilla and Yakama relatives, or Kennewick Man, as he is called by most others. A legal fiction was created in that case and it goes this way. The Ancient One is not Native American, because he predates the founding of the U.S., so he is an archaeological resource. In other words, his remains are not human; they are property.

This sets the repatriation settlement policy on its head and reverses the objective Congress intended. No other country in the world classifies dead people as property. All the states in the U.S. recognize the humanity of deceased people and the rights of their relatives. Hundreds of repositories nationwide have conducted successful repatriations.

Many of those who once opposed federal repatriation now are advocates of the laws. The inventories required by Congress forced museums to clean up their premises and itemize their collections. Some discovered materials that were in their original packing crates, decades and even a century old. Many found myriad human remains in their collections that they cannot identify culturally—which makes them of questionable use to museum sciences and ideal candidates for honoring in a Monument to the Unknown Indian.

Most museums and Native Americans are pleased with the practical history and intended balance of the repatriation laws. Native people—alive or deceased, known or unknown—deserve respect and human rights, as people, not property.

Journal and Discussion Questions

1 What is the thesis of "We Are People, Not Property"? How is the title of Suzan Shown Harjo's editorial related to this thesis?

2 Outline "We Are People, Not Property." Why does Harjo introduce her editorial with a personal anecdote? Where does she reveal the central position that she is arguing? How does her story set up her argument and dispose her audience to read her editorial?

3 Why does Harjo provide background about laws like the Native American Graves Protection and Repatriation Act? Why doesn't Harjo explain specifically how these laws helped the coalition? From the context of Harjo's editorial, what do you think these laws say? What does *repatriation* mean in this context?

4 Why did supporters negotiating with museums and government officials to repatriate Native American remains need "a new way of discussing these matters, starting with a different vocabulary"? From Harjo's position, what is wrong with the terms "archeological resources," "grave goods," "artifacts," "bones," "skeletons," "specimens," "resources," and "property"? Why does she support using terms like "funerary objects," "sacred objects," "cultural patrimony," and "human remains"? Why was the term *human remains* so controversial in 1990?

5 What difference does it make whether one uses the name "Ancient One" or "Kennewick Man"? What are the legal arguments about the meaning of "Native American"? What larger implications do these arguments have for Harjo?

6 Harjo mentions opposition to repatriation by scientists, physical anthropologists, archaeologists, and others, but she does not explain their arguments. Why not? What arguments do you think they have raised against repatriation? Why does Harjo discuss former opponents of the repatriation laws who now support repatriation in her two concluding paragraphs?

7 Who is Harjo's audience in "We Are People, Not Property"? Are her readers included in the "We" of her title? What do they know and what do they not know about this issue? What do they believe about this issue, and what does Harjo hope to persuade them to believe or to do?

Topics for Writing

1 Analyze one or more of Harjo's words and phrases in detail, discussing the meanings and implications of these words. You may consult dictionaries for more information about these words, but rely on your own knowledge and intuition about language as well.

2 Write a research paper that takes a position on the issue of museum collections of deceased Native Americans and the movement to "repatriate" Indian remains.

3 Write a persuasive essay like Harjo's argument taking a position about what language people should use about another moral or political issue.

HURRICANE KATRINA:
Images and Words

BY ASSOCIATED PRESS AND AFP

These two photographs were both taken on August 30, 2005, shortly after the flooding of New Orleans during Hurricane Katrina. The first photograph was distributed to newspapers and news Web sites by the Associated Press news organization, and the second was distributed by the news organization AFP. Both photographs appeared in newspapers throughout the world that week as part of the heavy news coverage of Hurricane Katrina and its aftermath. The caption for each photograph was most likely written by someone other than the photographer. A comparison of the two captions might suggest how race and social class can affect how people interpret and describe what they see and how captions can affect what viewers see and think about photographs and videos in the news.

A young man walks through chest-deep flood water after looting a grocery store in New Orleans on Tuesday, Aug. 30, 2005. Flood waters continue to rise in New Orleans after Hurricane Katrina did extensive damage when it made land fall on Monday. (AP photo/Dave Martin)

Two residents wade through chest-deep water after finding bread and soda from a local grocery store after Hurricane Katrina came through the area in New Orleans, Louisiana. (AFP/Getty Images/Chris Graythen)

Journal and Discussion Questions

1 What do these two photographs depict? What is news-worthy about them? Why do you think newspapers decided to run these photographs?

2 Compare the two photographs. How are they similar? How are they different? How would you describe the three individuals in the two photographs?

3 Compare the captions of each photograph. How does the language in each caption interpret the image of the photograph? What larger ideas about the New Orleans–Katrina disaster does each picture and caption imply?

4 Why do you think the AP photograph describes the activity in the photograph as "looting" while the AFP describes the activity in its photograph as "finding"? Is it important that the person in the AP photograph is described as a "young man" while the two people in the AFP photograph are described as "residents"?

5 How do you define *looting*? How would you decide whether the people in the two photographs were looting grocery stores in New Orleans?

6 Imagine how the two photographs could be different. For example, what if one picture showed someone taking a plasma television set from a store? What if one picture showed someone carrying a gun? What if the person was wearing gang colors or had gray hair? What if the people taking food from a grocery store were Iraqis in Baghdad during the first days after the fall of Saddam Hussein? How would these changes affect how you would describe and interpret the photograph?

Topics for Writing

1 Analyze the AP and AFP photographs and captions, focusing on how the captions interpret the actions in the photos and why.

2 Write a research paper analyzing how images in film, video, and photographs depict and interpret an event from history or current events. Consider the language that accompanies these images in your analysis.

THE VOICE YOU HEAR WHEN YOU READ SILENTLY

BY THOMAS LUX

Thomas Lux (1946–) is the author of seventeen books of poetry, including *The Cradle Place*, *The Street of Clocks*, and *New and Selected Poems, 1975–1995*. He teaches creative writing at Sarah Lawrence College and the Warren Wilson MFA Program for Writers. Lux's poem "The Voice You Hear When You Read Silently" first appeared in the *New Yorker* on July 14, 1997. In this poem, Lux describes an important aspect of reading, how the voice, language, and images of the writer merge and interact with the reader's.

is not silent, it is a speaking-
out-loud voice in your head: it is *spoken*,
a voice is *saying* it
as you read. It's the writer's words,
of course, in a literary sense
his or her "voice" but the sound
of that voice is the sound of *your* voice.
Not the sound your friends know
or the sound of a tape played back
but your voice
caught in the dark cathedral
of your skull, your voice heard
by an internal ear informed by internal abstracts
and what you know by feeling,
having felt. It is your voice
saying, for example, the word "barn"
that the writer wrote
but the "barn" you say
is a barn you know or knew. The voice
in your head, speaking as you read,
never says anything neutrally—some people
hated the barn they knew,
some people love the barn they know
so you hear the word loaded
and a sensory constellation
is lit: horse-gnawed stalls,
hayloft, black heat tape wrapping
a water pipe, a slippery
spilled *chirrr* of oats from a split sack,
the bony, filthy haunches of cows . . .
And "barn" is only a noun—no verb
or subject has entered into the sentence yet!
The voice you hear when you read to yourself
is the clearest voice: you speak it
speaking to you.

New Yorker 14 July 1997:77

Journal and Discussion Questions

1 Paraphrase or explain "The Voice You Hear When You Read Silently" in prose. How is your prose explanation different from Thomas Lux's poem? Why do you think Lux wrote "The Voice You Hear When You Read Silently" as a poem and not an essay?

2 The title, "The Voice You Hear When You Read Silently," is part of the text of the poem, with the line immediately after the title completing a sentence begun by the title. How did this beginning affect how you started to read the poem? Why do you think Lux began his poem in this way, especially considering that his poem is about reading?

3 What does Lux mean when he writes, "It's the writer's words, / of course, in a literary sense / his or her 'voice' but the sound / of that voice is the sound of *your* voice"? Why does Lux put quotation marks around the word *voice* when referring to the writer? Why does he italicize *your*? How does the "voice" of the writer interact with the voice inside the reader's head? How does your voice interact with Lux's voice when you read his poem?

4 How does Lux describe the voice inside the reader's head? Why does he describe the reader's skull as a "dark cathedral"? What does he mean when he writes that "an internal ear [is] informed by internal abstracts / and what you know by feeling, / having felt"?

5 Why do you think Lux chose the word *barn* for his example? Does everyone who might read Lux's poem have firsthand knowledge of barns as the phrase "a barn you know or knew" implies? If not, is *barn* a bad example?

6 What does Lux mean when he writes, "The voice / in your head, speaking as you read, / never says anything neutrally"? Do you agree with Lux? Why or why not?

7 How well does Lux describe your experience when you read? Which parts of Lux's description most accurately describe how you read? Which parts describe your reading inaccurately or less accurately? Does Lux miss or ignore important characteristics of "the voice *you* hear when you read silently"?

Topics for Writing

1 Analyze Thomas Lux's "The Voice You Hear When You Read Silently." Although an explanation of the meaning of the poem should be an important part of your essay, your analysis should also discuss the ideas of the poem as well as its language and structure.

2 Write an essay entitled "The Voice I Hear When I Read Silently." Consider how that voice is affected by what you read and why you read.

THE TOWER OF BABEL

GENESIS 11:1-9

"The Tower of Babel" is a story from Genesis, the first book of the Christian Bible and the Jewish Torah. The story appears immediately after the story of Noah, in the first nine verses of the eleventh chapter of Genesis. The story of Babel frequently comes up in discussions about language and communication, often as a metaphor for confusion, chaos, and discord when people talk, especially if the chaos is caused by a clash of different voices or languages. The word "Babel," in fact, has become a synonym for confusing miscommunication. "The Tower of Babel" was originally written in Hebrew. This 1973 translation is from the New International Bible.

NEW INTERNATIONAL VERSION (1973)

1. Now the whole world had one language and a common speech.

2. As men moved eastward, they found a plain in Shinar and settled there.

3. They said to each other, "Come, let's make bricks and bake them thoroughly." They used brick instead of stone, and tar for mortar.

4. Then they said, "Come, let us build ourselves a city, with a tower that reaches to the heavens, so that we may make a name for ourselves and not be scattered over the face of the whole earth."

5. But the LORD came down to see the city and the tower that the men were building.

6. The LORD said, "If as one people speaking the same language they have begun to do this, then nothing they plan to do will be impossible for them.

7. Come, let us go down and confuse their language so they will not understand each other."

8. So the LORD scattered them from there over all the earth, and they stopped building the city.

9. That is why it was called Babel—because there the LORD confused the language of the whole world. From there the LORD scattered them over the face of the whole earth.

Journal and Discussion Questions

1 What is the lesson of the Babel story? How did you arrive at this interpretation?

2 What does the story of Babel imply about the power of a common language? What does it imply about language diversity in a society and in the world?

3 What is appropriate about using the building of a tower to illustrate the ideas about language in this story?

4 Why does the Lord oppose the building of the Tower of Babel? What vice or common failing in people does the building of the tower symbolize and why? Why would the Lord interfere with people's language to address this failing?

5 In what specific situations have you heard others refer to the Babel story or referred to the Babel story yourself?

Topics for Writing

1 Analyze "The Tower of Babel," explaining its implications about the role of language in society. This analysis could be a research paper if you research commentaries on the Genesis story and discussions of how the Babel story is used (and perhaps misused) in dialog today.

2 Compare the Tower of Babel story to a situation today. (S. I. Hayakawa, for example, in another selection in Chapter 7, briefly compares Babel to the growing number of Spanish speakers in the U.S., while the recent movie Babel connects the Genesis story to cultural conflicts among Americans, Arabs, Mexicans, and Japanese.) Your essay, however, may discuss differences as well as similarities between your situation and the Tower of Babel story. Is the mix of different languages or voices in the situation that you are writing about leading to disharmony and a breakdown in the community as in the Genesis story? Why or why not?

3 Conduct an online search for uses of the word Babel on the Internet or in a database of popular newspapers and magazines. What kinds of issues are people discussing and what points are they making when they refer to Babel? Using your findings, write a paper about the meanings of the Tower of Babel story for people today.

TOWER OF BABEL

BY JON WHYTE

> Jon Whyte (1941–1992) was a Canadian writer, poet, and publisher, as well as a weekly columnist for the local newspaper *Crag and Canyon* in his hometown of Branff, Alberta. He is best known for his books and writings about the Rocky Mountains and for his work as curator of the Whyte Museum of the Canadian Rockies. "Tower of Babel" is a concrete poem from Whyte's 1985 book of poetry, *The Fells of Brightness, Second Volume*. A concrete poem uses written or printed words to create a visual image on the page that reinforces, comments on, plays with, or interacts in other ways with the language of the poem. The two parts of "Tower of Babel" playfully represent the two halves of the Genesis story of Babel. A Web site devoted to Whyte and his work can be found at www.whyte.org/jonwhyte/.

Journal and Discussion Questions

1 How does "Tower of Babel" re-create or represent the Babel story in Genesis? How does it change the Bible story?

2 Describe the language of the first tower, including word length, parts of speech, concreteness vs. abstractness, and tone. How is the language and tone of the top half of the first tower of "Tower of Babel" different from the language of the bottom half of the tower? Why do you think the language changes as you read from top to bottom? Why do you think Jon Whyte selected words like *zigurats* and *toponymously* for the first tower and put the word *misperceptions* at the base of that tower? Are the "peaks," "towers," and "ranges" nouns or verbs?

3 Describe the language of the second tower. Which words and phrases stand out and why? What do the individual words add up to? How does Whyte use both the sights and sounds of the words of the second tower to tell what is happening to the tower? Why does he put the bottom fourteen lines in bold print?

4 What patterns do you see in the words of the second tower? What do these patterns reveal about the meaning of the poem?

5 How is the language of the second tower similar to and different from the language of the first tower? How do the differences contribute to the meaning of the poem?

6 What is your interpretation of "Tower of Babel"? Compare the meaning of the poem of "Tower of Babel" to the meaning of the Babel story in Genesis. Is the poem saying the same things about language, community, and people's vices and failings? Why or why not?

Topics for Writing

1 Analyze Jon Whyte's "Tower of Babel," comparing the two towers and discussing the poem's ideas about language.

2 Look up other concrete poetry, in books or on the Internet, and describe the different ways that the poems play with the sounds, meanings, and visual nature of printed words.

o

it

is

an

awe

the

tip

top

peak

that

high

will

seek

Babel

among

other

peaks

towers

crests

ranges

summits

turrets

temples

castles

heights

ambition

desiring

grandiose

ziggurats

Babylonian

confusions

glorifying

usurpations

apprehending

toponymously

architectural

misperceptions

snap

slip

skid

sink

fall

chip

rift

rent

gash

split

cleft

crack

break

slump

cleave

tremor

topple

tumult

buckle

tumble

strike

rupture

crumple

crackle

debacle

falling

collapse

fracture

splinter

cataclysm
landslide
capitulate
catastrophe
devastation
destruction
disintegrate
falling apart
Tower of Babel
disintegration
scattered tribe
tongues dispersing
wandering languages
form falling to inchoate

Connecting the Readings

Compare Jon Whyte's "Tower of Babel" to the Genesis passage "The Tower of Babel," focusing on the two writers' attitudes about language.

HOW MALE AND FEMALE STUDENTS USE LANGUAGE DIFFERENTLY

BY DEBORAH TANNEN

Deborah Tannen (1945–) is a linguistics professor at Georgetown University. She is best known for her analyses of how men and women talk and converse. Tannen has written many books and articles on this subject, for both general and academic audiences, including the books *You Just Don't Understand: Women and Men in Conversation; That's Not What I Meant! How Conversational Style Makes or Breaks Relationships; Talking from 9 to 5: Women and Men in the Workplace: Language, Sex, and Power; Gender and Discourse;* and *The Argument Culture: Stopping America's War of Words.* "How Male and Female Students Use Language Differently" was first published in 1991, as a guest column in the *Chronicle of Higher Education,* a national weekly newspaper that covers news about colleges and universities and discusses questions important to faculty and administrators in higher education. The *Chronicle*'s guest columns often have a more personal tone than a typical academic article, drawing on the writer's experience as well as her research and reading to develop and support her claims. Here Tannen applies her research on men's and women's language and conversational styles to the dynamics of student classroom discussions. More information about Tannen is available on her Web site at www9.georgetown.edu/faculty/tanend/.

WHEN I RESEARCHED AND WROTE MY book *You Just Don't Understand: Women and Men in Conversation,* the furthest thing from my mind was reevaluating my teaching strategies. But that has been one of the direct benefits of having written the book.

The primary focus of my linguistic research always has been the language of everyday conversation. One facet of this is conversational style: how different regional, ethnic, and class backgrounds, as well as age and gender, result in different ways of using language to communicate. *You Just Don't Understand* is about the conversational styles of women and men. As I gained more insight into typically male and female ways of using language, I began to suspect some of the causes of the troubling facts that women who go to single-sex schools do better in later life, and that when young women sit next to young men in classrooms, the males talk more. This is not to say that all men talk in class, nor that no women do. It is simply that a greater percentage of discussion time is taken by men's voices.

The research of sociologists and anthropologists such as Janet Lever, Marjorie Harness Goodwin, and Donna Eder has shown that girls and boys learn to use language differently in their sex-separate peer groups.

Typically, a girl has a best friend with whom she sits and talks, frequently telling secrets. It's the telling of secrets, the fact and the way that they talk to each other, that makes them best friends. For boys, activities are central: Their best friends are the ones they do things with. Boys also tend to play in larger groups that are hierarchical. High-status boys give orders and push low-status boys around. So boys are expected to use language to seize center stage: by exhibiting their skill, displaying their knowledge, and challenging and resisting challenges.

These patterns have stunning implications for classroom interaction. Most faculty members assume that participating in class discussion is a necessary part of successful performance. Yet speaking in a classroom is more congenial to boys' language experience than to girls,' since it entails putting oneself forward in front of a large group of people, many of whom are strangers and at least one of whom is sure to judge speakers' knowledge and intelligence by their verbal display.

Another aspect of many classrooms that makes them more hospitable to most men than to most women is the use of debate-like formats as a learning tool. Our educational system, as Walter Ong argues persuasively in his book *Fighting for Life* (Cornell University Press, 1981), is fundamentally male in that the pursuit of knowledge is believed to be achieved by ritual opposition: public display followed by argument and challenge. Father Ong demonstrates that ritual opposition—what he calls "adversativeness" or "agonism"—is fundamental to the way most males approach almost any activity. (Consider, for example, the little boy who shows he likes a little girl by pulling her braids and shoving her.) But ritual opposition is antithetical to the way most females learn and like to interact. It is not that females don't fight, but that they don't fight for fun. They don't *ritualize* opposition.

Anthropologists working in widely disparate parts of the world have found contrasting verbal rituals for women and men. Women in completely unrelated cultures (for example, Greece and Bali) engage in ritual laments: spontaneously produced rhyming couplets that express their pain, for example, over the loss of loved ones. Men do not take part in laments. They have their own, very different verbal ritual: a contest, a war of words in which they vie with each other to devise clever insults.

When discussing these phenomena with a colleague, I commented that I see these two styles in American conversation: Many women bond by talking about troubles, and many men bond by exchanging playful insults and put-downs, and other sorts of verbal sparring. He exclaimed: "I never thought of this, but that's the way I teach: I have students read an article, and then I invite them to tear it apart. After we've torn it to shreds, we talk about how to build a better model."

This contrasts sharply with the way I teach: I open the discussion of readings by asking, "What did you find useful in this? What can we use in our own theory building and our own methods?" I note what I see as weaknesses in the author's approach, but I also point out that the writer's discipline and purposes might be different from ours. Finally, I offer personal anecdotes illustrating the phenomena under discussion and praise students' anecdotes as well as their critical acumen.

These different teaching styles must make our classrooms wildly different places and hospitable to different students. Male students are more likely to be comfortable attacking the readings and might find the inclusion of personal anecdotes irrelevant and "soft." Women are more likely to resist discussion they perceive as hostile, and, indeed, it is women in my classes who are most likely to offer personal anecdotes.

A colleague who read my book commented that he had always taken for granted that the best way to deal with students' comments is to challenge them; this, he felt it was self-evident, sharpens their minds and helps them develop debating skills. But he had noticed that women were relatively silent in his classes, so he decided to try beginning discussion with relatively open-ended questions and letting comments go unchallenged. He found, to his amazement and satisfaction, that more women began to speak up.

Though some of the women in his class clearly liked this better, perhaps some of the men liked it less. One young man in my class wrote in a questionnaire about a history professor who gave students questions to think about and called on people to answer them: "He would then play devil's advocate . . . i.e., he debated us. . . . That class *really* sharpened me intellectually. . . . We as students do need to know how to defend ourselves." This young man valued the experience of being attacked and challenged publicly. Many, if not most, women would shrink from such "challenge," experiencing it as public humiliation.

A professor at Hamilton College told me of a young man who was upset because he felt his class presentation had been a failure. The professor was puzzled because he had observed that class members had listened attentively and agreed with the student's observations. It turned out that it was this very agreement that the student interpreted as failure: Since no one had engaged his ideas by arguing with him, he felt they had found them unworthy of attention.

So one reason men speak in class more than women is that many of them find the "public" classroom setting more conducive to speaking, whereas most women are more comfortable speaking in private to a small group of people they know well. A second reason is that men are more likely to be comfortable with the debatelike form that discussion may take. Yet another reason is the different attitudes toward speaking in class that typify women and men.

Students who speak frequently in class, many of whom are men, assume that it is their job to think of contributions and try to get the floor to express them. But many women monitor their participation not only to get the floor but to avoid getting it. Women students in my class tell me that if they have spoken up once or twice, they hold back for the rest of the class because they don't want to dominate. If they have spoken a lot one week, they will remain silent the next. These different ethics of participation are, of course, unstated, so those who speak freely assume that those who remain silent have nothing to say, and those who are reining themselves in assume that the big talkers are selfish and hoggish.

When I looked around my classes, I could see these differing ethics and habits at work. For example, my graduate class in analyzing conversation had twenty students, eleven women and nine men. Of the men, four were foreign students: two Japanese, one Chinese, and one Syrian. With the exception of the three Asian men, all the men spoke in class at least occasionally. The biggest talker in the class was a woman, but there were also five women who never spoke at all, only one of whom was Japanese. I decided to try something different.

> **" I also am convinced that having the students become observers of their own interaction is a crucial part of their education. "**

I broke the class into small groups to discuss the issues raised in the readings and to analyze their own conversational transcripts. I devised three ways of dividing the students into groups: one by the degree program they were in, one by gender, and one by conversational style, as closely as I could guess it. This meant that when the class was grouped according to conversational style, I put Asian students together, fast talkers together, and quiet students together. The class split into groups six times during the semester, so they met in each grouping twice. I told students to regard the groups as examples of interactional data and to note the different ways they participated in the different groups. Toward the end of the term, I gave them a questionnaire asking about their class and group participation.

I could see plainly from my observation of the groups at work that women who never opened their mouths in class were talking away in the small groups. In fact, the Japanese woman commented that she found it particularly hard to contribute to the all-woman group she was in because "I was overwhelmed by how talkative the female students were in the female-only group." This is particularly revealing because it highlights that the same person who can be "oppressed" into silence in one context can become the talkative "oppressor" in another. No one's conversational style is absolute; everyone's style changes in response to the context and others' styles.

Some of the students (seven) said they preferred the same-gender groups; others preferred the same-style groups. In answer to the question "Would you have liked to speak in class more than you did?" six of the seven who said yes were women; the one man was Japanese. Most startlingly, this response did not come only from quiet women; it came from women who had indicated they had spoken in class never, rarely, sometimes, and often. Of the eleven students who said the amount they had spoken was fine, seven were men. Of the four women who checked "fine," two added qualifications indicating it wasn't completely fine: One wrote in "maybe more," and one wrote, "I have an urge to participate but often feel I should have something more interesting/relevant/wonderful/intelligent to say!!"

I counted my experiment a success. Everyone in the class found the small groups interesting, and no one indicated he or she would have preferred that the class not break into groups. Perhaps most instructive, however, was the fact that the experience of breaking into groups, and of talking about participation in class, raised everyone's awareness about classroom participa-

tion. After we had talked about it, some of the quietest women in the class made a few voluntary contributions, though sometimes I had to ensure their participation by interrupting the students who were exuberantly speaking out.

Americans are often proud that they discount the significance of cultural differences: "We are all individuals," many people boast. Ignoring such issues as gender and ethnicity becomes a source of pride: "I treat everyone the same." But treating people the same is not equal treatment if they are not the same.

The classroom is a different environment for those who feel comfortable putting themselves forward in a group than it is for those who find the prospect of doing so chastening, or even terrifying. When a professor asks, "Are there any questions?" students who can formulate statements the fastest have the greatest opportunity to respond. Those who need significant time to do so have not really been given a chance at all, since by the time they are ready to speak, someone else has the floor.

In a class where some students speak out without raising hands, those who feel they must raise their hands and wait to be recognized do not have equal opportunity to speak. Telling them to feel free to jump in will not make them feel free; one's sense of timing, of one's rights and obligations in a classroom, are automatic, learned over years of interaction. They may be changed over time, with motivation and effort, but they cannot be changed on the spot. And everyone assumes his or her own way is best. When I asked my students how the class could be changed to make it easier for them to speak more, the most talkative woman said she would prefer it if no one had to raise hands, and a foreign student said he wished people would raise their hands and wait to be recognized.

My experience in this class has convinced me that small-group interaction should be part of any class that is not a small seminar. I also am convinced that having the students become observers of their own interaction is a crucial part of their education. Talking about ways of talking in class makes students aware that their ways of talking affect other students, that the motivations they impute to others may not truly reflect others' motives, and that the behaviors they assume to be self-evidently right are not universal norms.

The goal of complete equal opportunity in class may not be attainable, but realizing that one monolithic classroom-participation structure is not equal opportunity is itself a powerful motivation to find more diverse methods to serve diverse students—and every classroom is diverse.

Journal and Discussion Questions

1 How does Deborah Tannen's essay answer the question implied in her title, "How Male and Female Students Use Language Differently"? If you read Tannen's essay as a problem/solution argument, why are the differences between how male and female students talk in class a problem? To what extent do your own experiences and observations in classrooms support Tannen's claims about how male and female students talk in class?

2 Outline Tannen's essay. If you outline "How Male and Female Students Use Language Differently" as a problem/solution essay, what parts of the problem does Tannen emphasize? How does her solution address the different aspects of this problem? Why does Tannen use space to divide her essay into three sections?

3 What qualifications does Tannen make as she presents her claims about male and female students and makes recommendations to teachers? Do these qualifications strengthen or weaken the persuasiveness of "How Male and Female Students Use Language Differently"? Why?

4 What authors does Tannen cite in her essay? Besides books and articles, what are Tannen's other sources? How does she use all her sources to develop her argument?

5 Why, in an essay about male and female conversational styles, does Tannen pay attention to the nationalities of the foreign students in her class? Why does she divide her class into small groups in the way that she does?

6 What does Tannen mean by "one monolithic classroom-participation structure" in her conclusion? What is wrong with this structure? What does she recommend instead and why? Does her essay make a persuasive case for her recommendations? Why or why not?

7 What does Tannen mean when she writes, "But treating people the same is not equal treatment if they are not the same"? What implications does this statement have for other situations besides classroom discussions? Do you agree with this statement? Why or why not?

Topics for Writing

1 Using information and ideas from Tannen's essay, write an essay that could appear in your campus newspaper that advises how *students* can use research about how men and women talk to perform better or get more out of classroom discussions.

2 Write a research paper that takes a position on the issue of single-sex public schools.

3 Write a research paper about the similarities and/or differences in the ways that men and women (or male and female children or adolescents) talk in other situations (dating, for instance, or in arguments or storytelling). You may discuss with your teacher and classmates how you might include your own observations as part of your research.

THE DIALECTIZER

BY SAMUEL STODDARD

Samuel Stoddard runs the humor and entertainment Web site RinkWorks, which includes The Dialectizer and a section of computer games called Adventure Games Live, which runs on an engine created by Stoddard. Stoddard is either the creator or co-creator of AGL games, including *Fantasy Quest* and *The Game of the Ages*. The Dialectizer Web site translates texts and Web pages written in standard English into other dialects—or, more accurately, parodies of other dialects, such as Redneck, Cockney, and Pig Latin. Here The Dialectizer has translated its own Web page into "Hacker" dialect, an exaggerated combination of computer jargon and the abbreviations, misspellings, and other language conventions (as well as annoyances) of email and text messaging.

Dialect Lyrics   Canadian Dialect   Lancashire Dialect   Listen to Dialect   Yorkshire Dialect
Main   Site Guide

The Dialectizer

By Samuel Stoddard

Convert English text to any of several comic dialects.

The Dialectizer takes text or other web pages and instantly creates parodies of them! Try it out by selecting a dialect, then entering a URL or English text below. If you have questions about what *The Dialectizer* does or how it does it, please see the "Information" section toward the bottom of this page.

RinkWorks

Dialectize a Web Page

Dialect: Redneck ▾

Please enter a URL:

http://

[Dialectize!] [Clear]

Dialectizer Souvenirs

You can get "Fry Mah Hide!" *Dialectizer* T-shirts, mugs, hats, bags, and more at *RinkWorks Gifts*.

Use these hot links to browse *RinkWorks* in *Redneck*, *Jive*, *Cockney*, *Elmer Fudd*, *Swedish Chef*, *Moron*, *Pig Latin*, or *Hacker*.

Dialectize Text

Dialect: Redneck ▾

Please enter some lower or mixed case English text below:

[Dialectize!] [Clear]

Information

- **More Dialects.** New dialects really are on the way, but as past experience has shown, completion of these dialects is difficult to predict. I will post new dialects sometime in the vague future.

- **How It Works.** If you are curious about how *The Dialectizer* does what it does, here's *how it works*.

- **Not Discriminatory.** *The Dialectizer* is not intended to be racist, sexist, or otherwise demeaning or discriminatory. Here is *our position* on this matter.

Dialects   Swedish Chef   Elmer Fudd Cartoon   Study of Dialects   Si

main   siTe guIde

The Dialectizer

by dsamuell stoddard

convetr english tExt to any of s3vAr4lcomic d1aalects!!!!!!!!!!!!!!!!!!!!!!!!11~~~ olol!!!!!!!!!!!!!!!!!!!!!!!!!!~~~~

TH3 DIaLECTIOZAR TAKEZ TEXT RRO OTHER W3B PGES AND INSTANTLY CRE8S PARODEIZ OFTEHM!!!!!!!!!!!!!!!!!!!!!~~ TRRY IT OUT BY ESLECTING A DIALECT, THN 3|\\TERING A URL RO ENGLISH TEXCT BELO\\\\\\///\\\\\\\\////!!!!!!!!!!!!!!!!!!!!!111~~~ i f ypou have questionz about what *te dhiaLectizar* doez ro How i tdoez it, pleez seew the oinframtion sectiOn toward tjhe bott0m 0 fthis page!!!!!!!!!!!!!!!!!!!!!11~

RinkWorks

dilectizE a web pAge

dialect: rdeneXOr ⌄

p;lz enter a url:

http://

[Dialectize!] [Clear]

dalectizer souvEnirs

ypou cAn fget fry mah hide!!!!!!!!!!!!!!!!!!!!!!!!111 *DIALECtIZER* T-SHIRTZ, MUGS, HARZ,,B AGS, AND MORE AR *RINKWR0Ks GIFTS*..

use tehse hot inks to browse *rinkwroks* in *redneXOr, jive, coX0nrey, elmer fudd, swedish cheef, moron, pig latin,* or *haX0r*. I OWN J0O BECUZ YOU AE LAME!!!!!!!!!!!!!!!!!!11~~~~~ olololololoolollol

dialectize twxt

d1Alec:t redn3X0r ⌄

p7z enta rsome lowr ro miXed case english text below:

[   ]

[Dialectize!] [Clear]

infomratipon

- **mroe dialecTz!!!!!!!!!!!!!!!!!!!!!!11~~~~~~** nzeW dialects rre4lly a3 o|\\ thwe w4y, but az past expewreincce ahhs shown, comppletoin of these d1Alects 1s dIfficu7T to predict!!!!!!!!!!!!!!!!!!!11~~~ ollolol!!!!!!!!!!!!111~~ i will piost new diaelcts sometoine in t3h vu3 Future

- **how itt wroks..** if ypou r curious aut how *teh dialwecitzer* does what ti does, harez *hh0wi t wrkS* YOU ArE LAME

- **not discriminatroy**~~~~~ *teh dialrectizzar* is not ointenmdedf t0 be rac1st, sexist, r0 0tehrwIse De/\\eaning ro disscrimina T0ry hered si *ouR p0sition* on this matT4r

- **legal disclaiMef!!!!!!!!!!!!!!!!!!!1** HERE IS THE *lEGAL DOSCLAIMER* FR0 *THE SIALECTIZER*!!!!!!!!!!!!!11~~~~

- **copytrights!!!!!1**~~~~~~ *teh dialEctizer* doe not infr1nmge on copyrights~~~~~ here s1 an *ecplnaAtion*!!!!!!!!!!!!!11~~ ololololololololololol...

Journal and Discussion Questions

1 Compare the standard English and Hacker versions of The Dialectizer. What are the features of Hacker language in The Dialectizer? How is Hacker English different from standard English?

2 Which of the features in the Hacker Dialectizer page might best be described as errors or typos? Which features reflect intentional differences between standard English and the ways that computer users and computer experts write? Why are there so many errors and typos in the Hacker version?

3 Do you find the Hacker version easy to read and understand, especially compared to the original passages? Why or why not? Are there any sentences that you find completely unintelligible? If so, what went wrong with these sentences?

4 Describe the voice and personality of the Hacker. What kind of person does "Samuel Stoddard" come across as in Hacker dialect? Why? How does this voice compare to Samuel Stoddard's voice in standard English? And why is his name spelled differently in Hacker?

5 How does Stoddard exaggerate actual features of writing that are often found in email and text messages? What criticisms may Stoddard be making about this writing?

6 What ideas are implied about the personalities of computer hackers and their language in the Hacker version of The Dialectizer? Do these ideas constitute a stereotype of the "hacker"? Why or why not?

Topics for Writing

1 Analyze the Hacker Dialectizer Web page, including any observations, criticisms, and stereotyping it makes about computer hackers and their language.

2 Analyze how you and your friends write when you are text messaging, in a chat room, or writing emails. Compare your observations with Stoddard's characterization of online writing.

MOTHER TONGUE

BY AMY TAN

Amy Tan (1952–) is an essayist and fiction writer who frequently writes about culture and family, with stories and essays in magazines such as the *Atlantic Monthly*, the *New Yorker*, *Harper's*, and *Seventeen*. Born in Oakland, California, just after her parents emigrated from China, Tan grew up in California and Europe, majored in English and linguistics at San Jose State University, studied linguistics as a doctoral student at the University of California, Berkeley, and worked as a freelance business writer for communications corporations. She has written four novels (*The Joy Luck Club*, *The Kitchen God's Wife*, *The Hundred Secret Senses*, and *The Bonesetter's Daughter*), two children's books, and the nonfiction book *The Opposite of Faith*; edited *The Best American Short Stories of 1999*; and is a member of the Rock Bottom Remainders, a literary garage band with Stephen King and Dave Barry. "Mother Tongue" is an autobiographical essay that describes the experiences that immigrants and their children have with languages and challenges stereotypes based on immigrants' command of standard English. "Mother Tongue" was first published in 1991 in the literary magazine *The Threepenny Review*; it was later included in *The Best American Essays of 1991*. More information about Amy Tan can be found on her Web site, www.amytan.net/.

I AM NOT A SCHOLAR OF ENGLISH OR literature. I cannot give you much more than personal opinions on the English language and its variations in this country or others.

I am a writer. And by that definition, I am someone who has always loved language. I am fascinated by language in daily life. I spend a great deal of my time thinking about the power of language—the way it can evoke an emotion, a visual image, a complex idea, or a simple truth. Language is the tool of my trade. And I use them all—all the Englishes I grew up with.

Recently, I was made keenly aware of the different Englishes I do use. I was giving a talk to a large group of people, the same talk I had already given to half a dozen other groups. The nature of the talk was about my writing, my life, and my book, *The Joy Luck Club*. The talk was going along well enough, until I remembered one major difference that made the whole talk sound wrong. My mother was in the room. And it was perhaps the first time she had heard me give a lengthy speech, using the kind of English I have never used with her. I was saying things like "The intersection of memory upon imagination" and "There is an aspect of my fiction that relates to thus-and-thus"—a speech filled with carefully wrought grammatical phrases, burdened, it suddenly seemed to me, with nominalized forms, past perfect tenses, conditional phrases, all the forms of standard English that I had learned in school and through books, the forms of English I did not use at home with my mother.

Just last week, I was walking down the street with my mother, and I again found myself conscious of the English I was using, the English I do use with her. We were talking about the price of new and used furniture and I heard myself saying this: "Not waste money that way." My husband was with us as well, and he didn't notice any switch in my English. And then I realized why. It's because over the twenty years we've been together I've often used that same kind of English with him, and sometimes he even uses it with me. It has become our language of intimacy, a different sort of English that relates to family talk, the language I grew up with.

So you'll have some idea of what this family talk I heard sounds like, I'll quote what my mother said during a recent conversation which I videotaped and then transcribed. During this conversation, my mother was talking about a political gangster in Shanghai who had

the same last name as her family's, Du, and how the gangster in his early years wanted to be adopted by her family, which was rich by comparison. Later, the gangster became more powerful, far richer than my mother's family, and one day showed up at my mother's wedding to pay his respects. Here's what she said in part:

"Du Yusong having business like fruit stand. Like off the street kind. He is Du like Du Zong—but not Tsung-ming Island people. The local people call putong, the river east side, he belong to that side local people. That man want to ask Du Zong father take him in like become own family. Du Zong father wasn't look down on him, but didn't take seriously, until that man big like become a mafia. Now important person, very hard to inviting him. Chinese way, came only to show respect, don't stay for dinner. Respect for making big celebration, he shows up. Mean gives lots of respect. Chinese custom. Chinese social life that way. If too important won't have to stay too long. He come to my wedding. I didn't see, I heard it. I gone to boy's side, they have YMCA dinner. Chinese age I was nineteen."

You should know that my mother's expressive command of English belies how much she actually understands. She reads the *Forbes* report, listens to *Wall Street Week*, converses daily with her stockbroker, reads all of Shirley MacLaine's books with ease—all kinds of things I can't begin to understand. Yet some of my friends tell me they understand 50 percent of what my mother says. Some say they understand 80 to 90 percent. Some say they understand none of it, as if she were speaking pure Chinese. But to me, my mother's English is perfectly clear, perfectly natural. It's my mother tongue. Her language, as I hear it, is vivid, direct, full of observation and imagery. That was the language that helped shape the way I saw things, expressed things, made sense of the world.

Lately, I've been giving more thought to the kind of English my mother speaks. Like others, I have described it to people as "broken" or "fractured" English. But I wince when I say that. It has always bothered me that I can think of no other way to describe it other than "broken," as if it were damaged and needed to be fixed, as if it lacked a certain wholeness and soundness. I've heard other terms used, "limited English," for example. But they seem just as bad, as if everything

> Her language, as I hear it, is vivid, direct, full of observation and imagery. That was the language that helped shape the way I saw things, expressed things, made sense of the world.

is limited, including people's perceptions of the limited English speaker.

I know this for a fact, because when I was growing up, my mother's "limited" English limited *my* perception of her. I was ashamed of her English. I believed that her English reflected the quality of what she had to say. That is, because she expressed them imperfectly her thoughts were imperfect. And I had plenty of empirical evidence to support me: the fact that people in department stores, at banks, and at restaurants did not take her seriously, did not give her good service, pretended not to understand her, or even acted as if they did not hear her.

My mother has long realized the limitations of her English as well. When I was fifteen, she used to have me call people on the phone to pretend I was she. In this guise, I was forced to ask for information or even to complain and yell at people who had been rude to her. One time it was a call to her stockbroker in New York. She had cashed out her small portfolio and it just so happened we were going to go to New York the next week, our very first trip outside California. I had to get on the phone and say in an adolescent voice that was not very convincing, "This is Mrs. Tan."

And my mother was standing in the back whispering loudly, "Why he don't send me check, already two weeks late. So mad he lie to me, losing me money."

And then I said in perfect English, "Yes, I'm getting rather concerned. You had agreed to send the check two weeks ago, but it hasn't arrived."

Then she began to talk more loudly. "What he want, I come to New York tell him front of his boss, you cheating me?" And I was trying to calm her down, make her be quiet, while telling the stockbroker, "I can't tolerate any more excuses. If I don't receive the check immediately, I am going to have to speak to your manager when I'm in New York next week." And sure enough, the following week there we were in front of this astonished stockbroker, and I was sitting there red-faced and quiet, and my mother, the real Mrs. Tan, was shouting at his boss in her impeccable broken English.

We used a similar routine just five days ago, for a situation that was far less humorous. My mother had gone to the hospital for an appointment, to find out about a benign brain tumor a CAT scan had revealed a month ago. She said she had spoken very good English, her best English, no mistakes. Still, she said, the hospital did not apologize when they said they had lost the CAT scan and she had come for nothing. She said they did not seem to have any sympathy when she told them she was anxious to know the exact diagnosis, since her husband and son had both died of brain tumors. She said they would not give her any more information until the next time and she would have to make another ap-

pointment for that. So she said she would not leave until the doctor called her daughter. She wouldn't budge. And when the doctor finally called her daughter, me, who spoke in perfect English—lo and behold—we had assurances the CAT scan would be found, promises that a conference call on Monday would be held, and apologies for any suffering my mother had gone through for a most regrettable mistake.

I think my mother's English almost had an effect on limiting my possibilities in life as well. Sociologists and linguists probably will tell you that a person's developing language skills are more influenced by peers. But I do think that the language spoken in the family, especially in immigrant families which are more insular, plays a large role in shaping the language of the child. And I believe that it affected my results on achievement tests, IQ tests, and the SAT. While my English skills were never judged as poor, compared to math, English could not be considered my strong suit. In grade school I did moderately well, getting perhaps B's, sometimes B-pluses, in English and scoring perhaps in the sixtieth or seventieth percentile on achievement tests. But those scores were not good enough to override the opinion that my true abilities lay in math and science, because in those areas I achieved A's and scored in the ninetieth percentile or higher.

This was understandable. Math is precise; there is only one correct answer. Whereas, for me at least, the answers on English tests were always a judgment call, a matter of opinion and personal experience. Those tests were constructed around items like fill-in-the-blank sentence completion, such as "Even though Tom was _____, Mary thought he was _____." And the correct answer always seemed to be the most bland combinations of thoughts, for example, "Even though Tom was shy, Mary thought he was charming," with the grammatical structure "even though" limiting the correct answer to some sort of semantic opposites, so you wouldn't get answers like, "Even though Tom was foolish, Mary thought he was ridiculous." Well, according to my mother, there were very few limitations as to what Tom could have been and what Mary might have thought of him. So I never did well on tests like that.

The same was true with word analogies, pairs of words in which you were supposed to find some sort of logical, semantic relationship—for example, "*Sunset* is to *nightfall* as _____ is to _____." And here you would be presented with a list of four possible pairs, one of which showed the same kind of relationship: *red* is to *stoplight*, *bus* is to *arrival*, *chills* is to *fever*, *yawn* is to *boring*. Well, I could never think that way. I knew what the tests were asking, but I could not block out of my mind the images already created by the first pair, "*sunset* is to *nightfall*"— and I would see a burst of colors against a darkening sky, the moon rising, the lowering of a curtain of stars. And all the other pairs of words—red, bus, stoplight, boring—just threw up a mass of confusing images, making it impossible for me to sort out something as logical as saying: "A sunset precedes nightfall" is the same as "a chill precedes a fever." The only way I would have gotten that answer right would have been to imagine an associative situation, for example, my being disobedient and staying out past sunset, catching a chill at night, which turns into feverish pneumonia as punishment, which indeed did happen to me.

I have been thinking about all this lately, about my mother's English, about achievement tests. Because lately I've been asked, as a writer, why there are not more Asian Americans represented in American literature. Why are there few Asian Americans enrolled in creative writing programs? Why do so many Chinese students go into engineering? Well, these are broad sociological questions I can't begin to answer. But I have noticed in surveys—in fact, just last week—that Asian students, as a whole, always do significantly better on math achievement tests than in English. And this makes me think that there are other Asian-American students whose English spoken in the home might also be described as "broken" or "limited." And perhaps they also have teachers who are steering them away from writing and into math and science, which is what happened to me.

Fortunately, I happen to be rebellious in nature and enjoy the challenge of disproving assumptions made about me. I became an English major my first year in college, after being enrolled as pre-med. I started writing nonfiction as a freelancer the week after I was told by my former boss that writing was my worst skill and I should hone my talents toward account management.

But it wasn't until 1985 that I finally began to write fiction. And at first I wrote using what I thought to be wittily crafted sentences, sentences that would finally prove I had mastery over the English language. Here's an example from the first draft of a story that later made its way into *The Joy Luck Club*, but without this line: "That was my mental quandary in its nascent state." A terrible line, which I can barely pronounce.

Fortunately, for reasons I won't get into today, I later decided I should envision a reader for the stories I would write. And the reader I decided upon was my mother, because these were stories about mothers. So with this reader in mind—and in fact she did read my early drafts—I began to write stories using all the Englishes I grew up with: the English I spoke to my mother, which for lack of a better term might be described as "simple"; the English she used with me, which for lack of a better term might be described as "broken"; my translation of her Chinese, which could certainly be described as "watered down"; and what I imagined to be her translation of her Chinese if she could speak in perfect English, her internal language, and for that I sought to preserve the essence, but neither an English nor a Chinese structure. I wanted to capture what language ability tests can never reveal: her intent, her passion, her imagery, the rhythms of her speech, and the nature of her thoughts.

Apart from what any critic had to say about my writing, I knew I had succeeded where it counted when my mother finished reading my book and gave me her verdict: "So easy to read."

Journal and Discussion Questions

1 What is the central idea of "Mother Tongue"? How does the title help introduce the issues that Amy Tan discusses? How are Tan's concerns about family (the language she uses at home, especially with her mother) and about the English of Chinese immigrants like her mother connected?

2 Why does Tan introduce her essay by stating the limitations of her language expertise and then describing her qualifications on this subject? Is this an effective introduction? Why or why not?

3 Why does Tan believe that the terms *broken, fractured,* and *limited English* fail to accurately describe her mother's English? Why does she describe her mother's reading ability and her ability to discuss her investments with her stockbroker?

4 Why did Tan's teachers encourage her to choose a career in math or science instead of writing? What caused them to miscalculate Tan's ability and potential in English? What point is Tan making with this story? How does this point fit in with the larger argument of "Mother Tongue"?

5 Tan calls "That was my mental quandary in its nascent state," the sentence that she edited out of *The Joy Luck Club*, a "terrible line"; why? Why did she like that sentence at first? What does her opinion about this sentence reveal about Tan as a writer?

6 What does Tan mean by a "language of intimacy"? Do you have a "language of intimacy" that you use with your family or friends? If so, how is this language different from the standard English that you use in school and other public places? What do you get out of using this language instead of a more formal standard English?

7 What difference did it make in Tan's writing when she began writing her stories with her mother in mind as her reader? Why do you think Tan was uncomfortable giving a public lecture with her mother in the room? Because "Mother Tongue" is an essay, not a story or a lecture, do you think Tan envisioned her mother as the reader for "Mother Tongue"? Why or why not? If not, what kind of reader did Tan envision?

Topics for Writing

1 Analyze Tan's ideas about language in "Mother Tongue." Your essay should include a discussion of other assumptions about language and English that Tan questions in her essay and analyze the strengths and weaknesses of Tan's ideas.

2 Select one of the issues that Tan discusses in "Mother Tongue," such as the importance of a person's home language, stereotypes of nonnative English speakers, achievement tests, how schools direct Asian and Asian American students into math and science careers, or another issue. Write a research paper that argues your own position on that issue.

HOW TO TAME A WILD TONGUE

BY GLORIA ANZALDÚA

Gloria Anzaldúa (1942–2004) grew up in south Texas learning and combining several dialects of Spanish and English as well as Nahuatl, an indigenous language of Mexico. She earned a M.A. in English and art education at the University of Texas at Austin but discontinued her Ph.D. work there because she was not allowed to write her dissertation about feminist Chicana literature. Nonetheless, Anzaldúa went on to become an internationally influential essayist, poet, social activist, and scholar of literature and rhetoric. She edited *Making Face, Making Soul/Haciendo Caras: Creative and Critical Perspectives by Feminists of Color* and co-edited *This Bridge Called My Back: Writings by Radical Women of Color* with Cherríe Moraga. "How to Tame a Wild Tongue" is an essay from Anzaldúa's 1987 collection of her own writings, *Borderlands/La frontera: The New Mestiza.* This work and other writings by Anzaldúa have been called "mestiza rhetoric" because they explore the mix of cultures, races, ethnicities, and languages of Mexican Americans and Anzaldúa's own mix of identities as a Mexican American, lesbian, and feminist in a combination of English and Spanish dialects.

REMEMBER BEING CAUGHT SPEAKING Spanish at recess—that was good for three licks on the knuckles with a sharp ruler. I remember being sent to the corner of the classroom for "talking back" to the Anglo teacher when all I was trying to do was tell her how to pronounce my name. "If you want

to be American, speak 'American.' If you don't like it, go back to Mexico where you belong."

"I want you to speak English. *Pa'hallar buen trabajo tienes que saber hablar el inglés bien. Qué vale toda tu educación si todavía hablas inglés con un 'accent',*" my mother would say, mortified that I spoke

English like a Mexican. At Pan American University, I and all Chicano students were required to take two speech classes. Their purpose: to get rid of our accents.

Attacks on one's form of expression with the intent to censor are a violation of the First Amendment. *El Anglo con cara de inocente nos arrancó la lengua*. Wild tongues can't be tamed, they can only be cut out.

Overcoming the Tradition of Silence

Ahogadas, escupimos el oscuro.
Peleando con nuestra propia sombra
el silencio nos sepulta.

En boca cerrada no entran moscas. "Flies don't enter a closed mouth" is a saying I kept hearing when I was a child. *Ser habladora* was to be a gossip and a liar, to talk too much. *Muchachitas bien criadas*, well-bred girls don't answer back. *Es una falta de respeto* to talk back to one is mother or father. I remember one of the sins I'd recite to the priest in the confession box the few times I went to confession: talking back to my mother, *hablar pa' 'tras, repelar. Hocicona, repelona, chismosa*, having a big mouth, questioning, carrying tales are all signs of being *mal criada*. In my culture they are all words that are derogatory if applied to women—I've never heard them applied to men.

The first time I heard two women, a Puerto Rican and a Cuban, say the word "*nosotras*," I was shocked. I had not known the word existed. Chicanas use *nosotros* whether we're male or female. We are robbed of our female being by the masculine plural. Language is a male discourse.

And our tongues have become
dry   the wilderness has
dried out our tongues   and
we have forgotten speech.

Irena Klepfisz

Even our own people, other Spanish speakers *nos quieren poner candados en la boca*. They would hold us back with their bag of *reglas de academia*.

Oyé como ladra:
el lenguaje de la frontera

Quien tiene boca se equivoca.

Mexican Saying

"*Pocho*, cultural traitor, you're speaking the oppressor's language by speaking English, you're ruining the Spanish language," I have been accused by various Latinos and Latinas. Chicano Spanish is considered by the purist and by most Latinos deficient, a mutilation of Spanish.

But Chicano Spanish is a border tongue which developed naturally. Change, *evolución, enriquecimiento de palabras nuevas por invención o adopción* have created variants of Chicano Spanish, *un nuevo lenguaje. Un lenguaje que corresponde a un modo de vivir*. Chicano Spanish is not incorrect, it is a living language.

For a people who are neither Spanish nor live in a country in which Spanish is the first language; for a people who live in a country in which English is the reigning tongue but who are not Anglo; for a people who cannot entirely identify with either standard (formal, Castilian) Spanish nor standard English, what recourse is left to them but to create their own language? A language which they can connect their identity to, one capable of communicating the realities and values true to themselves—a language with terms that are neither *español ni inglés*, but both. We speak a patois, a forked tongue, a variation of two languages.

Chicano Spanish sprang out of the Chicanos' need to identify ourselves as a distinct people. We needed a language with which we could communicate with ourselves, a secret language. For some of us, language is a homeland closer than the Southwest—for many Chicanos today live in the Midwest and the East. And because we are a complex, heterogeneous people, we speak many languages. Some of the languages we speak are

1. Standard English
2. Working class and slang English
3. Standard Spanish
4. Standard Mexican Spanish
5. North Mexican Spanish dialect
6. Chicano Spanish (Texas, New Mexico, Arizona, and California have regional variations)
7. Tex-Mex
8. *Pachuco* (called *caló*)

My "home" tongues are the languages I speak with my sister and brothers, with my friends. They are the last five listed, with 6 and 7 being closest to my heart. From school, the media, and job situations, I've picked up standard and working class English. From Mamagrande Locha and from reading Spanish and Mexican literature, I've picked up Standard Spanish and Standard Mexican Spanish. From *los recién llegados*, Mexican immigrants, and *braceros*, I learned the North Mexican dialect. With Mexicans I'll try to speak either Standard Mexican Spanish or the North Mexican dialect. From my parents and Chicanos living in the Valley, I picked up Chicano Texas Spanish, and I speak it with my mom, younger brother (who married a Mexican and who rarely mixes Spanish with English), aunts, and older relatives.

With Chicanas from *Nuevo México* or *Arizona* I will speak Chicano Spanish a little, but often they don't understand what I'm saying. With most California

> **❝ In childhood we are told that our language is wrong. Repeated attacks on our native tongue diminish our sense of self. The attacks continue throughout our lives. ❞**

Chicanas I speak entirely in English (unless I forget). When I first moved to San Francisco, I'd rattle off something in Spanish, unintentionally embarrassing them. Often it is only with another Chicana *tejano* that I can talk freely.

Words distorted by English are known as anglicisms or *pochismos*. The *pocho* is an anglicized Mexican or American of Mexican origin who speaks Spanish with an accent characteristic of North Americans and who distorts and reconstructs the language according to the influence of English. Tex-Mex, or Spanglish, comes most naturally to me. I may switch back and forth from English to Spanish in the same sentence or in the same word. With my sister and my brother Nune and with Chicano *tejano* contemporaries I speak in Tex-Mex.

From kids and people my own age I picked up *Pachuco*. *Pachuco* (the language of the zoot suiters) is a language of rebellion, both against Standard Spanish and Standard English. It is a secret language. Adults of the culture and outsiders cannot understand it. It is made up of slang words from both English and Spanish. *Ruca* means girl or woman, *vato* means guy or dude, *chale* means no, *simón* means yes, *churro* is sure, talk is *periquiar; pigionear* means petting, *que gacho* means how nerdy, *ponte águila* means watch out, death is called *la pelona*. Through lack of practice and not having others who can speak it, I've lost most of the *Pachuco* tongue.

CHICANO SPANISH. Chicanos, after 250 years of Spanish/Anglo colonization, have developed significant differences in the Spanish we speak. We collapse two adjacent vowels into a single syllable and sometimes shift the stress in certain words such as *maíz/maiz, cohete/cuete*. We leave out certain consonants when they appear between vowels: *lado/lao, mojado/mojao*. Chicanos from South Texas pronounce *f* as *j* as in *jue (fue)*. Chicanos use "archaisms," words that are no longer in the Spanish language, words that have been evolved out. We say *semos, truje, haiga, ansina*, and *naiden*. We retain the "archaic" *j*, as in *jalar*, that derives from an earlier *h* (the French *halar* or the Germanic *halon* which was lost to standard Spanish in the sixteenth century), but which is still found in several regional dialects such as the one spoken in South Texas. (Due to geography, Chicanos from the Valley of South Texas were cut off linguistically from

other Spanish speakers. We tend to use words that the Spaniards brought over from Medieval Spain. The majority of the Spanish colonizers in Mexico and the Southwest came from Extremadura—Hernán Cortés was one of them—and Andalucía. Andalucians pronounce *ll* like a *y*, and their *d*'s tend to be absorbed by adjacent vowels: *tirado* becomes *tirao*. They brought *el lenguaje popular; dialectos y regionalismos*.)

Chicanos and other Spanish speakers also shift *ll* to *y* and *z* to *s*. We leave out initial syllables, saying *tar* for *estar, toy* for *estoy, hora* for *ahora* (*cubanos* and *puertorriqueños* also leave out initial letters of some words). We also leave out the final syllable such as *pa* for *para*. The intervocalic *y*, the *ll* as in *tortilla, ella, botella*, gets replaced by *tortia* or *tortiya, ea, botea*. We add an additional syllable at the beginning of certain words: *atocar* for *tocar, agastar* for *gastar*. Sometimes we'll say *lavaste las vacijas*, other times *lavates* (substituting the *ates* verb endings for the *aste*).

We used anglicisms, words borrowed from English: *bola* from ball, *carpeta* from carpet, *máchina de lavar* (instead of *lavadora*) from washing machine. Tex-Mex argot, created by adding a Spanish sound at the beginning or end of an English word such as *cookiar* for cook, *watchar* for watch, *parkiar* for park, and *rapiar* for rape, is the result of the pressures on Spanish speakers to adapt to English.

We don't use the word *vosotros/as* or its accompanying verb form. We don't say *claro* (to mean yes), *imaginate*, or *me emociona*, unless we picked up Spanish from Latinas, out of a book, or in a classroom. Other Spanish-speaking groups are going through the same, or similar, development in their Spanish.

LINGUISTIC TERRORISM

> *Deslenguadas. Somos los del español deficiente.* We are your linguistic nightmare, your linguistic aberration, your linguistic *mestisaje*, the subject of your *burla*. Because we speak with tongues of fire we are culturally crucified. Racially, culturally, and linguistically *somos huérfanos*—we speak an orphan tongue.

Chicanas who grew up speaking Chicano Spanish have internalized the belief that we speak poor Spanish. It is illegitimate, a bastard language. And because we internalize how our language has been used against us by the dominant culture, we use our language differences against each other.

Chicana feminists often skirt around each other with suspicion and hesitation. For the longest time I couldn't figure it out. Then it dawned on me. To be close to another Chicana is like looking into the mirror. We are afraid of what we'll see there. *Pena*. Shame. Low estimation of self. In childhood we are told that our language is wrong. Repeated attacks on our native tongue diminish our sense of self. The attacks continue throughout our lives.

Chicanas feel uncomfortable talking in Spanish to Latinas, afraid of their censure. Their language was not outlawed in their countries. They had a whole lifetime of being immersed in their native tongue; generations, centuries in which Spanish was a first language, taught in school, heard on radio and TV, and read in the newspaper.

If a person, Chicana or Latina, has a low estimation of my native tongue, she also has a low estimation of me. Often with *mexicanas y latinas* we'll speak English as a neutral language. Even among Chicanas we tend to speak English at parties or conferences. Yet, at the same time, we're afraid the other will think we're *agringadas* because we don't speak Chicano Spanish. We oppress each other trying to out-Chicano each other, vying to be the "real" Chicanas, to speak like Chicanos. There is no one Chicano language just as there is no one Chicano experience. A monolingual Chicana whose first language is English or Spanish is just as much a Chicana as one who speaks several variants of Spanish. A Chicana from Michigan or Chicago or Detroit is just as much a Chicana as one from the Southwest. Chicano Spanish is as diverse linguistically as it is regionally.

By the end of this century, Spanish speakers will comprise the biggest minority group in the United States, a country where students in high schools and colleges are encouraged to take French classes because French is considered more "cultured." But for a language to remain alive it must be used. By the end of this century English, and not Spanish, will be the mother tongue of most Chicanos and Latinos.

So, if you want to really hurt me, talk badly about my language. Ethnic identity is twin skin to linguistic identity—I am my language. Until I can take pride in my language, I cannot take pride in myself. Until I can accept as legitimate Chicano Texas Spanish, Tex-Mex, and all the other languages I speak, I cannot accept the legitimacy of myself. Until I am free to write bilingually and to switch codes without having always to translate, while I still have to speak English or Spanish when I would rather speak Spanglish, and as long as I have to accommodate the English speakers rather than having them accommodate me, my tongue will be illegitimate.

I will no longer be made to feel ashamed of existing. I will have my voice: Indian, Spanish, white. I will have my serpent's tongue—my woman's voice, my sexual voice, my poet's voice. I will overcome the tradition of silence.

My fingers
move sly against your palm
Like women everywhere, we speak in code.

Melanie Kaye/Kantrowttz

"Vistas," corridos, y comida:

MY NATIVE TONGUE. In the 1960s, I read my first Chicano novel. It was *City of Night* by John Rechy, a gay Texan, son of a Scottish father and a Mexican mother. For days I walked around in stunned amazement that a Chicano could write and could get published. When I read *I Am Joaquin* I was surprised to see a bilingual book by a Chicano in print. When I saw poetry written in Tex-Mex for the first time, a feeling of pure joy flashed through me. I felt like we really existed as a people. In 1971, when I started teaching High School English to Chicano students, I tried to supplement the required texts with works by Chicanos, only to be reprimanded and forbidden to do so by the principal. He claimed that I was supposed to teach "American" and English literature. At the risk of being fired, I swore my students to secrecy and slipped in Chicano short stories, poems, a play. In graduate school, while working toward a Ph.D., I had to "argue" with one adviser after the other, semester after semester, before I was allowed to make Chicano literature an area of focus.

Even before I read books by Chicanos or Mexicans, it was the Mexican movies I saw at the drive-in—the Thursday night special of $1.00 a carload—that gave me a sense of belonging. "*Vámonos a las vistas*," my mother would call out and we'd all—grandmother, brothers, sister, and cousins—squeeze into the car. We'd wolf down cheese and bologna white bread sandwiches while watching Pedro Infante in melodramatic tearjerkers like *Nosotros los pobres*, the first "real" Mexican movie (that was not an imitation of European movies). I remember seeing *Cuando los hijos se van* and surmising that all Mexican movies played up the love a mother has for her children and what ungrateful sons and daughters suffer when they are not devoted to their mothers. I remember the singing-type "westerns" of Jorge Negrete and Miquel Aceves Mejía. When watching Mexican movies, I felt a sense of homecoming as well as alienation. People who were to amount to something didn't go to Mexican movies, or *bailes*, or tune their radios to *bolero*, *rancherita*, and *corrido* music.

The whole time I was growing up, there was *norteño* music sometimes called North Mexican border music, or Tex-Mex music, or Chicano music, or *cantina* (bar) music. I grew up listening to *conjuntos*, three- or four-piece bands made up of folk musicians playing guitar, *bajo sexto*, drums, and button accordion, which Chicanos had borrowed from the German immigrants who had come to Central Texas and Mexico to farm and build breweries. In the Rio Grande Valley, Steve Jordan and Little Joe Hernández were popular, and Flaco Jiménez was the accordion king. The rhythms of Tex-Mex music are those of the polka, also adapted from the Germans, who in turn had borrowed the polka from the Czechs and Bohemians.

I remember the hot, sultry evenings when *corridos*—songs of love and death on the Texas-Mexican borderlands—reverberated out of cheap amplifiers from the local *cantinas* and wafted in through my bedroom window.

Corridos first became widely used along the South Texas/Mexican border during the early conflict between Chicanos and Anglos. The *corridos* are usually about Mexican heroes who do valiant deeds against the Anglo oppressors. Pancho Villa's song, "*La cucaracha*," is the most famous one. *Corridos* of John F. Kennedy and his death are still very popular in the Valley. Older Chicanos remember Lydia Mendoza, one of the great border *corrido* singers who was called *la Gloria de Tejas*. Her "*El tango negro*," sung during the Great Depression, made her a singer of the people. The ever-present *corridos* narrated one hundred years of border history, bringing news of events as well as entertaining. These folk musicians and folk songs are our chief cultural mythmakers, and they made our hard lives seem bearable.

I grew up feeling ambivalent about our music. Country-western and rock-and-roll had more status. In the fifties and sixties, for the slightly educated and *agringado* Chicanos, there existed a sense of shame at being caught listening to our music. Yet I couldn't stop my feet from thumping to the music, could not stop humming the words, nor hide from myself the exhilaration I felt when I heard it.

There are more subtle ways that we internalize identification, especially in the forms of images and emotions. For me food and certain smells are tied to my identity, to my homeland. Woodsmoke curling up to an immense blue sky; woodsmoke perfuming my grandmother's clothes, her skin. The stench of cow manure and the yellow patches on the ground; the crack of a .22 rifle and the reek of cordite. Homemade white cheese sizzling in a pan, melting inside a folded *tortilla*. My sister Hilda's hot, spicy *menudo*, *chile colorado* making it deep red, pieces of *panza* and hominy floating on top. My brother Carito barbequing *fajitas* in the backyard. Even now and 3,000 miles away, I can see my mother spicing the ground beef, pork, and venison with *chile*. My mouth salivates at the thought of the hot steaming *tamales* I would be eating if I were home.

Si le preguntas a mi mamá, "¿Qué eres?"

> Identity is the essential core of who
> we are as individuals, the conscious
> experience of the self inside.
>
> *Cershen Kaufman*

Nosotros los Chicanos straddle the borderlands. On one side of us, we are constantly exposed to the Spanish of the Mexicans, on the other side we hear the Anglos' incessant clamoring so that we forget our language. Among ourselves we don't say *nosotros los americanos*, *o nosotros los españoles*, *o nosotros los hispanos*. We say *nosotros los mexicanos* (by *mexicanos* we do not mean citizens of Mexico; we do not mean a national identity, but a racial one). We distinguish between *mexicanos del otro lado* and *mexicanos de este lado*. Deep in our hearts we believe that being Mexican has nothing to do with which country one lives in. Being Mexican is a state of soul—not one of mind, not one of citizenship. Neither eagle nor serpent, but both. And like the ocean, neither animal respects borders.

> *Dime con quien and as y te diré quien eres.*
> (Tell me who your friends are and I'll tell you
> who you are.)
>
> *Mexican Saying*

Si le preguntas a mi mamá, "¿Qué eres?" te dirá, "*Soy mexicana.*" My brothers and sister say the same. I sometimes will answer "*soy mexicana*" and at others will say "*soy Chicana*" *o* "*soy tejana*." But I identified as "*Raza*" before I ever identified as "*mexicana*" or "*Chicana*."

As a culture, we call ourselves Spanish when referring to ourselves as a linguistic group and when copping out. It is then that we forget our predominant Indian genes. We are 70–80 percent Indian. We call ourselves Hispanic or Spanish-American or Latin American or Latin when linking ourselves to other Spanish-speaking peoples of the Western hemisphere and when copping out. We call ourselves Mexican-American to signify we are neither Mexican nor American, but more the noun "American" than the adjective "Mexican" (and when copping out).

Chicanos and other people of color suffer economically for not acculturating. This voluntary (yet forced) alienation makes for psychological conflict, a kind of dual identity—we don't identify with the Anglo-American cultural values and we don't totally identify with the Mexican cultural values. We are a synergy of two cultures with various degrees of Mexicanness or Angloness. I have so internalized the borderland conflict that sometimes I feel like one cancels out the other and we are zero, nothing, no one. *A veces no soy nada ni nadie. Pero hasta cuando no lo soy, lo soy*.

When not copping out, when we know we are more than nothing, we call ourselves Mexican, referring to race and ancestry; *mestizo* when affirming both our Indian and Spanish (but we hardly ever own our Black) ancestry; Chicano when referring to a politically aware people born and/or raised in the United States; *Raza* when referring to Chicanos; *tejanos* when we are Chicanos from Texas.

> ❝
> **Now that we had a name, some of the fragmented pieces began to fall together—who we were, what we were, how we had evolved. We began to get glimpses of what we might eventually become.**
> ❞

Chicanos did not know we were a people until 1965 when Cesar Chavez and the farmworkers united and *I Am Joaquín* was published and *la Raza Unida* party was formed in Texas. With that recognition, we became a distinct people. Something momentous happened to the Chicano soul—we became aware of our reality and acquired a name and a language (Chicano Spanish) that reflected that reality. Now that we had a name, some of the fragmented pieces began to fall together—who we were, what we were, how we had evolved. We began to get glimpses of what we might eventually become.

Yet the struggle of identities continues, the struggle of borders is our reality still. One day the inner struggle will cease and a true integration take place. In the meantime, *tenémos que hacer la lucha. ¿Quién está protegiendo los ranchos de mi gente? ¿Quién está tratando de cerrar la fisura entre la india y el blanco en nuestra sangre? El Chicano, si, el Chicano que anda como un landrón en su propia casa.*

Los Chicanos, how patient we seem, how very patient. There is the quiet of the Indian about us. We know how to survive. When other races have given up their tongue we've kept ours. We know what it is to live under the hammer blow of the dominant *norteamericano* culture. But more than we count the blows, we count the days the weeks the years the centuries the aeons until the white laws and commerce and customs will rot in the deserts they've created, lie bleached. *Humildes* yet proud, *quietos* yet wild, *nosotros los mexicanos-Chicanos* will walk by the crumbling ashes as we go about our business. Stubborn, persevering, impenetrable as stone, yet possessing a malleability that renders us unbreakable, we, the *mestizas* and *mestizos*, will remain.

Journal and Discussion Questions

1 What is the thesis of Gloria Anzaldúa's "How to Tame a Wild Tongue"? How are the title and Anzaldúa's introductory anecdotes related to this thesis?

2 "How to Tame a Wild Tongue" does not have a straightforward, "logical" organization, and Anzaldúa does not consistently begin each section of her essay with a heading. Outline Anzaldúa's essay. What is Anzaldúa's central concern in each section? How is her discussion in each section related to her discussion in the next section? Why do you think Anzaldúa put her sections in this order rather than follow an organization more familiar to readers?

3 Anzaldúa devotes much of "How to Tame a Wild Tongue" to discussing people's attitudes toward different languages and dialects and the people who use these languages. Whose attitudes is she interested in and why? What stereotypes does she challenge? Why do you think she is interested in the attitudes of Spanish speakers and not just the attitudes of Anglos who know only English?

4 Political discussions about the Spanish language in the United States often describe the situation as a choice between two languages—English or Spanish. How does Anzaldúa describe the mix of languages in the U.S.–Mexican borderlands, especially among Chicanos? Why do you think Anzaldúa considers this knowledge important to discussions of language policy in the U.S.?

5 According to Anzaldúa, why is language so important to the identity or self-image of individuals and of groups? How are gender and race involved in how identity and language intertwine with each other? How do current attitudes and policies about Spanish in the U.S. affect Chicano identity?

6 What are the problems with, or limitations of, the different names used to identify Chicanos—Chicano, Spanish, Hispanic, Mexican, Mexican-American, *mestizo*, Spanish-American, Latin, Latin American, etc.? What does Anzaldúa mean by "copping out" in her discussions of identity and names?

7 *Borderlands/La frontera*, the title of the book that includes "How to Tame a Wild Tongue," suggests that "borders" and "borderlands" are important metaphors for Anzaldúa. What do these metaphors mean to Anzaldúa, especially in the last section of her essay?

Topics for Writing

1 Analyze "How to Tame a Wild Tongue," focusing on one facet of Anzaldúa's essay, such as how the essay develops one of its ideas, how it is organized and why, or how Anzaldúa mixes Spanish and English in her essay and why.

2 Describe how language is involved in forming and maintaining identity. Your essay may focus on Chicanos and the varieties of English and Spanish that they use, or you may write about another group of people and how the language(s) that they use contributes to who they are and how they think of themselves and of each other.

3 Write a research paper discussing how language affects the lives and cultures on the U.S.–Mexican border.

THE FRENCH LANGUAGE:
The Heart of Louisiana

BY KALYN GUIDRY

Kalyn Guidry (1987–) is a student at the University of Louisiana at Lafayette. She wrote "The French Language: The Heart of Louisiana" in Connor Chauveaux's English 102 class in the spring of 2007. Guidry's research paper describes the importance of the French language to the Cajun culture of South Louisiana and supports efforts to preserve and promote the speaking of French in Louisiana. Guidry's research topic enabled her to make use of her knowledge of her local culture as a Cajun and to learn more about her Acadian heritage.

Kalyn Guidry

English 102

Connor Chauveaux

2 May 2007

The French Language: The Heart of Louisiana

The near disappearance of the French language is one of the most tragic events in Louisiana history. Nearly every youth of Cajun descent can name an elderly family member who speaks French, yet a youth in Louisiana who speaks French is a rare find. The French language is deeply rooted in Acadian history, culture, and heritage. The Acadian people have been suffering for years trying to uphold their culture and have overcome many attempts to devastate it. From the time the Cajuns lived in Canada in a colony called Acadia, their French language and unique culture has been under attack. Since arriving in Louisiana, the French language has become nearly extinct. The Cajun culture itself has managed to survive, if not flourish, throughout the Americanization of the Cajun people. But unfortunately, its language, which has been spoken by Cajuns in Louisiana for nearly three hundred years and is arguably the most important aspect of its culture, is fighting to prevent extinction in this generation. Barry Ancelet, a professor at the University of Louisiana at Lafayette, said to a newspaper, "The miracle is that, with all the attempts to kill it, there is anyone still speaking French at all. I think it has to do with the ferocious sense of independence here" (Tutwiler 13). Along with that independence Acadians have determination, and in reaction to this tragedy, many Cajuns in South Louisiana are becoming very active in the movement to uphold our heritage's French-speaking ancestors. French immersion programs are the most important outcome of this movement. French immersion programs in South Louisiana today are aiding in the survival of a four-hundred-year-old culture, and at the same time upholding Acadiana's unique and precious heritage.

The history of the Acadian people is extremely important in understanding why so many Cajuns want to maintain their culture. The first word that comes to mind is pride. The Acadians, since settling in a colony founded in 1604 known as Acadia, have been the victims of British cruelty. They were stuck in the middle of a power struggle between Great Britain and France that they wanted nothing to do with, and only desired to be allowed to express their culture, practice their Catholic religion, and speak their French language. Yet they suffered the most in this battle and were not granted any of the above requests. After a century of fighting, the deportations of Acadians began in the 1750's. Families were taken prisoners in their own lands by the British and deported to nearly ten different locations, sometimes five or six times over. By 1816, the Acadian migrations were finally over, and Acadian families, some separated, were dispersed all over the map. Many were sent to New England colonies where they weren't welcomed or understood, and were greatly criticized for not speaking English. A large majority of Acadians tried to return to Nova Scotia or

Prince Edward Island, but most were unsuccessful. Of the fifteen thousand Acadians who were deported, nearly three thousand took refuge in Louisiana, and they called their new region Acadiana, after their precious prior home Acadia in Canada (Condow 1-6).

Upon reaching Louisiana, the Cajuns faced new challenges when forced to "Americanize." With the beginning World War II, the Cajuns of Louisiana who had finally settled peacefully in the country were forced once again to come out of isolation, thus beginning the Americanization process. Mixed with Americans in the war, Cajuns experienced immense discrimination and criticism for their speech, culture, and names. Earl Comeaux, a soldier in the 1950's, expressed that he experienced "prejudice against me personally for the first time. I never thought of myself as a Cajun until then" (Bernard 28). But possibly the most harmful change to the Cajun-French culture was the classroom environment. Cajuns were spoken of extremely poorly in textbooks, as seen in *The People of Louisiana*, a book published in 1951, which described the Cajuns as "an unsophisticated agrarian people, slow in adopting 'American' ways," which were considered "the values and standards of their English speaking neighbors" (Bernard 32). Not stopping at that, the state textbook went on to blame the French-speaking region for why the population of southern Louisiana had such a poor educational standing, "just as the Spanish-speaking population of New Mexico is responsible for that state's low ranking educationally" (Bernard 33).

Not surprisingly, the French language was not only discouraged at this point, but children were punished severely when they used it. Paul L. Landry of Calcasieu Parish recalled teachers "locking violators (students who spoke French) in a closet or forcing them to wear nooses around their necks—a symbolic death for anyone who dared to speak their native tongue in the classroom" (Bernard 33). This "Americanization" of the Cajun people was nearly the death of their culture altogether. Where 83% of Cajuns spoke French as their primary language at the beginning of the twentieth century, only 21% of those born between 1956 and 1960 spoke it (Bernard 34). Yet despite all blows that the Acadian people have taken in the past four hundred years, today the Cajun culture is alive and kicking. And it is principally the history of this culture that keeps it alive. Because it has endured so much, the descendants of the French-speaking people of Acadia have immense respect and pride in their heritage and culture, and are still fighting to keep it alive today.

However, although the Cajun culture is still thriving in Louisiana today, the French language is still suffering from the effects that the past had on it. Where half a million people responded to speaking French as a native language in 1970, the census taken in 1990 reported that number to have dropped to two hundred thousand (Tutwiler 14). It is the spirit, pride, and desire to be fully Cajun which so many Acadians have that brought about the rise of French immersion programs in Louisiana.

Probably the most influential group leading the way in French immersion today is CODOFIL, the Council for the Development of French in Louisiana. CODOFIL was created in 1968 and by Legislative Act #409 given the power to "do any and all things necessary to accomplish the development, utilization, and preservation of the French language as found in Louisiana for the cultural, economic and touristic benefit of the state" ("CODOFIL"). CODOFIL has worked extremely hard in the past to reverse the psychological belief that French is inferior and unworthy of learning. This council is the first of many who unite a community with one goal: to preserve the French language and the Cajun French heritage. Another organization is CAFA, the Confederation of Associations of Families Acadian. Among their objectives is to promote the genealogy and culture of Acadian families, and their immediate goal is "Doing our utmost to supplement Foreign Language Classes in our area schools with supplies and funding to perpetuate the French Language" ("Who Is CAFA?"). Yet another organization is Action Cadienne, whose manifesto is "Because it is impossible to conceive of a culture without being able to speak its language" ("Manifesto"). With all these successful organizations popping up, it is clear that the issue of maintaining the French language with immersion programs in Louisiana is a very important matter to Cajuns today. It has been approximated that nine hundred students are now enrolled in French immersion programs in Lafayette Parish.

There are so many benefits to speaking one's heritage language. Grace Cho, a student at California State University, conducted a study into the benefits of speaking both one's native language and the language of their ancestors. One of her sociocultural findings was that those who speak their heritage language aided greatly in maintaining a better relationship with the generation before them who spoke their heritage language. She also found that those who had heritage language competence had a strong sense of identity and took great pride in, as well as had a better understanding of their culture (Cho). Morgan Calhoun, an eighth grader at Paul Breaux in the French immersion program agrees with Cho's findings, saying, "My step-dad's parents love it that I can speak French with them" (Tutwiler 14). In addition to speaking with one's elderly community members, it is also a great benefit to be able to communicate with those who speak French from other countries. Oliver Marteau, who came from France three years ago without knowing much English, now has a Thursday radio show on KRVS 88.7. He connected with this, saying, "I was struggling in English, and people, when they knew I really spoke French, they would speak to me in French. I met so many people the first year in Lafayette; I didn't really develop my English" (Tutwiler 14). So speaking French, and being bilingual in general, is proven to be extremely beneficial in connecting with both one's own community and culture as well as other French cultures throughout the world.

Probably the most important argument for the importance of French immersion in Louisiana today is simply that the Acadian people, both now and in the past, have had such a passion for their culture. It is more than a culture, it's a family which includes both Acadians here in Louisiana and Acadians who are still dispersed throughout the world as a result of the Grand Deportation which began in the 1750s. Leonie Comeau Poirier, an Acadian from Nova Scotia, in her book *My Acadian Heritage* expressed,

Acadians have strong historical ties. We're like a large family. I have been called "cousin" by people living in France whose ancestors were deported from Grand Pré in 1755. Their homes are open to me whenever I visit France. I have just returned from Southern Louisiana where a Cajun—formerly an Arsenault whose ancestors were also exiled by Governor Lawrence—received us as part of her family. Although the language spoken is mostly English, the names of the old Acadia and the historical ties are very strong" (Comean Poirier 88).

For nearly four hundred years now, the Acadian people have been struggling to live the simple life that they so desired in which they had few requests: to express their culture, practice their religion, and speak their language. As Huey Balfa, a renowned Acadian musician from the 1970's, put it, "My culture is not better than anybody else's culture. My people were not better than anybody else. And yet I will not accept it as a second-class culture. It's my culture. It's the best culture for me. Now I would expect, if you have a different culture, that you would feel the same about yours as I feel about mine" ("Who Is CAFA"). Finally the Acadian people are allowed to do just that, and, thanks to French immersion programs in South Louisiana, the Acadian's language still has hope at survival. As Mary Tutwiler said in her article in *The Independent Weekly*, "Language is at the heart of what makes Acadiana a unique place" (Tutwiler 12), and it is the obligation of Cajuns today to keep that spirit and family alive.

[NEW PAGE]

Works Cited

Bernard, Shane K. *The Cajuns: Americanization of a People*. Jackson: UP of Mississippi, 2003. Print.

Cho, Grace. *The Role of Heritage Language in Social Interactions and Relationships: Reflections from a Language Minority Group*. California State U, Fullerton, 2000. Web. 25 Apr. 2007.

"CODOFIL: Education." *CODOFIL*. Council for the Development of French in Louisiana, n.d. Web. 25 Apr. 2007.

Comeau Poirier, Leonie. *My Acadian Heritage*. Hantsport: Lancelot, 1985. Print.

Condow, James E. *The Deportations of the Acadians*. Ottawa: Minister of Supply Services Canada, 1986. Print.

"The Manifesto." *Action Acadianne*. Actionacadianne.org, n.d. Web. 2 May 2007.

Tutwiler, Mary. "The French Connection." *Independent Weekly* 9 Aug. 2006: 12–15. Print.

"Who Is CAFA?" *CAFA*. Confederation of Associated Families Acadian, 1 Apr. 2008. Web. 2 May 2007.

Journal and Discussion Questions

1 What is Kalyn Guidry's thesis in "The French Language: The Heart of Louisiana"? Why, according to Guidry, is French important to Cajuns, their culture, and their sense of identity?

2 How does Guidry's history of the Acadian people in Canada and Louisiana support her claims about the importance of French in Louisiana? What reasons motivated efforts to discourage or eliminate the speaking of French in Louisiana?

3 What roles have schools played in Cajuns' struggle to preserve the French language in their culture? What does Guidry's discussion of schools' attitudes and actions regarding the speaking of French indicate about how educators' ideas about schools' relationships to the local culture and language have changed?

4 What efforts to preserve French in South Louisiana does Guidry describe? Why does she support these efforts?

5 How does Guidry use her sources to develop her argument? Which of her sources provide "insider" perspectives about Cajun culture, by Cajuns themselves, and which sources provide outsider views? Why do you think she chose sources with a mix of perspectives about Cajuns? Why does Guidry discuss Grace Cho's study of Spanish speakers in California to develop Guidry's claims about the French language in South Louisiana?

6 What does Guidry's discussion of French language in Cajun culture suggest about the relationship between culture and language in general? What does the situation she describes have in common with other cultures with two or more native languages? What seems unique about the language situation of Acadiana?

7 Are you persuaded by "The French Language: The Heart of Louisiana"? Why or why not?

Topics for Writing

1 Analyze Kalyn Guidry's "The French Language: The Heart of Louisiana" as a research paper. Evaluate her sources, how she uses her sources to develop and support her ideas, and the strength and persuasiveness of her arguments.

2 Using Guidry as a source, argue whether governments and schools should work to promote languages other than English in the U.S. or whether they should devote their resources only to English instruction.

3 Write a research paper describing a program like CODOFIL that seeks to preserve a language in danger of dying, such as the French language in Louisiana or the Irish language in Ireland. Discuss the motives behind the program and assess its chances of success.

Connecting the Readings

Compare Gloria Anzaldúa's discussion of the importance of Spanish in the U.S./Mexican border country in "How to Tame a Wild Tongue" with Kalyn Guidry's discussion of the importance of French in South Louisiana in "The French Language: The Heart of Louisiana."

BILINGUALISM IN AMERICA: English Should Be the *Official* Language

BY S. I. HAYAKAWA

S. I. Hayakawa (1906–1992) was a naturalized U.S. citizen who was born in Vancouver, Canada, to Japanese parents. As a professor of linguistics at several universities, Hayakawa made important contributions to the development of semantics and to the teaching of writing and propaganda analysis with books such as *Our Language and Our World* and *Language and Society*. He became a national political figure when he cracked down on student rioters in 1968 as interim president of San Francisco State University and was elected to one term in the U.S. Senate in 1976 as a Republican from California. Hayakawa introduced a constitutional amendment in the Senate to make English the official language of the United States, and, after he left office in 1983, he helped found the organization U.S. English to continue to argue this position. Hayakawa argues how American citizens would benefit from a constitutional amendment making English the official national language of the U.S. in "Bilingualism in America," a July 1989 guest editorial in the national daily newspaper *USA Today*.

DURING THE DARK DAYS OF WORLD War II, Chinese immigrants in California wore badges proclaiming their original nationality so they would not be mistaken for Japanese. In fact, these two immigrant groups long had been at odds with each other. However, as new English-speaking generations came along, the Chinese and Japanese began to communicate with one another. They found they had much in common and began to socialize. Today, they get together and form Asian-American societies.

Such are the amicable results of sharing the English language. English unites us as American-immigrants and native-born alike. Communicating with each other in a single, common tongue encourages trust, while reducing racial hostility and bigotry.

My appreciation of English has led me to devote my retirement years to championing it. Several years ago, I helped to establish U.S. English, a Washington, D.C.-based public interest group that seeks an amendment to the U.S. Constitution declaring English our official language, regardless of what other languages we may use unofficially.

As an immigrant to this nation, I am keenly aware of the things that bind us as Americans and unite us as a single people. Foremost among these unifying forces is the common language we share. While it is certainly true that our love of freedom and devotion to democratic principles help to unite and give us a mutual purpose, it is English, our common language, that enables us to discuss our views and allows us to maintain a well-informed electorate, the cornerstone of democratic government.

Because we are a nation of immigrants, we do not share the characteristics of race, religion, ethnicity, or native language which form the common bonds of society in other countries. However, by agreeing to learn and use a single, universally spoken language, we have been able to forge a unified people from an incredibly diverse population.

Although our 200-year history should be enough to convince any skeptic of the powerful unifying effects of a common language, some still advocate the official recognition of other languages. They argue that a knowledge of English is not part of the formula for responsible citizenship in this country.

Some contemporary political leaders, like the former mayor of Miami, Maurice Ferre, maintain that "Language is not necessary to the system. Nowhere does our Constitution say that English is our language." He also told the *Tampa Tribune* that, "Within ten years there will not be a single word of English spoken [in Miami]—English is not Miami's official language—[and] one day residents will have to learn Spanish or leave."

The U.S. Department of Education also reported that countless speakers at a conference on bilingual education "expounded at length on the need for and eventually of, a multilingual, multicultural United States of America with a national language policy citing English and Spanish as the two 'legal languages.'"

As a former resident of California, I am completely familiar with a system that uses two official languages, and I would not advise any nation to move in such a direction unless forced to do so. While it is true that India functions with ten official languages, I haven't heard anyone suggest that it functions particularly well because of its multilingualism. In fact, most Indians will concede that the situation is a chaotic mess which has led to countless problems in the government's efforts to manage the nation's business. Out of necessity, English still is used extensively in India as a common language.

Belgium is another clear example of the diverse effects of two officially recognized languages in the same nation. Linguistic differences between Dutch- and French-speaking citizens have resulted in chronic political instability. Consequently, in the aftermath of the most recent government collapse, legislators are working on a plan to turn over most of its powers and responsibilities to the various regions, a clear recognition of the diverse effects of linguistic separateness.

There are other problems. Bilingualism is a costly and confusing bureaucratic nightmare. The Canadian government has estimated its bilingual costs to be nearly $400,000,000 per year. It is almost certain that these expenses will increase as a result of a massive expansion of bilingual services approved by the Canadian Parliament in 1988. In the United States, which has ten times the population of Canada, the cost of similar bilingual services easily would be in the billions.

We first should consider how politically infeasible it is that our nation ever could recognize Spanish as a second official language without opening the floodgates for official recognition of the more than 100 languages spoken in this country. How long would it take, under such an arrangement, before the United States started to make India look like a model of efficiency?

Even if we can agree that multilingualism would be a mistake, some would suggest that official recognition of English is not needed. After all, our nation has existed for over 200 years without this, and English as our common language has continued to flourish.

I could agree with this sentiment had government continued to adhere to its time-honored practice of operating in English and encouraging newcomers to learn the language. However, this is not the case. Over the last few decades, government has been edging slowly towards policies that place other languages on a par with English.

In reaction to the cultural consciousness movement of the 1960s and 1970s, government has been increasingly reluctant to press immigrants to learn the English language, lest it be accused of "cultural imperialism." Rather than insisting that it is the immigrant's duty to learn the language of this country, the government has acted instead as if it has a duty to accommodate an immigrant in his native language.

A prime example of this can be found in the continuing debate over Federal and state policies relating to bilingual education. At times, these have come dangerously close to making the main goal of this program the maintenance of the immigrant child's native language, rather than the early acquisition of English.

> As an immigrant to this nation, I am keenly aware of the things that bind us as Americans and unite us as a single people.

As a former U.S. senator from California, where we spend more on bilingual education programs than any other state, I am very familiar with both the rhetoric and reality that lie behind the current debate on bilingual education. My experience has convinced me that many of these programs are shortchanging immigrant children in their quest to learn English.

To set the record straight from the start, I do not oppose bilingual education *if it is truly bilingual*. Employing a child's native language to teach him (or her) English is entirely appropriate. What is not appropriate is continuing to use the children of Hispanic and other immigrant groups as guinea pigs in an unproven program that fails to teach English efficiently and perpetuates their dependency on their native language.

Under the dominant method of bilingual education used throughout this country, non-English-speaking students are taught all academic subjects such as math, science, and history exclusively in their native language. English is taught as a separate subject. The problem with this method is that there is no objective way to measure whether a child has learned enough English to be placed in classes where academic instruction is entirely in English. As a result, some children have been kept in native language classes for six years.

Some bilingual education advocates, who are more concerned with maintaining the child's use of their native language, may not see any problem with such a situation. However, those who feel that the most important goal of this program is to get children functioning quickly in English appropriately are alarmed.

In the Newhall School District in California, some Hispanic parents are raising their voices in criticism of its bilingual education program, which relies on native language instruction. Their children complain of systematically being segregated from their English-speaking peers. Now in high school, these students cite the failure of the program to teach them English first as the reason for being years behind their classmates.

Even more alarming is the Berkeley (Calif.) Unified School District, where educators have recognized that all-native-language instruction would be an inadequate response to the needs of their non-English-speaking pupils. Challenged by a student body that spoke more than four different languages and by budgetary constraints, teachers and administrators responded with innovative language programs that utilized many methods of teaching English. That school district is now in court answering charges that the education they provided was inadequate because it did not provide transitional bilingual education for every non-English speaker. What was introduced twenty years ago as an experimental project has become—despite inconclusive research evidence—the only acceptable method of teaching for bilingual education advocates.

When one considers the nearly 50 percent dropout rate among Hispanic students (the largest group receiving this type of instruction), one wonders about their ability to function in the English-speaking mainstream of this country. The school system may have succeeded wonderfully in maintaining their native language, but if it failed to help them to master the English language fully, what is the benefit?

ALTERNATIVES. If this method of bilingual education is not the answer, are we forced to return to the old, discredited, sink-or-swim approach? No, we are not, since, as shown in Berkeley and other school districts, there are a number of alternative methods that have been proven effective, while avoiding the problems of all-native-language instruction.

Sheltered English and English as a Second Language (ESL) are just two programs that have helped to get children quickly proficient in English. Yet, political recognition of the viability of alternate methods has been slow in coming. In 1988, we witnessed the first

crack in the monolithic hold that native language instruction has had on bilingual education funds at the Federal level. In its reauthorization of Federal bilingual education, Congress voted to increase the percentage of funds available for alternate methods from 4 to 25 percent of the total. This is a great breakthrough, but we should not be satisfied until 100 percent of the funds are available for any program that effectively and quickly can get children functioning in English, regardless of the amount of native language instruction it uses.

My goal as a student of language and a former educator is to see all students succeed academically, no matter what language is spoken in their homes. I want to see immigrant students finish their high school education and be able to compete for college scholarships. To help achieve this goal, instruction in English should start as early as possible. Students should be moved into English mainstream classes in one or, at the very most, two years. They should not continue to be segregated year after year from their English-speaking peers.

Another highly visible shift in Federal policy that I feel demonstrates quite clearly the eroding support of government for our common language is the requirement for bilingual voting ballots. Little evidence ever has been presented to show the need for ballots in other languages. Even prominent Hispanic organizations acknowledge that more than 90 percent of native-born Hispanics currently are fluent in English and more than half of that population is English monolingual.

Furthermore, if the proponents of bilingual ballots are correct when they claim that the absence of native language ballots prevents non-English-speaking citizens from exercising their right to vote, then current requirements are clearly unfair because they provide assistance to certain groups of voters while ignoring others. Under current Federal law, native language ballots are required only for certain groups: those speaking Spanish, Asian, or Native American languages. European or African immigrants are not provided ballots in their native language, even in jurisdictions covered by the Voting Rights Act.

As sensitive as Americans have been to racism, especially since the days of the civil rights movement, no one seems to have noticed the profound racism expressed in the amendment that created the "bilingual ballot." Brown people, like Mexicans and Puerto Ricans; red people, like American Indians; and yellow people, like the Japanese and Chinese, are assumed not to be smart enough to learn English. No provision is made, however, for non-English-speaking French-Canadians in Maine or Vermont, or Yiddish-speaking Hasidic Jews in Brooklyn, who are white and thus presumed to be able to learn English without difficulty.

Voters in San Francisco encountered ballots in Spanish and Chinese for the first time in the elections of 1980, much to their surprise, since authorizing legislation had been passed by Congress with almost no debate, roll-call vote, or public discussion. Naturalized Americans, who had taken the trouble to learn English to become citizens, were especially angry and remain so. While native language ballots may be a convenience to some voters, the use of English ballots does not deprive citizens of their right to vote. Under current voting law, non-English-speaking voters are permitted to bring a friend or family member to the polls to assist them in casting their ballots. Absentee ballots could provide another method that would allow a voter to receive this help at home.

Congress should be looking for other methods to create greater access to the ballot box for the currently small number of citizens who cannot understand an English ballot, without resorting to the expense of requiring ballots in foreign languages. We cannot continue to overlook the message we are sending to immigrants about the connection between English language ability and citizenship when we print ballots in other languages. The ballot is the primary symbol of civic duty. When we tell immigrants that they should learn English—yet offer them full voting participation in their native language—I fear our actions will speak louder than our words.

If we are to prevent the expansion of policies such as these, moving us further along the multilingual path, we need to make a strong statement that our political leaders will understand. We must let them know that we do not choose to reside in a "Tower of Babel." Making English our nation's official language *by law* will send the proper signal to newcomers about the importance of learning English and provide the necessary guidance to legislators to preserve our traditional policy of a common language.

Journal and Discussion Questions

1 Summarize S. I. Hayakawa's argument. What would have to happen for English to become the official language of the U.S.? What are some of the changes that Hayakawa wants to bring about with this law? Outline "Bilingualism in America." What does your outline reveal about how Hayakawa organizes and develops his argument?

2 What reasons and evidence do you find most persuasive in Hayakawa's argument? Why? What reasons and evidence are least persuasive? Why?

3 Where does Hayakawa discuss opposing arguments to his position? What are these arguments? How does Hayakawa counter these arguments?

4 What does Hayakawa mean when he identifies "the common language we share" as one of the most important "unifying forces" "that bind us as Americans and unite us as a single people"? How does a common language unify a people? How does Hayakawa explain and support this idea?

5 What does Hayakawa mean by "bilingual education"? What problems does he describe with bilingual education? What are the arguments in favor of bilingual education? What changes does Hayakawa advocate in the education of immigrant children who do not know English? What does Hayakawa mean—and why does he use italics—when he writes, "I do not oppose bilingual education *if it is truly bilingual*"?

6 Why does Hayakawa oppose bilingual ballots? What are the arguments in favor of bilingual ballots, and how does Hayakawa respond to these arguments?

7 Where does Hayakawa bring research into his argument? What are his sources of information? How does Hayakawa use this research to persuade his readers and develop his arguments? Hayakawa quotes only one source, Maurice Ferre, the only individual named in his editorial. Why does Hayakawa single out Ferre?

Topics for Writing

1 Argue about one of the issues in "Bilingualism in America"—whether English should be made the official language of the U.S., whether a country or a community needs one common language for stability and unity, whether the U.S. should have bilingual ballots for voters who read English poorly, or whether public schools should offer bilingual education. Your essay may argue against Hayakawa, or you may agree with Hayakawa and further develop his arguments with new reasons and evidence.

2 Discuss why the issues of making English the official language of the U.S., how immigrant children should learn English, and bilingual ballots frequently cause Americans to engage in emotional, divisive debates. Why do Americans feel so strongly about this issue, on both sides of the debate?

3 According to Hawakawa writing in 1989, the effectiveness of bilingual education programs were "unproven." Conduct research about educational programs for children who are not native speakers of English used in schools today and write a research paper that evaluates how well these programs work.

SHOULD ENGLISH BE THE LAW?

BY ROBERT D. KING

Robert D. King (1936–) is a professor of Asian studies, German, and linguistics at the University of Texas at Austin, with a Ph.D. in German linguistics from the University of Wisconsin. He has published numerous articles about language in academic journals and in magazines for general audiences such as *Society*, the *Texas Observer*, and the *National Review*. In "Should English Be the Law?" King compares the movement to make English the official language of the U.S. to official language laws and movements in other countries and questions the ability of a national language to unify the people of a nation. "Should English Be the Law?" was first published in the *Atlantic Monthly* in April 1997.

WE HAVE KNOWN RACE RIOTS, draft riots, labor violence, secession, antiwar protests, and a whiskey rebellion, but one kind of trouble we've never had: a language riot. Language riot? It sounds like a joke. The very idea of language as a political force—as something that might threaten to split a country wide apart—is alien to our way of thinking and to our cultural traditions.

This may be changing. On August 1 of last year the U.S. House of Representatives approved a bill that would make English the official language of the United States. The vote was 259 to 169, with 223 Republicans and thirty-six Democrats voting in favor and eight Republicans, 160 Democrats, and one independent voting against. The debate was intense, acrid, and partisan. On March 25 of last year the Supreme Court agreed to review a case involving an Arizona law that would require public employees to conduct government business only in English. Arizona is one of several states that have passed "Official English" or "English Only" laws. The appeal to the Supreme Court followed a 6-to-5 ruling, in October of 1995, by a federal appeals court striking down the Arizona law. These events suggest how divisive a public issue language could become in America—even if it has until now scarcely been taken seriously.

Traditionally, the American way has been to make English the national language—but to do so quietly, locally, without fuss. The Constitution is silent on language: the Founding Fathers had no need to legislate that English be the official language of the country. It has always been taken for granted that English is the national language, and that one must learn English in order to make it in America.

To say that language has never been a major force in American history or politics, however, is not to say that politicians have always resisted linguistic jingoism. In 1753 Benjamin Franklin voiced his concern that German immigrants were not learning English: "Those [Germans] who come hither are generally the most ignorant Stupid Sort of their own Nation . . . . they will soon so out number us, that all the advantages we have will not, in My Opinion, be able to preserve our language, and even our government will become precarious." Theodore Roosevelt articulated the unspoken American linguistic-melting-pot theory when he boomed, "We have room for but one language here, and that is the English language, for we intend to see that the crucible turns our people out as Americans, of American nationality, and not as dwellers in a polyglot boarding house." And: "We must have but one flag. We must also have but one language. That must be the language of the Declaration of Independence, of Washington's Farewell address, of Lincoln's Gettysburg speech and second inaugural."

OFFICIAL ENGLISH. TR's linguistic tub-thumping long typified the tradition of American politics. That tradition began to change in the wake of the anything-goes attitudes and the celebration of cultural differences arising in the 1960s. A 1975 amendment to the Voting Rights Act of 1965 mandated the "bilingual ballot" under certain circumstances, notably when the voters of selected language groups reached five percent or more in a voting district. Bilingual education became a byword of educational thinking during the 1960s. By the 1970s linguists had demonstrated convincingly—at least to other academics—that black English (today called African-American vernacular English or Ebonics) was not "bad" English but a different kind of authentic English with its own rules. Predictably, there have been scattered demands that black English be included in bilingual-education programs.

It was against this background that the movement to make English the official language of the country arose. In 1981 Senator S. I. Hayakawa, long a leading critic of bilingual education and bilingual ballots, introduced in the U.S. Senate a constitutional amendment that not only would have made English the official language but would have prohibited federal and state laws and regulations requiring the use of other languages. His English Language Amendment died in the Ninety-seventh Congress.

In 1983 the organization called U.S. English was founded by Hayakawa and John Tanton, a Michigan ophthalmologist. The primary purpose of the organization was to promote English as the official language of the United States. (The best background readings on America's "neolinguisticism" are the books *Hold Your Tongue*, by James Crawford, and *Language Loyalties*, edited by Crawford, both published in 1992.) Official English initiatives were passed by California in 1986, by Arkansas, Mississippi, North Carolina, North Dakota, and South Carolina in 1987, by Colorado, Florida, and Arizona in 1988, and by Alabama in 1990. The majorities voting for these initiatives were generally not insubstantial: California's, for example, passed by 73 percent.

It was probably inevitable that the Official English (or English Only—the two names are used almost interchangeably) movement would acquire a conservative, almost reactionary undertone in the 1990s. Official English is politically very incorrect. But its cofounder John Tanton brought with him strong liberal credentials. He had been active in the Sierra Club and Planned Parenthood, and in the 1970s served as the national president of Zero Population Growth. Early advisers of U.S. English resist ideological pigeonholing: they included Walter Annenberg, Jacques Barzun, Bruno Bettelheim, Alistair Cooke, Denton Cooley, Walter Cronkite, Angier Biddle Duke, George Gilder, Sidney Hook, Norman Podhoretz, Arnold Schwarzenegger, and Karl Shapiro. In 1987 U.S. English installed as its president Linda Chávez, a Hispanic who had been prominent in the Reagan Administration. A year later she resigned her position, citing "repugnant" and "anti-Hispanic" overtones in an internal memorandum written by Tanton. Tanton, too, resigned, and Walter Cronkite, describing the affair as "embarrassing," left the advisory board. One board member, Norman Cousins, defected in 1986, alluding to the "negative symbolic significance" of California's Official English initiative, Proposition 63. The current chairman of the board and CEO of U.S. English is Mauro E. Mujica, who claims that the organization has 650,000 members.

The popular wisdom is that conservatives are pro and liberals con. True, conservatives such as George Will and William F. Buckley Jr. have written columns supporting Official English. But would anyone characterize as conservatives the present and past U.S. English board members Alistair Cooke, Walter Cronkite, and Norman Cousins? One of the strongest opponents of bilingual education is the Mexican-American writer Richard Rodríguez, best known for his eloquent autobiography, *Hunger of Memory* (1982). There is a strain of American liberalism that defines itself in nostalgic devotion to the melting pot.

For several years relevant bills awaited consideration in the U.S. House of Representatives. The Emerson Bill (H.R. 123), passed by the House last August, specifies English as the official language of government, and requires that the government "preserve and enhance" the official status of English. Exceptions are made for the teaching of foreign languages; for actions necessary for public health, international relations, foreign trade, and the protection of the rights of criminal defendants; and for the use of "terms of art" from languages other than English. It would, for example, stop the Internal Revenue Service from sending out income-tax forms and instructions in languages other than English, but it would not ban the use of foreign languages in census materials or documents dealing with national security. "*E Pluribus Unum*" can still appear on American money. U.S. English supports the bill.

What are the chances that some version of Official English will become federal law? Any language bill will face tough odds in the Senate, because some western senators have opposed English Only measures in the past for various reasons, among them a desire by Republicans not to alienate the growing number of Hispanic Republicans, most of whom are uncomfortable with mandated monolingualism. Texas Governor George W. Bush, too, has forthrightly said that he would oppose any English Only proposals in his state. Several of the Republican candidates for President in 1996 (an interesting exception is Phil Gramm) endorsed versions of Official English, as has Newt Gingrich. While governor of Arkansas, Bill Clinton signed into law an English Only bill. As President, he has described his earlier action as a mistake.

Many issues intersect in the controversy over Official English: immigration (above all), the rights of minorities (Spanish-speaking minorities in particular), the pros and cons of bilingual education, tolerance, how best to educate the children of immigrants, and the place of cultural diversity in school curricula and in American society in general. The question that lies at the root of most of the uneasiness is this: Is America threatened by the preservation of languages other than English? Will America, if it continues on its traditional path of benign linguistic neglect, go the way of Belgium, Canada, and Sri Lanka—three countries among many whose unity is gravely imperiled by language and ethnic conflicts?

LANGUAGE AND NATIONALITY. Language and nationalism were not always so intimately intertwined. Never in the heyday of rule by sovereign was it a condition of employment that the King be able to speak the language of his subjects. George I spoke no English and spent much of his time away from England, attempting to use the power of his kingship to shore up his German possessions. In the Middle Ages nationalism was not even part of the picture: one owed loyalty to a lord, a prince, a ruler, a family, a tribe, a church, a piece of land, but not to a nation and least of all to a nation as a language unit. The capital city of the Austrian Hapsburg empire was Vienna, its ruler a monarch with effective control of peoples of the most varied and incompatible ethnicities, and languages, throughout Central and Eastern Europe. The official language, and the lingua franca as well, was German. While it stood—and it stood for hundreds of years—the empire was an anachronistic relic of what for most of human history had been the normal relationship between country and language: none.

The marriage of language and nationalism goes back at least to Romanticism and specifically to Rousseau, who argued in his *Essay on the Origin of Languages* that language must develop before politics is possible and that language originally distinguished nations from one another. A little-remembered aim of the French Revolution—itself the legacy of Rousseau— was to impose a national language on France, where regional languages such as Provençal, Breton, and Basque were still strong competitors against standard French, the French of the Ile de France. As late as 1789, when the Revolution began, half the population of the south of France, which spoke Provençal, did not understand French. A century earlier the playwright Racine said that he had had to resort to Spanish and Italian to make himself understood in the southern French town of Uzìs. After the Revolution nationhood itself became aligned with language.

In 1846 Jacob Grimm, one of the Brothers Grimm of fairy-tale fame but better known in the linguistic establishment as a forerunner of modern comparative and historical linguists, said that "a nation is the totality of people who speak the same language." After midcentury, language was invoked more than any other single criterion to define nationality. Language as a political force helped to bring about the unification of Italy and of Germany and the secession of Norway from its union with Sweden in 1905. Arnold Toynbee observed—unhappily—soon after the First World War that "the growing consciousness of Nationality had attached itself neither to traditional frontiers nor to new geographical associations but almost exclusively to mother tongues."

The crowning triumph of the new desideratum was the Treaty of Versailles, in 1919, when the allied victors of the First World War began redrawing the map of Central and Eastern Europe according to nationality as best they could. The magic word was "self-determination," and none of Woodrow Wilson's Fourteen Points mentioned the word "language" at all. Self-determination was thought of as being related to "nationality," which today we would be more likely to call "ethnicity"; but language was simpler to identify than nationality or ethnicity. When it came to drawing the boundary lines of various countries—Czechoslovakia, Yugoslavia, Romania, Hungary, Albania, Bulgaria, Poland—it was principally language that guided the draftsman's hand. (The main exceptions were Alsace-Lorraine, South Tyrol, and the German-speaking parts of Bohemia and Moravia.) Almost by default language became the defining characteristic of nationality.

And so it remains today. In much of the world, ethnic unity and cultural identification are routinely defined by language. To be Arab is to speak Arabic. Bengali identity is based on language in spite of the division of Bengali-speakers between Hindu India and Muslim Bangladesh. When eastern Pakistan seceded from greater Pakistan in 1971, it named itself Bangladesh: *desa* means "country"; *bangla* means not the Bengali people or the Bengali territory but the Bengali language.

Scratch most nationalist movements and you find a linguistic grievance. The demands for independence of the Baltic states (Latvia, Lithuania, and Estonia) were intimately bound up with fears for the loss of their respective languages and cultures in a sea of Russianness. In Belgium the war between French and Flemish threatens an already weakly fused country. The present atmosphere of Belgium is dark and anxious, costive; the metaphor of divorce is a staple of private and public discourse. The lines of terrorism in Sri Lanka are drawn between Tamil Hindus and Sinhalese Buddhists—and also between the Tamil and Sinhalese languages. Worship of the French language fortifies the movement for an independent Quebec. Whether a united Canada will survive into the twenty-first century is a question too close to call. Much of the anxiety about language in the United States is probably fueled by the "Quebec problem": unlike Belgium, which is a small European country, or Sri Lanka, which is halfway around the world, Canada is our close neighbor.

Language is a convenient surrogate for nonlinguistic claims that are often awkward to articulate, for they amount to a demand for more political and economic power. Militant Sikhs in India call for a state of their own: Khalistan ("Land of the Pure" in Punjabi). They frequently couch this as a demand for a linguistic state, which has a certain simplicity about it, a clarity of motive—justice, even, because states in India are normally linguistic states. But the Sikh demands blend religion, economics, language, and retribution for sins both punished and unpunished in a country where old sins cast long shadows.

Language is an explosive issue in the countries of the former Soviet Union. The language conflict in Estonia has been especially bitter. Ethnic Russians make up almost a third of Estonia's population, and most of them do not speak or read Estonian, although Russians have lived in Estonia for more than a generation. Estonia has passed legislation requiring knowledge of the Estonian language as a condition of citizenship. Nationalist groups in independent Lithuania sought restrictions on the use of Polish—again, old sins, long shadows.

In 1995 protests erupted in Moldova, formerly the Moldavian Soviet Socialist Republic, over language and the teaching of Moldovan history. Was Moldovan history a part of Romanian history or of Soviet history? Was Moldova's language Romanian? Moldovan—earlier called Moldavian—*is* Romanian, just as American English and British English are both English. But in the days of the Moldavian SSR, Moscow insisted that the two languages were different, and in a piece of linguistic nonsense required Moldavian to be written in the Cyrillic alphabet to strengthen the case that it was not Romanian.

The official language of Yugoslavia was Serbo-Croatian, which was never so much a language as a political accommodation. The Serbian and Croatian languages are mutually intelligible. Serbian is written in the Cyrillic alphabet, is identified with the Eastern Orthodox branch of the Catholic Church, and borrows its high-culture words from the east—from Russian and Old Church Slavic. Croatian is written in the Roman alphabet, is identified with Roman Catholicism, and borrows its high-culture words from the west—from German, for example, and Latin. One of the first things the newly autonomous Republic of Serbia did, in 1991, was to pass a law decreeing Serbian in the Cyrillic alphabet the official language of the country. With Croatia divorced from Serbia, the Croatian and Serbian languages are diverging more and more. Serbo-Croatian has now passed into history, a language-museum relic from the brief period when Serbs and Croats called themselves Yugoslavs and pretended to like each other.

Slovakia, relieved now of the need to accommodate to Czech cosmopolitan sensibilities, has passed a law making Slovak its official language. (Czech is to Slovak pretty much as Croatian is to Serbian.) Doctors in state hospitals must speak to patients in Slovak, even if another language would aid diagnosis and treatment. Some 600,000 Slovaks—more than 10 percent of the population—are ethnically Hungarian. Even staff meetings in Hungarian-language schools must be in Slovak. (The govern-

ment dropped a stipulation that church weddings be conducted in Slovak after heavy opposition from the Roman Catholic Church.) Language inspectors are told to weed out "all sins perpetrated on the regular Slovak language." Tensions between Slovaks and Hungarians, who had been getting along, have begun to arise.

The twentieth century is ending as it began—with trouble in the Balkans and with nationalist tensions flaring up in other parts of the globe. (Toward the end of his life Bismarck predicted that "some damn fool thing in the Balkans" would ignite the next war.) Language isn't always part of the problem. But it usually is.

> ## "
> # Language isn't always part of the problem. But it usually is.
> ## "

UNIQUE OTHERNESS. Is there no hope for language tolerance? Some countries manage to maintain their unity in the face of multilingualism. Examples are Finland, with a Swedish minority, and a number of African and Southeast Asian countries. Two others could not be more unlike as countries go: Switzerland and India.

German, French, Italian, and Romansh are the languages of Switzerland. The first three can be and are used for official purposes; all four are designated "national" languages. Switzerland is politically almost hyperstable. It has language problems (Romansh is losing ground), but they are not major, and they are never allowed to threaten national unity.

Contrary to public perception, India gets along pretty well with a host of different languages. The Indian constitution officially recognizes nineteen languages, English among them. Hindi is specified in the constitution as the national language of India, but that is a pious postcolonial fiction: outside the Hindi-speaking northern heartland of India, people don't want to learn it. English functions more nearly than Hindi as India's lingua franca.

From 1947, when India obtained its independence from the British, until the 1960s blood ran in the streets and people died because of language. Hindi absolutists wanted to force Hindi on the entire country, which would have split India between north and south and opened up other fracture lines as well. For as long as possible Jawaharlal Nehru, independent India's first Prime Minister, resisted nationalist demands to redraw the capricious state boundaries of British India according to language. By the time he capitulated, the country had gained a precious decade to prove its viability as a union.

Why is it that India preserves its unity with not just two languages to contend with, as Belgium, Canada, and Sri Lanka have, but nineteen? The answer is that India, like Switzerland, has a strong national identity. The two countries share something big and almost mystical that holds each together in a union transcending language. That something I call "unique otherness."

The Swiss have what the political scientist Karl Deutsch called "learned habits, preferences, symbols, memories, and patterns of landholding": customs, cultural traditions, and political institutions that bind them closer to one another than to people of France, Germany, or Italy living just across the border and speaking the same language. There is Switzerland's traditional neutrality, its system of universal military training (the "citizen army"), its consensual allegiance to a strong Swiss franc—and fondue, yodeling, skiing, and mountains. Set against all this, the fact that Switzerland has four languages doesn't even approach the threshold of becoming a threat.

As for India, what Vincent Smith, in the *Oxford History of India*, calls its "deep underlying fundamental unity" resides in institutions and beliefs such as caste, cow worship, sacred places, and much more. Consider *dharma, karma, and maya*, the three root convictions of Hinduism; India's historical epics; Gandhi; *ahimsa* (nonviolence); vegetarianism; a distinctive cuisine and way of eating; marriage customs; a shared past; and what the Indologist Ainslie Embree calls "Brahmanical ideology." In other words, "We are Indian; we are different."

Belgium and Canada have never managed to forge a stable national identity; Czechoslovakia and Yugoslavia never did either. Unique otherness immunizes countries against linguistic destabilization. Even Switzerland and especially India have problems; in any country with as many different languages as India has, language will never not be a problem. However, it is one thing to have a major illness with a bleak prognosis; it is another to have a condition that is irritating and occasionally painful but not life-threatening.

History teaches a plain lesson about language and governments: there is almost nothing the government of a free country can do to change language usage and practice significantly, to force its citizens to use certain languages in preference to others, and to discourage people from speaking a language they wish to continue to speak. (The rebirth of Hebrew in Palestine and Israel's successful mandate that Hebrew be spoken and written by Israelis is a unique event in the annals of language history.) Quebec has since the 1970s passed an array of laws giving French a virtual monopoly in the province. One consequence—unintended, one wishes to believe—of these laws is that last year kosher products imported for Passover were kept off the shelves, be-

cause the packages were not labeled in French. Wise governments keep their hands off language to the extent that it is politically possible to do so.

We like to believe that to pass a law is to change behavior; but passing laws about language, in a free society, almost never changes attitudes or behavior. Gaelic (Irish) is living out a slow, inexorable decline in Ireland despite enormous government support of every possible kind since Ireland gained its independence from Britain. The Welsh language, in contrast, is alive today in Wales in spite of heavy discrimination during its history. Three out of four people in the northern and western counties of Gwynedd and Dyfed speak Welsh.

I said earlier that language is a convenient surrogate for other national problems. Official English obviously has a lot to do with concern about immigration, perhaps especially Hispanic immigration. America may be threatened by immigration; I don't know. But America is not threatened by language.

The usual arguments made by academics against Official English are commonsensical. Who needs a law when, according to the 1990 census, 94 percent of American residents speak English anyway? (Mauro E. Mujica, the chairman of U.S. English, cites a higher figure: 97 percent.) Not many of today's immigrants will see their first language survive into the second generation. This is in fact the common lament of first-generation immigrants: their children are not learning their language and are losing the culture of their parents. Spanish is hardly a threat to English, in spite of isolated (and easily visible) cases such as Miami, New York City, and pockets of the Southwest and southern California. The everyday language of south Texas is Spanish, and yet south Texas is not about to secede from America.

But empirical, calm arguments don't engage the real issue: language is a symbol, an icon. Nobody who favors a constitutional ban against flag burning will ever be persuaded by the argument that the flag is, after all, just a "piece of cloth." A draft card in the 1960s was never merely a piece of paper. Neither is a marriage license.

Language, as one linguist has said, is "not primarily a means of communication but a means of communion." Romanticism exalted language, made it mystical, sublime—a bond of national identity. At the same time, Romanticism created a monster: it made of language a means for destroying a country.

America has that unique otherness of which I spoke. In spite of all our racial divisions and economic unfairness, we have the frontier tradition, respect for the individual, and opportunity; we have our love affair with the automobile; we have in our history a civil war that freed the slaves and was fought with valor; and we have sports, hot dogs, hamburgers, and milk shakes—things big and small, noble and petty, important and trifling. "We are Americans; we are different."

If I'm wrong, then the great American experiment will fail—not because of language but because it no longer means anything to be an American; because we have forfeited that "willingness of the heart" that F. Scott Fitzgerald wrote was America; because we are no longer joined by Lincoln's "mystic chords of memory."

We are not even close to the danger point. I suggest that we relax and luxuriate in our linguistic richness and our traditional tolerance of language differences. Language does not threaten American unity. Benign neglect is a good policy for any country when it comes to language, and it's a good policy for America.

Journal and Discussion Questions

1 At what point in his argument does Robert D. King answer his title question, "Should English Be the Law?" Why do you think King waits until this point to answer this question? Does the essay hint at or otherwise indicate what King's answer will be before he states his position? If so, where and how?

2 Outline "Should English Be the Law?" How does King organize his reasons and evidence to support his thesis? Why do you think King divides his essay with the headings "Language and Nationality" and "Unique Otherness"?

3 Much of "Should English Be the Law?" provides history and background, often about countries that speak languages other than English or Spanish. In what ways does this history support King's position about English Only laws? Do you find his argument persuasive? Why or why not?

4 Where does King present arguments and evidence supporting opposing positions? What are these arguments, and how does King try to refute them? Is King fair in how he presents opposing arguments? Are his refutations persuasive? Why or why not?

5 King often mentions writers such as Jean-Jacques Rousseau (an influential French philosopher and political theorist of the eighteenth century), Jean-Baptiste Racine (a seventeenth-century French playwright), and Arnold Toynbee (a well-known British historian of the twentieth century) without identifying who they are and sometimes without even mentioning their first names. What do references like these tell you about King's intended audience for "Should English Be the Law?" How else would you describe King's intended readers?

6 What sources does King cite in "Should English Be the Law?" How do these sources contribute to the information and arguments that King presents? What other information in "Should English Be the Law?" did King probably find by reading? Why doesn't he cite these texts?

7 King disagrees that language is an important source of national unity. What does King say is the source of national unity? How does he try to show that this source is more important than language in creating and maintaining a sense of national unity? Did you find these arguments persuasive? Why or why not?

Topics for Writing

1 Write a research paper about one of the language issues (Ireland's efforts to preserve Gaelic or Belgium's political and language conflicts, for example) that King brings up in "Should English Be the Law?" Or write a research paper about a similar language issue (e.g., efforts to keep alive Native American languages, Cajun French, or other languages in the U.S. or the politics of language in a multilingual post-colonial African nation).

2 King writes that the "unique otherness" that creates "a bond of national identity" for Americans consists of elements such as "the frontier tradition, respect for the individual, and opportunity" as well as "our love affair with the automobile," the Civil War, "sports, hot dogs, hamburgers, and milk shakes." Write an essay about how—or whether—one of these factors (or the English language or something else) contributes to Americans' sense of unity and national identity.

Connecting the Readings

Argue whether the United States needs a law or constitutional amendment making English the national language, considering the arguments in S. I. Hayakawa's "Bilingualism in America: English Should Be the *Official* Language" and Robert D. King's "Should English Be the Law?"

WHO CAN SAY 'NIGGER'? . . . AND OTHER CONSIDERATIONS

BY RANDALL L. KENNEDY

Randall L. Kennedy (1954–) is an African American professor at Harvard Law School who frequently writes about race, language, and legal issues in articles and books such as *Sellout: The Politics of Racial Betrayal*; *Race, Crime,* and *the Law*; and *Interracial Intimacies: Sex, Marriage, Identity, and Adoption*. "Who Can Say 'Nigger'? . . . And Other Considerations" was published in the Winter 1999/2000 issue of the academic periodical *The Journal of Blacks in Higher Education*, while Kennedy was completing his most controversial book, *Nigger: The Strange Career of a Troublesome Word*. In this article, as in other of his writings, Kennedy examines people's uses of and attitudes toward language in historic documents, recent popular culture, and court cases to argue a controversial complex position about "who can say 'nigger'" and under what circumstances and what meanings the "N-word" has for different people. A complete bibliography of Kennedy's publications and links to other articles available online can be found at www.law.harvard.edu/faculty/directory/facdir.php?id=36.

NIGGER IS A KEY WORD IN THE lexicon of race relations and thus an important term in American politics. Cultural literacy demands knowledge of it. Indeed, nigger is such an important term that to be ignorant of its functions, connotations, effects, and even of the way it might be confused with similar sounding but unrelated words, such as "niggardly,"[1] is to make oneself vulnerable to all manner of peril—the loss of one's equilibrium, one's reputation, one's job, even one's life.

To illuminate the significance of nigger, I analyze an array of disputes. The disputes that I shall address arise from questions such as these: What does nigger mean? What should it mean? Is nigger more, or less, hurtful as a racial epithet than competitors such as "kike," "wop," "wetback," "mick," "chink," or "gook"? Should certain people (say, blacks) be able to use the term in ways forbidden to others (say, whites)? Under what circumstances should relevant testimony about a person's use of the term nigger be excluded from the hearing of a jury? Should the law view nigger as a possible provocation that reduces the criminal culpability of a person who responds violently to it? What methods are useful for removing venomous power from

words like nigger when they are deployed as weapons of racial insult?

Let's begin with history. Leading etymologists believe that nigger was derived from a Northern English word—"neger"—that was itself derived from "Negro," the Spanish word for black.[2] No one knows precisely how it attained its pejorative, abusive meaning. The linguist Robin Lakoff speculates that nigger became a slur when users of the term became aware that it was a mispronunciation of Negro and decided to continue using the mispronunciation as a signal of contempt—much as individuals sometimes choose to insult others by deliberately mispronouncing their names.[3] Precisely when the term became a slur is unknown. We do know, however, that by the first third of the nineteenth century nigger had already become a familiar and influential insult. In his 1837 treatise on *The Condition of the Colored People of the United States: and the Prejudice Exercised Towards Them*,[4] Hosea Easton, who described himself as "a colored man," devoted considerable attention to the nefarious pedagogical purposes to which the term nigger was put by many of his fellow Americans. "Nigger," he observed, "is an opprobrious term, employed to impose contempt upon [blacks] as an inferior race. . . . The term in itself would be perfectly harmless were it used only to distinguish one class of society from another, but it is not used with that intent; the practical definition is quite different in England to what it is here, for here it flows from the fountain of purpose to injure."[5] Easton goes on to observe that often the earliest instruction that white adults gave to white children prominently featured the N-word. "The universality of this kind of instruction," he wrote, "is well known to the observing."[6] White adults reprimanded white children for being worse than niggers, for being ignorant as niggers, for having no more credit than niggers. And white adults disciplined their children by telling them that unless they behaved they would be carried off by "the old nigger" or be made to sit with niggers, or be consigned to the nigger seat which was, of course, a place of shame.[7]

> **White parents told their children that unless they behaved they would be carried off by 'the old nigger.'**

Since at least the early nineteenth century, then (and probably earlier), nigger has served as a way of referring derogatorily, contemptuously, and often menacingly to blacks. Over the years, it has become undoubtedly the best known of the American language's many racial insults, evolving into the paradigmatic epithet. Precisely because nigger bears this dubious distinction it is often adapted for more generalized used. Hence the coinage of the term "sand nigger" to refer to the Arab[8] or "timber nigger" to refer to the Native American.[9]

Many observers make strong claims on behalf of the special status of nigger as a racial insult. The journalist Farai Chideya describes nigger as "the all-American trump card, the nuclear bomb of racial epithets."[10] The Ninth Circuit Court of Appeals recently concurred in a case that involved the authority of a school district to assign to high school students Mark Twain's *Huckleberry Finn*. A parent of one of the few black children in the school objected to the assignment on the grounds that nigger appears in that novel 215 times and that the presence of that book in the curriculum distressed black students and prompted white ones to engage in acts of racial harassment. In the course of dismissing the parent's complaint on First Amendment grounds, the Ninth Circuit described nigger as "the most noxious racial epithet in the contemporary American lexicon." Elaborating, Judge Stephen Reinhardt asserted that "the word nigger as applied to blacks is uniquely provocative and demeaning and that there is probably no word or phrase that could be directed at any other group that could cause comparable injury."[11]

Another assertion of the unique status of nigger was voiced in the midst of the infamous O.J. Simpson murder trial in the most highly publicized discussion of a racial epithet in American history. "Nigger," prosecutor Christopher Darden maintained in a heated exchange with defense attorney Johnny Cochran, is the "filthiest, dirtiest, nastiest word in the English language."[12]

Asserting that nigger is the superlative racial epithet—the *most* hurtful, the *most* fearsome, the *most* dangerous, the *most* noxious—draws one into the difficult and delicate matter of comparing oppressions, measuring collective injuries, prioritizing victim status. Some observers scoff at this enterprise. Declining to enter a discussion comparing the Holocaust to American slavery, a friend of mine once remarked that he refused to become an accountant of atrocity. One can understand this impulse to avoid comparisons. Sometimes the process of comparison degenerates into divisive competitions between minority groups that insist upon jealously defending claims to victim status. Writing about the cult of victimhood Ian Buruma observes that "sometimes it is as if everyone wants to compete with the Jewish tragedy, in what an Israeli . . . once called the Olympics of suffering."[13] Hence Iris Chang describes the Japanese army's Rape of Nanking, China, during World War II as "The Forgotten Holocaust."[14] Hence Larry Kramer titles his reportage on the early days of the AIDS crisis "Reports From the Holocaust."[15] Hence Toni Morrison dedicates *Beloved*, her novel about enslaved African Americans, to the "60 million and more"—a number undoubtedly calculated to play off of 6 million, the number of Jews generally thought to have perished at the hands of the Nazis.[16]

It would be possible, I suppose, to avoid comparisons. Instead of saying that the Holocaust was the *worst* atrocity of the twentieth century, one could say simply that the Holocaust was a terrible event. Instead of saying that nigger has been the most socially destructive racial epithet in the American language, one could say that, used derogatorily, nigger is *a* socially destructive epithet—no more or less evil than the wide variety of racial epithets that dot the American language. But neither all epithets nor all atrocities are equal. There is a difference between the massacre that kills 500 as distinct from 5,000 as distinct from 50,000. By the same token, as Judge Reinhardt recognized, in the United States there is a stratification in the stigmatizing power of various racial insults that roughly mirrors the hierarchy of racial groups within the society—a tragic stratification in which the power of nigger complements the superdegraded status of the African American.

The comedian Paul Mooney made this point vividly in a comedy sketch dramatized by Richard Pryor and Chevy Chase on *Saturday Night Live*. Chase interviews Pryor for a job as a janitor and administers to him a word-association test that goes like this:

"White," says Chase.

"Black," Pryor replies.

"Bean.

"Pod."

"Negro."

"Whitey," Pryor replies lightly.

"Tarbaby."

"What did you say," Pryor asks, puzzled.

"Tarbaby," Chase repeats, monotone.

"Ofay," Pryor says sharply.

"Colored."

"Redneck!"

"Junglebunny!"

"Peckerwood," Pryor yells.

"Burrhead!"

"Cracker."

"Spearchucker!"

"White Trash!"

"Junglebunny!"

"Honky!"

"Spade!"

"Honky, Honky!

"Nigger," says Chase smugly, aware that, when pushed, he can use that trump card.

"Dead Honky!" Pryor growls resorting to a threat of violence now that he has been outgunned in the verbal game of racial insult.[17]

I am not saying that, hurled as an insult, nigger inflicts upon individual targets more distress than other racial epithets. Persons beset by thugs who hate them on a racial basis may well feel equally terrified regardless of whether the thugs are screaming "kill the honky" or "kill the nigger." And in any event, I know no way to compare the terror individual victims feel in those circumstances. I am saying, however, that in the aggregate, nigger is and has long been *the* outstanding racial insult on the American social landscape.

Consider, for example, the striking difference in incidence that distinguishes nigger from other racial epithets in reported court opinions.[18] Between 1988 and 1998 plaintiffs cited use of the term "kike" as evidence of anti-Jewish animus in the United States in only five opinions issued by federal courts.[19] During the same period, plaintiffs cited usage of "wetback" as evidence of anti-Latino animus in 36 opinions,[20] cited usage of "chink" or "gook" as evidence of anti-Asian animus in

17 opinions,[21] cited usage of "honky" as evidence of anti-white animus in 20 opinions.[22] These cases reveal cruelty, terror, brutality, and heartache.

There exists, though, a striking difference between the volume of cases generated by databanks when the key word punched into the computer is "kike" or "gook" or "wetback" or "honky" and the volume generated when the key word punched in is "nigger." Between 1988 and 1998, plaintiffs cited usage of nigger as evidence of anti-black prejudice in several hundred opinions.[23]

Reported court opinions do not offer a perfect reflection of social life in America; they offer merely an opaque reflection that poses real difficulties of interpretation. The social meaning of litigation is ambiguous. It may signal a search for remedying real injury. Or it may signal cynical exploitation of increased intolerance for racism. Bringing a lawsuit may express a sense of empowerment. But declining to bring a lawsuit may do so as well, signaling that a person or group has ways other than cumbersome litigation to settle scores or vindicate rights. That there is more litigation in which the term nigger appears could mean that usage of that term is more prevalent than usage of analogous epithets, that usage is associated with more dramatic injuries, that targets of nigger are more aggrieved, or more willing and able to sue, or that authorities—police, prosecutors, judges, or juries—are more receptive to this group of complaints. One cannot confidently know which of these hypotheses best explains the salience of nigger in the jurisprudence of racial epithets. What cannot plausibly be doubted, however, is the fact of that salience—a fact which is best understood, I believe, as a sign of the continuing and malevolent primacy of nigger in the lexicon of American racial insult.

> ## " The word nigger to colored people is like a red rag to a bull. "

Nigger first appears in the reports of the United States Supreme Court in a decision announced in 1871 during the tumultuous era of Reconstruction when African Americans were simultaneously cloaked with new federal civil rights and ruthlessly targeted by reactionaries who abhorred the very idea of racial equality. The case *Blyew v. United States*,[24] dealt with the prosecution for murder of two white men who, for racial reasons, hacked to death several members of a black family. According to a witness, one of the codefendants stated that "there would soon be another war about the niggers" and that when it came he "intended to go to killing niggers."[25]

In subsequent years, hundreds of cases in federal and state courts have arisen in which nigger figured as a constant refrain in episodes of racially motivated violence, threats, and arson. One with a particularly memorable factual background involved the successful prosecution of Robert Montgomery for violating various federal criminal civil rights statutes.[26] In 1988 in Indianapolis, Indiana, a residential treatment center was established for convicted child molesters in an all-white neighborhood known as "The Valley." From the center's opening until mid-1991, when all of the residents of the center were white, residents of the Valley evinced no objection to the presence of the felons. In June 1991, however, the center was converted into a shelter for approximately 40 homeless veterans, 25 of whom were black. Soon thereafter trouble erupted as a group of whites, including Montgomery, opposed to the presence of "niggers," burned a cross and vandalized a car to dramatize their feelings. An all-white cadre of child molesters was tolerable. But because of the presence of blacks a racially integrated cadre of homeless veterans was intolerable. Such is what one finds on the byways lit by the N-word in our federal and state judicial records.[27]

These and numerous other cases explain why what Langston Hughes observed in 1940 often obtains today. "The word nigger to colored people," Hughes averred, "is like a red rag to a bull. Used rightly or wrongly, ironically or seriously, of necessity for the sake of realism, or impishly for the sake of comedy, it doesn't matter. Negroes do not like it in any book or play whatsoever, be the book or play ever so sympathetic in its treatment of the basic problems of the race. Even though the book or play is written by a Negro, they still do not like it. The word *nigger*, you see, sums up for us who are colored all the bitter years of insult and struggle in America."[28]

Nigger, however, is much more than an insult. In 1925 Carl Van Vechten reported that nigger was "freely used by Negroes among themselves, not only as a term of opprobrium, but also actually as a term of endearment."[29] Since he was a white man, however, Van Vechten's testimony will be suspect to some. So for purposes of substantiation, let's turn to the black journalist Roi Ottley, who wrote in 1943 that "the term nigger is used by Negroes quite freely when out of the earshot of whites."[30] Let's turn as well to the black writer Clarence Major, who discussed nigger in his *Dictionary of Afro-American Slang* published in 1970. "When used by a white person in addressing a black person," he noted nigger is usually "offensive and disparaging." Major quickly added, however, that when "used by black people among themselves, [nigger] is a racial term with undertones of warmth and good will—reflecting . . . a tragicomic sensibility that is aware of black history."[31]

In 1977, in her book *Talkin' and Testifyin': The Language of Black America*, Geneva Smitherman ob-

served that blacks attach at least four different meanings to nigger. It may simply identify black folks as in "All the nigguhs in the Motor City got rides" (a sentence she translates as "All persons of African descent that live in the city of Detroit have automobiles"). It may express disapproval of a person's actions, as in "Stop acting like a nigger." It may designate a person who is "identifying with and sharing the values and experiences of black people: "James Brown is a 'shonuff nigger.'" Or, finally, according to Smitherman, it may be a term of personal affection or endearment, as in "He my main nigguh," meaning, "He's my best friend."[32]

A few commentators have expressed appreciation for the linguistic and political complexity of nigger. Jarvis Deberry maintains that nigger is "beautiful in its multiplicity of functions. I am not aware," he observes, "of any other word capable of expressing so many contradictory emotions. . . . [I]t might just be the most versatile and most widely applied intensifier in the English language."[33]

Many observers, however, condemn any ambiguous or comedic or ironic use of nigger, fearful that any blurring of the lines that define it as an insult will generate needless confusion that will ultimately function to de-stigmatize the term and thus facilitate its acceptability. Writing in the *Los Angeles Times*, Halford H. Fairchild argues that "everyone should refrain from [using the N-word] and provide negative sanctions on its use by others." What about the fact that many blacks use the term ironically as a term of affection? "The persistent viability of the N-word in the black community," Fairchild writes, "is a scar from centuries of cultural racism."[34] Articulating the same message, Ron Nelson, an editor of the University of North Carolina's student newspaper *The Daily Tar Heel*, writes that while "most blacks . . . understand the implications and the racist history of the word nigger, it has somehow dangerously and disturbingly found its way into everyday language. . . ." Castigating blacks' playful use of the N-word as "self-defeating," "hypocritical," and "absurd," Nelson asserts that that usage "creates an atmosphere of acceptance. . . . After all, if blacks themselves do it, why can't others?"[35]

This view is echoed by the Pulitzer Prize-winning journalist E.R. Shipp. In a column for the *New York Daily News* revealingly titled "N-Word Just as Vile When Uttered by Blacks," Shipp declares that "there needs to be no confusion . . . the N-word has no place in contemporary life or language."[36]

Bill Cosby takes a similar position, arguing that black comedians who tell nigger jokes evince a deplorable lack of self-regard or racial pride. He therefore urges his fellow black comedians to stop employing the

N-word in their comedy routines. Some have heeded his advice. Even Richard Pryor, whose best album is entitled *That Nigger's Crazy*, stopped using the N-word (at least for a while).

Cosby's prestige and popularity, however, has been insufficient to stop, much less roll back, the continued usage of nigger by large numbers of black Americans. Indeed, over the past quarter century, largely in conjunction with the dissemination of the hip-hop culture, the term nigger has grown in usage and popularity. What is truly compelling about nigger, Professor Todd Boyd observes, is that many blacks "have chosen to adopt a nuanced form of the word as a vital aspect of their own cultural identity."[37] One aspect of the nuance is linguistic. The blacks to whom Boyd refers have changed nigger to "nigga" or "niggaz." More fundamentally, they have continued the tradition that redefines nigger from a term of abuse to a term of affection. What many gays and lesbians have done with "queer" and "dyke" is what many African Americans have done with nigger—transformed it from a sign of shame to be avoided if possible into a sign of pride to be worn assertively.[38] That is why the opinionated basketball star Charles Barkley called himself a "90s nigga," why one of the most important groups in the recent history of American popular music titled itself NWA—"Niggas With Attitude," why nigger suffuses the raps of Ice Cube, Ice T, Tupac Shakur, Dr. Dre, and Snoop Doggy Dog, and why its presence is large in all episodes of *Def Comedy Jam*.

Some maintain that use of the N-word by blacks is a testament to the power of white racism to insinuate itself within black minds. There is something to this argument. It is undoubtedly true that in some instances blacks' use of nigger is indicative of an antiblack, self-hating animus. My first awareness of the term arose in an all-black setting—my household in Columbia, South Carolina—in which older relatives routinely disparaged what they perceived as the racial traits of Negroes—vices such as tardiness, dishonesty, and ignorance. The phrase that crystallized this disparagement is a phrase still very much in evidence in the psyches of all too many Americans, including black Americans. The phrase is this: "Niggers ain't shit."

But antiblack prejudice is an implausible explanation for why many assertive, self-aware, politically progressive African Americans continue to use nigger in the ways to which Shipp and Cosby object. These are African Americans who maintain that they use nigger not in subjection to racial subordination but in triumphant defiance to it, a defiance that includes saying what one pleases regardless of how it strikes the sensibilities of E.R. Shipp, Bill

Cosby, Tipper Gore, L. Delores Tucker, William Bennett, or any other would-be arbiters of taste and respectability.

Cosby, Shipp, and others contend that nigger should have no place in contemporary American language. Does it mean that the title of this article, or perhaps the article itself, should have no place? Or, does it mean that people should follow the lead of educators such as John Wallace who recommends that high schools exclude from their curriculums *Huckleberry Finn* and *To Kill a Mockingbird* because they contain the N-word?[39] If so, one can only shudder to think of the bowdlerization that might await Richard Wright's *Black Boy*, Ralph Ellison's *Invisible Man*, Malcolm X's *Autobiography*, Dick Gregory's *Nigger!* or H. Rap Brown's *Die! Nigger Die!*

In 1936 the bureaucrat in charge of black schools in Washington, D.C., recommended barring from the schools a magazine that printed the N-word in its pages. What was that magazine? None other than *Opportunity*, the organ of the National Urban League, and for years one of the leading platforms for the publication of serious literature by black American writers.[40]

What Shipp and others who wish to eradicate nigger fail adequately to recognize is the term's linguistic richness and the extraordinary extent to which it has insinuated itself—for bad but also for good—across the wide expanse of the American cultural landscape. To eliminate nigger from the American language would require erasing too much from too many valuable pages, including those found in such classics of Afro-American literature as Richard Wright's *Native Son* and Malcolm X's *Autobiography*.

But perhaps some of those who want to deprive nigger of a place in contemporary American culture mean something considerably more limited. Perhaps they mean simply that they want the term confined to the past, that they want people to know what the term meant historically—and thus are willing to permit its use for that narrow purpose—but that they also want people to shun its use otherwise. They want, in other words, for the N-word to be limited to a place in the museum of language, while denying it viability as part of our living and evolving speech. Proponents of this view favor exhibiting nigger as a linguistic fossil but absolutely nothing more.

I would oppose both positions, though the latter is a less terrible alternative than the former. I say this partly out of concern about the dangers of overweening public or private power. But I say this also because I enjoy, and sometimes admire, a considerable portion of the cultural work in which nigger is embedded. Much of this work—novels, plays, jokes,

> **There is no compelling justification for presuming that black usage of nigger is permissable while white usage is objectionable.**

songs—would have to be bowdlerized if not censored altogether in order to achieve the aim of depriving nigger of an existence in contemporary American life. I find pleasure in the routines of satirists like Chris Rock and others who deploy the N-word in ways that some critics of nigger find mightily upsetting. I savor these performances and think that without them our culture would be significantly diminished without attaining benefits that would warrant the sacrifice.

Rock, however, is black. What about whites deploying nigger? For many persons, nigger takes on a completely different complexion when uttered by someone who is black in contrast to someone who is white.[41] Some whites "still wonder why black people can say nigger and they can't," the comedian Chris Rock notes. "Believe it or not," he continues, "it's a very common question. I hear it all the time."[42] That is not surprising. After all, Rock's signature act is one in which he declares: "I love black people, but I hate niggers." It is the part of his act that received the loudest applause from the mostly black audience that served as the backdrop to his filmed concert *Bring on the Pain*. In a subsequent album, Rock adds a skit in which a white man comes up to him after the show and expresses his admiration for Rock's performance, especially his satire on the N-word.[43] After assuring Rock that he is not racist, the white guy actually uses the N-word himself. The next thing one hears is the white man getting punched. Rock apparently intends for the lesson of that punch to be that blacks can properly use nigger, at least in certain circumstances, while whites cannot.

Another person who strongly supports this notion is the filmmaker Spike Lee. Lee complains, for example, that the white filmmaker Quentin Tarantino has acted wrongly in using nigger in his films, especially the movies *Pulp Fiction* and *Jackie Brown*. When someone noted that Lee himself deploys the N-word extensively in some of his films, Lee responded by saying that "as an African American, I have more right to use that word."[44] Lee's belief corresponds to a popular intuition that blacks can permissibly talk about blacks in ways that nonblacks cannot.[45]

This racial distinction, however, like all racial distinctions, ought to raise eyebrows. It ought not be

authorized without a compelling justification of the sort that I have yet to hear. The intuition animating this racial distinction largely stems from the sense that when blacks use nigger they are generally using it in some positive fashion and that when whites use the term they are generally using it in some negative fashion.[46] Even if this intuition is empirically sound, however, we ought nonetheless to eschew policies or decisions made on the basis of racial proxies unless compelled by an emergency to do so. We ought to reject racial distinction-making on that basis in order to inculcate a habit for seeing people more carefully as distinctive, particular, sovereign individuals as opposed to predetermined agents or subjects of this or that racial group.[47] Presumptions can be effective shortcuts. Sometimes we should use them. But given our racial situation and the situation that we should attain, we should be wary of indulging in racial presumptions unless we are forced to do so by compelling reasons. There is no compelling justification for presuming that black usage of nigger is permissible while white usage is objectionable. The most fervent opponents of nigger agree with this point. They then go on to contend that public opinion should make nigger out of bounds to *everyone* in *every* setting. But the prospect of a wholesale eradication of nigger—with or without the aid of state power—poses a threat to valuable artistic and political expression. I therefore suggest proceeding in a different direction. I suggest that people presumptively frown upon the deployment of nigger regardless of the race of the speaker because the N-word is still so often associated with ugly, unjustified, racial disparagement. But I also suggest that everyone be offered an opportunity to rebut this presumption, even in those cases in which whites are the speakers and blacks the objects of the language in question.

Consider the following case.[48]

In 1991 Central Michigan University hired Keith Dambrot to be its varsity men's basketball coach. At the same time, the university gave him the title of assistant professor. Presumably, his subject was basketball. On January 20, 1993, the University of Miami of Ohio played Central Michigan University in a basketball game. At halftime, the coach tried to focus and inspire his players, 11 blacks and three whites. Before proceeding, Coach Dambrot asked his players for permission to use with them a term that they often used with one another—the N-word. They nodded assent, at which point Coach Dambrot said, as he recalls it: "We need to be tougher, harder-nosed, and play harder. . . . We need to have more niggers on the team."[49] He then referred admiringly to one white member of the team as a nigger and went around the room referring by name to players as either nigger or half-nigger. The niggers were the players who were doing their jobs well. The half-niggers or non-niggers were the ones who needed to work harder. Coach Dambrot later explained that he used the term nigger "for instructional purposes with the permission of my African-American players, and I used the term in the sense in which it is used by my African-American players . . . to connote a person who is fearless, mentally strong, and tough."[50]

Despite the halftime talk, Central Michigan lost the game. But that was just the beginning of Coach Dambrot's problems.

Somehow word spread on campus about Coach Dambrot's locker room speech. He must have become aware of this and that some observers might take offense because he requested the university's athletic director to talk about the incident with the members of the team. None of them indicated that they objected to what the coach had said. Nonetheless, the athletic director told Dambrot that, regardless of intentions or context, the use of nigger was "extremely inappropriate."[51] The director then warned the coach that if he used that term again he would be fired.

Soon thereafter a student who had previously quit the basketball team complained about the coach's language to the university's affirmative action officer. This person, a white woman, demanded that the coach be punished. She insisted that a formal reprimand be placed in his personnel file, that he be suspended without pay for five days, and that during the suspension he arrange for a sensitivity trainer to visit the team to explain why the use of nigger and like terms is always inappropriate. She also required that attendance for this sensitivity training session be mandatory, that Coach Dambrot "help assure that the team is not hostile to the training," and that the coach "convey his support of this training session to the players and the staff."[52]

The coach did not resist, hoping that the incident would blow over quietly. His hopes, however, were dashed. Publicity triggered two demonstrations at which 80 to 100 protested against the coach's purported "racism." The president of the university responded by announcing that the coach had been disciplined and by declaring that "the term [nigger] is inappropriate under any circumstances," and that he

was "deeply sorry about the hurt, anger, [and] embarrassment its use had caused individuals as well as the entire university community."[53] By that time, however, critics of the university, including state legislators, were voicing demands for harsher punishments that were soon forthcoming.

On April 12, 1993, the university administration fired Coach Dambrot on the grounds that "public reaction to the incident [had] created an environment that makes it impossible for the university to conduct a viable basketball program under [his] leadership."[54]

He responded by suing the university in federal court, claiming that his discharge constituted a violation of his First Amendment rights. Members of the basketball team sued the university as well, claiming that the university speech code violated their First Amendment rights.

The students prevailed. A federal district court, affirmed by a court of appeals, invalidated Central Michigan's speech code on the grounds that it violated the First Amendment. The coach, however, did not prevail. The district court, affirmed by the court of appeals, ruled that the university's termination of Dambrot was permissible. As an employee of a public institution, he was directly protected by the First Amendment. As interpreted by the Supreme Court, however, the First Amendment does not insulate from employer sanction all speech that is uttered by public employees. Speech that touches upon a matter of public concern is protected. Therefore, if the coach had been talking to his team at halftime about racist uses of the term nigger or about the NCAA's scandalous exploitation of athletes, his comments would probably have been deemed to be protected by the First Amendment. But in the view of the court of appeals, Dambrot's speech did not touch upon a matter of public concern. Thus there existed no federal constitutional bar to the university's firing Dambrot for reasons that stemmed from his locker room exhortation.

Here I am not so much interested in the courts' conclusion that the university had the authority to fire the coach—a legal conclusion that seems to me to have been correct. Rather, I am interested in the judgment that the university officials exercised pursuant to that authority. That judgment, or more accurately misjudgment, casts a revealing light on our society's continuously grappling with nigger and the cultural dynamics that surround it. The initial response by the athletic director ordering the coach to desist from using nigger seems to me to have been proper. On the one hand, it recognized the unjustifiable risk that the coach's words might be hurtful to his players or the wider community. True, the coach did ask for the players' permission to use the N-word and the players apparently gave it. But a disapproving player might understandably be hesitant to express disapproval of a coach's request in a locker room at halftime when the team is losing and when other players are signaling their approval. Moreover, the players are merely students—young people needing and presumably desiring guidance from wiser elders. If the deployment of the N-word is an evil activity, the mere permission of the players, even if genuine, could not make it innocent. As I have indicated, I don't believe that every deployment of the word nigger is evil. Sometimes it can be used humorously—see the comedy routines of *Def Comedy Jam*—and sometimes it can be used as a tool of antiracist education. (See its use in the protest fiction of Richard Wright.) In this case, however, using the N-word was in no sense essential to what the coach was attempting to accomplish. As Judge Keith rightly noted in his opinion for the court of appeals, "The point of [the coach's] speech was not related to his use of the N-word but to his desire to have his players play harder"[55]—an aim that could have been easily and effectively advanced by some other means less susceptible to misunderstanding and hurt feelings. In short, Coach Dambrot was imprudent in his choice of motivational strategy and the athletic director was correct in giving him firm instructions on the matter.

Subsequent actions taken by university officials, however, were mistaken. First, the one-dimensional character of the sensitivity training that the affirmative action officer envisioned (namely a session that would brook no debate over the propriety of nigger), requiring mandatory attendance, and directing the coach to pacify his players' possible resistance to the sensitivity training and to convey his support for it is reflective of just the sort of overreaching, overzealous, overconfident coercive conduct by educational officials that has, unfortunately, tarnished the reputation of multiculturalist reformism. Second, prior to firing Coach Dambrot, university officials appear to have made little effort to clarify the controversy, to indicate that this was a situation in which underlying realities were considerably more ambiguous than surface appearances. The fact is that this coach, imprudent though he may have been, was clearly employing nigger according to a usage embraced by his players—a usage in which the term was a compliment, not an insult.[56] Sometimes it may be wise, albeit tragic, for a university administration to sacrifice a deserving employee to mollify public anger that might otherwise pose a threat to a university's future. In this case, though, the authorities at Central Michigan University capitulated too

quickly to the formulaic rage of affronted blacks, the ill-considered sentimentality of well-meaning whites, and their own crass opportunism.

Thus far I have turned repeatedly to lawyerly texts—mainly opinions written by federal and state judges—for examples of the problem under investigation. Judicial opinions, however, can sometimes do more than provide facts as grist for analysis; they can also provide illumination. That is certainly true with respect to our grapplings with what nigger means. Three of the leading jurists of this century—Roger Traynor, Benjamin Cardozo, and Oliver Wendell Holmes Jr.—wrote opinions that stress a point that is absolutely essential for the proper resolution of the definitional problems under consideration. That point is that the meaning of words, all words, including nigger, are contingent, changeable, context-specific. "The meaning of particular words," Traynor wrote, "varies with the . . . verbal context and surrounding circumstances and purposes in view of the linguistic education and experiences of their users and their hearers or readers."[57] "The law," Cardozo maintained in a sentence that Coach Dambrot would have appreciated, "has outgrown its primitive stage of formalism when the precise word was the sovereign talisman, and every slip was fatal."[58] Holmes, though, is the one who puts the point most memorably and who should be listened to most closely as fights over the future of nigger unfold in years to come. "A word," Holmes wrote, "is not a crystal, transparent and unchanged, it is the skin of a living thought and may vary greatly in color and content according to the circumstances and the time in which it is used."[59]

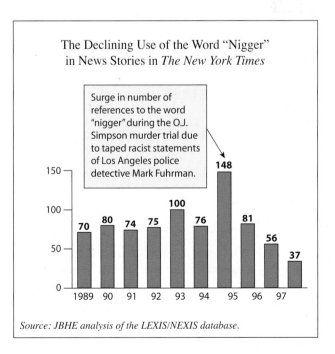

The Declining Use of the Word "Nigger" in News Stories in *The New York Times*

Surge in number of references to the word "nigger" during the O.J. Simpson murder trial due to taped racist statements of Los Angeles police detective Mark Fuhrman.

Source: JBHE analysis of the LEXIS/NEXIS database.

[1]In January 1999 a white official in Washington, D.C., resigned his post when black coworkers complained about his use of the term "niggardly." They wrongly believed that the word, which means miserly, is related to the word "nigger." The mayor of the District of Columbia initially accepted the resignation but later, after much criticism in the press, offered the official another post. See Michael Janofsky, "About-Face in Washington Furor on Misunderstood Word," *Washington Post*, February 4, 1999.

[2]See J.A. Simpson and E.S.C. Weiner III, eds., *The Oxford English Dictionary*, Second Edition (1989); H.L. Mencken (abridged with annotations and new material by Raven I. McDavid Jr. with the assistance of David W. Maurer), *The American Language: An Inquiry Into the Development of English in the United States*, 383–384 (1979).

[3]Robin Lakoff, "The N-Word: Still There, Still Ugly," *Newsday*, September 28, 1995.

[4]See Hosea Easton, *A Treatise on the Intellectual Character and Civil and Political Condition of the Colored People of the United States, and the Prejudice Exercised Towards Them* (1837).

[5]Id. at 40.

[6]Id.

[7]Id. at 41.

[8]*Hussein v. Oshkosh Motor Truck Co.*, 816 F. 2d. 348 (CA 7 1987).

[9]*DuFlambeau v. Stop Treaty Abuse*. 991 F. 2d 1249 (CA 7 1993).

[10]See *The Color of Our Future* (1999).

[11]See *Monteiro v. Tempe Union High School District*, 158 F. 3d 1022 (CA 9 1998).

[12]Quote in Margaret M. Russell. "Representing Race: Beyond 'Sellouts' and 'Race Cards': Black Attorneys and the Straitjacket of Legal Practice," 95 *Michigan Law Review* 765 (1997).

[13]See Ian Buruma, "Joys of Victimhood," *New York Review*, April 8, 1999.

[14]See Iris Chang, *The Rape of Nanking: The Forgotten Holocaust of World War II* (1997).

[15]See Larry Kramer, *Reports From the Holocaust: The Making of an AIDS Activist* (1989).

[16]See Toni Morrison, *Beloved* (1987). See also Stanley Crouch, reviewing *Beloved* in *The New Republic*, October 19, 1987.

[17]See Joseph Boskin, *Rebellious Laughter* 161–162 (1997); Mel Watkins, *On the Real Side: A History of African-American Comedy* (1999).

[18]In April 1999 I used the LEXIS database to determine the extent to which "nigger" and kindred terms were used in court opinions. I requested the citations for all cases in which these terms appeared and then read the cases.

[19]See, e.g., *In re Peia*, 1997 U.S. Dist. Lexis 16853 (D.C. Ct. 1997); *Goldberg v. City of Philadelphia*, 1994 U.S. Dist. Lexis 8969 (D.C. E.D. Pa. 1994). Several other cases in which the term kike appears involves alleged acts of bigotry abroad. See, e.g., *Korablina v. INS*, 158 F. 3d 1038 (CA 9 1998).

[20]See, e.g., *United States v. Makowski*, 120 F. 3d 1078 (CA 9 1997); *Vigil v. City of Las Cruces*, 119 F. 3d 871 (CA 10 1997); *United States v. Reese*, 2 F.3d 870 (CA 9 1993).

[21]See, e.g., *United States v. Piche*, 981 F. 2d 706 (CA 4 1992); *Nguyen v. Venson Toyota*, 1997 U.S. Dist. Lexis 4073 (E.D. La. 1997); *Chua v. St. Paul Fed. Bank*, 1996 U.S. Dist. Lexis 7874 (N.D. III. 1996).

[22]See, e.g., *Huckabay v. Moore*, 142 F. 3d 233 (CA 5 1998); *United States v. Thomas, 1993 U.S. App. Lexis 30976 CA 9 1993); Conrad v. P.T.O. Servs.*, 1996 U.S. Dist. Lexis 4441 (D.C. N.D. III. 1996).

[23]See, e.g., *Gant v. Wallingford Bd. of Education*, 69 F. 3d 669 (CA 2 1995); *United States v. Sowa*, 34 F. 3d 447 (CA 7 1994); *United States v. Ramey*, 24 F. 3d 602 (CA 4 1994); *United States v. Juve-*

nile Male J.H.H., 22 F. 3d 821 (CA 8 1994); *United States v. McInnis*, 976 F. 2d 1226 (CA 9 1992).

[24]80 U.S. 585 (1871). See also Robert D. Goldstein, "*Blyew*: Variations on a Jurisdictional Theme," 41 *Stanford Law Review* 469 (1988).

[25]80 U.S. at 589.

[26]*United States v. Montgomery*, 23 F. 3d 1130 (CA 7 1994).

[27]Nigger was also present at the terrible tragedy in Littleton, Colorado, at the Columbine High School, the site of a terrible mass killing. According to witnesses, a black student, Isaiah Shoels, was referred to as a "nigger" right before he was murdered by a gun-wielding racist. See, e.g., Sam Howe Nerhovek. "Terror in Littleton," *New York Times*, April 22, 1999: Arianna Huffington, "Behind the Facade of Littleton's Paradise." *Sacramento Bee*, April 30, 1999.

[28]See Langston Hughes, *The Big Sea* (1940).

[29]See Carl Van Vechten, *Nigger Heaven* (1925).

[30]See Roi Ottley, *New World A-Coming: Inside Black America*, 1943.

[31]See Clarence Major, *Dictionary of Afro-American Slang* 85 (1970).

[32]Geneva Smitherman, *Talkin' and Testifying': The Language of Black America* (1977). Today, most serious lexicographers continue to evince a recognition that nigger has meanings beyond the limits of the racist slur, though doing so sometimes attracts protests from those who want the term to be defined simply as a racial insult.

[33]Jarvis Deberry, "Keeping a Hateful Word Inside a Dictionary," *The [New Orleans] Times-Picayune*, June 23, 1998.

[34]See Halford H. Fairchild, "N Word Should be Odious From Anyone," *Las Angeles Times*, September 16, 1987.

[35]"The Word 'Nigga' is Only for Slaves and Sambos," *Journal of Blacks in Higher Education*, Autumn 1998.

[36]See E.R. Shipp, "N Word Just as Vile When Uttered by Blacks," *New York Daily News*, January 21, 1998. See also Mary A. Mitchell, "N Word OK for Blacks but Not for Whites?" *Chicago Sun Times*, December 28, 1997: "The word is so vile and loathsome, so dehumanizing and so steeped in racial hatred and disrespect that it can never be used—by whites or blacks—without betraying its roots." "It is self-loathing that gives this racial slur breath. That makes blacks the only race that has adopted the insults of its oppressors and embraced those insults as its own."

[37]See Todd Boyd, *Am I Black Enough For You? Popular Culture from the Hood and Beyond* 31 (1997).

[38]For another example of this phenomenon, see Inga Muscio, *Cunt: A Declaration of Independence* (1998).

[39]Wallace is a leading figure in the campaign to remove *Huckleberry Finn* from high school curriculums. His most publicized episode of attempted suppression occurred, ironically, at the Mark Twain Intermediate School in Fairfax, Virginia. Wallace has produced an edition of *Huckleberry Finn* in which the words nigger and hell are removed. It should be noted, though, that Wallace's opposition to reading unexpurgated editions of *Huckleberry Finn* extends only to primary and secondary schooling. He approves of assigning it at the collegiate level. See James S. Leonard, Thomas A. Tenney, and Thadious M. Davis, *Satire or Evasion? Black Perspectives on* Huckleberry Finn 274 (1992). Of special note in this valuable compilation is John H. Wallace, "The Case Against *Huck Finn*," a frightening exhibition of what can happen to thought in the absence of any sense of irony.

[40]See Mencken, supra note 3, at 382. The Harvard University library catalogue notes the presence of over a hundred items featuring nigger in the title. The list includes Joseph Conrad's *The Nigger of the "Narcissus."* Carl Van Vechten's *Nigger Heaven*, Thomas Carlyle's *Occasional Discourses on the Nigger Question*, Flannery O'Connor's *The Artificial Nigger and Other Tales*, and Cecil Brown's *The Life and Loves of Mr. Jiveass Nigger*.

[41]See, e.g., Stan Simpson, "In Defining the N-Word, Let Meaning Be Very Clear," *Hartford Courant*, November 3, 1997: "What would happen if a white friend were to come up to me and say [as does my black brother], 'Hey, Nigger! How are you doing?' Well, excuse my ebonics, but we be fightin'."

[42]See Chris Rock, *Rock This* 20 (1997).

[43]See, or rather, listen to, Chris Rock, "Niggers vs. Black People." *Roll With the New* (1997).

[44]See Kevin Merida, "Spike Lee, Holding Court: the Director Talks Movies, Hollywood, Basketball, and, Oh, Yes, Controversy," *Washington Post*, May 1, 1998.

[45]See Chris Rock, *Rock This*, 20 (1997): "Any black person can say 'nigger' and get away with it . . . . It's like calling your kid an idiot. Only *you* can call your kid that. Someone else calls your kid an idiot, there's a fight."; Larry G. Meeks, "Ethnically Speaking: Boy Should Know That Using Demeaning Names to Describe Own Race is Wrong," *The Detroit News*, June 4, 1997: "Almost every group has names that are only considered appropriate use by its members"; Michael Eric Dyson, "Nigger Gotta Stop," *The Source*, June 1999: "Most white folk attracted to black culture know better than to cross a line drawn in the sand of racial history. Nigger has never been cool when spit from white lips."

But see "Samuel L. Jackson Blasts Spike Lee for Criticizing Him for Using N-Word in *Jackie Brown*, *Jet*, March 9, 1998. Observing that some "black artists think they are the only ones allowed to use the word." Jackson responds, "Well, that's bull." Quentin Tarantino asserts that he is being unfairly attacked for realistically portraying the way that some people use the word nigger: "I am telling the truth. I would not be questioned if I [Tarantino] was black. . . . And I resent the question [being asked] because I'm white." Millner, "The N-Word for Whites, It's Still 'No.' And That's Not Bad Advice for Blacks Either," *Daily News*, January 11, 1998.

[46]That this intuition is so powerful and, for many, so persuasive, indicates the extent to which antidiscrimination norms have failed adequately to grip popular opinion. In many contexts, we eschew the notion that racial discrimination can rightly be predicated upon sociological generalizations even if they are empirically sound. Hence, we do not allow life insurance companies to charge blacks and whites different rates even though, from the point of view of profit maximization, it would be quite rational to do so, since, in fact, whites tend to live longer than blacks. The law demands that insurance companies assess applicants solely on the basis of their individual records. The companies are not permitted to use racial proxies—statistical generalizations distinguishing racial groups en masse—as analytical shortcuts, even though doing so might be considered an efficient mode of proceeding that could produce savings for the companies and, by extension, savings for consumers. Yet in other areas of American life, public morality accedes to decision making by racial proxy. In the Southwestern United States, law enforcement officials prevalently act upon their view that apparent Mexican heritage is a useful proxy for an increased risk that a given suspect is engaged in the transport of illegal aliens. Throughout the United States, law enforcement officials prevalently act upon their view that blackness is a useful proxy for an increased risk that a given suspect is engaged in drug dealing. See Randall Kennedy, *Race, Crime, and the Law*, 136–167 (1997).

[47]See Paul Brest, Foreword: "In Defense of the Antidiscrimination Principle," 90 *Harvard Law Review* 1 (1976).

[48]*Dambrot v. Central Michigan University*, 55 F. 3d 1177 (CA 6 1995). See, also, Michael P. Pompeo, Constitutional Law—First Amendment— Athletic coach's Locker Room Speech Is Not Protected Under First Amendment, Even Though University Policy is Found Unconstitutional, *Dambrot v. Central Michigan University*,

55 F 3d 1177 (6th Cir. 1995), 6 *Seton Hall Journal of Sport Law* 277 (1996). My understanding of *Dambrot* has also been enriched by conversations I have had with Professor Robert A. Sedler who represented Coach Dambrot on appeal.

[49]See First Brief of Plaintiffs-Appellants-Cross-Appellees in *Dambrot v. Central Michigan University* at 6 (quoting Complaint of Keith Dambrot).

[50]Id. Coach Dambrot also said on one occasion prior to the locker room incident that his players should not be "niggers in the classroom." Questioned later about that comment, the coach said that he was trying to express his feeling that "you can't be aggressive, tough, hard-nosed in class, especially at a school like Central Michigan University where the faculty members don't understand a lot about black people or have many black people in class." 55 F. 3rd at 1181.

[51]First Brief of Plaintiffs-Appellants, supra note 50, at 10 n.4.

[52]Id. at 11–12 n. 7.

[53]Id. at 12–13 n. 9.

[54]Id. at 13, n. 11.

[55]55 F. 3d at 1187.

[56]Other coaches have used nigger in the way that Dambrot did. For example, testifying on Dambrot's behalf, Adele Young, an African-American basketball coach, maintained that "a coach is around the players seven days a week, nine months of the year. The players are a part of the coach's family. A coach can pick up the players' language and speech patterns without being aware of a change. . . . My players, both African American and white, use [nigger] freely as I do in the coach setting. When used in this way, nigger means a tough, hard player. Coach Dambrot understood the way players use nigger and when he used it, he used it the very same way they did." First Brief of Plaintiffs-Appellants, supra note 50, at 9. For a case in which a coach at a public high school was dismissed for using nigger, see *Holthaus v. Board of Education, Cincinnati Public Schools*, 986 F. 2d 1044 (CA 6 1993).

[57]See *Pacific Gas & Electric Co. v. G.W. Thomas Dreyage & Rigging Co.*, 69 Cal. 33, 38 (1968) (quoting Arthur Corbin, "The Interpretation of Words and the Penal Evidence Rule," 50 *Cornell Law Quarterly* 161, 187 (1965)).

[58]*Wood v. Lucy, Lady Duff-Gordon*, 222 N.Y. 88, 91 (1917).

[59]*Towne v. Eisner, Collector of Internal Revenue for the Third District of New York*, 245 U.S. 418, 425 (1918).

The Declining Use of the Word "Nigger" in the World's Major Newspapers

Number of Times the Word "Nigger" Appeared in 70 Major Newspapers Worldwide

Surge in number of references to the word "nigger" during the O.J. Simpson murder trial due to taped racist statements of Los Angeles police detective Mark Fuhrman.

Year	Count
1992	1418
93	1737
94	1435
95	2115
96	1244
97	1080
	1045

Source: JBHE analysis of the LEXIS/NEXIS database.

Journal and Discussion Questions

1 What is Randall L. Kennedy's answer to the question raised in his title, "Who Can Say 'Nigger'? . . . And Other Considerations"? Where does Kennedy finally give his answer to the title question? Why does he wait so long to reveal his position?

2 Outline "Who Can Say 'Nigger'? . . . And Other Considerations." Where does Kennedy explain opposing arguments to his position? How does he answer each of these arguments? How does Kennedy try to build audience support for his position considering many readers' strong objections to his thesis?

3 According to Kennedy, what are the different meanings of the word *nigger*, today and in the past? What determines what *nigger* means to different people and in different contexts? What, if anything, does the spelling of *nigger* or *nigga* matter in determining the word's meaning? How does Kennedy's discussion of these different meanings support his overall argument?

4 What different kinds of sources does Kennedy cite? How does he use each type of source to develop his analysis of how people use the word *nigger* and what meanings the word has? Why does he reproduce a comedy routine on *Saturday Night Live* in a long block quotation on page 246? How does the information about *nigger* in *The Oxford English Dictionary* support or hurt his argument? Look up *nigger* in *The Oxford English Dictionary* for other information about the word. How does this information support or harm Kennedy's argument?

5 Find sentences in which Kennedy uses "N-word" instead of "nigger." Why do you think he uses this euphemism in these passages? Why doesn't he use a less offensive substitute like *N-word* or *n——-r* throughout his text, including his title, when he knows that many of his readers will be offended and hurt by the word *nigger*? Do you agree with his decisions about when to write *nigger* and when to write *N-word*? Why or why not?

6 Why does Kennedy conclude the body of his article with an extended description and analysis of the story of the Central Michigan University football coach's halftime talk? What points does Kennedy make with this long example? How does the rest of his article prepare readers for thinking about this case? Do you agree with all of Kennedy's opinions about the actions taken by the Central Michigan coach, students, athletic director, affirmative action officer, and president in this story and Kennedy's opinions about the court decisions? Why or why not?

7 Why does Kennedy conclude his article with Oliver Wendell Holmes' statement "A word is not a crystal, transparent and unchanged, it is the skin of a living thought and may vary greatly in color and content according to the circumstances and the time in which it is used"? How does this quotation support Kennedy's concluding claim, "[The] point is that the meaning of words, all words, including nigger, are contingent, changeable, context-specific"? Why does he end his article with this argument?

Topics for Writing

1 Argue in support of or opposition to Randall Kennedy's position in "Who Can Say 'Nigger'? . . . And Other Considerations" that *nigger* can be used for antiracist purposes and that whites as well as blacks should be encouraged to use the word *nigger* in positive ways.

2 Kennedy discusses a number of controversial issues involving the word *nigger*, including whether schools should teach or censure Mark Twain's *The Adventures of Huckleberry Finn*, whether colleges and universities should have "hate speech" regulations that prohibit students and faculty from using racist and sexist epithets, and whether the use of the word *nigga* by hip-hop artists and African American comedians is wrong and harmful. Write a research paper that argues your opinion while examining other positions on one of the controversies discussed by Kennedy.

3 On page 248, Kennedy mentions that some people are trying to redefine *nigga* "from a term of abuse to a term of affection" as others are trying to redefine other insulting epithets like "queer" and "dyke" so that the words lose their power to demean and hurt people. Write a research paper about the attempts to redefine one of these words or another racial, ethnic, or sexist epithet, including the arguments of people who oppose these attempts.

Suggestions for Essays on LANGUAGE

1 Write an essay comparing the ideas about language difference in "The Tower of Babel" to the positions about language difference in two or more of the following essays by Anzaldúa, Tan, Guidry, Hayakawa, King, and The Dialectizer Web site.

2 Considering "The Gettysburg PowerPoint Presentation" and the *Non Sequitur* comic strip about text messaging, write an essay describing and evaluating the fears and complaints that people have about how computer technologies are affecting people's use of language.

3 Examine how well or how poorly Nunberg's ideas about politics and language account for the language differences in the two Hurricane Katrina photographs or in Harjo's discussion of language about Native American "remains."

4 Compare and evaluate the different ideas about language education in Malcolm X, Guidry, Hayakawa, and King. Consider what each writer says and assumes about what purposes language education should serve and about how people learn to read and write most successfully.

5 Discuss what roles, if any, there should be for languages other than English in the U.S. considering at least three of the selections by Tan, Anzaldúa, Guidry, Hayakawa, and King.

08 Education

TUNE INTO A TELEVISION OR RADIO newscast; skim a newspaper, newsmagazine, or news Web site; or browse around a bookstore or library, and you will find skads of books, articles, and reports dealing with education issues. Education has perhaps become the most important issue in political campaigns—candidates for president, Congress, governor, state legislature, mayor, city council, and school board all emphasize education in their speeches and commercials, and education is often the central issue of ballot initiatives.

Here are just a few of the questions that students, educators, political officials, and journalists are investigating and debating now.

- What kinds of education and courses should schools and college and universities be offering and requiring? What is the primary purpose of an education—for example, to prepare people for a career; to teach moral values; to make educated democratic citizens; or to pass on the knowledge and traditions of history, art, science, and culture to the next generation?

- What emphasis should education place on memorization of facts? On creativity? On problem solving? On developing students' self-esteem?

- How should schools and colleges address the different needs of students of different cultures and ethnicities, different incomes and social classes, different genders, different ages, different religions, and different abilities and handicaps?

- Are we spending enough money on education? Too much? What should be done about demands to better fund schools for children of low-income families? To improve teacher salaries and provide better pay and working conditions for part-time college faculty? To pay for school programs in sports, art, and music? To reduce the need for students to work outside jobs while attending college?

- How should schools deal with problems such as discrimination, racism, sexism, and homophobia?

GAINS AND LOSSES

BY RICHARD RODRIGUEZ

Richard Rodriguez (1944–) is an award-winning essayist and cultural commentator best known for his works on Latino culture, education, and politics in the United States. Rodriguez is a contributing editor for *Harper's Magazine*, the Sunday "Opinion" section of the *Los Angeles Times*, and New America Media in San Francisco. He is the author of three books, including *Days of Obligation: An Argument with My Mexican Father* and *Brown: The Last Discovery of America*, and of many articles for magazines such as *Time, Harper's, Reader's Digest*, and *Mother Jones*. He is a regular essayist on the PBS television show *NewsHour with Jim Lehrer*; these essays are archived at www.pbs.org/newshour/essays/richard_rodriguez.html. "Gains and Losses" is a selection from "Aria: A Memoir of a Bilingual Childhood," an essay first published in *The American Scholar* in 1980 and later incorporated into Richard Rodriguez's 1982 book, *Hunger of Memory: The Education of Richard Rodriguez*. "Gains and Losses" is a familiar essay that reflects on Rodriguez's early schooling and his learning of English; it is also an argument against bilingual education programs. Rodriguez relies almost entirely on his personal experiences as evidence for his arguments, generalizing from these experiences to argue about what kind of language education should be provided for children who speak Spanish.

SUPPORTERS OF BILINGUAL EDUCATION today imply that students like me miss a great deal by not being taught in their family's language. What they seem not to recognize is that, as a socially disadvantaged child, I considered Spanish to be a private language. What I needed to learn in school was that I had the right—and the obligation—to speak the public language of *los gringos*. The odd truth is that my first-grade classmates could have become bilingual, in the conventional sense of that word, more easily than I. Had they been taught (as upper-middle-class children are often taught early) a second language like Spanish or French, they could have regarded it simply as that: another public language. In my case such bilingualism could not have been so quickly achieved. What I did not believe was that I could speak a single public language.

Without question, it would have pleased me to hear my teachers address me in Spanish when I entered the classroom. I would have felt much less afraid. I would have trusted them and responded with ease. But I would have delayed—for how long postponed?—having to learn the language of public society. I would have evaded—and for how long could I have afforded to delay?—learning the great lesson of school, that I had a public identity.

Fortunately, my teachers were unsentimental about their responsibility. What they understood was that I needed to speak a public language. So their voices would search me out, asking me questions. Each time I'd hear them, I'd look up in surprise to see a nun's face frowning at me. I'd mumble, not really meaning to answer. The nun would persist, 'Richard, stand up. Don't look at the floor. Speak up. Speak to the entire class, not just to me!' But I couldn't believe that the English language was mine to use. (In part, I did not want to believe it.) I continued to mumble. I resisted the teacher's demands. (Did I somehow suspect that once I learned public language my pleasing family life would be changed?) Silent, waiting for the bell to sound, I remained dazed, diffident, afraid.

Because I wrongly imagined that English was intrinsically a public language and Spanish an intrinsically private one, I easily noted the difference between classroom language and the language of home. At school, words were directed to a general audience of listeners. ('Boys and girls.') Words were meaningfully ordered. And the point was not self-expression alone but to make oneself understood by many others. The teacher quizzed: 'Boys and girls, why do we use that word in this sentence? Could we think of a better word to use there? Would the sentence change its meaning if the words were differently arranged? And wasn't there a better way of saying much the same thing?' (I couldn't say. I wouldn't try to say.)

Three months. Five. Half a year passed. Unsmiling, ever watchful, my teachers noted my silence. They began to connect my behavior with the difficult progress my older sister and brother were making. Until one Saturday morning three nuns arrived at the house to talk to our parents. Stiffly, they sat on the blue living room sofa. From the doorway of another room, spying the visitors, I noted the incongruity—the clash of two worlds, the faces and voices of school intruding upon the familiar setting of home. I overheard one voice gently wondering, 'Do your children speak only Spanish at home, Mrs. Rodriguez?' While another voice added, 'That Richard especially seems so timid and shy.'

That Rich-heard!

With great tact the visitors continued, 'Is it possible for you and your husband to encourage your children to practice their English when they are home?' Of course, my parents complied. What would they not do for their children's well-being? And how could they have questioned the Church's authority which those women represented? In an instant, they agreed to give up the language (the sounds) that had revealed and accentuated our family's closeness. The moment after the visitors left, the change was observed. '*Ahora*, speak to us *en inglés*,' my father and mother united to tell us.

> ❝
> **I did not realize that they were talking in Spanish however until, at the moment they saw me, I heard their voices change to speak English. Those *gringo* sounds they uttered startled me. Pushed me away.**
> ❞

At first, it seemed a kind of game. After dinner each night, the family gathered to practice 'our' English. (It was still then *inglés*, a language foreign to us, so we felt drawn as strangers to it.) Laughing, we would try to define words we could not pronounce. We played with strange English sounds, often over-anglicizing our pronunciations. And we filled the smiling gaps of our sentences with familiar Spanish sounds. But that was cheating, somebody shouted. Everyone laughed. In school, meanwhile, like my brother and sister, I was required to attend a daily tutoring session. I needed a full year of special attention. I also needed my teachers to keep my attention from straying in class by calling out; *Rich-heard*—their English voices slowly prying loose my ties to my other name, its three notes, *Ri-car-do*. Most of all I needed to hear my mother and father speak to me in a moment of seriousness in broken—suddenly heartbreaking—English. The scene was inevitable: One Saturday morning I entered the kitchen, where my parents were talking in Spanish. I did not realize that they were talking in Spanish however until, at the moment they saw me, I heard their voices change to speak English. Those *gringo* sounds they uttered startled me. Pushed me away. In that moment of trivial misunderstanding and profound insight, I felt my throat twisted by unsounded grief. I turned quickly and left the room. But I had no place to escape to with Spanish. (The spell was broken.) My brother and sisters were speaking English in another part of the house.

Again and again in the days following, increasingly angry, I was obliged to hear my mother and father: 'Speak to us *en inglés*.' *(Speak.)* Only then did I determine to learn classroom English. Weeks after, it happened: One day in school I raised my hand to volunteer an answer. I spoke out in a loud voice. And I did not think it remarkable when the entire class understood. That day, I moved very far from the disadvantaged child I had been only days earlier. The belief, the calming assurance that I belonged in public, had at last taken hold.

> " Hearing him, sometimes, I wasn't sure if he was pronouncing the Spanish word *gringo* or saying gringo in English. "

Shortly after, I stopped hearing the high and loud sounds of *los gringos*. A more and more confident speaker of English, I didn't trouble to listen to how strangers sounded, speaking to me. And there simply were too many English-speaking people in my day for me to hear American accents anymore. Conversations quickened. Listening to persons who sounded eccentrically pitched voices, I usually noted their sounds for an initial few seconds before I concentrated on *what* they were saying. Conversations became content-full. Transparent. Hearing someone's *tone* of voice—angry or questioning or sarcastic or happy or sad—I didn't distinguish it from the words it expressed. Sound and word were thus tightly wedded. At the end of a day, I was often bemused, always relieved, to realize how 'silent,' though crowded with words, my day in public had been. (This public silence measured and quickened the change in my life.)

At last, seven years old, I came to believe what had been technically true since my birth: I was an American citizen.

But the special feeling of closeness at home was diminished by then. Gone was the desperate, urgent, intense feeling of being at home; rare was the experience of feeling myself individualized by family intimates. We remained a loving family, but one greatly changed. No longer so close; no longer bound tight by the pleasing and troubling knowledge of our public separateness. Neither my older brother nor sister rushed home after school anymore. Nor did I. When I arrived home there would often be neighborhood kids in the house. Or the house would be empty of sounds.

Following the dramatic Americanization of their children, even my parents grew more publicly confident. Especially my mother. She learned the names of all the people on our block. And she decided we needed to have a telephone installed in the house. My father continued to use the word *gringo*. But it was no longer charged with the old bitterness or distrust. (Stripped of any emotional content, the word simply became a name for those Americans not of Hispanic descent.) Hearing him, sometimes, I wasn't sure if he was pronouncing the Spanish word *gringo* or saying gringo in English.

Matching the silence I started hearing in public was a new quiet at home. The family's quiet was partly due to the fact that, as we children learned more and more English, we shared fewer and fewer words with our parents. Sentences needed to be spoken slowly when a child addressed his mother or father. (Often the parent wouldn't understand.) The child would need to repeat himself. (Still the parent misunderstood.) The young voice, frustrated, would end up saying. 'Never mind'—the subject was closed. Dinners would be noisy with the clinking of knives and forks against dishes. My mother would smile softly between her remarks; my father at the other end of the table would chew and chew at his food, while he stared over the heads of his children.

My *mother!* My *father!* After English became my primary language, I no longer knew what words to use in addressing my parents. The old Spanish words (those tender accents of sound) I had used earlier—*mamá* and *papá*—I couldn't use anymore. They would have been too painful reminders of how much had changed in my life. On the other hand, the words I heard neighborhood kids call their parents seemed equally unsatisfactory. *Mother* and *Father; Ma, Papa, Pa, Dad, Pap* (how I hated the all-American sound of that last word especially)—all these terms I felt were unsuitable, not really terms of address for *my* parents. As a result, I never used them at home. Whenever I'd speak to my parents, I would try to get their attention with eye contact alone. In public conversations, I'd refer to 'my parents' or 'my mother and father.'

My mother and father, for their part, responded differently, as their children spoke to them less. She grew restless, seemed troubled and anxious at the scarcity of words exchanged in the house. It was she who would question me about my day when I came home from school. She smiled at small talk. She pried at the edges of my sentences to get me to say something more. (What?) She'd join conversations she overheard, but her intrusions often stopped her children's talking. By contrast, my father seemed reconciled to the new quiet. Though his English improved somewhat, he retired into silence. At dinner he spoke very little. One night his children and even his wife helplessly giggled at his garbled English pronunciation of the Catholic Grace before Meals. Thereafter he made his wife recite the prayer at the start of each meal, even on formal occasions, when there were guests in the house. Hers became the public voice of the family. On official business, it was she, not my father, one would usually hear on the phone or in stores, talking to strangers. His children grew so accustomed to his silence that, years later, they would speak routinely of his shyness. (My mother would often try to explain:

259

Both his parents died when he was eight. He was raised by an uncle who treated him like little more than a menial servant. He was never encouraged to speak. He grew up alone. A man of few words.) But my father was not shy, I realized, when I'd watch him speaking Spanish with relatives. Using Spanish, he was quickly effusive. Especially when talking with other men, his voice would spark, flicker, flare alive with sounds. In Spanish, he expressed ideas and feelings he rarely revealed in English. With firm Spanish sounds, he conveyed confidence and authority English would never allow him.

The silence at home, however, was finally more than a literal silence. Fewer words passed between parent and child, but more profound was the silence that resulted from my inattention to sounds. At about the time I no longer bothered to listen with care to the sounds of English in public, I grew careless about listening to the sounds family members made when they spoke. Most of the time I heard someone speaking at home and didn't distinguish his sounds from the words people uttered in public. I didn't even pay much attention to my parents accented and ungrammatical speech. At least not at home. Only when I was with them in public would I grow alert to their accents. Though, even then, their sounds caused me less and less concern. For I was increasingly confident of my own public identity.

I would have been happier about my public success had I not sometimes recalled what it had been like earlier, when my family had conveyed its intimacy through a set of conveniently private sounds. Sometimes in public, hearing a stranger, I'd hark back to my past. A Mexican farmworker approached me downtown to ask directions to somewhere. "¿Hijito . . . ?" he said. And his voice summoned deep longing. Another time, standing beside my mother in the visiting room of a Carmelite convent, before the dense screen which rendered the nuns shadowy figures, I heard several Spanish-speaking nuns—their busy, singsong overlapping voices—assure us that yes, yes, we were remembered, all our family was remembered in their prayers. (Their voices echoed faraway family sounds.) Another day, a dark-faced old woman—her hand light on my shoulder—steadied herself against me as she boarded a bus. She murmured something I couldn't quite comprehend. Her Spanish voice came near, like the face of a never-before-seen relative in the instant before I was kissed. Her voice, like so many of the Spanish voices I'd hear in public, recalled the golden age of my youth. Hearing Spanish then, I continued to be a careful, if sad, listener to sounds. Hearing a Spanish-speaking family walking behind me, I turned to look. I smiled for an instant, before my glance found the Hispanic-looking faces of strangers in the crowd going by.

Journal and Discussion Questions

1 "Gains and Losses" discusses bilingual education, intimacy, and the relationship between public and private life. State the main idea of each topic in a single sentence. How are these three ideas related to each other in "Gains and Losses"? What would you say is the central idea or thesis of this piece? Why?

2 Richard Rodriguez analyzes his experiences in his first year of school to make generalizations about the lives and education of other Latino/Latina children. Summarize his most important ideas about his life and his most important generalizations. How are Rodriguez's personal reflections connected to his main argument?

3 "Gains and Losses" is built around a number of contrasts, for example, between private and public voice and between the experiences of Rodriguez's mother and father. Outline the essay and note all the important contrasts in the essay. How does Rodriguez use these contrasts to explain his ideas about his education and persuade his audience to take his view?

4 What is *bilingual education*? Why do you think some educators and activists support bilingual education for children who grew up speaking Spanish or another language other than English? How does "Gains and Losses" seem to respond to these opposing arguments?

5 How does Rodriguez describe the lives of other members of his family in "Gains and Losses," especially his father and mother. How do their experiences fit into Rodriguez's analysis of how English and Spanish can affect people's identities and relationships in a Mexican immigrant family in the U.S.?

6 What do Rodriguez and his family sacrifice for Rodriguez's education? Why does Rodriguez believe that he and his family needed to make these sacrifices for Rodriguez to succeed in school and in public life? Would Rodriguez's argument be stronger if he ignored these costs?

Topics for Writing

1 Conduct research on the pros and cons of bilingual education, and argue in support of or against Rodriguez with your additional arguments and evidence.

2 Analyze the relationship between your public life and your private life, considering how big a separation exists between these lives.

EDUCATION IN A MULTICULTURAL SOCIETY:
Our Future's Greatest Challenge

BY LISA D. DELPIT

Lisa D. Delpit is an African American scholar in education whose research often focuses on race, language, and ethnic diversity in urban schools. A former MacArthur fellow, Delpit is Executive Director of the Center for Urban Education and Innovation at Florida International University and the Benjamin E. Mays Chair of Urban Educational Leadership at Georgia State University. She is a co-editor of *The Real Ebonics Debate: Power, Language, and the Education of African-American Children* and a co-author of *The Skin That We Speak: Thoughts on Language and Culture in the Classroom*. "Education in a Multicultural Society: Our Future's Greatest Challenge" was originally given in 1991 as a public lecture and later revised and published as the last chapter in Delpit's award-winning 1995 book, *Other People's Children: Cultural Conflict in the Classroom*. An academic argument addressed to a mixed audience of education scholars, school teachers, parents, and others interested in improving education, "Education in a Multicultural Society" disagrees with many popular opinions about why African American children and other ethnic minorities have trouble in school. Delpit analyzes a range of problems that children and teachers experience in schools and argues that the cause of these problems is often cultural misunderstanding—children and parents not understanding the cultural expectations and practices of the school and teachers not recognizing and accounting for these misunderstandings.

N ANY DISCUSSION OF EDUCATION and culture, it is important to remember that children are individuals and cannot be made to fit into any preconceived mold of how they are "supposed" to act. The question is not necessarily how to create the perfect "culturally matched" learning situation for each ethnic group, but rather how to recognize when there is a problem for a particular child and how to seek its cause in the most broadly conceived fashion. Knowledge about culture is but one tool that educators may make use of when devising solutions for a school's difficulty in educating diverse children.

THE CULTURAL CLASH BETWEEN STUDENTS AND SCHOOL. The clash between school culture and home culture is actualized in at least two ways. When a significant difference exists between the stu-

dents' culture and the school's culture, teachers can easily misread students' aptitudes, intent, or abilities as a result of the difference in styles of language use and interactional patterns. Secondly, when such cultural differences exist, teachers may utilize styles of instruction and/or discipline that are at odds with community norms. A few examples: A twelve-year-old friend tells me that there are three kinds of teachers in his middle school: the black teachers, none of whom are afraid of black kids; the white teachers, a few of whom are not afraid of black kids; and the largest group of white teachers, who are *all* afraid of black kids. It is this last group that, according to my young informant, consistently has the most difficulty with teaching and whose students have the most difficulty with learning.

I would like to suggest that some of the problems may certainly be as this young man relates. Yet, from

> ❝ **If teachers are to teach effectively, recognition of the importance of student perception of teacher intent is critical.** ❞

my work with teachers in many settings, I have come to believe that a major portion of the problem may also rest with how these three groups of teachers interact and use language with their students. These differences in discourse styles relate to certain ethnic and class groups. For instance, many African-American teachers are likely to give directives to a group of unruly students in a direct and explicit fashion, for example, "I don't want to hear it. Sit down, be quiet, and finish your work NOW!" Not only is this directive explicit, but with it the teacher also displays a high degree of personal power in the classroom. By contrast, many middle-class European-American teachers are likely to say something like, "Would you like to sit down now and finish your paper?", making use of an indirect command and downplaying the display of power. Partly because the first instance is likely to be more like the statements many African-American children hear at home, and partly because the second statement sounds to many of these youngsters like the words of someone who is fearful (and thus less deserving of respect), African-American children are more likely to obey the first explicit directive and ignore the second implied directive.

The discussion of this issue is complex, but, in brief, many of the difficulties teachers encounter with children who are different in background from themselves are related to this underlying attitudinal difference in the appropriate display of explicitness and personal power in the classroom.

If teachers are to teach effectively, recognition of the importance of student perception of teacher intent is critical. Problems arising from culturally different interactional styles seem to disproportionately affect African-American boys, who, as a result of cultural influences, exhibit a high degree of physicality and desire for interaction. This can be expressed both positively and negatively, as hugging and other shows of affection or as hitting and other displays of displeasure. Either expression is likely to receive negative sanction in the classroom setting.

Researcher Harry Morgan documents in a 1990 study what most of us who have worked with African-American children have learned intuitively: that African-American children, more than white, and boys more than girls, initiate interactions with peers in the classroom in performing assigned tasks. Morgan con-

cludes that a classroom that allows for greater movement and interaction will better facilitate the learning and social styles of African-American boys, while one that disallows such activity will unduly penalize them. This, I believe, is one of the reasons that there recently has been such a movement toward developing schools specifically for African-American males. Black boys *are* unduly penalized in our regular classrooms. They *are* disproportionately assigned to special education. They do not have to be, and would not be, if our teachers were taught how to redesign classrooms so that the styles of African-American boys are accommodated.

I would like to share with you an example of a student's ability being misread as a result of a mismatch between the student's and teacher's cultural use of language. Second-grader Marti was reading a story she had written that began, "Once upon a time, there was an old lady, and this old lady ain't had no sense." The teacher interrupted her, "Marti, that sounds like the beginning of a wonderful story, but could you tell me how you would say it in Standard English?" Marti put her head down, thought for a minute, and said softly, "There was an old lady who didn't have any sense." Then Marti put her hand on her hip, raised her voice and said, "But this old lady ain't had *no* sense!" Marti's teacher probably did not understand that the child was actually exhibiting a very sophisticated sense of language. Although she clearly knew the Standard English form, she chose a so-called nonstandard form for emphasis, just as world-class writers Charles Chesnutt, Alice Walker, Paul Lawrence Dunbar, and Zora Neale Hurston have done for years. Of course, there is no standardized test presently on the market that can discern that level of sophistication. Marti's misuse of Standard English would simply be assessed as a "mistake." Thus, differences in cultural language patterns make inappropriate assessments commonplace.

Another example of assessment difficulties arising from differences in culture can be found in the Latino community. Frequently, Latino girls find it difficult to speak out or exhibit academic prowess in a gender-mixed setting. They will often defer to boys, displaying their knowledge only when in the company of other girls. Most teachers, unaware of this tendency, are likely to insist that all groups be gender-mixed, thus depressing the exhibition of ability by the Latino girls in the class.

A final example involves Native Americans. In many Native American communities there is a prohibition against speaking for someone else. So strong is this prohibition that to the question, "Does your son like moose?," an adult Native American man responded to what should have been asked instead: "*I* like moose." The consequence of this cultural interactional pattern may have contributed to the findings in Charlotte Basham's study of a group of Native American college students' writing. The students appeared unable to write summaries and, even when explicitly told not to, continued to write their opinions of various works rather than summaries of the authors' words. Basham concludes that the prohibition against speaking for others may have caused these students considerable difficulty in trying to capture in their own words the ideas of another. Because they had been taught to always speak for themselves, they found doing so much more comfortable and culturally compatible.

STEREOTYPING. There is a widespread belief that Asian-American children are the "perfect" students, that they will do well regardless of the academic setting in which they are placed. This stereotype has led to a negative backlash in which the academic needs of the majority of Asian-American students are overlooked. I recall one five-year-old Asian-American girl in a Montessori kindergarten class. Cathy was dutifully going about the task assigned to her, that of placing a number of objects next to various numerals printed on a cloth. She appeared to be thoroughly engaged, attending totally to the task at hand, and never disturbing anyone near her. Meanwhile, the teacher's attention was devoted to the children who demanded her presence in one form or another or to those she believed would have difficulty with the task assigned them. Small, quiet Cathy fit neither category. At the end of work time, no one had come to see what Cathy had done, and Cathy neatly put away her work. Her behavior and attention to task had been exemplary. The only problem was that at the end of the session no numeral had the correct number of objects next to it. The teacher later told me that Cathy, like Asian-American students she had taught previously, was one of the best students in the class. Yet, in this case, a child's culturally influenced, nondisruptive classroom behavior, along with the teacher's stereotype of "good Asian students," led to her not receiving appropriate instruction.

Another example of stereotyping involves African-American girls. Research has been conducted in classroom settings which shows that African-American girls are rewarded for nurturing behavior while white girls are rewarded for academic behavior. Though it is likely true that many African-American girls are excel-

lent nurturers, having played with or helped to care for younger siblings or cousins, they are penalized by the nurturing "mammy" stereotype when they are not given the same encouragement as white girls toward academic endeavors.

Another example of stereotyping concerns Native American children. Many researchers and classroom teachers have described the "nonverbal Indian child." What is often missed in these descriptions is that these children are as verbal and eager to share their knowledge as any others, but they need appropriate contexts—such as small groups—in which to talk. When asked inappropriate questions or called on to talk before the entire class, many Native American children will refuse to answer, or will answer in as few words as possible. Thus, teachers sometimes refrain from calling on Native American students to avoid causing them discomfort, and these children subsequently miss the opportunity to discuss or display their knowledge of the subject matter.

A primary source of stereotyping is often the teacher education program itself. It is in these programs that teachers learn that poor students and students of color should be expected to achieve less than their "mainstream" counterparts.

CHILD-DEFICIT ASSUMPTIONS THAT LEAD TO TEACHING LESS INSTEAD OF MORE. We say we believe that all children can learn, but few of us really believe it. Teacher education usually focuses on research that links failure and socioeconomic status, failure and cultural difference, and failure and single-parent households. It is hard to believe that these children can possibly be successful after their teachers have been so thoroughly exposed to so much negative indoctrination. When teachers receive that kind of education, there is a tendency to assume deficits in students rather than to locate and teach to strengths. To counter this tendency, educators must have knowledge of children's lives outside of school so as to recognize their strengths.

One of my former students is a case in point. Howard was in first grade when everyone thought that he would need to be placed in special education classes. Among his other academic problems, he seemed totally unable to do even the simplest mathematics worksheets. During the unit on money, determining the value of nickels and dimes seemed hopelessly beyond him. I agreed with the general assessment of him until I got to know something about his life outside of school. Howard was seven years old. He had a younger sister who was four and afflicted with cerebral palsy. His mother was suffering from a drug problem and was unable to adequately care for the children, so Howard was the main caretaker in the family. Each morning, he would get his sister up, dressed, and off to school. He also did the family laundry and much of the shopping. To do both those tasks, he had become expert at counting money and knowing when or if the local grocer was overcharging. Still, he was unable to complete what appeared to his teachers to be a simple worksheet. Without teachers having knowledge of his abilities outside of school he was destined to be labeled mentally incompetent.

This story also exposes how curriculum content is typically presented. Children who may be gifted in real-life settings are often at a loss when asked to exhibit knowledge solely through decontextualized paper-and-pencil exercises. I have often pondered that if we taught African-American children how to dance in school, by the time they had finished the first five workbooks on the topic, we would have a generation of remedial dancers!

If we do not have some knowledge of children's lives outside of the realms of paper-and-pencil work, and even outside of their classrooms, then we cannot know their strengths. Not knowing students' strengths leads to our "teaching down" to children from communities that are culturally different from that of the teachers in the school. Because teachers do not want to tax what they believe to be these students' lower abilities, they end up teaching less when, in actuality, these students need *more* of what school has to offer. This is not a new concept. In 1933 Carter G. Woodson discussed the problem in *The Mis-Education of the Negro*:

> The teaching of arithmetic in the fifth grade in a backward county in Mississippi should mean one thing in the Negro school and a decidedly different thing in the white school. The Negro children, as a rule, come from the homes of tenants and peons who have to migrate annually from plantation to plantation, looking for light which they have never seen. The children from the homes of white planters and merchants live permanently in the midst of calculation, family budgets, and the like, which enable them sometimes to learn more by contact than the Negro can acquire in school. Instead of teaching such Negro children less arithmetic, they should be taught much more of it than white children.

Teaching less rather than teaching more can happen in several ways. Those who utilize "skills-based" approaches can teach less by focusing solely on isolated, decontextualized bits. Such instruction becomes boring and meaningless when not placed in any meaningful context. When instruction allows no opportunity for children to use their minds to create and interpret texts, then children will only focus on low-level

thinking and their school-based intellect will atrophy. Skills-oriented approaches that feature heavy doses of readiness activities also contribute to the "teaching less" phenomenon. Children are typically assigned to these activities as a result of low scores on some standardized test. However, they end up spending so much time matching circles and triangles that no one ever introduces them to actually learning how to read. Should anyone doubt it, I can guarantee you that no amount of matching circles and triangles ever taught anyone how to read. Worse, these activities take time away from real kinds of involvement in literacy such as listening to and seeing the words in real books.

Teaching less can also occur with those who favor "holistic" or "child-centered" approaches. While I believe that there is much of value in whole language and process writing approaches, some teachers seem almost to be using these methodologies as excuses for not teaching. I am reminded of a colleague who visited a classroom in California designed around the state-mandated whole language approach. My colleague witnessed one child in a peer reading group who clearly could not read. When she later asked the teacher about this child, the teacher responded that it was "OK" that this fourth-grader could not read, because he would understand the content via the subsequent discussion. While it is great that the child would have the opportunity to learn through a discussion, it is devastating that no one was providing him with what he also needed—explicit instruction in learning how to read.

In some "process writing" classrooms, teachers unfamiliar with the language abilities of African-American children are led to believe that these students have no fluency with language. They therefore allow them to remain in the first stages of the writing process, producing first draft after first draft, with no attention to editing or completing final products. They allow African-American students to remain at the level of developing fluency because these teachers do not understand the language competence their students already possess. The key here is not the kind of instruction but the attitude underlying it. When teachers do not understand the potential of the students they teach, they will underteach them no matter what the methodology.

IGNORANCE OF COMMUNITY NORMS. Many school systems have attempted to institute "parent training" programs for poor parents and parents of color. While the intentions of these programs are good, they can only be truly useful when educators understand the realities with which such parents must contend and why they do what they do. Often, middle-class school professionals are appalled by what they see of poor parents, and most do not have the training or the ability to see past surface behaviors to the meanings behind parents' actions.

> ## The key here is not the kind of instruction but the attitude underlying it. When teachers do not understand the potential of the students they teach, they will underteach them no matter what the methodology.

In a preschool I have often visited, four-year-old David's young mother once came to his class to provide a birthday party for her son. I happened to hear the conversation of the teachers that afternoon. They said she came to school in a "bum costume" yelling, "Let's party!" and running around the room. She had presents for all the children and a cake she or someone else had baked for the occasion. The teachers were horrified. They said they could smell alcohol on her breath, that the children went wild, and that they attempted to get the children out to recess as quickly as possible.

From an earlier conversation, I happened to know that this woman cares deeply for her son and his welfare. She is even saving money to put him in private school—a major sacrifice for her—when he enters kindergarten. David's teachers, however, were not able to see that, despite her possible inappropriateness, his mother had actually spent a great deal of effort and care in putting together this party for her son. She also probably felt the need to bolster her courage a bit with a drink in order to face fifteen four-year-olds and keep them entertained. We must find ways for professionals to understand the different ways in which parents can show their concern for their children.

Another example of a cultural barrier between teacher understandings and parental understandings occurred at a predominantly Latino school in Boston. Even though the teachers continually asked them not to, the parents, primarily mothers, kept bringing their first graders into their classroom before the school day officially began. The teachers wanted all children to remain on the playground with a teacher's aide, and they also wanted all parents to vacate the school yard as soon as possible while the teachers readied the classrooms for the beginning of the day. When the parents continued to ignore the request, the teachers began locking the school doors. Pretty soon feelings escalated to the point of yelling matches, and the parents even approached the school board.

What the teachers in this instance did not understand was that the parents viewed six-year-olds as still being babies and in need of their mother's or their surrogate mother's (the teacher's) attention. To the parents, leaving children outside without one of their "mothers" present was tantamount to child abuse and exhibited a most callous disregard for the children's welfare. The situation did not have to have become so highly charged. All that was needed was some knowledge about the parents and community of the children they were teaching, and the teachers could have resolved the problem easily—perhaps by stationing one of the first-grade teachers outside in the mornings, or by inviting one of the parents to remain on the school grounds before the teachers called the children in to class.

INVISIBILITY. Whether we are immediately aware of it or not, the United States is surely composed of a plethora of perspectives. I am reminded of this every time I think of my friend Martha, a Native American teacher. Martha told me how tired she got of being asked about her plans for Thanksgiving by people who seemed to take no note that her perspective on the holiday might be a bit different than their own. One year, in her frustration, she told me that when the next questioner asked, "What are you doing for Thanksgiving?", she answered, "I plan to spend the day saying, 'You're welcome!'"

If we plan to survive as a species on this planet we must certainly create multicultural curricula that educate our children to the differing perspectives of our diverse population. In part, the problems we see exhibited in school by African-American children and children of other oppressed minorities can be traced to this lack of a curriculum in which they can find represented the intellectual achievements of people who look like themselves. Were that not the case, these children would not talk about doing well in school as "acting white." Our children of color need to see the brilliance of their legacy, too.

Even with well-intentioned educators, not only our children's legacies but our children themselves can become invisible. Many of the teachers we educate, and indeed their teacher educators, believe that to acknowledge a child's color is to insult him or her. In her book *White Teacher*, Vivian Paley openly discusses the problems inherent in the statement that I have heard many teachers—well-intentioned teachers—utter, "I don't see color, I only see children." What message does this statement send? That there is something wrong with being black or brown, that it should *not* be noticed? I would like to suggest that if one does not see color, then one does not really see children. Children made "invisible" in this manner become hard-pressed to see themselves worthy of notice.

ADDRESSING THE PROBLEMS OF EDUCATING POOR AND CULTURALLY DIVERSE CHILDREN.

To begin with, our prospective teachers are exposed to descriptions of failure rather than models of success. We expose student teachers to an education that relies upon name calling and labelling ("disadvantaged," "at-risk," "learning disabled," "the underclass") to explain its failures, and calls upon research study after research study to inform teachers that school achievement is intimately and inevitably linked with socioeconomic status. Teacher candidates are told that "culturally different" children are mismatched to the school setting and therefore cannot be expected to achieve as well as white, middle-class children. They are told that children of poverty are developmentally slower than other children.

Seldom, however, do we make available to our teacher initiates the many success stories about educating poor children and children of color: those institutions like the Nairobi Day-School in East Palo Alto, California, which produced children from poor African-American communities who scored three grade levels above the national average. Nor do we make sure that they learn about those teachers who are quietly going about the job of producing excellence in educating poor and culturally diverse students: teachers like Marva Collins of Chicago, Illinois, who has educated many African-American students considered uneducable by public schools; Jaime Escalante, who has consistently taught hundreds of Latino high school students who live in the poorest *barrios* of East Los Angeles to test their way into advanced-placement calculus classes; and many other successful unsung heroes and heroines who are seldom visible in teacher education classrooms.

Interestingly, even when such teaching comes to our consciousness, it is most often not by way of educational research but via the popular media. We educators do not typically research and document this "power pedagogy" (as Asa Hilliard calls it), but continue to provide, at worst, autopsies of failure and, at best, studies in minimalist achievement. In other words, we teach teachers rationales for failure, not visions of success. Is there any wonder that those who are products of such teacher education (from classroom teachers to principals to central office staff) water down the curriculum for diverse students instead of challenging them with more, as Woodson says, of what school has to offer?

A second reason problems occur for our culturally diverse students is that we have created in most schools institutions of isolation. We foster the notion that students are clients of "professional" educators who are met in the "office" of the classroom where their deficiencies are remediated and their intellectual "illnesses" healed. Nowhere do we foster inquiry into who our students really are or encourage teachers to develop links to the often rich home lives of students, yet teachers cannot hope to begin to understand who sits before them unless they can connect with the families and communities from which their students come. To do that, it is vital that teachers and teacher educators explore their own beliefs and attitudes about non-white and non-middle-class people. Many teachers—black, white, and "other"—harbor unexamined prejudices about people from ethnic groups or classes different from their own. This is partly because teachers have been so conditioned by the larger society's negative stereotypes of certain ethnic groups, and partly because they are never given the opportunity to learn to value the experiences of other groups.

I propose that a part of teacher education include bringing parents and community members into the university classroom to tell prospective teachers (and their teacher educators) what their concerns about education are, what they feel schools are doing well or poorly for their children, and how they would like to see schooling changed. I would also like to see teacher initiates and their educators go out to community gatherings to acquire such firsthand knowledge. It is unreasonable to expect that teachers will automatically value the knowledge that parents and community members bring to the education of diverse children if valuing such knowledge has not been modelled for them by those from whom they learn to teach.

Following a speech I made at a conference a few years ago, I have been corresponding with a very insightful teacher who works at a prestigious university lab school. The school is staffed by a solely European-American fac-

> **It is unreasonable to expect that teachers will automatically value the knowledge that parents and community members bring to the education of diverse children if valuing such knowledge has not been modelled for them by those from whom they learn to teach.**

ulty, but seeks to maintain racial and cultural balance among the student body. They find, however, that they continue to lose black students, especially boys. The teacher, named Richard, wrote to me that the school often has problems, both behavioral and academic, with African-American boys. When called to the school to discuss these problems, these children's parents typically say that they do not understand, that their children are fine at home. The school personnel interpret these statements as indications of the parents' "being defensive," and presume that the children are as difficult at home as at school, but that the parents do not want to admit it.

When Richard asked for some suggestions, my first recommendation was that the school should work hard to develop a multicultural staff. Of course, that solution would take a while, even if the school was committed to it. My next and actually most important suggestion was that the school needed to learn to view its African-American parents as a resource and not as a problem. When problems arise with particular African-American children, the school should get the parents of these children involved in helping to point out what the school might do better.

Richard wrote back to me:

The change though that has made me happiest so far about my own work is that I have taken your advice and I am asking black parents about stuff I never would have brought up before. . . . We do a lot of journal writing, and with the 6- to 8-year-olds I teach, encourage them to draw as well as write, to see the journal as a form of expression. I was having a conference with the mother of one black boy. . . . We looked at his journal and saw that he was doing beautiful intricate drawings, but that he rarely got more than a few words down on the page. I talked to his mother about how we were trying to encourage C. to do the writing first, but that he liked to draw.

During the conversation I started to see this as something like what you were talking about, and I asked C.'s mom how she would handle this at home. I only asked her about how she herself might deal with this, but she said, "In black families, we would just tell him write the words first." I passed that information on to C.'s reading teacher, and we both talked to him and told him he had to get the words down first. Suddenly he began making one- and two-page entries into his journal.

While this is pleasing in and of itself, it is an important lesson to us in terms of equity. C. is now getting equal access to the curriculum because he is using the journal for the reasons we intended it. All we needed was a culturally appropriate way to tell him how to do it.

I am not suggesting that excellent teachers of diverse students *must* be of their students' ethnicity. I have seen too many excellent European-American teachers of African-American students, and too many poor African-American teachers of African-American students to come to such an illogical conclusion. I do believe, however, that we should strive to make our teaching force diverse, for teachers who share the ethnic and cultural backgrounds of our increasingly diverse student bodies may serve, along with parents and other community members, to provide insights that might otherwise remain hidden.

The third problem I believe we must overcome is the narrow and essentially Eurocentric curriculum we provide for our teachers. At the university level, teachers are not being educated with the broad strokes necessary to prepare them properly for the twenty-first century. We who are concerned about teachers and teaching must insist that our teachers become knowledgeable of the liberal arts, but we must also work like the dickens to change liberal arts courses so that they do not continue to reflect only, as feminist scholar Peggy McIntosh says, "the public lives of white Western men." These new courses must not only teach what white Westerners have to say about diverse cultures, they must also share what the writers and thinkers of diverse cultures have to say about themselves, their history, music, art, literature, politics, and so forth.

If we know the intellectual legacies of our students, we will gain insight into how to teach them. Stephanie Terry, a first-grade teacher I have recently interviewed, breathes the heritage of her students into the curriculum. Stephanie teaches in an economically strapped community in inner-city Baltimore, Maryland, in a school with a 100 percent African-American enrollment. She begins each year with the study of Africa, describing Africa's relationship to the United States, its history, resources, and so forth. As her students learn each new aspect of the regular citywide curriculum, Stephanie connects this knowledge to aspects of their African ancestry: while covering a unit about libraries she tells them about the world's first libraries, which were established in Africa. A unit on health presents her with the opportunity to tell her students about the African doctors of antiquity who wrote the first texts on medicine. Stephanie does not replace the current curriculum; rather, she expands it. She also teaches about the contributions of Asian-Americans, Native Americans, and Latinos as she broadens her students' minds and spirits. All of Stephanie's students learn to read by the end of the school year. They also learn to love themselves, love their history, and love learning.

Stephanie could not teach her children the pride of their ancestry and could not connect it to the material they learn today were it not for her extraordinarily broad knowledge of the liberal arts. However, she told me that she did not acquire this knowledge in her formal education, but worked, read, and studied on her own to make such knowledge a part of her pedagogy.

Teachers must not merely take courses that tell them how to treat their students as multicultural clients, in other words, those that tell them how to identify differences in interactional or communicative strategies and remediate appropriately. They must also learn about the brilliance the students bring with them "in their blood." Until they appreciate the wonders of the cultures represented before them—and they cannot do that without extensive study most appropriately begun in college-level courses—they cannot appreciate the potential of those who sit before them, nor can they begin to link their students' histories and worlds to the subject matter they present in the classroom.

If we are to successfully educate all of our children, we must work to remove the blinders built of stereotypes, monocultural instructional methodologies, ignorance, social distance, biased research, and racism. We must work to destroy those blinders so that it is possible to really see, to really know the students we must teach. Yes, if we are to be successful at educating diverse children, we must accomplish the Herculean feat of developing this clear-sightedness, for in the words of a wonderful Native Alaskan educator: "In order to teach you, I must know you." I pray for all of us the strength to teach our children what they must learn, and the humility and wisdom to learn from them so that we might better teach.

Journal and Discussion Questions

1 What is the thesis of the article, the central argument that Lisa Delpit is making about schooling? How does Delpit develop, expand, and complicate this idea as the article continues?

2 Outline "Education in a Multicultural Society." What parts of the article's central problem does Delpit identify? How do the parts relate to each other? How do you think Delpit determined the order of the sections of her article?

3 Much of Delpit's article consists of brief anecdotes or stories, usually of a problem that a teacher or student experienced in school. Delpit usually presents a common interpretation of the cause of the problem and then analyzes the problem to come up with a different cause. Look closely at a couple of these stories. What does Delpit write to persuade readers that her interpretation is better? What stories do you have of misunderstanding a teacher or being misunderstood by a teacher? To what extent did cultural differences create this misunderstanding? What other causes for misunderstanding may have been in play?

4 Delpit begins her article with a qualification, that it is important for teachers to remember that all children are individuals and that they cannot be expected to fit into a "predetermined mode" because of their culture, race, and ethnicity. Why was it important for Delpit to say this before getting into her argument that teachers need to know the culture of their students in order to teach them effectively? How can teachers use this knowledge without creating new stereotypes? How can they see each student as an individual while also understanding the child as part of a culture?

5 Why does a "color blind" stance toward children ("I don't see color, I only see children") fail in trying to treat children fairly and individually, according to Delpit? What other approaches to teaching, liberal and conservative, does she criticize? Why? Does she represent her opponents' ideas fairly and accurately? Explain.

6 What solutions does Delpit propose to begin to solve the problems she describes? How can these solutions improve students' learning? What problems might there be in implementing these solutions? Can you come up with other solutions?

7 Because "Education in a Multicultural Society" was originally a speech, it does not have parenthetical documentation or a works cited page. What techniques and phrasings does Delpit use to acknowledge her print and interview sources? How does she use these sources to support and explain her ideas without letting them overshadow her own ideas?

Topics for Writing

1 Here's your chance! Write a letter to your teacher explaining what he or she needs to know about you and your culture and why.

2 Write a letter to the school board of your city or town that argues for some of the reforms discussed by Delpit.

3 Discuss how ignorance of other cultures can lead to misunderstandings outside school, for example, at work, in church, or in a dormitory. Part of your essay should suggest ways to prevent or overcome these misunderstandings.

Connecting the Readings

Compare the goals and purposes of education in Richard Rodriguez's "Gains and Losses" and Lisa D. Delpit's "Education in a Multicultural Society: Our Future's Greatest Challenge."

THE BOONDOCKS

BY AARON McGRUDER

The Universal Press Syndicate comic strip *The Boondocks* by Aaron McGruder (1974–) follows the lives of Huey and Riley Freeman, two preadolescent African American boys from inner-city Chicago who have moved into the white suburb of Woodcrest to live with their grandfather. McGruder milks humor and social commentary about race in America, U.S. politics, and African American culture from the conflicts between Huey's revolutionary aspirations, Riley's gangsta ambitions, the grandfather's traditional values, and the anxieties that Woodcrest residents feel about blacks moving into the neighborhood. This strip discusses multicultural education, specifically a national debate about Afrocentric vs. Eurocentric teaching of history, when Huey brings books such as *How Whitey Done Messed Everything Up* or *How to Tell If Your Teacher Is Brainwashing You with Eurocentrism* to his world history class and deliberately leaves his textbook at home. This strip appeared just a few months after *The Boondocks* debut on April 19, 1999, and it is reprinted in McGruder's first book, *The Boondocks: Because I Know You Don't Read the Newspapers*. *The Boondocks* official Web site can be found at www.theboondockstv.com/.

Journal and Discussion Questions

1   Why does Huey believe that books that argue the importance of Africans, African Americans, and Native Americans in history deserve "priority" over the class' world history textbook?

2   What does *The Boondocks* imply about what is included and excluded in the textbook? What does Aaron McGruder imply about how world history is taught in Huey's old school in Southside Chicago compared to his new school in an all-white suburb?

3   Why would Huey object to his history teacher's "stirring tribute to Christopher Columbus"?

4   What seems to be the teacher's attitude toward Huey's actions and objections? Why is the teacher not pictured? What does this portrayal of the teacher contribute to McGruder's commentary about Eurocentric vs. Afrocentric history instruction?

5   What is reasonable about Huey's stance with his teacher? What is unreasonable about his stance? What does his stance imply about McGruder's attitude toward some proponents of Afrocentric history?

6   What does McGruder seem to be saying about the debate about Eurocentric vs. Afrocentric history instruction? What appears to be McGruder's opinion about multicultural education? Why?

7   Why do people care about the issue portrayed in *The Boondocks*? What is important about how race is taught in social studies and history classes?

Topics for Writing

1   Analyze *The Boondocks* strip and what Aaron McGruder appears to be saying about the debate about Eurocentrism and Afrocentrism in history instruction.

2   Research the different sides of the debate about how history instruction should deal with race and racism and cover the experiences of whites and people of color in history. Argue your position in this debate.

A STAND AGAINST WIKIPEDIA

BY SCOTT JASCHIK

Scott Jaschik is one of two editors of *Inside Higher Ed* (www.insidehighered.com), an important daily online source of news and opinion on college and universities. According to his biography on *Inside Higher Ed*, he oversees the publication's "news content, opinion pieces, resources, and interactive features" in addition to writing articles such as "A Stand Against Wikipedia." Before co-founding *Inside Higher Ed* in 2004, Jaschik held various positions with *The Chronicle of Higher Education*, the leading weekly newspaper on U.S. colleges and universities, for many years, including four years as the newspaper's editor. A 1985 graduate of Cornell University, Jaschik has also published articles on higher education in news publications, such as the *New York Times*, the *Washington Post*, the *Boston Globe*, and *Salon*. "A Stand Against Wikipedia" is a news article published in *Inside Higher Ed* on January 26, 2007. Jaschik reports college faculty's different concerns about students' use of Wikipedia (and other sources) and some of the effects of the Internet on students' academic work. He also describes faculty's responses to some of the problems that new information technology poses to students and teachers.

AS WIKIPEDIA HAS BECOME MORE and more popular with students, some professors have become increasingly concerned about the online, reader-produced encyclopedia.

While plenty of professors have complained about the lack of accuracy or completeness of entries, and some have discouraged or tried to bar students from using it, the history department at Middlebury College is trying to take a stronger, collective stand. It voted this month to bar students from citing the Web site as a source in papers or other academic work. All faculty members will be telling students about the policy and explaining why material on Wikipedia—while convenient—may not be trustworthy.

"As educators, we are in the business of reducing the dissemination of misinformation," said Don Wyatt, chair of the department. "Even though Wikipedia may have some value, particularly from the value of leading students to citable sources, it is not itself an appropriate source for citation," he said.

The department made what Wyatt termed a consensus decision on the issue after discussing problems professors were seeing as students cited incorrect information from Wikipedia in papers and on tests. In one instance, Wyatt said, a professor noticed several students offering the same incorrect information, from Wikipedia.

There was some discussion in the department of trying to ban students from using Wikipedia, but Wyatt said that didn't seem appropriate. Many Wikipedia entries have good bibliographies, Wyatt said. And any absolute ban would just be ignored. "There's the issue of freedom of access," he said. "And I'm not in the business of promulgating unenforceable edicts."

Wyatt said that the department did not specify punishments for citing Wikipedia, and that the primary purpose of the policy was to educate, not to be punitive. He said he doubted that a paper would be rejected for having a single Wikipedia footnote, but that students would be told that they shouldn't do so, and that multiple violations would result in reduced grades or even a failure. "The important point that we wish to communicate to all students taking courses and submitting work in our department in the future is that they cite Wikipedia at their peril," he said.

He stressed that the objection of the department to Wikipedia wasn't its online nature, but its unedited nature, and he said students need to be taught to go for quality information, not just convenience.

The frustrations of Middlebury faculty members are by no means unique. Last year, Alan Liu, a professor of English at the University of California at Santa Barbara, adopted a policy that Wikipedia "is not appropriate as the primary or sole reference for anything that is central to an argument, complex, or controversial." Liu said that it was too early to tell what impact his policy is having. In explaining his rationale— which he shared with an e-mail list—he wrote that he had "just read a paper about the relation between structuralism, deconstruction, and postmodernism in which every reference was to the Wikipedia articles on those topics with no awareness that there was any need to read a primary work or even a critical work."

Wikipedia officials agree—in part—with Middlebury's history department. "That's a sensible policy," Sandra Ordonez, a spokeswoman, said in an e-mail interview. "Wikipedia is the ideal place to start your research and get a global picture of a topic, however, it is not an authoritative source. In fact, we recommend that students check the facts they find in Wikipedia against other sources. Additionally, it is generally good research practice to cite an original source when writing a paper, or completing an exam. It's usually not advisable, particularly at the university level, to cite an encyclopedia."

Ordonez acknowledged that, given the collaborative nature of Wikipedia writing and editing, "there is no guarantee an article is 100 percent correct," but she said that the site is shifting its focus from growth to improving quality, and that the site is a great resource for students. "Most articles are continually being edited and improved upon, and most contributors are real lovers of knowledge who have a real desire to improve the quality of a particular article," she said.

Experts on digital media said that the Middlebury history professors' reaction was understandable and reflects growing concern among faculty members about the accuracy of what students find online. But some worry that bans on citing Wikipedia may not deal with the underlying issues.

Roy Rosenzweig, director of the Center for History and New Media at George Mason University, did an analysis of the accuracy of Wikipedia for *The Journal of American History,* and he found that in many entries, Wikipedia was as accurate or more accurate than more traditional encyclopedias. He said that the quality of material was inconsistent, and that biographical entries were generally well done, while more thematic entries were much less so. Like Ordonez, he said the real problem is one of college students using encyclopedias when they should be using more advanced sources.

"College students shouldn't be citing encyclopedias in their papers," he said. "That's not what college is about. They either should be using primary sources or serious secondary sources."

In the world of college librarians, a major topic of late has been how to guide students in the right direction for research, when Wikipedia and similar sources are so easy. Some of those who have been involved in these discussions said that the Middlebury history department's action pointed to the need for more outreach to students.

Lisa Hinchliffe, head of the undergraduate library and coordinator of information literacy at the University of Illinois at Urbana-Champaign, said that earlier generations of students were in fact taught when it was appropriate (or not) to consult an encyclopedia and why for many a paper they would never even cite a popular magazine or non-scholarly work. "But it was a relatively constrained landscape," and students didn't have easy access to anything equivalent to Wikipedia, she said. "It's not that students are being lazy today. It's a much more complex environment."

When she has taught, and spotted footnotes to sources that aren't appropriate, she's considered that "a teachable moment," Hinchliffe said. She said that she would be interested to see how Middlebury professors react when they get the first violations of their policy, and said she thought there could be positive discussions about why sources are or aren't good ones. That kind of teaching, she said, is important "and can be challenging."

Steven Bell, associate librarian for research and instructional services at Temple University, said of the Middlebury approach: "I applaud the effort for wanting to direct students to good quality resources," but he said he would go about it in a different way.

"I understand what their concerns are. There's no question that [on Wikipedia and similar sites] some things are great and some things are questionable. Some of the pages could be by eighth graders," he said. "But to simply say 'don't use that one' might take students in the wrong direction from the perspective of information literacy."

Students face "an ocean of information" today, much of it of poor quality, so a better approach would be to teach students how to "triangulate" a source like Wikipedia, so they could use other sources to tell whether a given entry could be trusted. "I think our goal should be to equip students with the critical thinking skills to judge."

Journal and Discussion Questions

1 Why, according to Scott Jaschik's "A Stand Against Wikipedia," are some college faculty "concerned" about Wikipedia's popularity with students? Why does Jaschik focus on Wikipedia?

2 What action did the history department at Middlebury College take regarding student citations of Wikipedia? Why? Compare Middlebury's policy to other policies discussed in "A Stand Against Wikipedia." Why do you think Jaschik made Middlebury's new policy the focus of his news article?

3 Do you agree with Middlebury College's policy? Why or why not? Explain your opinion of the other Wikipedia policies mentioned in the article. What other policies or actions could faculty take to deal with the problems posed by Wikipedia?

4 As a source for student papers and exams, how is Wikipedia similar to and different from other online sources, print encyclopedias, and other nonscholarly sources? What do the people quoted by Jaschik seem to think makes a "good quality" source for college students' papers?

5 What are "the underlying issues" behind faculty's concerns about Wikipedia? Why might a college's rule against using Wikipedia as a source in an essay or exam fail to deal with these issues?

6 What does Steven Bell mean when he says, in the final paragraph, that students should be taught how to "triangulate" Wikipedia and similar sources? How would this ability develop students' critical thinking?

7 What sources did Jaschik cite in "A Stand Against Wikipedia"? Why would readers of *Inside Higher Ed* regard these sources as authorities? How did Jaschik use his sources' information and opinions to develop and support his picture of the Wikipedia citation issue? Why didn't Jaschik interview students for "A Stand Against Wikipedia"? How would student sources have improved or detracted from his report?

Topics for Writing

1 Argue what policy your class should have about students' use of Wikipedia as a source in their writing, considering the problems and solutions discussed in Scott Jaschik's "A Stand Against Wikipedia."

2 Interview several students and faculty members about their opinions about students citing Wikipedia as a source in their papers and exams. Compare your findings with Jaschik's news article and propose a campus-wide policy about using Wikipedia as a source. (This project could be expanded into a group project by working together to write and distribute a questionnaire about this issue.)

3 Write a research paper about how computers and other information are changing college education and how students or faculty should—and should not—make use of these technologies.

TAKING WOMEN STUDENTS SERIOUSLY

BY ADRIENNE RICH

Adrienne Rich (1929–) is a feminist poet and essayist who, as she discusses in this selection, taught composition, English literature, and women's studies at a number of colleges and universities. As she points out in a note, "Taking Women Students Seriously" was originally a speech for an audience of teachers of women at the New Jersey College and University Coalition on Women's Education on May 9, 1978. Rich published "Taking Women Students Seriously" a year later in her essay collection *On Lies, Secrets, and Silence: Selected Prose 1966–1978* and may have had a wider readership partly in mind as she composed her essay. "Taking Women Seriously" evaluates the education women typically receive in college and makes recommendations to improve the educational experiences of men as well as women. Rich has published five other books of prose: *Of Women Born: Motherhood as Experience and Institution*; *Blood, Bread and Poetry: Selected Prose, 1979–1986*; *What Is Found There: Notebooks on Poetry and Politics*; *Arts of the Possible: Essays and Conversations*; and *Poetry and Commitment: An Essay.* She has also written many books of poetry.

The talk that follows was addressed to teachers of women. . . . It was given for the New Jersey College and University Coalition on Women's Education, May 9, 1978.

I SEE MY FUNCTION HERE TODAY AS ONE of trying to create a context, delineate a background, against which we might talk about women as students and students as women. I would like to speak for awhile about this background, and then I hope that we can have, not so much a question period, as a raising of concerns, a sharing of questions for which we as yet may have no answers, an opening of conversations which will go on and on.

When I went to teach at Douglass, a women's college, it was with a particular background which I would like briefly to describe to you. I had graduated from an all-girls' school in the 1940s, where the head and the majority of the faculty were independent, unmarried women. One or two held doctorates, but had been forced by the Depression (and by the fact that they were women) to take secondary school teaching jobs. These women cared a great deal about the life of the mind, and they gave a great deal of time and energy—beyond any limit of teaching hours—to those of us who showed special intellectual interest or ability. We were taken to libraries, art museums, lectures at neighboring colleges, set to work on extra research projects, given extra

French or Latin reading. Although we sometimes felt "pushed" by them, we held those women in a kind of respect which even then we dimly perceived was not generally accorded to women in the world at large. They were vital individuals, defined not by their relationships but by their personalities; and although under the pressure of the culture we were all certain we wanted to get married, their lives did not appear empty or dreary to us. In a kind of cognitive dissonance, we knew they were "old maids" and therefore supposed to be bitter and lonely; yet we saw them vigorously involved with life. But despite their existence as alternate models of women, the *content* of the education they gave us in no way prepared us to survive as women in a world organized by and for men.

From that school, I went on to Radcliffe, congratulating myself that now I would have great men as my teachers. From 1947 to 1951, when I graduated, I never saw a single woman on a lecture platform, or in front of a class, except when a woman graduate student gave a paper on a special topic. The "great men" talked of other "great men," of the nature of Man, the history of Mankind, the future of Man; and never again was I to experience, from a teacher, the kind of prodding, the insistence that my best could be even better, that I had known in high school. Women students were simply not taken very seriously. Harvard's message to women was an elite mystification: we were, of course, part of Mankind; we were special, achieving women, or we would not have been there; but of course our real goal was to marry—if possible, a Harvard graduate.

In the late sixties, I began teaching at the City College of New York—a crowded, public, urban, multiracial institution as far removed from Harvard as possible. I went there to teach writing in the SEEK Program, which predated Open Admissions and which was then a kind of model for programs designed to open up higher education to poor, black, and Third World students. Although during the next few years we were to see the original concept of SEEK diluted, then violently attacked and betrayed, it was for a short time an extraordinary and intense teaching and learning environment. The characteristics of this environment were a deep commitment on the part of teachers to the minds of their students; a constant, active effort to create or discover the conditions for learning, and to educate ourselves to meet the needs of the new college population; a philosophical attitude based on open discussion of racism, oppression, and the politics of literature and language; and a belief that learning in the classroom could not be isolated from the student's experience as a member of an urban minority group in white America. Here are some of the kinds of questions we, as teachers of writing, found ourselves asking:

1. What has been the student's experience of education in the inadequate, often abusively racist public school system, which rewards passivity and treats a questioning attitude or independent mind as a behavior problem? What has been her or his experience in a society that consistently undermines the selfhood of the poor and the nonwhite? How can such a student gain that sense of self which is necessary for active participation in education? What does all this mean for us as teachers?

2. How do we go about teaching a canon of literature which has consistently excluded or depreciated nonwhite experience?

3. How can we connect the process of learning to write well with the student's own reality, and not simply teach her/him how to write acceptable lies in standard English?

When I went to teach at Douglass College in 1976, and in teaching women's writing workshops elsewhere, I came to perceive stunning parallels to the questions I had first encountered in teaching the so-called disadvantaged students at City. But in this instance, and against the specific background of the women's movement, the questions framed themselves like this:

1. What has been the student's experience of education in schools which reward female passivity, indoctrinate girls and boys in stereotypic sex roles, and do not take the female mind seriously? How does a woman gain a sense of her *self* in a system—in this case, patriarchal capitalism—which devalues work done by women, denies the importance and uniqueness of female experience, and is physically violent toward women? What does this mean for a woman teacher?

2. How do we, as women, teach women students a canon of literature which has consistently excluded or depreciated female experience, and which often expresses hostility to women and validates violence against us?

3. How can we teach women to move beyond the desire for male approval and getting "good grades" and seek and write their own truths that the culture has distorted or made taboo? (For women, of course, language itself is exclusive: I want to say more about this further on.)

In teaching women, we have two choices: to lend our weight to the forces that indoctrinate women to passivity, self-depreciation, and a sense of powerlessness, in which case the issue of "taking women students seriously" is a moot one; or to consider what we have to work against, as well as with, in ourselves, in our students, in the content of the curriculum, in the structure of the institution, in the society at large. And this means, first of all, taking ourselves seriously: Recognizing that central responsibility of a woman to herself, without which we remain always the Other, the defined, the object, the victim; believing that there is a unique quality of validation, affirmation, challenge, support, that one woman can offer another. Believing in the value and significance of women's experience, traditions, perceptions. Thinking of ourselves seriously, not as one of the boys, not as neuters, or androgynes, but *as women*.

Suppose we were to ask ourselves, simply: What does a woman need to know? Does she not, as a self-conscious, self-defining human being, need a knowledge of her own history, her much-politicized biology, an awareness of the creative work of women of the past, the skills and crafts and techniques and powers exercised by women in different times and cultures, a knowledge of women's rebellions and organized movements against our oppression and how they have been routed or diminished? Without such knowledge women live and have lived without context, vulnerable to the projections of male fantasy, male prescriptions for us, estranged from our own experience because our education has not reflected or echoed it. I would suggest that not biology, but ignorance of our selves, has been the key to our powerlessness.

But the university curriculum, the high-school curriculum, do not provide this kind of knowledge for women, the knowledge of Womankind, whose experience has been so profoundly different from that of Mankind. Only in the precariously budgeted, much-condescended-to area of women's studies is such knowledge available to women students. Only there can they learn about the lives and work of women other than the few select women who are included in the "mainstream" texts, usually misrepresented even when they do appear. Some students, at some institutions, manage to take a majority of courses in women's studies, but the message from on high is that this is self-indulgence, soft-core education: the "real" learning is the study of Mankind.

If there is any misleading concept, it is that of "coeducation": that because women and men are sitting in the same classrooms, hearing the same lectures, reading the same books, performing the same laboratory experiments, they are receiving an equal education. They are not, first because the content of education itself validates men even as it invalidates women. Its very message is that men have been the shapers and thinkers of the world, and that this is only natural. The bias of higher education, including the so-called sciences, is white and male, racist and sexist; and this bias is expressed in both subtle and blatant ways. I have mentioned already the exclusiveness of grammar itself: "The student should test himself on the above questions"; "The poet is representative. He stands among partial men for the complete man." Despite a few half-hearted departures from custom, what the linguist Wendy Martyna has named "He-Man" grammar prevails throughout the culture. The efforts of feminists to reveal the profound ontological implications of sexist grammar are routinely ridiculed by academicians and journalists, including the professedly liberal *Times* columnist, Tom Wicker, and the professed humanist, Jacques Barzun. Sexist grammar burns into the brains of little girls and young women a message that the male is the norm, the standard, the central figure beside which we are the deviants, the marginal, the dependent variables. It lays the foundation for androcentric thinking, and leaves men safe in their solipsistic tunnel-vision.

Women and men do not receive an equal education because outside the classroom women are perceived not as sovereign beings but as prey. The growing incidence of rape on and off the campus may or may not be fed by the proliferations of pornographic

> **"I would suggest that not biology, but ignorance of our selves, has been the key to our powerlessness."**

magazines and X-rated films available to young males in fraternities and student unions; but it is certainly occurring in a context of widespread images of sexual violence against women, on billboards and in so-called high art. More subtle, more daily than rape is the verbal abuse experienced by the woman student on many campuses—Rutgers for example—where, traversing a street lined with fraternity houses, she must run a gauntlet of male commentary and verbal assault. The undermining of self, of a woman's sense of her right to occupy space and walk freely in the world, is deeply relevant to education. The capacity to think independently, to take intellectual risks, to assert ourselves mentally, is inseparable from our physical way of being in the world, our feelings of personal integrity. If it is dangerous for me to walk home late of an evening from the library, *because I am a woman and can be raped*, how self-possessed, how exuberant can I feel as I sit working in that library? how much of my working energy is drained by the subliminal knowledge that, as a woman, I test my physical right to exist each time I go out alone? Of this knowledge, Susan Griffin has written:

> . . . more than rape itself, the fear of rape permeates our lives. And what does one do from day to day, with *this* experience, which says, without words and directly to the heart, *your existence, your experience, may end at any moment.* Your experience may end, and the best defense against this is not to be, to deny being in the body, as a self, to . . . avert your gaze, make yourself, as a presence in the world, less felt.

Finally, rape of the mind. Women students are more and more often now reporting sexual overtures by male professors—one part of our overall growing consciousness of sexual harassment in the workplace. At Yale a legal suit has been brought against the university by a group of women demanding an explicit policy against sexual advances toward female students by male professors. Most young women experience a profound mixture of humiliation and intellectual self-doubt over seductive gestures by men who have the power to award grades, open doors to grants and graduate school, or extend special knowledge and training. Even if turned aside, such gestures constitute mental rape, destructive to a woman's ego. They are acts of domination, as despicable as the molestation of the daughter by the father.

But long before entering college the woman student has experienced her alien identity in a world which misnames her, turns her to its own uses, denying her the resources she needs to become self-affirming, self-defined. The nuclear family teaches her that relationships are more important than selfhood or work; that "whether the phone rings for you, and how often," having the right clothes, doing the dishes, take precedence over study or solitude; that too much intelligence or intensity may make her unmarriageable; that marriage and children—service to others—are, finally, the points on which her life will be judged a success or a failure. In high school, the polarization between feminine attractiveness and independent intelligence comes to an absolute. Meanwhile, the culture resounds with messages. During Solar Energy Week in New York I saw young women wearing "ecology" T-shirts with the legend: CLEAN, CHEAP AND AVAILABLE; a reminder of the 1960s antiwar button which read: CHICKS SAY YES TO MEN WHO SAY NO. Department store windows feature female mannequins in chains, pinned to the wall with legs spread, smiling in positions of torture. Feminists are depicted in the media as "shrill," "strident," "puritanical," or "humorless," and the lesbian choice—the choice of the woman-identified woman—as pathological or sinister. The young woman sitting in the philosophy classroom, the political science lecture, is already gripped by tensions between her nascent sense of self-worth, and the battering force of messages like these.

Look at a classroom: look at the many kinds of women's faces, postures, expressions. Listen to the women's voices. Listen to the silences, the unasked questions, the blanks. Listen to the small, soft voices, often courageously trying to speak up, voices of women taught early that tones of confidence, challenge, anger, or assertiveness, are strident and unfeminine. Listen to the voices of the women and the voices of the men; observe the space men allow themselves, physically and verbally, the male assumption that people will listen, even when the majority of the group is female. Look at the faces of the silent, and of those who speak. Listen to a woman groping for language in which to express what is on her mind, sensing that the terms of academic discourse are not her language, trying to cut down her thought to the dimensions of a discourse not intended for her *(for it is not fitting that a woman speak in public)*; or reading her paper aloud at breakneck speed, throwing her words away, deprecating her

own work by a reflex prejudgment: *I do not deserve to take up time and space*.

As women teachers, we can either deny the importance of this context in which women students think, write, read, study, project their own futures; or try to work with it. We can either teach passively, accepting these conditions, or actively, helping our students identify and resist them.

We need to keep our standards very high, not to accept a woman's preconceived sense of her limitations; we need to be hard to please, while supportive of risk-taking, because self-respect often comes only when exacting standards have been met.

One important thing we can do is *discuss* the context. And this need not happen only in a women's studies course; it can happen anywhere. We can refuse to accept passive, obedient learning and insist upon critical thinking. We can become harder on our women students, giving them the kinds of "cultural prodding" that men receive, but on different terms and in a different style. Most young women need to have their intellectual lives, their work, legitimized against the claims of family, relationships, the old message that a woman is always available for service to others. We need to keep our standards very high, not to accept a woman's preconceived sense of her limitations; we need to be hard to please, while supportive of risk-taking, because self-respect often comes only when exacting standards have been met. At a time when adult literacy is generally low, we need to demand more, not less, of women, both for the sake of their futures as thinking beings, and because historically women have always had to be better than men to do half as well. A romantic sloppiness, an inspired lack of rigor, a self-indulgent incoherence, are symptoms of female self-depreciation. We should help our women students to look very critically at such symptoms, and to understand where they are rooted.

Nor does this mean we should be training women students to "think like men." Men in general think badly: in disjuncture from their personal lives, claiming objectivity where the most irrational passions seethe, losing, as Virginia Woolf observed, their senses in the pursuit of professionalism. It is not easy to think like a woman in a man's world, in the world of the professions; yet the capacity to do that is a strength which we can try to help our students develop. To think like a woman in a man's world means thinking critically, refusing to accept the givens, making connections between facts and ideas which men have left unconnected. It means remembering that every mind resides in a body; remaining accountable to the female bodies in which we live; constantly retesting given hypotheses against lived experience. It means a constant critique of language, for as Wittgenstein (no feminist) observed, "The limits of my language are the limits of my world." And it means that most difficult thing of all: listening and watching in art and literature, in the social sciences, in all the descriptions we are given of the world, for the silences, the absences, the nameless, the unspoken, the encoded—for there we will find the true knowledge of women. And in breaking those silences, naming our selves, uncovering the hidden, making ourselves present, we begin to define a reality which resonates to *us*, which affirms *our* being, which allows the woman teacher and the woman student alike to take ourselves, and each other, seriously: meaning, to begin taking charge of our lives.

Journal and Discussion Questions

1 In her first paragraph, Adrienne Rich describes her "function" as a speaker but does not state the thesis of her argument, and in the next four paragraphs, she provides a brief autobiography of her career as a teacher. What is the thesis of Rich's speech? Where does she first state that thesis? Why does she delay her thesis and instead begin her speech with her history as a teacher?

2 Rich presents six sets of questions that she and other teachers asked themselves in two of her teaching positions. Why does Rich repeat these questions rather than going right into her answers to them? Which questions does her essay answer, and which questions go unanswered?

3 Rich writes: "If there is any misleading concept, it is that of 'coeducation': that because women and men are sitting in the same classrooms, hearing the same lectures, reading the same books, performing the same laboratory experiments, they are receiving an equal education." How does Rich try to show that this commonsense idea is mistaken? Can you give examples from your own experiences as a student in which students in the same classroom received unequal educations?

4 What specific problems for women students in college does Rich identify? Why does she believe these problems are greater for women than for men? Do you agree? Why or why not?

5 Rich briefly suggests that the problems that she describes for women students are similar to the problems of "poor, black, and Third World students" in higher education. How are the problems of women students similar to the problems of these other students? How are they different? Do you agree with Rich? Why or why not?

6 In addition to her experiences teaching in universities and her observations of popular culture, Rich cites four writers in her essay: Wendy Martyna, Susan Griffin, Virginia Woolf, and Ludwig Wittgenstein. How does she use each source to explain and strengthen her argument? Why does she point out that Wittgenstein was "no feminist"?

7 Why does Rich argue that teachers need to discuss "context" to help improve the education of women? How would this emphasis change classes that you have taken? Based on this essay, what changes in men's education do you think Rich would advocate? Why?

Topics for Writing

1 Argue whether Adrienne Rich's arguments in "Taking Women Students Seriously," made in 1978, still apply today.

2 Considering Rich's arguments, propose and argue for changes to improve students' education on your campus. Your argument may focus on women students or another group of students, or it may concern all students at your school.

3 Rich points out a "polarization between feminine attractiveness and independent intelligence" in media advertising and slogans. Write a paper analyzing the media images of women today, exploring advertising, television, movies, popular magazines, and the Internet, perhaps revealing other attitudes toward women than those that Rich discusses. Or describe and analyze the media images of another group of people based on their ethnicity, age, occupation, or financial status.

4 Research efforts to reduce or eliminate sexism in language, examining the arguments—pro and con—that sexism in the English language harms women and society and describing the major changes in the language advocated to eliminate sexism in English. Argue whether these changes are necessary.

5 Research the dangers of rape or another safety issue on college campuses. Discuss how safe college campuses are today. What are colleges and universities doing to address students' fears and keep them safe?

FRESHMEN PAY, MENTALLY AND PHYSICALLY, AS THEY ADJUST TO LIFE IN COLLEGE

BY THOMAS BARTLETT

Thomas Bartlett is a reporter for *The Chronicle of Higher Education*, a weekly newspaper offering news stories, analysis, and editorials on higher education and read by college and university faculty and administrators. His February 2, 2002, news article "Freshman Pay, Mentally and Physically, as They Adjust to Life in College" identifies important problems that first-year students experience adjusting to college life and demands today based on the results of a nationwide survey of college freshmen. The report compared freshmen's responses to questions just before they started college to their responses to the same questions immediately after their freshman year.

THE FRESHMAN YEAR IS TAKING A real toll on students' physical and mental health. Colleges now have a better sense of that cost, based on the results of a new survey.

For more than 30 years, freshmen have been asked about their attitudes, behaviors and aspirations when they enter college. But until recently, researchers have ignored what is perhaps more crucial to college leaders concerned about the freshman experience: What happens to students during that transformative first year?

A new assessment tool tries to answer that question by surveying students in the spring and comparing the results with those gathered from the survey that students take at orientation.

The comparisons yield insights into how the first year affects students—and most of the news isn't good.

The survey is the brainchild of John Gardner, executive director of the Policy Center on the First Year of College, at Brevard College, in North Carolina. It was designed to offer a "more holistic portrait" of students new to college, he says. "What we know about freshmen up to this point has been mostly anecdotal. We haven't been able to look at broad data that are empirically verified."

The 2001 report, "Your First College Year," was conducted by the Higher Education Research Institute at the University of California at Los Angeles, which also administers the freshman-orientation survey. The report is based on the responses of 3,680 freshmen at 50 four-year institutions who were surveyed in the fall of 2000 and again the following year.

Some of the findings are troubling. For instance, 44.9 percent of freshmen rated their emotional health "above average" at the end of their first year of college—a significant drop from 52.4 percent at the beginning of the academic year. A similar decline in ratings of physical health over the course of the year—51.4 percent to 41.3 percent—may be linked to the fact that students are exercising less frequently. The percentage of students who said they didn't exercise at all during a typical week doubled, from 5.4 percent to 11.8 percent.

FEELING OVERWHELMED. Also worrisome is the increase in the number who reported feeling depressed at some point during the past year—from 8.2 to 16.3 percent. Likewise, many more students said they felt "overwhelmed by all that I had to do"—44.3 percent, compared with 31.6 percent. "We've heard it said so many times to students in orientation sessions that the freshman year is the time of your life," says Randy L. Swing, co-director of the Brevard research center. "Then you read these data, and it doesn't look like it's the time of anybody's life."

Other results provide insights into students' faith. The survey showed a big dip in the percentage of students who said they had attended a religious service during the past year (84.7 at orientation, 59.6 at the end of the first year). But more students said they considered "integrating spirituality" into their lives "essential" or "very important" at the end of their first year (56.7 percent) than at the beginning (47.7 percent).

"At first, those statistics seem to conflict," says Mary Stuart Hunter, director of the National Resource Center for the First-Year Experience and Students in Transition, at the University of South Carolina at Columbia. "But when you think about it, they really go hand in glove. Students aren't able to fall back on some of their old routines, like attending a religious service with their parents. They're searching for something else."

> ## The most recent version of the annual report, released last fall, revealed that many undergraduates studied only half as much as professors said was necessary, and that a fifth of those surveyed admitted 'frequently' coming to class unprepared.

Some of the findings mirror those of the National Survey of Student Engagement, which gauges how well colleges encourage learning. The most recent version of the annual report, released last fall, revealed that many undergraduates studied only half as much as professors said was necessary, and that a fifth of those surveyed admitted "frequently" coming to class unprepared.

Freshmen are no different. Although they study more than they did during their senior year of high school, 65.2 percent of them said they hit the books 15 hours or less during a typical week.

They are also struggling to stay awake in class. The freshman survey found that 39.5 percent of the respondents said they felt "bored in class"—an increase over the 36 percent who reported the same feeling during their senior year of high school. "That the boredom factor went up is really a red flag for me," says Mr. Gardner, of Brevard. "Colleges expect students to be more engaged, but this shows just the opposite. We need to do more than blame students. We need to try to figure out why this is happening."

Not all of the findings in the freshman survey are discouraging. Students showed greater interest in "developing a meaningful philosophy of life" (50.4 percent, compared with 42.3 percent when they arrived on campus) and in "helping to promote racial understanding" (38.4 percent, compared with 29.6 percent).

While part of the survey was designed as a follow-up to the orientation survey, other questions were new and focused on "engagement," a buzzword among educators.

There was a disparity between what students ranked as "very important" in helping them to learn and what actually happened in the classroom. Students ranked "group discussion" as more important than "extensive lecturing" but indicated that the latter was more frequent. And nearly half (46 percent) said "field experience or internships" were important to them, while only 4.7 percent said such activities took place at their colleges.

Brevard's Mr. Swing says professors should pay close attention to those statistics. "The mismatch between what students tell us they want and what is actually delivered is striking," he says.

The survey also offers a look at the not-so-rosy financial lives of first-year students. A majority (60.4 percent) said they had overspent their budgets, and a significant number (16.7 percent) reported accumulating "excessive" credit-card debt.

KEY OBJECTIVES. When asked about their objectives, students ranked "raising a family" (75.5 percent), "being very well-off financially" (73.2 percent) and "becoming an authority in my field" (66.4 percent) at the top of their lists. Fewer aspired to "become involved in programs to clean up the environment" (22.1 percent) or to "influence the political structure" (19.9 percent).

The next freshman-year survey, to be conducted this spring, will include more colleges—125 have signed up so far. "I'm interested to see if the trends continue over the next several years," Mr. Gardner says. "It's already given us greater clarity about what's going on during the freshman year on campuses, and about the kinds of questions college leaders need to be asking."

Journal and Discussion Questions

1 What are the main findings of the study reported in "Freshmen Pay, Mentally and Physically, as They Adjust to Life in College"? What information do you find surprising? What facts did you already know from your own experiences or other sources?

2 How do the findings of the survey compare to your own experiences of freshman year and to the experiences of other students in your class?

3 What causes does Thomas Bartlett suggest for the problems described here? What other causes can you suggest?

4 Newspaper articles are often organized roughly starting from the most important or most interesting information and ending with the least interesting. Compose an outline of this article. Why does the article save most of the positive news for the end?

5 What do you think faculty, advisors, and others who work with students should do with this information?

6 The research for this article consists solely of statistics based on student responses to a questionnaire. Why does Bartlett include information on who conducted the survey, how it was conducted, and where readers can find the full report? If you could interview some of the students in this survey, what would you ask them?

7 How would an article with this information be written for a campus newspaper or a magazine for college students?

Topics for Writing

1 Randy L. Swing, co-director of the Policy Center on the First Year of College at Brevard College, is quoted as saying, "The mismatch between what students tell us they want and what is actually delivered is striking." Write an essay describing what the students on your campus want (especially first-year students) and evaluating how well your school is providing what students want and need.

2 Find out whether the problems described here exist for first-year students on your campus by conducting interviews and/or asking students to fill out a questionnaire. This research might be conducted by the class as a whole or by a group of classmates. Write a report on the findings of your research.

3 Argue, perhaps in an editorial for your student newspaper, how your school can better help students with some of the problems described by Bartlett or what students can do to help themselves with these problems.

4 Pick one of the problems described in Bartlett's article and investigate what services your school offers to help students with this problem. Write an article for your campus newspaper informing students about this service and the help it provides.

COLLEGE AND ALLOWANCE

BY LAUREN SILVERMAN

Lauren Silverman was a junior in high school in Berkeley, California, when she composed and produced "College and Allowance" for Youth Radio, a national radio project run by and for high school students. Many of these commentaries, including "College and Allowance," can be found on the Web site YouthRadio.org. Silverman's commentary on how students cope with the high cost of attending college relies heavily on interviews with college students, and she spliced tapes from these interviews into her recorded commentary. Although Youth Radio's primary audience is high school students, its commentaries and features are sometimes broadcast on news programs on National Public Radio for general audiences. Silverman's commentary works as both an essay preparing future college students to deal with the financial demands of college and as an essay informing general listeners about the financial demands of college students today. Silverman received a 2005 Gracie Allen Award from American Women in Radio and Television for another Youth Radio commentary about her struggles with anorexia.

I DON'T GET AN OFFICIAL "ALLOWANCE." My parents give me money for food and train fare, but I'd rather use my own small paycheck for extras like earrings and hair dye. But I know there's an allowance in my future when I head to college in a couple of years.

My brother goes to Duke University, and I'm watching him make the transition from self-supporting high school student to broke college student calling the folks for money. And now *I'm* getting ready for the same thing, pumping my Dad for information about my future budget. I'm also attending every college party I can. I know it's hard to believe, but I really *am* scoping out the college allowance scene at these parties. The free food and cute boys are just a bonus.

Matt Renner, a friend's older brother, lives in a house with tons of roommates. I got hella free food over there one night. Here's what I found out from these guys while chowing down. First, not only does it look like I'm going to have to actually study at college, I'm going to act like a financial analyst. Matt has got it down. To get *his* allowance, he *itemizes* everything from internet charges to gas.

MATT (on tape)
I just make a spreadsheet. It gets complicated otherwise.)

LAUREN
A spreadsheet for your Dad?

MATT (on tape)
I actually bring him receipts for stuff—books and everything. So that we get it all on the books. Legitimately.

LAUREN
Keeping track of receipts. This sounds scary already. Matt's roommate Alexandra Ayoub goes through a *negotiation* process with *her* parents.

ALEXANDRA (on tape)
And if I'm spending a hundred dollars a month on like cell phones—he's like, "No I'll give you 50" and then I'll have to come up with the other 50, or change my plan or not talk as much or something.

LAUREN
Most of these roommates say their allowance covers the basics—rent, utilities, and food. Spending money is trickier. Concerts and clothes don't seem to be bankrolled by their parents.

Even with an allowance, everyone says they are still pinching pennies . . . especially when it comes to what's in the fridge. Nathaniel Loman is another roomie.

NATHANIEL (on tape)

We have a royal rumble way of working things out. My roommates have taken to counting slices of bread and marking milk jugs. Just the other day, Matt definitely put a threat up on the board for anybody who was taking sips out of his milk carton. The line had been crossed.

LAUREN

The college allowance tension goes beyond the kitchen. No one wants to admit the extent this happens, but there are stories . . . from people being left out of concerts and dinner plans because their allowance is small or non-existent, to the people who get a fat check and get teased about "daddy's money."

This is what I have to look forward to. And I'm already getting a taste of it now. When I attend college parties I have to abide by rules, like paying for every slice of pizza I eat so no one's wallet is hit.

You can't really look to your parents to feel sorry for you. All the roommates tell me their parents supported themselves completely in college. And Nathaniel's mom went even further. . . .

NATHANIEL (on tape)

She often took out additional student loans, because they were subsidized, to loan money to her parents. So through my mother, my grandparents were able to borrow money from the university at a reduced rate.

LAUREN

Somehow a lot of us have been able to convince our parents that paying for college *AND* an allowance is a reasonable investment—even with a 40 thousand dollar price tag. If I take a year off, I won't be getting ANY allowance. But as long as I'm enrolled in college, I'll be on the family bankroll just like my brother—sending most bills home for Mom and Dad to pay.

Journal and Discussion Questions

1 "College and Allowance" is structured as a problem–solution essay. What is the problem described in the essay? What solutions does the author, Lauren Silverman, offer?

2 Outline "College and Allowance." What are the major divisions of Silverman's essay? What is the main idea in each section? How did you decide where the divisions are?

3 "College and Allowance" depends mainly on examples that develop and support Silverman's ideas. What do the examples have in common? How are they different from each other? How representative of college students do you find Silverman's examples? Has she chosen strong examples for her subject? Why or why not?

4 Silverman's outside research comes entirely from interviews with college students. What questions do you think Silverman asked to get these statements from Matt, Alexandra, and Nathaniel? What questions would you have asked? If Silverman were writing a longer, more extensive paper on college student finances, what additional sources and interviews would be helpful for her to consult?

5 How do the details from Silverman's life and experiences contribute to her essay?

6 What are the main solutions to the problem of college expenses that Silverman discovers in her research? How does each solution help students keep their finances under control? Which solutions does she most recommend and why? Would these solutions work for you? Why or why not? What other solutions could Silverman have recommended?

7 In a sidebar to Silverman's commentary, the Youth Radio Web site states that in the 2004–05 school year, the average in-state tuition and fees increased by 10.5% to $5,132 at four-year state colleges and universities and by 6.0% to $20,082 at four-year private institutions. The overall cost of attending college increased by 7.8% to $11,354 for students at public institutions and by 5.6% to $27,516 for students at private colleges. What does this information add to Silverman's commentary? Considering the strict length requirements for radio commentaries, do you think Silverman should have cut part of her essay to make room for these statistics? Why or why not?

Topics for Writing

1 Write an essay for high school students from your perspective to inform them about and prepare them for the costs of higher education. You might compose this essay as a radio commentary.

2 Conduct additional research about the financial problems and pressures of college students, how students deal with these problems, and what solutions are available to college students. Interview students and counselors as part of your research. Write a problem–solution essay describing and analyzing the problem and arguing for the best solution to this problem.

3 Write and record a three-minute radio commentary on another subject, incorporating interviews as part of your essay.

Connecting the Readings

Drawing on Thomas Bartlett's "Freshmen Pay, Mentally and Physically, as They Adjust to Life in College" and Lauren Silverman's "College and Allowance," explain some of the stresses and problems that freshmen experience in college, how students deal with the stress, and suggestions for improving their adjustments to college life.

ADVERTISING HIGHER EDUCATION:
Magazine Advertisements for The University of Alabama, University of Richmond, and Grinnell College

The newsmagazine *U.S. News & World Report* devotes one issue a year to its rankings of the best colleges in the United States and other articles on getting into college. A number of colleges and universities take out full-page advertisements in this issue, knowing that it will be read by thousands of parents and high school students getting ready to apply to universities. The advertisements for The University of Alabama and University of Richmond appeared in the August 20, 2004 edition of *U.S. News & World Report*; the advertisement for Grinnell College appeared in the August 7, 2007, issue of *U.S. News & World Report*.

USA Today's
All-USA College Academic Team Members

Harvard 5, Alabama 4

Surprising? Not really–last year we came in first.

Four students from The University of Alabama have earned spots on *USA Today's* 2004 All-USA College Academic Team, continuing our students' excellent record of achievement and ranking us second in the nation, just behind Harvard and tied with Northwestern. (Last year, we led the nation with five members to Harvard's three.)

Thanks to the quality of our faculty and of our campus staff and facilities, the opportunities available to you at Alabama are limited only by your energy and imagination. See how far your dreams can take you when you start from a solid foundation of quality education with a global perspective!

The University of Alabama's 2004 USA Today All-USA College Academic Team members (l-r): Abigail Smith, speech communication; Cody Locke, biology; Rob Davis, aerospace engineering; Kristin Robinson, social work

THE UNIVERSITY OF ALABAMA

Undergraduate Admissions—alabama.ua.edu • For more information, e-mail alabama@ua.edu, or call 1-800-933-BAMA.

A curious mind thrives at Richmond.

Faculty who inspire. Students who challenge.
Incredible facilities. The latest technology.
More opportunities than you can imagine.

Ranked one of America's premier private
universities, we offer an intimate environment
where students explore a wide range of
academic possibilities. Our small classes
encourage intellectual debate, close interaction
with professors and hands-on research.

Satisfy your curiosity at Richmond.

UNIVERSITY OF RICHMOND

UNIVERSITY OF
RICHMOND

www.richmond.edu
1-888-270-5505
Richmond, Virginia

ARTS & SCIENCES • BUSINESS • LEADERSHIP STUDIES • LAW • CONTINUING STUDIES

Journal and Discussion Questions

1 What reasons do The University of Alabama, University of Richmond, and Grinnell College give prospective students for applying to these universities? Summarize each ad's central reasons in the form of a thesis statement.

2 Magazine advertisements are often organized in a "Z" pattern, with images and print designed to draw readers first to the upper left section of the advertisement, then across the page, then down the page, and finally coming to rest in the lower right section. Are the advertisements by The University of Alabama, University of Richmond, and Grinnell College organized in this way? What words and images are emphasized by each ad's design? Why? What parts of the advertisement are deemphasized? Why?

3 Compare the slogans in each advertisement. What initial impressions do the slogans create about the three universities and their students? How does each slogan appeal to the interests of parents and students reading *U.S. News & World Report*?

4 Compare the messages and the tone in the text or "copy" of each advertisement. How does the information in the copy develop the ideas and impressions suggested by the slogans? How does the tone of the language attempt to attract students and parents?

5 Compare the pictures in each advertisement. What impressions do these pictures create about each university, the students who go there, the kind of education the university provides, and the life of the students? What do the pictures emphasize about each university? How do the pictures work with the language in each ad?

6 What kinds of students do you think each advertisement is directed toward? What kinds of students might be persuaded by each ad to apply to the university or at least check out the university's Web site? Which ad do you find most persuasive? Why?

7 What ideas about a college education—its definition, its importance, its benefits, and what students should experience in college—are stated and implied in each advertisement? What similarities and differences do you find in the philosophy of education implied in each ad?

Topics for Writing

1 Compare the images of student life and a university education in The University of Alabama, University of Richmond, and Grinnell College advertisements. Discuss the reasons and priorities that each advertisement gives for students pursuing a college degree.

2 Argue which of the three advertisements is most persuasive.

3 Write a research paper about how colleges and universities sell higher education.

Suggestions for Essays on EDUCATION

1 Compare Rodriguez', Delpit's, and McGruder's arguments for dealing with multiculturalism in education.

2 Compare proposals for improving education in at least two of the selections written by Delpit, Rich, and Jaschik.

3 Write an essay discussing how schools serve—or should serve—their diverse population of students considering several of the selections by Rodriguez, Delpit, McGruder, and Rich.

4 Compare the images of college student life in Bartlett, Silverman, and the three advertisements.

5 Write an essay for entering freshmen about how they should prepare themselves for college life based on several of the following selections as well as your own observations and experiences: Rich, Jaschik, Bartlett, Silverman, and the magazine ads.

09 Work

MAYBE YOU HAVE ALREADY DECIDED ON the career that you want. Maybe you are weighing several possible career paths or reexamining a career decision that you now have some doubts about. Maybe a decision to begin a new career has prompted you to enroll in college. Or maybe you don't feel ready to decide on a career yet. But as a college student, you probably have a special appreciation of the importance of the subject of work and career.

Your career decision at this time is just one of the questions that you may be asking yourself about work. Almost certainly you are working out how best to prepare for your career, even if you don't know what that career will be. You are probably trying to cope with the work of being a college student and how to meet the responsibilities of a job you need to pay for college with your responsibilities as a student and how to balance all this work with your social life, your responsibilities to your family, and other demands and desires.

Browse through the magazines and newspapers at a library or do a search on the Internet about jobs and work, and you will find dozens, maybe hundreds of articles and Web sites that offer advice about these problems—and a few that analyze how useful this advice is. And if you start researching social, political, economic, and ethical issues involving work, you'll quickly find thousands of texts on the subject, from informational or entertaining articles about unusual kinds of jobs to editorials about minimum wage, job safety, and the impact of environmental and economic regulations on employment to movies, television shows, and comic strips like *North Country*, *The Office*, and *Dilbert* that comment on workplace issues such as office politics, sexual harassment, and tensions between management and labor.

Our jobs largely determine the structure of our lives, how we and our families live and spend our time. The work that we do, the meaning this work has for us, and how others value the work that we do greatly affects our view of ourselves and our

place in the world. Every workplace is a complicated, fascinating social setting that confronts people with complex political and ethical conflicts and
responsibilities. It is a place where workers have to
depend on each other while often competing with
each other for promotions, clients, and recognition. It is a place with an often complex power
structure in which some workers execute significant power over others. Yet it is also a place where
people form some of their closest personal relationships and loyalties.

In short, there are few subjects that are as rich and
complex or as important and interesting to readers as
work. Here are a few questions for you to think about
as you read and write about it.

- What should a person consider in choosing
  a career? How should someone prepare for a
  career?

- What kinds of work make you happy? What
  kinds of work do you find meaningful? Why?
  How important is the money you can earn in your
  career as compared to the personal importance
  and meaningfulness of your work?

- What does it mean to be successful in a career?
  How can one achieve such success?

- What's the difference between a good job and a
  bad job? Why are some people unhappy or dis-
  contented with their jobs?

- Why do people do the work that they do if
  they could earn more money doing something else or if they do not need the money?
  What satisfaction do people get out of work?
  What do you want to get out of the work that
  you do?

- Why do people work at activities that do not
  pay a salary, like raising a family, taking care
  of a home, doing charity work, or working
  hard to do well in an activity like amateur
  sports, dance, acting, painting, or writing
  poetry?

- What is the relationship between work and play
  (especially play that takes significant effort)?

- What rights do workers have on the job? What
  rights should they have?

- What responsibilities should employers assume
  about the well-being of their employees? What
  do workers owe to their jobs and employers?

- What constitutes fair pay and benefits for a
  job? What benefits should employees receive
  for their work?

- How do gender, social class, family, race, ethnicity, sexual orientation, and other aspects of identity affect the careers that people decide on, their
  working conditions, and how their work is perceived and valued?

Invitations for Journal Writing

1 Describe the jobs you have held. Discuss what you
learned from your work and what knowledge and abilities it
took to do your job well. Describe your working conditions and
whether you considered your job a "good" or "bad" job.

2 Discuss in what ways being a college student is a job and
in what ways it isn't. If you are working a job while going to
school, describe how your job affects your schoolwork and your
life at school. Compare how your job is preparing you for your
career to how college is preparing you for the future.

3 Discuss the kind of career you want and why. In addition to the kind of work, describe what you want from your
career and how your work should fit in with other aspects of
your life. Compare the working life that you want with the
working lives you have observed of family members, friends,
and others.

4 Discuss how important work is in your life and why.
Describe how your work has shaped who you are.

WORK, LABOR, AND PLAY

BY W. H. AUDEN

W. H. Auden (1907–1973) was one of the most celebrated poets of the twentieth century and a serious essayist. He was born in England, but he emigrated to the United States in 1939 and became a U.S. citizen. *The Dyer's Hand* is Auden's best known book of nonfiction, and his books of poetry include *New Year Letter*; *Nones*; *Homage to Clio*; *Thank You, Fog*; and *Age of Anxiety*, for which he won the 1947 Pulitzer Prize. The essay "Work, Labor, and Play" appeared in Auden's 1970 prose collection, *A Certain World: A Commonplace Book*. Like a response essay assigned in many college classes, "Work, Labor, and Play" begins by reflecting about an idea that he read in a book, *The Human Condition* by the philosopher Hannah Arendt. Auden uses Arendt's ideas as a jumping off point to develop his own thoughts about work, labor, and play.

SO FAR AS I KNOW, MISS HANNAH Arendt was the first person to define the essential difference between work and labor. To be happy, a man must feel, firstly, free and, secondly, important. He cannot be really happy if he is compelled by society to do what he does not enjoy doing, or if what he enjoys doing is ignored by society as of no value or importance. In a society where slavery in the strict sense has been abolished, the sign that what a man does is of social value is that he is paid money to do it, but a laborer today can rightly be called a wage slave. A man is a laborer if the job society offers him is of no interest to himself but he is compelled to take it by the necessity of earning a living and supporting his family.

The antithesis to labor is play. When we play a game, we enjoy what we are doing, otherwise we should not play it, but it is a purely private activity; society could not care less whether we play it or not.

Between labor and play stands work. A man is a worker if he is personally interested in the job which society pays him to do; what from the point of view of society is necessary labor is from his own point of view voluntary play. Whether a job is to be classified as labor or work depends, not on the job itself, but on the tastes of the individual who undertakes it. The difference does not, for example, coincide with the difference between a manual and a mental job; a gardener or a cobbler may be a worker, a bank clerk a laborer. Which a man is can be seen from his attitude toward leisure. To a worker, leisure means simply the hours he needs to relax and rest in order to work efficiently. He is therefore more likely to take too little leisure than too much; workers die of coronaries and forget their wives' birthdays. To the laborer, on the other hand, leisure means freedom from compulsion, so that it is natural for him to imagine that the fewer hours he has to spend laboring, and the more hours he is free to play, the better.

What percentage of the population in a modern technological society are, like myself, in the fortunate position of being workers? At a guess I would say sixteen per cent; and I do not think that figure is likely to get bigger in the future.

Technology and the division of labor have done two things: by eliminating in many fields the need for special strength or skill; they have made a very large number of paid occupations which formerly were enjoyable work into boring labor, and by increasing productivity they have reduced the number of necessary laboring hours. It is already possible to imagine a society in which the majority of the population, that is to say, its laborers, will have almost as much leisure as in earlier times was enjoyed by the aristocracy. When one recalls how aristocracies in the past actually behaved, the prospect is not cheerful. Indeed, the problem of dealing with boredom may be even more difficult for such a future mass society than it was for aristocracies. The latter, for example, ritualized their time; there was a season to shoot grouse, a season to spend in town, etc. The masses are more likely to replace an unchanging ritual by fashion which it will be in the economic interest of certain people to change as often as possible. Again, the masses cannot go in for hunting, for very soon there would be no animals left to hunt. For other aristocratic amusements like gambling, dueling, and warfare, it may be only too easy to find equivalents in dangerous driving, drug-taking, and senseless acts of violence. Workers seldom commit acts of violence, because they can put their aggression into their work, be it physical like the work of a smith, or mental like the work of a scientist or an artist. The role of aggression in mental work is aptly expressed by the phrase "getting one's teeth into a problem."

Journal and Discussion Questions

1 What is the central idea of "Work, Labor, and Play"? Outline "Work, Labor, and Play." How are the ideas of each section related to each other and to the central idea? What cues does W. H. Auden supply to emphasize his central idea over his other ideas in the essay?

2 Auden's essay develops his ideas by definition and comparison/contrast. How does Auden define "work," "labor," and "play." How does he use comparisons of the meanings of the three words to develop his main idea?

3 How do you think Auden arrived at his definitions? Do you think he consulted a dictionary for help with his definitions? Why or why not?

4 Auden's only source is Hannah Arendt's *The Human Condition*. What ideas does he borrow from her book? How does he use Arendt's ideas to arrive at his own thoughts? How can you tell where he stops summarizing Arendt and begins to discuss his own ideas?

5 What other set of job categories does Auden introduce? What is his purpose in raising a different classification system than his work, labor, and play categories?

6 The conclusion of Auden's essay is a cause-and-effect argument. What present and future effects does Auden argue are the result of technology and the division of labor? How do these causes lead to these effects? Do you find Auden's arguments persuasive? Why or why not?

7 Auden wrote "Work, Labor, and Play" before the invention of personal computers, laptops, cell phones, and the Internet. What technology was he referring to in his essay? Do his arguments apply to recent technologies?

Topics for Writing

1 Using Auden's concepts of work, labor, and play, analyze a job that you have had or a profession that you are considering for your career. Discuss what aspects of that job are labor and what aspects are play and why. Argue whether the job as a whole is work or labor.

2 Write a research paper arguing whether Auden is right about whether changes in technology and division of labor have made most jobs in modern society less interesting and gratifying.

3 Write a research paper about why Americans are spending more hours at their jobs than past generations. You may want to focus on a particular kind of job for this paper.

WORKING LIFE

BY NISHA RAMACHANDRAN

Nisha Ramachandran is a writer for *U.S. News & World Report* who often covers stories about economics and higher education. Her news article "Working Life" appeared in the April 17, 2006, issue of the newsmagazine *U.S. News & World Report*, in the magazine's Money & Business section under the heading "Paying for College." Like many articles in *U.S. News & World Report*, "Working Life" describes a national trend and focuses on practical information that readers can use in their lives. Here Ramachandran reports on a recent trend in part-time jobs for college students and discusses some of the problems for college students trying to balance work and studies.

JOSHUA HOWTON HAS RELIED ON loans, scholarships, and grants to pay for his five years at the University of Texas–Austin. But he has also put in long hours of hard work. The Dallas native filled orders for cappuccinos and café au laits his freshman year as a Starbucks barista. The next year, tired of commuting, Howton opted for an on-campus job as a tour guide. He traded that gig his junior year for a position in the university's career center, where he has stayed. "My family did not contribute to my education at all," says Howton, who will graduate this spring with a degree in communications. "By working, I was able to finance my living expenses and pay for books and clothes."

Working in college is familiar territory for many students. With total costs expected to average $32,000 this fall at private schools (and roughly half that at in-state public universities), more and more students are working to help pay the bills. A whopping 74 percent of full-time students juggle work and school, according to a study by the Higher Education Project of the State Public Interest Research Groups. Forty-six percent of them log 25 hours or more a week on the job, with 1 in 5 working full time.

KEEPING IT REAL. As the number of working students has grown, so has the emphasis on real-world work experience. "In my day, I was a summer camp counselor until the day I graduated," says Jody Queen-Hubert, executive director of co-op education and career services at Pace University in New York. "We recognize how competitive the world is. We are pushing students to get pre-professional experience before they graduate."

That's good news for cash-strapped students, who find that jobs requiring more experience or skills often pay well. The average undergraduate student at Pace who participated in a co-op program earned around $13.65 an hour and worked 15 to 20 hours a week.

Engineering students are paid particularly well. Caroline Monroe, a chemical engineering major, participated in a co-op program at Penn State University. She earned $18 to $19 an hour working full time for a vaccine manufacturer the spring semester of her junior year. With her earnings, Monroe quickly recouped the $871 cost of the co-op program, paid off about $3,000 of her semester's tuition at Penn State, and bought a 2005 Honda. And she learned the ins and outs of a plant, something that would have been impossible to do at Penn State itself. "It's not realistic for a campus to have that kind of equipment," says Monroe, who extended her stay to work full time during the summer. "It's a completely different world and industry."

Some companies offer tuition reimbursement to employees. UPS's Earn and Learn program provides between $2,000 and $3,000 for school costs for part-time workers, on top of wages. Kathleen O'Leary, 19, took advantage of the program to attend Jefferson Community and Technical College in Louisville, Ky. She works 25 to 30 hours a week at UPS headquarters, where she manages 11 employees who route packages, while attending school full time. O'Leary, who hopes to transfer to a four-year university and major in business after two years at Jefferson, expects that her work experience will also translate into a better job at UPS. "I want to keep moving up," she says. "I hope to move into a managerial position someday."

Even an on-campus job may afford the opportunity to build up a résumé while banking cash. "We are running a business," says Janice Sutera, director of the career center at George Mason University in Fairfax, Va. "With everything we need to make this place work, there is a potential for student workers." Jobs swiping meal cards and monitoring the library are still available, but those that require more training such as website design or maintenance often offer higher wages.

RESPONSIBILITIES. Take Howton, who doesn't simply answer phones or file papers at the University of Texas–Austin's career center. Over the past three years, he has designed and run advertising and marketing campaigns to draw more students to the center. After three years on the job, he now pulls in $10.50 an hour.

Still, most college students shouldn't expect—or even seek—riches while in school. Career coun-selors caution that most adults working full time, let alone students, would be hard-pressed to pay off upwards of $30,000 in annual costs. And while students who work 10 hours or less per week boast slightly higher grade-point averages than their peers do, studies show that those who work 25 hours or more a week often suffer academically, earning lower grades or dropping some classes alto-gether. Educational experts recommend that stu-dents who are finding it extremely difficult to make ends meet and working long hours should confer with a financial aid adviser to explore other funding options. After all, the primary job for those in col-lege is to be a student.

Journal and Discussion Questions

1 Outline Nisha Ramachandran's "Working Life." What is the article's central idea? How does Ramachandran develop this idea? Do the two headings in the article, "Keeping It Real" and "Responsibilities," reflect the actual structure of the article, or do they appear to be included mainly to break up the text to make it appear more appealing on the printed page?

2 What does Ramachandran mean by "real-world work experience"? How is this kind of job different from other jobs that college students often work? How are jobs that provide "real-world work experience" usually better than other part-time jobs?

3 What is the point of Joshua Howton's story? Why do you think Ramachandran decided to introduce her article with Howton's story? Why does she return to his story near the end of the article?

4 Who did Ramachandran interview for this article? Why do you think she selected these people for interviews? How do you think she decided which student interviews to include? Do you think she interviewed other people besides the ones named in her interview? Why or why not?

5 In addition to interviews, what other sources of informa-tion did Ramachandran consult for her article? How does the information from these sources fit into what she has to say?

6 How is the last paragraph connected to the rest of the article? Why do you think Ramachandran decided to conclude her article with a discussion of problems that part-time jobs create for college students? Do you agree with Ramachandran's last sentence, "After all, the primary job for those in college is to be a student"? Why or why not?

7 What pros and cons about working while going to col-lege does Ramachandran discuss? What advice does "Work-ing Life" seem to suggest to college students who need or want to work? Does this advice apply to your situation? Why or why not?

Topics for Writing

1 Conduct research about internships and other jobs like those described in "Working Life" available to students at your school, and write an informational article that could be published in the campus newspaper.

2 Write an editorial that could be published in the campus newspaper about how college students should try to balance work and school.

SLOUCHING AND DIGRESSING

BY HEATHER HUNSAKER

Heather Hunsaker was employed as a rhetoric associate in the writing center at Utah State University when she wrote "Slouching and Digressing." A double major in English literature and theatre arts, Hunsaker grew up in Barley, Idaho; tutored in the writing center for three years; and graduated from Utah State University in 2007. "Slouching and Digressing" appeared as a "Tutor's Column" in the February 2006 issue of the *Writing Lab Newsletter*, a monthly publication of articles for faculty and students who work in campus writing centers. The Tutor's Column each month is written by an undergraduate or graduate student who works as a writing center tutor or consultant. Many Tutor's Columns began as papers for a college course and were later revised for submission to the *Writing Lab Newsletter*, sometimes after the author presented a version of the paper at a conference for writing center tutors. Although Tutor's Columns often cite books and articles about tutoring students in writing centers, their arguments, as in "Slouching and Digressing," usually rely more heavily on the writer's experiences as a tutor. Here Hunsaker describes her approach to tutoring in Utah State's Writing Center and the importance of creating a comfortable atmosphere and a good working relationship with each writer. Hunsaker takes readers through a typical conference with a student to show tutors reading her column how they can use conversation and body language to relax students and have a productive discussion about a writer's paper.

THE OTHER DAY I WAS WITH ONE OF MY good friends discussing a large research paper that was coming up in our Survey of Western Theatre class. She sounded quite frightened about the upcoming due date. I naturally suggested to her that she might want to take her paper into the Writing Center to get some help on it. Her reply shocked me as she said, "That won't help, the last time that I went in they just checked my grammar and that was it." I was stunned! As a tutor at the Writing Center, I know that grammar is on the bottom of our priority list. This conversation spurred my thought process forward as I analyzed what I do in a session to send my students away feeling like my friend. Through this analysis I found that the number one thing that I try to control in my sessions is the atmosphere. There are certain tactics which I find helpful in creating a more comfortable atmosphere which, in turn, helps me guide my student to a better developed paper.

I concentrate heavily on atmosphere because I feel that no student can concentrate when they are nervous, so the best thing to do for a session is to relieve the tension in the room. I know that we have all had students who come in and their tension is palpable. They are clinging to their book like it is the last life-preserver on a sinking ship. When I can see the whites of their eyes, first thing I do is shoot them a smile. Enthusiastically introducing myself and asking them what they are working on helps to break the ice.

I like to sit back in my chair at the beginning of the session. I just slouch back in my chair with my legs sprawled in front of me and nod as they tell me about what they are worried about with their paper. When they see how relaxed I am by my tone and posture, they loosen up and really open up as to what their concerns are.

Once I get this introduction out of the way I step into the next gear. After they have told me

> **"When students, like my friend, feel more comfortable with the tutors to really talk about the big ideas of their paper, they will feel that their time at the writing center was relaxed, enjoyable, and productive."**

what their paper is about and what they want to really focus on, I lean forward to read the paper. It seems silly that this kind of posturing is so important, but it is. When the student reads me their paper, they are not looking at my face. They are looking at the paper on the table. If they can see in my body positioning that I am leaning forward, they get the sense that I am engaged in their paper. I like to make pencil marks during this time as to what I want to go back and talk about later, but I try not to disrupt the flow of their reading while I do this.

Once the paper has been read I take a breather. The student is out of breath, so they do not mind. I just take a second and collect my thoughts on the overall impression of the paper. At this moment the student has just put their work all out in front of me. They are rather vulnerable. Students often feel that a tutor is judging them somehow. Once again, I find that relaxed posture can help them not to feel so anxious about this exposure. While in this relaxed, laid-back atmosphere I feel free to digress for a few minutes.

Since we only have a short amount of time with the students and their papers, tutors often feel like they have to stay 100% on task. However, I often feel like digressions are the best part of the session. When I let myself explore a stream-of-consciousness that the student's paper has led me down, the student and I can banter back and forth about the big ideas of their paper. The student may find in this "big picture analysis" that the real thought of their paper did not come through. This automatically exposes any problems with the thesis statement, which is the next step in the process.

Once the digression has exhausted itself, then— and I make sure to wait until then, I get back to the actual paper. The digressing breather gives us both a short while to relax before jumping into the specifics of the paper.

When I jump back into the paper, I like to lean forward again. I go though the paper paragraph by paragraph with them and see if each paragraph fits into the big picture that we talked about or if it needs to be modified. Even though I am leaning forward and posturing that I am attentive, I make sure to not seem rigid. When I get excited I'll pull my feet up under me and shift around in my chair or jump up and pace if the mood strikes me. I hate feeling like the chair I sit in is a ball-and-chain, or worse, that the student feels like it is the Judgment Seat and I'm Chief Justice. This bohemian-type atmosphere is free from pressure and liberating for both the tutor and the student. They can tell that I am just a peer, totally on their level.

It is only after we get through these periods of digressions and idea discussions that I will move on, if we have time, to the minutiae of English such as punctuation and syntax.

I have found these planned breathers to be the best part of my sessions. They give me a chance to tell the student what their paper made me think about and really discuss their ideas. It allows us both to step back and look at the ideas in a lower pressure environment. Tutors need to feel free to slouch during the digression section. Slouching helps the students to see that we are non-judgmental peers. The persona of "I'm the tutor on this side of the table and you are the student on that side" gets broken down. This level of comfort can help the student to open up to their tutor and really discuss and defend their paper, rather than just wanting the tutor to "proofread" it so they can go. When students, like my friend, feel more comfortable with the tutors to really talk about the big ideas of their paper, they will feel that their time at the writing center was relaxed, enjoyable, and productive. This increased satisfaction will in turn make students want to come back to the writing center more often.

Journal and Discussion Questions

1   What is the main claim that Heather Hunsaker is arguing in "Slouching and Digressing"? How does she explain and support her argument?

2   Describe Hunsaker's work as a tutor. What is she trying to accomplish in a conference with a student? Why does she need to be concerned about what students are feeling when they come to Utah State University's Writing Center in order to accomplish her goals?

3   "Slouching and Digressing" can be read as a problem–solution essay. Outline Hunsaker's argument. What problem does Hunsaker describe? How does her organization bring out her specific recommendations to tutors for solving this problem? How does the organization bring out the reasons and evidence behind Hunsaker's recommendations?

4   A large portion of this article is a description of Hunsaker's process of conducting a conference with a writer. How does Hunsaker's description keep the focus on body language and digressing? What other activities in the conference (which might be important to the success of the conference) does Hunsaker deemphasize or ignore in order to emphasize her main ideas?

5   What does each change in Hunsaker's body language—leaning forward at times and slouching at other times, for example—communicate to the writer she is tutoring? Why do you think Hunsaker emphasizes body language in discussing how she tries to control "the atmosphere" of her sessions with writers?

6   Why does Hunsaker believe that frequently "digressions are the best part of the session" rather than the parts of the conference when she and the writer discuss "the specifics of the paper"? Why might these "stream-of-consciousness" discussions be more helpful to a writer than the more focused discussions of specific problems and questions about the paper? What objections might be raised about Hunsaker spending part of her conference talking about other subjects besides the student's paper? How does Hunsaker anticipate and address possible objections?

7   What ideas about communicating and dealing with clients' emotions in "Slouching and Digressing" could be applied to other jobs? What aspects of Hunsaker's work seem to be unique to the job of writing center tutor?

Topics for Writing

1   Analyze how Heather Hunsaker thinks about her work as a tutor in "Slouching and Digressing," including what her goals are in her job, what problems she faces in meeting these goals, and how she works out solutions to those problems.

2   Interview a student with a part-time job, a job that you have never held yourself. Write an essay describing the job, what challenges or problems are involved in the job, and what the student does to deal with those challenges.

3   Write a research paper about the importance of body language in other situations, such as job interviews, classes, or personal discussions with friends or family members.

Connecting the Readings

Compare Heather Hunsaker's work as a writing center tutor in "Slouching and Digressing" to the "real-world work experience" of college students' part-time jobs discussed in Nisha Ramachandran's "Working Life," including the possible educational benefits and career preparation offered by the jobs.

SERVING IN FLORIDA

BY BARBARA EHRENREICH

Barbara Ehrenreich (1941–) is a writer of feminist and social criticism, often focusing on labor issues. She has been a regular columnist for *The Progressive* and *Time*; has written articles in magazines such as *Atlantic Monthly, Ms., Z Magazine,* and *Salon*; and has authored or co-authored more than a dozen books. She also keeps a blog on ehrenreich.blogs.com. "Serving in Florida" is part of an essay that first appeared in *Harper's Magazine* in January 1999, but was written as a chapter in Ehrenreich's 2001 book, *Nickel and Dimed: On (Not) Getting by in America.* For this book, Ehrenreich researched low-paying, blue-collar jobs in different parts of the U.S. by spending a month living and working as a waitress, a house-cleaner, and a discount store clerk. She did similar research about low-paying, white-collar jobs in her 2005 book, *Bait and Switch: The (Futile) Pursuit of the American Dream.* "Serving in Florida" describes her month as a waitress in two restaurants in Key West. Written for a general audience, "Serving in Florida" is both a personal narration and an often biting social analysis of jobs that pay little more than minimum wage. This excerpt begins after Ehrenreich has described finding an affordable place to live, looking for a job, and working her first ten days as a waitress at "Hearthside," a "family restaurant."

I COULD DRIFT ALONG LIKE THIS, IN some dreamy proletarian idyll, except for two things. One is management. If I have kept this subject to the margins so far it is because I still flinch to think that I spent all those weeks under the surveillance of men (and later women) whose job it was to monitor my behavior for signs of sloth, theft, drug abuse, or worse. Not that managers and especially "assistant managers" in low-wage settings like this are exactly the class enemy. Mostly, in the restaurant business, they are former cooks still capable of pinch-hitting in the kitchen, just as in hotels they are likely to be former clerks, and paid a salary of only about $400 a week. But everyone knows they have crossed over to the other side, which is, crudely put, corporate as opposed to human. Cooks want to prepare tasty meals, servers want to serve them graciously, but managers are there for only one reason—to make sure that money is made for some theoretical entity, the corporation, which exists far away in Chicago or New York, if a corporation can be said to have a physical existence at all. Reflecting on her career, Gail tells me ruefully that she swore, years ago, never to work for a corporation again. "They don't cut you no slack. You give and you give and they take."

Managers can sit—for hours at a time if they want—but it's their job to see that no one else ever does, even when there's nothing to do, and this is why, for servers, slow times can be as exhausting as rushes. You start dragging out each little chore because if the manager on duty catches you in an idle moment he will give you something far nastier to do. So I wipe, I clean, I consolidate catsup bottles and recheck the cheesecake supply, even tour the tables to make sure the customer evaluation forms are all standing perkily in their places—wondering all the time how many calories I burn in these strictly theatrical exercises. In desperation, I even take the desserts out of their glass display case and freshen them up with whipped cream and bright new maraschino cherries; anything to look busy. When, on a particularly dead afternoon, Stu finds me glancing at a *USA Today* a customer has left behind, he assigns me to vacuum the entire floor with the broken vacuum cleaner, which has a handle only two feet long, and the only way to do that without incurring orthopedic damage is to proceed from spot to spot on your knees.

On my first Friday at Hearthside there is a "mandatory meeting for all restaurant employees," which I attend, eager for insight into our overall marketing strategy and the niche (your basic Ohio cuisine with a tropical twist?) we aim to inhabit. But there is no "we" at this meeting. Phillip, our top manager except for an occasional "consultant" sent out by corporate head-quarters, opens it with a sneer: "The break room—it's disgusting. Butts in the ashtrays, newspapers lying around, crumbs." This windowless little room, which also houses the time clock for the entire hotel, is where we stash our bags and civilian clothes and take our half-hour meal breaks. But a break room is not a right, he tells us, it can be taken away. We should also know that the lockers in the break room and whatever is in them can be searched at any time. Then comes gossip; there has been gossip; gossip (which seems to mean employees talking among themselves) must stop. Off-duty employees are henceforth barred from eating at the restaurant, because "other servers gather around them and gossip." When Phillip has exhausted his agenda of rebukes, Joan complains about the condition of the ladies' room and I throw in my two bits about the vacuum cleaner. But I don't see any backup coming from my fellow servers, each of whom has slipped into her own personal funk; Gail, my role model, stares sorrowfully at a point six inches from her nose. The meeting ends when Andy, one of the cooks, gets up, muttering about breaking up his day off for this almighty bullshit.

> ## "
> ### I haven't been treated this way—lined up in the corridor, threatened with locker searches, peppered with carelessly aimed accusations—since at least junior high school.
> ## "

Just four days later we are suddenly summoned into the kitchen at 3:30 P.M., even though there are live tables on the floor. We all—about ten of us—stand around Phillip, who announces grimly that there has been a report of some "drug activity" on the night shift and that, as a result, we are now to be a "drug-free" workplace, meaning that all new hires will be tested and possibly also current employees on a random basis. I am glad that this part of the kitchen is so dark because I find myself blushing as hard as if I had been caught toking up in the ladies' room myself: I haven't been treated this way—lined up in the corridor, threatened with locker searches, peppered with carelessly aimed accusations—since at least junior high school. Back on the floor, Joan cracks, "Next they'll be telling us we can't have *sex* on the job." When I ask Stu what happened to inspire the crackdown, he just mutters about "management decisions" and takes the opportunity to upbraid Gail and me for being too generous

with the rolls. From now on there's to be only one per customer and it goes out with the dinner, not with the salad. He's also been riding the cooks, prompting Andy to come out of the kitchen and observe—with the serenity of a man whose customary implement is a butcher knife—that "Stu has a death wish today."

Later in the evening, the gossip crystallizes around the theory that Stu is himself the drug culprit, that he uses the restaurant phone to order up marijuana and sends one of the late servers out to fetch it for him. The server was caught and she may have ratted out Stu, at least enough to cast some suspicion on him, thus accounting for his pissy behavior. Who knows? Personally, I'm ready to believe anything bad about Stu, who serves no evident function and presumes too much on our common ethnicity, sidling up to me one night to engage in a little nativism directed at the Haitian immigrants: "I feel like I'm the foreigner here. They're taking over the country." Still later that evening, the drug in question escalates to crack. Lionel, the busboy, entertains us for the rest of the shift by standing just behind Stu's back and sucking deliriously on an imaginary joint or maybe a pipe.

The other problem, in addition to the less-than-nurturing management style, is that this job shows no sign of being financially viable. You might imagine, from a comfortable distance, that people who live, year in and year out, on $6 to $10 an hour have discovered some survival stratagems unknown to the middle class. But no. It's not hard to get my coworkers talking about their living situations, because housing, in almost every case, is the principal source of disruption in their lives, the first thing they fill you in on when they arrive for their shifts. After a week, I have compiled the following survey:

> Gail is sharing a room in a well-known downtown flophouse for $250 a week. Her roommate, a male friend, has begun hitting on her, driving her nuts, but the rent would be impossible alone.

> Claude, the Haitian cook, is desperate to get out of the two-room apartment he shares with his girlfriend and two other, unrelated people. As far as I can determine, the other Haitian men live in similarly crowded situations.

> Annette, a twenty-year-old server who is six months pregnant and abandoned by her boyfriend, lives with her mother, a postal clerk.

Marianne, who is a breakfast server, and her boyfriend are paying $170 a week for a one-person trailer.

Billy, who at $10 an hour is the wealthiest of us, lives in the trailer he owns, paying only the $400-a-month lot fee.

The other white cook, Andy, lives on his dry-docked boat, which, as far as I can tell from his loving descriptions, can't be more than twenty feet long. He offers to take me out on it once it's repaired, but the offer comes with inquiries as to my marital status, so I do not follow up on it.

Tina, another server, and her husband are paying $60 a night for a room in the Days Inn. This is because they have no car and the Days Inn is in walking distance of the Hearthside. When Marianne is tossed out of her trailer for subletting (which is against trailer park rules), she leaves her boyfriend and moves in with Tina and her husband.

Joan, who had fooled me with her numerous and tasteful outfits (hostesses wear their own clothes), lives in a van parked behind a shopping center at night and showers in Tina's motel room. The clothes are from thrift shops.[1]

It strikes me, in my middle-class solipsism, that there is gross improvidence in some of these arrangements. When Gail and I are wrapping silverware in napkins—the only task for which we are permitted to sit—she tells me she is thinking of escaping from her roommate by moving into the Days Inn herself. I am astounded: how she can even think of paying $40 to $60 a day? But if I was afraid of sounding like a social worker, I have come out just sounding like a fool. She squints at me in disbelief: "And where am I supposed to get a month's rent and a month's deposit for an apartment?" I'd been feeling pretty smug about my $500 efficiency, but of course it was made possible only by the $1,300 I had allotted myself for start-up costs when I began my low-wage life: $1,000 for the first month's rent and deposit, $100 for initial groceries and cash in my pocket, $200 stuffed away for emergencies. In poverty, as in certain propositions in physics, starting conditions are everything.

There are no secret economies that nourish the poor; on the contrary, there are a host of special costs. If you can't put up the two months' rent you need to secure an apartment, you end up paying through the nose for a room by the week. If you have only a room, with a hot plate at best, you can't save by cooking up huge lentil stews that can be frozen for the week ahead. You eat fast food or the hot dogs and Styrofoam cups of soup that can be microwaved in a convenience store. If you have no money for health insurance—and the Hearthside's niggardly plan kicks in only after three months—you go without routine care or prescription drugs and end up paying the price. Gail, for example, was doing fine, healthwise anyway, until she ran out of money for estrogen pills. She is supposed to be on the company health plan by now, but they claim to have lost her application form and to be beginning the paperwork all over again. So she spends $9 a pop for pills to control the migraines she wouldn't have, she insists, if her estrogen supplements were covered. Similarly, Marianne's boyfriend lost his job as a roofer because he missed so much time after getting a cut on his foot for which he couldn't afford the prescribed antibiotic.

My own situation, when I sit down to assess it after two weeks of work, would not be much better if this were my actual life. The seductive thing about waitressing is that you don't have to wait for payday to feel a few bills in your pocket, and my tips usually cover meals and gas, plus something left over to stuff into the kitchen drawer I use as a bank. But as the tourist business slows in the summer heat, I sometimes leave work with only $20 in tips (the gross is higher, but servers share about 15 percent of their tips with the busboys and bartenders). With wages included, this amounts to about the minimum wage of $5.15 an hour. The sum in the drawer is piling up but at the present rate of accumulation will be more than $100 short of my rent when the end of the month comes around. Nor can I see any expenses to cut. True, I haven't gone the lentil stew route yet, but that's because I don't have a large cooking pot, potholders, or a ladle to stir with (which would cost a total of about $30 at Kmart, somewhat less at a thrift store), not to mention onions, carrots, and the indispensable bay leaf. I do make my lunch almost every day—usually some slow-burning, high-protein combo like frozen chicken patties with melted cheese on top and canned pinto beans on the side. Dinner is at the Hearthside, which offers its employees a choice of BLT, fish sandwich, or hamburger for only $2. The burger lasts longest, especially if it's heaped with gut-puckering jalapeños, but by midnight my stomach is growling again.

---

[1] I could find no statistics on the number of employed people living in cars or vans, but according to a 1997 report of the National Coalition for the Homeless, "Myths and Facts about Homelessness," nearly one-fifth of all homeless people (in twenty-nine cities across the nation) are employed in full- or part-time jobs.

So unless I want to start using my car as a residence, I have to find a second or an alternative job. I call all the hotels I'd filled out housekeeping applications at weeks ago—the Hyatt, Holiday Inn, Econo Lodge, HoJo's, Best Western, plus a half dozen locally run guest houses. Nothing. Then I start making the rounds again, wasting whole mornings waiting for some assistant manager to show up, even dipping into places so creepy that the front-desk clerk greets you from behind bullet-proof glass and sells pints of liquor over the counter. But either someone has exposed my real-life housekeeping habits—which are, shall we say, mellow—or I am at the wrong end of some infallible ethnic equation: most, but by no means all, of the working housekeepers I see on my job searches are African Americans, Spanish-speaking, or refugees from the Central European post-Communist world, while servers are almost invariably white and monolingually English-speaking. When I finally get a positive response, I have been identified once again as server material. Jerry's—again, not the real name—which is part of a well-known national chain and physically attached here to another budget hotel, is ready to use me at once. The prospect is both exciting and terrifying because, with about the same number of tables and counter seats, Jerry's attracts three or four times the volume of customers as the gloomy old Hearthside.

> **" Sinks everywhere are clogged with scraps of lettuce, decomposing lemon wedges, water-logged toast crusts. "**

Picture a fat person's hell, and I don't mean a place with no food. Instead there is everything you might eat if eating had no bodily consequences—the cheese fries, the chicken-fried steaks, the fudge-laden desserts—only here every bite must be paid for, one way or another, in human discomfort. The kitchen is a cavern, a stomach leading to the lower intestine that is the garbage and dishwashing area, from which issue bizarre smells combining the edible and the offal: creamy carrion, pizza barf, and that unique and enigmatic Jerry's scent, citrus fart. The floor is slick with spills, forcing us to walk through the kitchen with tiny steps, like Susan McDougal in leg irons. Sinks everywhere are clogged with scraps of lettuce, decomposing lemon wedges, water-logged toast crusts. Put your hand down on any counter and you risk being stuck to it by the film of ancient syrup spills, and this is unfortunate because hands are utensils here, used for scooping up lettuce onto the salad plates, lifting out pie slices, and even moving hash browns from one plate to another. The regulation poster in the single unisex rest room admonishes us to wash our hands thoroughly, and even offers instructions for doing so, but there is always some vital substance missing—soap, paper towels, toilet paper—and I never found all three at once. You learn to stuff your pockets with napkins before going in there, and too bad about the customers, who must eat, although they don't realize it, almost literally out of our hands.

The break room summarizes the whole situation: there is none, because there are no breaks at Jerry's. For six to eight hours in a row, you never sit except to pee. Actually, there are three folding chairs at a table immediately adjacent to the bathroom, but hardly anyone ever sits in this, the very rectum of the gastro-architectural system. Rather, the function of the peri-toilet area is to house the ashtrays in which servers and dishwashers leave their cigarettes burning at all times, like votive candles, so they don't have to waste time lighting up again when they dash back here for a puff. Almost everyone smokes as if their pulmonary well-being depended on it—the multinational mélange of cooks; the dishwashers, who are all Czechs here; the servers, who are American natives—creating an atmosphere in which oxygen is only an occasional pollutant. My first morning at Jerry's, when the hypoglycemic shakes set in, I complain to one of my fellow servers that I don't understand how she can go so long without food. "Well, I don't understand how *you* can go so long without a cigarette," she responds in a tone of reproach. Because work is what you do for others; smoking is what you do for yourself. I don't know why the antismoking crusaders have never grasped the element of defiant self-nurturance that makes the habit so endearing to its victims—as if, in the American workplace, the only thing people have to call their own is the tumors they are nourishing and the spare moments they devote to feeding them.

Now, the Industrial Revolution is not an easy transition, especially, in my experience, when you have to zip through it in just a couple of days. I have gone from craft work straight into the factory, from the air-conditioned morgue of the Hearthside directly into the flames. Customers arrive in human waves, sometimes disgorged fifty at a time from their tour buses, peckish and whiny. Instead of two "girls" on the floor at once, there can be as many as six of us running around in our brilliant pink-and-orange Hawaiian shirts. Conversations, either with customers or with fellow employees, seldom last more than twenty seconds at a time. On my first day, in fact, I am hurt by my sister servers' coldness. My mentor for the day is a supremely competent, emotionally uninflected twenty-three-year-old, and the others, who gossip a little among themselves about the real reason someone is out sick today and the size of the bail bond someone else has had to pay, ignore me completely. On my second day, I find out why. "Well, it's good to see *you* again," one of them says in greeting. "Hardly anyone comes back after the first day." I feel powerfully vindicated—a survivor—but it would take a long time, probably months, before I could hope to be accepted into this sorority.

I start out with the beautiful, heroic idea of handling the two jobs at once, and for two days I almost do it: working the breakfast/lunch shift at Jerry's from 8:00 till 2:00, arriving at the Hearthside a few minutes late, at 2:10, and attempting to hold out until 10:00. In the few minutes I have between jobs, I pick up a spicy chicken sandwich at the Wendy's drive-through window, gobble it down in the car, and change from khaki slacks to black, from Hawaiian to rust-colored polo. There is a problem, though. When, during the 3:00–4:00 o'clock dead time, I finally sit down to wrap silver, my flesh seems to bond to the seat. I try to refuel with a purloined cup of clam chowder, as I've seen Gail and Joan do dozens of times, but Stu catches me and hisses "No *eating*!" although there's not a customer around to be offended by the sight of food making contact with a server's lips. So I tell Gail I'm going to quit, and she hugs me and says she might just follow me to Jerry's herself.

But the chances of this are minuscule. She has left the flophouse and her annoying roommate and is back to living in her truck. But, guess what, she reports to me excitedly later that evening, Phillip has given her permission to park overnight in the hotel parking lot, as long as she keeps out of sight, and the parking lot should be totally safe since it's patrolled by a hotel security guard! With the Hearthside offering benefits like that, how could anyone think of leaving? This must be Phillip's theory, anyway. He accepts my resignation with a shrug, his main concern being that I return my two polo shirts and aprons.

Gail would have triumphed at Jerry's, I'm sure, but for me it's a crash course in exhaustion management. Years ago, the kindly fry cook who trained me to waitress at a Los Angeles truck stop used to say: Never make an unnecessary trip; if you don't have to walk fast, walk slow; if you don't have to walk, stand. But at Jerry's the effort of distinguishing necessary from unnecessary and urgent from whenever would itself be too much of an energy drain. The only thing to do is to treat each shift as a one-time-only emergency: you've got fifty starving people out there, lying scattered on the battlefield, so get out there and feed them! Forget that you will have to do this again tomorrow, forget that you will have to be alert enough to dodge the drunks on the drive home tonight—just burn, burn, burn! Ideally, at some point you enter what servers call a "rhythm" and psychologists term a "flow state," where signals pass from the sense organs directly to the muscles, bypassing the cerebral cortex, and a Zen-like emptiness sets in. I'm on a 2:00–10:00 P.M. shift now, and a male server from the morning shift tells me about the time he "pulled a triple"—three shifts in a row, all the way around the clock—and then got off and had a drink and met this girl, and maybe he shouldn't tell me this, but they had sex right then and there and it was like *beautiful*.

Journal and Discussion Questions

1 What overall impression does Barbara Ehrenreich create in her story about her work as a waitress? How do the details of her description of her month as a waitress support her thesis about waitress work?

2 What specific criticisms does Ehrenreich make about how restaurant workers are treated? How are these specific issues related to her overall thesis? How do you think the owners and managers of the restaurants and hotel where Ehrenreich worked might respond to her criticisms?

3 Why does Ehrenreich spend several pages describing her search for a job and for a place to live? What do these experiences have to do with the overall purpose of "Serving in Florida"?

4 "Serving in Florida" makes use of comparisons between Ehrenreich's work as a waitress at Hearthside and at Jerry's and probably the middle-class lives that she and most of her readers likely live. What are the most important similarities and differences that she finds in her comparisons? What similarities and differences do you think her readers find between their own lives and the lives Ehrenreich describes?

5 Ehrenreich describes many of her co-workers and managers at some length, often going into their lives outside the workplace. Which people particularly stand out for you? Why? How do these descriptions enhance her story and add to her arguments?

6 Ehrenreich introduces her library research for *Nickel and Dimed* mainly in footnotes. How does the information in the footnote on homeless people add to Ehrenreich's argument and analysis about restaurant work? Why did she confine this research to footnotes instead of including it in the main text of "Serving in Florida"?

7 Considering Ehrenreich's background and age, how typical is her experience as a waitress? How would you compare her experience to the experiences of students who work low-paying jobs like restaurant work?

Topics for Writing

1 Using "Serving in Florida" as your primary source, write an editorial about one of the labor issues raised in "Serving in Florida" (such as drug-testing, health care, low wages, bathroom breaks, managers' treatment of low-wage workers, or homelessness, among others). Your editorial may agree or disagree with one of Ehrenreich's positions or argue for a specific solution to a problem that Ehrenreich discusses.

2 Using "Serving in Florida" as a model, describe a job that you have held and evaluate the treatment of employees and their working conditions in that job.

3 Write a research paper about the salaries, benefits, and general working conditions of a specific occupation. Your sources might include interviews with people who have worked in that occupation as well as library sources such as those cited by Ehrenreich.

A WEEK IN THE LIFE OF A PART-TIME TEACHER

BY DIANA CLAITOR

Diana Claitor was a freelance writer and editor and adjunct English instructor at Austin Community College when she wrote "A Week in the Life of a Part-Time Teacher." She now writes fiction and works for Wexford Publishing. "A Week in the Life of a Part-Time Teacher" appeared in *Ghosts in the Classroom: Stories of College Adjunct Faculty—and the Price We All Pay*, a collection of personal essays by part-time college faculty about their lives and work. The purpose of *Ghosts in the Classroom* is to argue for better salaries, benefits, and working conditions for "adjunct" faculty. Claitor makes this argument with a detailed description of her work during one week as a part-time instructor at several schools.

EVA LEFT ME A NOTE AND A LITTLE gift that I found when I returned for the summer session. Eva is a Salvadoran, a mother of two who had been studying in the tutoring lab every day for months, struggling through the Comp I obstacle course. The card read: "Diana, thank you for so much help. I got the B!"

The other mail in my box was not nearly that pleasant—mostly memos about new titles, computer foul-ups and the general chaos created by the reorganization of Austin Community College. Worst of all, the department heads had been summarily fired, and there was nobody to go to with the unexpected questions that come at the beginning of each semester. What to do with the Chinese student who has a degree in engineering but who only speaks about 25 words of English? Who has the departmental entrance exam for our developmental writing classes? Where can I hide from the overly talkative paranoid schizophrenic who tells me she's been banned from all the other campuses but is now back on her meds?

At the same time, it turned out the tutoring labs were being placed under new departments. The labs, the mainstay for most of us who teach developmental classes, were in an uproar, and my lab already made one small but significant change: the file cabinet with folders for each instructor was being removed. Those files were the one reliable place we could leave tests or information for students. Since we adjuncts have variable hours and no separate offices of our own, whenever students missed a class, this was the place they could pick up materials. (And it got students into the lab, where they might get some individual help.)

The disappearance of the file cabinet seemed symbolic—one of the many ways part-timers were being cut loose.

Both of my classes had very low enrollment. I explained to the first group that we'd probably be canceled, and one student followed me out to my car with tears in her eyes.

"I've planned this for three years," she said. "I work nights. I got a deal worked out with Financial Aid. I got everything balanced just right, so I can go to school and do a good job but keep my job. This class is required, and I GOT to have it at this time of day."

I told her I'd carry her message to whatever higher authority I could find—and I did have some small hope since the college was supposed to give special consideration to these state-mandated courses without which many students are bounced out of school. In the meantime, I discovered that our departing department head had hired two new adjuncts to teach fall classes even though there weren't enough classes to sustain the instructors already here. I suppose that was her little way of saying "thanks" to the veteran teachers who'd put in years here.

It was storming at the first meeting of my other class, and shortly after I gave them the entrance exam, we were evacuated to a room on the ground floor. A tornado was ripping through a subdivision to the west of us. The entire population of the campus spent forty nervous minutes crammed together. When my students returned to our room, another class was sitting there. The room was double booked. The other teacher acted like an ass; I took my class to an empty room down the hall and finished the test there.

The next day I found a phone message from a student I'd tutored many times. Julia is an African American woman with three children and a huge smile. Two semesters ago, I supported her in a disagreement with an English professor over a grade. She had struggled hard to make the grades necessary to get into a nursing program, but one hurdle remained: the writing skills test. Julia was understandably nervous and wanted me to tutor her one last time. I told her the hours I'd be available in the lab.

Despite evidence of the students' need for my particular classes, the college canceled both sections. Of course,

it affected me as well: now my only income for the summer would be the tutoring along with any freelance journalism and research I could scare up. Since the administration cut the lab's budget, I probably wouldn't be able to work as many hours in the lab either.

That night, while drinking too much wine, I came to realize that no matter how much I loved teaching and tutoring here, my time at the college was coming to an end.

During the next week, I came in early and met with the division head (whose job had been eliminated but whose duties went on), and we tried to find ways for the nine students in my canceled classes to stay in school. Each one had a complicated schedule, and there were very few classes to offer them as an alternative to mine. I called the students, called the division head at home, and even made a special trip to another campus to fill out a special form so one student could jump a level and get a writing class at the right time at another campus. The division head thanked me for my efforts.

I ran into a student—a refrigerator-sized ex-football player with the face of a plump girl—whom I taught last semester. He said, "Hey, Miz Claitor, I'm going to take that next writing class in the fall. When are you teaching it?" I told him I wouldn't be teaching here in the fall. His sweet face fell. He asked, "Why?" I couldn't think how to sum up all the complicated reasons, and I didn't want him to lose confidence in the college, so I just said they couldn't offer me enough classes and wished him luck.

Julia showed up for the big finale tutoring session. Her little boy was with her because the two older kids couldn't keep him today; I wondered if she'd be able to concentrate. He had some crayons, and I got him a pile of used computer paper. Julia and I discussed the best way to "psyche yourself" for a test. I gave her a grammar pre-test, and later I saw that she was doing so well she could stop, but she wanted to do the whole thing. Beaming at me, she blurted, "Diana, I just LOVE learning."

Trying for matter-of-fact, I nodded and told her I felt exactly the same way. Then I went away so she could finish; when I returned, she said, "I think this is exactly what I needed to get ready. Thank you." I told her to pat herself on the back—she is the one who taught herself.

The following week, I went for my first interview for a "real job," meaning work with benefits and some degree of security and support. But to my mind, this use of the word "real" renders it meaningless. Teaching in a community college is as real as it gets—our students are real people with real needs, students who need committed teachers. It seems, however, that the teacher is no longer considered essential or deserving of respect. To those in power who somehow, against all logic, consider themselves educators—to those people, I was just not real.

Journal and Discussion Questions

1 What is the central idea of "A Week in the Life of a Part-Time Teacher"? How does Diana Claitor use description and narration about her work to make this argument?

2 What impression does Claitor create about herself? How do the details of her life contribute to this impression? How do her voice and tone as a writer contribute to this impression? How do you think this impression affects the persuasiveness of her essay?

3 Outline "A Week in the Life of a Part-Time Teacher." Why does Claitor introduce her essay with the story of Eva? How does each story in the essay contribute to Claitor's overall argument? Why do you think Claitor gives more space on Julia's story than any other story?

4 What does the disappearance of a file cabinet symbolize in the essay? Why?

5 Why does Claitor want to continue teaching despite her complaints about her job?

6 How do the problems that Claitor describes about her work affect the students that she teaches?

7 What are the causes of the problems that Claitor describes? Where in her essay does Claitor refer to these causes? What other causes might there be for the situation that she describes? What arguments might be made by someone opposing Claitor's argument?

Topics for Writing

1 Write an editorial about the use of part-time instructors in colleges and universities.

2 Write a research paper about Claitor's issue, why colleges and universities often depend on part-time faculty to teach many classes, whether complaints about poor pay and working conditions are justified, how students' education may be affected by this situation, and what, if anything, should be done about the problem.

3 Write a research paper about part-time jobs in another line of work. Why does this kind of work employ part-time workers? Why do people take part-time jobs? Are part-time workers rewarded and treated as well as full-time workers? Why or why not?

I WANT A WIFE

BY JUDY BRADY

Judy Brady (1937–) is a freelance writer and cancer activist who is best known for her writings on women's issues. She edited the books *Women and Cancer* and *One in Three: Women with Cancer Confront an Epidemic* and co-founded the Toxic Links Coalition. The essay "I Want a Wife" is a satirical essay that was first published in the feminist magazine *Ms.* in 1971 but has been republished in dozens of books and Web sites since then. As a satirical argument, "I Want a Wife" makes its criticisms about the work and status of wives indirectly, using irony to drive home Brady's points instead of straightforwardly laying out her claims, reasons, and evidence.

I BELONG TO THAT CLASSIFICATION OF people known as wives. I am A Wife. And, not altogether incidentally, I am a mother.

Not too long ago a male friend of mine appeared on the scene fresh from a recent divorce. He had one child, who is, of course, with his ex-wife. He is looking for another wife. As I thought about him while I was ironing one evening, it suddenly occurred to me that I, too, would like to have a wife. Why do I want a wife?

I would like to go back to school so that I can become economically independent, support myself, and, if need be, support those dependent upon me. I want a wife who will work and send me to school. And while I am going to school I want a wife to take care of my children. I want a wife to keep track of the children's doctor and dentist appointments. And to keep track of mine, too. I want a wife to make sure my children eat properly and are kept clean. I want a wife who will wash the children's clothes and keep them mended. I want a wife who is a good nurturant attendant to my children, who arranges for their schooling, makes sure that they have an adequate social life with their peers, takes them to the park, the zoo, etc. I want a wife who takes care of the children when they are sick, a wife who arranges to be around when the children need special care, because, of course, I cannot miss classes at school. My wife must arrange to lose time at work and not lose the job. It may mean a small cut in my wife's income from time to time, but I guess I can tolerate that. Needless to say, my wife will arrange and pay for the care of the children while my wife is working.

I want a wife who will take care of *my* physical needs. I want a wife who will keep my house clean. A wife who will pick up after my children, a wife who will pick up after me. I want a wife who will keep my clothes clean, ironed, mended, replaced when need be, and who will see to it that my personal things are kept in their proper place so that I can find what I need the minute I need it. I want a wife who cooks the meals, a wife who is a *good* cook. I want a wife who will plan the menus, do the necessary grocery shopping, prepare the meals, serve them pleasantly, and then do the cleaning up while I do my studying. I want a wife who will care for me when I am sick and sympathize with my pain and loss of time from school. I want a wife to go along when our family takes a vacation so that someone can continue to care for me and my children when I need a rest and change of scene.

I want a wife who will not bother me with rambling complaints about a wife's duties. But I want a wife who will listen to me when I feel the need to explain a rather difficult point I have come across in my course of studies. And I want a wife who will type my papers for me when I have written them.

I want a wife who will take care of the details of my social life. When my wife and I are invited out by my friends, I want a wife who will take care of the babysitting arrangements. When I meet people at school that I like and want to entertain, I want a wife who will have the house clean, will prepare a special meal, serve it to me and my friends, and not interrupt when I talk about things that interest me and my friends. I want a wife who will have arranged that the children are fed and ready for bed before my guests arrive so that the children do not bother us. I want a wife who takes care of the needs of my guests so that they feel comfortable, who makes sure that they have an ashtray, that they are passed the hors d'oeuvres, that they are offered a second helping of the food, that their wine glasses are replenished when necessary, that their coffee is served to them as they like it. And I want a wife who knows that sometimes I need a night out by myself.

I want a wife who is sensitive to my sexual needs, a wife who makes love passionately and eagerly when I feel like it, a wife who makes sure that I am satisfied. And, of course, I want a wife who will not demand sexual attention when I am not in the mood for it. I want a wife who assumes the complete responsibility for birth control, because I do not want more children. I want a wife who will remain sexually faithful to me so that I do not have to clutter up my intellectual life with jealousies. And I want a wife who understands that *my* sexual needs may entail more than strict adherence to monogamy. I must, after all, be able to relate to people as fully as possible.

If, by chance, I find another person more suitable as a wife than the wife I already have, I want the liberty to replace my present wife with another one. Naturally, I will expect a fresh, new life; my wife will take the children and be solely responsible for them so that I am left free.

When I am through with school and have a job, I want my wife to quit working and remain at home so that my wife can more fully and completely take care of a wife's duties.

My God, who *wouldn't* want a wife?

Journal and Discussion Questions

1 If Judy Brady were to directly state the thesis that she is arguing in "I Want a Wife," what would she say? Why doesn't she state her thesis directly? What reasons does Brady imply to support her thesis?

2 Outline "I Want a Wife." How does Brady group the different kinds of work that a wife is expected to do in her essay? What difference would it make in how you respond to her argument if the paragraphs in the body of her essay were sequenced in another way?

3 How does Brady's essay define the job of "wife"? Why do you think Brady decided to write that she wants "a wife" instead of writing that she wants "a husband" who will do all the work she describes? Is "I Want a Wife" a good title?

4 What does "I Want a Wife" have to say about the work of a wife and mother and how others value that work? Does Brady suggest why a wife's work is largely unnoticed and unappreciated? What other reasons could be given for the situation that she describes?

5 How many times does Brady begin a sentence with the four words of her title? Why does Brady make use of this repetition? Do you find this repetition effective? Why or why not? What does she do to prevent her use of repetition from getting monotonous and tiresome? Why does Brady repeatedly use the first-person pronoun *I* instead of writing about wives and husbands in general?

6 Like many arguments, "I Want a Wife" wants to make readers aware of a problem. What arguments do you think an opposing essay might offer? What do you think Brady might have identified as the causes of this problem? What solutions might she have proposed to improve or discourage the kind of marriage she describes? Would her argument be stronger if she had discussed opposing arguments, causes, and solutions? Why or why not?

7 If Brady had written "I Want a Wife" as a typical editorial column, with an explicit thesis, paragraphs that focused on reasons that support her thesis, and use of third person ("wives" and "husbands") instead of first person, how do you think it could have been organized? What would be lost if Brady had written her argument like this? What might be gained?

Topics for Writing

1 Write a research paper discussing to what extent Brady's 1971 description of how wives and husbands divide the work of maintaining a home is true today. What are the causes for how families decide how this work is divided and assigned? You might interview people who are or have been married as part of your research.

2 Pick a subject other than "wife" and write an "I Want a . . ." essay modeled after Brady's "I Want a Wife."

3 Since 1971, it has become commonplace for married women to have jobs and careers outside the home. As a consequence, many married women without outside jobs now complain that their work is disrespected even by other women, mothers who work outside the home are sometimes accused of being selfish at the expense of their children, and many married women—and their husbands—worry about how to balance their workloads and responsibilities inside and outside the home. Research one of these issues, and argue your position.

DILBERT

BY SCOTT ADAMS

Dilbert is syndicated in more than 2,000 daily newspapers, and cartoonist Scott Adams (1957–) has published more than twenty *Dilbert* books. Set in a mediocre software engineering company, *Dilbert* is a workplace comic that draws its humor by exaggerating and commenting on the behavior and office politics of engineers, managers, secretaries, salespeople, and other white-collar workers. On the *Dilbert* Web site (www.unitedmedia.com/comics/dilbert/), Adams writes that *Dilbert* emerged out of doodles and drawings based on his co-workers at "a number of jobs that defy description but all involve technology and finances." In this strip, the character Dogbert takes the role of an anthropologist observing and describing the workplace culture of managers and engineers in the firm where Dilbert works. This situation allows Adams to make satirical observations about the life and work of anthropologists as well as engineers and managers. The heading above the last panel refers to *Gorillas in the Mist*, a book by anthropologist Diane Fosse about her study of a community of gorillas, which was made into a movie starring Sigourney Weaver.

Journal and Discussion Questions

1 What kind of language does Dogbert use to describe the engineers and managers in Scott Adams' comic strip? What does his language reveal about Dogbert's attitude toward the people he observes? Would you say that Dogbert's analysis is "objective"? Why or why not?

2 Compare the drawings and bits of conversation in the strip with Dogbert's descriptions. How accurate are Dogbert's descriptions of each panel?

3 Using everyday language, rewrite Dogbert's observations in the first six panels.

4 What is the humor in comparing Dilbert's company to the book and movie *Gorillas in the Mist*?

5 What is Adams' attitude toward Dogbert here? To what extent do you think Dogbert represents Adams' attitude toward Dilbert and the people he works with? What criticisms might Adams be implying about the job of anthropologist and the studies anthropologists produce?

6 How would you describe Dilbert's workplace? What criticisms may Adams be suggesting about engineering firms and office work in general?

Topics for Writing

1 Analyze this *Dilbert* strip, discussing Scott Adams' use of humor and irony to represent and critique workplace culture.

2 Observe another workplace (you may treat classrooms as workplaces) and write a description and analysis of the behavior that you observe. Your essay may be written straightforwardly or ironically, but your descriptions and commentary must be based on what you observe even if you are striving for humor.

3 Create an eight-panel comic strip like Adams' about a place where you have worked.

4 Read a scholarly study of a workplace and write an analysis comparing the study's approach to Dogbert's approach in describing and understanding the workplace. Does Dogbert accurately represent how scholars observe and describe people at work, however much Adams exaggerates this work for humor?

U.S. ARMY RECRUITING ADVERTISEMENT:
From the Ballfield to the Battlefield

BY NEIL RAVITZ WITH ALEC MORRISON

The U.S. Army published this recruiting advertisement in *Sports Illustrated* on April 24, 2006. The heart of this ad is an essay by a soldier, Neil Ravitz, comparing his life and work as a soldier to his experiences as a college football player. The ad attempts to persuade readers to enlist in the Army in part by emphasizing the value and meaning of a U.S. soldier's work and by conveying a sense of the exciting life of a soldier.

Journal and Discussion Questions

1   How does the U.S. Army's advertisement represent the work of soldiers? What value and meaning does this work have, according to the advertisement?

2   What impression of Neil Ravitz as a person do you get from his essay and photographs in this advertisement? What details in the advertisement create this impression of Ravitz? Why are his character traits and values important in the work of a soldier? Why would the Army focus on these character traits to persuade readers of *Sports Illustrated* to join the Army?

3   How do Ravitz and the ad connect the experience of playing football to life in the Army? How does this comparison appeal to some readers of *Sports Illustrated*?

4   According to the caption for the photograph, Ravitz apparently fought in Iraq as a member of the Pennsylvania National Guard, after he had completed his period of active duty in the Army. Why do you think the Army chose Ravitz for this advertisement instead of someone who has made the Army his career? Why do you think Ravitz concluded his essay by writing, "It's funny—I didn't dream, growing up, of a military career. Now I can't imagine taking any other path"?

5   Why does Ravitz discuss his family and his regular job as a systems analyst in the next-to-last paragraph?

6   What do the two photographs in the advertisement suggest about Ravitz and his life? How do they support the ideas in his essay? What impressions and information do they add to the advertisement?

7   What reasons for joining the Army are stated and implied in the advertisement? Why doesn't the advertisement argue all these reasons more directly? How does the advertisement anticipate possible objections to its arguments caused by the increasing unpopularity of the war in Iraq?

Topics for Writing

1   Analyze how the U.S. Army advertisement represents the life and work of a soldier and the value and meaning of that work.

2   Analyze the appeals and arguments of the U.S. Army recruiting advertisement and how effective and ethical it is in its attempt to persuade readers to enlist in the Army.

FROM THE
BALLFIELD TO THE BATTLEFIELD

WHEN I PLAYED MY FINAL FOOTBALL GAME as a West Point cadet in 1998, the world looked much different than it does now. That fall I was a senior captain and offensive lineman, and my only concern was the annual Army-Navy game, the culmination of four years of hard work. My classmates and I wanted to go out as winners, and our 34–30 victory brings back fond, vivid memories today. Upon graduating, I would begin a career as an active Army officer, but I didn't really know what the future had in store for me.

by Neil Ravitz

When I attended last fall's Army-Navy game in Philadelphia, I couldn't help but contemplate what lay ahead for the game's graduating seniors. They're approaching a future far more demanding than the one I faced. Our nation is fighting a war on terror, and as I learned firsthand during a 12-month tour in Iraq, serving our country in these times comes with a remarkable sense of duty and purpose. Fortunately for me, my experience playing football at West Point only strengthened my ability to answer that call. That's what I would tell today's Army players too: On a smaller scale, they've already prepared for a lot of the challenges they're going to face upon leaving school. If they keep in mind the basics of leadership and how to act as human beings, they're going to succeed no matter the situation.

I probably did not realize just how strong the bonds of brotherhood and shared sacrifice were on my Army teams until I'd left. That's one of the rare experiences sports offers. Just look at this year's NCAA basketball tournament. Was George Mason the most talented team? No. They clicked because they'd become a tight-knit group, which doesn't happen overnight. The same was true when my unit was called to Iraq. I went over as a battery executive officer and the leader of a platoon of 36 guys. Every time we endured a new challenge, we grew

SENSE OF DUTY

In January 2004, Neil Ravitz, West Point '99, began a 12-month tour as a platoon leader in Iraq. Ravitz had served active duty for two years after college, then joined the Pennsylvania National Guard.

a little. You'd see guys becoming more confident, putting their arms around each other's shoulders. A bond started to grow. The stress of those challenges helped build it. There's a valuable lesson here: Whether you're playing football or leading a platoon, you must gain the respect of the people you work with. You have to build trust and act ethically.

We covered a lot of ground in Iraq, beginning in Baghdad running convoy security missions, helping to set up police stations and training personnel. Then we moved into the Sunni Triangle for more missions. Serving overseas is a surreal experience. I saw everything from people living in mud huts with no plumbing to the ornate palaces of Saddam's regime. In our travels, my fellow soldiers and I grew far closer than normal professional colleagues. I can only compare it to my old Army teams. Your lives become so tightly entwined, normal workplace boundaries disappear. Even now we all keep in close touch and care deeply about each other's lives and families.

Admittedly, I feel a much different sense of duty serving my country than I might in my regular job, as a systems analyst for BearingPoint. But I'm more thankful than ever to be home with my wife, Stefanie, and my baby daughter, Julia. Each day I try to appreciate the freedoms I have here.

Joining the military involves certain risks and dangers. Still, I believe it's one of the great opportunities in America today, no matter what your background is. The Army will treat you equally and give you the training to have a career. I recognize now more than ever the value of my experience attending West Point, playing football and serving my country.

It's funny—I didn't dream, growing up, of a military career. Now I can't imagine taking any other path.

HIGH-TECH JOBS ARE GOING ABROAD! BUT THAT'S OKAY

BY ROBERT B. REICH

Robert B. Reich (1946–) is a professor of public policy at the University of California at Berkeley and a former Secretary of Labor in the Clinton administration. He has written ten books, including *The Work of Nations: Preparing Ourselves for 21st Century Capitalism, Locked in the Cabinet, I'll Be Short: Essentials for a Decent Working Society,* and *Reason: Why Liberals Will Win the Battle for America.* Reich also writes frequently on public policy, economics, and labor for magazines and newspapers such as the *New Yorker, Slate,* the *Wall Street Journal,* and *American Prospect,* and the public radio business program *Marketplace.* "High-Tech Jobs Are Going Abroad! But That's Okay" is an editorial column that appeared in the *Washington Post* on November 2, 2003, when the United States was starting to recover from the economic recession that followed 9/11. Americans were beginning to worry about the "outsourcing" of middle-class, white-collar jobs. Although industry had moved many factory jobs out of the U.S. to cheaper labor markets in other countries, companies were taking advantage of cheap and speedy Internet communication to move many jobs that required a college education to countries like India. This practice was criticized for contributing to unemployment and lower salaries in high-tech and other white-collar jobs. Reich here disagrees with many of his liberal readers and colleagues and tries to change public perception and debates about the changing global and American job market. Many of Reich's articles and radio commentaries are available at www.robertreich.org/reich/biography.asp, and Reich keeps a blog on robertreich.blogspot.com/.

THERE'S GOOD NEWS AND NOT-SO-GOOD news in the American workplace. The good news is that the economy is growing and businesses are spending once again, on high technology. The Commerce Department reported last Thursday a sharp pickup in spending on equipment and software in the third quarter. Not so good is the news that high-tech jobs have not come back, at least not so far.

Jobs in America's sprawling information-technology (or IT, as it known in the info world) sector—including everything from software research, design and development to computer engineering—are down 20 percent from late 2000. Salaries are down, too. In 2000, senior software engineers earned $130,000. The same job now pays no more than $100,000. Meanwhile, a lot of high-tech jobs are moving offshore. Is that a cause for concern?

When I was labor secretary, I fought to preserve U.S. jobs. So you might well assume that I would see the number of high-tech jobs moving offshore as a troubling trend. And yet, I do not. I'll explain why in a moment.

But lots of people are worried about it. Indeed, those anxieties seem to be increasing:

- On Sept. 30, Congress let the cap on H-1B visas issued to foreign high-tech workers to shrink from 195,000 to its old level of 65,000. The ostensible reason: to make sure more high-tech jobs go to Americans.

- Bills are pending in several state legislatures barring state government projects from using offshore high-tech workers.

- High-tech workers are organizing against foreign outsourcing. One group of them—the Organization for the Rights of American Workers—has demonstrated outside conferences on "strategic outsourcing" in New York and Boston.

The fear is understandable.

More than half of all Fortune 500 companies say they're outsourcing software development or expanding their own development centers outside the United States. Sixty-eight percent of more than 100 IT executives who responded to a survey last spring by CIO magazine said their offshore contracts will increase this year. By the end of 2004, 10 percent of all information-technology jobs at American IT companies and 5 percent in non-IT companies will move offshore, according to Gartner Co., a research and analysis firm that specializes in high-technology trends. And by 2015, according to a study by Forrester Research in Cambridge, an estimated 3.3 million more American white-collar jobs will shift to low-cost countries, mostly to India.

The trend isn't surprising. American companies are under intense pressure to reduce costs, and foreigners can do a lot of high-tech jobs more cheaply than they can be done here. Already India has more than half a million IT professionals. It's adding 2 million college graduates a year, many of whom are attracted to the burgeoning IT sector. The starting salary of a software engineer in India is around $5,000. Experienced engineers get between $10,000 to $15,000. Top IT professionals there might earn up to $20,000.

Meanwhile, it's become far easier to coordinate such work from headquarters back in America. Overseas cable costs have fallen as much as 80 percent since 1999. With digitization and high-speed data networks, an Indian office park can seem right next door. Matthew Slaughter, associate professor of business administration at Dartmouth College, says information-technology work "will move faster [than manufacturing] because it's easier to ship work across phone lines and put consultants on airplanes than it is to ship bulky raw materials across borders and build factories and deal with tariffs and transportation."

With such ease of communicating, the squeeze on H1-B visas will do little to keep IT jobs out of the hands of non-Americans. "It doesn't make a difference for firms whose business model has people largely working offshore," Moksha Technologies Chairman Pawan Kumar told the Press Trust of India. "It . . . will make firms drive business where the technology workers are." Guatam Sinha, head of the Indian human-resource firm TVA Infotech, agrees. "In fact, lots of techies are coming back to India." India exported $9.6 billion worth of software last year. Such exports are expected to grow 26 percent this fiscal year.

So why don't I believe the outsourcing of high-tech work is something to lose sleep over?

First, the number of high-tech jobs outsourced abroad still accounts for a tiny proportion of America's 10-million-strong IT workforce. When the U.S. economy fully bounces back from recession (as it almost surely will within the next 18 months), a large portion of high-tech jobs that were lost after 2000 will come back in some form.

Second, even as the number of outsourced jobs increases, the overall percent of high-tech jobs going abroad is likely to remain relatively small. That's because outsourcing increases the possibilities of loss or theft of intellectual property, as well as sabotage, cyberterrorism, abuse by hackers, and organized crime. Granted, not much of this has happened yet. But as more IT is shipped abroad, the risks escalate. Smart companies will continue to keep their core IT functions in-house, and at home.

Outsourcing also poses quality-control problems. The more complex the job order and specs, the more difficult it is to get it exactly right over large distances with subcontractors from a different culture. In a Gartner survey of 900 big U.S. companies that outsource IT work offshore, a majority complained of difficulty in communicating and meeting deadlines. So it's unlikely that very complex engineering and design can be done more efficiently abroad.

As smart U.S. companies outsource their more standard high-tech work, they're simultaneously shifting their in-house IT employees to more innovative, higher value-added functions, such as invention, creation, integration, key R&D and basic architecture. These core creative activities are at the heart of these companies' competitive futures. They know they have to nourish them.

The third and most basic reason why high-tech work won't shift abroad is that high technology isn't a sector like manufacturing or an industry like telecommunications. High-tech work entails the process of innovating. It's about discovering and solving problems. There's no necessary limit to the number of high-tech jobs around the world because there's no finite limit to the ingenuity of the human mind. And there's no limit to human needs that can be satisfied.

Hence, even as the supply of workers around the world capable of high-tech innovation increases, the demand for innovative people is increasing at an even faster pace. Recessions temporarily slow such demand, of course, but the long-term trend is toward greater rewards to people who are at or near the frontiers of information technology—as well as biotechnology, nanotechnology and new-materials technologies. Bigger pay packages are also in store for the professionals (lawyers, bankers, venture capitalists, advertisers, marketers and managers) who cluster around high-tech workers and who support innovative enterprises.

In the future, some of America's high-tech workers will be found in laboratories but many more will act like management consultants, strategists and troubleshooters. They'll have intimate understandings of particular businesses so they can devise new solutions that meet those businesses' needs. They'll help decide which high-tech work can most efficiently be outsourced, and they'll coordinate work that goes offshore with work done in-house.

Don't get me wrong. None of this is an argument for complacency. It's crucial that America continues to be the world's leader in innovation. Our universities are the best in the world, but they can't remain that way when so many are starved for cash. Federal and state support for higher education must keep up with rising demand for people who are creative and adaptive.

Federal government investments in basic research and development are also vital. We need to guard against what is already a drift away from basic research toward applied research and development—that is, from the creation of new knowledge that can be put to many different uses versus R&D that's related to the commercialization of specific products, especially military-related aerospace, telecommunications and weapons.

And just as with laid-off manufacturing workers, we need to ensure that high-tech workers are adaptive and flexible. They should be able to move quickly and get the retraining they need. Pensions and health insurance should be more portable across jobs. High-tech workers who want to polish their skills or gain new ones should have access to tax credits that make it easy for them to go back to college for a time.

But it makes no sense for us to try to protect or preserve high-tech jobs in America or block efforts by American companies to outsource. Our economic future is wedded to technological change, and most of the jobs of the future are still ours to invent.

Journal and Discussion Questions

1 Outline "High-Tech Jobs Are Going Abroad! But That's Okay" and describe Robert B. Reich's intended audience. How does his editorial's organization serve his purposes and help to persuade his audience?

2 Reich expresses his thesis in the title and introduction of his editorial but announces in the third paragraph that he will delay explaining his central idea. What is his thesis? What are the reasons for this belief? Where does he begin to explain these reasons? Why does he wait so long to explain his position?

3 What idea about the outsourcing of high-tech jobs is Reich arguing against? What reasons and evidence lie behind this belief? Why does Reich develop his opponents' argument in such detail? Does this strategy make his overall argument more or less persuasive? Why or why not?

4 If outsourcing of American high-tech jobs is not a business and labor problem that we should be worrying about, according to Reich, what problems should we be worrying about? Why? What solutions does he propose to these problems? Are you persuaded by these arguments? Why or why not?

5 What sources does Reich draw on? Why does he cite Indian business executives as well as American experts? Where do you think Reich found his statistics? How does he make use of this research to build his argument?

6 According to Reich, how is technology changing business and jobs in the twenty-first century, for good and for bad? How does Reich explain and support his claims about technology? Which claims are most persuasive? Why? Which claims are least persuasive? Why?

7 What role does higher education have in Reich's vision of the twenty-first century job market? What changes in higher education does Reich propose and why? What other changes in colleges and universities might be implied by "High-Tech Jobs Are Going Abroad!"?

Topics for Writing

1 Analyze Robert B. Reich's "High-Tech Jobs Are Going Abroad! But That's Okay." How logical and persuasive are his arguments? How effectively does Reich appeal to liberals who strongly oppose the outsourcing of jobs to other countries? Do you think Reich's making a conservative argument, despite his liberal background and credentials? Why or why not?

2 Write a research paper arguing for or against Reich's claims about the effects of outsourcing on American jobs and the U.S. economy or about the effects of computer technologies on twenty-first century jobs and businesses.

3 For an audience of college students and faculty, write an argument about how colleges and universities should prepare students for careers in the new global economy, drawing on Reich's argument and other research. You may address this argument mainly to college students (how they should prepare themselves for the job market) or mainly to college and university faculty and administrators (how they should prepare students for the new economy).

WHY THE NEW JOBS GO TO IMMIGRANTS

BY DAVID R. FRANCIS

David R. Francis is a journalist who covers economic stories for the *Christian Science Monitor*. He wrote "Why the New Jobs Go to Immigrants" for the March 10, 2005, issue of the *Christian Science Monitor*. In this analysis, Francis argues that the millions of illegal immigrants working in the U.S. reduce the employment opportunities for American citizens.

WALL STREET CHEERED AND STOCK prices rose when the US Labor Department announced last Friday that employers had expanded their payrolls by 262,000 positions in February.

But it wasn't entirely good news. The statisticians also indicated that the share of the adult population holding jobs had slipped slightly from January to 62.3 percent. That's now two full percentage points *below* the level in the brief recession that began in March 2001.

Why the apparent contradiction? Reasons abound: population growth, rising retirements. But one factor that gets little attention is immigration.

In the past four years, the number of immigrants into the US, legal and illegal, has closely matched the number of new jobs. That suggests newcomers have, in effect, snapped up all of the new jobs.

"There has been no net job gain for natives," says Andrew Sum, an economist at Northeastern University.

Something similar has happened in Western Europe. Each year, about 500,000 to 800,000 illegal immigrants enter the 15 member nations of the European Union (not including the 10 new members as of last May), estimates Demetrios Papademetriou, president of the Migration Policy Institute in Washington. While it's more difficult for immigrants to get into Europe legally, once in they have more social and labor rights and protections than legal immigrants in the US do, says Mr. Papademetriou. And in Europe, illegal immigrants have a relatively bigger underground economy in which to find work.

If anything, the job outlook for native Europeans is bleaker than for Americans. Unemployment remains high in most of Europe. It hit 12.6 percent in Germany last month, the highest since World War II.

So with people from poor nations striving to get in and natives often losing out in the competition for many new jobs, the US and EU might be expected to have coherent immigration policies. Instead, chaos reigns.

Concerned with extremely low birthrates in Western Europe, the European Commission has suggested common policies to attract immigrants to fill longer-term needs for labor. Instead, national policies vary enormously.

In Italy, Spain, Portugal, and Greece, for instance, illegal immigrants flood across the borders, despite efforts to stop them, and then once inside are frequently legalized by government edicts.

"There is no rhyme nor reason to much of this," says Mr. Papademetriou.

In the US, President Bush calls for giving millions of illegal immigrants a kind of guest-worker status as a legal path to US citizenship. So far, no specific legislation to implement his suggestion has been put before Congress.

Meanwhile, US border patrols spend millions of dollars a year trying to keep illegals out. And yet, they keep coming, evidently little discouraged by recession or the 9/11 attacks. In the past four years alone, the number of immigrants ran some 2.5 million to 3 million, of which about half were illegal.

They come for jobs, of course. And the Bush administration makes barely any effort to enforce current law. In 2003, a total of 13 employers were fined for hiring undocumented employees.

In fact, neither Republicans nor Democrats have promoted enforcement of immigration law prohibiting the hiring of illegal immigrants, says Mr. Sum, head of Northeastern's Center for Labor Market Studies.

Of course, not every job filled by an immigrant is taken away from a native American, a native German, a French citizen, or other national.

Most immigrants take jobs at the bottom of the ladder, jobs which many natives won't seek because they are considered too hard, pay too little, or have lost status, Papademetriou notes.

> ## Teens used to take many of the entry level jobs offered by restaurants, retail stores, landscaping companies, factories, and other businesses. Now more teens are going to college, and many may not want or need to work.

And the people they do displace often have little political clout. Sum sees immigrants as one factor behind today's historical low employment rate among US teenagers. Barely more than a third hold jobs. Over the past four years, the number of employed teens has declined by nearly 1.3 million.

Teens used to take many of the entry level jobs offered by restaurants, retail stores, landscaping companies, factories, and other businesses. Now more teens are going to college, and many may not want or need to work. But a new study by Sum and his colleagues at Northeastern finds that 2.5 million teens last year were unemployed, underemployed, or had stopped looking for work in the past month. They faced severe competition for jobs from young adults, older women, and immigrants—most of whom are young.

That lack of employment has social implications. The study notes that youths who work more during their high school years have an easier time transitioning to the labor market upon high school graduation, especially those not going on to college. Jobless teenage women are more likely to get pregnant, and economically disadvantaged boys and girls are more likely to drop out of school if jobless.

In occupational fields with many immigrants, native-born workers tend to have higher jobless rates. The four occupations with the largest number of newly arrived immigrants (1.4 million in construction, food preparation, cleaning and maintenance, and production workers) employ 21.4 million natives, and have more than 2 million unemployed natives.

What employers really want in many cases by hiring immigrants is to hold down wage costs, experts say.

Journal and Discussion Questions

1 What is the thesis of "Why the New Jobs Go to Immigrants"? What reasons and evidence does David R. Francis provide to support this claim? What reasons and evidence are most persuasive? Why?

2 What specific problems about jobs does Francis discuss? How does he show that illegal immigration is an important cause for each of these problems? How does each problem that Francis discusses appeal to the people who may read his editorial and address their concerns?

3 Where in "Why the New Jobs Go to Immigrants" does Francis mention opposing arguments to his position? What are these opposing arguments? How does Francis answer these arguments? Do you find his refutations of opposing arguments persuasive? What other arguments might someone who disagrees with Francis raise?

4 Why does Francis introduce an editorial about unemployment problems with good news about employment? Why does he later discuss unemployment and immigration in the European Union? How does his comparison of the U.S. and the E.U. support his argument about immigration and employment in the U.S.?

5 How does Francis use research to support his arguments? What are his sources, and how does he assure readers that his sources are knowledgeable and credible?

6 What solutions does Francis discuss? How does each solution address the problems Francis has described?

7 Why does Francis focus on the effect of illegal immigration on entry-level jobs that usually employ teens? Do your own experiences and observations about jobs available for teens support Francis' claims? Why or why not?

Topics for Writing

1 Write an argument that either agrees or disagrees with the central thesis of "Why the New Jobs Go to Immigrants."

2 Propose and defend a solution to the problem that David R. Francis discusses.

3 Write a research paper about the job market for teens, either those in high school, those in college, or those who choose to get a job instead of going to college. What is the employment situation? What improvements, if any, are needed?

COST OF ILLEGAL IMMIGRATION MAY BE LESS THAN MEETS THE EYE

BY EDUARDO PORTER

Eduardo Porter is a journalist for the *New York Times*. He wrote the editorial "Cost of Illegal Immigration May Be Less Than Meets the Eye" for the April 16, 2006, issue of the *New York Times*. In his argument, Porter challenges claims that the wages and working conditions of American workers are hurt significantly because of competition from the large number of illegal immigrants working in the U.S.

CALIFORNIA MAY SEEM THE BEST place to study the impact of illegal immigration on the prospects of American workers. Hordes of immigrants rushed into the state in the last 25 years, competing for jobs with the least educated among the native population. The wages of high school dropouts in California fell 17 percent from 1980 to 2004.

But before concluding that immigrants are undercutting the wages of the least fortunate Americans, perhaps one should consider Ohio. Unlike California, Ohio remains mostly free of illegal immigrants. And what happened to the wages of Ohio's high school dropouts from 1980 to 2004? They fell 31 percent.

As Congress debates an overhaul of the nation's immigration laws, several economists and news media pundits have sounded the alarm, contending that illegal immigrants are causing harm to Americans in the competition for jobs.

Yet a more careful examination of the economic data suggests that the argument is, at the very least, overstated. There is scant evidence that illegal immigrants have caused any significant damage to the wages of American workers.

The number that has been getting the most attention lately was produced by George J. Borjas and Lawrence F. Katz, two Harvard economists, in a paper published last year. They estimated that the wave of illegal Mexican immigrants who arrived from 1980 to 2000 had reduced the wages of high school dropouts in the United States by 8.2 percent. But the economists acknowledge that the number does not consider other economic forces, such as the fact that certain businesses would not exist in the United States without cheap immigrant labor. If it had accounted for such things, immigration's impact would be likely to look less than half as big.

Mr. Katz was somewhat taken aback by the attention the study has received. "This was not intended," he said.

At first blush, the preoccupation over immigration seems reasonable. Since 1980, eight million illegal immigrants have entered the work force. Two-thirds of them never completed high school. It is sensible to expect that, because they were willing to work for low wages, they would undercut the position in the labor market of American high school dropouts.

This common sense, however, ignores half the picture. Over the last quarter-century, the number of people without any college education, including high school dropouts, has fallen sharply. This has reduced the pool of workers who are most vulnerable to competition from illegal immigrants.

In addition, as businesses and other economic agents have adjusted to immigration, they have made changes that have muted much of immigration's impact on American workers.

For instance, the availability of foreign workers at low wages in the Nebraska poultry industry made companies realize that they had the personnel to expand. So they invested in new equipment, generating jobs that would not otherwise be there. In California's strawberry patches, illegal immigrants are not competing against native workers; they are competing against pickers in Michoacán, Mexico. If the immigrant pickers did not come north across the border, the strawberries would.

"Immigrants come in and the industries that use this type of labor grow," said David Card, an economist at the University of California, Berkeley. "Taking all into account, the effects of immigration are much, much lower."

In a study published last year that compared cities that have lots of less educated immigrants with cities that have very few, Mr. Card found no wage differences that could be attributed to the presence of immigrants.

Other research has also cast doubt on illegal immigration's supposed damage to the nation's disadvantaged. A study published earlier this year by three economists—David H. Autor of the Massachusetts Institute of Technology, Mr. Katz of Harvard and Melissa S. Kearney of the Brookings Institution—observed that income inequality in the bottom half of the wage scale has not grown since around the mid-1980's.

Even economists striving hardest to find evidence of immigration's effect on domestic workers are finding that, at most, the surge of illegal immigrants probably had only a small impact on wages of the least-educated Americans—an effect that was likely swamped by all the other things that hit the economy, from the revolution in technology to the erosion of the minimum wage's buying power.

When Mr. Borjas and Mr. Katz assumed that businesses reacted to the extra workers with a corresponding increase in investment—as has happened in Nebraska—their estimate of the decline in wages of high school dropouts attributed to illegal immigrants was shaved to 4.8 percent. And they have since downgraded that number, acknowledging that the original analysis used some statistically flimsy data.

Assuming a jump in capital investment, they found that the surge in illegal immigration reduced the wages of high school dropouts by just 3.6 percent. Across the entire labor force, the effect of illegal immigrants was zero, because the presence of uneducated immigrants actually increased the earnings of more educated workers, including high school graduates. For instance, higher-skilled workers could hire foreigners at low wages to mow their lawns and care for their children, freeing time for these workers to earn more. And businesses that exist because of the availability of cheap labor might also need to employ managers.

> **Across the entire labor force, the effect of illegal immigrants was zero, because the presence of uneducated immigrants actually increased the earnings of more educated workers, including high school graduates.**

Mr. Borjas said that while the numbers were not large, the impact at the bottom end of the skill range was significant. "It is not a big deal for the whole economy, but that hides a big distributional impact," he said.

Others disagree. "If you're a native high school dropout in this economy, you've got a slew of problems of which immigrant competition is but one, and a lesser one at that," said Jared Bernstein of the Economic Policy Institute, a liberal research group.

Mr. Katz agreed that the impact was modest, and it might fall further if changes in trade flows were taken into account—specifically, that without illegal immigrants, some products now made in the United States would likely be imported. "Illegal immigration had a little bit of a role reinforcing adverse trends for the least advantaged," he said, "but there are much stronger forces operating over the last 25 years."

Journal and Discussion Questions

1 What is the central claim of "Cost of Illegal Immigration May Be Less Than Meets the Eye"? What are the main reasons and evidence that Eduardo Porter provides to support that thesis?

2 What is the point of Porter's introductory comparison of California and Ohio? Is this an effective introduction? Why or why not?

3 What opposing arguments and evidence does Porter consider? How does he answer these objections to his position? What other objections could be raised against Porter's arguments?

4 What is the central source for Porter's argument? How does he make use of and discuss this source? What other research does Porter bring into his editorial? How does each source contribute to his argument?

5 High school dropouts make up a very small percentage of the readers of the *New York Times,* so how does Porter try to persuade his readers that the effect of illegal immigration on the employment of high school dropouts is an important issue?

6 What do you think are the "stronger forces" that Porter mentions in his conclusion that he believes are having a greater effect on wages and jobs for high school dropouts and American workers in general than illegal immigration?

7 What policies regarding illegal immigration and employment for high school dropouts might Porter favor based on his argument? What policies and proposals do you think he would oppose? Should he have included ideas about immigration and employment programs as part of his editorial? Why or why not?

Topics for Writing

1 Analyze the strengths and weaknesses of Porter's arguments in "Cost of Illegal Immigration May Be Less Than Meets the Eye."

2 Write an argument arguing what should be done about illegal immigration.

3 Write a research paper about the causes and effects of illegal immigration.

Connecting the Readings

Considering the arguments in David R. Francis' "Why the New Jobs Go to Immigrants" and Eduardo Porter's "Cost of Illegal Immigration May Be Less Than Meets the Eye," write an argument about the effects of illegal immigration on jobs and the economy in the U.S.

A LAKE OF SLEEPING CHILDREN

BY LUIS ALBERTO URREA

Luis Alberto Urrea (1955–) was born in Tijuana, Mexico, to an American mother and a Mexican father. He worked as a relief worker on the U.S.–Mexico border in the late 1980s and early 1990s. He wrote a series of articles about what he observed for the *San Diego Reader* and other newspapers and collected these and other essays about life on the border in *Across the Wire: Life and Hard Times on the Mexican Border* (1993) and *By the Lake of Sleeping Children: The Secret Life of the Mexican Border* (1996). "A Lake of Sleeping Children" is the title essay of the latter book, and like many of Urrea's essays, it depicts life among the poor who make their living picking garbage in the giant dumps of Tijuana. Here Urrea goes into detail describing the dumps where children pick through garbage alongside adults, and he explains the rules and procedures that govern their work. Urrea has also published two novels, a book of poetry, a collection of short stories, and a memoir about his father. He teaches creative writing as a professor of English at the University of Illinois-Chicago and keeps a blog on his Web site at www.luisurrea.com.

JUST WHEN YOU THINK YOU'VE SEEN IT all, Tijuana comes up with something so unexpected that you may not, at first, be sure what you're seeing. And then, when you do figure it out, likely as not you'll be stunned into silence and have to just stand there, staring. It's happened again: Tijuana threw me a curveball.

Since I am lately seen as some kind of expert on Tijuana's poverty, I often find myself leading mini-safaris to the southland's favorite representation of hell. You know the drill by now: we go to some shacks, maybe stop at an orphanage or two, gobble fish tacos and go to Tacos El Paisano, then gird ourselves for the Tijuana dump. Everybody loves the dump—cameras fly out of purses, and wanderers walk into the trash, furtively glancing at me over their shoulders so they can be sure they're not *really* in danger.

If there aren't a million gulls, some living-dead pit-bull mongrel bitches, or overwhelming stenches rising in eye-watering clouds, the tourists feel cheated and blue. But the sight of an open and festering wound, say, on a garbage-picker's hand . . . well! That sends them right over the moon. Pus Polaroids for the apocalypse scrapbook.

It seems to me that the gringos at the King Kong Group, those sultans of NAFTA trash operating the dump and siphoning easy millions off the efforts of these hungry *basureros*, could open an amusement park ride right here. Hieronymus Bosch Land: The Garden of Earthly Delights Ride in 3-D Stinkovision!

And there I was, leading a small safari yet again. And when I got to the lake of sleeping children, it took me a while to see what I was looking at. And of course I'm exaggerating: it wasn't nearly a lake; it was a pond, a lagoon. And the smell was as vivid as we'd all hoped. And later, when I tried to sleep, I knew the thing had seeped into me. It gets into you, you know—it gets in through the eyes. You find pieces of it drifting in your head as you sleep, and you're infected. I dreamed, later, of the children. They were waking up. They were sitting up. The filthy water was cascading out of their eye sockets. They opened their mouths to call my name, and black water jetted out, like fountains.

And, my God, *they wanted to play with me.*

Those of us who worked with the poor all those years in Baja saw so many astounding things that we could each make a full album of them. Things at once horrific and sly, with a kind of Salvador Dalí sense of demonic humor. Droll sights, and almost metaphoric in their richness.

Like the day when I came across the refrigerator in the Barrio of Shallow Graves (near the blinking TV antennas you can see from San Diego, ghostly over the middle ground of Tijuana). I opened the door—it wasn't connected to any power source, just sitting on the edge of a dirty alley, more Magritte than Dalí—and sitting on the middle shelf, in the middle of the middle shelf, on a small tin serving tray, was one curled, perfectly formed human turd. Presented tastefully, as if it were some kind of evil finger sandwich.

Like the woman who swore she was suffering from the evil eye. And when the *curandera* came to cast out the demons, a small viper fell out of the straw seat of the kitchen chair she was sitting on and writhed in the dirt beneath her. "I feel better," the woman said.

Like the man who lived in a washing-machine box. He didn't like sleeping on the dirt, so he carpeted the floor with cast-off avocados. He slept in a blackening swamp of guacamole.

Like the time Negra was given a pair of pigs as a gift. Now, Negra is quite a farmer; she has a knack for growing flowers in the trash, for bringing up various creatures and selling them—dogs, cats, crows, geese, pigs. The pigs in question were those cute little potbellied fellows, about the size of small cats when she first got them. When I first saw them in the corner of her house, I mistook them for puppies. I was startled to pick one up and have it shriek, "Greet! Greeeeet!"

It never occurred to the giver, nor to me, that Negra and all her neighbors had never heard of a mini-pig. In fact, the very concept of a mini-pig was so extraordinary as to be indecipherable to them. When I tried to explain what kind of pigs these were, she looked at me as if I were crazy.

Needless to say, the pigs refused to grow into fat giant porkers. Negra fed and fed them—overfed them, in fact. Gave them vitamins. And then, when it was obvious that an evil curse had been put on these shoats ("They stay babies no matter what we do!" Negra said), she called in the handy witch-doctor, who used up most of her family savings casting spell after spell, trying to break the powerful black hoodoo curse that kept these potential bacon factories chained to infancy.

Tony, a United pilot and book dealer, was in town for his mother's wedding. We had met through the book business and were starting a friendship. Because of the nature of the writing life, you travel about once a month, or more, and end up in all kinds of unlikely places. You're seldom home, or at least I have been seldom home, and a United pilot is a good guy to have for a friend, since he's able to show up in many of the cities you're visiting. It is always good to see a friendly face—or, I should say, a face you know. All the faces are usually friendly: everybody but the Tijuana police, Pat Buchanan, and the Nestor Militia likes an author. (One night I was standing around in the lobby of a hotel in San Francisco, chatting with a bunch of really pleasant British bankers. All of them gray-haired, vaguely weathered, wearing jackets and Oxford shirts and saying "Lovely" and "Quite right." It was only when the elevator doors were closing that I realized I'd been chatting with Pink Floyd.)

And Tony had read about the *dompe* and wanted to see it. I think he may have wanted to compare it with his mental pictures of Saigon. I think his nose was secretly longing for that weird tropical rot you get stuck in there: mangoes and mud and something dead and some sewage mixed in with flowers.

The dump was quiet.

Once a gaping Grand Canyon, it gradually filled with the endless glacier of trash until it rose, rose, swelling like a filling belly. The canyon filled and formed a flat plain, and the plain began to grow in bulldozed ramps, layers, sections, battlements. New American garbology affected the basic Mexican nature of the place. From a disorderly sprawl of *basura* to a kind of Tower of Babel of refuse.

Still, the poor Mexicans, transformed now by NAFTA into a kind of squadron of human tractors, made their way through the dump, lifting, sifting, bagging, hauling, carting, plucking, cutting, recycling. The original *dompe* rules, a set of ordinances that sprang up organically from the people who have to work the garbage, prevailed. A set of rules, by the way, that are extraordinarily humane and sane.

In the midsection of the *dompe*, the big trucks drop off their loads, and the towering orange tractors, roaring and farting and crushing the mounds with nasty steel wheels sporting *Mad Max* knobs and spikes, pass by with the seeming arrogance of a *T. rex* hunting party.

There, of course, the best stuff is to be found. The strong and the young work this dangerous zone. Anything is possible here. The freshest produce, the undented cans, the unbroken televisions, the bursting bags, the brightest stenches, the runniest of the rotted wads of refuse, the startling explosions of dead dogs, cats, horses, jump out of the tumbling comic books and soda cans and soggy Pampers like some strange carnal jack-in-the-box.

You sometimes have to drop down into the trash. There are gaps in the piles. And if you get down into the gap, into the *basura* fault line, you have a side view of strata. You might find a six-pack of Dole pineapple juice lodged in there like trilobites. It's part mining, part farming, part archaeology. (Some visitors to Negra's house declined water on a hot day, so she graciously broke out some cool cans of orange juice. "Don't tell them," she said, "I got those out of the trash with a shovel.")

When you do drop down in there, you put up a pole with a rag tied at the end. This alerts the tractor-pilots, who would never see you otherwise, to veer away from your hole and spare your life.

Rule #1: Watch for heavy machinery. Those who do not become mulch.

Rule #2: No children in the trash.

Rule #3: Women are equal to men in the trash.

Rule #4: Old-timers and kids are allowed to work the outer edges of the trash, where the tractors push things down the slopes and the slopes themselves act as sifters, rolling the best things out across the face of the new King Kong pyramid.

Rule #5: A special safe area is set up by the healthy workers. This area is set apart, avoided by the trucks and the tractors. It has inviolate boundaries, could almost be roped off. And everybody honors it. The occasional truckload is directed over there, or young men carry a few bags there and toss them in. In this special section, the disabled and the old are allowed to do their share. They can work all day, safely, aside, not competed with or jostled or in harm's way. But working hard, nonetheless.

There is no welfare in the dump, but there is work, care, sweat, and dignity.

The dump could be described as a series of arcs.

There is the small arc of a hill that hides the dump from view. This hill sits between the dump and the view of San Diego. Running along the other side of this hill is a curving road that leads down to barrios at one end and Tijuana at the other.

Behind this hill, the next arc: the narrow village that has sprung up. These homes are where the majority of the modern garbage-pickers dwell. And Tony pointed out that it seemed a pretty well-off community. Certainly better off than Vietnam had been. *(Yeah, no napalm—yet.)* After all, there are chickens and dogs, kites rattling in the power lines; there are power lines!

The next arc: the potter's field. At the top of a rise the crematorium, and in the middle distance the adult graves, and then at the lower end the babies. The graves with cribs for headstones, where parents bring their small daughters and sons and scratch out their final beds in the yellow dirt. *Niña, 3 días,* the crooked wooden crosses say. Or *María de los Angeles, Julio 3–Julio 5.* Or *Hijo. Un día.* Or the cribs, forlorn and somehow frightening, still vaguely cheery in their colors as they come apart in the elements, fade, break, slump. Playpens. And a board hammered onto the side that bears the sad, minuscule life history of yet another *niña* or *niño.*

Then the final arc, a sort of bull's-eye: the dump.

> **" The whole area was full of nameless, abandoned, forgotten, sleeping little corpses. Plastic flowers faded from blue to pink by the sun. A toy or two. Cribs. "**

We walked along, looking, and then we saw the lake and stopped and it started to lap at the edges of our minds, the dark water, the realization of what it was we were seeing, the strange shore of a land so far from home, so far from Tijuana even, that we could have been glimpsing the lip of the underworld. We could have been wading in the feces-scented waters of the River Styx.

Miraculously peculiar things abound in the dump, too. If you have an eye for the perversely beautiful, you can have a wonderful day looking around. I have seen tornados of garbage rising thirty feet in the air. I have seen piles of money tumbling in the landslide of shattering windows and dancing shoes. Three-legged dogs? All the time. Try a two-legged dog, running at full speed balanced on his two legs and zooming into the distance like a living rollerblade.

One day I thought I was seeing little geysers or volcanoes. But Negra pointed out that a subterranean trash fire had started. But it hadn't remained in the trash: it had crept into the graves. And the dry carcasses of these dear people were igniting underground. Sometimes, when it rained, the ground actually broke open and flames leapt up for a moment.

This day, somehow, there had been a flood.

Tony the pilot first saw it. One end of the dump had been closed off by the new trash mountain. A small valley had been sealed at one end, where the runoff would have originally formed a nostalgic little waterfall into the little Edward Abbey desert canyon and run on to the sea. Deer would have frolicked at its base; jackrabbits, coyotes, foxes, hawks, owls, rattlesnakes, tarantulas, three kinds of daisies, locoweed, gourds, raccoons, lizards, tortoises, skunks, wild goats, cottonwoods, berries, grapes, small fish, crawdads, butterflies, pottery shards, arrowheads, lions, morning glories, corn, Queen Anne's lace, would have flourished along this glittering little creek. Now, however, the northern arm of the landfill had cut off the vale and the small bed of the waterway. The canyon itself, as we know, was long gone. Kotex, Keds, Kalimán comic books, and ketchup bottles frolicked there now.

The slopes of this vale, small as it was, were crowded with the sad wooden crosses of the dead children's graves. The whole area was full of nameless, abandoned, forgotten, sleeping little corpses. Plastic flowers faded from blue to pink by the sun. A toy or two. Cribs.

From somewhere this flood had come. And the vale filled with water. And the water ate away at the slope, the clay and sand coming loose and the little crosses toppling and falling into the water to float around like model sailboats. And other crosses, those in the bottom of the vale, stood in the water at angles, reflecting on the still surface. It looked like a Pink Floyd album cover, actually.

And all around the edge of this lake (I always think of it as a *lake*, not a pond, a pool) was stinking mud, and stuck to the mud at every angle were more crosses. Broken crosses. Crooked crosses. Scattered crosses. Fallen crosses. Names on some, peering up at me from the lapping water's edge: Juan, Hija, Nena, Linda.

At one side, three vast tractor tires. They marched into the water in a row. The one farthest out we couldn't see into. The middle one was empty, save for some dark water and some blown trash. The one on the shore had become an impromptu outhouse: it was well loaded, the shit falling on crosses. Shit on the painstakingly hand-painted letters: *Diciembre 21–Dic. 25; Mi Hijo; Alfonsina, 10 días y 4 horas.*

And crowding the shore, gulls. Many, many gulls. Gulls fighting, pushing, raising their wings but not flying. Fat and noisy gulls. We stood there watching them, this white snowdrift of gulls. And they'd waddle to the water and heave themselves into it. Filthy water. Black at first, but with a clear blue overlay of sky. Floating with wads of paper and bits of wood and these gulls and the reflections and shadows of the crosses standing out there like mangroves in a swamp.

And the gulls dipped their heads into the water and brought up small tidbits and flung their heads back and gulped.

And the water revealed small brown and green and reddish objects. A kind of layer beneath the surface, like seaweed. Like the clouds of stuff in miso soup. Like algae, but not algae. And we looked: looked at the shore, where the ground was swelling with this noxious water and crumbling. And we looked in, deep, where the bed of the lake was mud, and the mud was drifting up, and the rotten soil was broken, and the coffins, the cardboard boxes, the pillowcases, the wooden crates, the winding sheets, were coming up. They were coming up. The children themselves were rising, expanding into the water, and the gulls were eating them.

The gulls had grown too fat to fly on the flesh of these sleeping children.

The sky above was yet another perfect southern California blue. The blue of a stained glass window. Clouds as bright as electric signs over our heads. And that same sky, spreading farther than any of us can know, shading different colors in different places, covered the garbage dump in Mexico City, the garbage dump in Manila, the garbage dumps in El Salvador, Guatemala, Zaire, Rwanda, Honduras, Mexicali, Matamoros, Juárez, Belize, Ho Chi Minh City, Patpong, Calcutta, Sarajevo, Tripoli, New Jersey, and Three Mile Island, Pennsylvania.

Proposition 187? A new Berlin Wall at the border? California citizen identification cards? Microchips injected into the backs of our hands, read by circling Landsat spy satellites? Two thousand Border Patrol guards augmented by T-1000 Terminator Droids armed with nuclear shotguns and laser-sighting eyeballs?

You think they're going to work? You think they can possibly work? Swim in this lake for a minute, then tell me you can keep these people on its shore. Jump in— you own it: it's Lake Nafta.

Journal and Discussion Questions

1 Why does Luis Alberto Urrea choose to reveal what he saw in the lake gradually, with some details shortly after the introduction and a full description near the end of the essay? Why does he imagine what he saw as "an amusement park ride" that he calls "Hieronymus Bosch Land: The Garden of Earthly Delights Ride in 3-D Stinkovision"?

2 Outline "A Lake of Sleeping Children." In addition to the lake itself, what other topics does Urrea write about? What do these different topics have to do with each other? What is the central idea of "A Lake of Sleeping Children"?

3 Why does Urrea discuss his "mini-safaris" into Tijuana that he leads for "gringo" tourists as a lead-in to his description of the garbage dumps and the lake? What does this decision tell you about his essay's intended audience? What points is Urrea making about the perspectives of tourists, especially in encountering poverty in a foreign country?

4 How does Urrea describe the *dompe* and the people who live and work there? What stories and images stand out? How do these images challenge or reinforce images and stereotypes that Americans hold about the poor and about Mexicans?

5 Urrea spends much of "A Lake of Sleeping Children" describing how the garbage pickers work in the *dompe* and the rules they work by. How are people able to make a living from garbage? What does Urrea's description of their work reveal about them?

6 Why does "A Lake of Sleeping Children" conclude with a discussion of proposed laws to discourage or prevent illegal immigration from Mexico into the U.S.? Why does Urrea name the lake of sleeping children *Lake Nafta*, after the controversial North America Free Trade Act (NAFTA)? What does his description of life and work in the giant Tijuana garbage dumps have to do with the political issues of free trade and illegal immigrants?

7 Why do you think Urrea focuses on the Tijuana garbage pickers instead of other ways that the poor in Tijuana survive? What does his description of the culture of the garbage pickers suggest about poverty in general? What might it suggest about the relationship between the economies of the U.S. and Mexico?

Topics for Writing

1 Analyze "A Lake of Sleeping Children." Discuss one of the larger issues that Luis Urrea is interested in, such as NAFTA, illegal immigration, the culture of the U.S.–Mexico border, the relationship between U.S. and Mexican cultures, or the life and work of the poor. You might research one of these issues to expand this assignment for a research paper.

2 "A Lake of Sleeping Children" challenges images of the poor as idle people who don't want to work. Conduct your own research for a paper about the working poor, their incentives to work or not to work, the work that the poor do and the compensation that they receive, and programs and proposals that address the problems of the working poor.

IMAGES OF CHILD LABOR

A photograph with a brief caption can make a powerful argument. A number of photographers have used their art to publicize the problems of child labor, young children working long hours, usually for small wages and often subject to many dangers. By taking pictures of children at work, photographers try to inform viewers of a hidden phenomenon, convince them that the situation is a problem, and move them to actively support solutions for this problem. Below are three photographs with brief captions of children at work in Mexico, Afghanistan, and the United States.

THE FIRST PHOTOGRAPH, TAKEN BY physician and human rights activist David Parker in 1996, depicts a young Mexican garbage picker like those described in Luis Alberto Urrea's "A Lake of Sleeping Children." The photograph and caption appear in Parker's 1997 book of photographs, *Stolen Dreams*, and his online collection of photographs, "Stolen Dreams: Gallery of the Harvard School of Public Health," which include Parker's photographs of children at work from around the world, including the U.S., India, Indonesia, Turkey, Thailand, Morocco, Bangladesh, and Nepal. Parker's online collection "Stolen Dreams" can be found at www.hsph.harvard.edu/gallery/intro.html.

The second photograph, from 2002, is part of a photo essay by freelance photographer Chien-Min Chung entitled "Afghan Child Labor" that is displayed on *The Digital Journalist* Web site at www.digitaljournalist.org. Born in Taiwan but raised in the United States, Chung earned a bachelor's degree in photography from New York University and worked as a photographer in China for the Associated Press before going to Afghanistan in 2002. He now works in Beijing, China, as a freelance photographer for several magazines,

including *Time*. More of Chung's photographs can be found at www.china-pix.com.

The third photograph was taken by Lewis W. Hine (1874–1940), whose photo essays of child labor helped persuade Americans to pass and enforce strict child labor laws. Hine was already known for his photo essay of immigrants on Ellis Island when he left teaching in 1908 to work as an investigative photographer for the National Child Labor Committee. For four years he traveled across the U.S., taking pictures of children, some as young as three years old, working in farms, factories, mines, and other workplaces. This photograph of a Jewish family and their neighbors sewing garters, along with Hine's notation about the picture, is taken from an online gallery of Hine's photographs, "The History of Place: Child Labor in America 1908–1912" at www.history-place.com/unitedstates/childlabor/. Hine began publishing photos like this in 1909 in a series of photo essays about child labor in America. In his long career, Hine also published pictures and photo essays of adult laborers, most famously a photo essay about the construction of the Empire State Building, and documented World War I refugees for the American Red Cross.

Garbage picker, Mexico 1996

Children hunt for wood scraps at a brick factory in Kabul, February 9, 2002

Journal and Discussion Questions

1 Describe each photograph. What details are most striking to you? Why?

2 Lewis W. Hine's photographs are often noted for the facial expressions of his subjects, especially in his child labor pictures. Describe the expressions of the subjects in these three photographs. What do their faces seem to reveal about them? How do the expressions contribute to the emotional impact and persuasiveness of the photograph?

3 If you analyze each photograph as an argument, what would you say is the thesis of each argument? How do the photographs argue that child labor is wrong or harmful? What similarities and differences do you find in how each photographer makes his case to the viewer?

4 Describe the emotions that each photograph tries to evoke and how these emotions help persuade readers.

5 Do you find these photographs persuasive? Why or why not? Do they try to persuade only by appealing to viewers' emotions, or is there an informational or logical element to their arguments? Explain. Which photograph do you find most persuasive? Why?

6 Why does Hine mention that the family and neighbors sewing garters were Jewish? Consider that many of the child laws to limit and protect working children at the time were written specifically to exclude immigrant children.

7 Look up information about the Harvard School of Public Health and the National Child Labor Committee. Why would they want to publish these photographs?

A Jewish family and neighbors working until late at night sewing garters. This happens several nights a week when there is plenty of work. The youngest work until 9 PM. The others until 11 PM or later. On the left is Mary, age 7, and 10-year-old Sam, and next to the mother is a 12-year-old boy. On the right are Sarah, age 7, next is her 11-year-old sister, 13-year-old brother. Father is out of work and also helps make garters. (New York City)

Topics for Writing

1 Compare and contrast the photographs of the Mexican and Afghan children and what they suggest about child labor in Mexico and Afghanistan.

2 Write an argument about child labor that could be accompanied by at least one of these photographs. Or go online to find other child labor photographs for your essay. Be sure to credit the photographer and publisher of the photographs.

3 Write an argumentative research paper about a child labor issue, past or present, in the U.S. or another region. What are the economic causes for child labor? What cultural beliefs support the use of child labor? What protections exist and are being proposed to protect children in the workforce?

Suggestions for Essays on WORK

1 Use Auden's distinction between work and labor to analyze the jobs described by at least two of the following writers: Hunsaker, Ehrenreich, Claitor, Adams, or the Army recruitment advertisement.

2 Analyze the problems of working conditions described by at least two of the following writers: Ehrenreich, Claitor, Brady, or Adams.

3 Discuss the general talents, abilities, and attitudes that a content and effective worker should have considering Auden, Reich, Hunsaker, and Ravitz's personal essay in the Army advertisement.

4 Drawing on Ramachandran, Hunsaker, and Reich, write an essay arguing how college students should prepare for the jobs of the future.

5 Compare the picture of the job market and working conditions for citizens of other countries described by at least three of the following: Reich, Francis, Porter, Urrea, and Parker's, Chung's and Hine's photographs.

6 Drawing on Urrea, and the three photographs of child labor, write an essay analyzing the problems of child labor and the reasons why children are employed as workers and discussing the best solutions to this problem.

Wealth and Property

WRITING TEACHERS OFTEN SAY THAT students need to have a sense of ownership of their writings to do their best work. Pride of ownership in one's writing can be a strong incentive to work carefully and independently on a paper from planning to proofreading. The same instructors, however, also teach and enforce rules against plagiarism, and their discussions of crediting sources and determining what is "common knowledge" suggest that writings may not come entirely from the writer. As a writer, you must recognize the intellectual property rights of the writers that you quote, paraphrase, and summarize. The penalties for not respecting the intellectual property rights of others, by plagiarizing a paper or downloading a music or video file illegally, are severe—a failing grade, possible expulsion from school, even being sued by a record or movie company. So even writing a class essay that (let's face it) probably has little market value is wrapped up in complex social concepts, attitudes, and laws about ownership and property.

The idea of owning your papers as intellectual property illustrates how much our ideas about wealth and property affect society and how complicated these ideas can be. Here are some of the questions about wealth and property that the selections in this chapter address, directly and indirectly, questions that you may want to address in your writings and class discussions.

- Is it good for an individual to desire wealth and property? Is it good for American society to be driven by desires for wealth, property, and consumer goods? Why or why not?

- How do wealth and ownership affect people individually and as a society? What are the positive effects of wealth and property? What are the negative effects?

- What responsibilities come with wealth? What privileges should the wealthy enjoy?

- What causes poverty? What responsibilities should individuals and society take toward the poor?

- How should society define *intellectual property*? How should society reward creators of intellectual property—of new knowledge, inventions, art, music, literature, business practices, etc.—and at the same time encourage the free exchange of ideas that creativity depends on?

- "The commons" is a term often used to refer to public or common property, including public lands and parks, inventions that are no longer covered by patents, books and music in the public domain, and other forms of shared physical and intellectual property. What benefits do the commons provide society? How should society decide what property should be included in the commons?

- Should person-to-person (P2P) file sharing of certain computer files, such as music, movies, computer games, and other computer programs be illegal? What should the government do about P2P file sharing? What, if anything, should colleges and universities do about students who engage in illegal P2P file sharing?

- What constitutes plagiarism? Why is plagiarism unethical? Should all forms of plagiarism be defined as academic dishonesty? What policies should colleges and universities have regarding plagiarism?

Invitations for Journal Writing

1 How has property, or the lack of it, affected your life? Be concrete and specific here by focusing on the effects of owning or not owning your own car, computer, cell phone, television, etc.; having or not having a credit card; having your own bedroom growing up or having to share a room with a brother or sister. How would your life be different if you had lived in different economic circumstances? How might you be different?

2 What are your economic and career goals? How do these goals relate to your other life goals? How are these goals related to your education goals?

3 What is your position about free downloading of music and illegal forms of person-to-person file sharing?

DEFINING AN OWNERSHIP SOCIETY

BY DAVID BOAZ

David Boaz (1953–) is the executive vice president of the Cato Institute, an influential think tank of scholars who develop conservative, libertarian public policy ideas to influence public opinion, news media, and government officials. The Cato Institute published "Defining an Ownership Society" with the original title of "Ownership Society: Responsibility, Liberty, Prosperity" during the 2004 presidential campaign. In this editorial, Boaz supports President George W. Bush's call for an "ownership society" in his 2004 campaign, a concept that would become a central theme of Bush's Inaugural Address in 2005. Although the phrase is most often associated with Bush's proposal to use some Social Security funds to create private retirement investment accounts, Boaz discusses broad implications of the concept of "ownership society" and the ways in which personal ownership benefit society as well as individuals. Boaz has written and edited over a dozen books, including *Libertarianism: A Primer* and *The Libertarian Reader*. He has published articles on political and economic issues in newspapers and magazines, including the *Wall Street Journal*, the *National Review*, the *New York Times*, the *Washington Post*, *Slate*, and the *Los Angeles Times*, and frequently appears on radio and television news programs. Before he joined the Cato Institute in 1981, Boaz was editor of *New Guard* magazine and executive director of the Council for a Competitive Economy. Many of his commentaries can be found at www.davidboaz.com/.

PRESIDENT BUSH SAYS HE WANTS AMERICA to be an "ownership society." What does that mean?

People have known for a long time that individuals take better care of things they own. Aristotle wrote, "What belongs in common to the most people is accorded the least care: they take thought for their own things above all, and less about things common, or only so much as falls to each individually." And we all observe that homeowners take better care of their houses than renters do. That's not because renters are bad people; it's just that you're more attentive to details when you stand to profit from your house's rising value or to suffer if it deteriorates.

Just as homeownership creates responsible homeowners, widespread ownership of other assets creates responsible citizens. People who are owners feel more dignity, more pride, and more confidence. They have a stronger stake, not just in their own property, but in their community and their society. Geoff Mulgan, a top aide to British prime minister Tony Blair, explains, "The left always tended to underestimate the importance of ownership, and how hard it is for a democracy that does not have widespread ownership of assets to be truly democratic. . . . To escape from poverty you need assets—assets which you can put to work. There is a good deal of historical evidence . . . as well as abundant contemporary evidence, that ownership tends to encourage self-esteem and healthy habits of behaviour, such as acting more for the long term, or taking education more seriously."

Former prime minister Margaret Thatcher had that goal in mind when she set out to privatize Great Britain's public housing. Her administration sold 1.5 million housing units to their occupants, transforming 1.5 million British families from tenants in public housing to proud homeowners. She thought the housing would be better maintained, but more importantly she thought that homeowners would become more responsible citizens and see themselves as having a real stake in the future and in the quality of life in their communities. And yes, she thought that homeowners would be more likely to vote for lower taxes and less regulation—policies that would tend to improve the country's economic performance—and thus for the Conservative Party, or for Labour Party candidates only when they renounced their traditional socialism.

Margaret Thatcher saw that private ownership allows people to profit from improving their property by building on it or otherwise making it more valuable. People can also profit by improving themselves, of course, through education and the development of good habits, as long as they are allowed to reap the profits that come from such improvement. There's not much point in improving your skills, for instance, if regulations will keep you from entering your chosen occupation or high taxes will take most of your higher income.

The United States today has the most widespread property ownership in history. This year an all-time high of 68.6 percent of American households own their own homes. Even more significantly, increasing numbers of Americans are becoming capitalists—people who own a share of productive businesses through stocks or mutual funds. About half of American households qualify as stockholding in some form. That's up from 32 percent in 1989 and only 19 percent in 1983, a remarkable change in just 20 years. That means almost half of Americans directly benefited from the enormous market appreciation between 1982 and 2000 and are prepared to see their wealth increase again when the current stock market slump ends.

But it also means that about half of Americans are not benefiting as owners from the growth of the American economy (though of course they still benefit as wage-earners and consumers). In general, those are the Americans below the average income. The best thing we could do to create an ownership society in America is to give more Americans an opportunity to invest in stocks, bonds, and mutual funds so that they too can become capitalists. And the way to do that is obvious.

Right now, every working American is required to send the government 12.4 percent of his or her income (up to about $88,000) via payroll taxes. That's $4,960 on a salary of $40,000 a year. But that money is not invested in real assets, and it doesn't belong to the wage-earner who paid it. It goes into the Social Security system, where it's used to pay benefits to current retirees. If we want to make every working American an investor—an owner of real assets, with control of his own retirement funds and a stake in the growth of the American economy—then we should let workers put their Social Security taxes into private retirement accounts, like IRAs or 401(k)s. Then, instead of hoping someday to receive a meager retirement income from a Social Security system that is headed for bankruptcy, American workers would own their own assets in accounts that couldn't be reduced by Congress.

President Bush has talked about such a reform since his first campaign, and his President's Commission to Strengthen Social Security proposed three ways to achieve this goal. If he chooses to make Social Security reform part of his reelection campaign, then we may see congressional action in 2005. Sen. John F. Kerry has pledged never to "privatize Social Security." He should be asked why he thinks working-class Americans should not be allowed to invest their savings in stocks and bonds, as his family has done so successfully.

Other reforms that could enhance the ownership society include school choice—which would give parents the power to choose the schools their children attend—and wider use of Health Savings Accounts, which transfer control over health care decisions from employers, insurance companies, and HMO gatekeepers to individual patients.

Advancing an ownership society can also improve environmental quality. People take care of things they own, and they're more likely to waste or damage things that are owned by no one in particular. That's why timber companies don't cut all the trees on their land and instead plant new trees to replace the ones they do cut down. They may be moved by a concern for the environment, but the future income from the property is also a powerful incentive. In the socialist countries of Eastern Europe, where the government controlled all property, there was no real owner to worry about the future value of property; conse-

quently, pollution and environmental destruction were far worse than in the West. Vacláv Klaus, prime minister of the Czech Republic, said in 1995, "The worst environmental damage occurs in countries without private property, markets, or prices."

Another benefit of private property ownership, not so clearly economic, is that it diffuses power. When the government owns all property, individuals have little protection from the whims of politicians. The institution of private property gives many individuals a place to call their own, a place where they are safe from depredation by others and by the state. This aspect of private property is captured in the axiom, "A man's home is his castle." Private property is essential for privacy and for freedom of the press. Try to imagine "freedom of the press" in a country where the government owns all the presses and all the paper.

The many benefits of an ownership society are not always intuitively obvious. The famous Harvard economist John Kenneth Galbraith wrote a bestselling book in 1958 called *The Affluent Society*, in which he discussed the phenomenon of "private opulence and public squalor"—that is, a society in which privately owned resources were generally clean, efficient, well-maintained, and improving in quality while public spaces were dirty, overcrowded, and unsafe—and concluded, oddly enough, that we ought to move more resources into the public sector. Thousands of college students were assigned to read *The Affluent Society*, and Galbraith's ideas played a major role in the vast expansion of government during the 1960s and 1970s.

But Galbraith and American politicians missed the real point of his observation. The more logical answer is that if privately owned resources are better maintained, then we should seek to expand private ownership.

Widespread ownership of capital assets has many benefits for society: It means that property is better maintained and long-term values are higher, including environmental quality. It means that people have a greater stake in their community and thus become better citizens. It protects people from the arbitrary power of government and gives them more freedom and more confidence as citizens. It produces prosperity because markets can't work without private property. Private retirement accounts and reduced taxes on investment would encourage more ownership for all Americans.

> **People take care of things they own, and they're more likely to waste or damage things that are owned by no one in particular.**

Journal and Discussion Questions

1 How does David Boaz define an *ownership society*? What does he argue are the main benefits of an ownership society? Do you agree with Boaz about these benefits? Why or why not?

2 What government policies does Boaz advocate? How would these policies benefit individuals and society, according to Boaz? Which of Boaz's arguments seem directed especially to liberal readers? Why?

3 Outline "Defining an Ownership Society." Why does Boaz begin his discussion with home ownership? How do Boaz's arguments about home ownership prepare readers for his arguments about investment funds and social policies? Would the editorial be less persuasive if it focused only on the policy proposals? Why or why not?

4 Where does Boaz mention opposing arguments to the positions he takes? What are these arguments? How does Boaz refute these arguments? What other arguments might a liberal raise against Boaz's argument?

5 The introductory paragraph of "Defining an Ownership Society" is brief, even terse: "President Bush says he wants America to be an 'ownership society.' What does that mean?" Is this an effective introduction? Why or why not?

6 Boaz quotes and paraphrases a number of sources, and they come from different political ideologies, different nations, and, with Aristotle, even different periods of history. How do these sources strengthen the authority of Boaz's argument? Why does Boaz cite liberal John Kenneth Galbraith in support of his argument?

7 What statistics does Boaz use to support his argument? What ideas do these statistics support in his editorial? Why doesn't Boaz cite the sources of these statistics? Where do you think Boaz found these statistics? If "Defining an Ownership Society" were a student paper or an academic article, would it need to cite the sources for these statistics? Why or why not?

Topics for Writing

1 Analyze the strengths and weaknesses of David Boaz's concept of "ownership society" and consider how well it might apply to issues other than those Boaz considers.

2 Research one of the issues that Boaz discusses in "Defining an Ownership Society," such as Social Security reform, Health Savings Accounts, or school choice, and argue your position on this issue.

3 Research liberal and conservative proposals to increase property ownership, especially for low-income families. Compare these approaches, what they have in common, how they differ, and the strengths and weaknesses of each approach.

DISOWNED BY THE OWNERSHIP SOCIETY

BY NAOMI KLEIN

Naomi Klein (1970–) is a Canadian journalist, a former Miliband Fellow at the London School of Economics, and a well-known activist against the globalization of the economy and consumer culture. She is the author of three books—*No Logo: No Space, No Choice, No Jobs*; *Fences and Windows: Dispatches from the Front Lines of the Globalization Debate*; and *The Shock Doctrine: The Rise of Disaster Capitalism*—as well as articles in U.S. and Canadian publications. She and her husband, Avi Lewis, also directed *The Take*, a documentary about workers in Buenos Aires, Argentina, who converted a closed automobile factory into a worker's cooperative. "Disowned by the Ownership Society," Klein's analysis and commentary on President George W. Bush's ownership society policies, appeared in the February 18, 2008, issue of *The Nation*, an influential liberal news magazine.

REMEMBER THE "OWNERSHIP SOCIETY," fixture of major George W. Bush addresses for the first four years of his presidency? "We're creating . . . an ownership society in this country, where more Americans than ever will be able to open up their door where they live and say, welcome to my house, welcome to my piece of property," Bush said in October 2004. Washington think-tanker Grover Norquist predicted that the ownership society would be Bush's greatest legacy, remembered "long after people can no longer pronounce or spell Fallujah." Yet in Bush's final State of the Union address, the once-ubiquitous phrase was conspicuously absent. And little wonder: rather than its proud father, Bush has turned out to be the ownership society's undertaker.

Well before the ownership society had a neat label, its creation was central to the success of the right-wing economic revolution around the world. The idea was simple: if working-class people owned a small piece of the market—a home mortgage, a stock portfolio, a private pension—they would cease to identify as workers and start to see themselves as owners, with the same interests as their bosses. That meant they could vote for politicians promising to improve stock performance rather than job conditions. Class consciousness would be a relic.

It was always tempting to dismiss the ownership society as an empty slogan—"hokum" as former Labor Secretary Robert Reich put it. But the ownership society was quite real. It was the answer to a roadblock long faced by politicians favoring policies to benefit the wealthy. The problem boiled down to this: people tend to vote their economic interests. Even in the wealthy United States, most people earn less than the average income. That means it is in the interest of the majority to vote for politicians promising to redistribute wealth from the top down.

So what to do? It was Margaret Thatcher who pioneered a solution. The effort centered on Britain's public housing, or council estates, which were filled with die-hard Labour Party supporters. In a bold move, Thatcher offered strong incentives to residents to buy their council estate flats at reduced rates (much as Bush did decades later by promoting subprime mortgages). Those who could afford it became homeowners while those who couldn't faced rents almost twice as high as before, leading to an explosion of homelessness.

As a political strategy, it worked: the renters continued to oppose Thatcher, but polls showed that more than half of the newly minted owners did indeed switch their party affiliation to the Tories. The key was a psychological shift: they now thought like owners, and owners tend to vote Tory. The ownership society as a political project was born.

Across the Atlantic, Reagan ushered in a range of policies that similarly convinced the public that class divisions no longer existed. In 1988 only 26 percent of Americans told pollsters that they lived in a society bifurcated into "haves" and "have-nots"—

71 percent rejected the whole idea of class. The real breakthrough, however, came in the 1990s, with the "democratization" of stock ownership, eventually leading to nearly half of American households owning stock. Stock watching became a national pastime, with tickers on TV screens becoming more common than weather forecasts. Main Street, we were told, had stormed the elite enclaves of Wall Street.

Once again, the shift was psychological. Stock ownership made up a relatively minor part of the average American's earnings, but in the era of frenetic downsizing and offshoring, this new class of amateur investor had a distinct shift in consciousness. Whenever a new round of layoffs was announced, sending another stock price soaring, many responded not by identifying with those who had lost their jobs, or by protesting the policies that had led to the layoffs, but by calling their brokers with instructions to buy.

Bush came to office determined to take these trends even further, to deliver Social Security accounts to Wall Street and target minority communities—traditionally out of the Republican Party's reach—for easy homeownership. "Under 50 percent of African Americans and Hispanic Americans own a home," Bush observed in 2002. "That's just too few." He called on Fannie Mae and the private sector "to unlock millions of dollars, to make it available for the purchase of a home"—an important reminder that subprime lenders were taking their cue straight from the top.

Today, the basic promises of the ownership society have been broken. First the dot-com bubble burst; then employees watched their stock-heavy pensions melt away with Enron and WorldCom. Now we have the subprime mortgage crisis, with more than 2 million homeowners facing foreclosure on their homes. Many are raiding their 401(k)s—their piece of the stock market—to pay their mortgage. Wall Street, meanwhile, has fallen out of love with Main Street. To avoid regulatory scrutiny, the new trend is away from publicly traded stocks and toward private equity. In November Nasdaq joined forces with several private banks, including Goldman Sachs, to form Portal Alliance, a private equity stock market open only to investors with assets upward of $100 million. In short order yesterday's ownership society has morphed into today's members-only society.

The mass eviction from the ownership society has profound political implications. According to a September Pew Research poll, 48 percent of Americans say they live in a society carved into haves and have-nots—nearly twice the number of 1988. Only 45 percent see themselves as part of the haves. In other words, we are seeing a return of the very class consciousness that the ownership society was supposed to erase. The free-market ideologues have lost an extremely potent psychological tool—and progressives have gained one. Now that John Edwards is out of the presidential race, the question is, will anyone dare to use it?

Journal and Discussion Questions

1 What claim is Naomi Klein arguing in "Disowned by the Ownership Society"? How does it differ from President Bush's claim?

2 Outline "Disowned by the Ownership Society." What points does Klein make with her history of the ownership society? Why does she discuss Margaret Thatcher, British Prime Minister in the 1980s? How does Klein's discussion of the past prepare readers for her arguments about ownership today?

3 What is the meaning of Klein's title, "Disowned by the Ownership Society"? Who has been "disowned"? How? Is this a good title? Why or why not?

4 Why do you think Robert B. Reich called Bush's ownership society "hokum"? Why does Klein refuse "to dismiss the ownership society as an empty slogan"?

5 What positions about wealth and property does Klein seem to support in "Disowned by the Ownership Society"? How do you know? Do you agree with these ideas? Why or why not?

6 What research did Klein do for her article? How did she use her sources to support and develop her ideas? Why are her comparisons of 1988 and 2008 polls important to the central argument of "Disowned by the Ownership Society"?

7 Why does Klein conclude "Disowned by the Ownership Society" by referring to John Edwards' withdrawal from the race for the 2008 Democratic presidential nomination? What "extremely potent psychological tool" have liberals gained, according to Klein? Why does she seem to doubt that they would use this weapon in the 2008 election?

Topics for Writing

1 Analyze Naomi Klein's "Disowned by the Ownership Society," focusing on the strengths and weaknesses of her argument.

2 Klein writes that "it is in the interest of the majority to vote for politicians promising to redistribute wealth from the top down." Identify one policy that does this and write an argument defending or opposing this policy.

3 Write a research paper about the social effects of a government policy, past or present, that encouraged the "democratization" of stock ownership, the expansion of home ownership, or the redistribution of wealth "from the top down."

Connecting the Readings

Compare David Boaz's "Defining an Ownership Society" and Naomi Klein's "Disowned by the Ownership Society," focusing on their arguments about the social effects of individual ownership of homes and stocks.

EDITORIAL CARTOONS

BY STEVE BREEN AND ROB ROGERS

Steve Breen (1970–) is a Pulitzer Prize–winning political cartoonist for the *San Diego Union-Tribune*. His cartoons are syndicated nationally and often appear in the *New York Times*, *USA Today*, *U.S. News & World Report*, and other news publications. Breen also draws the comic strip *Grand Avenue*. Rob Rogers is an award-winning political cartoonist with the *Pittsburgh Post-Gazette*. His cartoons are also nationally syndicated, often appearing in *Newsweek*, *USA Today*, the *Washington Post*, and the *New York Times*. Rogers' Web site can be found at www.robrogers.com/.

Breen's political cartoon was originally published in November 2006. Rogers' cartoon first appeared in January 2007. Breen's cartoon examines some of the effects that ownership of communication technology is having on American children. Rogers considers how Americans' buying habits are affecting employment in the U.S. and abroad.

Journal and Discussion Questions

1   What argument is Steve Breen making in his cartoon? What argument is Rob Rogers' cartoon making? State their positions in two thesis statements.

2   Describe each cartoon. What details stand out? How do Breen and Rogers use images to communicate their ideas and attitudes?

3   Describe what is funny about each cartoon. What attitude do Breen and Rogers have about the problem that they are commenting on? Does the humor of the cartoons diminish the seriousness and urgency of the problem for you? Why or why not?

4   Compare the ideas about property and ownership in the two cartoons. How does what Americans buy and own affect their lives and the lives of others in these two cartoons? Do you think Breen and Rogers share similar ideas and attitudes about American consumerism? Why or why not?

5   Why do Breen and Rogers see what Americans buy and own as a social problem, as an issue for their newspapers' editorial pages, rather than as a strictly personal matter? Do you agree? Why or why not?

6   Which cartoon makes the better argument and commentary, Breen's or Rogers'? Why?

Topics for Writing

1   Analyze and compare Steve Breen's and Rob Rogers' political cartoons as visual arguments about the effects of some aspects of consumerism and ownership on American society.

2   Referring to Breen's or Rogers' cartoon, write an editorial that agrees or disagrees with the cartoon's position.

3   Research the issue in Breen's or Rogers' cartoon, and write a research paper discussing the problem.

DEBT SMOTHERS YOUNG AMERICANS

BY CHRISTINE DUGAS

Christine Dugas is an award-winning personal finance reporter for the national daily newspaper *USA Today*. She is the author of many articles on insurance, banking, and retirement issues at *USA Today* as well as the book *Fiscal Fitness: A Guide to Shaping Up Your Finances for the Rest of Your Life*. Before her *USA Today* job, Dugas was a business reporter at the New York City daily newspaper *Newsday* for six years and a high school English teacher in Columbia and El Salvador. "Debt Smothers Young Americans" was the cover story of the February 11, 2001, issue of *USA Today*. Dugas explains, "I tried to write the story even handedly. I didn't want to paint today's young people as a generation of spend thrifts. Clearly, there are many reasons for the debt problems, including the high cost of college tuition and the general lack of financial education in public schools. It seemed important to create more awareness about the problem, before bankruptcy becomes the only option."

> **" They often live paycheck to paycheck, using credit cards and loans to finance restaurant meals, high-tech toys and new cars they couldn't otherwise afford . . ."**

AS A FRESHMAN AT THE UNIVERSITY of Houston in 1995, Jennifer Massey signed up for a credit card and got a free T-shirt. A year later, she had piled up about $20,000 in debt on 14 credit cards.

Paige Hall, 34, returned from her honeymoon in 1997 to find herself laid off from her job at an Atlanta mortgage company. She was out of work for four months. She and her husband, Kevin, soon were trying to figure out how to pay $18,200 in bills from their wedding, honeymoon and furnishings for their new home.

By the time Mistie Medendorp was 29, she had $10,000 in credit card debt and $12,000 in student loans.

Like no other generation, today's 18- to 35-year-olds have grown up with a culture of debt—a product of easy credit, a booming economy and expensive lifestyles. They often live paycheck to paycheck, using credit cards and loans to finance restaurant meals, high-tech toys and new cars they couldn't otherwise afford, according to market researchers, debt counselors and consumer advocates.

"Lenders are much more willing to take a risk on people under 25 than they were 15 years ago," says Nina Prikazsky, a vice president at student loan corporation Nellie Mae. "They will give out credit cards based on a college student's expected ability to repay the bills."

And young people are taking advantage of the offers. A study out today from Nellie Mae shows that the average credit card debt among undergraduate students soared by nearly $1,000 in the past two years. On average they owed $2,748 last year, up from $1,879 in 1998.

At a time when they could be setting aside money for a down payment on a home, many young people are mortgaging their financial future. Instead of getting a head start on saving for retirement, they are spending years digging themselves out of debt.

"I knew for a while that I had a problem. I wouldn't say I was living high on the hog, but when I wanted clothes, I'd buy a new outfit," says Medendorp, an Atlanta resident. "I'd go out to eat and charge it on my cards. There were a bunch of small expenses that added up and got out of control."

Massey, Hall and Medendorp each ended up seeking help from a local consumer credit counseling service. Hundreds of thousands more young people like them are turning to credit counseling or bankruptcy because they can no longer juggle their bills. In 1999 alone, an estimated 461,000 Americans younger than 35 sought protection from their creditors in bankruptcy, up from about 380,000 in 1991, according to Harvard Law School professor Elizabeth Warren, principal researcher in a national survey of debtors who filed for bankruptcy.

At the Consumer Credit Counseling Service of Greater Denver, more than half of all the clients are 18 to 35 years old, says Darrin Sandoval, director of operations. On average, they have 30% more debt than all other age groups, he says.

"By the time they begin to settle into a suburban lifestyle, they are barely able to meet their debt obligations," says Sandoval. "If there is a job loss, an unexpected medical expense, or the birth of a child, they supplement their income with credit cards. Soon they are being financially crushed."

DEBT HEADS. Unlike the baby boom generation—raised by Depression-era parents—young Americans today are often unfazed by the amount of debt they carry. "This generation has lived through a time when everything was on the upswing," says J. Walker Smith, president of Yankelovich Partners, a market research firm. "There is no sense of worry about being overleveraged. It all seems to work out."

Kevin Jackson, a 32-year-old software engineer in Denver, has about $8,000 in credit card debt and a $20,000 home equity loan. He doesn't believe he has a debt problem, though his goal is to reduce his credit card balance to $2,000.

"You learn to live with a certain amount of debt," he says. "It's a means to an end. There is something to be said for paying for everything and something to be said for enjoying life, as long as you do it responsibly."

Unfortunately, enjoying life can be expensive, especially for many young Americans who feel it's essential to have the latest high-tech products and services, such as a cellphone, pager, voice mail, a computer with a second phone line or a DSL connection, an Internet Service Provider and a Palm Pilot.

Jackson just bought a DVD player and a big-screen TV. "I try to control costs," he says. "I easily could have spent $5,000 on the TV, but instead I paid $2,000 and I got a one-year, no-interest deal."

Movies, TV shows and advertising only reinforce the idea that young people are entitled to have an affluent lifestyle. "We're encouraged to overspend," says Jason Anthony, 31, co-author of *Debt-free by 30*, a book he wrote with a friend after they found themselves drowning in debt. "We all see shows like *Melrose Place* and *Beverly Hills 90210*. It creates tremendous pressure to keep up. I'm one of the few persons who think a recession will be good for my generation. Our expectations are so elevated. In the frenzy to keep up, we've gotten into financial trouble."

THE PERILS OF PLASTIC. Consumers like Massey, who get bogged down in credit card debt before they even graduate from college, learn the hard way about managing money. Now 24 and married, Massey has a good job in marketing. She has cut up her credit cards and is gradually repaying her debts. But there have been consequences: She had to explain to her boss that without a credit card, she cannot travel for work if it involves renting a car or booking a hotel reservation on her own. She had to tell her husband about her debt problems before they were married.

"I lack confidence now," Massey says. "I'm hard on myself because of my mistakes. But I blame the credit card companies and the university for allowing them to promote the cards on campus without educating students about credit."

The percentage of undergraduate college students with a credit card jumped from 67% in 1998 to 78% last year, according to the Nellie Mae study. And many of them are filling their wallets with cards. Last year, 32% said they had four or more cards, up from 27% two years earlier.

Although graduate students have an even bigger appetite for credit, they are starting to show some signs of restraint. Their average debt declined slightly from $4,925 in 1998 to $4,776 last year, Nellie Mae says.

Many young people will be saddled with credit card debts for years, experts say. Among all age groups, credit card holders younger than 35 are the least likely to pay their bills in full each month, according to Robert Manning, author of *Credit Card Nation*.

Though credit cards and uncontrolled spending are a combustible combination, many young people are pushed to the financial edge by the staggering cost of college. The average annual tuition at a four-year private university jumped to $16,332 last year, from $7,207 in 1980, according to the College Board. Between 1991 and 2000, the average student loan burden among households under 35 increased nearly 142% to $15,700, according to an exclusive analysis of the finances of 18- to 34-year-olds for *USA Today* by Claritas, a San Diego-based market research firm.

And those who choose to go on and get a graduate degree pay an even higher price. Another Nellie Mae study found that those who borrow for graduate work, and specifically those in expensive professional programs in law and medicine, are likely to have unusually high debt burdens that are not always offset by comparably high salaries.

Karen Mann didn't need a survey to come to that conclusion. Her husband, Michael, is about to start his career as an orthopedic surgeon after racking up $400,000 in loans during four years of undergraduate school, four years of medical school, one year in an MBA program and a five-year residency program. During his residency and a subsequent fellowship, they have deferred payments and some of the interest on his student loans. But soon they'll have to begin paying them off.

The interest payment alone is now $20,000 a year.

The Manns are not extravagant. "I've always saved, and I have a budget," says Karen, 31. "I'd love to buy a house, but there's no way. We haven't been able to afford kids yet. The loans are so awesome that you do get crazy."

PAYING FOR EVERYTHING WITH CASH. The Manns are not alone in having to defer important goals because of heavy debt loads. Medendorp, a social worker in Decatur, Ga., now lives on a budget and is diligently paying her bills with the help of a Consumer Credit Counseling Service debt-management plan. She pays for everything with cash. There are many things she'd like to do but can't afford, like having laser eye surgery, going back to school and buying a home.

"When you get in a tar pit, forget about buying a home," says author Anthony. "Instead of saving for a down payment, you're making credit card payments."

At a time when the overall U.S. homeownership rate has risen to historic highs, young Americans are less likely than people their age 10 years ago to buy a home. The homeownership rate for heads of households younger than 35 has declined from 41.2% in 1982 to 39.7% in 1999, according to the U.S. Census Bureau. And if they own a home, young people tend to make smaller down payments or borrow against what equity they have. As a result, the average amount of equity accumulated by homeowners younger than 35 has shrunk to about $49,200 in 1999, from $57,100 10 years earlier, according to a study from the Consumer Federation of America.

Although they may have a lot of debt, they also are very focused on saving and investing, especially through 401(k)-type retirement accounts.

"For middle-income Americans, the most important form of private savings is home equity," says Stephen Brobeck, executive director of the Consumer Federation of America. "It's essential to have paid off a mortgage by retirement so that living expenses are lower and one has an asset that can be borrowed on or sold if necessary."

By almost every measure, young people are falling behind. Between 1995 and 1998, the median net worth of families rose for all age groups except for the under-35 group. Their median net worth declined from $12,700 to $9,000, according to the Federal Reserve.

That is not to say that young people today are slackers and deadbeats, as they have sometimes been characterized. They work hard and often make good incomes. Although they may have a lot of debt, they also are very focused on saving and investing, especially through 401(k)-type retirement accounts. Jackson, for example, contributes the maximum to his 401(k) plan.

"They want to protect themselves against future uncertainty," Smith says. "They absolutely don't expect that Social Security will be around for them."

But it's hard to save money if you are head over heels in debt. Massey earns $32,000 a year. With her husband, their annual income is more than $100,000. "But we're still broke trying to pay our bills," she says.

Journal and Discussion Questions

1 What debt problems does Christine Dugas describe in "Debt Smothers Young Americans"? What are the causes of young adults' heavy debt? What effects does this debt have on their lives?

2 *USA Today* uses headings to divide Dugas' story into four parts but does not set off the introduction and conclusion from the rest of the story. Outline "Debt Smothers Young Americans." How does Dugas introduce and conclude her story? How does Dugas order her discussion of the different causes and effects of young adults' debt problem? Why do you think she chose this organization? What do the headings have to do with the discussion in each section?

3 How does Dugas compare the attitudes of college students today about acquiring debt to those of their parents' generation? What does this comparison contribute to Dugas' overall argument?

4 What sources does Dugas use to construct her portrait of young adults' debt problems? What does each source contribute to this picture? How do the charts support or add to Dugas' text?

5 How relevant is Dugas' 2001 news story today? What is similar about young Americans' debt situation today? How has the debt situation for college students and young adults changed since "Debt Smothers Young Americans" first appeared?

6 Do you agree with Dugas' portrait of young Americans and debt? Why or why not?

7 What preventative measures can college students take to avoid or minimize the debt problems described by Dugas? What actions can young adults take when they have taken on too much debt? What can high schools and colleges do to address this problem?

Topics for Writing

1 Analyze Christine Dugas' "Debt Smothers Young Americans," focusing on how Dugas weighs the different causes for the rising debt situation and considers possible solutions. Do you agree with Dugas' analysis of the problem? Why or why not?

2 Write an editorial for your campus newspaper arguing what students and/or your school should do to address the problem of rising student debt.

3 Write a research paper discussing whether or not the debt situation for young Americans has changed since Dugas' story in 2001.

IDENTIFYING PRODUCTS WITH BUYERS IN MAGAZINE ADVERTISEMENTS:
Rolex, John Deere, and Fair Instant Coffee

Like many advertisements, the three following advertisements, Rolex watches, John Deere equipment, and Fair Instant coffee, persuade largely by identifying the product with the potential buyer. The product says something to him or herself and to others about the person who owns it or uses it. The advertiser tries to create an emotional relationship between the consumer and the product, often along with logical reasons for buying the product. The advertisements that follow identify the product and the consumer in different ways. The John Deere advertisement appeared in the June/July 2007 issue of *Mother Earth News*, a "green" magazine with a strong environmentalist ethic. The ads for Rolex watches and for Fair Instant coffee were published in various magazines in 2008.

OYSTER PERPETUAL LADY-DATEJUST
PERFECTLY ACCESSORISED WITH PURPLE SEA FAN.

Knowing when to quit.
That's the hard part.

C'mon, admit it. Deep down, you can't get enough. Just look at the place. It's as obvious as the reason you want John Deere equipment and implements. Whether it's hauling plants, tending paddocks or simply mowing acre upon acre, John Deere gets the job done. And gets it done right. Anything else would feel like a compromise. And what's the fun in that? Your Land is Your World.

www.JohnDeere.com   Nothing Runs Like A Deere™   JOHN DEERE

Coffee with a bigger heart.

Every cup of Fair Instant coffee has real heart. Not only Fairtrade at a Fair Price, but also 20p from every jar goes to Save the Children education projects in coffee growing regions. So now every time you make a cup of coffee you can make a real difference. Available now.

FFi FAIR INSTANT

Also in GOLD Freeze Dried

FAIR TRADE, FAIR PRICE, FAIR INSTANT.

www.fair-instant.co.uk

Journal and Discussion Questions

1 Describe each advertisement. What reasons does each ad give readers for buying its product? How are the pictures in the ads related to the ads' verbal arguments?

2 What kind of person wears a Rolex watch, uses John Deere equipment, or drinks Fair Instant coffee, as stated and implied in each ad? How does each ad flatter consumers? How is the John Deere ad designed to appeal to the readers of *Mother Earth News*? What magazines might publish the Rolex and Fair Instant coffee ads? Why?

3 What does the picture of a model floating in a designer dress at the bottom of the ocean say about Rolex watches and the people who buy them? Why does the advertiser rely almost entirely on the image of the watch and the model with very few words about the watch? Why isn't the picture of the watch bigger? Why is the watch pictured alone against a black background?

4 Why is the photograph in the John Deere ad round? What objects are highlighted in this photo? How does the photo connect to the slogan that ends the text of the ad, "Your Land is Your World"? What meaning (or meanings) does this slogan suggest?

5 How does the Fair Instant coffee advertisement explain and develop the meaning of its slogan, "Coffee with a Bigger Heart"? How does the product's association with the Fair Trade movement and Save the Children education programs help sell Fair Instant coffee?

6 What emotions does each ad try to evoke about its product? How?

Topics for Writing

1 Compare the advertisements for Rolex watches, John Deere, and Fair Instant coffee, focusing on how each advertisement creates an identification between the product and the consumer and how the advertiser connects the product with buyers' desired images of themselves. What does owning or buying the product say about the consumer, according to the ads?

2 Analyze an advertisement or commercial for another product, discussing how the ad tries to establish a relationship between the product and the buyer and how it appeals to the consumer's self-image and aspirations.

KEYNOTE SPEECH AT THE PROGRESS AND FREEDOM FOUNDATION CONFERENCE

BY LAMAR SMITH

Lamar Smith (1947–) has been the Congressional Representative of the 21st District of Texas since 1986. A Republican and an attorney, Smith is a member of the House Judiciary Committee and former chairman of that committee's Subcommittee on Courts, the Internet, and Intellectual Property. Smith has made several political speeches, like this one, on intellectual property law and illegal file sharing, and he sponsored a bill in April 2006 that would expand copyright protection of computer software, a proposal that was opposed by "digital rights" supporters who want to encourage more sharing of software and information. This speech was given at George Mason University on June 10, 2003, at a conference of the Progress and Freedom Foundation, a think tank of scholars that, as Smith mentions, tries to influence and "educate elected officials, opinion leaders and the public about issues associated with technological change." Congressman Smith has a copy of this speech on his Web site, http://lamarsmith.house.gov.

TODAY, I'D LIKE TO DO SOMETHING I DON'T do very often, and that is to speak from a written text. It is said of William F. Buckley that he "pays the audience the ultimate tribute of a prepared talk." I'd like to do the same as we address the issues of this conference, many of which I have a special interest in as chairman of the House Judiciary Intellectual Property Subcommittee.

There is a good reason why those who wrote the Constitution embraced the concept of intellectual property protection. The Founding Fathers realized that if creators cannot gain from their creations, they won't bother to create.

Article One, Section Eight, of the Constitution reads "The Congress shall have Power . . . To promote the Progress of Science and useful Arts, by securing for limited Times to Authors and Inventors the exclusive Right to their respective Writings and Discoveries."

Intellectual property laws allow people to hold a particular bundle of rights pertaining to their creativity, innovation, and in some cases, brilliance, in a similar way that they own physical property. Through these rights, the IP owner is rewarded in the market-

place, and this encourages further creativity, innovation and brilliance. That benefits us all.

Some believe that once something is created, it should be released into the public arena for anyone to use. At the other end of the spectrum, others believe that the creator should retain exclusive control over how their creation is used, forever.

Of course, these views are extreme, but they illustrate the range of different bundles of rights attached to various kinds of intellectual property.

Intellectual property is essential to a thriving market. And a thriving market encourages the creation of intellectual property. One cannot function without the other.

In looking for ways to protect both intellectual property and free exchange in the marketplace, there are currently a number of critical issues Congress must consider: piracy, the broadcast flag, patent rights, counterfeiting in the software industry, and a standard of "fair use" that protects consumer rights.

For instance, some believe the profitability of intellectual property can be protected using extended private licensing strategies. But we must be careful that such licensing agreements do not improperly

> **"Depending on the circumstances, students engaged in illegal file sharing should face penalties that include a loss of university-supported computer privileges or suspension."**

assert intellectual property and thus have a negative effect on the markets or consumer interests.

One thing I hope all of us can agree on is that there is no way to completely protect an intellectual property right. Look at what is happening on our university campuses. University students illegally download music, sometimes on publicly supported computers.

When encouraged to exercise disciplinary measures, too many university administrators react with relative indifference: kids will be kids, they say. Yet these same university administrators pursue research and development projects as champions of a strong patent law. It's a curious inconsistency.

A similar dynamic applies to a major, high tech firm located in the state of Washington that produces a product called Windows. It's certainly an understatement to say this company is a holder of intellectual property rights. That's like saying Babe Ruth hit a baseball.

To some, there appears to be a major difference between *intellectual* property rights and *physical* property rights.

For example, some employees of this same company are aligned with anti-private property rights movements in the Northwest, such as those fighting landowners over forest use and endangered species.

This company has invoked intellectual property rights to defend itself against a Department of Justice antitrust prosecution, yet often opposes the rights of private property owners, especially landowners.

I use these examples not to single out academia or private companies but to illustrate the complexity and scope of the issues we discuss today, and the fact that intellectual property rights are not always crystal clear.

Intellectual property represents the single largest sector of the economy, employing more than 4 million Americans. It is vital that we encourage its continued growth and protection.

The rise of the Internet and new digital media has changed how we live and do business. One of the advantages of digital formats is that they offer extremely high quality reproduction of audio and video. A major disadvantage is that digital formats make the works very susceptible to piracy since every digital copy offers a perfect reproduction.

The problem is only exacerbated by Peer-to-Peer file-sharing networks, which were the focus of the

first hearing held by my Subcommittee. The hearing addressed file sharing on university campuses.

The ready access to file-sharing sites and the ease with which files can be downloaded by broadband connections has emboldened American university students to engage in piracy. This is a serious problem that seeks to undermine the protections provided by the Constitution.

While Peer-to-Peer technology has many benefits, it also permits the widespread and massive distribution of digital music, movies, and software files, which often results in copyright infringement. Industry officials estimate that there are billions of illegal file downloads every week.

Some staggering statistics illustrate the magnitude of the problem. Research of Fast Track, a Peer-to-Peer file-sharing service, showed that 16% of all the files available at any given moment are located at Internet Provider addresses managed by U.S. educational institutions. It's unlikely that this amount of file-sharing activity is in furtherance of class assignments.

I've seen the millions of file downloads take place. During a 9:30 a.m. demonstration last year, the KaZaa website already had over 5 million users logged in. The result of these transactions is lost sales to businesses and lost royalties to artists and copyright owners.

So what do we do about illegal file sharing, particularly on university campuses? Given the recent news reports, there's been a shift in the seriousness of the problem. Harvard University policy now suspends students for a second violation. The Naval Academy recently disciplined 92 Midshipmen. Both cases offer good signs of progress.

I hope to see additional progress from a committee examining file sharing on campuses, which is headed by Pennsylvania State University President Graham Spanier.

This process begins with education and ends with disciplinary action. Depending on the circumstances, students engaged in illegal file sharing should face penalties that include a loss of university-supported computer privileges or suspension.

Generally, as a solution to illegal file sharing, I am skeptical of government mandates on the technology industry. They are hard to write, easy to ignore and hard to repeal if unintended consequences harm the marketplace. Until evidence shows otherwise, I believe existing copyright law is adequate. It simply needs to be enforced.

Keep in mind that exports and foreign sales of U.S. copyrighted products total $100 billion. Copyrighted works are a result of American creativity. When properly commercialized, these works lead to jobs, profits, and a more enjoyable quality of life.

Of course in looking at piracy, we have to tackle the problem not only of stealing music over the Internet but also of manufacturing illegal CD's and selling them for profit. This was the subject of another hearing held by my Subcommittee this year.

Physical piracy is a serious problem not only here in the United States, but abroad. This fact has plagued the software industry in recent years. Globally, four out of 10 software programs—or 40 percent—are pirated.

If we could lower the piracy rate by just 10% around the world, the information technology industry would see an additional $400 billion in economic growth.

The software industry is under siege by professional pirates primarily due to the counterfeiting of authentication features on software, like the certificates of authenticity, or COAs. Thieves steal or counterfeit these COAs and affix them to pirated products to deceive consumers into thinking they are getting the real product.

The worldwide losses suffered by American copyright-based industries due to piracy are enormous: $9 billion in 56 countries. Half of those losses affected the music industry. In fact, there was one pirated music product for every three sold worldwide.

In 2000, the annual seizure of pirated discs for the Motion Picture Association was 1.9 billion units. By the close of 2002, it was up to 6.1 billion units. In just two years, the annual piracy rate had increased three times.

In some places, such as Asia, and parts of the former Soviet Union, pirated software accounts for nearly 90 percent of the software used. At the close of 2002, seizures of pirated Microsoft products alone exceeded $1.7 billion.

A recent article in *Time Europe* noted that an average drug dealer pays $47,000 for a kilo of cocaine with an estimated street value of $94,000, which yields a 100% profit. For that same $47,000 investment, a pirate could buy or produce 1,500 pirated copies of Microsoft's "Office 2000, Professional" software and resell it for a profit of 900%.

> **Intellectual property represents the single largest sector of the economy, employing more than 4 million Americans. It is vital that we encourage its continued growth and protection.**

In other words, the overhead for pirating copyrighted material relative to other illegal economic activities is minimal, the profits are exceptional, and the relative risk level of attracting the attention of law enforcement officials is low. Low risk and high profit is how criminals view piracy.

In the end, it doesn't matter whether the pirates are individuals or crime organizations, one thing is clear: their activity is rising and it must be addressed.

On one level, my Subcommittee seeks to ensure that new technologies designed to prevent piracy do not limit the public's ability to make fair use of copyrighted works. On another level, we continue our efforts to support private industry efforts to curb piracy of their products.

We are in the midst of a transition to digital television. As early as 2006, all broadcasts must be aired in digital format. This presents opportunities for American consumers, businesses, and copyright owners. As with many technological advances, the DTV transition has been frustrated by both technological and legal hurdles.

There is a great danger of massive piracy of unprotected broadcasts once the transition to DTV is complete. Pirates can easily copy and redistribute millions of digital files in a matter of seconds. In the absence of protection against unauthorized redistribution, it is unlikely that content owners will make high-value programming available to broadcasters.

The broadcast flag is one solution strongly supported by copyright owners and broadcasters. It is a sequence of digital bits embedded in a television program that signals that the program must be protected from unauthorized redistribution.

Last August, the Federal Communications Commission adopted a notice of proposed rulemaking on digital broadcast copy protection. My Subcommittee has great interest in the FCC's action because the agency might issue rules that impact the Copyright Act and therefore involve my Subcommittee's jurisdiction.

I know controversy continues over what the broadcast flag will and will not do. And whether it will have an adverse affect on the ability of consumers to make "fair use" of copyrighted broadcast television.

We know fair use is a defense that may limit any of the copyright owner's exclusive rights. The Copyright Act states that fair use of a copyrighted work for purposes such as criticism, comment, news reporting, teaching, scholarship, or research does not constitute infringement. Fair use is determined on a case-by-case basis.

For example, in Sony Corp. v. Universal City Studios, the Supreme Court held that the practice of taping free television broadcasting for later viewing was a fair use.

It is important that the transition to DTV and any implementation of rules requiring the use of the broadcast flag technology does not have an adverse affect on how consumers may legitimately use lawfully acquired entertainment products.

The wisdom of our Country's founders regarding intellectual property issues still rings true today. The authors of the Constitution understood that the incentive to create would greatly benefit the public. And

underlying that wisdom was an appreciation of the marketplace. Intellectual property only has meaning in the context of the market.

And more than two centuries after the fact, our lives have been enriched as a result.

Whether it be a bicycle or a baseball, an old Betamax or my Blackberry, intellectual property has infused American life. These products—along with millions of others—are the reason why we are here today.

I want to thank the Progress and Freedom Foundation and George Mason University for inviting me to this luncheon. Your mission to educate elected officials, opinion leaders and the public about issues associated with technological change goes back to the first days of the Internet Revolution. Thank you for all you have done.

Journal and Discussion Questions

1 What thesis is Lamar Smith arguing in this speech? What are the main reasons that he gives to support this thesis? Which reasons do you find most persuasive? Why? Which reasons are least persuasive? Why?

2 Write an outline of Smith's speech. How many major sections make up the body of Smith's argument? Why do you think Smith chose this order for these sections?

3 What statistical evidence does Smith provide? How do these statistics support his reasons? Why does Smith rely so heavily on statistical evidence?

4 Smith did not give his speech a formal title. What might be a good title for this speech? What revisions in his introduction and other parts of his speech would you recommend if he were revising this speech into a guest editorial for a newspaper?

5 Smith cites several sources in his speech, including the U.S. Constitution. Locate each source. What purpose does each source have in persuading Smith's listeners?

6 Smith identifies his position as a moderate one between two extremes. What are the two extreme positions? What is moderate about Smith's position? What is persuasive about representing his position as a moderate position between two extreme positions?

7 Where does Smith mention opposing arguments to his positions? How does he answer these objections?

Topics for Writing

1 Write an editorial for a campus newspaper responding to Lamar Smith's argument to crack down on college students and administrators to reduce illegal file sharing on college and university campuses.

2 Research policies governing students' file sharing at several college and university campuses, such as those mentioned in Smith's speech. Evaluate the fairness and effectiveness of your school's policies or compose a new policy proposal for your campus.

3 Research the hearings mentioned by Smith conducted by the Courts, the Internet, and Intellectual Property Subcommittee of the U.S. House of Representatives Judiciary Committee in government documents and news reports. Write a research paper arguing how government should deal with one of the five "critical issues" that Smith names on page 344.

SOME LIKE IT HOT

BY LAWRENCE LESSIG

Lawrence Lessig (1961–) is a law professor at Stanford Law School and founder of Stanford's Center for Internet and Society. He is a prominent advocate for changes in copyright, piracy, and intellectual property laws, with numerous technical and popular articles and books on this subject, including *The Future of Ideas* and *Other Laws of Cyberspace*. "Some Like It Hot" is an excerpt from his 2004 book, *Free Culture: How Big Media Uses Technology and the Law to Lock Down Culture and Control Creativity*. It is a controversial argument to significantly reduce copyright restrictions on person-to-person file sharing and other protections of intellectual property in order to promote sharing, creativity, and common property. This excerpt was published as an article in *Wired Magazine*, a popular magazine for readers who are interested in computer technologies and the Internet and are particularly sympathetic to arguments against restrictions in their use. In "Some Like It Hot," Lessig describes the legal history of copyright law and piracy in the U.S. entertainment industry to influence his readers' views about intellectual property, piracy, and file sharing. Lessig keeps a blog at www.lessig.org/blog/.

IF PIRACY MEANS USING THE CREATIVE property of others without their permission, then the history of the content industry is a history of piracy. Every important sector of big media today—film, music, radio, and cable TV—was born of a kind of piracy. The consistent story is how each generation welcomes the pirates from the last. Each generation—until now.

The Hollywood film industry was built by fleeing pirates. Creators and directors migrated from the East Coast to California in the early 20th century in part to escape controls that film patents granted the inventor Thomas Edison. These controls were exercised through the Motion Pictures Patents Company, a monopoly "trust" based on Edison's creative property and formed to vigorously protect his patent rights.

California was remote enough from Edison's reach that filmmakers like Fox and Paramount could move there and, without fear of the law, pirate his inventions. Hollywood grew quickly, and enforcement of federal law eventually spread west. But because patents granted their holders a truly "limited" monopoly of just 17 years (at that time), the patents had expired by the time enough federal marshals appeared. A new industry had been founded, in part from the piracy of Edison's creative property.

Meanwhile, the record industry grew out of another kind of piracy. At the time that Edison and Henri Fourneaux invented machines for reproducing music (Edison the phonograph; Fourneaux the player piano), the law gave composers the exclusive right to control copies and public performances of their music. Thus, in 1900, if I wanted a copy of Phil Russel's 1899 hit, "Happy Mose," the law said I would have to pay for the right to get a copy of the score, and I would also have to pay for the right to perform it publicly.

But what if I wanted to record "Happy Mose" using Edison's phonograph or Fourneaux's player piano? Here the law stumbled. If I simply sang the piece into a recording device in my home, it wasn't clear that I owed the composer anything. And more important, it wasn't clear whether I owed the composer anything if I then made copies of those recordings. Because of this gap in the law, I could effectively use someone else's song without paying the composer anything. The composers (and publishers) were none too happy about this capacity to pirate.

In 1909, Congress closed the gap in favor of the composer and the recording artist, amending copyright law to make sure that composers would be paid for "mechanical reproductions" of their music. But rather than simply granting the composer complete control over the right to make such reproductions, Congress gave recording artists a right to record the music, at a price set by Congress, after the composer allowed it to be recorded once. This is the part of copyright law that makes cover songs possible. Once a composer authorizes a recording of his song, others

> **“ Many kinds of piracy are useful and productive, either to create new content or foster new ways of doing business. Neither our tradition, nor any tradition, has ever banned all piracy. ”**

are free to record the same song, so long as they pay the original composer a fee set by the law. So, by limiting musicians' rights—by partially pirating their creative work—record producers and the public benefit.

A similar story can be told about radio. When a station plays a composer's work on the air, that constitutes a "public performance." Copyright law gives the composer (or copyright holder) an exclusive right to public performances of his work. The radio station thus owes the composer money.

But when the station plays a record, it is not only performing a copy of the *composer's* work. The station is also performing a copy of the *recording artist's* work. It's one thing to air a recording of "Happy Birthday" by the local children's choir; it's quite another to air a recording of it by the Rolling Stones or Lyle Lovett. The recording artist is adding to the value of the composition played on the radio station. And if the law were perfectly consistent, the station would have to pay the artist for his work, just as it pays the composer.

But it doesn't. This difference can be huge. Imagine you compose a piece of music. You own the exclusive right to authorize public performances of that music. So if Madonna wants to sing your song in public, she has to get your permission.

Imagine she does sing your song, and imagine she likes it a lot. She then decides to make a recording of your song, and it becomes a top hit. Under today's law, every time a radio station plays your song, you get some money. But Madonna gets nothing, save the indirect effect on the sale of her CDs. The public performance of her recording is not a "protected" right. The radio station thus gets to pirate the value of Madonna's work without paying her a dime.

No doubt, one might argue, what the promotion artists get is worth more than the performance rights they give up. Maybe. But even if that's the case, this is a choice that the law ordinarily gives to the creator. Instead, the law gives the radio station the right to take something for nothing.

Cable TV, too: When entrepreneurs first started installing cable in 1948, most refused to pay the networks for the content that they hijacked and delivered to their customers—even though they were basically selling access to otherwise free television broadcasts.

Cable companies were thus Napsterizing broadcasters' content, but more egregiously than anything Napster ever did—Napster never charged for the content it enabled others to give away.

Broadcasters and copyright owners were quick to attack this theft. As then Screen Actors Guild president Charlton Heston put it, the cable outfits were "free-riders" who were "depriving actors of compensation."

Copyright owners took the cable companies to court. Twice the Supreme Court held that the cable companies owed the copyright owners nothing. The debate shifted to Congress, where almost 30 years later it resolved the question in the same way it had dealt with phonographs and player pianos. Yes, cable companies would have to pay for the content that they broadcast, but the price they would have to pay was not set by the copyright owner. Instead, lawmakers set the price so that the broadcasters couldn't veto the emerging technologies of cable. The companies thus built their empire in part upon a piracy of the value created by broadcasters' content.

As the history of film, music, radio, and cable TV suggest, even if some piracy is plainly wrong, not all piracy is. Or at least, not in the sense that the term is increasingly being used today. Many kinds of piracy are useful and productive, either to create new content or foster new ways of doing business. Neither our tradition, nor any tradition, has ever banned all piracy.

This doesn't mean that there are no questions raised by the latest piracy concern—peer-to-peer file-sharing. But it does mean that we need to understand the harm in P2P sharing a bit more before we condemn it to the gallows.

Like the original Hollywood, P2P sharing seeks to escape an overly controlling industry. And like the original recording and radio industries, it is simply exploiting a new way of distributing content. But unlike cable TV, no one is selling the content that gets shared on P2P services. This difference distinguishes P2P sharing. We should find a way to protect artists while permitting this sharing to survive.

Much of the "piracy" that file-sharing enables is plainly legal and good. It provides access to content that is technically still under copyright but that is no longer commercially available—in the case of music, some 4 million tracks. More important, P2P networks enable sharing of content that copyright owners want shared, as well as work already in the public domain. This clearly benefits authors and society.

Moreover, much of the sharing—which is referred to by many as piracy—is motivated by a new way of spreading content made possible by changes in the technology of distribution. Thus, consistent with the tradition that gave us Hollywood, radio, the music industry, and cable TV, the question we should be asking about file-sharing is how best to preserve its benefits while minimizing (to the extent possible) the wrongful harm it causes artists.

The question is one of balance, weighing the protection of the law against the strong public interest in continued innovation. The law should seek that balance, and that balance will be found only with time.

Journal and Discussion Questions

1 What is the thesis of "Some Like It Hot"? What reasons does Lawrence Lessig give to support his thesis?

2 "Some Like It Hot" uses bold print to divide it into three sections. Outline the essay. What is the main idea of each section? What transitional devices does Lessig use to connect the three sections? How do the three sections fit together to support Lessig's thesis?

3 How does the title, "Some Like It Hot," serve Lessig's argument? *Wired Magazine* constructed a photograph of Marilyn Monroe being kissed by a pirate from two separate photographs to accompany this essay. How does this image and the way it was constructed reinforce Lessig's argument?

4 Lessig begins with a definition: "If piracy means using the creative property of others without their permission, [. . .] ." Why is this definition of piracy important to Lessig's argument? Do you think Lessig accepts this definition of *piracy*? What do the quotation marks around the word piracy on page 349 and the phrase "much of the sharing—which is referred to by many as piracy" on this page suggest about Lessig's attitude about the word *piracy*?

5 Lessig compares a series of copyright violations in the history of the entertainment industry to the controversy of MP3 file-sharing and other P2P file sharing today. How do these comparisons support his argument? How is today's file-sharing situation different from the other copyright violation situations? Do these differences weaken Lessig's argument? Why or why not?

6 Lessig quotes only one source in "Some Like It Hot," Charlton Heston on page 349. How does this quotation—and the fact that Heston said it—contribute to Lessig's argument? What other research appears in "Some Like It Hot"? If Lessig was writing an argument for a law school journal, what additional citations would appear? Why are these citations missing in an article for *Wired*?

7 What changes in copyright law does Lessig advocate? Why? What kinds of "piracy" does Lessig oppose? Why? How does Lessig's article apply to your downloading of music and movies for personal use?

Topics for Writing

1 Argue for or against the policy changes advocated in Lawrence Lessig's "Some Like It Hot," weighing the benefits and problems that Lessig's proposals would create.

2 Research the laws and regulations of your college or university regarding the legal and illegal downloading of music, movies, and other computer files. Write an editorial for your campus newspaper about the fairness of these laws and regulations.

3 Research other Lessig writings on intellectual property and pro and con responses to his arguments, such as reviews of his books. Form your own position on one of his issues and write a research paper arguing that position.

Connecting the Readings

Discuss how intellectual property rights should be balanced against society's needs and rights for knowledge, considering Lamar Smith's and Lawrence Lessig's arguments. Or argue that intellectual property laws do not pose a threat to society's creativity and knowledge gathering.

DOONESBURY

BY GARRY TRUDEAU

Garry Trudeau (1948–) has used the Pulitzer Prize-winning comic strip *Doonesbury* as a venue for social and political commentary since 1970. *Doonesbury* is published in over 1400 newspapers, in dozens of books, and on the Web site www.doonesbury.com/. Trudeau has also written plays and television scripts (*Tanner '88, Tanner on Tanner*); has worked as a contributing essayist for *Time* and as an occasional columnist for the *New York Times*; and has published articles in magazines such as *Harper's, The New Yorker, Rolling Stone*, and the *New Republic*. Music file sharing is the subject of several *Doonesbury* strips. Trudeau generally writes from a liberal perspective, although in this strip the character Michael Doonesbury agrees with Republican Congressman Lamar Smith's position on Internet piracy. Unlike some political cartoonists, Trudeau sometimes uses his strip to provide a dialogue on an issue, as he does here.

Journal and Discussion Questions

1 What positions on music file sharing do Michael Doonesbury and his daughter, Alex, hold? Whose position does Garry Trudeau seem to support? Why?

2 Which position do you most agree with? Why?

3 Why do you think Trudeau puts this argument in the mouths of a middle-aged father and his teenage daughter? What do the details in the strip—clothing, hair styles, newspaper, kitchen setting—suggest about this family? What, if anything, do these details suggest about what type of people care about the issue of illegal file sharing?

4 Why does Trudeau emphasize the different term each character uses to describe the daughter's actions—"sharing" vs. "stealing"? What do these two verbs tell you about how Michael and Alex define and view illegal file sharing?

5 Trudeau suggests that the baby-boomer generation and the current high school- and college-age population hold differing moralities. Do you think this is true? Why or why not?

Topics for Writing

1 Analyze this *Doonesbury* strip as an analysis and argument about intellectual property rights and music file sharing, discussing how Garry Trudeau represents the two sides of the debate, what position he sympathizes with, and why he presents this debate between a middle-class father and daughter.

2 Research the different sides of the debate about free person-to-person sharing of music and video files, and analyze the language in the arguments, the key terms for each side of the debate, how the language of each side reflects its attitudes and assumptions, and how both sides use language to influence audiences' attitudes and opinions.

PLAGIARISM A PROBLEM FOR WSU STUDENTS

BY BRANDI TRAPP

Brandi Trapp was a student at Wayne State University in Detroit and news editor of the campus newspaper, *The South End Newspaper*, when she wrote this article for the paper's December 12, 2006, edition. "Plagiarism a Problem for WSU Students" investigates the problem of student plagiarism not only at Wayne State University but throughout the nation, even mentioning a story from the American University of Beirut. Plagiarism is an intellectual property issue because the words, ideas, and information in a text are considered the intellectual property of the writer and plagiarism is often defined as stealing from another writer. Trapp's article discusses some of the causes of plagiarism and some of the measures that colleges and universities are taking to catch and punish plagiarists.

FINALS ARE APPROACHING AND papers are due. After hours or even days of sleep deprivation a student might consider buying a prewritten paper from a Web site like 1millionpapers.com for $9.95 a page or just swiping a free essay from cheathouse.com or planetpapers.com, even though the repercussions could result in expulsion.

A survey conducted by the Center for Academic Integrity revealed that nearly 80 percent of college students have admitted to cheating at least once, and a study published in *Education Week* found that 54 percent of students plagiarize from the Internet.

Some students can get away with plagiarizing because teachers don't want to research every paper turned in.

A Stanford University professor told TechWeb.com, "Who wants to sit around looking for websites trying to find out if a paper is plagiarized or not . . . pretty soon you're a private investigator."

Victoria Anderson, ombudsperson at WSU, said students may plagiarize by accident because they are not familiar with the university's Policy on Academic Dishonesty. "They think if they re-word information they've avoided plagiarizing."

The WSU undergraduate bulletin includes plagiarism in its description of academic dishonesty as "any activity that tends to compromise the academic integrity of the institution or subvert the education process," and "any act of intentionally using or attempting to use, or intentionally providing or attempting to provide, unauthorized materials, information or assistance in any academic exercise."

This means that a student can be accused of plagiarism if they get any information from a source without citation, re-word information from a source (paraphrasing) without acknowledgement, or accidentally use information from a source without citing it.

WSU history professor Jeff Powell said "If you use words or ideas and present them as your own it qualifies as plagiarism."

Over the years Powell has noticed students don't realize that paraphrasing counts as plagiarism. "Even if they re-word something they read from a text they are still passing off the idea as their own," Powell said.

A safe way to avoid plagiarism is by citing all references used as research. Professors can tell if a student has plagiarized by simply Googling a suspicious sentence or paragraph.

"Students often forget that if they can find it, I can find it," Powell said.

A plagiarism warning sign is if a student has grammatical and syntax errors in an essay, then has a sentence or paragraph that is grammatically correct.

Powell said he doesn't mind being a private investigator when it comes to plagiarism. He has to confront students for it every year.

"It's pervasive," he said. "Every year plagiarism, not just borderline plagiarism, but blatant plagiarism, is evident in the classroom."

Penalties for plagiarism range from failing an assignment or class, to expulsion.

"If re-wording other people's work is plagiarism then yes, I've done it," said an anonymous senior.

"I didn't know that re-wording someone's work counted as plagiarism," said another anonymous senior.

"I thought I was doing OK but I guess I'm not doing as good as I thought."

"I've done it in high school," said Stephen King-Monroe, a WSU junior majoring in electrical engineering. "Honestly, I didn't know re-wording something was plagiarism."

Students interviewed were aware of anti-plagiarism software. "I'm scared to plagiarize," said another anonymous senior. "I know a lot of teachers can use computer programs to see if you've copied something."

If a professor suspects plagiarism he or she can enter the essay in an anti-plagiarizing program like Turnitin, and compare the essay to other essays and sources.

Some anti-plagiarism software, like Turnitin's, has been criticized. Turnitin's database is filled with archived essays from students. Once a professor uploads an essay it becomes part of the database.

Professors at the American University of Beirut (AUB) uploaded an authentic senior thesis onto Turnitin's software only to be surprised when Turnitin claimed the entire essay was plagiarized.

According to the AUB Web site there is an intrinsic flaw in the program that doesn't make a distinction between plagiarized and properly quoted text.

If WSU students are still unsure of how they can identify plagiarism, they can visit www.lisp.wayne.edu and take the plagiarism quiz.

Powell thinks plagiarism is a sign of laziness.

"Students can do quality work but for some reason they think they need to plagiarize," said Powell.

Journal and Discussion Questions

1 What is the thesis or central claim of "Plagiarism a Problem for WSU Students"? How does Brandi Trapp support this claim?

2 How big a problem is plagiarism on college campuses? What causes does Trapp identify for this problem? What possible causes are missing from her article?

3 How does ignorance about plagiarism contribute to the problem? What aspects of plagiarism are some students ignorant about? Why do you think students are ignorant or confused about what constitutes plagiarism?

4 What measures do professors take to discover plagiarism in their students' papers? What are the penalties for plagiarism at Wayne State University? Why do professors believe that plagiarism is a serious offense deserving of these penalties?

5 What sources does Trapp use in her article? What does each source contribute to her depiction of the problem of plagiarism on college campuses?

6 Why does Trapp mention criticisms of Turnitin.com and the problem with Turnitin at the American University of Beirut?

Topics for Writing

1 Compare Wayne State University's problems with plagiarism and its policies for detecting and punishing plagiarism with the plagiarism problem and policies on your campus. You may need to conduct interviews or a survey for this essay.

2 Explain why college students are often ignorant about what constitutes plagiarism and discuss how colleges should take this ignorance into account in their plagiarism policies.

3 Write a research paper about the intellectual property issues of plagiarism.

THE COPYCAT SYNDROME: Plagiarists at Work

BY MEGHAN O'ROURKE

Meghan O'Rourke (1976–) is the culture editor for *Slate*, an online magazine with a focus on politics and culture; a poetry editor for the *Paris Review*; and a former writer and editor at *The New Yorker*. Her poetry and essays have appeared in periodicals, such as the *New York Book Review*, the *Kenyon Review*, *The Nation*, and the *New Republic*, and she is the author of a book of poems, *Halflife*. "The Copycat Syndrome: Plagiarists at Work" appeared in *Slate* on January 11, 2007. A recent charge that two passages of Ian McEwan's novel *Atonement* were plagiarized from another book prompted O'Rourke to write this essay, but she uses McEwan's situation to explore the nature of plagiarism and why it upsets people. O'Rourke considers arguments that plagiarism violates another writer's intellectual property rights in her discussion of the role of market forces and the value our culture places on originality, but she argues that our attitudes about labor may be more important in explaining why we consider plagiarism a serious offense.

WE MAY KNOW PORNOGRAPHY when we see it, but the same can't be said of plagiarism. Ever since it was revealed last month that several passages in Ian McEwan's *Atonement* closely resemble sections of Lucilla Andrews' World War II memoir, *No Time For Romance*, critics have debated whether the similarities constitute wholesale "plagiarism" or mere literary "discourtesy." The one thing everyone does agree on, apparently, is the necessity of policing plagiarism, whatever it may be. A partial list of authors recently accused (rightly or wrongly) includes Dan Brown, Yann Martel, Kaavya Viswanathan, J.K. Rowling, playwright Bryony Lavery, Doris Kearns Goodwin, Stephen Ambrose, and Alan Dershowitz. In an op-ed in early 2003, Condoleezza Rice even cited Saddam Hussein's habitual plagiarism as evidence of the leader's fundamental treachery.

Our distaste for plagiarism is usually framed in terms of our affection for originality. "We prize originality above everything and place a high value on novelty of expression," Robert McCrum wrote in the *Observer*, examining the outcry over McEwan. In *The*

Little Book of Plagiarism, an engaging new study of the concept, law professor and Judge Richard A. Posner attributes today's "increasing attention" to plagiarism largely to a "cult of originality" first shaped by the Romantics—who venerated individual genius—and further intensified by a 21st-century modern market economy that values novelty in its "expressive works." Obviously, originality does have something to do with all the fuss: Most of us expect writers—especially novelists and poets—to have a distinctive voice and literary style. We carve out exceptions for writers like Shakespeare—a plagiarist by modern-day standards—because they are creative in their use of borrowed material; such copying isn't "slavish" but inventive, or, as Posner puts it, "The imitation is producing value." Those who don't recontextualize borrowed work—like Kaavya Viswanathan—we censure.

But the rhetoric of creative originality doesn't fully explain our preoccupation with footnoting and credit—or the recent accusations against Dershowitz, Goodwin, and Ambrose. The historians were attacked for using language from other historians—in Ambrose's case, from a writer he cited in the book's notes—without quotation marks. Dershowitz was accused in 2003 by Norman Finkelstein of "fraud, falsification, plagiarism" for having borrowed many of the citations in *The Case For Israel* directly from another contemporary book—in other words, for using them without having checked the primary sources himself. (As evidence, Finkelstein pointed to Dershowitz's verbatim reproduction of errors in citation made by the original author, Joan Peters.) Judging by the "originality" standard, what Dershowitz did hardly seems like plagiarism. He did not copy Peters' actual words or pass the quoted authors' works off as his own; he just took a shortcut. In the case of Kearns, adding quotation marks to the passages she had borrowed wouldn't have made her work more original. It just would have given credit where credit was due.

These examples help bring a crucial issue of plagiarism into focus. Behind the talk of originality lurks another preoccupation, less plainly voiced: a concern about the just distribution of labor. In plenty of instances of so-called plagiarism, what bothers us isn't so much a lack of originality as the fact that the plagiarizer has stolen someone else's *work*—the time it took to write the words or do the necessary research. The cribbed student essay—which Posner views as a particularly insidious form of plagiarism, committed by approximately one-third of high-school and college students—isn't an academic crime because a C student has tried to pass himself as a Matthew Arnold in the making. It's an academic crime because the student who buys his thesis from a paper mill has shirked the labor that his fellow students actually perform.

In fact, labor and plagiarism were entwined from the start. The word derives from the Latin *plagiarius*, referring to "kidnapper." Around the first century A.D., Roman satirist Martial gave us its modern sense when he wrote an epigram complaining that another man (whom he labeled a "plagiarius") had kidnapped his writings (which he metaphorically labeled his slaves) and was passing them off as his own. What had been a metaphor for a slave-stealer—someone who got labor for free—became a symbolic expression for the theft of words. As Glenn Reynolds and Peter Morgan observed in a 2002 essay, the ancients who gave us the notion of plagiarism didn't object to creative imitation. On the contrary, they encouraged it, knowing that there are only a limited number of good ideas in the world: "Imitation was bad only when it was disguised, or a symptom of laziness. It was not denounced simply on grounds of being 'unoriginal.'" And in his excellent book *Stolen Words: Forays Into the Origins and Ravages of Plagiarism*, Thomas Mallon notes that writers didn't care about plagiarism much "until they thought of writing as their trade."

It may be less obvious that issues of labor lurk behind our anxieties when it comes to fiction. But even the McEwan affair, when you think about it, boils down to a concern that he cut corners at someone else's expense. At this juncture, McEwan has published roughly a dozen works of fiction, most of them critically acclaimed, and is revered for his distinctive prose style. In the case of *Atonement*, it can hardly be said that the presence of two cribbed passages, comprising a few hundred words, profoundly alters our perception of McEwan's overall literary "originality." For one thing, *Atonement* is hundreds of pages long. For another, McEwan didn't exactly hide his borrowing: Andrews is acknowledged in the book. Why, exactly, do we care if a few sentences resemble a historical source? And what do we think would be gained from his having painstakingly substituted different words from those Andrews had used? The answer, clearly, has to do with work; it seems unfair that Andrews had to sit at her desk and painstakingly consider how to describe cleaning a soldier's wounds, while McEwan could merely sit down and effectively copy out her sentences, moving on to the rest of his story (while getting paid more than she did, presumably).

> ❝
> **In plenty of instances of so-called plagiarism, what bothers us isn't so much a lack of originality as the fact that the plagiarizer has stolen someone else's *work*—the time it took to write the words or do the necessary research.**
> ❞

Posner may be right to connect our obsession with plagiarism to the rise of a market economy that values individualism in cultural works. But perhaps it also stems from a collision of contemporary ideas about what accomplishment really is: the result of effortless gifts, or the fruition of hard labor? Americans are fond of the myth of hard work. As preternaturally gifted distance runner Steve Prefontaine puts it in the 1998 biopic *Without Limits*, "Talent is a myth." And recent studies have shown that the old joke about how to get to Carnegie Hall is based in quantifiable fact: The top tier of 20-year-old violinists, it turns out, practiced on average 2,500 hours more than violinists the next rank down. Yet contemporary culture pays quite a lot of lip service to the myth of innate talent, wildly overestimating, for instance, the contributions of single employees to companies.

Clearly, our post-Romantic awe at individual talent still lives on. But it is also clear, as Posner points out, that we don't actually believe art must be sui generis to be great. Plenty of good Hollywood movies, to take just one example, are highly imitative. Martin Scorsese's acclaimed new film *The Departed* is a remake of the 2002 Hong Kong film *Infernal Affairs*. But critics didn't hold that against Scorsese; after all, he did the work of translating the film to a contemporary Boston setting. (This makes the film different from its predecessor, but hardly "original.") What really bothers us about plagiarism isn't the notion of influence itself, but the notion that a piece of writing has been effortless for the thief in question. Instead of worrying whether writers who borrow from other artists are fakers, perhaps we should be asking if they're slackers. It might make it easier to decide which kinds of influence to condone and which to condemn.

Journal and Discussion Questions

1 What thesis is Meghan O'Rourke arguing in "The Copycat Syndrome: Plagiarists at Work"? Outline "The Copycat Syndrome." How does O'Rourke use comparison/contrast to develop her main idea?

2 At what point does O'Rourke identify her thesis? Why does she delay identifying her main idea about plagiarism?

3 What does *originality* have to do with plagiarism? How does O'Rourke connect the importance of originality to plagiarism with the emergence of market capitalism, individualism, and writing as a trade or occupation? What does she think of this explanation for what makes plagiarism a serious offense?

4 Why does O'Rourke argue that distribution of labor is a more important issue with plagiarism than originality? How does she use the plagiarism of prominent writers like Ian McEwan, Alan Dershowitz, and Stephen Ambrose to support this claim?

5 What, according to O'Rourke, does slavery have to do with plagiarism? What does her discussion of the origins of the word *plagiarism* and how plagiarism was viewed in ancient Rome contribute to her argument?

6 O'Rourke provides links to most of her sources in the original online text of "The Copycat Syndrome" in *Slate*. What sources does she cite in her essay? What does each source contribute to her argument?

7 What implications does "The Copycat Syndrome" have for the issue of plagiarism on high school and college campuses?

Topics for Writing

1 Compare plagiarism in college classes with the plagiarism committed by published authors in "The Copycat Syndrome: Plagiarists at Work," and discuss the implications of Meghan O'Rourke's essay for college students.

2 Write a research paper about the legal penalties when plagiarism is proved in court and other harm caused by plagiarism, analyzing the reasons for treating plagiarism as a serious offense.

3 Research one of the plagiarism cases that O'Rourke mentions in her introduction or another prominent plagiarism charge against an author, a songwriter, or a newspaper or magazine. Write an essay arguing whether the situation fits the definition of *plagiarism* and the seriousness of the charge or the offense.

Connecting the Readings

Drawing on Brandi Trapp's "Plagiarism a Problem for WSU Students" and Meghan O'Rourke's "The Copycat Syndrome: Plagiarists at Work," analyze the nature and problem of plagiarism on college campuses and in publishing.

Suggestions for Essays on WEALTH AND PROPERTY

1 Analyze and compare the policy recommendations regarding private and public ownership in selections by at least three of the writers: Boaz, Klein, Smith, and Lessig.

2 Compare and analyze the emotional appeals and effects of buying and owning property in at least two selections by Boaz, Klein, Dugas, Breen, and the advertisers for Rolex, John Deere, and Fair Instant coffee.

3 Discuss the relationship between wealth and property and moral behavior and responsibilities, drawing on Boaz, Klein, and the advertisers for Rolex, John Deere, and Fair Instant coffee.

4 Analyze the attractions, benefits, and problems of modern consumer culture considering the arguments about consumerism by Dugas, Breen, and Rogers and your analyses of the three advertisements.

5 Analyze how the lives of college students are complicated by property issues considering the ideas in Dugas, Smith, and Trapp.

6 Argue what responsibilities, if any, people should assume toward the poor and starving, drawing on Klein and the Fair Instant coffee advertisement.

7 Discuss the problems of balancing the rights and needs of the creators and owners of intellectual property with the rights and needs of those who want to make use of intellectual property in at least two of the selections by Smith, Lessig, Trudeau, Trapp, and O'Rourke.

Folk and Popular Culture

IN THE YEARS FOLLOWING THE PREMIERE of *National Lampoon's Animal House*, college students dressed in bedsheets and, in their own ways, recreated the rituals and debaucheries of Bluto and Otter at fraternity toga parties. These toga parties suggest how a local folk culture can interact with national commercial and media-driven popular culture. The creators of *Animal House* used memories of their college fraternity cultures to create a hit movie about a fraternity in the early 1960s that spent its days and nights conducting panty raids, food fights, and beer bashes while sleeping through classes and flunking out of college. In turn, the movie changed the cultures of fraternities and fraternity parties throughout the country, as Greek organizations created their own rituals for toga parties.

The movie, the fraternity parties and culture it was loosely based on, and the fraternity toga parties it spawned all might interest a culture critic. What was college and fraternity life for the filmmakers really like? How did they represent and transform their experiences in *Animal House*? What made *Animal House* and toga parties so popular? How did fraternities adapt the movie's toga party scene for their own parties in the late 1970s? What do fraternity parties of the early 1960s and late 1970s reveal about the culture and values of college students and American society in general?

The selections in this chapter examine popular culture and what might be called "folk culture." Popular culture, or "pop culture," refers to television, movies, pop music, bestselling books, computer games, advertising, tourist events, and other cultural artifacts and events that are mass marketed, commercially driven, and usually made available through mass media. What makes this culture "popular" is that it has a large, general audience, not a small, elite audience.

Folk culture refers to cultural events and art that are created by a specific group of people. The indigenous music, stories, legends, jokes, food, and celebrations of a local or regional community or ethnic group make up a folk culture.

Both popular and folk culture are often contrasted with the "high culture" of elite, well-educated audiences, which includes classical music, opera, classic works of literature, and the art in fine art museums. Interestingly, the lines between these three cultures can be fuzzy. A work of art can win high praise as great art and become widely popular, and sometimes the work of a folk artist wins praise and study as high art. Oprah Winfrey's book club can turn a classic work of literature into a popular best seller. William Shakespeare mixed folk beliefs about fairies with Greek mythology to create *A Midsummer Night's Dream*, while Baz Luhrman made a hit move of Shakespeare's classic *Romeo and Juliet* using a rock music soundtrack, with south Los Angeles as the setting, and popular young actors, Leonardo de Caprio and Claire Danes, in the lead roles. Rock and roll, hip-hop, punk rock, and country music all began as the music of regional cultures but became part of the national popular culture when record producers recognized each genre's national sales potential for records, CDs, and concerts.

People study popular and folk culture partly because they want to learn about, read about, and write about what they enjoy—horror movies, Tex-Mex food, romance novels, fantasy baseball, Barbie dolls, rodeos, reality TV shows, gay pride festivals, hip-hop music, family reunions, sorority initiation ceremonies. They enjoy exploring something that intrigues them, such as graffiti artists, "polar bear clubs," Hong Kong action films, or tattoos. Newspapers and magazines often publish articles about local and national popular culture—from trends in action movies to a portrait of a local ice sculptor—because editors know that people are fascinated by folk and popular culture. But a more serious purpose is to understand what an aspect of popular culture reflects about the culture at large—what it reveals about the people who create and consume that culture and how the popular culture may be influencing society, changing people's values, and influencing their images of the world and their expectations and desires.

Here are a few general questions that writers like those in this chapter might ask to explore folk and popular culture. You might ask yourself these questions when you write.

- What different kinds of folk and popular culture (such as art, music, stories, celebrations, movies, food, clothing, rituals) exist? How can each be described?

- Who creates a particular work of culture? How? Why?

- Who consumes the work (watches the movie, listens to the music, eats the food, participates in the celebration, etc.)? What do they get out of this experience?

- What does commercial popular culture reveal about the people who consume it? What does it reveal about the people who create and distribute it?

- What values and ideology does popular culture promote?

- How does the media and other popular culture shape and influence the culture? Is this influence beneficial or harmful? Why?

- How does commercialism influence both folk and popular culture? What is beneficial and what is harmful about this influence?

- What does folk culture reveal about the culture and character of a community, whether it is a family, a local neighborhood, a city or town, a regional community, an ethnic group, or another group? What makes folk culture important to its people? How does it relate to and is it influenced by the culture of the larger society?

Invitations for Journal Writing

1 What kinds of commercial popular culture do you particularly enjoy (music, movies, television, computer games, etc.)? Describe one of these forms of entertainment. What do you enjoy about it? Why? What does your interest in this form of popular culture reveal about you and your values? Why do you think this example of popular culture is popular with many people?

2 What kinds of local or folk popular culture do you enjoy or participate in? These might include family or local festivals, parties, or rituals (such as a city ethnic celebration, a 4th of July parade, Thanksgiving dinner, or the first day of deer-hunting season); student-organized activities (tail-gating before a football game, a fraternity or sorority ritual); preparing and eating certain kinds of food associated with your family, region, or ethnic group (Tex-Mex dishes, gumbo, burgoo soup) or associated with a specific occasion (Easter eggs, birthday cake, turkey dinner). Describe one of these events or activities. Why do you get involved in this activity? Why is it important to the family, group, or local culture? What does this example of popular culture reveal about you and the culture that created or developed it?

3 Describe a popular or folk culture artifact or activity that you object to or have problems with, perhaps something that you used to enjoy but no longer find entertaining or meaningful. What problems do you have with it? What causes these problems? Why is this part of the culture still popular with people despite these problems?

FOLKLORE AND MUSIC

BY ZORA NEALE HURSTON

Zora Neale Hurston (1891–1960) was a fiction writer, essayist, and scholar of African American and Caribbean folklore and an important figure of the Harlem Renaissance, a particularly creative and significant African American movement of art and culture in the mid-twentieth century. Hurston wrote "Folklore and Music" for *The Florida Negro*, an unfinished and unpublished folklore project that Hurston researched, collecting folk tales and folk songs from African Americans in Florida, when she worked for the Federal Writers' Project in Florida in 1938. "Folklore and Music" was finally published in a 1995 anthology of Hurston's writings entitled *Hurston: Folklore, Memoirs, and Other Writings.* Hurston grew up in Eatonville, Florida, the first incorporated Negro township in the United States, and moved to New York City in 1925, where she became the first black female student at Barnard College. Although she once had her picture on the cover of the *Saturday Review*, Hurston died in obscurity, her writings largely forgotten until she was rediscovered in the 1970s. Hurston is now one of the most famous American writers of the twentieth century, and her novels (*Their Eyes Were Watching God, Seraph on the Suwanee*), her books on African American folklore (*Mules and Men, Tell My Horse*), her autobiography (*Dust Tracks on a Road*), and her essays and short stories are widely studied and enjoyed.

FOLKLORE IS THE BOILED-DOWN juice of human living. It does not belong to any special time, place, nor people. No country is so primitive that it has no lore, and no country has yet become so civilized that no folklore is being made within its boundaries.

Folklore in Florida is still in the making. Folk tunes, tales, and characters are still emerging from the lush glades of primitive imagination before they can be finally drained by formal education and mechanical inventions.

A new folk hero has come to be in the Florida prison camps, and his name is Daddy Mention. It is evident that he is another incarnation of Big John de Conquer or, that hero of the slavery days who could out-smart Ole Massa, God, and the Devil. He is the wish-fulfillment projection. The wily Big John compensated for the helplessness of the slave in the hands of the master, and Daddy Mention does the same for the convict in the prison camp.

In folklore, as in everything else that people create, the world is a great, big, old serving-platter, and all the local places are like eating-plates. Whatever is on the plate must come out of the platter, but each plate has a flavor of its own because the people take the universal stuff and season it to suit themselves on the plate.

And this local flavor is what is known as originality. So when we speak of Florida folklore, we are talking about that Florida flavor that the story- and song-makers have given to the great mass of material that has accumulated in this sort of culture delta. And Florida *is* lush in material because the State attracts such a variety of workers to its industries.

Thinking of the beginnings of things in a general way, it could be said that folklore is the first thing that man makes out of the natural laws that he finds around him—beyond the necessity of making a living. After all, culture and discovery are forced marches on the near and the obvious. The group mind uses up a great part of its life-span trying to ask infinity some questions about what is going on around its door-steps. And the more that the group knows about its own doorstep, the more it can bend and control what it sees there, the more civilized we say it is. For what we call civilization is an accumulation of recognitions and regulations of the common place. How many natural laws of things have been recognized, classified, and utilized by these people? That is the question that is being asked in reality when the "progress" of a locality is being studied. Every generation or so some individual with extra keen perception grasps something of the obvious about us and hitches the human

> **"Folklore is the arts of the people before they find out that there is any such thing as art, and they make it out of whatever they find at hand."**

race forward slightly by a new "law." For instance, millions of things had been falling on and about men for thousands of years before the falling apple hit Newton on the head and made him see the attraction of the earth for all unsupported objects heavier than air. So we have the law of gravity.

In the same way, art is a discovery in itself. Seen in detail it is a series of discoveries, perhaps intended in the first instance to stave off boredom. In a long range view, art is the setting up of monuments to the ordinary things about us, in a moment and in time. Examples are the great number of representations of men and women in wood and stone at the moment of the kill or at the bath; or a still moment of a man or beast in the prime of strength, or a woman at the blow of her beauty. Perhaps the monument is made in word and tune, but anyway, such is the urge of art. Folklore is the arts of the people before they find out that there is any such thing as art, and they make it out of whatever they find at hand.

Way back there when Hell wasn't no bigger than Maitland, man found out something about the laws of sound. He had found out something before he even stood erect to think. He found out that sounds could be assembled and manipulated and that such a collection of sound forms could become as definite and concrete as a war-axe or a food-tool. So he had language and song. Perhaps by some happy accident he found out about percussion sounds and spacing the intervals for tempo and rhythm. Anyway, it is evident that the sound-arts were the first inventions and that music and literature grew from the same root. Somewhere songs for sound-singing branched off from songs for story-telling until we arrive at prose.

The singing grew like this: First a singing word or syllable repeated over and over like frogs in a pond; then followed sung phrases and chanted sentences as more and more words were needed to portray the action of the battle, the chase, or the dance. Then man began to sing of his feelings or moods, as well as his actions, and it was found that the simple lyre was adequate to walk with the words expressing moods. The Negro blues songs, of which Florida has many fine examples, belong in the lyric class; that is, feelings set to strings. The oldest and most typical form of Negro blues is a line stating the mood of the singer repeated

three times. The stress and variation is carried by the tune and the whole thing walks with rhythm.

Look at the "East Coast Blues" and see how:

> Love ain't nothing but the *easy-going* heart disease;
> *Love* ain't nothing but the easy-going heart *disease;*
> Oh, *love* ain't *nothing* but the *easy-going heart disease*.

The next step going up is still a three-line stanza. The second line is a repetition of the first so far as the words go, but the third line is a "flip" line that rhymes with the others. The sample that follows is from a widespread blues song that originated in Palm Beach:

> When you see me coming h'ist your window high;
> When you see me coming h'ist your window high;
> Done got blood-thirsty, don't care how I die.

Incidentally, this is the best known form as far as the commercial blues is concerned because in the early days of the commercial blues, Porter Grainger, who wrote most of these songs, followed this pattern exclusively.

The blues song, "Halimuhfack," is still more complicated as to word-pattern. The title is a corruption of Halifax. The extra syllables are added for the sake of rhythm:

> You may leave and go to Halimuhfack,
> But my slow drag will-uh bring you back;
> Well, you may go, but this will bring you back.

Literary progress in construction is even more evident in "Angeline." Here is seen a pattern of a stanza of a rhymed couplet which also rhymes with the succeeding couplet. In addition, it carries out connected thought.

> Oh, Angeline! Oh, Angeline!
> Oh, Angeline that great, great gal of mine!
>
> And when she walk, and when she walk,
> And when she walk, she rocks and reels behind;
>
> You feel her legs, you feel her legs,
> You feel her legs, and you want to feel her thighs;
>
> You feel her thighs, you feel her thighs,
> You feel her thighs, then you want to go on high;
>
> You go on high, you go on high,
> You go on high, then you fade away and die;

Oh, Angeline! Oh, Angeline!
Oh, Angeline that great, great gal of mine!

"Uncle Bud," that best loved of Negro working songs is a rhymed couplet with a swinging refrain:

Uncle Bud is a man, a man in full;
His back is strong like a Jersey bull.

Refrain:
Uncle Bud, Uncle Bud, Uncle Bud, Uncle Bud,
    Uncle Bud.

'Tain't no use in you raising sand,
You got to take that crap off of grandpa's land.

Refrain:
Uncle Bud's got cotton ain't got no squares;
Uncle Bud's got gal ain't got no hairs.

Folk song making has become rather well developed when it arrives at the stage of the ballad. "Delia," from around Fernandina, and "John Henry," from who knows where, are good examples:

DELIA

Coonie told Delia on a Christmas eve night,
If you tell me 'bout my mama I'm sho going to
    take your life,
She's dead, she's dead and gone.

(Coonie shoots Delia to death during the
course of several verses)

Coonie in the jail-house drinking out a silver cup
Poor Delia in the graveyard don't care if she
    never wake up
She's dead, she's dead and gone

(Coonie justifies his killing of Delia)

Mama, Oh mama, how could I stand
When all round my bedside was full of
    married men
So she's dead, she's dead and gone

JOHN HENRY

John Henry driving on the right hand side,
Steam drill driving on the left,
Says before I'll let your steam drill beat me down,
I'll hammer my fool self to death, lawd!
Hammer my fool self to death.

John Henry told his captain,
Says when you go to town,
Please bring me back a nine-pound hammer,
And I'll drive your steel on down, Lawd!
Drive your steel on down.

John Henry went upon the mountain
Just to whip a little steel,
But the rocks so tall, John Henry so small,
He laid down his hammer and he cried, lawd!
He laid down his hammer and he cried.

John Henry had a little woman,
The dress she wore was red,
Says I'm going down the track and
    she never looked back
I'm going where John Henry fell dead, lawd!
Going where John Henry fell dead.

A ballad catches the interest of everybody in that it is more or less a story that is sung. The power of the group to create and transmit a story is increased. Before, there was music mostly for music's sake. But in the ballad the storyteller is merely using the vehicle of music to carry a tale. The interest of the listener has shifted from sound and rhythm to characterization and action. The music has become the servant of the words. Looping back to the more primitive forms, it is evident that the often meaningless words are mere excuses for repeating the haunting tune. But in the ballad the words make the tune. Take "John Henry," for example, and it is plain that the words and the music are one and the same thing. Read the words aloud and you have the tune. The stresses and lack of stresses all come where they would naturally be if the story were told without music. In other words, the ballad is the prelude to prose.

The ballad is, however, not the only road to prose. Among the other progressions are the folk-rhymes. In biology it is generally accepted that the evolution of an organism is reviewed in the embryo. In folk literature it is the same. Anyone who has been around children knows that they pass through various phases from the mere repeating of pleasing single notes to the phase of rhyme-making. This usually occurs when they are between six and eight years old. These verses seldom make sense. They are made for the sake of sound. The child is discovering sound laws for himself. The adult primitive does the same thing on his way to prose. So, rhyme for the sake of sound, furnishes evidence of the youth of literature. The second step is a combination of sound and sense. Every nation and race has a large body of observations on life coupled with rhyme for the sake of sound. Here is a sample from the Florida area:

1.

Love is a funny thing, love is a blossom;
If you want your finger bit, poke it at a possum.

. . .

In each of these rhymes there is a sense line and a sound line. The speaker might easily have said what was necessary without the rhyme, but it was felt that the couplet was more forceful and beautiful than the simple statement, but the real significance of these rhymes is that there is no thought of vocal or instrumental accompaniment—just a talking sentence. So that brings it right next door to prose.

FOLK TALES. The age of prose in every locality and among all races overlaps the twilight of poetry. Like song, prose grows from the short and often pointless tale to the long and complicated story with a smashing climax. All this is quite evident in the folk tales of the Negro-American. A single incident, or even a vivid description, is often offered as a story. Here are some samples of this from various parts of Florida.

· · ·

12.

(Big John de Conquer is the culture hero of the American Negro folk tales. He is the Jason, or Ulysses, of the Greeks; Baldur of the Norse tales; Jack-the-Giant-Killer of European mythology. He is the success story that all weak people create to compensate for their weakness. He is a projection of the poor and humble into the realms of the mighty. By cunning or by brute might he overcomes the ruling class and utterly confounds its strength. He is among men what Brer Rabbit is among the animals. In the Ole Massa tales he compensates the slave for his futility. He even outwits the Devil, who in Negro mythology is smarter than God.)

Ole Massa had a nigger named John, you know. Ole Massa lakted (liked) John because he learned everything Ole Massa tried to teach him and he never forgot nothing you told him. Ole Big John used to go and stand in the chimney corner every night at the big house and listen to see what Ole Massa talked about. Then he would go back and tell the other niggers in the quarters that he could tell fortunes. If he hear Ole Massa tell Ole Miss that he was going to kill hogs next day, John would come back and tell them, "Well, Ole Massa is going to kill hogs tomorrow." Them others would ask, "What make you say that, John?" "I'm a fortune teller and nothing ain't hid from me." So sure enough when Ole Massa come out next morning he would tell everybody to get ready for the big hog killing. It kept on like that until they all believed John when he said anything.

The way he fooled Ole Massa and Ole Miss was he was hanging round the back door when he seen the water throwed out that Ole Miss had done bathed in and he seen her diamond ring get throwed out in the water. John seen a turkey gobler grab up that ring and swallow it down. So when Ole Miss looked for her ring and couldn't find it she started to cry and say that somebody had done stole her diamond ring that Ole Massa give her for a birthday present. John he come tole Ole Massa that he could find the ring for Ole Miss. So Massa told him to find it if he could and he would give John a fine shoat. So John told him to kill that certain turkey gobler and he would find the ring. Ole Massa told him not to fool him into killing his prize turkey rooster, do he aimed to kill ole John. When he killed the gobler there was the ring sure enough, so then Ole Massa believed everything John told him.

One day when Ole Massa was talking with some more betting white folks he told them, "I got a nigger that can tell fortunes." One man told him, "No, he can't tell no fortunes, neither!" Massa told him, "I'll bet you forty acres of bottom land that Big John can tell fortunes." The man told Ole Massa, "Why don't you back your judgment with your money? Bet me something! I'll bet you my whole plantation that nigger can't tell no fortunes. I'll bet you every inch of land I own."

Ole Massa had him where he wanted him, so he reared back and said, "I didn't know you was going to make a betting thing out my statement, but since I see you do, let's make it worth my time. I'm a fighting dog, you know, and my hide is worth money. I bet you my whole plantation against yours, and every horse and every mule and every hog and every nigger on the place that my nigger John *can* tell fortunes." So they took paper and signed up the bet. They made arrangements to prove the thing out a week from that day. Massa come home and told John what he done done, and he told John, too, "John I done bet everything I got in the world on you and you better not make me lose everything I got, do I sure will kill you."

> John looked at the pot and he walked all around it three or four times but he couldn't get the least inkling of what was under that pot.

The day of the bet come and Ole Massa told John the night before to be ready bright and soon to go to the betting ground with him to prove out the thing. Ole Massa used to ride a fine prancing horse, and John used to ride a fat mule right along with Massa everywhere he went. He used to be up every morning and have Massa's saddle horse at the door before Massa get out of bed. But this morning Massa was up and had done saddled his own horse and had to go wake John up. John was so scared because he knowed he couldn't tell no fortunes and he knowed that he was going to make Ole Massa lose everything he had and then Massa was going to shoot him. So he hung way back behind Massa on the way to where they was holding the bet.

When they got to the place, why, everybody was there from all over the world because they had done heard about this big bet. John and Ole Massa got there and Ole Massa lit down from his horse real spry, but John just sort of slid off of that mule and stood there. The man that was betting against Ole Massa had the privilege to fix the proof, so John was carried off a little piece and when he come back he seen a great big old iron washpot turned down over something and the man told John to tell them what was under that washpot. Ole Massa told him he better think good 'cause he sure meant to kill him if he didn't tell it right and make him lose his place. It was very still because all of them had seen what was under the pot except John, and they was all waiting to see what he had to say. John looked at the pot and he walked all around it three or four times but he couldn't get the least inkling of what was under that pot. He begin to sweat and to scratch his head and Ole Massa looked at John and he begin to sweat, too. Finally John decided he might just as well give up and let Ole Massa kill him and be done with it. So he said, "Well, you got the old 'coon at last." When he said that, Ole Massa throwed his hat up in the air and let out a whoop. Everybody whooped except the man that was betting against Massa, because that was what was under the pot, a big old 'coon (raccoon). So none of them never did know that John didn't know what was under that pot. Massa give John his freedom and a hundred dollars, and Massa went off to Philadelphia to celebrate and left John in charge of everything.

13.

When Massa went off to celebrate his bet, he left John in charge of everything. So soon as him and Ole Miss got on the train to go, John sent word round to all the plantations to ask his friends to a big eating and drinking. "Massa is gone to Philly-mah-York (corruption of New York and Philadelphia) and won't be back in three weeks. He done left everything in my charge. Come on over for a big time." He sent word round to all the niggers on all the plantations like that. While some of them was gone to carry out the invitations, he told some more to go into Massa's lot and kill hogs until you could walk on them.

So that night everybody come to eat and to drink and John really had done spread a table. Everybody that could get hold of the white folks clothes had them on that night. John, he opened up the whole house and took Ole Massa's big rocking chair and put it up on

Massa's big bed and then he got up in it to sit down so he could be sitting high when he called the figures for the dance. He was sitting up in his high seat with a box of Massa's fine cigars under his arm and one in his mouth: "Ladies right! First couple to the floor! Sashay all!" When he seen a couple of poor-looking white folks come in. John looked at them and said, "Take them poor folks out of here and carry them back to the kitchen where they belong. Give them plenty to eat, but don't allow them back up front again. Nothing but quality up here."

You see, John didn't know that was Ole Massa and Ole Miss done slipped back to see what he would do in their absence. So they ate some of the good meat first and then they washed the dirt off their faces and come back into the room where John was sitting up in the rocking chair in the bed.

"John," Massa told him, "now you done smoked up my fine cigars and killed up my hogs and got all these niggers in my house carrying on like they crazy when I trusted you with my place. Now I am going to take you out to that big persimmon tree and kill you. You needs a good hanging and that is just what you are going to get."

John asked him, "Massa, will you grant me one little favor before you kill me?" Massa told him yes, but hurry up because he was anxious to hang a man who would cut the capers that John had cut. John called his friend Ike to one side and told him, "Ike, Ole Massa is going to take me out to the pessimmon tree to hang me. I want you to get up in that tree with a box of matches and every time I ask God for a sign, you strike a match. That is the only way to save my life." So Ike run ahead and got up in the tree with the box of matches. After while here come Massa with John and a rope to hang him. He throwed the rope over a high limb and tied one end around John's neck. At that time John said, "Massa, will you let me pray before you kill me?" Massa told him to go ahead and pray, but he better pray fast because he was tired of waiting to hang him. So John got down and said, "O Lord, if you mean to stop Massa from hanging me, give me a sign." When he said that, Ike struck a match and when Massa see that light up the tree, he begin to get scared. John made out he didn't see Massa flinch and he kept right on praying. "O Lord, if you mean to kill Ole Massa tonight, give me another sign." Ike struck another match. Ole Massa said, "That's all right, John, don't pray no more." John kept right on praying. "O Lord, if you mean to put Massa to death tonight with his wife and all his chillun, give me another sign." Ike struck a whole heap of matches at that and Old Massa lit out from there, running just as fast as he could. And after that he give John and everybody else they freedom and that is how Negroes got their freedom—because John fooled Ole Massa so bad.

BIG JOHN TODAY. There are numerous other stories of John's doings with Ole Massa, of his tricking strong men out of contests, of his visits to heaven and hell, and his victories over the Devil. Casual listeners have confused John de Conquer with John Henry, but this is far from correct. John Henry is celebrated for one single act of bravery and strength, in the manner of Casey Jones. While John de Conquer is a hero cycle yet unfinished. The strongest herb used in hoodoo is called Big John de Conquer root. Nothing is supposed to stand against it. There have been no stories of John's death, except the ones told in order to show him carrying on in heaven. He is up to his old tricks there also.

DADDY MENTION. Just when or where Daddy Mention came into being, none of the guests at the Duval County (Florida) Blue-Jay (prison farm) seem to know. Only one thing is certain about this wonder-working prisoner: Every other prisoner claims to have known him.

Not that any of his former friends can describe Daddy Mention to you, or even tell you very many close details about him. They agree, however, that he has been an inmate of various and sundry Florida jails, prison camps, and road farms for years.

In fact, it is this unusual power of omnipresence that first arouses the suspicions of the listeners: was Daddy Mention perhaps a legendary figure? Prisoners will insist that he was in the Bartow jail on a 90-day sentence, "straight up," when they were doing time there. Then another will contradict and say it must have been some other time, because that was the period when Daddy was in Marion County, "making a bit in the road gang." The vehemence with which both sides argue would seem to prove that Daddy was in neither place, and that very likely he was nowhere.

Legendary though Daddy Mention may be, however, the tales of his exploits are vividly told by the prisoners. All the imagination, the color, and the action of the "John" stories of other sections are duplicated in Daddy's activities; it is peculiar that the exploits, far-fetched though they may seem, seldom fall on unbelieving ears. A selection of the Daddy Mention tales appear in *Florida: A Guide to the Southernmost State*.

On the west coast, from Key West to Tampa, there is a tremendous addition of Cuban music, tales and folk ways. On the east coast, from Fort Pierce to Key West, there is an even stronger element seeping into Negro folk ways. This is something brought into the United States by the flood of Negro workers from the Bahamas. The Negro music is more dynamic and compelling than that of the American Negro, and the dance movements are more arresting; perhaps because the Bahaman offerings are more savage. The Bahaman, and the West Indian Negro generally, has had much less contact with the white man than the American Negro. As a result, speech, music, dancing, and other modes of expression are definitely nearer the African. Thus the seeker finds valuable elements long lost to the American Negro. This is because the Negro slave on the continent of North America, unlike the island slave, was never allowed to remain in tribal groups. This is both to prevent uprisings and to speed up his Americanization. Also on American soil the slave came into direct contact with the master and the master's family almost daily, whereas the system of absentee ownership was prevalent in the West Indies, and the slave owner might not visit his plantations once in ten years. There might be three hundred slaves under the care of one white overseer, who could not concern himself with the personal contact that most masters relish with their own property.

> **Legendary though Daddy Mention may be, however, the tales of his exploits are vividly told by the prisoners.**

Bahaman drum rhythms are truly magnificent. The songs are nearly all dance songs and the words are mere excuses to introduce the tunes. A rhythmic phrase is repeated until the fire-tuned drum grows cold and slack in the head and must be tuned and tightened by fire again. Then another tune is introduced.

Of the dance tunes, there are two main types: the jumping dance and the ring dance. The jumping dance tune is short and repetitious. As soon as a dancer chooses a partner, it begins all over again. The length varies. There are "one move" rhythms, two moves, and so on. For instance, in a three-move dance, the dancer "cuts pork": enters the circle and does a solo dance; chooses a partner and retires.

"LIME, OH, LIME"

Lime, Oh, lime, (cutting pork, a preliminary
    movement)
Juice and all;
Lime, Oh, lime, Dessa hold your back (Leaps
    into ring);
Oh, Dessa! (one move) Oh Dessa! (two moves)
    Oh Dessa!, etc.

The ring play is more elaborate and florid, though it is actually less difficult to do. The dancer chosen enters the ring at the first syllable of the verse and moves around the ring in search of a partner. All dancers in the ring clap their hands loudly throughout the movement. The selected partner steps out of the ring when a rhythmic moment arrives.

"BONE FISH"

> Good morning, Father Fisher; good morning
>   Father Brown;
> Have you any sea-crabs, sell me one or two.
> Bone fish is biting, have no bait to catch him;
> Every married man got his own bone fish.
>
> (The circling ceases and the dancer faces his
>   choice.)
>
> Eh, eh, looy loo! (The two dance out to the
>   center of the ring)
> Eh, eh, lolly loo, eh, eh, lolly loo! (This
>   continues until the original dancer leaves
>   the ring so that the other may in turn
>   choose a partner. Then, the verse begins
>   all over again.)

One is astonished to find that all of the Bahaman tunes have an African tribal origin. Let the dancers but hear an air and they can instantly tell you to which tribe it belongs. This is a Nago, that an Ibo, another a Congo, another a Yoruba (the proudest and most arrogant of all the Negro tribes in the West Indies). One hears such screams of outrage, "What! A Congo man stands in the face of a Yoruba and talks such! Don't you cheek me, Congo!"

Nightly in Palm Beach, Fort Pierce, Miami, Key West and other cities of the Florida east coast, the hot drum heads throb and the African-Bahaman folk arts seep into the soil of America.

Also in Florida are the Cuban-African and the Bahaman-African folk tales. It is interesting to note that the same Brer Rabbit tales of the American Negro are told by these islanders. One also finds the identical tales in Haiti and the British West Indies. Since it is not possible for these same stories to have arisen in America and become so widely distributed through the western world wherever the Negro exists, the wide distribution denotes a common origin in West Africa. It has been noted by Carita Doggett Corse that these same tales are told by the Florida Indians. But this does not mean that they are purely Indian tales as those recorded by John R. Swanson (*Myths and Tales of the Southeastern Indians,* Bulletin 88, Bureau of Am. Eth. Smithsonian Inst.). On the contrary, it merely accentuates the amount of contact which the Negroes have had with Southeastern Indians in the past. Since it is well known that runaway slaves fled to the Indian communities of southern Georgia and Florida in great numbers, the explanation of the Brer Rabbit tales among the Indians is obvious.

One fact stands out as one examines the Negro folk tales which have come to Florida from various sources. There is no such thing as a Negro tale which lacks point. Each tale brims over with humor. The Negro is determined to laugh even if he has to laugh at his own expense. By the same token, he spares nobody else. His world is dissolved in laughter. His "bossman," his woman, his preacher, his jailer, his God, and himself, all must be baptized in the stream of laughter. A case in point is the explanation of why Negroes are black.

"You know God didn't make people all of a sudden. He made them by degrees when He had some spare time from the creating He was doing. First start off He took a great big hunk of clay and stomped it all out until it was nice and smooth. Then He cut out all the human shapes and stood them up against His long gold fence to dry. Then when they was all dried, He blowed the breath of life into them and they walked on off. That had took God two or three working days to do that. Then one day He told everybody to come up and get their eyes. So they all come up and got eyes. Another day when He had some spare time He called everybody to come up and get their noses and mouths, and they all come got them. Then one day He give out toe-nails and so on till people was almost finished. The last thing He called everybody and told them, 'Tomorrow morning at seven o'clock I am going to give out color.

> **❝ So they all jumped up from where they was and went running on up to the throne hollering about, 'Give us our color! We want our color!' ❞**

I want everybody here on time because I got plenty creating to do tomorrow and I don't want to lose no time.'

"Next morning at seven o'clock God was sitting on his throne with His high gold crown on. He looked north, He looked west, He looked east, and He looked Australia; and blazing worlds was falling off His teeth. There was the great multitude standing there before Him. He begin to give out color right away. He looked at a great big multitude over at His left hand and said, 'Youse yellow folks.' They said 'Thank you, Massa,' and walked off. He looked at another squaddle and told them 'Youse red people.' They thanked Him and went on off. He told the next crowd say, 'Youse white people.' They said, 'Thank you, Jesus,' and they went on off. God looked around on his other hand and told Gabriel, 'Look like I miss some multitudes.' Gabriel looked all around the throne and said, 'Yes sir, it is some multitudes missing. I reckon they will be along after while.' So God set there a whole hour and a half without doing a thing. After that He said, 'Look here, Gabriel, you go and find them multitudes that ain't got their color yet and you tell them I say they better come on here and get their color because when I get up from here today I am never to give out no more color. And if they don't hurry and come on here pretty soon they won't get none now.'

"Gabriel went off and way after while he found great multitudes that didn't have no color. Gabriel told them they better come on up there and get their color before God changed His mind. He was getting mighty tired of waiting. So they all jumped up from where they was and went running on up to the throne hollering about, 'Give us our color! We want our color! We got just as much right to have some color as anybody else.'

"The first one that got to the throne couldn't stop because those behind kept on pushing and shoving until the throne was careening way over one side and God got vexed and hollered, 'Get back! Get back!' But they misunderstood Him and thought He said 'get black,' so they just got black, and we been keeping the thing up ever since."

This will to humor and building to a climax which is so universal in the American Negro tales is sadly lacking in Negro tales elsewhere. This proves that what has always been thought of as native Negro humor is in fact something native to American soil. But anyway, if the other elements that go to fill up the Florida plate of Negro folklore do not possess the humor of the native American Negro, still their contributions certainly are important in other ways, so that Florida has the most tempting, the most highly flavored Negro plate around the American platter.

Biddy, biddy bend, my story is end.
Turn loose the rooster and hold the hen.

Journal and Discussion Questions

1 How does Zora Neale Hurston define *folklore* in "Folklore and Music"? Why does she believe folklore is an important part of every culture? How do her examples of folk songs and folk tales support her claims about folklore?

2 Outline "Folklore and Music." What major points does Hurston make about Negro folk songs and folk tales? How does the organization of Hurston's essay help develop these ideas?

3 According to Hurston, what features do folk songs and folk tales have in common? What distinguishes a simple song or story from a more complex and sophisticated example of the genre? How do Hurston's examples support these claims?

4 It's usually a bad practice in research papers to include a number of block quotations, especially without commenting on or analyzing the quotations, but in her original essay Hurston repeats thirteen folk tales from her research, one after another. What do these tales reveal about African American folk tales? Do you think Hurston made a good decision as a writer by simply repeating these tales? Why or why not?

5 Why do you think Hurston concludes "Folklore and Music" by retelling and analyzing a folk tale that explains why Negroes are black? What point does this story make?

6 Why does Hurston compare Big John de Conquer and Daddy Mention? What do they have in common? What do recent stories about John de Conquer and Daddy Mention suggest about changes in African American life and folklore in the twentieth century?

7 What do the songs and stories that Hurston has collected reveal about African American life and culture?

Topics for Writing

1 Analyze one of the folk songs or folk tales in Zora Neale Hurston's "Folklore and Music," explaining how the piece supports Hurston's descriptions of African American folklore and discussing what the work reveals about black culture in Florida and the entire U.S.

2 Write a research paper about the relationship between African American culture and a group of African American folk songs or folk tales (perhaps the Big John de Conquer or Daddy Mention tales).

3 Select a group of folk songs, folk tales, or legends from another culture and write a research paper about what this folklore reveals about the people of this culture.

SOME ACCOUNTS OF WITCH RIDING

BY PATRICIA K. RICKELS

Patricia K. Rickels (1923–), a folklorist and civil rights activist, is a professor emeritus in English at the University of Louisiana at Lafayette (formerly the University of Southwestern Louisiana), where she directed the Honors Program until 2007. "Some Accounts of Witch Riding" first appeared in a 1961 issue of *Louisiana Folklore Miscellany*, a journal that publishes academic articles about Louisiana folk culture, such as the indigenous music, folktales, food, and celebrations of Louisiana.

AT THE TIME OF THE NEW ENGLAND witch trials, no charge was more common than that the accused had "ridden people," that is, leaped upon them as they slept and "grievously oppressed them."[1] The word nightmare, commonly used today to mean merely a bad dream, is also defined by *The American College Dictionary* as a "monster or evil spirit formerly supposed to oppress persons during sleep." Here the word *formerly* implies that witch-riding is extinct in America. The fact that it survives in American Negro folk tradition is recognized by Richard Dorson when he speaks of "the luminous ghosts who alarm colored folk at dusk dark, and the shape shifting witches who straddle them in bed."[2] That it survived among Louisiana Negroes a generation ago is attested by two brief mentions of witch riding in *Gumbo Ya Ya*.[3] The accounts presented here will demonstrate that the belief is still both widespread and deeply entrenched among Negroes in the French-Catholic culture area of southwestern Louisiana.

At the suggestion of Wayland Hand, president of the American Folklore Society, I began in 1958 to collect folklore from my students at the University of Southwestern Louisiana. Such a project is bound to be full of surprises; my first was discovering a student who had been ridden by a witch.

A serious-minded Negro in his mid twenties, a native of Abbeville, a Catholic, he speaks both French and English. His full account is given below, just as he wrote it, because he represents a paradox perhaps not found in America since the seventeenth century. Like Cotton Mather, he is intelligent, literate, sophisticated about most things, but full of a simple faith in the "wonders of the invisible world," wonders which he describes in direct, concrete, and often colloquial language, though employing generally a finished prose style.

PROLOGUE. Few people are willing to admit that superstition has some truth in it. Those who believe in such far fetched ideas are regarded as ignorant. Whether I am called ignorant or not, I do believe to a greater degree than most people. I have good reason to believe in witches, however, as you will discover when you read this story. The story is true, believe it or not, as you may.

THE RIDE OF THE WITCH. My grandfather was regarded as the best storyteller in our community. Almost every night the boys and girls in our neighborhood would assemble in the parlor of our home to listen to the old man.

One evening, while grandfather was in the midst of about ten small children and getting ready to begin his session of storytelling, I tip-toed into the room inconspicuously, for I did not want to interrupt his guests. In the meantime, he had begun to tell the tale of the witch. He described her as being tall and bony. She had a mouth almost bare of teeth, with the exception of one long tooth in the center of the upper part of her bridge; a long nose with several pimples scattered around and near the tip; long, gray, stringy hair which resembled the threads of a soiled mop; fingernails about an inch long, and a complexion as white as a sheet. She was attired in a dingy black dress and wore a pointed black hat.

Grandfather went on to say that her evil duty, among others, was to sneak into the homes of bad

---

[1] *Narratives of the Witchcraft Cases, 1648–1706*, ed. George Lincoln Burr (Charles Scribner's Sons, New York, 1914), pp. 225–227 and *passim*.
[2] Richard Dorson, *American Folklore* (University of Chicago Press, Chicago, 1959), p. 185.
[3] Lyle Saxon and others, *Gumbo Ya Ya* (Houghton Mifflin Company, Boston, 1945), pp. 258, 545.

boys and girls and haunt them while they slept. This occurred usually after midnight when she was certain that everyone was asleep.

This is how she went about her task of haunting; first, after entering a home, she would go from room to room in search of a victim to ride, but the only way she could ride the victim was to find him sleeping on his stomach; second, if the conditions were contrary to her expectations, she would then use force to roll the sleeping person over. The moment the witch rolled him over, she would pounce on his back and ride the daylights out of him. This was surely an experience he would never forget.

The only way to get her off your back was to pray, said grandfather. The witch was afraid of prayers. If one had the power to make the sign of the cross or utter a prayer, she would immediately leave the house. The prayers, however, had to be heard by the witch or otherwise they were of no use. She fought with all her might to prevent the mere thought of someone saying a prayer.

After grandfather had finished telling spine-tingling tales, the children were too afraid to go to their homes. It was dark, and they were afraid that the witch would attack them if they dared to venture alone in the night. He told them that if they would run fast and make a lot of noise the witch would not attack them; so finally they decided to leave. You should have seen them run. We could hear their noise blocks away.

I retired to my room and prepared for bed, but after putting out the light, I could imagine that I was seeing all sorts of eerie things around my room. Then I saw something weird coming toward me, crouching and lifting its arms high above its head. It was the witch! She made a wild leap for me, clutching desperately for my head; made a loud screeching noise which sounded like the noise of a bird of prey, preparing to attack its victim. I screamed! I immediately pulled the blankets over my head in a vain attempt to blot out the vision of that horrible creature. But she kept diving in on me, again and again. She tried with all her strength to roll me over, but she could not manage to do it. The bed was wet with the sweat from my body as I lay there helpless and pleading.

Several hours later, when everything had quieted down, the witch led me to believe that she had gone. I was too scared to believe that she had really left the room, and too tired to uncover my head. So, I remained motionless under the blankets until I could find strength to move the tired muscles in my body.

My weariness led me into a deep slumber, and somehow, during a bad dream I happened to roll over on my stomach and she hopped me just as fast as ever. Realizing that in my position I could not defend myself, I resorted to making outcries for help, but no one heard me, because no matter how wide I opened my mouth to yell, no sounds would come out of me. If you could but imagine how horrible a situation such as that could be, you would pray that this would never happen to you.

Two nights of those vicious attacks by the witch and I was almost a nervous wreck. In the meantime, however, I had told my mother about all the things that had happened to me. My mother was despondent and she did not know what to do. I begged for her help, but did not know what possible assistance she could give me, except perhaps, to keep a constant watch over me during the nights that followed.

> "
> I resorted to making outcries for help, but no one heard me, because no matter how wide I opened my mouth to yell, no sounds would come out of me.
> "

On the third night the witch jumped me again, but that time I gave her a run for her money. I fought her like a savage with all the strength I could muster, but I could not shake her off of my back. She pinned my arms to my sides and used them as reins to subdue all the fight within me. I made a vain attempt to pray out loud, but that only provoked her to a greater degree of contempt for me. She became more violent than ever, and rode me completely out of my bed onto the floor; then steering me toward the stairs, she proceeded to guide me to the very top. There was an opened window, screenless, just above the landing. Her intention was to ride me completely out of the house through that window. Death loomed over me like a dark cloud, waiting cautiously to engulf me. I did not want to die and I pleaded with her to set me free. But she was determined to take me with her. Her mind was made up and there was nothing I could do or say to change it.

Meanwhile, my mother had pulled a bed check on me. When she could not find me in bed she began a mad search through the house for me. By the time she found me I was almost ready to jump out of the window. Upon seeing this, mother became almost hysterical; screaming at the top of her voice she came running to aid me, and reached me in the nick of time, for a minute more and I would have been a goner.

As I stood there staring blankly into space, Mother held my hands and cried piteously, for the witch had almost cost me my life. Now I am a grown man and I am still plagued by the witch. However, through experiences I have learned to cope with her. That is, I don't sleep on my stomach any more. And if I have occasions to roll over during a bad dream, and she should hop on me, well, the story is different now. I have found the strength to make the sign of the cross and utter a vociferous prayer.

I asked this man why the witch chose him to ride. His answer was, "The only reason I know is that I was sleeping on my stomach." I asked him whether he had ever told the priest about the witch. "No," he replied, "I never thought about mentioning it to my confessor."

This turned out not to be an isolated case. When my American literature class next read Cotton Mather's account of Bridget Bishop, I asked whether the stories of her riding people reminded them of anything they knew. Everyone looked blank except the one Negro in the class—a French major, an ex-seminarian, and an excellent student. He said, "Why, it sounds like *cauchemar*." He went on to explain that he knew people who believed in a spirit that rode sleeping persons and agreed to make inquiries about it in his home town, St. Martinville, Louisiana. The following is his English version of a story told to him *in* French by an eighty-six year old Negress, a native of St. Martinville.

"My husband had been living a bad life. A bad woman called Big Marie had hoodooed him in his coffee. He stopped going to church and would come home after twelve almost every night. I knew that he was coming from Big Marie's house, so I would make him sleep alone in another room.

"One night I heard him straining and coughing and trying to call for help. I lit the lamp and ran to his room. He was trying to push someone away from him.

"I knew that Cauchemar must have had him. So I turned him on his side. Soon as I turned him on his side, Cauchemar left him. So he tried to show me that Cauchemar was leaving out of the door, but only he could see him, I could not. I told him to say his prayers and go back to sleep, but he was too scared to sleep. He sprinkled holy water all around his bed and spent the whole night with the lamp lit.

"What do you think would have happened if you had not waked your husband?" I asked. "Cauchemar would have choked him to death," she replied. Upon being asked if she knew of anyone whom Cauchemar had choked to death, she said that many people who are thought to have died in their sleep of natural causes were in reality strangled by Cauchemar.

"Do you know of anyone else who was caught by Cauchemar?" I asked. "That used to happen to a lot of people a long time ago," she replied. "But people have screen doors today. And, you see, Cauchemar has to count every little hole in the screen before he can enter the house. If he makes a mistake he has to start all over again. That's why he doesn't bother people any more."

"Did he ever bother you?" I questioned. "Oh, yes," she said. "But as soon as I feel him getting on me from my feet, I just turn on my side and he leaves me alone."

"Why doesn't he bother you on your side?"

"I don't know, but he can only catch you when you are lying on your back. If you are fast enough you can roll on your side before he gets a good grip on you and he will have to go."

"But what does he do? How does it feel when he is at you? Does he touch your whole body?" She paused in amazement at my apparent ignorance.

"Oh, yes, he touches you all over—even your head. In whatever position he finds you, he will try to hold you. If he gets a good grip, no matter how hard you try you cannot move. You may try to scream, but no sound comes out. Sometimes when he would catch my brother, my brother would strain so much that his neck would be stiff the next day. That's why it's so good to have someone sleeping with you, so he can wake you up."

We might note here in passing that just about everybody in this family was witch-ridden at one time or another.

Still another student in another class had something to report. This one, an eighteen year old Catholic Negro girl from Carencro, Louisiana, says she understands French but cannot speak it. She wrote the following account in a remedial English course.

One night a friend of mines came to my house to sleep with me. During the middle of the night it seemed as though I had awaken and heard a voice through the window, which was up, asking a question in a soft voice 'Which one it is?' I tried to call my mother but the words couldn't come out. All I could have done was stay in one place and trimble. A few minutes after I heard the voice again asking the same question. After I really woke up I started thinking that it must have been a *Quesma* because I was sleeping on my back and when I heard the voice I couldn't get up or call anybody. That happened about three summers ago.

My white students do not seem to know this tradition, though they are ready enough to report their beliefs in other supernatural phenomena. One Youngsville, Louisiana, girl does remember her grandfather's speaking of *cauchemar* as "a spirit that colored people believe in." And among Negroes around Lafayette, the belief persists everywhere. I asked two older colored persons and both of them were full of information. The first is a woman of about fifty who has lived all her life in Breaux Bridge, Louisiana, speaks English and French with equal ease, and can read and write fairly well. She works as a servant, her husband as a carpenter's helper, and between them they maintain a high standard of living, sending all their children through high school and some on to college. She is not sure whether *cauchemar* is anything more than a bad dream but is inclined to believe, because she has had other experiences with the spirit world. For instance, her mother, when she had been dead for twenty-two years, once got into bed with her and her husband. They could not see her but could touch her and hear her voice. "*Cauchemar*," she says, "is the spirit of an unbaptized person that chokes you in the night. It comes to scare Catholics who need to go to Communion. It happens when you are lying on your back." "If it happened to you, would you tell the priest," I asked. "Oh, no," she replied. "Those priests don't like hoodoo! They're always talking against it. They say if you fool with hoodoo, you're fooling with the devil. Just last week the priest said, when he preached the Gospel, 'All you peoples that got a dime in your leg—that's hoodoo!' All the people laughed, because plenty of them got a dime in their leg right then! No, ma'am, I wouldn't tell that priest anything—just go on to Communion." (Notice here the curiously confused theology: a spirit sent, presumably by God, for the edification and reformation of the victim, is at the same time interpreted as a manifestation of voodooism, forbidden by the Church.) I read her the account of one of Bridget Bishop's victims, written down in Salem, in 1693, and she approved it as "Just right." When I told her that some of my students believed an attack by the *cauchemar* did not mean you

had done anything wrong, she took this as just one more example of the younger generation's flippancy which will bring about their ruin.

I also discussed cauchemar with an "old style" Negress, an elderly woman who lives with her tenant farmer husband in the country, near Milton, Louisiana, has no new-fangled ideas, and has never been to school. She speaks English well but calls herself a Creole. She boasts that she "can't even understand Cajun" but talks "better Creole than Mayor Morrison on T.V." She has had experience with *cauchemar* and knows many others who have also. It is the spirit of an unbaptized person who jumps on Catholics who have been remiss about their prayers. The spirit takes the form of an old grey haired woman. It is visible only to the victim, whom it attacks when he is in bed but

> **"My white students do not seem to know this tradition, though they are ready enough to report their beliefs in other supernatural phenomena."**

"Cauchemar stops everything." At last one can outwrestle the thing, manage to say a prayer, and hope to avoid further encounters by being faithful in his prayers from then on. I asked her whether a person's leading an immoral life would bring the attack of the spirit. She had never heard of that. I asked if she had ever told the priest about her experience with *cauchemar* and she said, no. I asked whether *cauchemar* was the same as a witch. "Well," she said, rather dubiously, "some peoples calls it a 'wench'." The word was obviously not familiar to her.

Richard Dorson has remarked that some Negro tales of witch riding "strongly echo the Salem witchcraft records of seventeenth-century New England."[4] A number of such resemblances might be cited in the accounts I have collected. The basic similarity is obvious: one of the faithful is attacked in his sleep by a mysterious being who chokes off his breath until repelled by the force of prayer or until a second person takes hold of the victim. And many of the details are strikingly reminiscent of Salem: the appearance as an ugly old woman, the entry through a window, the stopping of the power of speech of the victim, the invisibility of the witch to all but the victim. But the differences from Salem accounts are about as striking. Most important, in New England, the witch was an identifiable person in the community, in league with the powers of evil. From this fact arose the whole quality of the witchcraft cases in Salem. They were matters of public interest, ecclesiastically and legally. There was a criminal to be brought to justice under the edict "Thou shalt not

---

[4]p. 185.

suffer a witch to live." The accounts I have presented clearly show *cauchemar* to be unconnected with persons known to the victim. It may be a good, rebuking spirit, or a bad, malicious spirit. But it is a spirit, not a person in league with the devil. Thus there is no legal problem. The experience is a private one, so private that even one's priest is not ordinarily told of it, much less an officer of the law. There are other notable differences from the Salem pattern. The emphasis placed by all my informants on the importance of the position of the sleeper has no parallel that I have been able to discover. And this is the one condition insisted upon in all five accounts. Whatever else brings a witch to ride you, you must be lying in a certain position or the spirit will be unsuccessful. There is no mention of shape-shifting or of animal familiars in any of the accounts. The Catholic sacramentals—the sign of the cross, the holy water—are certainly not echoes of Cotton Mather's Salem. One of the most interesting contrasts between Salem and Southwest Louisiana witches is their color. The witches who plagued white New Englanders were often black. The devil was dark-skinned, and so were those who dealt with him.[5] Conversely, the witch who rides Louisiana Negroes is white. The sociological implications here may be illustrated by the remark of a New Orleans Negress quoted in *Gumbo Ya Ya*: "I seen plenty of witches, too. Them things ride you at night. . . . I think lots of white peoples is witches. Others is just plain bitches."[6] Finally, we might note the enormous difference in emotional attitude between the witch ridden of 17th century Massachusetts and 20th century Louisiana. Hysteria was the order of the day there and then. Yet only a few persons were bewitched in New England, whereas many in Louisiana seem to be troubled by *cauchemar* at one time or another. And we cannot quite accept the view expressed by Christina Hole that "to-day what was once a universal creed has, for most people, sunk to a shamefaced and only half-acknowledged superstition, shorn of its worst terrors, and never again . . . to influence our lives in any serious manner."[7] My informants were not shamefaced, and two of them believe that *cauchemar* can kill his victim.

Whatever its likenesses to and differences from the classic New England pattern, the witch-riding tradition in Louisiana must, like every folk tradition, serve some need in order to survive. Kittredge remarks that all the theology of witchcraft has the same origin: the need to explain bad things that actually happen to people.[8]

Cauchemar functions in just this way. It provides an acceptable explanation for otherwise mysterious phenomena: bad dreams, sleep-walking, waking up with a stiff neck, or even death in sleep. Witch-riding is adequate as an explanation of all these things. But the motivation of the witch is sketchy in most of these cases. Logically a witch should have a reason for riding a victim. The primary reason in Salem was personal revenge or spite, but the absence here of any attempt to identify the witch with a known person rules out that motive. There was an elaborate mythology connected with witchcraft in Western Europe, and to a lesser degree in England and New England. Both the doctrine of the *incubus* or *succubus* and that of the Witches' Sabbath were apparently related to witch-riding. The *incubus*, a male spirit, and the *succubus*, a female spirit, descended on sleeping persons for the purpose of having sexual intercourse with them. There is no direct survival of this belief in local witch riding tales; however, a remnant of the *incubus-succubus* tradition may perhaps be preserved in the insistence on the importance of the position in which the victim lies. Since a man is attacked when lying on his stomach, a woman when lying on her back, this could be a relic of the tradition underlying the etymology of *incubus* (one who lies on) and *succubus* (one who lies under).

A clearer connection may perhaps be made with the Witches' Sabbath. There seems to be a survival in the first account given here of the tradition that witches sometimes use their victims for transportation to the Witches' Sabbath, often, but not always, turning them into horses by means of a magic bridle. The victim recalls: "She pinned my arms to my sides and used them as reins to subdue all the fight within me. . . . She became more violent than ever, and rode me completely out of my bed onto the floor; then steering me toward the stairs, she proceeded to guide me to the very top. . . . Her intention was to ride me completely out of the house through that window." He was afraid for his life, because he assumed he would fall and be killed. Here we have the idea of being ridden like a horse without the logical accompanying idea of a destination which the witch needs a mount to reach. Negro witch-riding stories from other parts of the South often have this element more clearly defined, even when the Witches' Sabbath is not the specific destination. Mark Twain has Jim in *Huckleberry Finn* tell how "the witches bewitched him and put him in a trance, and rode him all over the State, and then set him under the trees again, and hung his hat on a limb to show who done it. And next time Jim told it he said they rode him down to New Orleans; and, after that, every time he told it he spread it more and more, till by and by he said they rode him all over the world, and tired him most to death, and his back was all over saddle-boils.

---

[5]*Narratives of the Witchcraft Cases*, pp. 261, 298, 312, 326, 344, 355, etc.

[6]p. 298.

[7]Christina Hole, *Witchcraft in England* (Charles Scribner's Sons, New York, 1947), p. 19.

[8]George Lyman Kittredge, *Witchcraft in Old and New England* (Russell & Russell, New York, 1956), pp. 4–6.

Jim was monstrous proud about it, and he got so he wouldn't hardly notice the other niggers."[9] There is a Virginia Negro ballad about a victim being ridden by witches to a fox hunt.[10] My informant has apparently kept the terminology of mount and rider but not the idea of purpose in the ride beyond mere malice on the witch's part. He has never heard of the Witches' Sabbath as such.

The source of our local witch-riding tradition is a complex problem. Dorson insists on a European rather than an African origin on the basis of Christian elements. If we accept this premise, it is still difficult to fix a European source.[11] Spain, England, and France all brought witchcraft with them to the New World. That the belief lingered long in Spanish America is shown by the burning of two witches in Mexico as late as 1874.[12] The Catholicism of southwestern Louisiana seems to argue against penetration of the New England Puritan witchcraft beliefs. It seems most likely that the French brought witch-riding to Louisiana as they did that other, and perhaps related, survival from the middle ages, the *loupgarous*, the werewolf of the bayous. And African origin of some aspects of the local tradition cannot be entirely dismissed. The Negroes concerned clearly connect *cauchemar* with voodoo, and their instinct in this may not be altogether wrong, for the African tradition of the *loa* has much in common with *cauchemar*. The *loa* is a spirit which possesses a human being, though usually with his consent and when he is awake. The similar use of equestrian images to express the relation between possessed and spirit is especially striking. The *loa* is said to take a person as a "mount" and to "ride" him.[13] Puckett, in his *Folk Beliefs of the Southern Negro*, notes that "the beliefs relating to burial, ghosts, and witches show certain broad similarities both in Europe and Africa."[14] He believes that Afro-American beliefs result from contact between these two cultures.

The reason why Negroes and not whites preserve the belief may be simple cultural lag, perhaps reinforced by voodooism. Puckett found in his investigation that southern Negroes were "in part, at least, custodians of former belief of the whites."[15] Especially among illiterate Negroes in rural areas he discovered many fragments of earlier European thought. The witch-riding tradition, though still a very lively one in our Negro-French-Catholic cultural community, is losing its moral force. The older generation believes *cauchemar* has a real significance: to punish or warn against wrong doing. The younger generation believes the experience is just something that happens without any real reason or meaning. Probably the next step will be for witches to stop riding altogether.

[9]Chapter 2.
[10]R. Meikleham, "A Negro Ballad." *Journal of American Folklore*, VI (1893), 300.
[11]p. 185.
[12]Henry Charles Lea, *Materials Toward a History of Witchcraft*, ed. Arthur C. Howland (T. Yoseloff, New York, 1939), III, 1528.

[13]Alfred Metraux, *Voodoo in Haiti*, trans. Hugo Charteris (Oxford University Press, New York, 1959), pp. 120–122. Also, in this connection Newbell Niles Puckett notes that in New Orleans and parts of Mississippi a "voodoo doctor" is sometimes spoken of as a "horse." *Folk Beliefs of the Southern Negro* (University of North Carolina Press, Chapel Hill, 1926), p. 159.
[14]p. 165.
[15]p. 2.

Journal and Discussion Questions

1 Summarize Patricia K. Rickels' "Some Accounts of Witch Riding" for someone who has not read it. What do you think is the main idea of the article?

2 Rickels' opening paragraph combines two approaches for introductions: a discussion of the definition and derivation of a key word in her article and a brief survey of previous works written about the article's topic, witch riding, with an argument that the writer has discovered something important about the subject that no one else has written about. The second strategy, often called a *boost*, is common in academic articles. Why does Rickels discuss an old definition of *nightmare* to introduce the topic of witch riding? How does she show that she has something new and significant to say about her topic?

3 Outline "Some Accounts of Witch Riding," paying attention to each account. Why do you think Rickels organized her article as a narration, giving a chronological account of her research? What does each new account add to Rickels' knowledge of witch riding? What elements are constant with each story? What elements vary?

4 Why does Rickels mention how she began collecting folklore from her students? Why might college students be good sources about local culture? What is important about the background information she provides about her informants? What does the library research add to her understanding of witch riding folklore in southwestern Louisiana?

5   Although Rickels mentions that many people regard a belief in witches as "superstition," she refers to her students' stories about witch riding as "folklore," not "superstition." Why? What attitudes are implied by the terms *superstition* and *folklore*? Why doesn't Rickels emphasize the possibility, implied by the terms *nightmare* and *cauchemar*, that people who report being ridden by a witch are actually dreaming and sleep walking?

6   Why does Rickels conclude her article by comparing witch riding folklore in Louisiana to similar folklore in other cultures and by discussing why witch riding was part of the folklore of blacks in Louisiana at the time but not whites? Why does Rickels mention that her white students have supernatural beliefs although they do not believe in witch riding? Considering Rickels' work in the civil rights movement and that the controversies over the integration of state universities in the South when Rickels conducted this research, what political purposes may have led her to research African American folklore with her students?

7   What do you think the folklore about witch riding suggests about south Louisiana culture in the 1950s and 1960s? Why?

Topics for Writing

1   Using Rickels' sources, summarize the Louisiana folklore about witch riding in a brief essay, as if you were writing a brief online encyclopedia article on the subject. Explain the variations in people's accounts about this legend as well as the common elements among most of the accounts. Try to be entertaining as well as informative.

2   Relate a story or experience that reveals something about your culture. Local legends and celebrations, rituals, and games that are important to your region, neighborhood, or family are particularly good subjects for this assignment. Your essay should include detailed descriptions and commentary about the meaning and significance of the experience or story.

3   Conduct research on beliefs and legends about witches in Puritan New Salem and other cultures, past and present. Write a research paper describing and analyzing folklore about witches in different cultures.

EVERYDAY USE

BY ALICE WALKER

Alice Walker (1944–) is probably best known for her Pulitzer Prize–winning novel, *The Color Purple*, but she is also a prolific writer of essays, poetry, fiction, children's books, and criticism, and is an ardent political activist for civil rights, feminism, environmentalism, and animal rights. She has published well over 20 books, including *In Search of Our Mothers' Gardens: Womanist Prose*; *Warrior Marks*; *Revolutionary Petunias and Other Poems*; *The Temple of My Familiar*; and *By the Light of My Father's Smile*. She was born the youngest of eight children in a family of poor sharecroppers but earned a bachelor of arts degree at Sarah Lawrence College in 1965, after a year as an exchange student in Africa. Walker has taught at Wellesley College and Yale University. "Everyday Use" was first published in Alice Walker's 1973 collection of short stories, *In Love and Trouble: Stories of Black Women*.

For Your Grandmama

WILL WAIT FOR HER IN THE YARD that Maggie and I made so clean and wavy yesterday afternoon. A yard like this is more comfortable than most people know. It is not just a yard. It is like an extended living room. When the hard clay is swept clean as a floor and the fine sand around the edges lined with tiny, irregular grooves anyone can come and sit and look up into the elm tree and wait for the breezes that never come inside the house.

Maggie will be nervous until after her sister goes: she will stand hopelessly in corners homely and ashamed of the burn scars down her arms and legs, eyeing her sister with a mixture of envy and awe. She thinks her sister has held life always in the palm of one hand, that "no" is a word the world never learned to say to her.

You've no doubt seen those TV shows where the child who has "made it" is confronted, as a surprise, by her own mother and father, tottering in weakly from backstage. (A pleasant surprise, of course: What would they do if parent and child came on the show only to curse out and insult each other?) On TV mother and child embrace and smile into each other's faces. Sometimes the mother and father weep, the child wraps them in her arms and leans across the table to tell how she would not have made it without their help. I have seen these programs.

Sometimes I dream a dream in which Dee and I are suddenly brought together on a TV program of this sort. Out of a dark and soft-seated limousine I am ushered into a bright room filled with many people. There I meet a smiling, gray, sporty man like Johnny Carson who shakes my hand and tells me what a fine girl I have. Then we are on the stage and Dee is embracing me with tears in her eyes. She pins on my dress a large orchid, even though she has told me once that she thinks orchids are tacky flowers.

In real life I am a large, big-boned woman with rough, man-working hands. In the winter I wear flannel nightgowns to bed and overalls during the day. I can kill and clean a hog as mercilessly as a man. My fat keeps me hot in zero weather. I can work outside all day, breaking ice to get water for washing; I can eat pork liver cooked over the open fire minutes after it comes steaming from the hog. One winter I knocked a bull calf straight in the brain between the eyes with a sledge hammer and had the meat hung up to chill before nightfall. But of course all this does not show on television. I am the way my daughter would want me to be: a hundred pounds lighter, my skin like an uncooked barley pancake. My hair glistens in the hot bright lights. Johnny Carson has much to do to keep up with my quick and witty tongue.

But that is a mistake. I know even before I wake up. Who ever knew a Johnson with a quick tongue? Who can even imagine me looking a strange white man in the eye? It seems to me I have talked to them always with one foot raised in flight, with my head turned in whichever way is farthest from them. Dee, though. She would always look anyone in the eye. Hesitation was no part of her nature.

"How do I look, Mama?" Maggie says, showing just enough of her thin body enveloped in pink skirt and red blouse for me to know she's there, almost hidden by the door.

"Come out into the yard," I say.

Have you ever seen a lame animal, perhaps a dog run over by some careless person rich enough to own a car, sidle up to someone who is ignorant enough to be kind to him? That is the way my Maggie walks. She has been like this, chin on chest, eyes on ground, feet in shuffle, ever since the fire that burned the other house to the ground.

Dee is lighter than Maggie, with nicer hair and a fuller figure. She's a woman now, though sometimes I forget. How long ago was it that the other house burned? Ten, twelve years? Sometimes I can still hear the flames and feel Maggie's arms sticking to me, her hair smoking and her dress falling off her in little black papery flakes. Her eyes seemed stretched open, blazed open by the flames reflected in them. And Dee. I see her standing off under the sweet gum tree she used to dig gum out of, a look of concentration on her face as she watched the last dingy gray board of the house fall in toward the red-hot brick chimney. Why don't you do a dance around the ashes? I'd wanted to ask her. She had hated the house that much.

I used to think she hated Maggie, too. But that was before we raised the money, the church and me, to send her to Augusta to school. She used to read to us without pity; forcing words, lies, other folks' habits, whole lives upon us two sitting trapped and ignorant underneath her voice. She washed us in a

> **" She washed us in a river of make-believe, burned us with a lot of knowledge we didn't necessarily need to know. "**

river of make-believe, burned us with a lot of knowledge we didn't necessarily need to know. Pressed us to her with the serious way she read, to shove us away at just the moment, like dimwits, we seemed about to understand.

Dee wanted nice things. A yellow organdy dress to wear to her graduation from high school; black pumps to match a green suit she'd made from an old suit somebody gave me. She was determined to stare down any disaster in her efforts. Her eyelids would not flicker for minutes at a time. Often I fought off the temptation to shake her. At sixteen she had a style of her own: and knew what style was.

I never had an education myself. After second grade the school was closed down. Don't ask me why: in 1927 colored asked fewer questions than they do now. Sometimes Maggie reads to me. She stumbles along good-naturedly but can't see well. She knows she is not bright. Like good looks and money, quickness passed her by. She will marry John Thomas (who has mossy teeth in an earnest face) and then I'll be free to sit here and I guess just sing church songs to myself. Although I never was a good singer. Never could carry a tune. I was always better at a man's job. I used to love to milk till I was hooked in the side in '49. Cows are soothing and slow and don't bother you, unless you try to milk them the wrong way.

I have deliberately turned my back on the house. It is three rooms, just like the one that burned, except the roof is tin; they don't make shingle roofs any more. There are no real windows, just some holes cut in the sides, like the port-holes in a ship, but not round and not square, with rawhide holding the shutters up on the outside. This house is in a pasture, too, like the other one. No doubt when Dee sees it she will want to tear it down. She wrote me once that no matter where we "choose" to live, she will manage to come see us. But she will never bring her friends. Maggie and I thought about this and Maggie asked me, "Mama, when did Dee ever *have* any friends?"ᵗ

She had a few. Furtive boys in pink shirts hanging about on washday after school. Nervous girls who never laughed. Impressed with her they worshiped the well-turned phrase, the cute shape, the scalding humor that erupted like bubbles in lye. She read to them.

When she was courting Jimmy T she didn't have much time to pay to us, but turned all her faultfinding power on him. *He flew* to marry a cheap gal from a family of ignorant flashy people. She hardly had time to recompose herself.

When she comes I will meet—but there they are!

Maggie attempts to make a dash for the house, in her shuffling way, but I stay her with my hand. "Come back here," I say. And she stops and tries to dig a well in the sand with her toe.

It is hard to see them clearly through the strong sun. But even the first glimpse of leg out of the car tells me it is Dee. Her feet were always neat-looking, as if God himself had shaped them with a certain style. From the other side of the car comes a short, stocky man. Hair is all over his head a foot long and hanging from his chin like a kinky mule tail. I hear Maggie suck in her breath. "Uhnnnh," is what it sounds like. Like when you see the wriggling end of a snake just in front of your foot on the road. "Uhnnnh."

Dee next. A dress down to the ground, in this hot weather. A dress so loud it hurts my eyes. There are yellows and oranges enough to throw back the light of the sun. *I* feel my whole face warming from the heat waves it throws out. Earrings, too, gold and hanging down to her shoulders. Bracelets dangling and making noises when she moves her arm up to shake the folds of the dress out of her armpits. The dress is loose and flows, and as she walks closer, I like it. I hear Maggie go "Uhnnnh" again. It is her sister's hair. It stands straight up like the wool on a sheep. It is black as night and around the edges are two long pigtails that rope about like small lizards disappearing behind her ears.

"Wa-su-zo-Tean-o!" she says, coming on in that gliding way the dress makes her move. The short stocky fellow with the hair to his navel is all grinning and he follows up with "Asalamalakim, my mother and sister!" He moves to hug Maggie but she falls back, right up against the back of my chair. I feel her trembling there and when I look up I see the perspiration falling off her chin.

"Don't get up," says Dee. Since I am stout it takes something of a push. You can see me trying to move a second or two before I make it. She turns, showing white heels through her sandals, and goes back to the car. Out she peeks next with a Polaroid. She stoops down quickly and lines up picture after picture of me sitting there in front of the house with Maggie cowering behind me. She never takes a shot without making sure the house is included. When a cow comes nibbling around the edge of the yard she snaps it and me and Maggie *and* the house. Then she puts the Polaroid in the back seat of the car, and comes up and kisses me on the forehead.

Meanwhile Asalamalakim is going through the motions with Maggie's hand. Maggie's hand is as limp as a fish, and probably as cold, despite the sweat, and she keeps trying to pull it back. It looks like Asalamalakim wants to shake hands but wants to do it

> **❝ It is hard to see them clearly through the strong sun.**
> **But even the first glimpse of leg out of the car tells me it is Dee. ❞**

fancy. Or maybe he don't know how people shake hands. Anyhow, he soon gives up on Maggie.

"Well," I say. "Dee."

"No, Mama," she says. "Not Dee, Wangero Lee-wanika Kemanjo!"

"What happened to 'Dee'?" I wanted to know.

"She's dead," Wangero said. "I couldn't bear it any longer being named after the people who oppress me."

"You know as well as me you was named after your aunt Dicie," I said. Dicie is my sister. She named Dee. We called her "Big Dee" after Dee was born.

"But who was *she* named after?" asked Wangero.

"I guess after Grandma Dee," I said.

"And who was she named after?" asked Wangero.

"Her mother," I said, and saw Wangero was getting tired. "That's about as far back as I can trace it," I said. Though, in fact, I probably could have carried it back beyond the Civil War through the branches.

"Well," said Asalamalakim, "there you are."

"Uhnnnh," I heard Maggie say.

"There I was not," I said, "before 'Dicie' cropped up in our family, so why should I try to trace it that far back?"

He just stood there grinning, looking down on me like somebody inspecting a Model A car. Every once in a while he and Wangero sent eye signals over my head.

"How do you pronounce this name?" I asked.

"You don't have to call me by it if you don't want to," said Wangero.

"Why shouldn't I?" I asked. "If that's what you want us to call you, we'll call you."

"I know it might sound awkward at first," said Wangero.

"I'll get used to it," I said. "Ream it out again."

Well, soon we got the name out of the way. Asalamalakim had a name twice as long and three times as hard. After I tripped over it two or three times he told me to just call him Hakim-a-barber. I wanted to ask him was he a barber, but I didn't really think he was, so I didn't ask.

"You must belong to those beef-cattle peoples down the road," I said. They said "Asalamalakim" when they met you, too, but they didn't shake hands. Always too busy: feeding the cattle, fixing the fences, putting up saltlick shelters, throwing down hay. When the white folks poisoned some of the herd the men stayed up all night with rifles in their hands. I walked a mile and a half just to see the sight.

Hakim-a-barber said, "I accept some of their doctrines, but farming and raising cattle is not my style." (They didn't tell me, and I didn't ask, whether Wangero [Dee] had really gone and married him.)

We sat down to eat and right away he said he didn't eat collards and pork was unclean. Wangero, though, went on through the chitlins and corn bread, the greens and everything else. She talked a blue streak over the sweet potatoes. Everything delighted her. Even the fact that we still used the benches her daddy made for the table when we couldn't afford to buy chairs.

"Oh, Mama!" she cried. Then turned to Hakim-a-barber. "I never knew how lovely these benches are. You can feel the rump prints," she said, running her hands underneath her and along the bench. Then she gave a sigh and her hand closed over Grandma Dee's butter dish. "That's it!" she said. "I knew there was something I wanted to ask you if I could have." She jumped up from the table and went over in the corner where the churn stood, the milk in it clabber by now. She looked at the churn and looked at it.

"This churn top is what I need," she said. "Didn't Uncle Buddy whittle it out of a tree you all used to have?"

"Yes," I said.

"Uh huh," she said happily. "And I want the dasher, too."

"Uncle Buddy whittle that, too?" asked the barber.

Dee (Wangero) looked up at me.

"Aunt Dee's first husband whittled the dash," said Maggie so low you almost couldn't hear her. "His name was Henry, but they called him Stash."

"Maggie's brain is like an elephant's," Wangero said, laughing. "I can use the churn top as a centerpiece for the alcove table," she said, sliding a plate over the churn, "and I'll think of something artistic to do with the dasher."

When she finished wrapping the dasher the handle stuck out. I took it for a moment in my hands. You didn't even have to look close to see where hands pushing the dasher up and down to make butter had left a kind of sink in the wood. In fact, there were a lot of small sinks; you could see where thumbs and fingers had sunk into the wood. It was beautiful light yellow wood, from a tree that grew in the yard where Big Dee and Stash had lived.

After dinner Dee (Wangero) went to the trunk at the foot of my bed and started rifling through it. Maggie hung back in the kitchen over the dishpan. Out came Wangero with two quilts. They had been pieced by Grandma Dee and then Big Dee and me had hung them on the quilt frames on the front porch and quilted them. One was in the Lone Star pattern. The other was Walk Around the Mountain. In both of them were scraps of dresses Grandma Dee had worn fifty and more years ago. Bits and pieces of Grandpa Jarrell's Paisley shirts. And one teeny faded blue piece, about the size of a penny matchbox, that was from Great Grandpa Ezra's uniform that he wore in the Civil War.

"Mama," Wangero said sweet as a bird. "Can I have these old quilts?"

I heard something fall in the kitchen, and a minute later the kitchen door slammed.

"Why don't you take one or two of the others?" I asked. "These old things was just done by me and Big Dee from some tops your grandma pieced before she died."

"No," said Wangero. "I don't want those. They are stitched around the borders by machine."

"That'll make them last better," I said.

"That's not the point," said Wangero. "These are all pieces of dresses Grandma used to wear. She did all this stitching by hand. Imagine!" She held the quilts securely in her arms, stroking them.

"Some of the pieces, like those lavender ones, come from old clothes her mother handed down to her," I said, moving up to touch the quilts. Dee (Wangero) moved back just enough so that I couldn't reach the quilts. They already belonged to her.

"Imagine!" she breathed again, clutching them closely to her bosom.

"The truth is," I said, "I promised to give them quilts to Maggie, for when she marries John Thomas."

She gasped like a bee had stung her.

"Maggie can't appreciate these quilts!" she said. "She'd probably be backward enough to put them to everyday use."

"I reckon she would," I said. "God knows I been saving 'em for long enough with nobody using 'em. I hope she will!" I didn't want to bring up how I had offered Dee (Wangero) a quilt when she went away to college. Then she had told me they were old-fashioned, out of style.

"But they're *priceless!*" she was saying now, furiously; for she has a temper. "Maggie would put them on the bed and in five years they'd be in rags. Less than that!"

"She can always make some more," I said. "Maggie knows how to quilt."

Dee (Wangero) looked at me with hatred. "You just will not understand. The point is these quilts, *these* quilts!"

"Well," I said, stumped. "What would *you* do with them?"

"Hang them," she said. As if that was the only thing you *could* do with quilts.

Maggie by now was standing in the door. I could almost hear the sound her feet made as they scraped over each other.

"She can have them, Mama," she said, like somebody used to never winning anything, or having anything reserved for her. "I can 'member Grandma Dee without the quilts."

I looked at her hard. She had filled her bottom lip with checkerbeny snuff and it gave her face a kind of dopey, hangdog look. It was Grandma Dee and Big Dee who taught her how to quilt herself. She stood there with her scarred hands hidden in the folds of her skirt. She looked at her sister with something like fear but she wasn't mad at her. This was Maggie's portion. This was the way she knew God to work.

When I looked at her like that something hit me in the top of my head and ran down to the soles of my feet, just like when I'm in church and the spirit of God touches me and I get happy and shout. I did something I never had done before: hugged Maggie to me, then dragged her on into the room, snatched the quilts out of Miss Wangero's hands and dumped them into Maggie's lap. Maggie just sat there on my bed with her mouth open.

"Take one or two of the others," I said to Dee.

But she turned without a word and went out to Hakim-a-barber.

"You just don't understand," she said, as Maggie and I came out to the car.

"What don't I understand?" I wanted to know.

"Your heritage," she said. And then she turned to Maggie, kissed her, and said, "You ought to try to make something of yourself, too, Maggie. It's really a new day for us. But from the way you and Mama still live you'd never know it."

She put on some sunglasses that hid everything above the tip of her nose and her chin.

Maggie smiled; maybe at the sunglasses. But a real smile, not scared. After we watched the car dust settle I asked Maggie to bring me a dip of snuff. And then the two of us sat there just enjoying, until it was time to go in the house and go to bed.

Journal and Discussion Questions

1 Summarize "Everyday Use." What is the significance of the title, "Everyday Use"? Find the passage in the story from which the title is taken. What is the significance of this passage in the story?

2 What do Alice Walker's physical descriptions of Mama, Dee, and Maggie reveal about them? Why does Mama imagine herself thinner in her fantasy about appearing on television with Dee? Why does Walker tell the story "Everyday Use" from Mama's point of view rather than another character's point of view?

3 According to Mama, Dee "used to read to us without pity; forcing words, lies, other folks' habits, whole lives upon us two, sitting trapped and ignorant under her voice. She washed us in a river of make-believe, burned us with a lot of knowledge we didn't necessarily need to know." What do you think Dee was reading? Why was her reading a point of contention between Dee and Mama?

4 Why are Dee and Hakim-a-barber so interested in African culture? How do they express this interest? Why doesn't Mama understand their interest in Africa?

5 Why does Dee take a photograph of the house making sure that Mama, Maggie, and a cow are in the picture? Why does Dee want the churn, the butter dish, the bench, and especially the quilts? What do the quilts mean, or symbolize, to Dee, to Mama, and to Maggie? Why does Mama think it important to remember that Dee hated the old house and refused Mama's gift of a quilt when she went to college?

6 What does the final exchange between Mama and Dee reveal about what "heritage" means to each of them? Why does Mama object to Dee's desire to display the quilts? Why does Dee think Mama doesn't understand her heritage? What criticisms does the story imply about these two views?

7 Considering the similarities between Walker and her character Dee—both from poor rural backgrounds, well-educated readers, and interested in African history and culture—why does Walker's story seem so critical of Dee?

Topics for Writing

1 Compare and evaluate the two views of African American folk culture represented by Mama and Dee in "Everyday Use."

2 Describe a possession that has meaning because it is related to the history, culture, or heritage of your family, neighborhood, or another community to which you belong. Discuss what the object symbolizes to the community, how its meaning may have changed over time, and whether members of the community find different meaning in that object.

THREE QUILTS

As Dee realizes in Alice Walker's "Everyday Use," quilts are an important kind of folk art. Movies such as *How to Make an American Quilt* and *Stepmom* prominently feature quilt-making as an important way for people, women especially, to express themselves and to pass on something about themselves to their children. Museums often feature displays of quilts, and there are dozens of Web sites that display quilts or provide support and materials to quilt-makers.

For the last two centuries, quilts have been an especially important folk art form for women, African Americans, and Native Americans, especially when they were discouraged or prevented from practicing "higher" forms of visual arts, such as painting and sculpture. Unlike Mama's quilts in "Everyday Use," the three quilts in this section were made to be displayed.

Harriet Powers, Bible Quilt

THE "BIBLE QUILT" WAS FINISHED AROUND 1886 BY HARRIET POWERS (b. 1837), a former slave from Clark County, Georgia, who used "traditional African applique technique" to make quilts that incorporated Bible stories, astronomical events, and local legends. The Bible Quilt and other quilts by Powers are on display in the Smithsonian Institute. When her family needed money, Powers reluctantly sold the Bible Quilt to Jennie Smith, who had wanted to buy it when she first saw it on display at the 1886 Athens Cotton Fair. Powers insisted on explaining each frame of the quilt to Smith before giving it up. Smith described the Bible Quilt in her diary, with quotations from Powers.

No. 1 represents Adam and Eve in the Garden of Eden, naming the animals, and listening to the subtle whisper of the "sarpent which is degiling Eve." It will be noticed that the only animal represented with feet is the only animal that has no feet. The elephant, camel, leviathan, and ostrich appear in this scene.

No. 2 is a continuation of Paradise but this time Eve has "conceived and bared a son" though he seems to have made his appearance in pantaloons, and has made a pet of the fowl. The bird of Paradise in the right lower corner is resplendent in green and white calico.

No. 3 is "Satan amidst the seven stars," whatever that may mean, and is not as I first thought, a football player. I am sure I have never seen a jauntier devil.

No. 4 is where Cain "is killing his brother Abel, and the stream of blood which flew over the earth" is plainly discernible. Cain being a shepherd is accompanied by sheep.

No. 5 Cain here goes into the land of Nod to get him a wife. There are bears, leopards, elks, and a "kangaroo hog" but the gem of the scene is an orange colored calico lion in the center, who has a white tooth sticking prominently from his lower lip. The leading characteristic of the animal is its large neck and fierce manner. This lion has a tiny neck and a very meek manner and coy expression.

No. 6 is Jacob's dream "when he lied on the ground" with the angel ascending or descending the ladder. She has rather a stylish appearance.

No. 7 is the baptism of Christ. The bat-like creature swooping down is "the Holy Sperret extending in the likeness of a dove."

No. 8 "Has reference to the crucifixion." The globular objects attached to the crosses like balloons by a string represent the darkness of the earth and the moon turning into blood, and is stitched in red and black calico.

No. 9 This is Judas Ascariot and the thirty pieces of silver. The silver is done in green calico. The large disc at his feet is "the star that appeared in 1886 for the first time in three hundred years."

No. 10 is the Last Supper, but the number of disciples is curtailed by five. They are all robed in white spotted cloth, but Judas is clothed in drab, being a little off-color in character.

No. 11 "The next history is the Holy Family; Joseph, the Vargint and the infant Jesus with the stare of Bethlehem over his head. Them is the crosses which he had to bear through his undergoing. Anything for wisement. We can't go back no further than the Bible."

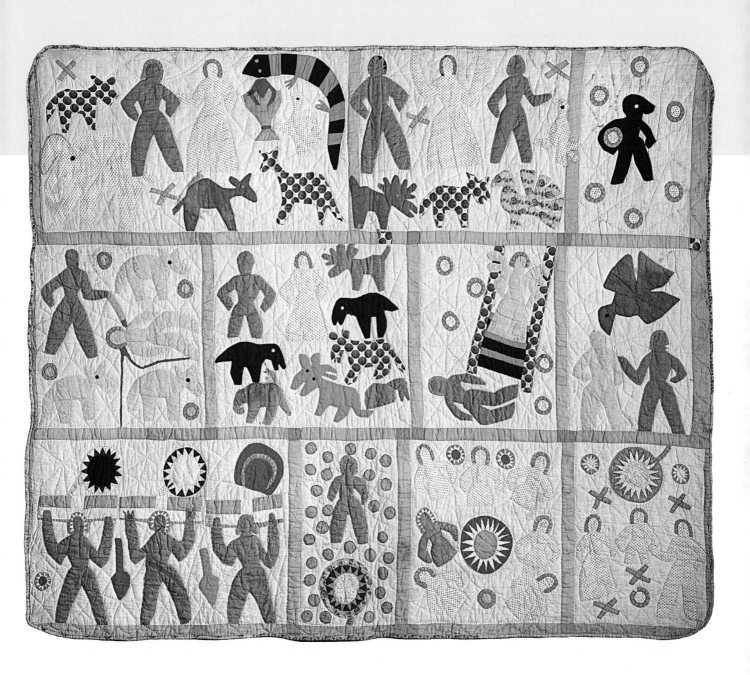

Polly Calistro, Around America

POLLY CALISTRO'S QUILT "AROUND AMERICA" IS PART OF THE LIBRARY OF Congress American Memory collection "Quilts and Quiltmaking in America: 1978–1996" at memory .loc.gov/ammem/qlthtml/qlthome.html. Calistro's quilt won a New Hampshire State award sponsored by Land's End in 1992. A quilt-maker for more than 15 years, Calistro has written that she learned to quilt by "Reading, asking questions, by doing (learning from my own mistakes)." Rather than base her "Around America" quilt on a traditional pattern, "I was looking at photo albums of 3 family vacations and thought I could use cloth to duplicate the photos. [. . .] I began with using what I had on hand, then added as I went along as all my blocks are all different."

The AIDS Memorial Quilt

BEGUN IN 1987 TO RAISE AWARENESS ABOUT THE AIDS EPIDEMIC, THE "AIDS Memorial Quilt" is "the largest ongoing community arts project in the world," according to its official Web site (www.aidsquilt.org), and it continues to grow. Each of the more than 40,000 3′x 6′ panels was made by a different contributor to remember someone who died of AIDS. The "AIDS Memorial Quilt" is sponsored by the NAMES Project Foundation, which raises money to maintain and display the quilt and to contribute to AIDS research. The NAMES Project Foundation also keeps an archive of photographs and letters about the people memorialized by the quilt. Pictured here is a reproduction of the first block of panels in the "AIDS Memorial Quilt."

Journal and Discussion Questions

1 What may have been Harriet Powers' intentions in retelling stories from the Bible in her quilt? Why do you think Powers chose these particular stories? What is the significance of the last panel in the quilt?

2 What sections of Jennie Smith's diary entry on Harriet Powers' "Bible Quilt" are the most insightful? Why? What sections appear less insightful? Why? What can you add to her observations and insights?

3 Why do you think the Smithsonian Institution decided to display Powers' "Bible Quilt"? What is significant about the "Bible Quilt"? Is it important to know that Powers was a former slave from rural Georgia to fully appreciate the "Bible Quilt"? Why or why not?

4 Try to identify all the images in Polly Calistro's "Around America" quilt. Why do you think Calistro chose these images? What impressions of the United States are provided in "Around America"? What is the overall image of America in this quilt?

5 Considering that Calistro selected her images from photographs of family vacations, what does the "Around America" quilt suggest to you about American vacations and how we use photographs to remember our vacations?

6 Why do you think the NAMES Project Foundation decided to use a quilt rather than another art form to represent the victims of AIDS? What panels from the AIDS Memorial Quilt here are most surprising, interesting, or unusual? What do you think the intention was behind these panels?

7 What do you know about the people who are memorialized in the first block of the AIDS Memorial Quilt? What does each panel reveal about the person who constructed the panel? What overall impression about the people who died of AIDS does the AIDS Memorial Quilt create?

8 Conduct some research about the debates about AIDS in 1987, when the AIDS Memorial Quilt was begun. What position do you think the AIDS Memorial Quilt was arguing in this debate? How do you think the message of the AIDS Memorial Quilt may have changed since 1987?

Topics for Writing

1 Write an essay comparing and contrasting Harriet Powers' "Bible Quilt," Polly Calistro's "Around America" quilt, and the first block of the AIDS Memorial Quilt and what they express about American culture.

2 Using Jennie Smith's diary entry on page 380 as a model, write a journal explaining Polly Calistro's "Around America" or the first block of the AIDS Memorial Quilt, panel by panel. Or, on paper, design a quilt of ten to fifteen panels and write an essay explaining your quilt. Your quilt could tell a story, represent you or someone you know, represent America or another region, or express something else.

3 Imagine that Jennie Smith was asked to write an article about Harriet Powers' "Bible Quilt" for one of the new women's magazines of the 1880s. If she used her diary as her prewriting for this article, what would the article say? How would it be organized?

4 Conduct research on the art and history of quilting (perhaps including interviews with quiltmakers) and write a research paper on the importance of quilting. Or conduct research on another type of folk art and write a research paper on that art for readers who are unfamiliar with it.

Connecting the Readings

Considering Alice Walker's "Everyday Use," Harriet Powers' "Bible Quilt," Polly Calistro's "Around America" quilt, and the "AIDS Memorial Quilt" (and perhaps further research on quilts), write an essay discussing the significance of quilts in American culture.

LET THE GOOD TIMES ROLL

BY CHRIS ROSE

Chris Rose (1960–) is a columnist for the New Orleans newspaper, *The Times-Picayune*, and he also gives commentary on *The NewsHour with Jim Lehrer* on PBS and *Morning Edition* on National Public Radio. Rose contributed to the Pulitzer-Prize–winning coverage of the destruction and trauma that New Orleans endured after Hurricane Katrina struck the city on August 29, 2005, and the area's difficult, slow recovery. Rose and his wife and three children evacuated New Orleans on August 29, but, like most of the newspaper's staff, he returned a few days later while the city was still flooded and without power and other services to write essays about his personal observations and experiences of the city and surrounding area. "Let the Good Times Roll" first appeared as one of Rose's *Times– Picayune* columns on December 13, 2005, and was reprinted in Rose's book, *1 Dead in Attic: After Katrina*, a collection of his 2005 and 2006 columns about post-Katrina Louisiana.

MARDI GRAS. IT'S NOT ON THE table. It's not a point of negotiation or a bargaining chip.

We're going to have it, and that's that. End of discussion.

Folks in faraway places are going to feel the misery of missing it, and that is a terrible thing. In the past, I have missed the season a couple of times because of story assignments elsewhere, and it sucked to be away from the center of the universe and not be a part of this city's fundamental, quintessential, and indelible cultural landmark.

But we can't turn off the lights and keep the costumes in storage and ladders in the shed for another year just because we are beaten and broken and so many of us are not here.

In fact, we have to do this because we are beaten and broken and so many of us are not here.

Katrina has proved, more than ever, that we are resilient. We are tougher than dirt. Certainly tougher than the dirt beneath our levees.

The social and celebratory nature of this event defines this city, and this is no time to lose definition. The edges are too blurry already.

Some folks say it sends the wrong message, but here's the thing about that: New Orleans is in a very complicated situation as far as "sending a message" goes these days. It's a tricky two way street.

On the one hand, it is vital to our very survival that the world outside here understand just how profoundly and completely destroyed this city is right now, with desolate power grids and hundreds of thousands of residents living elsewhere and in limbo.

Jobs, businesses, and the public spirit are all about as safely shored as the 17th Street Canal floodwall. We're leaking. And we could very well breach in the coming year or two.

We very well could.

On the other hand, we need to send a message that we are still New Orleans. We are the soul of America. We embody the triumph of the human spirit. Hell, we *are* Mardi Gras.

And Zulu can say they're only playing if they get it their way and Rex can say nothing at all and the mayor—our fallen and befuddled rock star—can say that he wants it one day and he doesn't want it the next day, but the truth is: It's not up to any of them. It's up to me now. And we're having it.

And here's a simple, not-so-eloquent reason why: If we don't have Mardi Gras, the terrorists win. The last thing we need right now is to divide ourselves over our most cherished event.

If the national news wants to show people puking on Bourbon Street as a metaphor for some sort of displaced priorities in this town, so be it. The only puking I've seen at Mardi Gras in the past ten years is little babies throwing up on their mothers' shoulders after a bottle.

To encapsulate the notion of Mardi Gras as nothing more than a big drunk is to take the simple and stupid way out, and I, for one, am getting tired of staying stuck on simple and stupid.

Mardi Gras is not a parade. Mardi Gras is not girls flashing on French Quarter balconies. Mardi Gras is not an alcoholic binge.

Mardi Gras is bars and restaurants changing out all the CDs in their jukeboxes to Professor Longhair and the Neville Brothers, and it is annual front-porch crawfish

boils hours before the parades so your stomach and attitude reach a state of grace, and it is returning to the same
street corner, year after year, and standing next to the
same people, year after year—people whose names you
may or may not even know but you've watched their kids
grow up in this public tableau and when they're not
there, you wonder: Where are those guys this year?

It is dressing your dog in a stupid costume and cheer-
ing when the marching bands go crazy and clapping and
saluting the military bands when they crisply snap to.

Now that part, more than ever.

It's mad piano professors converging on our city
from all over the world and banging the 88s until dawn
and laughing at the hairy-shouldered men in dresses
too tight and stalking the Indians under the Claiborne
overpass and thrilling the years you find them and
lamenting the years you don't and promising yourself
you will next year.

It's wearing frightful color combinations in public
and rolling your eyes at the guy in your office who—
like clockwork, year after year—denies that he got the
baby in the king cake and now someone else has to
pony up the ten bucks for the next one.

Mardi Gras is the love of life. It is the harmonic convergence of our food, our music, our creativity, our eccentricity, our neighborhoods, and our joy of living. All at once.

And it doesn't really matter if there are superpa-
rades or even any parades at all this year. Because some
group of horn players will grab their instruments and
they will march down the Avenue because that's what
they do, and I, for one, will follow.

If there are no parades, I'm hitching a boom box to
a wagon, putting James Booker on the CD player, and
pulling my kids down the Avenue and you're welcome
to come along with me and where more than two
tribes gather, there is a parade.

We are the parade. We are Mardi Gras. We're
Whoville, man—you can take away the beads and the
floats and all that crazy stuff, but we're still coming
out into the street. Cops or no cops. Postparade garbage pickup or no garbage pickup—as if anyone could
tell the friggin' difference!

If you are stuck somewhere else, in some other
town, bring it to them. If you've got a job somewhere
else now, take off that Tuesday and get all the New Orleanians you know and gather in a park somewhere
and cook up a mass of food and put some music on a
box and raise a little hell.

And raise a glass to us, brothers and sisters, because we're in here fighting this fight and we'll raise a
glass to you because you cannot be here with us and
we know you want to. Let the whole damn country
hear Al Johnson yelling "It's Carnival time" and let
them know we're not dead and if we are dying, we're
going to pretend we're not.

Fly the flag. Be in that number. This is our battle to
win or lose. Hopefully, of one mind and one message.
That we are still here. And that we are still New Orleans.

Journal and Discussion Questions

1 Outline "Let the Good Times Roll." What position is Chris
Rose arguing in "Let the Good Times Roll"? What reasons does
he state and imply in support of this position?

2 Why does Rose state his position in such a stubborn tone
in the introduction to "Let the Good Times Roll"? Why does he
end the second paragraph with the fragment "End of discussion" but then go on to discuss his position on Mardi Gras for
another 27 paragraphs?

3 Why, according to Rose, is Mardi Gras especially important to New Orleanians as they struggle to recover from
Hurricane Katrina? How do the locals' experiences of Mardi
Gras differ from the Mardi Gras experience for national news
reporters and tourists? How does Rose use this comparison
to explain and support his central argument?

4 Why didn't Rose raise a popular argument at the time,
that New Orleans should celebrate Mardi Gras in 2006 to
bring badly needed tourist dollars into the city? Why did he
barely mention the opinions of the mayor of New Orleans and
the Zulu and Rex krewes, two of the city's most important
Mardi Gras organizations? Would Rose's argument be stronger
if he considered more people's positions about celebrating
Mardi Gras? Why or why not?

5 "Let the Good Times Roll" is the English translation of a
French motto, *Laissez les bon temps rouler*, for the party-loving
spirit of New Orleans and French Louisiana. Why did Rose
choose this expression for his title?

6 What does Rose have to say to evacuated New Orleanians who are unable to return home for Mardi Gras? Why does
Rose conclude "Let the Good Times Roll" by directly addressing
these readers?

Topics for Writing

1 Analyze Chris Rose's "Let the Good Times Roll" and what the Mardi Gras celebration in New Orleans means both to its residents and to the tourists and college students who travel to New Orleans for the festivities and how the meanings of Mardi Gras were changed by Hurricane Katrina. This writing project may be expanded into a research paper if you look up news and academic articles about Mardi Gras and representations of Mardi Gras on Web sites like YouTube.

2 Drawing on Rose's "Let the Good Times Roll," argue whether New Orleans should have celebrated Mardi Gras less than seven months after Hurricane Katrina and the flooding and evacuation of the city.

3 Write a research paper about another community festival or holiday celebration analyzing how the celebration has been influenced by factors such as the community's ethnic makeup, economic considerations such as tourism, and changes in the community. Interviews with people who remember earlier celebrations or who have insider knowledge about the planning and organization of the celebration could be part of your research.

SANTA CLAUS

BY HOWARD NEMEROV

Howard Nemerov (1920–1991) was the Poet Laureate of the United States in 1963–1964 and again in 1988–1989 and won many awards for his poetry, including the National Book Award and membership in the American Academy of Poets. From 1969 until his death, Nemerov was the Distinguished Poet in Residence at Washington University in St. Louis. Although best known for his poetry, Nemerov also wrote fiction, essays, and literary criticism. His books include *The Howard Nemerov Reader; Trying Conclusions: New and Selected Poems, 1961–1991; Journal of the Fictive Life; Figures of Thought: Speculations on the Meaning of Poetry and Other Essays;* and the novels *Homecoming Game* and *Melodramatists.* "Santa Claus" was published in Nemerov's 1962 book of poetry, *The Next Room of the Dream,* as well as the 1975 Pulitzer Prize–winning *The Collected Poems of Howard Nemerov.* Written in iambic pentameter, "Santa Claus" displays an acid wit in condemning how materialism and commercialism have changed the celebration of Christmas.

Somewhere on his travels the strange Child
Picked up with this overstuffed confidence man,
Affection's inverted thief, who climbs at night
Down chimneys, into dreams, with this world's goods.
Bringing all the benevolence of money,
He teaches the innocent to want, thus keeps
Our fat world rolling. His prescribed costume,
White flannel beard, red belly of cotton waste,
Conceals the thinness of essential hunger,
An appetite that feeds on satisfaction;

Or, pregnant with possessions, he brings forth
Vanity and the void. His name itself
Is corrupted, and even Saint Nicholas, in his turn,
Gives off a faint and reminiscent stench,
The merest soupçon, of brimstone and the pit.

Now, at the season when the Child is born
To suffer for the world, suffer the world,
His bloated Other, jovial satellite
And sycophant, makes his appearance also
In a glitter of goodies, in a rock candy glare.
Played at the better stores by bums, for money,
This annual savior of the economy
Speaks in the parables of the dollar sign:
Suffer the little children to come to Him.

At Easter, he's anonymous again,
Just one of the crowd lunching on Calvary.

Journal and Discussion Questions

1 What is the central theme of "Santa Claus"? How does Howard Nemerov develop this theme stanza by stanza?

2 How does the poem describe Santa Claus? Compare this description with traditional descriptions of Santa Claus, such as in the poem "The Night Before Christmas." What do Nemerov's details reveal about the character of Santa Claus? Why does Nemerov give the reader two conflicting choices about the meaning of Santa's costume and fat "red belly" in lines 8–12?

3 What does Nemerov mean, literally and metaphorically, when he writes, "His name itself / Is corrupted," in lines 12–13? Why does Nemerov write that even the name "Saint Nicholas" "Gives off a faint and reminiscent stench, / The merest soupçon, of brimstone and the pit." at the end of the first stanza?

4 Make a two-column list comparing and contrasting Santa Claus and the Child in the poem. What do the two figures symbolize about the celebration of Christmas in "Santa Claus"?

5 What religious terms appear in the second stanza of "Santa Claus"? What are the meanings of these terms in the poem? Why does Nemerov use the Bible quote, "Suffer the little children to come to Him." at the end of the second stanza?

6 What do lines 22–23, "Played at the better stores by bums, for money, / This annual savior of the economy," say about the economic role of Santa Claus and Christmas?

7 Arguments condemning the commercialization of Christmas are very common. Santa Claus is the central opponent of the commercialization of Christmas, even as he works for Macy's Department Store, in the 1946 Christmas movie classic *Miracle on 34th Street*. What do Nemerov's criticisms about commercialism in "Santa Claus" have in common with other arguments you have heard and read? How are Nemerov's criticisms of the commercialization of Christmas different from other anticommercialism arguments?

Topics for Writing

1 Write an essay analyzing Howard Nemerov's "Santa Claus" as a criticism of modern celebrations of Christmas.

2 Write an essay defending Santa Claus from Nemerov's criticisms.

3 Write a research paper about Christmas and the economy. Possible topics include the economic importance of Christmas in the U.S., how gift-giving became an important part of the Christmas celebration, and how the commercial importance of Christmas has changed the way people celebrate Christmas.

4 Write a research paper about how economic and commercial factors have affected another part of popular culture, such as a festival or celebration or a piece of popular music.

ASSAULTS ON TV MISDIRECTED

BY MICHAEL MEDVED

Michael Medved (1948–) is a conservative radio commentator, writer, and film critic who writes frequently about politics, popular culture, and religion. He has written or co-written ten books, including What Really Happened to the Class of '65, Hollywood vs. America, *and—with his wife, Diane Medved—*Saving Childhood: Protecting Our Children from the National Assault on Innocence. *"Assaults on TV Misdirected" is an editorial column that first appeared in the national newspaper* USA Today *on May 23, 2005. In this column, Medved examines a familiar complaint about television— that it often underrepresents or stereotypes minorities and other groups—and discusses the merits of this complaint. More writings by Medved can be found on his Web site, MichaelMedved.com.*

COMPLAINTS BY SPECIAL-INTEREST GROUPS ignore the real power of the public—selectively choosing what we watch.

Savvy observers occasionally note television's resemblance to the weather: Everybody loves to complain about it, but nobody can do anything to fix it.

This important insight, however, has done nothing to diminish the ardor of activists who regularly assault the nation's most influential medium of communications for real or imagined crimes. In a single week in April, for instance, representatives of three interest groups complained simultaneously of their under-representation in the TV world.

The National Asian Pacific American Legal Consortium released results of a study showing that Asian-Americans represented only 2.7% of regular characters on prime time TV, despite comprising nearly 5% of the national population. Karen Narasaki, president of the consortium, also lamented the fact that the networks reinforced stereotypes by showing Asians as smart and successful, while giving insufficient attention to dysfunctional individuals and families.

Meanwhile, a group of black TV professionals gathered at a session at the National Association of Television Program Executives to voice very different complaints. While acknowledging that African-Americans are slightly over-represented on TV screens, the producers worried about the absence of people of color in "decision-making positions" within the broadcast industry. Karla Winfrey (no relation to Oprah) of Stone Mountain, Ga., said, "It's difficult when you have people who make decisions who are not able or willing to accept the fact that not everybody is a hip-hopper or an athlete. There are people in our communities who are teachers, doctors, businesspeople, and we have great stories."

Meanwhile, another significant segment of the population fretted over its shabby treatment by a major network. Conservatives, despite their increasingly powerful presence on cable TV and talk radio, feel excluded and disregarded by the longstanding preponderance of liberal voices on public television. Ken Tomlinson, president of the Corporation for Public Broadcasting, is committed to greater balance and diversity on PBS—efforts that carry special urgency because of taxpayer funding for public television.

Do any—or all—of these complaints from Asian-Americans, blacks and conservatives deserve serious consideration?

On the one hand, the importance of televised imagery can't be ignored. The average American invests nearly 30 hours a week watching the tube, so a typical citizen will spend more time with TV fictional characters than with his own neighbors. TV portrayals of minority groups can achieve real world consequences: Most social critics would agree, for example, that the more frequent and sympathetic treatment of gay characters in prime time has encouraged the vastly greater acceptance of homosexuality.

In the case of Asian-Americans, it's hard to imagine how favorable stereotyping or slight under-representation have damaged a segment of the population already enjoying disproportionate educational and economic success. If the networks suddenly provided one-out-of-20 TV characters who were recognizably Asian (instead of today's one out of 37), the programming might provide a marginally more accurate reflection of reality. But who would benefit?

Meanwhile, an increased presence of African-Americans in network executive suites might enhance the power of a tiny handful of black producers. But given the fact that black viewers already watch more TV than any other portion of the public, raising viewership to even higher levels probably would harm, rather than help, the African-American community. Most educational experts agree that excessive engagement with TV leads to an array of negative outcomes, including diminished school performance, lack of exercise, obesity and other problems. For the black community at the moment, the biggest challenge isn't the low quality of TV, but the high quantity that most children watch.

As for complaints from conservatives about PBS, fairness argues against any use of government money to advance a one-sided agenda. Nevertheless, even the most indignant activists can't claim that sparsely viewed liberal shows on struggling public TV stations across the country somehow pose a serious threat to the current Republican hegemony in Washington.

In other words, the complaints by interest groups illustrate the same unfortunate tendency to emphasize supply-side solutions, rather than demand-side solutions, to the problems of TV's impact. We spend too much time fretting over the way the industry produces programming, and too little worrying about the way the public consumes it. Statistical analysis shows that black characters are over-represented on TV, while Asians are under-represented. But that hardly means that the medium is good for blacks and bad for Asians. The influence of broadcast images depends on how selectively consumers choose to watch, not the ethnically based casting decisions executives agree to make.

Ultimately, the only television schedule the public and activists reliably can control is the schedule of what we watch. We might not be able to determine what the industry makes, but we always make the final decision on what we take. In short, complaining about the weather may do nothing to change it, but you always have the option to come in out of the rain.

Journal and Discussion Questions

1 What is the central position that Michael Medved is arguing in "Assaults on TV Misdirected"? How do the other positions that he argues support this position?

2 Outline "Assaults on TV Misdirected." Where does Medved present opposing arguments? Where does he refute those arguments? Is "Assaults on TV Misdirected" effectively organized? Why or why not?

3 Medved examines complaints about the representation of Asian Americans, African Americans, and conservatives in television. Summarize each complaint. Why would the National Asian Pacific American Legal Consortium object to positive stereotyping of Asian Americans? What is Medved's response to each complaint? Which complaint seems most serious to Medved? Why?

4 Medved argues that increasing the number of African Americans in network executive positions would harm the black community. What is his reasoning? How do you think the black executives who made the complaint would respond to Medved's argument?

5 Explain the fairness argument that Medved offers regarding conservative representation on PBS. Why does Medved, a conservative, disagree with conservative activists' call for more representation on PBS?

6 What does Medved mean by "supply-side" and "demand-side" solutions? Why are supply-side solutions superior to demand-side solutions, according to Medved? Do you agree? Why or why not?

7 Medved refers to a well known saying about the weather in his introduction and conclusion. What point is he making with this saying? Does his conclusion say anything different than the introduction in this reference? How effective are the introduction and the conclusion? Why?

8 What sources does Medved use in his argument? How do these sources make his editorial more credible and persuasive? Where do you think Medved found the statistic that Americans on average watch television almost 30 hours a week?

Topics for Writing

1 Write an editorial that agrees or disagrees with one of Michael Medved's arguments in "Assaults on TV Misdirected." If you agree with Medved, try to develop his reasons further or come up with additional reasons.

2 Conduct your own research about how a group or a profession is represented on television, and argue whether television represents this group fairly and accurately, and what, if anything, should be done about any unfair stereotyping.

3 Medved makes a couple of claims about the effects that television viewing has had for gays and for blacks while expressing skepticism about the political influence of public television. Research one of these claims or another claim about the effects of television viewing on society and write a research paper arguing for or against this claim.

BAMBOOZLED DVD COVER

Spike Lee's movie *Bamboozled*, which premiered in 2000, is a scathing critique of how African Americans are represented in popular culture and a harsh satire of recent situation comedies with predominantly African American casts. The protagonist in *Bamboozled*, played by Damon Wayans, is an African American television writer who is angry that TV networks will no longer air sitcoms that portray positive images of black families like the 1980s series *The Cosby Show* and *The Fresh Prince of Bel Air*. In frustration, Wayans creates a comedy that revives the black stereotypes of minstrel shows. But instead of white actors in black face, his show stars African American comedians wearing very black makeup. To the surprise and consternation of the writer and actors, the series becomes an instant hit. The cover for the *Bamboozled* DVD itself expresses some of Lee's critique of American popular culture's portrayal of blacks today.

Journal and Discussion Questions

1 Describe the *Bamboozled* DVD cover. How does it exploit black stereotypes? What does the cover tell you about Spike Lee's movie and his ideas about the images of African Americans in popular culture?

2 What specific television series do you think Lee has in mind with his criticisms? Why? How do some black comic characters in movies and on TV resemble minstrel show stereotypes? How are they different? Is Lee fair in comparing these characters to minstrel shows? Why or why not?

3 How does the DVD cover use exaggeration to make its point? Is exaggeration an effective technique for Lee's argument? Why or why not?

4 Who is the audience for the DVD cover? Lee would expect people who enjoyed his other films on African American life, such as *Do the Right Thing, Jungle Fever, 4 Little Girls,* and *School Daze,* to be offended by the stereotypes pictured on this poster. Why would he approve a DVD cover that might offend people that he hopes will buy tickets to *Bamboozled*? How do these images sell his movie?

5 In its design, the DVD cover resembles posters that advertised live minstrel shows in the nineteenth and early twentieth century. What features are taken from these old posters? Why did the artist of the DVD cover imitate posters that most movie-goers have never seen?

6 Does the DVD cover interest you in seeing *Bamboozled*? Why or why not?

Topics for Writing

1 Watch Spike Lee's *Bamboozled*, and analyze the *Bamboozled* poster, discussing how well it represents what Lee's movie is about and how effectively it persuades audiences to see his film.

2 Conduct research on the minstrel shows that Lee refers to, and write a research paper comparing the minstrel show images of African Americans to their portrayals in popular culture today.

3 Review *Bamboozled* or another movie or television show that critiques television, movies, music, or another genre of popular culture (e.g. the movies *Network* and *Broadcast News*, satirical skits of popular culture on *Saturday Night Live* or *Mad TV*, or a song that comments on a trend in music or pop culture). Your review should focus on the work's criticism of popular culture.

Connecting the Readings

Compare and evaluate Michael Medved's and Spike Lee's critiques of how American television portrays African Americans and other groups. Discuss whether you agree with their criticisms—and why or why not—based on your observations of at least three different television shows.

A DROP IN THE OCEAN

BY JOHN POWERS

John Powers (1951-) writes about popular culture, film, and politics for *Vogue* and the National Public Radio program *Fresh Air* with Terry Gross. He is the author of *Sore Winners: American Idols, Patriotic Shoppers, and Other Strange Species in George Bush's America.* "A Drop in the Ocean" appeared in Powers' regular "On" column in *L. A. Weekly* in January 2005, shortly after the giant tsunami in the Indian Ocean killed thousands of people in southern Asia on December 29, 2004.

Victims suggest innocence. And innocence, by the inexorable logic that governs all relational terms, suggests guilt.

—SUSAN SONTAG

TV MAY NOT HAVE A CLUE HOW TO cover the death of a famous intellectual, but an epochal tsunami sure makes it feel right at home. Within hours of last week's calamity in Asia, the cable networks had already launched into megadeath overkill. CNN gave its coverage the tag line "Tsunami Disaster" (replacing its initial attempt, "Asia Tsunami," which sounded more like a porn actress than a catastrophe). Reporters began churning out human-interest stories, from the ersatz "Sophie's Choice" of the water-buffeted Aussie mum who had to decide which of her sons to let go (unlike in the novel, both kids survived) to reports that Jet Li had injured his toe protecting his daughter in the Maldives—don't laugh, he *acts* with that foot! Hour after hour, the networks recycled each fresh snippet of footage: waves pummeling beaches, graying tourists clinging to balconies, children's small bodies lying in heartbreaking rows. While pedants explained the difference between tsunamis and tidal waves, anchors kept warning us that we might be disturbed by the upcoming footage—as if we weren't wishing they'd shut up so we could see whatever you called it.

And really, who could blame anyone for being riveted? The number of casualties was so staggering—150,000 dead, another half-million badly injured—that you could watch for hours without getting your mind around it. The vast majority of casualties were locals, yet as in the 2002 Bali bombing, our media paid disproportionate attention to Western tourists. This was a pity, for nothing in English was more harrowingly poetic than the testimony of a woman, Chanjira Sangkarak, from the demolished Thai village of Nam Khem, who told *New York Times* reporter Seth Mydans that she'd always been afraid of ghosts. But barely living through the tidal wave had changed her. "Now, I wasn't afraid," she said. "I wasn't afraid of ghosts and I wasn't afraid of the dead because I was dead already, too, and I had survived."

Still, the focus on tourists wasn't mere ethnocentrism. Viewers desperately wanted to hear precisely what happened, and most poor Sri Lankans or Indonesians don't speak English. It was fascinating to witness the emotional abyss separating studio talking heads, forced to spend hours screwing their faces into looks of compassionate concern, from shell-shocked European holidaymakers like the British woman who, six full days after the tsunami, sat in a wheelchair sobbing guiltily for not dying: "It's not fair on the people who didn't make it."

The Indonesians and Sri Lankans who did make it must reckon themselves lucky that there were tourists to help publicize the event. It will bring them billions of dollars in relief that didn't go to, say, Bangladesh back in 1991 when a typhoon killed more than 130,000 souls whose deaths barely registered on the international radar. Be honest. Had you ever heard of it? Here, the tourists served as our surrogates, our there-but-for-the-grace-of-God-go-I's. While most of us can't imagine dying of starvation or being hacked to pieces by one's neighbors, we've all stood on the beach and pictured what it might be like to see a tsunami coming. Hey, this could've happened to *me*.

I myself spent hours watching TV, then went on the Internet to get riper footage, and not because I was getting off on the suffering. I just wanted to see the damn wave. Like most people, all I'd previously known of tsunamis came from Hollywood disaster pictures or those Japanese prints with huge curling waves. Who knew the problem wasn't the wall of water's height, but that it roared forward like a runaway train? No, wait. That's a lousy metaphor. For what makes a tsunami so awesome is precisely the fact that it's *natural*. Unlike Darfur or Fallujah, last week's calamity was not man-made. As the Israeli daily *Haaretz* editorialized, such a natural disaster is a crushing reminder to security-mad nations like Israel (and, one could add, the U.S.) that "absolute existential security" is out of the question.

Not that we ought to genuflect before such acts of God like stupefied peasants or insurance companies. Back when the *Titanic* sank, Thomas Hardy wrote a famous poem, "Convergence of the Twain," in which, with characteristic cosmic fatalism, he pinned the catastrophe on "The Immanent Will that stirs and urges everything." Maybe so. Then again, while no human being was responsible for putting that iceberg in the ocean liner's path, countless passengers died because the ship's owners hadn't put lifeboats on the lower decks that served "the lower orders." The victims died as much from class bias as from Immanent Willfulness.

The same thing happened with the Indian Ocean tsunami, although it, too, had its cosmic apologists. "This is a moment to feel deeply bad," wrote *The New York Times*' normally chirpy David Brooks, "for the dead and for those of us who have no explanation." Well, yeah. But as we wallow in how incomprehensible the tragedy was, it's worth remembering that we *can* explain why tens of thousands lost their lives. There are the Thai authorities who, having apparently studied DVDs of *Jaws* to see how to do it wrong, didn't release warnings of possible trouble because it was the height of the tourist season. There are the slipshod Asian governments that, despite the area's famously dangerous fault lines, never spent the $20 million or so it would take to install the kind of tsunami detectors that monitor the Pacific Ocean. And, of course, there are the wealthy elites of South and Southeast Asia who, greedy for all the spoils of modernity, remain content to let most of their fellow citizens live without proper roads, proper shelter, proper communications.

In America, anyway, these foreign leaders took less public abuse than President Bush, whose response to the catastrophe was actually less cold than shockingly clueless. Within hours of the tsunami, everybody I knew was talking about how these terrible events could be parlayed into a PR bonanza for the U.S. Surely the administration would capitalize on this unhappy chance to show the world, especially the Muslim world, that we will use our enormous resources to save lives, especially Muslim lives. After all, this was a White House communications team so brilliant that it framed Dubya's head next to Mount Rushmore during a speech in South Dakota and transformed his stumbling inability to discuss the Iraq occupation into proof of steely resolve.

But evidently Karl Rove's genius at image–making doesn't travel beyond the U.S. border, nor is the Bush administration as good at seeming generous as at talking tough. (When Undersecretary of State John Bolton was asked about a possible carrot-and-stick approach to Iran, he memorably replied, "I don't do carrots.") The vacationing Bush didn't show up to offer condolences for 72 hours, the administration's initial offer of $15 million in relief was embarrassingly paltry (Bush's inauguration will cost $40 million), and Colin "What have I done to deserve this?" Powell spent his final days at State defending the U.S. against U.N. official Jan Egeland's charge that the Western nations were being "stingy." By the time it finally got into gear, the White House was behind the PR curve. Indeed, at a time when oil-rich Arab nations were doing shamefully little to help their fellow Muslims, it was America that appeared shamed into generosity.

And maybe we were. Possibly because we see so much suffering on our TV screens, it's become a national delusion that America is singularly benevolent in doling out foreign aid. More than half the country thinks we give nearly a quarter of our GNP to help other, less prosperous countries. In fact, we are amazingly cheap: We actually give less than one-half of one percent of our GNP. (They also skimp in France and Britain, whose sanctimony about America becomes nauseating once you see the figures.) Although every single American has spent $531 for the war in Iraq, he or she gives a mere $73 a year through the government in foreign aid. And lest we think this, like everything wicked, is George W. Bush's fault, it's worth noting that he actually pushed through the biggest increase in foreign aid since JFK.

Sadly, we are no more generous as private citizens. The U.S. is the most prosperous country in history. Even those on our welfare rolls enjoy a standard of living many times higher than the average worker in

> I myself spent hours watching TV, then went on the Internet to get riper footage, and not because I was getting off on the suffering. I just wanted to see the damn wave.

Meulaboh, the western Sumatra city where nearly half of its 50,000 residents were killed by the tidal wave. Although our wealth and their poverty are connected, the average American gives only slightly more than $17 a year to foreign aid (the average Frenchman only $3!). And when you consider that moguls like Bill Gates boost the per capita average by giving away, oh, $5 billion or so a year, that means the rest of us are giving only three or four bucks—frappuccino money!—to fight the hunger, disease and dehumanizing nullity that menace billions like an invisible tsunami.

Although our newscasts now ring with encouraging tales of international aid for the tidal wave's victims—on Monday, the two Bushes and Bill Clinton stood together like the Three Tenors—it would be even more heartening if it didn't take nature's capricious cruelty to make us share our bounty with those who spend their days on the cusp of death and disaster. After all, just because the universe is arbitrary and unfair, that doesn't mean we ought to follow its lead.

Journal and Discussion Questions

1 What is the thesis of John Powers' "A Drop in the Ocean"? Outline "A Drop in the Ocean." How many multi-paragraph blocks is "A Drop in the Ocean" organized into? What is the main idea of each block? How does each of these ideas support Powers' thesis?

2 Susan Sontag, who died shortly before the tsunami, is the "famous intellectual" that Powers alludes to in his lead sentence. How does the epigraph contribute to Powers' essay? Why do you think Powers compares television coverage of Sontag's death and the tsunami in his lead?

3 Powers begins paragraph 3 by writing, "Still, the focus on tourists wasn't mere ethnocentrism"? What was ethnocentric about American news coverage's focus on tourists who experienced the tsunami? How does Powers make this point in paragraph 2? How does he qualify this criticism in paragraph 3?

4 Why does Powers offer a metaphor describing the tsunami in paragraph 5 and then write, "No, wait. That's a lousy metaphor"? What is "lousy" about the metaphor? Why didn't Powers simply leave out this metaphor or replace it with another metaphor when he revised his column?

5 Powers often makes brief allusions and comparisons in his column, including the allusions to Sontag, Darfur, Fallujah, and Hollywood. List Powers' allusions to people and events that are not directly related to the tsunami. What do the allusions tell you about the audience Powers has in mind for his column? What does each allusion contribute to Powers' arguments?

6 Who does Powers quote in "A Drop in the Ocean" and why? Do you think he included a good variety of people to quote? Why or why not? What other people might Powers have quoted? How would his essay be different if he had quoted these people? Why does Powers quote Thomas Hardy's poem about the *Titanic*?

7 Powers's discussion turns to issues of the image and generosity of the United States in his conclusion. What is the main point of this conclusion? How does the discussion of tsunami news coverage lead up to this discussion of broader issues? Is the conclusion effective? Why or why not?

Topics for Writing

1 Based on John Powers' "A Drop in the Ocean," analyze the strengths and weaknesses of news coverage of the December 29, 2004, Indian Ocean tsunami.

2 Analyze and compare the coverage of a single news story by two or three news sources—newspapers, newsmagazines, cable news networks, broadcast news shows on television or radio, or internet news sites. What does the news coverage reveal about the interests, values, and world view of the news sources and perhaps of their audiences?

GANGSTERS— REAL AND UNREAL

BY NELSON GEORGE

Nelson George (1957–) is an African American who writes fiction, screenplays, magazine articles, and cultural criticism, often of popular music. He is a former editor of the music magazines *Record World* and *Billboard*, wrote a column in the *Village Voice* for several years, and authored several books, including *The Michael Jackson Story* and *The Death of Rhythm and Blues*. In "Gangsters—Real and Unreal," a chapter from George's 1998 book, *Hip Hop America*, George analyzes the relationship of hip-hop music (and other works of popular culture) with economic developments and crime and drug trends in urban African American society while composing a complex description and definition of gangsta rap.

People are usually the product of where they come from. The bonds that you made, the codes that were there, all have an influence on you later in life. You can reject them. You can say "Okay, those codes don't exist for me, because I'm not of that world anymore." But the reason for those codes—why people live that way—are very strong lessons. The most important reason is survival. It comes down to that. That struggle of the human form, the corporal, the flesh, to survive—anything to survive. I think those things you carry with you the rest of your life.

—Martin Scorsese, *Rolling Stone, 1990*

IN THE WAKE OF THE CIVIL RIGHTS Movement black middle-class families, and many working-class families, finally had the freedom to live wherever they could afford. Of course racism still kept them out of certain areas, but a lot of people up and down the economic ladder got enough capital—and guts—to finally get out of the old, embattled neighborhoods. Not just doctors and lawyers moved out of these black neighborhoods. So did bus drivers, teachers, and bureaucrats with new gigs in municipal governments. Ironically, the enhanced mobility of black wage earners left the old neighborhoods wide open to increased crime, which led to an increase in white flight. White merchants, vilified as exploiters by many of their Africa-American customers, were either burned out by urban riots or chased out by crime.

And the majority of that crime was instigated by drugs. As was tellingly illustrated by Allen and Albert Hughes in *Dead Presidents*, the change happened with a lethal quickness. In their film, a black GI leaves for Vietnam from a tough, yet still hopeful neighborhood

and returns to a meaner, more desperate and heroin-saturated ghetto. In fact, GIs contributed to this tragic change both as victims and predators.

In 1971, the U.S. Army estimated that 10 percent of our soldiers used heroin while in 'Nam and that 5 percent were hardcore junkies. Some black GIs, returning home to an uncertain future, brought heroin back with them as a hedge against unemployment. In so doing they participated in inaugurating a new wave of black criminal entrepreneurship—a street-corner response to President Nixon's rhetoric encouraging black capitalism in lieu of government aid.

The heroin invasion, while partially orchestrated by the Mafia and other established crime syndicates, brought new forces into American crime (Asian and South American traffickers) and empowered a new, vicious kind of black gangster. Heroin emboldened the black criminal class, which had been clustered in numbers running, prostitution, fencing, and robbery, to expand and become more predatory.

Prior to heroin's mass marketing in the late '60s, the prototypical black criminal was the numbers runner, a creature of the northern ghettos with a pedigree that went back to the '30s. Numbers runners were viewed as a necessary evil who, in the best-case scenario, acted as community bankers, processing daily investments from their customers. Less romantically, numbers runners were also unreliable liars who skimmed profits from winners and conveniently disappeared when someone hit big, though too much inconsistency in payment endangered his or her livelihood (and life). As drug dealers would later, the numbers runners profited off the community's poorest. They sold dreams and, in dribs and drabs, drained money out of black America.

Of course running numbers wasn't selling an inherently lethal product—just elusive big money dreams, the same as horse racing and other games of chance. Numbers running employed people in a network of criminal activity that was condoned by the community and the police because it provided hope and, on occasion, large sums of money to its customers. Numbers were, in fact, part of the glue that held together many poor African-American neighborhoods, a shared enthusiasm that sustained daily life at the same time it undercut it.

Alongside the numbers runner in the pantheon of preheroin black criminality were the pimp and the wino. While obviously an exploiter of women and male sexual desire, the pimp has been, in the mind of many men and more women than would admit it, a figure of fascination, a certain awe, and suppressed respect. At the core of this interest is the pimp's ability to control others. Any man who can, through business savvy, sexual prowess, understanding of human psychology, and yes, violence, get others to perform the most intimate sexual acts and give him the money titillates many at some undeniably base level.

In a warped and unhealthy way the pimp's ability to control his environment (i.e., his stable of women) has always been viewed as a rare example of black male authority over his domain. Despite decades of moral censure from church leaders and those incensed by his exploitation of women, the pimp endures as an antihero among young black males. The pimp's garb, slang, and persona influences the culture to this day and shows no signs of abating.

In contrast to the potent, romanticized pimp, the wino was the precursor to the heroin addict as the embodiment of urban tragedy. Heroin junkies weren't new to the black community in the '60s. It's just that, in the rarified world of jazz and music, they were more isolated, while the victims of cheap wine and alcohol had haunted street corners since African-Americans moved North. The sale of Ripple, Wild Irish Rose, and other juice-flavored poisons in poor and black neighborhoods foreshadowed the target marketing of malt liquor in the '80s and '90s.

Through black pop culture of the '60s and '70s one can experience the evolution in black criminal culture. In Richard Pryor's classic routine "The Wino and the Junkie," from his *That Nigger's Crazy* album, the great comedian depicts the wino as a city-living country wit and the junkie as a wasted young urban zombie. The split is significant in that Pryor, an artist/cocaine addict himself, provided nuance to the difference between addiction to heroin and alcohol and to how it would eventually affect the entire black community.

The Holloway House novels of Iceberg Slim and Donald Goines, published throughout the '60s and '70s, memorably documented the transition in black crime from pimping, numbers running, and grifting to selling smack. Slim (Robert Beck), a fair-skinned con man who often passed for white, wrote lovingly of country-bred hustlers who traveled to the big cities employing various psychological gambits to get women to prostitute themselves (as in *Pimp: The Story of My Life*) and to swindle men out of their hard-earned cash (as in *Trick Baby*). Goines, who succeeded Slim as essential black barbershop reading, was a longtime heroin addict gunned down in 1974, along with his wife, apparently while at his typewriter. During his tortured thirty-nine years on earth, Goines ground out sixteen novels about lost, mentally diseased people existing in squalid conditions, in blunt, brutal prose that, early in his career, possessed the ugly poetry of bracing pulp fiction.

In the real world, African-American heroin empires grew during the '70s around the country: in Chicago under the rule of the violent El Rukins gang; in the District of Columbia run by Rayfield Edmonds, Sr.; in New York City, first by Frank Matthews and later by "Mr. Untouchable"—Leroy "Nicky" Barnes. They all established large distribution networks and, in the case of Barnes, made international contacts for importation that superseded traditional white ethnic control. Just as many blaxploitation movie scenarios revolved around struggles to control crime in black neighborhoods, these real-life black kingpins found themselves in high-pitched short-term battles with the fading Italian and Irish syndicates—in the long run new forces would come to replace the Italians. The long stable hierarchy of American crime crumbled when new drugs, such as angel dust and cocaine, became popular in the streets.

> ## "
> ## There was little inspiration in grown men begging for quarters, stealing car radios, and sleeping curled up in doorways.
> ## "

Heroin's growth as a mass market commodity ended the drug's romantic association with black musicians. The idea of Charlie Parker and other musicians as "beautiful losers" rather than as what they were—gifted people with a debilitating addiction—largely collapsed as the squalid junkie lifestyle became clear on America's streets. There was little inspiration in grown men begging for quarters, stealing car radios, and sleeping curled up in doorways.

Heroin couldn't have run wild in the streets without widespread police and political corruption aiding its dissemination. Hand in hand with this moral failure, the federal government under President Nixon cut back on Democratic antipoverty programs and systematically ignored the economic development pleas of America's urbanites, whose jobs were fleeing to the suburbs.

There are all kinds of conspiracy theories about why heroin flowed so intensely into black neighborhoods. There is evidence that the CIA was involved in the Asian "golden triangle," purchasing and helping distribute heroin as a way to fund assassinations and other covert operations. This fact has evolved into the theory that heroin was imported into black communities by government forces (including the virulent, racist Federal Bureau of Investigation honcho J. Edgar Hoover) to undermine the civil rights movement. This theory of government conspiracy provided the premise to Melvin Van Peebles's screenplay for son Mario's 1995 film *Panther*. Sure, there's an edge of paranoia there, but the more you learn about the counterintelligence program (COINTELPRO) that the FBI and Justice Department targeted at black leaders, the easier it is to give these theories some credence.

It is a fact that in the '70s agent-provocateurs infiltrated Black Panther chapters around the nation, often rising to positions of authority where they helped sabotage an already high-strung organization. The police shooting of Chicago's Fred Hampton in 1969, instigated by a government informer in that Panther chapter, is just one of many documented episodes of internal espionage aimed at the period's black activists.

In August 1996, the *San Jose Mercury News,* a California daily, ran a series called "Dark Alliance" that connected the CIA with the importation of crack into Southern California during the '80s. African-American activists like Dick Gregory and Congresswoman Maxine Waters of South Central Los Angles embraced the report and stuck by its conclusions even after the CIA aggressively debunked the story and the *Mercury News* itself finally backed off most of its original conclusions.

African-American belief in government duplicity toward them is deep-seated and even sometimes overly paranoid, yet there is an evil history that gives these conspiracies real credibility. From the Tuskegee syphilis experiment that poisoned the bodies of poor Alabama men with a venereal disease for over forty years at U.S. expense to the FBI putting microphones under Dr. Martin Luther King's bed to record his sex life and COINTELPRO's subversion of black radical organizing, elements of this country's law enforcement branches have been performing nefarious deeds on its African-American citizens for decades.

While the crack-CIA connection seems a dead end now, who knows what information will come to light in the next century?

Whether a covert government conspiracy or just the product of everyday law-enforcement corruption and neglect, the growth of the urban drug culture stifled the civil rights movement around the country. It wore down white goodwill toward blacks' noble striving, particularly among big-city Jews and liberals. By the early '70s it was crime, not equality, that became the focus of discussion between blacks and Jews, ultimately driving a wedge between these longtime allies that may never be smoothed over.

Heroin use declined in the early '80s due to a slackening of the supply, but the illegal drug industry, which has proven to be one of the most adaptable enterprises in our country, aimed a new product line at the nation's drug aficionados—angel dust aka PCP (phencyclidine). This manmade psychoactive drug produces hallucinations that can cause severe psychological trauma. Usually sprinkled on a regular or marijuana cigarette, angel dust can drive its users to uncontrollable violent reactions. Someone "dusty" is always dangerous, because you never know what the next puff can lead to. Local news broadcasts of the early '80s regularly led off the six o'clock news with footage of cops and hospital personnel struggling to subdue someone "beaming up to Scotty." Angel dust is, in effect, a lethal form of ghetto LSD, which many kids experimented with to enter a vibrant, animated dream world. In my experience, angel dust was particularly popular with people with rich fantasy lives who ignored the danger in exchange for high-intensity pleasure. I remember one dusty homie was always seeing space ships hovering over Harlem.

During the early days of hip hop, angel dust was the drug of choice at parties. It was cheap, fast, and readily available. Many rap stars and their fans attended hip hop events extremely dusty and, as a result, angel dust became a creative stimulant in hip hop culture. But while angel dust ruled the streets, a more potent form of cocaine was quietly trickling down from the Wall Street elite.

CRACK. In the "Superfly" '70s, coke was sniffed or snorted (choose your verb) in powder form from tabletops, album covers, and parts of other folks' bodies. In inner-city neighborhoods, coke users wishing to socialize with those of similar appetites gathered at after-hours clubs to separate themselves from marijuana smokers and heroin junkies. Back in 1979, I interviewed a dealer who said that "coke sniffers were Kings and Queens and heads of state"—as opposed to "the low rent people" he sold marijuana to.

By the early '80s, cocaine consumption turned toward smoking freebase, which is cocaine at its basic alkaloid level. Like many folks, I'd never heard of freebasing until Richard Pryor ran in a fiery ball out of his California home on June 9, 1980. Coke had always been an expensive drug and this "cooking" to create a smokable version just seemed another occupation of the bored rich.

In freebasing, the cocaine is boiled in water and the residue is placed in cold water where it forms "base" or "freebase." The chipped-off pieces are called "crack" because it often makes a crackling sound as it burns. The popularity of this form of cocaine coincided with a dramatic increase in the growth of coca leaves in Bolivia, Peru, and Colombia that drove down the price of manufactured cocaine.

According to sociologist Terry Williams's insightful 1992 book about the crack lifestyle, *Crackhouse: Notes from the End of the Line*, the price dropped from $50,000 a kilo in 1980 to $35,000 in 1984 to $12,000 in 1992. Crack took cocaine away from high rollers and put it within reach of poorer addicts. For as little as $2, crack became available in plastic vials with red, blue, yellow, or green caps that denoted a particular dealer's territory or a particular dealer's product line. Often dealers named their brands after some pop culture artifact such as the movie *Lethal Weapon* or the band P-Funk.

The first references to mass market freebase came in two rap records—"White Lines" by Grandmaster Flash & the Furious Five, featuring Melle Mel, in 1983 and "Batterram" by Toddy Tee in 1985, which described a mini-tank the LAPD was using to break "rock houses." Soon the American media landscape would be littered with references to, and discussions of, crack. From those initial street reports, hip hop would chronicle, celebrate, and be blamed for the next level of drug culture development.

The crack industry became able employers of teenagers, filling the economic vacuum created by the ongoing loss of working-class jobs to the suburbs and then to poor Third World countries. Teenagers and adolescents were zealously recruited to provide the unskilled labor needed for manufacturing, packaging, and selling illegal drugs. By 1992 it was estimated that as many as 150,000 people were employed in New York City's drug trade. Similarly large numbers could be found in most major cities. MC Guru was not joking when he termed dealing "a daily operation," since the financial life of significant portions of the American economy suddenly became driven not by the stock market but by the crack industry.

Drug addiction has always been an equal opportunity exploiter. It strikes old, rich, white, and black. Yet there was something profoundly disheartening about crack's impact on young women. Williams estimated that 40 percent of all crackhouse denizens were female. It was maddening to see how many young mothers abandoned their children in pursuit of another hit. Often these women were forced to give sexual favors to support their dependencies.

During the eight years of Reagan's presidency, the ripple effect of crack flowed through all the social service agencies of our country—welfare, child care, Medicaid, you name the area of concern and crack's impact could be felt in it. At Family Court on any given day you'd see grandmothers struggling to hold families together by taking custody of their neglected or abandoned grandchildren. It was a tragedy that robbed grandparents of their rightful rest, strained their meager financial resources, and shortened their lives. In this multigenerational chaos few could raise their head above water or plan intelligently for the future.

For those who felt the fallout from crack's addictive power—the children of crackheads, their immediate families, friends, and neighbors—hope became a very hollow word. The world became defined by the 'hood, the block, or the corner where the search for drugs or their addicted loved one went on every day. As the '80s rolled on, the physical and moral decay begun by heroin was accelerated by angel dust and then the McDonaldization of crack.

As a consequence for many, materialism replaced spirituality as the definer of life's worth. An appreciation for life's intangible pleasures, like child rearing and romantic love, took a beating in places where children became disposable and sex was commodified. The go-go capitalism of Reagan's America (and its corporate greed) flowed down to the streets stripped of its jingoistic patriotism and fake piety. The unfettered free market of crack generated millions and stoked a voracious appetite for "goods," not good.

CRACK UP

> In my neighborhood you were either in a gang or a group—most were in both.
>
> —*Smokey Robinson, 1997*

Gangsta rap (or reality rap or whatever descriptive phrase you like) is a direct by-product of the crack explosion. Unless you grasp that connection nothing else that happened in hip hop's journey to national scapegoat will make sense. This is not a chicken-or-the-egg riddle—first came crack rocks, then gangsta rap.

Because the intense high of crack fades quickly, crack turned ordinary drug dealers into kingpins. After shooting up or snorting heroin, an addict resides in dreamland for hours; a crack addict experiences a brief, incredible rush, then five minutes later desires another

> **" The dirty little secret of mainstream America is that kids of every age, particularly in high school and junior high, have access to a medley of controlled substances. "**

rock. Crack created a fast-food economy of quick product turnover. Because it was so addictive and profitable, competition within impromptu urban enterprise zones (i.e., urban street corners) grew fierce. With the money crack generated from its increasingly ghostly clientele, bigger and more lethal guns filled our cities. Entering the '80s, the Saturday Night Special, a .45 caliber automatic, had long been America's death inducer of choice; by the end of the decade a medley of higher caliber weapons (the Israeli Uzi and Desert Eagle, the Austrian Glock, even the good old American Mossburg 12-gauge shotgun) pushed murder totals in Washington, D.C; Los Angeles; Detroit; Gary, Indiana; and scores of other cities to record levels.

As dealers used these guns indiscriminately, residents in the drug-ravaged communities armed themselves as well, seeking protection from dealers and crackheads, and the climate of immorality they represented. Police impotence in cleaning neighborhoods of drug trafficking and our government's failure in drug interdiction (or complicity in the trade) produce cynicism and alienation in this nation that made Nancy Reagan's "Just Say No" campaign a joke and left her husband's "Morning in America" rife with gunsmoke from the night before.

Gangsta rap first appeared in the mid-'80s. It exploded at the end of that decade and has leveled off—just like crack use—in the '90s. The majority of this subgenre's sales are made in the suburbs. A lot of this has to do with the rebel credentials of hard rappers with teenage kids . . . and with the true nature of the contemporary teenage suburban experience.

Suburban kids—no longer just stereotypically white, but black, Asian, and Hispanic—have, since the '60s, always known a lot more about drugs than civic leaders have ever acknowledged. (Although there aren't as many drive-bys in suburban counties, they do indeed happen. Drug dealers don't necessarily all congregate on green lawns, but they have never met a mall they didn't love.) The dirty little secret of mainstream America is that kids of every age, particularly in high school and junior high, have access to a medley of controlled substances. The romance of the outlaw mystique of drugs and dealing is not foreign to young people—another reason why gangsta records, supposedly

so distant from the white teen experience, are in fact quite familiar. Even the urban context of the records is not as mysterious or exotic, as commentators assert, since many suburban dealers and addicts use urban 'hoods as drive-through windows.

Another consequence of the crack plague was an evil increase in the numbers of incarcerated black males. In February 1990 a Washington, D.C.–based nonprofit organization, the Sentencing Project, issued a frightening report titled *Young Black Men and the Criminal Justice System: A Growing National Problem*. The report stated that one in four African-American males between twenty and twenty-nine—610,000 men in total—was either behind bars or on probation. In comparison, only 436,000 were enrolled in higher education.

The reasons for this number were legion—the crack trade, the aggressive sentencing for low-level drug offenses such as possession, the eroded economic base for urban America, a profound sense of hopelessness, ineffective school systems. The social repercussions, however, were sometimes less obvious. With so many young men in jail or monitored by law enforcement, most African-Americans had someone in their family or a friend involved with the justice system, both as perpetrator and victim. It is not surprising then that narratives dealing with crime and its consequences—from the reality TV show *Cops* to urban movies like *Boyz N the Hood* and *Juice*, and, of course, hip hop records that talk of jail culture—have a special appeal.

More profoundly, the mentality of back culture was deeply affected. The kind of dispassionate view of violence and overall social alienation that incarceration fosters was spread by prisoners and infected the rest of the community. Jail became not a cruel punishment but a rite of passage for many that helped define one's entry into manhood. And what being a man meant could be perversely shaped by imprisonment. For many young men, their sexual and romantic dealings were forever altered by the sexual activity that goes on behind bars.

While homosexuality is widely condemned in the black community, the committing of homosexual acts behind bars is rarely commented on. Because they often occur through rape or psychological coercion they are not viewed as acts of sexual orientation but as manifestations of control and domination, both reflections consistent with a "gangsta mental" or gangster mentality. If sex is taken, from this viewpoint, it is not an act of love but power. Whatever the justification, it suggests that there's a homoerotic quality to this culture's intense male bonding. As an example of how values shaped by prison influence behavior outside it, sex becomes about power, not affection. You bond with other men, not simply out of shared interest and friendship, but as protector and to gain predator power. For some men, in and out of jail since adolescence, jail begins to supersede the presence of all other environments.

Suspicion of women, loyalty to the crew, adoption of a stone face in confronting the world, hatred of authority—all major themes of gangsta rap—owe their presence in lyrics and impact on audiences to the large number of African-American men incarcerated in the '90s.

CRIMINAL MINDED. Whenever people rail about the evils of gangsta rap, my mind floats back to a particular record and an interview that never happened.

In 1985, New York's KISS-FM had a Friday night rap show, I'd either write with it on in the background or lie in bed listening. However, every week there was one record that stubbornly refused to be background music. Whenever the station played Schoolly D's "PSK—What Does It Mean?" the mood of my night changed. A first-person narrative about being a vicious stick-up kid and a member of PSK (Parkside Killers) in Philadelphia, it wasn't just Schoolly D's words that got me. His cold-blooded delivery and the bracing, taunting track always chilled me. The intensity of my reaction of "PSK" has been matched by only two other listening experiences: hearing Robert Johnson's devilish Delta blues for the first time and experiencing Tricky's dense pre-millennium dread at a New York concert in 1997.

Though as an artist Schoolly D is not on the same level as the legendary Johnson or the innovative trip-hop pioneer Tricky, the Philly homeboy channeled something tortured and warped when he laid down "PSK." When I hear people talk of being repulsed by gangsta rap's cartoony brutality I understand it by invoking the unease "PSK" induced in me. Back in that more innocent age, Schoolly D's nonjudgmental attitude toward violence (as opposed to the cautionary tone of "The Message") was unusual and even shocking.

My second early gangsta memory involves my sole encounter with Boogie Down Production's cofounder Scott LaRock (Scott Sterling). It was backstage at Madison Square Garden during a huge, arena-sized rap show. The flavors of mid-'80s black pop culture were in effect: the teen star of America's then number-one sitcom, *The Cosby Show's* Malcolm-Jamal Warner, sat in the wings watching L.L. Cool J rock the crowd;

Mike Tyson, the then heavyweight champ from my native Brownsville and unrepentant bully, hit a girl with his forearm as he passed her and chuckled.

A moment later I was introduced to LaRock, who had just emerged as one of the hottest producer-entrepreneurs in hip hop. As part of Boogie Down Productions, LaRock had helped mastermind the brilliant *Criminal Minded*. Fronted by the brutal rhymes and oddly whimsical vocals of ex-homeless teen KRS-One (Kris Parker), this was the first album-length exploration of the crack-fueled criminality of Reagan's America.

Criminal Minded had been released in 1987 on the black-owned, Bronx-based B-Boy Records, which KRS-One took every opportunity he had in the press to trash. B-Boy controlled Boogie Down Productions for only one album. As a result, everybody in the business was after BDP, but Jive's Barry Weiss and Ann Carli closed the deal. I told LaRock I wanted an interview for *Billboard*. He took my notepad and wrote down his name and number. I said I'd call next week. That weekend on August 26, 1987, LaRock was murdered in the kind of gun-related stupidity we now take for granted.

Before he began his hip hop career, LaRock had earned his keep as a counselor at homeless shelters, which is how he'd hooked up with Parker. One of the young men in the BDP collective was D-Nice (Derrick Jones), a shy, attractive, and gifted fifteen-year-old DJ being mentored by Parker and LaRock. D-Nice's boyish good looks had attracted the unwanted attention of a drug dealer's girlfriend in the Bronx and her unamused boyfriend threatened Derrick with harm. On the Saturday afternoon after the Garden concert, LaRock, D-Nice, and a couple of BDP members drove to the dealer's 'hood hoping to squash the beef. Apparently the dealer or some of his associates knew BDP were coming. Aware of *Criminal Minded's* violent content, perhaps they anticipated trouble, but LaRock was actually seeking a sit-down. As the Jeep containing BDP members arrived on the dealer's street, a shot rang out and the bullet that entered the vehicle struck Scott LaRock dead. As with so much urban violence, no one was ever indicted for the murder.

The question of whether BDP's rep played any part in this preemptive strike will likely never be answered, but whenever someone equates rap and gangsterism LaRock's death comes back to me. Looking back at his shooting, it seems a harbinger of a future where reality and rhyme often would tragically intersect, LaRock was not a violent man. He, in fact, spent much of his life trying to mediate conflicts in shelters where hopelessness ruled. The day he died he was on a peace mission for a friend. Yet with *Criminal Minded*, LaRock, as a musician and entertainer, had already tapped into the furiously self-destructive materialism of his age.

It is the irony of LaRock's life and death that makes me question simplistic explanations of gangsta rap. Not all rappers who write violent lyrics have lived the words. Most exercise the same artistic license to write violent tales as do the makers of Hollywood flicks. A few of those who do write violent lyrics have lived the tales or have friends who have. Within any collection of rap songs—either by those making it up or those who have lived it—a wide range of narrative strategies are employed. Many violent rhymes are just cartoons, with images as grounded in reality as the Road Runner. The outrageous words of Eazy-E and Kool G Rap fit this category. Some are cautionary tales that relate the dangers inherent to street life—Melle Mel and Duke Bootee's words in "The Message" are the prototype. Some are first-person narratives told with an objective, almost cinematic eye, by masters of the style like Ice Cube and KRS-One. Some end with the narrator in bold, bloody triumph, techniques both Scarface and Ice-T employ well. A bold few end with the narrator dead and work as stories told from the grave, an approach both Tupac Shakur and the Notorious B.I.G. favored in sadly prophetic recordings.

Some violent rhymes are poetically rendered and novelistically well observed, as in the more nuanced work of Chuck D. Rakim, and Nas. Too Short and Luther Campbell can, in contrast, be as crude as the bathroom humor of Jim Carrey's *Dumb & Dumber*. Some are morally complicated by the narrator's possible insanity, which is a specialty to Houston's Scarface. Some are so empty and rote that only the most reactionary listeners would think they could incite anything beyond contempt. My point is that most MCs who've been categorized as gangsta rappers are judged thoughtlessly without any understanding of the genuine stylistic differences between them.

Besides, what's gangsta rap anyway? Listen to any of N.W.A.'s albums, as well as Eazy-E's solo efforts, Dr. Dre's *The Chronic* and Snoop Doggy Dogg's *Doggystyle*. In their celebration of gatts, hoes, gleeful nihilism, and crack as the center of their economic universe, these albums darkly display everything people fear about gangsta rap. But outside of this collection of records—most of them with brilliantly modulated vocals supervised by Dr. Dre—I'd be hard-pressed to agree to label any other major rap star a gangsta rapper. For example, the work of Ice Cube (except for his insipid West Coast Connection project) and Scarface is way too diverse and eclectic to fit a simplistic mass media stereotype.

The martyrs of '90s hip hop—Tupac Shakur and the Notorious B.I.G. (Christopher Wallace)—were quickly tagged gangsta rappers *after* their demise, though crack and crime were not their only topics. A lot of drivel has been written about these two dead young black men. Heroes for a generation. Victims of their violent recordings. Martyrs. Villains. Whatever. For a moment let's just discuss them as artists. If, over twenty years after it evolved out of the Bronx, hip hop is an art form, then these men built profoundly on that foundation. Far from being simple oppositional figures in an East Coast-West Coast soap opera, Pac and Biggie complemented each other, though outwardly they seem mismatched.

Biggie was round and spoke in a thoughtful Brooklyn-meets-the-Caribbean drawl he derived from his articulate mother, a Jamaican-born schoolteacher. Tupac was taut and spoke with an activist's urgency and an actor's sense of drama, a by-product of his mother's militant background and his theatrical training in high school. Biggie covered himself in layers of expensive clothing and the regal air that led him to be dubbed the "King of New York" after the '90s gangsta film. Tupac always seemed to have his shirt off, better to expose his six-pack abdominals, wiry body, and the words "Thug 4 Life" tattooed across his belly.

But inside, both young men possessed lyrical dexterity, a writer's strong point of view, and a bitter, street-hardened sense of irony. Ultimately, Tupac and Biggie, like most of the controversial and best rappers who came after Public Enemy's political spiels, were both poets of negation, a stance that always upsets official cultural gatekeepers and God-fearing folks within black America. African-Americans have always been conflicted by art that explores the psychologically complex, even evil aspects of their existence, feeling it plays into the agenda of white oppression. On a very direct, obvious level they have a point. Black people saying bad things about themselves can serve to reinforce racist attitudes among non-blacks.

Yet, without a doubt, political and social conditions must not, cannot, and will not circumscribe the vision of true artists. Tupac and Biggie were artists who looked at the worst things in their world and reveled in describing their meanest dreams and grossest nightmares. They embraced the evil of crack America and articulated it with style—but highlighting is not the same as celebrating. The celebrated work of director Martin Scorsese parallels this artistic impulse. His violent masterworks—*Mean*

> **A bold few end with the narrator dead and work as stories told from the grave, an approach both Tupac Shakur and the Notorious B.I.G. favored in sadly prophetic recordings.**

Streets, Raging Bull, and *GoodFellas*—are undeniable artful yet morally twisted and deeply troubling in what they depict about the Italian-American soul in particular and the human capacity for violence in general—yet no one accuses him of being a self-glorifying predator.

Scorsese is considered, perhaps, the greatest living American filmmaker; Tupac and Biggie were labeled gangsta rappers in their obituaries. Yet the homicidal characters depicted by Joe Pesci and Robert DeNiro in *GoodFellas* could walk into any of Tupac's or the Notorious B.I.G.'s records and feel right at home, Tupac and the Notorious B.I.G. didn't make records for the NAACP; they made harsh, contemplative, graphic, deliberately violent American pulp art.

Tupac's hip hop Jimmy Cagney and the Notorious B.I.G.'s Edward G. Robinson didn't die for their sins or the one's they rhymed about; they died for their lives—the lives they chose and the lives that chose them. Rap lyrics that describe violence are a natural consequence of a world where a sixteen-year-old is shot at close range over his jacket by classmates, where a fifteen-year-old boy is fatally stabbed by another teen over his glasses, where a seventeen-year-old is stabbed to death after hitting another teen with an errant basketball pass. In a world where crack-empowered gangs run on a philosophy of old-fashioned, excessive, insatiable, and unending revenge—one that is supported by the plots of American classics from *The Searchers* to *Star Wars*—gangsta rap is just further exploration of this theme.

There is an elemental nihilism in the most controversial crack-era hip hop that wasn't concocted by the rappers but reflects the mentality and fears of young Americans of every color and class living an exhausting, edgy existence, in and out of big cities. Like crack dealing, this nihilism may die down, but it won't disappear, because the social conditions that inspired the trafficking and the underlying impulse that ignited nihilistic rap have not disappeared. And because, deep in the American soul, it speaks to us and we like the sound of its voice.

Journal and Discussion Questions

1 What is the subject of Nelson George's "Gangsters—Real and Unreal"? What is the central point that George is arguing? How does George develop this idea, and how does he try to persuade readers to believe him?

2 Outline "Gangsters—Real and Unreal." How does George use headings to organize "Gangsters"? Why does George delay mentioning rap music until page 398? What does his history of urban black society have to do with his ideas about hip-hop music?

3 What changes in American society, especially urban African American society, does George describe? What caused these changes, according to George? How did each of these changes help create and shape gangsta rap? Are you persuaded by his analysis of the rise of gangsta rap? Why or why not?

4 What does George mean by the phrase "the McDonaldization of crack"? How does he compare the fast-food industry to the illegal drug business? Do you agree with this comparison? Why or why not?

5 What research did George conduct for "Gangsters—Real and Unreal"? Where does George mention his sources? How does he use his research to build his analysis of gangsta rap's place in American culture?

6 Why does George, in the "Criminal Minded" section (page 401), switch to first-person narrative and describe his personal experiences listening to gangsta rap? What do his individual experiences have to do with the national experiences that he is analyzing? Is his use of the first-person pronoun *I* appropriate here? Why or why not?

7 George complains that hip hop became a "national scapegoat" (page 399) and that many explanations of gangsta rap are "simplistic" (page 402). What ideas about hip-hop music in general and gangsta rap in particular does George disagree with? Why? What view of gangsta rap is George arguing? What evidence does he give to support his arguments? Do you think his arguments would persuade someone who believes gangsta rap is harmful and offensive? Why or why not?

Topics for Writing

1 Write an argument that agrees or disagrees with Nelson George's depiction of hip-hop music in "Gangsters–Real and Unreal" or that argues whether George's depiction of rap music in 1998 holds true today.

2 Compare the role of hip-hop music in American culture today to the influence it had in American society in the 1980s and 1990s, as described by George.

3 Choose a genre of popular music like gangsta rap for a research paper discussing how the music reflects the culture or how it has influenced the culture. Like "Gangsters—Real and Unreal," your paper should discuss individual performers to support your claims about the music.

RHYME AND RESIST: Organizing the Hip-Hop Generation

BY ANGELA ARDS

Angela Ards is sometimes described as an "advocacy journalist" who frequently writes about community organizing, national social movements, the politics of race and gender, and art and culture. She is a youth activist as well as a regular contributor to *The Village Voice*, *The Nation*, and RadioNation and has published essays in magazines such as *Ms.* and *The Crisis* and books such as *Step into a World: A Global Anthology of the New Black Literature* and *Still Lifting, Still Climbing: Contemporary African American Women's Activism.* "Rhyme and Resist: Organizing the Hip-Hop Generation" appeared in the July 26, 1999, issue of the liberal news magazine *The Nation*.

"YOU'LL TURN AROUND IF THEY put you in jail," a young black man quips to a peer as counselor LaTosha Brown belts out the classic freedom song.

It's the kickoff of the 21st Century Youth Leadership Movement's annual winter summit, held last December at Tuskegee University in Alabama. In 1985 former SNCC activists and their children founded 21st Century on the anniversary of the Selma marches, which ushered in the 1965 Voting Rights Act. Three times a year the group convenes camps to teach movement history to a generation with little appreciation of its accomplishments. They've heard of sit-ins but little of SNCC. Media soundbites provide piecemeal knowledge of Malcolm X and Martin Luther King, but who was Ella Baker? 21st Century seeks to fill in the gaps before this generation slips through. Yet the paradoxical pull of preparing for the future by building a bridge to the past reveals just how wide the chasm has grown.

"When spirits got low, the people would sing," Brown explains: "The one thing we did right/Was the day we started to fight/Keep your eyes on the prize/Oh, Lord." Her rich contralto, all by itself, sounds like the blended harmonies of Sweet Honey in the Rock, but it's not stirring this crowd of 150 Southern youth. Two fresh-faced assistants bound on stage to join in like cheerleaders at a pep rally. Most of the others, however, take their cues from the older teens, slouched in their seats in an exaggerated posture of cool repose. Brown hits closer to their sensibilities when she resorts to funk. "Say it loud," she calls. "I'm black and

I'm proud," they respond. But a brash cry from the back of the room speaks more to their hearts. "Can we sing some Tupac?" Another cracks, "Y'all wanna hear some Busta Rhymes?"

By the weekend's close, 21st Century co-founder Rose Sanders is voicing a sentiment activists who work with young people increasingly share. "Without hip-hop," says Sanders, 53, "I don't see how we can connect with today's youth."

In *Hiphop America*, cultural critic Nelson George writes that this post–civil rights generation may be the first black Americans to experience nostalgia. Although it's proverbial that you can't miss what you never had, or what never truly was, romantic notions of past black unity and struggle—despite the state violence that created the sense of community—magnify the despair of present realities. Public schools are almost as segregated today as at the time of the 1954 *Brown v. Board of Education* ruling. "Jail, no bail"—the civil-disobedience tactic used by sixties activists to dismantle Southern apartheid—could just as easily refer to the contemporary incarceration epidemic, ushered in by mandatory minimum sentencing, three-strikes-you're-out laws and the "war on drugs." The voter registration campaigns for which many Southern blacks lost jobs, land and lives are now mocked by the fact that 13 percent of African-American men—1.4 million citizens—cannot vote because of criminal records meted out by a justice system proven to be neither blind nor just.

Hip-hop was created in the mid-seventies as black social movements quieted down, replaced by electoral politics. It has deep sixties cultural and political roots; Gil Scott-Heron and The Last Poets are considered the forebears of rap. But once the institutions that supported radical movements collapsed or turned their attention elsewhere, the seeds of hip-hop were left to germinate in American society at large—fed by its materialism, misogyny and a new, more insidious kind of state violence.

Under the watch of a new establishment of black and Latino elected officials, funding for youth services, arts programs and community centers was cut while juvenile detention centers and prisons grew. Public schools became way stations warehousing youth until they were of prison age. Drugs and the violence they attract seeped into the vacuum that joblessness left. Nowhere was this decay more evident than in the South Bronx, which came to symbolize urban blight the way Bull Connor's Birmingham epitomized American racism—and black and Latino youth in the Boogie Down made it difficult for society to pretend that it didn't see them.

In the tradition of defiance, of creating "somethin' outta nothin'," they developed artistic expressions that came to be known as hip-hop. Rapping, or MCing, is now the most well-known, but there are three other defining elements: DJing, break dancing and graffiti writing. For most of the seventies hip-hop was an underground phenomenon of basement parties, high school gyms and clubs, where DJs and MCs "took two turntables and a microphone," as the story has come to be told, creating music from the borrowed beats of soul, funk, disco, reggae and salsa, overlaid with lyrics reflecting their alienated reality. On city streets and in parks, hip-hop crews—the peaceful alternative to gangs—sought to settle disputes through lyrical battles and break-dancing competitions rather than violence. On crumbling city walls and subways, graffiti writers left their tags as proof that they'd passed that way, or that some friend had passed on. Eventually, all of these mediums shaped in New York morphed into regional style defined by the cities in which they arose—Los Angeles, Oakland, Chicago, Philadelphia, Atlanta.

Underground tapes showcasing a DJ's skills or an MC's rhymes were all the outside world knew of rap music until 1979, when the Sugar Hill Gang released "Rapper's Delight" on a small independent black label. It wasn't the first rap album; many of the lyrics were recycled from artists with more street credibility. But it was a novelty to the mainstream. The record reached No. 36 on US charts and was a huge international hit, purchased largely by young white males, whose tastes have dictated the way rap music has been marketed and promoted ever since. From those classic "a hip hip-pin to the hip hip hop" lyrics and risqué "hotel-motel" rhymes, rap music has gone through various phases— early eighties message raps, late-eighties Afro-centricity, early nineties gangsta rap, today's rank materialism— and shows no signs of stopping.

This past February, *Time* trumpeted hip-hop on its cover: "After 20 years—how it's changed America." In the past year it has been the subject of at least five academic conferences—from Howard to Harvard to Princeton to UCLA to NYU. In January 2000, the Postal Service plans to issue a hip-hop stamp. *Nation* colleague Mark Schapiro reports that in Macedonian refugee camps, Kosovar Albanian youth shared tapes of homegrown hip-hop, raging against life in prewar Kosovo. This creation of black and Latino youth whom America discounted is now the richest—both culturally and economically—pop cultural form on the planet.

Given hip-hop's social origins and infectious appeal, there's long been a hope that it could help effect social change. The point of the music was always to "move the crowd," for DJs to find the funkiest part of the record—the "break beat"—and keep it spinning until people flooded the dance floor and the energy raised the roof. In the late eighties, Chuck D of Public Enemy declared rap "the black CNN" and argued that the visceral, sonic force that got people grooving on the dance floor could, along with rap's social commentary, get them storming the streets.

If nothing else, rapping about revolution did raise consciousness. Public Enemy inspired a generation to exchange huge gold rope chains, which the group likened to slave shackles, for Malcolm X medallions. From PE and others like KRS-ONE, X-Clan and the Poor Righteous Teachers, urban youth were introduced to sixties figures like Assata Shakur and the Black Panther Party, then began to contemplate issues like the death penalty, police brutality, nationalism and the meaning of American citizenship.

These "old school hip-hop headz," in the parlance of the culture, have come of age along with the music. Many of them are activists, artists, educators, academics, administrators, entrepreneurs, hoping to use hip-hop to awaken a younger generation in the way it began to politicize them. Much of this "hip-hop activism" is in New York, emanating from the culture's Bronx birthplace, but flashes of organizing are being seen in San Francisco, Los Angeles, Washington, Atlanta and cyberspace.

Last September former Nation of Islam minister Conrad Muhammad launched A Movement for CHHANGE (Conscious Hip Hop Activism Necessary for Global Empowerment) and its Youth Voter Registration Drive. El Puente Academy for and Justice in

Williamsburg, Brooklyn, has a Hip Hop 101 that borrows from Paulo Freire's teaching model: Educate to liberate. In 1993 the Central Brooklyn Partnership, which has trained people since 1989 to organize for economic justice, opened the first "hip-hop credit union" in Bedford-Stuyvesant to offer low-interest loans. The Prison Moratorium Project, a coalition of student and community activists dedicated to ending prison growth and rebuilding schools, is producing *No More Prisons*, a hip-hop CD featuring Hurricane G, The Coup and Cornel West. In Atlanta, the Youth Task Force works with rap artists Goodie Mobb to teach youth about environmental justice and political prisoners. In the Bay Area, the Third Eye Movement, a youth-led political and arts organization, has initiated a grassroots campaign against police brutality that combines action, policy reform and hip-hop concerts that serve as fundraisers, voter education forums and mass demonstrations. The New York chapter of the Uhuru Movement, a black nationalist organization that promotes communal living and self-determination, has as its president Mutulu Olugbala, M1 of the rap group Dead Prez. In cyberspace, Davey D's Hip-Hop Corner, produced by an Oakland radio personality, keeps aficionados up to date on the latest industry trends and issues affecting urban youth. On his own Web site, Chuck D is waging a campaign to get rap artists to plunge into the new MP3 technology, which offers musicians creative control and immediate access to a global audience, bypassing corporate overhead and earning more profits for themselves and, potentially, their communities.

For many activists, the creation of hip-hop amid social devastation is in itself a political act. "To—in front of the world—get up on a turntable, a microphone, a wall, out on a dance floor, to proclaim your self-worth when the world says you are nobody, that's a huge, courageous, powerful, exhilarating step," says Jakada Imani, a civil servant in Oakland by day and a co-founder of the Oakland-based production company Underground Railroad. Concerted political action will not necessarily follow from such a restoration of confidence and self-expression, but it is impossible without it. Radical movements never develop out of despair.

It's too early to say whether the culture can truly be a path into politics and not just a posture, and, if it can, what those politics might be. But what is emerg-

ing throughout the country—when the influence of the black church has diminished, national organizations seem remote from everyday life and, in some sense, minority youth have to start from scratch—is an effort to create a space where youth of color can go beyond pain to resistance, where alternative institutions, and alternative politics, can develop.

As Tricia Rose, professor of Africana studies and history at New York University and author of *Black Noise: Rap Music and Black Culture in Contemporary America*, puts it, "The creation, and then tenacious holding on, of cultural forms that go against certain kinds of grains in society is an important process of subversion." It is "about a carving out of more social space, more identity space. This is critical to political organizing. It's critical to political consciousness." Because of its osmotic infusion into the mainstream, Rose argues, hip-hop culture could be used to create a conversation about social justice among young people, much as black religious culture influenced the civil rights discourse of the sixties.

> Come on, baby, light my fire/Everything you drop is so tired/Music is supposed to inspire/ How come we ain't getting no higher?
>
> —*Lauryn Hill, "Superstar"*

The parallel may stop with broad social appeal. There are critical distinctions between black religious culture and hip-hop that make using hip-hop for social change a complicated gesture, suggests Richard Yarborough, English professor and director of the Center for African-American Studies at UCLA. "Black religious culture didn't threaten mainstream white liberals the way hip-hop does," notes Yarborough. "It grew directly out of black social institutions, while hip-hop has few sustained institutional bases. Black religious culture never became fodder for the mainstream commodity economy the way hip-hop has. It provided a central role for black women, while the role of women in hip-hop is still problematic. Black religious culture was associated with the moral high ground, while hip-hop is too often linked to criminality."

Indeed, Davey D dubbed 1998 "The Year of the Hip-Hop Criminal." Scores of artists, from Busta Rhymes and DMX to Ol' Dirty Bastard and Sean "Puffy" Combs, were arrested that year on charges

> " **It's too early to say whether the culture can truly be a path into politics and not just a posture, and, if it can, what those politics might be.** "

ranging from assault to drug and weapons possession to domestic and sexual violence. Given the hip-hop mandate to "keep it real," to walk the talk of rap music, the inescapable question becomes, What kind of perspectives are youth tapping into and drawing on in hip-hop music?

At the 21st Century youth camp, students are attending the workshop "Hip-Hop 2 Educate." Discussion facilitator Alatunga asks the students to list the music's major themes, prompting a lugubrious litany, in this order: death, pain, drugs, sex, alcohol, gangbanging, guns, struggling in life, reality, murder and childbirth (an odd inclusion, perhaps provoked by Lauryn Hill's joyful ode to her firstborn). The young woman who offers "childbirth" then suggests "love." A fan of Kirk Franklin's hip-hop-inflected gospel says "God." It is Alatunga who suggests "politics." The students duly note it on their list.

For the next exercise, he has each person name a "positive" rapper. The first to respond cite the obvious: Lauryn Hill, Goodie Mobb, Outkast. The rest struggle, coming up with current, though not necessarily politically conscious, chart toppers: Jay-Z, DMX, the whole No Limit family. Gospel singer Fred Hammond is allowed because Kirk Franklin was before. Tupac gets in because everyone feels bad he died before fulfilling his potential. Master P, chief exec of the No Limit label, raises some eyebrows because of his hustler image but slides in because it's argued that the distribution contract he negotiated with Priority Records, which secures him 80 percent of the sales revenue, upsets the classic master-slave relationship between the industry and artists. Alatunga finally draws the line at master marketer Puff Daddy, reminding the group that by "positive" he means political, not just "getting paid."

It's a tricky business fitting culture into politics. Adrienne Shropshire, 31, is a community organizer in Los Angeles with AGENDA (Action for Grassroots Empowerment and Neighborhood Development Alternatives), which came together after the 1992 "Rodney King riots." "Oftentimes the music reinforces the very things that we are struggling against," she says. "How do we work around issues of economic justice if the music is about 'getting mine'? How do we promote collective struggle when the music is about individualism?"

In 1995, AGENDA tried using hip-hop culture in its organizing efforts against Prop 209, the anti–affirmative action ballot measure that eventually passed. Organizers hoped to get youth involved in canvassing around voter education and peer education workshops in schools through open-mike poetry nights. The organizers succeeded in creating a space to talk about so-cial justice issues. They also were able to introduce themselves to artists whom they often failed to reach doing campus-based work. And the events were fun, balancing the unglamorous work of organizing.

Overall, though, Shropshire said, "people didn't make the leap" between raising issues and taking action. They would attend the Friday night poetry reading but pass on the Saturday morning rally. "The attitude was 'If I'm rapping about social justice, isn't that enough?' They wanted to make speeches on the mike, but there was not a critical mass who could take the next step in the process."

This failed experiment forced AGENDA organizers to return to more tried and true techniques: door-to-door canvassing; editorials for local, college and high school newspapers; educational workshops on campuses; collaboration with on-campus student organizations. At their meetings they passed out "action cards" for people to note the areas in which they had expertise: media, outreach, fundraising, event security, etc. And they came to understand that the solid core of people who remained were not the dregs of the hip-hop open-mikes but the die-hard troops who could be counted on over the long haul of a campaign.

As AGENDA learned firsthand, the pitfall organizers have to avoid is becoming like advertisers, manipulating youth culture for their own ends. About a decade ago, Tricia Rose recalls, Reynolds Wrap had a campaign with a cartoon figure reciting rhymes over corny beats about using the plastic wrap. Since teenagers rarely purchase Reynolds Wrap, the commercial was rather odd and largely unsuccessful. "But once the advertisers moved into the realm of youth products," says Rose, "then the fusion was complete. There was no leap. You could do sneakers, soda, shoes, sunglasses, whatever, because that's what they're already consuming."

> We don't pull no rabbits from a hat/we pull rainbows/from a trash can/we pull hope from the dictionary/n teach it how to ride the subway/we don't guess the card in yo hand/we know it/aim to change it/yeah/we know magic/and don't be so sure that card in yo hand/is the Ace
>
> —*Ruth Forman, "We Are the Young Magicians"*

"I believe in magic," poet/actor Saul Williams chants into the mike at CBGB in New York's East Village, backed up by a live band with violin, viola, drum, bass and electric guitars, and accompanied by a "live performance painting" by Marcia Jones, his partner. In 1996 Williams won the Grand Slam Championship, a competition among spoken-word artists who bring a hip-hop aesthetic to poetry. "Magic,"

Williams riffs, "not bloodshed," will bring on "the revolution." The transformative power of art is the theme of his hit movie *Slam*, in which Williams plays a street poet cum drug dealer incarcerated for selling marijuana. Through his poetry, and beautiful writing teacher, the protagonist transforms himself and fellow inmates. At the movie's end, he raps, "Where my niggas at?" both demanding to know where all the troops are who should be fighting against injustice, and lamenting that they are increasingly in jail. At CBGB, when Williams asks, "Where my wizards at?" the challenge to the hip-hop community to transform society through art is clear.

Later, Williams predicted a "changing of the guard" in hip-hop, from a commodity culture to an arts renaissance that reconnects with hip-hop's sixties Black Arts Movement roots. There are plenty of skeptics. Last September, at a festival of readings, panels and performances in Baltimore and College Park, Maryland, sixties poet Mari Evans argued that while the Black Arts Movement was the cultural arm of a political movement, the work of contemporary artists is "an expression of self rather than the community."

> ❝
>
> **Today, what look like mere social events may represent a prepolitical phase of consciousness building that's integral to organizing.**
>
> ❞

Considering that these are not the sixties and there is not yet a movement to be the arm of, a better analogy would be to the Beat poets of the fifties, whose subversive art prefigured the political tumult that would arise only a few years later, even if they didn't anticipate it. Today, what look like mere social events may represent a prepolitical phase of consciousness building that's integral to organizing. Often, these open-mike nights and poetry slams have politically conscious themes that the poets address in their rhymes. They are also increasingly used for education and fundraising. For instance, Ras Baraka, son of Black Arts father Amiri Baraka, used the proceeds from his weekly Verse to Verse poetry nights in Newark to raise money for his political campaigns for mayor in 1994 and city council in 1998. (He lost both races narrowly, in runoffs.)

Others are developing companies, curriculums and performance spaces to institutionalize hip-hop and reclaim it as a tool for liberation. Mannafest, a performance company, seeks to develop the voice of black London by creating a space where people can

express their ideas on political and social issues. This fall the Brecht Forum in New York will sponsor a nine-week "course of study for hip-hop revolutionaries." Akila Work-songs, an artist-representation company, evolved out of president April Silver's work in organizing the first national hip-hop conference at Howard University in 1991. One of its missions is to "deglamorize" hip-hop for school-age kids. About the responsibility of artists, Silver says, "You can't just wake up and be an artist. We come from a greater legacy of excellency than that Artists don't have the luxury to not be political."

At the Freestyle Union (FSU) in Washington, DC, artist development isn't complete without community involvement. That philosophy grew out of weekly "cipher workshops," in which circles of artists improvise raps under a set of rules: no hogging the floor, no misogyny, no battling. The last of those, which defies a key tenet of hip-hop, has outraged traditionalists, who see it feminizing the culture. What this transformation has created is a cadre of trained poet-activists, the Performance Corps, who run workshops and panels with DC-based universities, national educational conferences, the Smithsonian Institution and the AIDS Project, on issues ranging from domestic violence to substance abuse and AIDS prevention. This summer FSU and the Empower Program are holding a twelve-week Girls Hip-Hop Project, which tackles violence against women.

Obviously, as Tricia Rose points out, this stretching of the culture, even if it does raise political consciousness, "is not the equivalent of protesting police brutality, voting, grassroots activism against toxic waste dumping, fighting for more educational resources, protecting young women from sexual violence." Toni Blackman, the founder of FSU, admits as much. "As artists," she says, "we're not necessarily interested in being politicians. We are interested in making political statements on issues that we care about. But how do you give young people the tools to decide how to spend their energy to make their lives and the world better?"

It's a good question, but activist/artist Boots of the Oakland-based rap group The Coup laid the challenge far more pointedly in an interview with Davey D in 1996: "Rappers have to be in touch with their communities no matter what type of raps you do, otherwise people won't relate. Political rap groups offered solutions only through listening. They weren't part of a movement, so they died out when people saw that their lives were not changing. On the other hand, gangsta groups and rappers who talk about selling drugs are a part of a movement. The drug game has been around for years and has directly impacted lives, and for many it's been positive in the sense that it earned people some money. Hence gangsta rap has a home. In order for political rap to be around, there has to be a movement that will be around that will make people's lives better in a material sense. That's what any movement is about, making people's lives better."

> In order to have a political movement, you have to have education and consciousness. It's very difficult to mix education and consciousness with capitalism. And most people, when confronted with an option, will pick money over everything else.
>
> —*Lisa Williamson,* a k a *Sister Souljah*

> It's all about the Benjamins, baby.
>
> —*Sean "Puffy" Combs,* a k a *Puff Daddy,* No Way Out

Organizing the hip-hop generation is "an idea whose time has come," says Lisa Sullivan, president of LISTEN (Local Initiative Support Training Education Network), a youth development social change organization in Washington. "But there's no reason to believe that it will happen naturally."

No organizing ever does. The grassroots work that is going on around the country is mostly small, diffuse and underfunded. For it ever to reach a mass scale, Sullivan argues, there will have to be an independent infrastructure to support close-to-the-ground organizing. That means training, coordination and leadership building. It also means money. There is plenty of that among the most successful rappers—for the uninitiated, "the Benjamins" refers to $100 bills—but for the most part they, and the projects they get behind, are in thrall to the corporate ideology that made them stars.

Consider Rock the Vote's Hip-Hop Coalition, designed to register black and Latino youth for the 1996 presidential election using the same model by which rock artists have tried to convince white youth that voting is relevant to their lives. The brainchild of rapper LL Cool J, the Hip-Hop Coalition was led by former Rock the Vote executive director Donna Frisby and involved artists Chuck D, Queen Latifah and Common Sense, among others, registering almost 70,000 youth of color, versus hundreds of thousands of white youth.

This media strategy didn't succeed as Frisby had hoped, so the coalition took its show on the road, staging political forums where rap artists and local politicians talked to teenagers about the political process. What was clear from these open forums was that besides the political apathy characteristic of most young people, there is a deeper sense of alienation. "African-American and low-income youth feel that the Constitution and the Declaration of Independence were not created with us in mind," says Frisby. "So people felt, the system isn't doing anything to help me, why should I participate in it?"

From these experiences Frisby learned that not only will programs for minority youth always be given short shrift by mainstream underwriters—the Hip-Hop Coalition never got the media support of its white counterpart—but they won't even reach their audience unless they are specifically designed for youth of color. Now she and Chuck D have a new venture, Rappers Educating All Curricula through Hip-Hop (REACH). Building on the Hip-Hop Coalition, REACH is recruiting a cadre of artists as "conduits of learning," making public appearances at schools, juvenile detention centers, community centers. In nurturing more conscious artists, Chuck D and Frisby hope more conscious art will result. The group also plans to develop educational tools incorporating hip-hop songs. "Hip-hop is first and foremost a communication tool," says Chuck D. "For the last twenty years hip-hop has communicated to young people all across the world, people in different time zones, who speak different languages, teaching them more about English, or black hip-hop lingo, quicker than any textbook can." REACH aims to narrow the cultural and generational gap between teachers and students in the public schools, and to promote the idea that "being smart is being cool."

As described by Chuck D, however, REACH seems in many ways to be an if-you-can't-beat-'em-join-'em approach. To compete for the short attention spans of youth, he says, social change organizations have to be like corporations. "A lot of organizations that have been out there for a long time are not really on young people's minds. In the information age, there are so many distractions. Organizations have to market themselves in a way so that they are first and foremost on young people's minds and supply the answers and options that they might need."

But political organizing isn't about supplying "answers." As Sister Souljah puts it, "Just because you have the microphone doesn't mean you know what you're talking about. Just because you can construct a rhyme doesn't mean that you know how to organize a movement or run an organization." Souljah came to broad public attention during the 1992 presidential campaign when Bill Clinton, gunning for Jesse Jackson to woo the conservative vote, distorted a statement she had made about the LA riots. But before there was Sister Souljah, rap icon, there was Lisa Williamson, activist. At Rutgers University, she was involved in campaigns against apartheid and police brutality. With the United Church of Christ's Commission for Racial Justice, she mobilized young people for various events in the black community and organized a star-studded concert at Harlem's Apollo Theater to fund a summer camp she'd developed. Impressed with her organizing skills, Chuck D christened her "Sister Souljah" and designated her minister of information for Public Enemy.

Today, Souljah is executive director of Daddy's House—the nonprofit arm of Puffy's rap empire, Bad Boy Entertainment—which runs a summer camp for urban youth and provides meals for the homeless during the holidays. "The stars we choose to celebrate are reflections of who we are as a people," she says. "Right now we celebrate those with money, but that has nothing to do with understanding history, culture or understanding your future. And I think that's missing in hip-hop right now."

Last November in an *Essence* profile, Combs said that he wanted to use his popularity and influence to galvanize his generation to exercise their political power in the 2000 presidential election. Last September Master P's nonprofit foundation helped finance the Million Youth March. Rap artists are clearly not political leaders—they might be better described as representatives of their record labels than of their communities—but they do have one obvious role to play if they want to foster activism. While Sullivan embodies the idea of organizing as a fundamentally grassroots undertaking, she knows that it can't survive on sweat alone. "Hip-hop is a billion-dollar industry," she says, "and there are people who can play a venture philanthropist role. But that would require educating them about different ways to be philanthropists." No doubt, Master P and Puffy get capitalism. In 1998, the two were the top-selling rap artists, with Master P earning $57 million and Combs $54 million. But "the $64,000 Question," says Sullivan, "is could [they] become what Sidney Poitier and Harry Belafonte were for the civil rights movement? Those two guys actively financed how people got from Mississippi to Atlantic City," she recalls, referring to the historic all-black Mississippi State delegation, led by Fannie Lou Hamer, that demanded to be seated at the 1964 Democratic convention in place of the state's white segregationists.

"Sullivan was the field coordinator of the Children's Defense Fund and, until 1996, manager of its Black Student Leadership Network, a service and child advocacy program. Her subsequent stint as a consultant at the Rockefeller Foundation convinced her that a movement of the hip-hop generation will have to fund itself. "Traditional foundations are not going to support this work. You have a couple of program officers in the arts and humanities who get how important youth culture is to reaching alienated young people. While they tend to be radical and politicized, the institutions that they money-out from are not anywhere comfortable supporting what a mature hip-hop political agenda could be."

For Sullivan, such an agenda would address three issue areas. Top on the list is the criminal justice system, including police brutality and the incarceration epidemic. "It's the whole criminalization of poor, urban youth," she says. "That's a policy area that folks have got to get a handle on quickly. And it's also a place where our constituency numbers—our power—if organized well, could move the policy agenda away from its current punitive, negative stance." Public education is agenda item number two: "People are being set up. This is the system that is the most dysfunctional in the country, and something drastic has to occur so that people acquire the skills and have a fighting chance in terms of the economic future. A bad public education system feeds a whole generation of young people into the criminal justice system." Finally, activists need to address people losing the vote because of incarceration: "This is about the health of American democracy. What is happening to the hip-hop community around the loss of citizenship is permanently preventing many of us from ever being able to participate in the democratic process."

> If you ain't talkin' about endin' exploitation/ then you just another sambo in syndication/ always sayin' words that's gon' bring about elation/never doin' shit that's gon' bring us vindication/and while we getting strangled by the slave-wage grippers/you wanna do the same,/ and say we should put you in business?/so you'll be next to the ruling class, lyin' in a ditch/cuz when we start this revolution all you prolly do is snitch.
>
> *—The Coup, "Busterismology"*

Once all this activism matures, it's hard to say whether it will resemble hip-hop, or the left, as we know it. But a few operations on the ground suggest some necessary features. First off, it has to be youth led and defined.

At the weekly rally for A Movement for CHHANGE, everyone is frisked as they enter the National Black Theater in Harlem, women on the left, men on the right. "Hip-hop minister" Conrad

> **" A mature hip-hop political movement will have more than a race-based political analysis of the issues affecting urban youth. "**

Muhammad, the motive force behind the group, is waging a mass voter registration drive in preparation for 2001, when he hopes to sponsor a convention to announce a bloc of young urban voters with the political clout to influence the mayoral agenda. The minister's roots lie in the Nation of Islam, but at the rally he sounds more like a Southern Baptist preacher.

"Would you, please, brother, register today?" Muhammad pleads with a dreadlocked black man sitting with his wife. Their new baby just had a harrowing hospital stay. They're relieved that the baby is healthy and that insurance will pay for the visit, but initially neither was a certainty. After the minister's hourlong pitch, the man is still unconvinced that casting a ballot and then hounding politicians, of any color, will assure strong black communities of healthcare, good schools and intact families.

Voter registration is an odd, and hard, sell coming from a man who, until three years ago, never cast a ballot and, while minister of the Nation of Islam's Mosque #7 in Harlem, preached against it. But Muhammad, 34, tries. It's mid-November 1998, the same week Kwame Ture, *a k a* Stokeley Carmichael, died and the Madd Rapper, *a k a* Deric "D-Dot" Angeletti, ambushed and battered the then–editor in chief of the hip-hop magazine *Blaze*. Someone, Muhammad figures, ought to be the bridge between the civil rights tradition and the hip-hop generation, and it might as well be him.

He appeals to that sense of competition supposedly at the core of hip-hop: "If Kwame at 21 could go down to Lowndes County and register his people to vote, so can we." He appeals to a sense of shame: "This is the talented tenth that Du Bois said was supposed to come up with solutions to the problems of our people, and here they are fighting and killing each other up in corporate offices. Brothers and sisters, you know we got to make a change from that kind of craziness." He goads: "Talkin' 'bout you a nationalist, you don't believe in the system. You're a part of the system!" He suggests outright poverty: "Somebody had to say, 'I'll forgo the riches of this world to make sure that my people are in power.' If Stokeley died with $10 in his pocket I'd be surprised." He pushes the willingness-to-suffer motif that characterized the early civil rights movement:

"James Meredith decided to have a march against fear. We need one of those today in the 'hood, where dope is being sold, people are destroying themselves, frivolity and ignorance are robbing this generation of its substance. Meredith marched by himself—of course, he was shot down. You make that kind of stand, you're going to be shot down." At long last, he gets to his point: "If A Movement for CHHANGE can organize the youth, get them off these street corners, get them registered, make them conscious, active players in the political landscape, maybe we can vote Sharpton into office as mayor or Jesse as President."

The grandmothers of the amen gallery in the audience punctuate each exhortation with cheers, and a few raised fists. The young folks quietly mull over the prospects: poverty, suffering, Sharpton, Jesse. At one point, a 17-year-old decked in the "ghetto fabulous" hip-hop style—baggy jeans, boots, black satin do-rag, huge rhine-stone studs weighing down each lobe—challenges the voter registration model of political empowerment. "They [politicians] always say things, do things, but soon as they get in office, they don't say and do what they're supposed to. The community that I live in is mostly, like, a drug environment. And they're always talking about, we're going to get the drug dealers, we're going to bust them, we're going to stop all the gangs, we're going to stop all the black-on-black crime, we're going to have our own businessmen. And they never follow their word, so what's the sense in voting?"

"Let's put you in office," says Muhammad. "In 2001, when forty-two City Council seats come up [in New York City], let's run you."

"Run me?" the young brother asks incredulously, biting a delighted grin. He is clearly interested in the idea of being involved, even a leader, in his community. But if these are the terms, he and his peers don't seem so sure.

Secondly, a mature hip-hop political movement will have more than a race-based political analysis of the issues affecting urban youth. Increasingly, the face of injustice is the color of the rainbow, so a black-white racial analysis that pins blame on some lily-white power structure is outdated. At the 21st Century meeting in Tuskegee the theme of the weekend was mis-education and tracking. In the Selma public schools, however, more than 90 percent of the students are black, so whatever the remedial tracking, it is happening along class lines, instituted by black teachers, principals and superintendents. "All teachers except for the whites told me that I wasn't going to be anybody," says a heavyset, dark, studious young man, who transferred from the public school system to a Catholic school. When he asked many of the black teachers for help, the response was often flip and cutting: "Your mama's smart, figure it out."

Ras Baraka tells of how Black NIA F.O.R.C.E., the protest group he founded while at Howard University in the late eighties, descended on a Newark City Council meeting to oppose an ordinance banning citizens from speaking at its sessions. They were arrested for disrupting city business on the orders of Donald Tucker, a black councilman. "Stuff like 'the white man is a devil' is anachronistic," Baraka says. "The white man didn't make Donald Tucker call the police on us. He did that on his own."

In explaining his actions, Tucker invoked his own history in civil rights sit-ins. "That's their disclaimer to justify doing anything," Baraka says. "If it were white people [jailing peaceful demonstrators], the people would be outraged. The irony is that we went down there singing civil rights songs. We thought we would call the ghosts of Martin Luther King and Medgar Evers and Kwame Ture on their asses, but it didn't even faze them. They have more in common now with the people who oppress us than with us. In that sense the times are changing so our level of organizing has to change."

Like many activists working on a range of issues across the left in this country, these organizers are beginning to shift focus from civil rights to human rights. As Malaika Sanders, the current executive director of 21st Century, puts it, "Civil rights is based on the state and what the state has defined as the rights of the people." Human rights, on the other hand, is based on the rationale that "no matter who or where I am, I have some basic rights, so it's not about voting rights or what the law is." She argues that human rights presents a more motivating rationale for activism. Whereas a civil rights philosophy—focused on a finite set of principles that define citizenship—can lead to despair as those rights are never fully attained or are subject to the mood of the times, "a human rights approach allows a vision that's bigger than your world or what you think on a day-to-day basis."

On the West Coast, the Third Eye Movement has developed a theory of organizing that goes from civil rights to human rights, from nationalism to internationalism. It couples grassroots organizing with programs and policy analysis, using hip-hop culture not just to educate and politicize but to help young people express their concerns in their own language, on their own terms. Third Eye activists used rap and song to testify before the San Francisco Police Commission in 1997 after Officer Marc Andaya stomped and pepper-sprayed to death Aaron Williams, an unarmed black man. By the sixth week of these appearances, three of the five commissioners had resigned. Their replacements fired Andaya for his brutal police record shortly after being seated. Third Eye also worked recently on the case of Sheila DeToy, a 17-year-old white girl shot in the back of the head by police.

"They've taken hip-hop where it's never been before. They've taken hip-hop ciphers to the evening news," boasts Van Jones, executive director of the Ella Baker Center for Human Rights in San Francisco, one of the principals of Third Eye. Mixed with hip-hop's aggressive attitude, the political message can get "scary," he says. "You won't find it in a traditional civics-class curriculum: We're willing to take issues into our hands if the system won't work. As scary as people thought gangsta rap was, it's nothing compared to young people using hip-hop to express what they're going through and targeting the people who are really responsible."

Jones says he founded the Ella Baker Center—named to honor the soul mother of SNCC—in response to the failures of the civil rights establishment, which had become "too tame and too tired." "I don't believe the true power of the people can be confined to a ballot box," he says, but must express itself in strikes, boycotts, pickets, civil disobedience. "We need to be about the whup-ass. Somebody's fucking up somewhere. They have names and job descriptions. You have to be creative about how you engage the enemy, because if you do it on his terms, the outcome is already known."

Most important, a mature hip-hop movement will have to deal with the irony of using hip-hop. Organizing for social change requires that people tap into their mutual human vulnerability and acknowledge their common oppression before they can bond, and band, together in solidarity. Though born in and of alienation and extreme social vulnerability, hip-hop culture is not eager to boast of it. Whereas the blues embraced pain to transcend it, hip-hop builds walls to shield against further injury. So getting to that place where the music might once again speak of individual frailty and collective strength is a difficult task.

At a December 12 rally for Mumia Abu-Jamal—co-sponsored by Third Eye and STORM (Standing Together to Organize a Revolutionary Movement), among others—students from the Bay Area crowd the steps of Oakland's City Hall. It's the kind of rally a traditional leftist would recognize. White radicals pass out socialist papers, petitions to end the death penalty and "Free Mumia" decals. Placards and banners quote Malcolm X, Assata Shakur, Che Guevara. The difference is that hip-hop headz take center stage, leaving older white lefties on the periphery with their pamphlets.

It is not exactly a changing of the guard. The rally begins on a shaky note. The Ella Baker Center's youth coordinator, Jasmin Barker, steps to the mike and calls for a moment of silence. Minutes before, the sound system was blaring what might be called less than conscious rap. It's difficult for some to make the switch from the gangsta lyrics to a spirit of solidarity with Mumia. Barker persists like a schoolmarm and finally gets the reverence she demands. She then calls for a "moment of noise" to put the city government on notice. But it's Saturday. City Hall is closed. Downtown Oakland is empty. If mass demonstrations are for the onlookers, at first glance it seems as if these young activists have made the most basic of organizing errors: staging an action for a targeted constituency that's not even around. But soon enough it's evident that the objective here, this day, is to assert a generational identity, a collective sense of political possibility.

"Chill with the sellin' papers while the rally's goin' on," a young brother named Ryan scolds a man passing out *Workers Vanguard* during a step routine by seven Castlemont High School students. They are wearing blue jeans, sneakers, white T-shirts and fluorescent orange decals that say "Free Mumia," distrib-

uted by Refuse and Resist. They stand at attention, in single file, each girl holding two empty aluminum cans end to end. The lead girl sets the beat with a syncopated chant: "Mu-miiiiii-aa! Free Mumia, yeah! Mu-miiiiii-aa!" The other six chime in, and the line begins to move like a locomotive, with hands and legs clapping and stomping to recreate the diasporan rhythms that are at the heart of hip-hop.

Speakers pass the mike. Castlemont junior Muhammad, 15, explains the uses of the criminal justice system, from police brutality to the death penalty, to uphold the interests of the ruling class in his own hip-hop lingo. Latifah Simon, founder of the Center for Young Women's Development in San Francisco, relates Mumia's predicament to their lives: "If they should kill Mumia what will they do to you? If they should kill a revolutionary, people got to be in the streets screaming. It was young people like the ones here," she reminds the 300 on the steps of City Hall, "who made the civil rights movement happen." A white kid named Michael Lamb, with UC Berkeley's Poetry for the People collective, pays tribute to Saul Williams and *Slam* in reciting a rap with the refrain "Where my crackers at?" suggesting that the struggle for true democracy in America needs to be an equal opportunity affair.

It is Dontario Givens, 15, who best illustrates the impact a burgeoning hip-hop movement could have on a generation so long alienated. His favorite record at the movement is Outkast's tribute to Rosa Parks, the mother of the civil rights movement. But when his social studies teacher asked him to speak at the rally on behalf of Mumia, his first response was pure hip-hop. "Why should I care?" It took him three weeks to sort through his initial resistance before hitting on that space of empathy and recognition that is the cornerstone of organizing. "What would I want the world to do if I was Mumia?" he asked himself. "Come together and make the revolution."

> Organizing for social change requires that people tap into their mutual human vulnerability and acknowledge their common oppression before they can bond, and band, together in solidarity.

Journal and Discussion Questions

1   What reasons does Angela Ards give for using hip-hop music to try to involve youth in political and social movements? What problems in trying to use rap music for political purposes does Ards discuss? What overall idea is Ards arguing about using hip-hop music to organize young people around social causes in "Rhyme and Resist: Organizing the Hip-Hop Generation"?

2   Outline "Rhyme and Resist." Why does Ards intersperse *epigrams*—quotations from other writers set apart from the rest of "Rhyme and Resist"—to introduce her essay and several of its major sections? How do these quotations prepare readers for what Ard has to say in the section that follows?

3   What does each example of political activists or social programs that have used hip-hop music reveal about the political potential and the political problems of using rap music in social causes? How does the opening anecdote about Ella Baker and the 21st Century Youth Leadership Movement rally prepare readers for what Ards has to say in "Rhyme and Resist"? Why does Ards conclude "Rhyme and Resist" with a story about the rally for Mumia Abu-Jamal and a discussion about fifteen-year-old Dontario Givens?

4   What are the important similarities and differences between the civil rights generation of the 1950s and 1960s and the post-civil rights generation of today, according to Ards? How does Ards use this comparison to develop her ideas in "Rhyme and Resist"? Why does Ards switch from this comparison to a comparison with the Beat poets of the 1950s?

5   How does the background that Ards provides about the history of hip-hop music help develop Ards' argument? According to Ards, what did rap music have to do with what was happening in the U.S., especially the youth culture of inner-city blacks and Latinos?

6   What are Ards' criticisms about the "rank materialism" and "misogyny" of much hip-hop music? How, according to Ards, is rap music able to express and encourage negative attitudes and behavior and social consciousness about themes like drugs, violence, and racism at the same time? How can activists, especially feminists, use hip-hop music to raise social consciousness without sending sexist and selfishly materialistic messages?

7   Do you agree with Ards' description and analysis of hip-hop music? What do you think she has gotten right about it? What does she get wrong? What does she ignore or seem ignorant about?

Topics for Writing

1   Drawing from "Rhyme and Resist," discuss the pros and cons of using popular music to raise public consciousness about social problems and to help organize people to take action to solve these problems.

2   Analyze the values promoted by rap music. You may want to focus on the music of a single artist, record label, genre (such as gangsta rap), or period of hip-hop music.

3   "Given hip-hop's social origins and infectious appeal," Ards writes, "there's long been a hope that it could help effect social change." Argue whether hip-hop music has brought about social change since Ards published "Rhyme and Resist" in the summer of 1999. Be specific about the social changes that rap music has helped bring about.

4   Write a research paper discussing the social impact of other music, in the past or present.

Connecting the Readings

Drawing on Nelson George's "Gangsters—Real and Unreal" and Angela Ards' "Rhyme and Resist: Organizing the Hip-Hop Generation," analyze hip-hop music's relationship to urban African American culture or to American youth culture. Discuss how hip-hop music both reflects and influences cultures in the U.S.

I DEMAND REPARATIONS!

BY CLAY JONES

Political cartoonist Clay Jones, according to his biography in *Slate*, "calls himself 'an unreliable conservative,' and believes it is his daily goal to lampoon authority and make it look as ridiculous as possible. 'My cartoons do not tell readers what they should believe. I hope they simply challenge people to think.'" Jones works for the Fredericksburg, Virginia, newspaper, the *Free Lance-Star*. His cartoons have appeared in *Newsweek*, *USA Today*, and other newspapers, and he has a book of cartoons entitled *Knee-Deep in Mississippi*. The political cartoon "I Demand Reparations!" first appeared in the *Free Lance-Star* in July 2006, and was republished in the online news magazine *Slate*.

Journal and Discussion Questions

1 What is the main point of Clay Jones' political cartoon? How do the details of the cartoon communicate this idea?

2 Why do you think the African American in the cartoon objects to the teenager? What reasons can you offer to defend the teenager?

3 What is Jones' attitude toward hip-hop dress and language? How do you know?

4 Why is the issue of slavery reparations mentioned in the cartoon? Why does Jones compare this issue to the issue of whites adopting hip-hop language, dress, and music? What attitude do you think Jones has about slavery reparations? Why?

5 Is Jones' portrait of the white hip-hop teenager a fair and accurate portrayal of young people who are into hip-hop culture? Why or why not? Do you think Jones means to be fair and accurate? Why or why not?

6 Think of other examples in popular culture when whites have adopted or appropriated something from the culture of another group of people (music, fashion, art). What might be wrong or dangerous about whites or American popular culture adopting phenomena from black culture or the cultures of other minorities or countries? What might be healthy or positive about this?

Topics for Writing

1 Analyze the argument of Clay Jones' political cartoon and respond to Jones' ideas.

2 Write a research paper describing and evaluating how American culture has adopted or appropriated a part of black culture or the culture of another people.

3 Draw a political cartoon about another debate in popular culture.

MOVIE REVIEW: *Junebug*

BY ANDREA KRETCHMER

Andrea Kretchmer is student at Pomona College and a writer and movie critic for *The Student Life*, the campus newspaper at Pomona College. According to the newspaper's masthead, *The Student Life* began in 1889, making it "the oldest college newspaper in southern California." Kretchmer's movie review of *Junebug* appeared in the February 10, 2006, issue of *The Student Life*.

PHIL MORRISON'S CRITICALLY acclaimed and award-winning film *Junebug*, playing at Rose Hills this weekend, is a charming and bittersweet tale of coming home. Classy Chicago art gallery owner Madeline (*Bridget Jones's Diary*'s Embeth Davidtz) travels down to Bible-belt North Carolina to woo an "amazing" artist—a wacky southerner who paints ridiculous wartime scenes. Coincidentally, her handsome husband of six months, George (*Mansfield Park*'s Alessandro Nivola), was a former North Carolina bumpkin. So, the journey becomes a meet-the-parents adventure for the two of them.

The Johnston family and the town they live in contrasts greatly with metropolitan Chicago. George's family consists of his pushy, controlling, mother (Celia Weston) and his quiet and reserved father (Scott Wilson). Also living at home are George's angry younger brother, Johnny (*The OC*'s Ben McKenzie), and his perky, pregnant wife, Ashley (*Catch Me If You Can*'s Amy Adams). Johnny works at a dishware-packing factory while trying to get through school, while Ashley waits around the house, wishing their love was what it used to be. When Madeline and George arrive, Ashley is the only family member who seems to be slightly excited to see them. She is in awe of Madeline's worldliness. Immediately hugging her and saying "I want to know everything there is to know about you. I want you to tell us every little thing." You can't help but pity Ashley, with her eagerness and desire to be appreciated. In one scene, while Ashley and Madeline are relaxing on the sofa, Ashley painting Madeline's nails, the mother comes in and scolds her for sitting on the couch: "I don't want your water breaking. We just had the upholstery cleaned."

Although *Junebug* moves rather slowly, it has a sweet and quirky humor to it, poking fun at the family and Madeline's shock at their life. Ashley is obsessed with meercats, the mother's lipstick is never on correctly, and to top it off the artist's paintings are just awful. As Madeline attends baby showers and church dinners, her perception of who her husband is and where he came from completely changes. As she grows to love the family, the family also learns to let down their guard and welcome her.

Junebug has an *About Schmidt* quality to it—the film will make you laugh one moment and make you misty the next. Its simplicity makes its message much more compelling. Amy Adams, just nominated for an Oscar for her role, is fantastic. Her eagerness, innocence, and desire to be appreciated will break your heart. McKenzie also delivers a fantastic performance as a kid trying to do good but with no idea how. *Junebug* was not widely released but rightfully won acclaim from critics and awards ceremonies. For less than what it would cost to rent it at Blockbuster, *Junebug* is definitely worth checking out this weekend. Even if you do not like the story, the *non sequitur* scene of North Carolinians yodeling, the catchy "Yo La Tengo" song that appears twice in the film, and the sight of Ryan Atwood with a hick mustache are worth the two bucks.

Journal and Discussion Questions

1 According to Andrea Kretchmer, what are the strengths and weaknesses of *Junebug*? Why does she recommend the movie? How does Kretchmer support and illustrate her opinions about *Junebug*? Which claims about the strengths and weaknesses of *Junebug* are especially well explained and supported?

2 What points about the movie does Kretchmer make or support by quoting two bits of dialogue from *Junebug*?

3 Who is the intended audience for Kretchmer's movie review? What kind of student does she seem to think would be interested in seeing *Junebug*? How can you tell?

4 Writing teachers often warn students to be cautious about using *the generalized you* in their writing, using *you* instead of nouns like *people* or *viewers* or *movie-goers*. Why do you think Kretchmer decided to use *you* in several sentences, such as "You can't help but pity Ashley, with her eagerness and desire to be appreciated"? Was this a good decision? Why or why not?

5 Kretchmer mentions several other movies and one television series in her review, even though she cannot assume that all her readers have seen these films and shows. Why do you think she makes these references? What does she mean when she writes, "*Junebug* has an *About Schmidt* quality to it—the film will make you laugh one moment and make you misty the next"? Is the sentence clear to someone who hasn't seen *About Schmidt*?

6 If you have seen *Junebug*, do you agree with Kretchmer's review? Why or why not? If you haven't seen *Junebug*, does her review make you want to see the movie? Why or why not? Do you think this is a well-written movie review? Why or why not?

7 If Kretchmer were writing a paper analyzing *Junebug* for a film or literature class, how would it be different from her movie review? What in this movie review might fit in an analytical paper about a film? Why?

Topics for Writing

1 Rent *Junebug* and write a response to Andrea Kretchmer's review, agreeing or disagreeing with her.

2 Write a review of another movie that could appear in your campus newspaper.

Suggestions for Essays on FOLK AND POPULAR CULTURE

1 Analyze the importance of regional cultural events, stories, and beliefs on the people in that region, drawing on several of the selections by Hurston, Rickels, Walker, Rose, George, Ards, and Calistro's quilt.

2 Discuss the effects that popular culture can have on people's moral beliefs and behavior considering some of the ideas of George, Ards, Medved, Nemerov, the Bible Quilt, the AIDS Memorial Quit, and the *Bamboozled* DVD cover.

3 Write an argument about the value of hip-hop music and culture and the influence it is having on American society, considering the arguments by Hurston, George, Ards, and Jones.

4 Write an essay discussing the roles college students can have as contributors or critics of folk and popular culture, considering Kretchmer's movie review, Jones' cartoon, and the essay on witch-riding by the student in Rickels's article.

5 Analyze the ways that the commercial cultures of mass media and tourism influence and are influenced by local and regional cultures, considering Nemerov, Rose, and George.

6 Write an essay analyzing the influence that family and popular culture have on each other, discussing the selections by Rickels and Walker.

7 Discuss how folk and popular culture influence people's sense of identity drawing on several of the selections by Hurston, Rickels, Walker, Medved, George, Ards, Powers, the *Bamboozled* DVD cover, and the three quilts in this chapter.

12 War, Terrorism, and Protest

EVER SINCE AL QUAEDA'S ATTACKS ON the World Trade Center and the Pentagon on September 11, 2001, people have been discussing and writing about war, terrorism, and protest with a greater sense of importance and urgency. The events of 9/11 and the wars in Afghanistan and Iraq have made us more aware that questions about war, terrorism, and protest are intertwined and often inseparable. The rise of radical Islamic terrorist groups cannot be explained without discussing previous wars in the Middle East, including the 1976 Arab–Israeli war, the Soviet Union's invasion of Afghanistan in 1980, and the 1990 Persian Gulf War that followed Iraq's invasion of Kuwait. The 9/11 attacks prompted President George W. Bush to declare a "war on terror," to invade Afghanistan, and to lay out a policy of preemptive war that justifies going to war, without being attacked, in order to prevent terrorist actions. President Bush invoked this policy when the U.S. invaded Iraq to bring down the government of Saddam Hussein. Terrorist tactics, such as car bombings and suicide bombings, became important components of the military campaigns and civil war that followed the fall of Hussein in Iraq. Opponents of the war in Iraq have staged protests worldwide, first, to persuade the U.S. government not to invade Iraq and then to remove its troops from Iraq, even as some supporters of the war questioned the patriotism of the protesters and staged counter-demonstrations in support of the war and President Bush.

The Iraq War and the war on terror have generated countless arguments about the morality, legality, and effectiveness of various military, diplomatic, and domestic laws, tactics, and policies that the U.S. government has used in the wars in Iraq and Afghanistan and against terrorist suspects. As the wars have continued, we have argued about the very definitions of *torture*, *terrorism*, and *war*. We have argued about how we should and should not express our opinions about the war and even whether we should be arguing at all, if debating the war might encourage our enemies and discourage our troops.

Of course, people have been arguing about war, political violence, and peoples' rights to oppose or even rebel against government almost since the beginnings of civilization and the establishment of governments. Few subjects receive as much attention as war because the moral, political, psychological, economic, environmental, and humanitarian stakes of war are so complex and serious. Few subjects receive more attention than political protest and political violence because of the complicated ethical, political, and practical risks and problems involved whenever individuals or groups consider opposing their government or another powerful institution. We continue to discuss and debate past wars, social movements, and rebellions, questioning whether the U.S. should have dropped atomic bombs on Hiroshima and Nagasaki, what went wrong with the Vietnam War, why Gandhi's nonviolent campaign for India's independence worked, why Malcolm X opposed Martin Luther King Jr.'s doctrine of nonviolent civil disobedience, and what the student demonstrations in the 1960s achieved. We revisit the past partly in the hope that time and distance can give us a better understanding of what happened and that we can use that understanding to guide our decisions today.

Many issues of war, protest, and terrorism are related to issues that writers face in less dramatic situations because people engage in war, terrorism, and demonstrations for the same basic reason that people write—to influence people's minds and actions. Most academic writing assignments assume a rough equality between writers and their readers. When you write an argument in a college class, you usually assume that your audience will consider your words carefully and is willing to change their minds, even though you realize that some audiences are more difficult to persuade than others. The rhetorical situation is usually different when a government or a group is considering war, political protest, or terrorism. Protesters and terrorists usually are trying to change the minds of a group or institution much more powerful than themselves. Governments and political groups usually consider violence—military action, war, terrorism—only when persuasion and diplomacy have failed, when they are convinced that their opponents will not listen to arguments.

Many of the problems that we consider in trying to understand the ethics, motives, and tactics of war, terrorism, and protest are similar to the problems that we think about when we try to persuade others—especially the ethical problems. How can one change another person's mind, especially when he is stubbornly holding to a position, or even persuade him to listen? How should ethics guide and restrict one's tactics and strategies for persuading others? Do the ends sometimes justify means of persuasion that may be morally questionable?

Here are some important questions that you may ask yourself when you write about issues of war,

protest, and terrorism. As you write about particular subjects, you may want to adapt these questions to the particular subject that you are writing about ("Should we call the U.S. campaign against terrorism a war?" for "What constitutes war?"; "Was World War II avoidable?" for "Is war inevitable?").

- What constitutes a war?

- Why do nations go to war? Is war an inevitable part of human existence?

- Is there such a thing as a just war? Why or why not? If so, what makes a war just?

- When should or must a nation go to war? What alternatives should a nation pursue instead of, or before, declaring war?

- What should the rules of warfare be? Does war justify any act, including torture, the killing of civilians, or the use of nuclear and biological weapons, that might help defeat the enemy? Why or why not?

- Is it accurate to use the word *war* to describe the U.S. campaign against terrorism? Why or why not?

- What is terrorism? Is any act of violence in support of a political cause an act of terrorism? Is a hate crime an act of terrorism? Why or why not?

- What are the causes of terrorism? Why do people resort to terrorism?

- How can terrorism be discouraged or eliminated?

- Why do people engage in political protests? Why don't more people engage in political protests when they strongly disagree with or are harmed by government or corporate actions?

- What forms of political protest are most effective? Why?

- What circumstances would justify the following tactics sometimes used by protesters: flag burning, blocking abortion clinics, labor strikes, disrupting traffic, withholding taxes? How do you decide whether the end justifies the means in political protest?

- Are some forms of protest always inappropriate or wrong, no matter what the cause? Is violence ever justified or necessary to try to end oppression or another evil?

- How are the Internet and information technologies changing political activism? How can technology be used effectively to support a political or moral cause?

- Is civil disobedience—breaking the law in support of a moral or political cause—ever justified? Why or why not? If so, when is it justified?

Invitations for Journal Writing

1 Discuss your thoughts about a particular war, past or present—such as the wars in Iraq or Afghanistan, the Persian Gulf War, the Vietnam War, World War II, or the Civil War. Discuss whether you think the war was justified, whether it was a successful war, and how you arrived at your opinions.

2 Describe a specific war-related image or story that you find meaningful or powerful. You might choose an image or story that you encountered in the news or popular culture (a photograph, a movie, a news story, even a video game), that you learned about from someone you know, or that you experienced yourself. Discuss why you chose this image or story and what meaning it has for you.

3 Describe where you were when you learned about the attacks of September 11, 2001. What were your thoughts and reactions in the first days or weeks after the attacks? How have your thoughts and feelings changed in the years since then? Why?

MILITARY-INDUSTRIAL COMPLEX SPEECH

BY DWIGHT D. EISENHOWER

Dwight D. Eisenhower (1890–1969) was Supreme Commander of the victorious Allied forces in Europe in World War II and President of the United States from 1953 to 1961. As a Republican president, Eisenhower is credited with negotiating an end to the Korean War, beginning NASA and the interstate highway system, and generally maintaining peace during the Cold War while working with a Democratically controlled Congress for six of his eight years in office. On January 17, 1961, just before the end of his second term, Eisenhower appeared on television to give this farewell address, now known as his military-industrial complex speech. By mentioning his "half a century in the service of our country," Eisenhower refers both to his two terms as President and his long career in the Army, during which Eisenhower rose to the rank of five-star general. This speech was given at the height of the Cold War against the Soviet Union when fears of communism and of a nuclear World War III that could end the world dominated western politics. In the speech, Eisenhower warns that economic, political, and technological changes in the United States created a climate that encouraged political and military leaders to go to war rather than try to work out peaceful solutions to international conflicts.

MY FELLOW AMERICANS:

I.

Three days from now, after half a century in the service of our country, I shall lay down the responsibilities of office as, in traditional and solemn ceremony, the authority of the Presidency is vested in my successor.

This evening I come to you with a message of leave-taking and farewell, and to share a few final thoughts with you, my countrymen.

Like every other citizen, I wish the new President, and all who will labor with him, Godspeed. I pray that the coming years will be blessed with peace and prosperity for all.

Our people expect their President and the Congress to find essential agreement on issues of great moment, the wise resolution of which will better shape the future of the Nation.

My own relations with the Congress, which began on a remote and tenuous basis when, long ago, a member of the Senate appointed me to West Point, have since ranged to the intimate during the war and immediate post-war period, and, finally, to the mutually interdependent during these past eight years.

In this final relationship, the Congress and the Administration have, on most vital issues, cooperated well, to serve the national good rather than mere partisanship, and so have assured that the business of the Nation should go forward. So, my official relationship with the Congress ends in a feeling, on my part, of gratitude that we have been able to do so much together.

II.

We now stand ten years past the midpoint of a century that has witnessed four major wars among great nations. Three of these involved our own country. Despite these holocausts America is today the strongest, the most influential and most productive nation in the world. Understandably proud of this pre-eminence, we yet realize that America's leadership and prestige depend, not merely upon our unmatched material progress, riches and military strength, but on how we use our power in the interests of world peace and human betterment.

III.

Throughout America's adventure in free government, our basic purposes have been to keep the peace; to fos-

ter progress in human achievement, and to enhance liberty, dignity and integrity among people and among nations. To strive for less would be unworthy of a free and religious people. Any failure traceable to arrogance, or our lack of comprehension or readiness to sacrifice would inflict upon us grievous hurt both at home and abroad.

Progress toward these noble goals is persistently threatened by the conflict now engulfing the world. It commands our whole attention, absorbs our very beings. We face a hostile ideology—global in scope, atheistic in character, ruthless in purpose, and insidious in method. Unhappily the danger it poses promises to be of indefinite duration. To meet it successfully, there is called for, not so much the emotional and transitory sacrifices of crisis, but rather those which enable us to carry forward steadily, surely, and without complaint the burdens of a prolonged and complex struggle—with liberty the stake. Only thus shall we remain, despite every provocation, on our charted course toward permanent peace and human betterment.

Crises there will continue to be. In meeting them, whether foreign or domestic, great or small, there is a recurring temptation to feel that some spectacular and costly action could become the miraculous solution to all current difficulties. A huge increase in newer elements of our defense; development of unrealistic programs to cure every ill in agriculture; a dramatic expansion in basic and applied research—these and many other possibilities, each possibly promising in itself, may be suggested as the only way to the road we wish to travel.

But each proposal must be weighed in the light of a broader consideration: the need to maintain balance in and among national programs—balance between the private and the public economy, balance between cost and hoped for advantage—balance between the clearly necessary and the comfortably desirable; balance between our essential requirements as a nation and the duties imposed by the nation upon the individual; balance between actions of the moment and the national welfare of the future. Good judgment seeks balance and progress; lack of it eventually finds imbalance and frustration.

The record of many decades stands as proof that our people and their government have, in the main, understood these truths and have responded to them well, in the face of stress and threat. But threats, new in kind or degree, constantly arise. I mention two only.

> **" Good judgment seeks balance and progress; lack of it eventually finds imbalance and frustration. "**

IV.

A vital element in keeping the peace is our military establishment. Our arms must be mighty, ready for instant action, so that no potential aggressor may be tempted to risk his own destruction.

Our military organization today bears little relation to that known by any of my predecessors in peacetime, or indeed by the fighting men of World War II or Korea.

Until the latest of our world conflicts, the United States had no armaments industry. American makers of plowshares could, with time and as required, make swords as well. But now we can no longer risk emergency improvisation of national defense; we have been compelled to create a permanent armaments industry of vast proportions. Added to this, three and a half million men and women are directly engaged in the defense establishment. We annually spend on military security more than the net income of all United States corporations.

This conjunction of an immense military establishment and a large arms industry is new in the American experience. The total influence—economic, political, even spiritual—is felt in every city, every State house, every office of the Federal government. We recognize the imperative need for this development. Yet we must not fail to comprehend its grave implications. Our toil, resources and livelihood are all involved; so is the very structure of our society.

In the councils of government, we must guard against the acquisition of unwarranted influence, whether sought or unsought, by the military-industrial complex. The potential for the disastrous rise of misplaced power exists and will persist.

We must never let the weight of this combination endanger our liberties or democratic processes. We should take nothing for granted. Only an alert and knowledgeable citizenry can compel the proper meshing of the huge industrial and military machinery of defense with our peaceful methods and goals, so that security and liberty may prosper together.

Akin to, and largely responsible for the sweeping changes in our industrial-military posture, has been the technological revolution during recent decades.

In this revolution, research has become central; it also becomes more formalized, complex, and costly. A steadily increasing share is conducted for, by, or at the direction of, the Federal government.

Today, the solitary inventor, tinkering in his shop, has been overshadowed by task forces of scientists in laboratories and testing fields. In the same fashion, the free university, historically the fountainhead of free ideas and scientific discovery, has experienced a revolution in the conduct of research. Partly because of the huge costs involved, a government contract becomes virtually a substitute for intellectual curiosity. For every old blackboard there are now hundreds of new electronic computers.

The prospect of domination of the nation's scholars by Federal employment, project allocations, and the power of money is ever present and is gravely to be regarded.

Yet, in holding scientific research and discovery in respect, as we should, we must also be alert to the equal and opposite danger that public policy could itself become the captive of a scientific-technological elite.

It is the task of statesmanship to mold, to balance, and to integrate these and other forces, new and old, within the principles of our democratic system—ever aiming toward the supreme goals of our free society.

V.

Another factor in maintaining balance involves the element of time. As we peer into society's future, we—you and I, and our government—must avoid the impulse to live only for today, plundering, for our own ease and convenience, the precious resources of tomorrow. We cannot mortgage the material assets of our grandchildren without risking the loss also of their political and spiritual heritage. We want democracy to survive for all generations to come, not to become the insolvent phantom of tomorrow.

VI.

Down the long lane of the history yet to be written America knows that this world of ours, ever growing smaller, must avoid becoming a community of dreadful fear and hate, and be instead, a proud confederation of mutual trust and respect.

Such a confederation must be one of equals. The weakest must come to the conference table with the same confidence as do we, protected as we are by our moral, economic, and military strength. That table, though scarred by many past frustrations, cannot be abandoned for the certain agony of the battlefield.

Disarmament, with mutual honor and confidence, is a continuing imperative. Together we must learn how to compose differences, not with arms, but with intellect and decent purpose. Because this need is so sharp and apparent I confess that I lay down my official responsibilities in this field with a definite sense of disappointment. As one who has witnessed the horror and the lingering sadness of war—as one who knows that another war could utterly destroy this civilization which has been so slowly and painfully built over thousands of years—I wish I could say tonight that a lasting peace is in sight.

Happily, I can say that war has been avoided. Steady progress toward our ultimate goal has been made. But, so much remains to be done. As a private citizen, I shall never cease to do what little I can to help the world advance along that road.

VII.

So—in this my last good night to you as your President—I thank you for the many opportunities you have given me for public service in war and peace. I trust that in that service you find some things worthy; as for the rest of it, I know you will find ways to improve performance in the future.

You and I—my fellow citizens—need to be strong in our faith that all nations, under God, will reach the goal of peace with justice. May we be ever unswerving in devotion to principle, confident but humble with power, diligent in pursuit of the Nation's great goals.

To all the peoples of the world, I once more give expression to America's prayerful and continuing aspiration:

We pray that peoples of all faiths, all races, all nations, may have their great human needs satisfied; that those now denied opportunity shall come to enjoy it to the full; that all who yearn for freedom may experience its spiritual blessings; that those who have freedom will understand, also, its heavy responsibilities; that all who are insensitive to the needs of others will learn charity; that the scourges of poverty, disease and ignorance will be made to disappear from the earth, and that, in the goodness of time, all peoples will come to live together in a peace guaranteed by the binding force of mutual respect and love.

Journal and Discussion Questions

1 The printed text of the military-industrial complex speech in Eisenhower's presidential papers divides his speech into seven sections of different lengths. Outline Eisenhower's "Military-Industrial Complex Speech" with a sentence summarizing the central idea of each section. Is the military-industrial complex the main subject of his speech? If it is, how are the other topics that Eisenhower discusses related to his central topic? If the military-industrial complex isn't the central subject of this speech, what is?

2 What is the thesis of President Eisenhower's speech? What reasons and evidence does he provide to support this argument?

3 Explain the principles of government and foreign policy that Eisenhower argues in the third section of his speech. What does he mean by "balance," and why do you think he saves this principle for the longest and final explanation in this section? How are the principles of government that Eisenhower discussed in section III connected to Eisenhower's discussion of the two threats to the U.S. that he describes in sections IV and V?

4 Summarize the changes in the U.S. military that Eisenhower describes. What are the causes for these changes? What are the advantages of these changes? What dangers or problems are posed by these changes?

5 What does Eisenhower mean by "the military-industrial complex"? What brought about its existence? What dangers does it pose to the U.S. and the world? In a draft of his speech, Eisenhower used the phrase "military-industrial-congressional complex" but decided on "military-industrial complex" for his final draft. How does adding the word *congressional* change the meaning of the key phrase of Eisenhower's speech? Considering Eisenhower's statements about Congress in his introduction, why do you think he made this revision? Was this a good revision?

6 What are Eisenhower's fears about research and the technological revolution in his discussion of the military-industrial complex? What are his concerns about universities with the growth of military research? Do you think his fears have been borne out? Why or why not?

7 How does President Eisenhower's ethos and reputation—who he is and what his audience thinks and feels about him—affect his speech and its persuasiveness with readers? How might this speech be different if it were given by someone without Eisenhower's military and political experience?

Topics for Writing

1 Research the historical context of Eisenhower's "Military-Industrial Complex Speech"—such as the changes in the military that occurred after World War II during the Cold War, the growth of military research and technology in the 1950s, the role of the U.S. in international affairs, and perceived foreign threats to the U.S.—and write a research paper analyzing Eisenhower's argument about the military-industrial complex in the U.S.

2 Write a research paper discussing the influence of the military-industrial complex after Eisenhower's speech, for example, in the Cuban missile crisis, the Vietnam War, the Gulf War, or the war in Iraq. Argue whether the war or military crisis of your paper supports Eisenhower's argument, shows that his fears were unjustified, or shows that his words were heeded.

APRIL 29, 2005— MEMORIES OF DEATH

BY ZACHARY SCOTT-SINGLEY

Many soldiers who have fought in Iraq and Afghanistan have written blogs describing their experiences and expressing their thoughts and feelings about the war. Some soldiers have sought a wide audience for their blogs and wished to be a part of the ongoing public discussions about the war. Zachary Scott-Singley's blog, *A Soldier's Thoughts* (misoldierthoughts.blogspot.com), is one of these blogs. Scott-Singley (1981–) was a sergeant in the 3rd Infantry Division, stationed in Tikrit, Iraq, when he began writing *A Soldier's Thoughts*. Like many blogs, each entry can be read as a short essay. "April 29, 2005—Memories of Death" is the first essay in a selection of five entries from Scott-Singley's blog that were recognized as the "Best American Excerpt from a Military Blog" in *The Best American Nonrequired Reading 2006*, edited by Dave Eggers. Scott-Singley's blog provides an insider's view of how war changes the character of soldiers and the complicated relationship that U.S. soldiers have with Iraqi civilians. "Memories of Death" asks difficult personal questions about the motives and morality of the killing that soldiers do in a war.

THERE IS GOOD OUT THERE EVEN though at times it all seems bleak. There is also death. How many have dealt in death? Some would call it murder. Well, I have a confession to make, my platoon and I have had over 192 confirmed kills during our first deployment here (during the war on our way to capture Baghdad). We targeted people and then they just disappeared. Why? They were going to kill me. I had my orders and they had theirs. We were mortal enemies because we were told that we were. There are some who would tell me to not think about what I had to do, or it will drive you insane.

For me, however, I can't help but think about it. They were men like me. Some of them were even conscripted into military service. What made them fight? Were they more scared of their leader than of us? What has become of their families? How could I forget or not think about all that I have done? Should I wash my hands

of it all like Pontius Pilate? I think not. My choices have been made, my actions irreversible. So live I will, for we were the victors, right? The ones who survived. It is our victory, and our burden to carry, and I bear it with pride and with the greatest of remorse. Do you think that there is a special place in hell for people like me? Or will God judge me to have been a man of honor and duty?

When they told us how many we had killed my first thought was pride. Pride for such a high number. How does one feel pride for killing? Two years later and my thoughts are changed, transformed if you will. Those were just numbers so long ago when I first heard them. Now, however, I know that they were men with families like mine. It is crazy that we humans can be so destructive. There are people out there lining up to become martyrs, to kill themselves in order to kill others, and yet you still have people who fight tooth and nail to live for just one more minute longer.

> "There are people out there lining up to become martyrs, to kill themselves in order to kill others, and yet you still have people who fight tooth and nail to live for just one more minute longer."

We are an oxymoron, humanity that is. What makes someone look down the sights of a rifle to take aim on a fellow human being? What does it take to pull the trigger? I have done those things. I have done them and would do it again if it meant returning to my wife and children again. Some of you may think that I am a beast and you are probably right. I am. I will kill, I will take aim and fire, I will call fire upon you from afar with rockets and bombs or anything I can get my hands on if it means that I will see my family one more time.

But, I will also choose to dwell on and live with my choices. I chose to enlist as a soldier. My time has been served and now it is becoming overtime, but I won't just run away. As much as I would love to just be done (and rightly so now that I have been involuntarily extended). One thing is all I ask of you. I ask that you not judge me. Let me be my own judge, for my judgment is harsher than any you could give me anyway. For I will always have those memories to remind me of what I have done and what I am. Please know that I pray for peace every day, that and to see my family again.

Journal and Discussion Questions

1 What is the central question of "April 29, 2005—Memories of Death"? How does Zachary Scott-Singley answer that question? Why doesn't he mention the political reasons behind the U.S. decision to go to war in Iraq?

2 Is "April 29, 2005—Memories of Death" an argument that tries to persuade readers to accept Scott-Singley's opinion or an exploratory essay that asks questions and explores Scott-Singley's conflicting answers without coming to a definite conclusion? Explain.

3 In "Memories of Death," Scott-Singley writes, "There are some who would tell me to not think about what I had to do, or it will drive you insane. For me, however, I can't help but think about it." What does Scott-Singley mean by "what I had to do" here? Why would some people counsel soldiers not to think about this? Why does Scott-Singley ignore the advice? Do you agree with Scott-Singley's decision to think and write about "what I had to do"? Why or why not?

4 What does *A Soldier's Thoughts* have to say about the relationships between war and family, for both American soldiers and for the Iraqis that the soldiers are fighting and protecting? How do Scott-Singley's thoughts about family both motivate his actions and complicate his life as a soldier?

5 How have Scott-Singley's thoughts changed about his first deployment in the war in Iraq in the two years between conducting that mission and writing this blog? What are the reasons for this change?

6 How does Scott-Singley compare himself to other soldiers fighting the war in Iraq, on both sides of the conflict? What do these comparisons suggest about how he sees and judges himself and how he will live with his actions and decisions?

7 What does Scott-Singley mean when he writes, "We are an oxymoron, humanity that is," in "Memories of Death"? What conclusions does Scott-Singley come to about humanity and the human condition in his blog? Why?

Topics for Writing

1 Analyze "April 29, 2005—Memories of Death," focusing on one or more of Zachary Scott-Singley's questions or uncertainties about the war. How does Scott-Singley think through each side of the issue that he is considering? Why does he find it difficult to settle on one answer or position? How has his thinking developed during his service in Iraq? Considering Scott-Singley's own uncertainties, what should readers learn from his blog?

2 Find three other blogs about the war in Iraq and Afghanistan, by soldiers and other participants in or witnesses to the war, and write an essay comparing their different experiences and different perspectives about the war.

3 Write a research paper comparing soldiers' experiences in the war in Iraq with soldiers' experiences in an earlier war, such as the Kuwait War, the Vietnam War, or World War II. Your research should include journals and memoirs written by soldiers.

IMAGES OF WAR

Eugène Delacroix, *Liberty Leading the People*

EUGÈNE DELACROIX (1798–1863) WAS AN IMPORTANT ARTIST IN THE FRENCH Romantic movement, and some of his greatest works, like *Massacre at Chios*, depicted the horrors of war while also supporting revolutions against oppressive governments. Many of his later paintings depicted Arabic and Jewish culture, often based on sketches that he made while traveling in Spain and North Africa. Delacroix also illustrated books by William Shakespeare, Sir Walter Scott, and Johann Wolfgang von Goethe, and he earned a reputation as a writer on art and other subjects for his *Journals*. His painting *Liberty Leading the People* commemorates France's three-day July Revolution in 1830 when the Trois Glorieuses, a coalition of workers and the middle classes, deposed King Charles X and established a constitutional monarchy under King Louis-Philippe. The July Revolution was prompted by four proclamations signed by Charles that dissolved the National Assembly, ended freedom of the press, and created an electoral system that gave the aristocracy more power. *Liberty Leading the People* combines realism and allegory, with Liberty personified as both a mythical figure or goddess and a woman of the people leading the rebels on the bloodiest day of the revolution. Delacroix created this painting for a May 1831 exhibit celebrating the revolution at the Salon in Paris. But because government officials feared that Delacroix's painting would encourage more insurrections, *Liberty Leading the People* was exhibited only rarely after the Salon until it entered the Louvre in 1874. Now Delacroix's painting is associated with patriotism for the French Republic, so much so that the portrait appeared on the back of the hundred-franc note for fifteen years.

Journal and Discussion Questions

1 Describe *Liberty Leading the People*. What ideas about war and rebellion are implied by *Liberty Leading the People*? How does the painting communicate these ideas?

2 Describe the figure of Liberty. Why is Liberty a woman? Why is she bare-breasted? What does her personification tell you about Delacroix's concept of liberty?

3 Describe the other fighters. What does their clothing signify about them? Who do the fighters represent? What impression does Delacroix create about these fighters?

4 How does Delacroix depict the death and violence of war in *Liberty Leading the People*? Why does he have Liberty and the other rebels marching on the dead bodies of the government's soldiers?

5 Describe the rebels' attitudes about the death and destruction that occurred in the revolution. Does Delacroix share their attitudes? How does his painting consider the means and ends of revolution?

6 Why do you think the French government viewed Delacroix's *Liberty Leading the People* as a threatening, subversive painting and did not display it for several decades? Why do you think the painting has become a patriotic icon of the French Republic that the government has displayed on money and stamps?

Topics for Writing

1 Analyze Eugéne Delacroix's *Liberty Leading the People*, focusing on the painting's arguments and attitudes about war and rebellion. You might expand this paper into a research paper by consulting sources about Delacroix and about the three-day revolution.

2 Write a research paper about representations of war and revolution in other paintings and visual art.

Pablo Picasso, *Guernica*

PABLO PICASSO OF SPAIN (1881–1973) IS THE MOST FAMOUS ARTIST OF the twentieth century, and his painting *Guernica* is the century's most famous artistic condemnation of war. The giant black-and-white oil painting, which is $11\frac{1}{2}$ feet tall and almost 26 feet wide, depicts the massacre of the small Basque village of Guernica in northern Spain during the Spanish Civil War. Sixteen hundred civilians were killed or wounded, and the village burned for three days after fascist forces supporting General Franco bombed Guernica on April 27, 1937. Over a million people participated in May Day demonstrations against this massacre in Paris four days later. Inspired by photographs of the atrocities at Guernica, Picasso's painting was the centerpiece of the Spanish Pavilion exhibit at the Paris International Exposition in July 1937. Funded by the Spanish republican government that opposed Franco and the fascists in the civil war, the Spanish Pavilion exhibit was meant to critique the Paris Exposition's celebration of modern technology. *Guernica* has been displayed throughout the world since then and is currently displayed in Reina Sofia, Spain's national museum of modern art.

Journal and Discussion Questions

1 Describe the different figures in *Guernica*. What story is Pablo Picasso telling with his painting? How do Picasso's images communicate this story? What thoughts and emotions does Picasso's painting evoke in you?

2 Why does Picasso depict animals in *Guernica*—a horse being gored by a bull, another bull watching a mother and child, and a bird? What images seem hidden in the drawing of the horse? What do the horse and the images within it contribute to Picasso's painting and its persuasive and emotional impact?

3 Why does Picasso set the events of his painting inside, confining the people and animals to a single room?

4 Describe the eyes in *Guernica*, including the overhead light in the shape of an eye. How does Picasso draw attention to the eyes in his mural? How does his emphasis on eyes affect the meaning of *Guernica*?

5 Describe what is "unrealistic" or "distorted" about Picasso's depictions of the people, animals, and other images of the massacre. How do these distortions affect the meaning and emotional impact of *Guernica*? How would the impact of *Guernica* be different if Picasso had painted these realistically?

6 What arguments about the massacre at Guernica and about modern war in general is Picasso making in *Guernica*? How persuasive are these arguments?

Topics for Writing

1 Analyze Pablo Picasso's *Guernica*, focusing on the arguments Picasso is making about the massacre in Guernica and about modern warfare. You may expand this analysis into a research paper by researching art criticism about Picasso and *Guernica* and books, articles, and photographs about the massacre at Guernica and about the Spanish Civil War and its aftermath.

2 Considering Picasso's critique of twentieth-century technological warfare, write a research paper about how modern technology has changed how wars are fought. You might limit your paper to the effects of one invention (airplanes, tanks, land mines, missiles, or computers, for example).

Joe Rosenthal, Soldiers Raising the American Flag at Iwo Jima, 23 Feb. 1945

THIS PHOTOGRAPH OF FIVE MARINES AND ONE NAVY HOSPITAL CORPSMAN raising the American flag over Mount Suribachi during the Battle of Iwo Jima may be the most reproduced photograph in history. Associated Press photographer Joe Rosenthal (1911–2006) won the Pulitzer Prize for this picture, and the photograph immediately became an icon for American patriotism, helping to persuade a war-weary American public that the U.S. would eventually defeat Japan in World War II. In 1954, this image was memorialized with a statue for the Marine Corps War Memorial outside Arlington National Cemetery. Rosenthal took this photograph on February 23, 1945, five days into one of the bloodiest battles of World War II. When the U.S. took control of the small Pacific island of Iwo Jima 30 days later, the Japanese military lost the most important island in their early warning system for notifying mainland Japan about approaching American bombers. As depicted in Clint Eastwood's movie *Flags of Our Fathers*, very few of the millions who saw Rosenthal's photograph in newspapers across the U.S. knew that the six soldiers were actually replacing the original flag placed on top of Mount Suribachi, hours after American forces had taken control of the mountain with heavy casualties. Three of the soldiers in the photograph, Harlon Block, Franklin Sousley, and Michael Strank, later died on Iwo Jima. The other three soldiers, Rene Gagnon, Ira Hayes, and John Bradley, became national celebrities in a campaign to sell war bonds and bolster support for the war. After the war, from 1945 until his retirement in 1980, Rosenthal was a photographer with the *San Francisco Chronicle*. You can find more information and photographs on the Battle of Iwo Jima at www.iwojima.com.

Journal and Discussion Questions

1   What story about the soldiers and the Battle of Iwo Jima does Joe Rosenthal's photograph seem to be telling? How?

2   What makes Rosenthal's photograph such a powerful patriotic image, even generations after World War II? What virtues and other qualities does the photograph suggest about the soldiers raising the flag? What details suggest the character of the soldiers?

3   Why is it important that the soldiers are raising the American flag? How does the meaning of the photograph depend on the symbolism of the American flag? Would the photograph be as powerful if it had caught the soldiers a few seconds later, when the flag was erect? Why or why not?

4   If you view Rosenthal's photograph as a visual argument, what is its thesis? What ideas and attitudes about war are suggested by the photograph? What details in the photograph communicate these ideas and attitudes?

5   In Clint Eastwood's 2006 film about this photograph, *Flags of Our Fathers*, the character Rosenthal worries, correctly, that he didn't get the faces of the soldiers in the picture. Would his photograph be more powerful or meaningful if their faces were visible? Why or why not?

6   Does the knowledge that the soldiers in the photograph were replacing the original flag hours after the battle for Mount Suribachi had ended change the meaning of the photograph? Why or why not?

Topics for Writing

1 Analyze Joe Rosenthal's photograph, discussing what the photograph says about soldiers, warfare, and patriotism, and what makes it a powerful icon.

2 Write a research paper analyzing the meanings of different reproductions and uses of Rosenthal's photograph, such as at the Marine Corps War Memorial, in the film *Flags of Our Fathers*, on a U.S. postage stamp, and in books, on posters, or on Web sites about Iwo Jima, World War II, and the U.S. Marine Corps.

3 Research the story of Rosenthal's photograph and the soldiers it depicts, and write a research paper analyzing what the story reveals about the meaning and persuasive power of the photograph. Your essay may discuss ideas about the photograph in Clint Eastwood's film, *Flags of Our Fathers*, and compare his version of the story to your research.

Nick Ut, Girl Fleeing Napalm Attack Near Trang Bang, Vietnam, 8 June 1972

THIS PHOTOGRAPH OF A NINE-YEAR-OLD VIETNAMESE GIRL RUNNING away from the incendiary bombing of her village, Trang Bang, on June 8, 1972, may be the most memorable photograph of the Vietnam War. Associated Press (AP) photographer, Huynh Cong Út (1951–), better known as Nick Ut, won the Pulitzer Prize for this picture. AP decided to release the photograph despite its policy against publishing photographs with full frontal nudity. Most people who initially saw the photograph knew little of the story behind it. Trang Bang was destroyed by incendiary bombs of white phosphorous and napalm, an oily substance that sticks to the skin, dropped by two South Vietnamese aircraft. North Vietnamese and Vietcong soldiers had abandoned the village hours before the bombing, so civilians were the only victims. The girl, Phan Thi Kim Phúc, was badly burned and eventually would have 17 operations, but she survived thanks to Ut, who brought her to a hospital and saw that she had treatment. Ut's photograph quickly became a powerful icon for the antiwar movement in the U.S. and internationally. More information about the photograph, Ut, and Phúc can be found at digitaljournalist.org/issue0008/ng2.htm.

Journal and Discussion Questions

1 Why do you think people have found Nick Ut's photograph a powerful statement against the Vietnam War? Summarize the argument implied by his photograph. Do you think the photograph's message is about the Vietnam War or that it has a wider application? Why?

2 What story does Ut's photograph tell? How does the photograph communicate this story?

3 Although multiple people appear in Ut's photograph, the picture is remembered because of the image of the crying naked nine-year-old girl, Phan Thi Kim Phúc. Describe the girl. What does her image say about war? Would the photograph be less powerful if Kim Phúc were clothed? Why or why not?

4 What do you notice about the other children in the photograph (including Kim's brother, at the left edge of the picture)? Is it important that the villagers fleeing Trang Bang in the photograph are all children? How does the position of the camera—the fact that the children are running directly to the camera—contribute to the emotions and perspective of someone viewing the photograph?

5 Describe the soldiers in Ut's photograph. Compare how they and the children are leaving the burning village. What does the presence of the soldiers add to Ut's photograph?

6 Describe the scene behind and around the people in the photograph. What does the scene add to the photograph?

Topics for Writing

1 Analyze Nick Ut's photograph, focusing on what it argues about war.

2 Write a research paper about the effects of images of war in photographs, television, film, and art on Americans' support and opinions of war. Your essay might focus on a particular war, such as propaganda in World War II or television coverage of the Vietnam War or the Gulf War, but your essay might also compare the visual arguments about two or more wars.

Connecting the Readings

Compare the visual arguments about war in at least two of the following: Eugéne Delacroix's *Liberty Leading the People*, Pablo Picasso's *Guernica*, Joe Rosenthal's photograph of soldiers raising the flag at Iwo Jima, and Nick Ut's photograph of children fleeing a napalm attack on Trang Bang, Vietnam.

THE LAW OF WAR IN THE WAR ON TERROR

BY KENNETH ROTH

Kenneth Roth is Executive Director of the Human Rights Watch, a liberal, independent organization that conducts human rights investigations throughout the world, promotes political freedom, opposes discrimination and abuse of government powers, and tries to protect people from inhumane conduct in times of war. Before joining the HRW in the late 1980s, Roth was a federal prosecutor who gained fame for his work in the government's investigation of the Iran-Contra scandal during the Reagan administration. Roth has published more than eighty articles in *Foreign Affairs*, the *New York Times*, the *Washington Post*, the *New York Review of Books*, and other political magazines and newspapers. "The Law of War in the War on Terror" was first published in the January/February 2004 issue of *Foreign Affairs*, which may be the most influential journal on U.S. foreign policy and international affairs. *Foreign Affairs* is published by the nonpartisan Council on Foreign Relations, an organization whose members include U.S. Presidents, cabinet secretaries, other government officials, members of human rights associations, scholars, business leaders, and members of the news media. "The Law of War in the War on Terror" makes a legal argument by applying definitions of war and international laws governing nations' conduct at war to specific examples in the U.S. "war on terror." Roth's analysis leads him to challenge the idea that we should view the U.S. campaign against radical Islamist terrorism as a war.

WHAT ARE THE BOUNDARIES OF THE BUSH administration's "war on terrorism?" The recent battles fought against the Afghan and Iraqi governments were classic wars between organized military forces. But President George W. Bush has suggested that his campaign against terrorism goes beyond such conflicts; he said on September 29, 2001, "Our war on terror will be much broader than the battlefields and beachheads of the past. The war will be fought wherever terrorists hide, or run, or plan."

This language stretches the meaning of the word "war." If Washington means "war" metaphorically, as when it speaks about a "war" on drugs, the rhetoric would be uncontroversial, a mere hortatory device intended to rally support for an important cause. Bush, however, seems to think of the war on terrorism quite literally—as a real war—and this concept has worrisome implications. The rules that bind governments are much looser during wartime than in times of peace. The Bush administration has used war rhetoric precisely to give itself the extraordinary powers enjoyed by a wartime government to detain or even kill suspects without trial. In the process, the administra-

tion may have made it easier for itself to detain or eliminate suspects. But it has also threatened the most basic due process rights.

LAW AT PEACE, LAW AT WAR. By literalizing its "war" on terror, the Bush administration has broken down the distinction between what is permissible in times of peace and what can be condoned during a war. In peacetime, governments are bound by strict rules of law enforcement. Police can use lethal force only if necessary to meet an imminent threat of death or serious bodily injury. Once a suspect is detained, he or she must be charged and tried. These requirements—what one can call "law-enforcement rules"—are codified in international human rights law.

In times of war, law-enforcement rules are supplemented by a more permissive set of rules: namely, international humanitarian law, which governs conduct during armed conflict. Under such "war rules," unlike during peacetime, an enemy combatant can be shot without warning (unless he or she is incapacitated, in custody, or trying to surrender), regardless of any imminent threat. If a combatant is captured, he or she can be held in custody until the end of the conflict, without any trial.

These two sets of rules have been well developed over the years, both by tradition and by detailed international conventions. There is little law, however, to explain exactly when one set of rules should apply instead of the other. For example, the Geneva Conventions—the principal codification of war rules—apply to "armed conflict," but the treaties do not define the term. Fortunately, in its commentary on them, the International Committee of the Red Cross (ICRC), the conventions' official custodian, has provided some guidance. One test that the ICRC suggests can help determine whether wartime or peacetime rules apply is to examine the intensity of hostilities in a given situation. The Bush administration, for example, has claimed that al Qaeda is at "war" with the United States because of the magnitude of its attacks on September 11, 2001, its bombings of the U.S. embassies in Kenya and Tanzania, its attack on the U.S.S. Cole in Yemen, and the bombing of residential compounds in Saudi Arabia. Each of these attacks was certainly a serious crime warranting prosecution. But technically speaking, was the administration right to claim that they add up to a war? The ICRC's commentary does not provide a clear answer.

In addition to the intensity of hostilities, the ICRC suggests considering factors such as the regularity of armed clashes and the degree to which opposing forces are organized. Whether a conflict is politically motivated also seems to play an unacknowledged role in deciding whether it is a "war" or not. Thus organized crime or drug trafficking, although methodical and bloody, are generally understood to fall under law-enforcement rules, whereas armed rebellions, once sufficiently organized and violent, are usually seen as "wars." The problem with these guidelines, however, is that they were written to address political conflicts rather than global terrorism. Thus they do not make it clear whether al Qaeda should be considered an organized criminal operation (which would not trigger the application of war rules) or a rebellion (which would).

Even in the case of war, another factor in deciding whether law-enforcement or war rules should be applied is the nature of a given suspect's involvement. Such an approach can be useful because war rules treat as combatants only those who are taking an active part in hostilities. Typically, this category includes members of a military who have not laid down their arms as well as others who are fighting or approaching a battle, directing an attack, or defending a position. Under this rule, even civilians who pick up arms and start fighting can be considered combatants and treated accordingly. But this definition is difficult to apply to terrorism, where roles and activities are clandestine and a person's relationship to specific violent acts is often unclear.

HARD CASES. Given that so much confusion exists about whether to apply wartime or law-enforcement rules to a given situation, a better approach would be to make the decision based on its public policy implications. Unfortunately, the Bush administration seems to have ignored such concerns. Consider, for example, the cases of Jose Padilla and Ali Saleh Kahlah al-Marri. Federal officials arrested Padilla, a U.S. citizen, in May 2002 when he arrived from Pakistan at Chicago's O'Hare Airport, allegedly to scout out targets for a radiological ("dirty") bomb. As for al-Marri, a student from Qatar, he was arrested in December 2001 at his home in Peoria, Illinois, for allegedly being a "sleeper" agent: an inactive terrorist who, once activated, would help others launch attacks. President Bush, invoking war rules, has declared both men to be "enemy combatants," allowing the U.S. government to hold them without charge or trial until the end of the war against terrorism—whenever that is.

But should Padilla and al-Marri, even if they have actually done what the government claims, really be considered warriors? Aren't they more like ordinary criminals? A simple thought experiment shows how dangerous are the implications of treating them as combatants. The Bush administration has asserted that the two men planned to wage war against the United States and therefore can be considered de facto soldiers. But if that is the case, then under war rules, the two men could have been shot on sight, regardless of whether they posed any immediate danger to the United States (although they might have been spared under what is known as the doctrine of "military necessity," which holds that lethal force should not be used if an enemy combatant can be neutralized through lesser means). Under the administration's logic, then, Padilla could have been gunned down as he stepped off his plane at O'Hare, and al-Marri as he left his home in Peoria. That, after all, is what it means to be a combatant in time of war.

But the Bush administration has not claimed that either suspect was anywhere near to carrying out his alleged terrorist plan. Neither man, therefore, posed the kind of imminent threat that would justify the use of lethal force under law-enforcement rules. Given this fact, it would have been deeply disturbing if they were shot as enemy soldiers. Of course, the White House has not proposed killing them; instead, it plans to detain the two men indefinitely. But if Padilla and al-Marri should not be considered enemy combatants for the purpose of killing them, they should not be considered enemy combatants for the purpose of detaining them, either.

> **" Each of these attacks was certainly a serious crime warranting prosecution. But technically speaking, was the administration right to claim that they add up to a war? "**

A similar classification problem, although with a possibly different result, arose in the case of Qaed Salim Sinan al-Harethi. Al-Harethi, who Washington alleges was a senior al Qaeda official, was killed by a drone-fired missile in November 2002 while driving in a remote tribal area of Yemen. Five of his companions, including a U.S. citizen, also died in the attack, which was carried out by the CIA. The Bush administration apparently considered al-Harethi to be an enemy combatant for his alleged involvement in the October 2000 U.S.S. Cole bombing. In this instance, the case for applying war rules was stronger than with Padilla or al-Marri (although the Bush administration never bothered to spell it out). Al-Harethi's mere participation in the 2000 attack on the Cole would not have made him a combatant in 2002, since he could have subsequently withdrawn from al Qaeda; war rules permit attacking only current combatants, not past ones. And if al-Harethi were a civilian, he could not have legally been attacked unless he was actively engaged in hostilities at the time. But the administration alleged that al-Harethi was a "top bin Laden operative in Yemen," implying that he was in the process of preparing future attacks. If true, this would have made the use of war rules against him more appropriate. And unlike in the cases of Padilla and al-Marri, arresting al-Harethi may not have been an option. The Yemeni government has little control over the tribal area where he was killed; indeed, 18 Yemeni soldiers had reportedly died in an earlier attempt to arrest him.

Although there may have been a reasonable case for applying war rules to al-Harethi, the Bush administration has applied these rules with far less justification in other episodes outside the United States. For example, in October 2001, Washington sought the surrender of six Algerian men in Bosnia. At first, the U.S. government followed law-enforcement rules and secured the men's arrest. But then, after a three-month investigation, Bosnia's Supreme Court ordered the suspects released for lack of evidence. Instead of providing additional evidence, however, Washington simply switched to war rules. It pressured the Bosnian government to hand the men over

anyway and whisked them out of the country—not to trial, but to indefinite detention at the U.S. naval base at Guantánamo Bay.

The administration followed a similar pattern in June 2003, when five al Qaeda suspects were detained in Malawi. Malawi's high court ordered local authorities to follow the law and either charge or release the five men, all of whom were foreigners. Ignoring local law, the Bush administration then insisted that the men be handed over to U.S. security forces instead. The five were spirited out of the country to an undisclosed location—not for trial, but for interrogation. The move sparked riots in Malawi. The men were released a month later in Sudan, after questioning by Americans failed to turn up any incriminating evidence.

A BAD EXAMPLE. These cases are not anomalies. In the last two and a half years, the U.S. government has taken custody of a series of al Qaeda suspects in countries such as Indonesia, Pakistan, and Thailand. In many of these cases, the suspects were not captured on a traditional battlefield. Yet instead of allowing the men to be charged with a crime under local law-enforcement rules, Washington had them treated as combatants and delivered to a U.S. detention facility.

There is something troubling about such a policy. Put simply, using war rules when law-enforcement rules could reasonably be followed is dangerous. Errors, common enough in ordinary criminal investigations, are all the more likely when a government relies on the kind of murky intelligence that drives many terrorist investigations. If law-enforcement rules are used, a mistaken arrest can be rectified at trial. But if war rules apply, the government is never obliged to prove a suspect's guilt. Instead, a supposed terrorist can be held for however long it takes to win the "war" against terrorism. And the consequences of error are even graver if the supposed combatant is killed, as was al-Harethi. Such mistakes are an inevitable hazard of the battlefield, where quick life-and-death decisions must be made. But when there is no such urgency, prudence and humanity dictate applying law-enforcement standards.

Washington must also remember that its conduct sets an example for governments around the world. After all, many other states would be all too eager to find an excuse to eliminate their enemies through war rules. Israel, to name one, has used this rationale to justify its assassination of terrorist suspects in Gaza and the West Bank. It is not hard to imagine Russia doing the same to Chechen leaders in Europe, Turkey using a similar pretext against Kurds in Iraq, China against Uighurs in Central Asia, or Egypt against Islamists at home.

Moreover, the Bush administration should recognize that international human rights law is not indifferent to the needs of a government facing a security crisis. Criminal trials risk disclosure of sensitive information, as the administration has discovered in prosecuting Zacarias Moussaoui. But under a concept known as "derogation," governments are permitted to suspend certain rights temporarily when they can show that it is necessary to meet a "public emergency threatening the life of the nation." The International Covenant on Civil and Political Rights, which the United States has ratified, requires governments seeking derogation to file a declaration justifying the move with the UN secretary-general. Among the many governments to have done so are Algeria, Argentina, Chile, Colombia, Peru, Poland, Russia, Sri Lanka, and the United Kingdom. Yet the United States, determined to avoid the formal scrutiny involved, has not bothered.

The Justice Department has defended the administration's use of war rules by citing a U.S. Supreme Court decision from World War II, Ex Parte Quirin. In that case, the Court ruled that German army saboteurs who landed in the United States could be tried as enemy combatants before military commissions. The Court distinguished its ruling from an earlier Civil War-era case, Ex Parte Milligan, which held that a civilian resident of Indiana could not be tried in military court because local civil courts remained open and operational. Noting that the German saboteurs had entered the United States wearing at least parts of their uniforms, the Court in Quirin held that the Milligan protections applied only to people who are not members of an enemy's armed forces.

There are several reasons, however, why Quirin does not justify the Bush administration's broad use of war rules. First, the saboteurs in Quirin were agents of a government—Germany's—with which the United States was obviously at war. Whether the United States is actually at "war" with al Qaeda, however, remains uncertain under the law. Second, although the Court in Quirin defined a combatant as anyone operating with hostile intent behind military lines, the case has arguably been superseded by the 1949 Geneva Conventions (ratified by the United States), which, as noted

above, rule that people are combatants only if they either are members of an enemy's armed force or are taking active part in hostilities. Quirin thus does not help determine whether, under current law, people such as Padilla and al-Marri should be considered civilians (who, under Milligan, must be brought before civil courts) or combatants (who can face military treatment). Moreover, Quirin only establishes who can be tried before a military tribunal. The Bush administration, however, has asserted that it has the right to hold Padilla, al-Marri, and other detained "combatants" without a trial of any kind—in effect, precluding serious independent assessment of the grounds for potentially lifelong detention. Finally, whereas the government in Quirin was operating under a specific grant of authority from Congress, the Bush administration has acted on its own in taking the difficult decision to treat Padilla and al-Marri as combatants, without allowing the popular input that a legislative debate would provide.

STAY SAFE. The United States should not lightly suspend due process rights, as the Bush administration has done with its "enemy combatants"—particularly when a mistake could result in death or lengthy detention without charge or trial. Law-enforcement rules should presumptively apply to all suspects in the "war" on terror, and the burden should fall on those who want to invoke war rules to demonstrate that they are necessary and appropriate.

The best way to determine if war rules should apply would be through a three-part test. To invoke war rules, Washington should have to prove, first, that an organized group is directing repeated acts of violence against the United States, its citizens, or its interests with sufficient intensity that it can be fairly recognized as an armed conflict; second, that the suspect is an active member of an opposing armed force or is an active participant in the violence; and, third, that law enforcement means are unavailable.

Within the United States, the third requirement would be nearly impossible to satisfy—as it should be. Given the ambiguities of terrorism, we should be guided more by Milligan's affirmation of the rule of law than by Quirin's exception to it. Outside the United States, Washington should never resort to war rules away from a traditional battlefield if local authorities can and are willing to arrest and deliver a suspect to an independent tribunal—regardless of how the tribunal then rules. War rules should be used in such cases only when no law-enforcement system exists (and the other conditions of war are present), not when the rule of law happens to produce inconvenient results. Even if military forces are used to make an arrest in such cases, law-enforcement rules can still apply; only when attempting an arrest is too dangerous should war rules be countenanced.

This approach would recognize that war rules have their place—but that, given the way they inherently compromise fundamental rights, they should be used sparingly. Away from a traditional battlefield, they should be used, even against a warlike enemy, as a tool of last resort—when there is no reasonable alternative, not when a functioning criminal justice system is available. Until there are better guidelines on when to apply war and law-enforcement rules, this three-part test, drawn from the policy consequences of the decision, offers the best way to balance security and civil rights. In the meantime, the Bush administration should abandon its excessive use of war rules. In attempting to make Americans safer, it has made all Americans, and everyone else, less free.

Journal and Discussion Questions

1 What is the central thesis that Kenneth Roth is arguing in "The Law of War in the War on Terror"? What is important about the issue that Roth is arguing about? List the reasons Roth gives to support his thesis. Which reasons seem most important? Why?

2 Outline "The Law of War in the War on Terror." How does Roth organize his ideas and information to build a persuasive argument? How well do the article's headings guide you through Roth's argument?

3 Why does Roth introduce "The Law of War in the War on Terror" with a discussion of literal and metaphorical meanings of the word *war*? Why is the meaning of the word *war* in the phrase *war on terror* important?

4 According to Roth, what is the difference between *rules of war* and *rules of law enforcement*? How does Roth use comparison/contrast of these two sets of laws in his overall analysis and argument? How does this comparison lead up to Roth's concluding discussion of a "three-part test" for deciding on the rules that should govern the American government's antiterrorism campaign?

5 List the cases and examples that Roth discusses in "The Law of War in the War on Terror." Why does Roth select these particular examples? What does he conclude in his commentary of each example? What does his analysis of these cases contribute to his argument?

6 According to Roth, what is the Bush administration's argument? Does Roth describe this argument fairly and accurately? Why or why not? What concessions does Roth make to the Bush administration's position? What counterarguments does Roth offer against Bush's arguments?

7 What sources does Roth mention in "The Law of War in the War on Terror"? Where do you think he learned about the cases that he analyzes and about the rules of law and definitions of war?

Topics for Writing

1 Analyze Kenneth Roth's "The Law of War in the War on Terror," focusing on his use of definition and legal arguments to persuade readers. You may want to research other arguments on this issue to help you analyze how Roth represents and refutes opposing arguments and evidence.

2 Write an editorial for your local newspaper arguing whether the U.S. campaign against international terrorism should be described and conducted as a war. Your editorial may focus on strategic questions or ethical questions about the war on terrorism or both.

3 Write a research paper about the meanings and uses of the word *war* and other words associated with warfare in a specific context, such as the wars on drugs, on poverty, on crime, or on cancer, or the use of war metaphors in sports. Discuss how and why people use the metaphor of war and whether that metaphor is appropriate and useful in discussions of this topic or whether it is harmful and misleading.

LAWS OF WAR NEED TO CHANGE TO DEFEAT 'UNCIVILIZED' ENEMY

BY JAMES ZUMWALT

James Zumwalt is a retired Marine Corps lieutenant colonel and a veteran of the U.S. wars in Vietnam and the Persian Gulf. Zumwalt earned a law degree from Villanova University in 1979, served under President George W. Bush as a senior advisor to the assistant secretary of state on human rights and humanitarian affairs, and was a signatory of the controversial Swift Boat Veterans for Truth that challenged Senator John Kerry's war record during the 2004 presidential campaign. Today Zumwalt works as a private investment consultant to foreign and domestic clients in global markets and frequently contributes political and military commentary to newspapers and television. His editorial "Laws of War Need to Change to Defeat 'Uncivilized' Enemy" first appeared in December 2005, in the *Army Times*, an independent, nongovernmental magazine about military news and issues written for active and retired soldiers. Here Zumwalt argues that international rules of warfare like the Geneva Convention did not envision wars against terrorism and need to be changed.

IT MIGHT BE TIME TO REVISIT THE laws of war if we want to provide coalition forces with the appropriate tools to maximize their fighting capabilities.

Case in point: The Oct. 30 attack by Pakistani helicopter gunships on a religious school that killed 80 alleged terrorists, but an earlier opportunity by U.S. forces to conduct such an attack against known terrorists in Afghanistan was not allowed to go forward.

In July, aerial reconnaissance in Afghanistan observed 190 Taliban fighters in the open. No civilians were present, so an attack would have avoided collateral damage and the loss of innocent lives. Yet the enemy combatants could not be targeted under existing laws of war because they were assembled for a funeral.

Both situations involved enemy combatants in locations protected by the laws of war and thus not targetable unless an exception, based on enemy activity, removes the protection. In Pakistan, the terrorists were in a religious school; in Afghanistan, a cemetery. In Pakistan, intelligence revealed the school was being used as a terrorist training camp, thus removing it from protected status. Clearly, terrorists have learned to take advantage of protected sites in violation of the laws of war and were most likely doing so in this instance.

But what if the school was also being used periodically for its intended and protected purpose? If such were the case, arguably, protection would have vacillated with usage. Similarly, the Taliban in the cemetery were protected while burying a fallen comrade, but what if they lingered afterward to discuss combat operations, as was most assuredly done? If targetability turns on enemy intentions, that is a difficult qualifier for a distant observer to ascertain.

The laws of war reflect the Golden Rule of doing unto your enemy as you would have him do unto you. These laws have evolved over time out of a sense of conviction and hope that enemies sharing diverse cultural mind-sets can, nonetheless, adhere to a battlefield culture of mutual respect for various time-tested principles in the conduct of combat operations.

But battlefield conditions have required revisions to the laws of war.

Five years after Sept. 11, it should be clear to us that we are encountering an enemy unlike any other we have ever engaged. The Islamo-fascist has no concept of the warrior culture of mutual respect for human life under certain battlefield conditions and is incapable, because of the cultural mind-set in which he was bred, of understanding it. In fact, his lack of respect for human life is wielded as a new tactic with which to instill fear in his enemy. While evolution of the laws of war recognizes that cultural differences between opposing forces on the battlefield can result in occasional violations, it is doubtful that it ever envisioned an enemy using such violations as an outright strategy in fighting a war.

For this reason, initiative should be taken to review the laws, with an eye toward providing more liberal interpretations to enhance the capabilities of civilized forces in combating uncivilized ones. Failing to do so only limits our war-fighting capabilities while furthering those of an enemy who respects us even less for our attempts to preserve human life in combat.

Critics will suggest that an expansion of enemy targetability dilutes our higher, principled beliefs, making us no better than the barbarian we fight.

Such arguments are meaningless to the families of victims killed by the 190 Taliban who went on to fight what has since been described as "the most intensive conduct of the war." Because we felt honor-bound not to attack, these thugs lived to fight and kill another day.

A popular 1980s TV police show would begin each weekly episode with the sergeant briefing his officers. Concluding his brief with an admonition about the bad guys, the sergeant would say, "Let's do it to them before they do it to us." This is exactly what we need to be doing for our troops—fully empowering them under the laws of war in our fight against an uncivilized enemy who honors no bounds.

Journal and Discussion Questions

1   What is the thesis of James Zumwalt's "Laws of War Need to Change to Defeat 'Uncivilized' Enemy"? What reasons and evidence does he provide to support this thesis?

2   For much of his argument, Zumwalt relies on his description and analysis of examples from the war on terrorism. List these examples. Why does Zumwalt choose these particular examples? How does each example support his position?

3   According to Zumwalt, where do the laws of war come from? How does his view of the origins and status of rules for conducting warfare affect his arguments? What view about these rules might a critic of Zumwalt hold?

4   Why does Zumwalt wait until the next-to-last paragraph to discuss critics' likely objections to his argument? Does he present these objections fairly, and does he refute them convincingly? Has he anticipated the most important objections that critics might have? What other objections could be offered?

5   Why do you think Zumwalt concludes his editorial with an allusion to an old television cop show? Is this an effective conclusion? Why or why not?

6   Does Zumwalt's background as a retired Marine colonel who fought in the Vietnam War affect the persuasiveness of his argument? Why or why not?

7   What indicates that Zumwalt's argument is addressed to the readers of the *Army Times*? What changes might he need to make if he were writing a newspaper article for a civilian audience?

Topics for Writing

1   Agree or disagree with James Zumwalt's position about the laws of war in the war against terrorism in "Laws of War Need to Change to Defeat 'Uncivilized' Enemy."

2   Write a research paper describing and evaluating the Geneva Convention rules of war or another attempt to establish legal or moral standards for how wars should be fought, such as religions' definitions of a "just war."

Connecting the Readings

Write an argument about what measures the U.S. military should or should not take in its campaign against international terrorism, considering the arguments of Kenneth Roth's "The Law of War in the War on Terror" and James Zumwalt's "Laws of War Need to Change to Defeat 'Uncivilized' Enemy."

GENDER, TERRORISM, AND WAR

BY SUSAN J. BRISON

An associate professor of philosophy, Susan J. Brison has been on the faculty at Dartmouth College since 1985 and has worked as visiting faculty at Tufts University, Princeton University, and New York University, where she served as a Mellon Fellow. She has authored two books, *Aftermath: Violence and the Remaking of a Self* and *Speech, Harm, and Conflicts of Rights*, as well as academic articles in a number of books and philosophy journals. "Gender, Terrorism, and War" first appeared in 2002 in *Signs: Journal of Women in Culture and Society*, an important academic journal that publishes articles on women's and gender studies by scholars in many disciplines. It was published as part of a roundtable discussion of short essays on gender and language issues about war and terrorism following the terrorist attacks on the World Trade Center and the Pentagon on September 11, 2001.

E MONDE PROCLAIMED, "WE ARE all New Yorkers." "We are all Yankees," said a baseball fan in Chicago. After September 11, there seemed to be a sudden, if short-lived, consensus about who "we" were: we saw the same things at the time of the attacks, and we remembered the same images. And when an airliner crashed in Queens on November 12, we thought it, too, was a terrorist attack. As a commentator on Cable News Network pointed out that afternoon, "We can't help but see it that way." The appearance of a unified group identity forged by the memory of September 11 quickly dissipated with the resurgence of *other* cultural memories—particularly those inflected by nationality, race, and religion. But gender was not mentioned much, at least in public responses to the attacks. Amid all the attention to the apparent religious and political motivations for the attacks, the media didn't find it particularly significant that the perpetrators were all men. I suppose I shouldn't have been surprised; since wars and terrorist attacks are virtually always initiated and carried out by men, this was not exactly news. But wasn't it noteworthy that young male Muslim suicide bombers "are usually . . . told that they will be greeted by 70 dark-eyed virgins in heaven?"[1] That the three hijackers who were at a Daytona Beach strip club and sports bar on Monday night and who had attracted FBI attention by allegedly saying "'Wait until tomorrow, America is going to see bloodshed'" had just "spent a few hundred dollars on lap dances and drinks"?[2] *USA Today* commented on the apparent hypocrisy of Islamic fundamentalists engaging in such decadent Western behavior but not on what such behavior means when routinely engaged in by "our" men. Why, I wondered, was so much attention being paid to the influence of Islam on the suicide hijackers and virtually none paid to the influence of gender norms? The perpetrators were Muslim men. Why did women of color in the United States have to fear being victims of hate crimes if they identified themselves as Muslim by wearing scarves in public, while white men here felt free, as always, to go wherever they wanted?

Of course, I am not suggesting that all men are somehow more culpable than women in this attack, any more than I would suggest that all Muslims are more culpable than non-Muslims. Although only men were apparently implicated in this attack, to hold all men responsible would be just as misguided as the

---

[1]Kevin Sacks, with Jim Yardley, "After the Attacks: The Suspects; U.S. Says Hijackers Lived in the Open with Deadly Secret," *New York Times* (September 14, 2001), 1.

[2]Jodi Wilgoren, "After the Attacks: The Hijackers; A Terrorist Profile Emerges That Confounds the Experts," *New York Times* (September 15, 2001), 1.

view of those who considered the attack to justify perpetrating hate crimes at home—and waging war abroad—against Muslims.

> ## Although only men were apparently implicated in this attack, to hold all men responsible would be just as misguided . . .

This is not to say that we should ignore the gendered aspects of the attack and our responses to it: the *Times* of London reported, on October 9, in an article titled "Elated Airmen Feel like Football Heroes," that "for one U.S. airman, dropping some of the first bombs on Afghanistan from a B1 bomber was 'like being a football player on Super Bowl day,'" and that "an aircraft commander described the start of the war as 'pretty doggone exciting.'"[3] In a November 23 article in *USA Today*, we learned that "the Miami Dolphins cheerleaders arrived Wednesday to sign autographs, pose for pictures and dance on the ship's hangar deck."[4] When I was in high school, during the final years of the Vietnam War, football was talked about as if it were war ("Kill Rahway!" "Kill Rahway!" shouted the cheerleaders at the pep rallies). Now war is talked about as if it were football.

Afghan fighters' ideals of masculinity were also in evidence: when Kabul fell, the *New York Times* ran a series of photos of a captured Taliban who had been tortured, beaten, shot, and beaten some more: although it was not mentioned, one photo showed him naked and bloody from the waist down—clearly the victim of sexual violence, most likely castration. The accompanying article said there was some concern on the part of U.S. officials that the Northern Alliance *might* be getting a little out of hand. And on December 11, *USA Today* reported that the battered al-Qaida soldiers remained "cocky and belligerent"— "My dear brothers, your sisters could fight better than you!" blared a voice over a walkie-talkie, an insult conveyed to the anti-Taliban forces.[5]

That "boys will be boys" in a time of war was taken for granted, although journalists did seem to see the misogyny in Mohammed Atta's suicide note, and Robert McElvaine, a history professor, wrote in the *Washington Post* that "a kind of religion motivates the Taliban, but the religion in question, I'd say, is not Islam [but] insecure masculinity. These men are terrified of women."[6]

But if the enemy's masculinity was "insecure," back home in the United States, masculinity, having been sorely tested, emerged newly secure and celebrated. What women *really* want, we were told, is brawny firefighters and police officers—strong men to protect them (against whom? other strong men?). Michael Kimmel, in a piece in the *Chronicle*, observed that these masculine men, who were so recently maligned by feminists for excluding women from their ranks, turned out to be heroes, saving lives, risking and losing their own.[7] Yes, *and* they also fought long and hard to keep women out of their ranks. Why can't we keep these two thoughts in our heads at once?

I don't really think we're all New Yorkers, and I'm not a fan of the Yankees or any other sports team for that matter. But I do think that all of us—including the women who were kept out of the firehouses and the 343 firefighters who were killed by the suicide hijackers, the Taliban and the Northern Alliance, and the lap dancers and the fighter pilots—are victims of oppressive gender norms. Some of us are murdered because of them. I can't help but see it that way.

---

[3]Damien Whitworth, *Times* (October 9, 2001), 9.
[4]Andrea Stone, "No Turkey on Carrier until Bombing Day Is Through," *USA Today* (November 23, 2001), 4A.
[5]Jack Kelley, "'Chaos' in War's Final Push," *USA Today* (December 11, 2001), 1.
[6]See Maureen Dowd, "Liberties: Cleopatra and Osama," *New York Times* (November 18, 2001), Sec. 4, 13.
[7]Michael Kimmel, "Declarations of War," *Chronicle of Higher Education* (October 26, 2001), B18–B19.

Journal and Discussion Questions

1 Summarize the central claim of Susan J. Brison's "Gender, Terrorism, and War" in a single sentence and then outline "Gender, Terrorism, and War." How does Brison organize her argument about the influence of gender on people's decisions and attitudes about war and terrorism?

2 Why does Brison begin the introduction and the conclusion of "Gender, Terrorism, and War" by referring to the quotations "We are all New Yorkers" and "We are all Yankee fans" that were made immediately after the terrorist attacks of September 11, 2001? How are these quotations relevant to her argument? Why does she disagree with these statements?

3 Why isn't Brison surprised that "the media didn't find it particularly significant that the perpetrators [of the 9/11 attacks] were all men"? Why does Brison use the entire second paragraph to clarify that she does not "hold all men responsible" for the attacks on the World Trade Center and the Pentagon? Why is it easier to discuss the influences of "nationality, race, and religion" in terrorism and war today than assumptions about gender? How does Brison deal with this problem?

4 How does Brison compare the influence of religion to the influence of gender norms and attitudes in discussions of war and terrorism after September 11, 2001? How do the gendered images and language of Americans and of Arabians affect their attitudes about war and terrorism? How does Brison use these comparisons to develop her argument?

5 Why are references to sports—the New York Yankees, the Miami Dolphin cheerleaders, and comparisons of war to football—important to Brison? What do references to sports in discussions of war and terrorism reveal about society's assumptions about war and gender?

6 What sources does Brison use in her argument? How does she use these sources to support her claims?

7 How does Brison take the interests and assumptions of the readers of *Signs* into account in her argument? Would "Gender, War, and Terrorism" persuade readers who are not strongly committed feminists? Why or why not? What changes would she need to make in her essay if she were to revise "Gender, Terrorism, and War" for a men's magazine like *Esquire*?

Topics for Writing

1 Write an argument agreeing or disagreeing with Susan J. Brison's "Gender, Terrorism, and War" about the importance of American and Arabic assumptions about gender in the wars and terrorist actions since September 11, 2001.

2 Collect at least a dozen passages and images that reveal connections between people's assumptions about gender and their positions about war or terrorism in recent newspapers, magazines, Web sites, political speeches, art, photography, or other texts and images. Using "Gender, Terrorism, and War" as a model, write a research paper analyzing the influence of gender attitudes in images and discussions of war since September 11, 2001. You may want to focus on one specific source or set of sources, such as cable news networks, congressional speeches, pro- or antiwar Web sites, or political humor for this essay.

3 Write a research paper about the ways news reports, propaganda, and arguments about a war in the past revealed or exploited people's assumptions about the nature of men and women.

LETTER FROM BIRMINGHAM JAIL

BY MARTIN LUTHER KING, JR.

Dr. Martin Luther King, Jr. (1929–1968), is the most famous and influential of the many activists in the civil rights movement of the 1950s and 1960s. A Baptist minister with a doctoral degree in theology from Boston University and recipient of the 1964 Nobel Peace Prize, King was an inspiring preacher who crafted a politics of nonviolent resistance and civil disobedience to oppose racism and oppression. His assassination in Memphis was mourned throughout the world. "Letter from Birmingham Jail" is an open letter nominally addressed to eight white clergymen from Birmingham, Alabama, who published a public letter in the *Birmingham News* that opposed peaceful demonstrations for civil rights for African Americans after a judge ordered an end to political demonstrations in Birmingham. King's letter is, in part, a refutation of the clergymen's letter. But because "Letter from Birmingham Jail" is a public letter, it is written for a much wider audience than the eight clergymen, and readers do not need to be familiar with the clergymen's letter in order to understand King's argument.

MY DEAR FELLOW CLERGYMEN:

While confined here in the Birmingham city jail, I came across your recent statement calling my present activities "unwise and untimely." Seldom do I pause to answer criticism of my work and ideas. If I sought to answer all the criticisms that cross my desk, my secretaries would have little time for anything other than such correspondence in the course of the day, and I would have no time for constructive work. But since I feel that you are men of genuine good will and that your criticisms are sincerely set forth, I want to try to answer your statement in what I hope will be patient and reasonable terms.

I think I should indicate why I am here in Birmingham, since you have been influenced by the view which argues against "outsiders coming in." I have the honor of serving as president of the Southern Christian Leadership Conference, an organization operating in every southern state, with headquarters in Atlanta, Georgia. We have some eighty-five affiliated organizations across the South, and one of them is the Alabama Christian Movement for Human Rights. Frequently we share staff, educational, and financial resources with our affiliates. Several months ago the affiliate here in Birmingham asked us to be on call to engage in a nonviolent direct-action program if such

were deemed necessary. We readily consented, and when the hour came we lived up to our promise. So I, along with several members of my staff, am here because I was invited here. I am here because I have organizational ties here.

But more basically, I am in Birmingham because injustice is here. Just as the prophets of the eighth century B.C. left their villages and carried their "thus saith the Lord" far beyond the boundaries of their home towns, and just as the Apostle Paul left his village of Tarsus and carried the gospel of Jesus Christ to the far corners of the Greco-Roman world, so am I compelled to carry the gospel of freedom beyond my own home town. Like Paul, I must constantly respond to the Macedonian call for aid.

Moreover, I am cognizant of the interrelatedness of all communities and states. I cannot sit idly by in Atlanta and not be concerned about what happens in Birmingham. Injustice anywhere is a threat to justice everywhere. We are caught in an inescapable network of mutuality, tied in a single garment of destiny. Whatever affects one directly, affects all indirectly. Never again can we afford to live with the narrow, provincial "outside agitator" idea. Anyone who lives inside the United States can never be considered an outsider anywhere within its bounds.

You deplore the demonstrations taking place in Birmingham. But your statement, I am sorry to say, fails to express a similar concern for the conditions that brought about the demonstrations. I am sure that none of you would want to rest content with the superficial kind of social analysis that deals merely with effects and does not grapple with underlying causes. It is unfortunate that demonstrations are taking place in Birmingham, but it is even more unfortunate that the city's white power structure left the Negro community with no alternative.

In any nonviolent campaign there are four basic steps: collection of the facts to determine whether injustices exist; negotiation; self-purification; and direct action. We have gone through all these steps in Birmingham. There can be no gainsaying the fact that racial injustice engulfs this community. Birmingham is probably the most thoroughly segregated city in the United States. Its ugly record of brutality is widely known. Negroes have experienced grossly unjust treatment in the courts. There have been more unsolved bombings of Negro homes and churches in Birmingham than in any other city in the nation. These are the hard, brutal facts of the case. On the basis of these conditions, Negro leaders sought to negotiate with the city fathers. But the latter consistently refused to engage in good-faith negotiation.

Then, last September, came the opportunity to talk with leaders of Birmingham's economic community. In the course of the negotiations, certain promises were made by the merchants—for example, to remove the stores' humiliating racial signs. On the basis of these promises, the Reverend Fred Shuttlesworth and the leaders of the Alabama Christian Movement for Human Rights agreed to a moratorium on all demonstrations. As the weeks and months went by, we realized that we were the victims of a broken promise. A few signs, briefly removed, returned; the others remained.

As in so many past experiences, our hopes had been blasted, and the shadow of deep disappointment settled upon us. We had no alternative except to prepare for direct action, whereby we would present our very bodies as a means of laying our case before the conscience of the local and the national community. Mindful of the difficulties involved, we decided to undertake a process of self-purification. We began a series of workshops on nonviolence, and we repeatedly asked ourselves: "Are you able to accept blows without retaliating?" "Are you able to endure the ordeal of jail?" We decided to schedule our direct-action program for the Easter season, realizing that except for Christmas, this is the main shopping period of the year. Knowing that a strong economic-withdrawal program would be the by-product of direct action, we felt that this would be the best time to bring pressure to bear on the merchants for the needed change.

Then it occurred to us that Birmingham's mayoral election was coming up in March, and we speedily decided to postpone action until after election day. When we discovered that the Commissioner of Public Safety, Eugene "Bull" Connor, had piled up enough votes to be in the run-off, we decided again to postpone action until the day after the run-off so that the demonstrations could not be used to cloud the issues. Like many others, we wanted to see Mr. Connor defeated, and to this end we endured postponement after postponement. Having aided in this community need, we felt that our direct-action program could be delayed no longer.

> **The purpose of our direct-action program is to create a situation so crisis-packed that it will inevitably open the door to negotiation.**

You may well ask, "Why direct action? Why sit-ins, marches, and so forth? Isn't negotiation a better path?" You are quite right in calling for negotiation. Indeed, this is the very purpose of direct action. Nonviolent direct action seeks to create such a crisis and foster such a tension that a community which has constantly refused to negotiate is forced to confront the issue. It seeks so to dramatize the issue that it can no longer be ignored. My citing the creation of tension as part of the work of the nonviolent-resister may sound rather shocking. But I must confess that I am not afraid of the word "tension." I have earnestly opposed violent tension, but there is a type of constructive, nonviolent tension which is necessary for growth. Just as Socrates felt that it was necessary to create a tension in the mind so that individuals could rise from the bondage of myths and half-truths to the unfettered realm of creative analysis and objective appraisal, so must we see the need for nonviolent gadflies to create the kind of tension in society that will help men rise from the dark depths of prejudice and racism to the majestic heights of understanding and brotherhood.

The purpose of our direct-action program is to create a situation so crisis-packed that it will inevitably open the door to negotiation. I therefore concur with you in your call for negotiation. Too long has our beloved Southland been bogged down in a tragic effort to live in monologue rather than dialogue.

One of the basic points in your statement is that the action that I and my associates have taken in Birmingham is untimely. Some have asked: "Why didn't you give the new city administration time to act?" The only answer that I can give to this query is that the new Birmingham administration must be prodded about as much as the outgoing one, before it will act. We are sadly mistaken if we feel that the election of Albert Boutwell as mayor will bring the millennium to Birmingham. While Mr. Boutwell is a much more gentle person than Mr. Connor, they are both segregationists, dedicated to maintenance of the status quo. I have hoped that Mr. Boutwell will be reasonable enough to see the futility of massive resistance to desegregation. But he will not see this without pressure from devotees of civil rights. My friends, I must say to you that we have not made a single gain in civil rights without determined legal and nonviolent pressure. Lamentably, it is an historical fact that privileged groups seldom give up their privileges voluntarily. Individuals may see the moral light and voluntarily give up their unjust posture, but, as Reinhold Niebuhr has reminded us, groups tend to be more immoral than individuals.

We know through painful experience that freedom is never voluntarily given by the oppressor; it must be demanded by the oppressed.

We know through painful experience that freedom is never voluntarily given by the oppressor; it must be demanded by the oppressed. Frankly, I have yet to engage in a direct-action campaign that was "well timed" in the view of those who have not suffered unduly from the disease of segregation. For years now I have heard the word "Wait!" It rings in the ear of every Negro with piercing familiarity. This "Wait" has almost always meant "Never." We must come to see, with one of our distinguished jurists, that "justice too long delayed is justice denied."

We have waited for more than 340 years for our constitutional and God-given rights. The nations of Asia and Africa are moving with jet-like speed toward gaining political independence, but we still creep at horse-and-buggy pace toward gaining a cup of coffee at a lunch counter. Perhaps it is easy for those who have

never felt the stinging darts of segregation to say, "Wait." But when you have seen vicious mobs lynch your mothers and fathers at will and drown your sisters and brothers at whim; when you have seen hate-filled policemen curse, kick, and even kill your black brothers and sisters; when you see the vast majority of your twenty million Negro brothers smothering in an airtight cage of poverty in the midst of an affluent society; when you suddenly find your tongue twisted and your speech stammering as you seek to explain to your six-year-old daughter why she can't go to the public amusement park that has just been advertised on television, and see tears welling up in her eyes when she is told that Funtown is closed to colored children, and see ominous clouds of inferiority beginning to form in her little mental sky, and see her beginning to distort her personality by developing an unconscious bitterness toward white people; when you have to concoct an answer for a five-year-old son who is asking, "Daddy, why do white people treat colored people so mean?"; when you take a cross-country drive and find it necessary to sleep night after night in the uncomfortable corners of your automobile because no motel will accept you; when you are humiliated day in and day out by nagging signs reading "white" and "colored"; when your first name becomes "nigger," your middle name becomes "boy" (however old you are) and your last name becomes "John," and your wife and mother are never given the respected title "Mrs."; when you are harried by day and haunted by night by the fact that you are a Negro, living constantly at tiptoe stance, never quite knowing what to expect next, and are plagued with inner fears and outer resentments; when you are forever fighting a degenerating sense of "nobodiness"—then you will understand why we find it difficult to wait. There comes a time when the cup of endurance runs over, and men are no longer willing to be plunged into the abyss of despair. I hope, sirs, you can understand our legitimate and unavoidable impatience.

You express a great deal of anxiety over our willingness to break laws. This is certainly a legitimate concern. Since we so diligently urge people to obey the Supreme Court's decision of 1954 outlawing segregation in the public schools, at first glance it may seem rather paradoxical for us consciously to break laws. One may well ask: "How can you advocate breaking some laws and obeying others?" The answer lies in the fact that there are two types of laws: just and unjust. I would be the first to advocate obeying just laws. One has not only a legal but a moral responsibility to obey just laws. Conversely, one has a moral responsibility to disobey unjust laws. I would agree with St. Augustine that "an unjust law is no law at all."

Now, what is the difference between the two? How does one determine whether a law is just or unjust? A just law is a man-made code that squares with the moral law or the law of God. An unjust law is a code that is out of harmony with the moral law. To put it in the terms of St. Thomas Aquinas: An unjust law is a human law that is not rooted in eternal law and natural law. Any law that uplifts human personality is just. Any law that degrades human personality is unjust. All segregation statutes are unjust because segregation distorts the soul and damages the personality. It gives the segregator a false sense of superiority and the segregated a false sense of inferiority. Segregation, to use the terminology of the Jewish philosopher Martin Buber, substitutes an "I-it" relationship for an "I-thou" relationship and ends up relegating persons to the status of things. Hence segregation is not only politically, economically, and sociologically unsound, it is morally wrong and sinful. Paul Tillich has said that sin is separation. Is not segregation an existential expression of man's tragic separation, his awful estrangement, his terrible sinfulness? Thus it is that I can urge men to obey the 1954 decision of the Supreme Court, for it is morally right; and I can urge them to disobey segregation ordinances, for they are morally wrong.

Let us consider a more concrete example of just and unjust laws. An unjust law is a code that a numerical or power majority group compels a minority group to obey but does not make binding on itself. This is *difference* made legal. By the same token, a just law is a code that a majority compels a minority to follow and that it is willing to follow itself. This is *sameness* made legal.

Let me give another explanation. A law is unjust if it is inflicted on a minority that, as a result of being denied the right to vote, had no part in enacting or devising the law. Who can say that the legislature of Alabama which set up that state's segregation laws was democratically elected? Throughout Alabama all sorts of devious methods are used to prevent Negroes from becoming registered voters, and there are some counties in which, even though Negroes constitute a majority of the population, not a single Negro is registered. Can any law enacted under such circumstances be considered democratically structured?

Sometimes a law is just on its face and unjust in its application. For instance, I have been arrested on a charge of parading without a permit. Now, there is nothing wrong in having an ordinance which requires a permit for a parade. But such an ordinance becomes unjust when it is used to maintain segregation and to deny citizens the First-Amendment privilege of peaceful assembly and protest.

I hope you are able to see the distinction I am trying to point out. In no sense do I advocate evading or defying the law, as would the rabid segregationist. That would lead to anarchy. One who breaks an unjust law must do so openly, lovingly, and with a willingness to accept the penalty. I submit that an individual who breaks a law that conscience tells him is unjust, and who willingly accepts the penalty of imprisonment in order to arouse the conscience of the community over its injustice, is in reality expressing the highest respect for law.

Of course, there is nothing new about this kind of civil disobedience. It was evidenced sublimely in the refusal of Shadrach, Meshach, and Abednego to obey the laws of Nebuchadnezzar, on the ground that a higher moral law was at stake. It was practiced superbly by the early Christians, who were willing to face hungry lions and the excruciating pain of chopping blocks rather than submit to certain unjust laws of the Roman Empire. To a degree, academic freedom is a reality today because Socrates practiced civil disobedience. In our own nation, the Boston Tea Party represented a massive act of civil disobedience.

We should never forget that everything Adolf Hitler did in Germany was "legal" and everything the Hungarian freedom fighters did in Hungary was "illegal." It was "illegal" to aid and comfort a Jew in Hitler's Germany. Even so, I am sure that, had I lived in Germany at the time, I would have aided and comforted my Jewish brothers. If today I lived in a Communist country where certain principles dear to the Christian faith are suppressed, I would openly advocate disobeying that country's anti-religious laws.

I must make two honest confessions to you, my Christian and Jewish brothers. First, I must confess that over the past few years I have been gravely disappointed with the white moderate. I have almost reached the regrettable conclusion that the Negro's great stumbling block in his stride toward freedom is not the White Citizen's Counciler or the Ku Klux Klanner, but the white moderate, who is more devoted to "order" than to justice; who prefers a negative peace which is the absence of tension to a positive peace which is the presence of justice; who constantly says, "I agree with you in the goal you seek, but I cannot agree with your methods of direct action"; who paternalistically believes he can set the timetable for another man's freedom; who lives by a mythical concept of time and who constantly advises the Negro to wait for a "more convenient season." Shallow understanding from people of good will is more frustrating than absolute misunderstanding from people of ill will. Lukewarm acceptance is much more bewildering than outright rejection.

I had hoped that the white moderate would understand that law and order exist for the purpose of establishing justice and that when they fail in this purpose they become the dangerously structured dams that block the flow of social progress. I had hoped that the white moderate would understand that the present tension in the South is a necessary phase of the transition from an obnoxious negative peace, in which the Negro passively accepted his unjust plight, to a substantive and positive peace, in which all men will respect the dignity and worth of human personality. Actually, we who engage in nonviolent direct action are not the creators of tension. We merely bring to the surface the hidden tension that is already alive. We bring it out in the open, where it can be seen and dealt with. Like a boil that can never be cured so long as it is covered up but must be opened with all its ugliness to the natural medicines of air and light, injustice must be exposed, with all the tension its exposure creates, to the light of human conscience and the air of national opinion, before it can be cured.

In your statement you assert that our actions, even though peaceful, must be condemned because they precipitate violence. But is this a logical assertion? Isn't this like condemning a robbed man because his possession of money precipitated the evil act of robbery? Isn't this like condemning Socrates because his unswerving commitment to truth and his philosophical inquiries precipitated the act by the misguided populace in which they made him drink hemlock? Isn't this like condemning Jesus because his unique God-consciousness and never-ceasing devotion to God's will precipitated the evil act of crucifixion? We must come to see that, as the federal courts have consistently affirmed, it is wrong to urge an individual to cease his efforts to gain his basic constitutional rights because the quest may precipitate violence. Society must protect the robbed and punish the robber.

I had also hoped that the white moderate would reject the myth concerning time in relation to the struggle for freedom. I have just received a letter from a white brother in Texas. He writes: "All Christians know that the colored people will receive equal rights eventually, but it is possible that you are in too great a religious hurry. It has taken Christianity almost two thousand years to accomplish what it has. The teachings of Christ take time to come to earth." Such an attitude stems from a tragic misconception of time, from the strangely irrational notion that there is something in the very flow of time that will inevitably cure all ills. Actually, time itself is neutral; it can be used either destructively or constructively. More and more I feel that the people of ill will have used time much more effectively than

have the people of good will. We will have to repent in this generation not merely for the hateful words and actions of the bad people, but for the appalling silence of the good people. Human progress never rolls in on wheels of inevitability; it comes through the tireless efforts of men willing to be co-workers with God, and without this hard work, time itself becomes an ally of the forces of social stagnation. We must use time creatively, in the knowledge that the time is always ripe to do right. Now is the time to make real the promise of democracy and transform our pending national elegy into a creative psalm of brotherhood. Now is the time to lift our national policy from the quicksand of racial injustice to the solid rock of human dignity.

You speak of our activity in Birmingham as extreme. At first I was rather disappointed that fellow clergymen would see my nonviolent efforts as those of an extremist. I began thinking about the fact that I stand in the middle of two opposing forces in the Negro community. One is a force of complacency, made up in part of Negroes who, as a result of long years of oppression, are so drained of self-respect and a sense of "somebodiness" that they have adjusted to segregation; and in part of a few middle-class Negroes who, because of a degree of academic and economic security and because in some ways they profit by segregation, have become insensitive to the problems of the masses. The other force is one of bitterness and hatred, and it comes perilously close to advocating violence. It is expressed in the various black nationalist groups that are springing up across the nation, the largest and best-known being Elijah Muhammad's Muslim movement. Nourished by the Negro's frustration over the continued existence of racial discrimination, this movement is made up of people who have lost faith in America, who have absolutely repudiated Christianity, and who have concluded that the white man is an incorrigible "devil."

I have tried to stand between these two forces, saying that we need emulate neither the "do-nothingism" of the complacent nor the hatred and despair of the black nationalist. For there is the more excellent way of love and nonviolent protest. I am grateful to God that, through the influence of the Negro church, the way of nonviolence became an integral part of our struggle.

If this philosophy had not emerged, by now many streets of the South would, I am convinced, be flowing with blood. And I am further convinced that if our white brothers dismiss as "rabblerousers" and "outside agitators" those of us who employ nonviolent direct action, and if they refuse to support our nonviolent efforts, millions of Negroes will, out of frustration and despair, seek solace and security in black-nationalist ideologies—a development that would inevitably lead to a frightening racial nightmare.

> **" We will have to repent in this generation not merely for the hateful words and actions of the bad people, but for the appalling silence of the good people. "**

Oppressed people cannot remain oppressed forever. The yearning for freedom eventually manifests itself, and that is what has happened to the American Negro. Something within has reminded him of his birthright of freedom, and something without has reminded him that it can be gained. Consciously or unconsciously, he has been caught up by the *Zeitgeist*, and with his black brothers of Africa and his brown and yellow brothers of Asia, South America, and the Caribbean, the United States Negro is moving with a sense of great urgency toward the promised land of racial justice. If one recognizes this vital urge that has engulfed the Negro community, one should readily understand why public demonstrations are taking place. The Negro has many pent-up resentments and latent frustrations, and he must release them. So let him march; let him make prayer pilgrimages to the city hall; let him go on freedom rides—and try to understand why he must do so. If his repressed emotions are not released in nonviolent ways, they will seek expression through violence; this is not a threat but a fact of history. So I have not said to my people, "Get rid of your discontent." Rather, I have tried to say that this normal and healthy discontent can be channeled into the creative outlet of nonviolent direct action. And now this approach is being termed extremist.

But though I was initially disappointed at being categorized as an extremist, as I continued to think about the matter I gradually gained a measure of satisfaction from the label. Was not Jesus an extremist for love: "Love your enemies, bless them that curse you, do good to them that hate you, and pray for them which despitefully use you, and persecute you." Was not Amos an extremist for justice: "Let justice roll down like waters and righteousness like an ever-flowing stream." Was not Paul an extremist for the Christian gospel: "I bear in my body the marks of the Lord Jesus." Was not Martin Luther an extremist: "Here I stand; I cannot do otherwise, so help me God." And John Bunyan: "I will stay in jail to the end of my days before I make a butchery of my conscience." And Abraham Lincoln: "This nation cannot survive half slave and half free." And Thomas Jefferson: "We hold these truths to be self-evident, that all men are created equal. . . ." So the question is not whether we will be extremists, but what kind of extremists we will be. Will we be extremists for hate or for love? Will we be extremists for the preservation of injustice or for the extension of

justice? In that dramatic scene on Calvary's hill three men were crucified. We must never forget that all three were crucified for the same crime—the crime of extremism. Two were extremists for immorality, and thus fell below their environment. The other, Jesus Christ, was an extremist for love, truth, and goodness, and thereby rose above his environment. Perhaps the South, the nation, and the world are in dire need of creative extremists.

I had hoped that the white moderate would see this need. Perhaps I was too optimistic; perhaps I expected too much. I suppose I should have realized that few members of the oppressor race can understand the deep groans and passionate yearnings of the oppressed race, and still fewer have the vision to see that injustice must be rooted out by strong, persistent, and determined action. I am thankful, however, that some of our white brothers in the South have grasped the meaning of this social revolution and committed themselves to it. They are still all too few in quantity, but they are big in quality. Some—such as Ralph McGill, Lillian Smith, Harry Golden, James McBridge Dabbs, Ann Braden, and Sarah Patton Boyle—have written about our struggle in eloquent and prophetic terms. Others have marched with us down nameless streets of the South. They have languished in filthy, roach-infested jails, suffering the abuse and brutality of policemen who view them as "dirty nigger-lovers." Unlike so many of their moderate brothers and sisters, they have recognized the urgency of the moment and sensed the need for powerful "action" antidotes to combat the disease of segregation.

Let me take note of my other major disappointment. I have been so greatly disappointed with the white church and its leadership. Of course, there are some notable exceptions. I am not unmindful of the fact that each of you has taken some significant stands on this issue. I commend you, Reverend Stallings, for your Christian stand on this past Sunday, in welcoming Negroes to your worship service on a nonsegregated basis. I commend the Catholic leaders of this state for integrating Spring Hill College several years ago.

But despite these notable exceptions, I must honestly reiterate that I have been disappointed with the church. I do not say this as one of those negative critics who can always find something wrong with the church. I say this as a minister of the gospel, who loves the church; who was nurtured in its bosom; who has been sustained by its spiritual blessings and who will remain true to it as long as the cord of life shall lengthen.

When I was suddenly catapulted into the leadership of the bus protest in Montgomery, Alabama, a few years ago, I felt we would be supported by the white church. I felt that the white ministers, priests, and rabbis of the South would be among our strongest allies. Instead, some have been outright opponents, refusing to understand the freedom movement and misrepresenting its leaders; all too many others have been more cautious than courageous and have remained silent behind the anesthetizing security of stained glass windows.

In spite of my shattered dreams, I came to Birmingham with the hope that the white religious leadership of this community would see the justice of our cause and, with deep moral concern, would serve as the channel through which our just grievances could reach the power structure. I had hoped that each of you would understand. But again I have been disappointed.

I have heard numerous southern religious leaders admonish their worshipers to comply with a desegregation decision because it is the law, but I have longed to hear white ministers declare: "Follow this decree because integration is morally right and because the Negro is your brother." In the midst of blatant injustices inflicted upon the Negro, I have watched white churchmen stand on the sideline and mouth pious irrelevancies and sanctimonious trivialities. In the midst of a mighty struggle to rid our nation of racial and economic injustice, I have heard many ministers say: "Those are social issues, with which the gospel has no real concern." And I have watched many churches commit themselves to a completely otherworldly religion which makes a strange, un-Biblical distinction between body and soul, between the sacred and the secular.

I have traveled the length and breadth of Alabama, Mississippi, and all the other southern states. On sweltering summer days and crisp autumn mornings I have looked at the South's beautiful churches with their lofty spires pointing heavenward. I have beheld the impressive outlines of her massive religious-education buildings. Over and over I have found myself asking: "What kind of people worship here? Who is their God? Where were their voices when the lips of Governor Barnett dripped with words of interposition and nullification? Where were they when Governor Wallace gave a clarion call for defiance and hatred? Where were their voices of support when bruised and weary Negro men

and women decided to rise from the dark dungeons of complacency to the bright hills of creative protest?"

Yes, these questions are still in my mind. In deep disappointment I have wept over the laxity of the church. But be assured that my tears have been tears of love. There can be no deep disappointment where there is not deep love. Yes, I love the church. How could I do otherwise? I am in the rather unique position of being the son, the grandson, and the great-grandson of preachers. Yes, I see the church as the body of Christ. But, oh! How we have blemished and scarred that body through social neglect and through fear of being nonconformists.

There was a time when the church was very powerful—in the time when the early Christians rejoiced at being deemed worthy to suffer for what they believed. In those days the church was not merely a thermometer that recorded the ideas and principles of popular opinion; it was a thermostat that transformed the mores of society. Whenever the early Christians entered a town, the people in power became disturbed and immediately sought to convict the Christians for being "disturbers of the peace" and "outside agitators." But the Christians pressed on, in the conviction that they were "a colony of heaven," called to obey God rather than man. Small in number, they were big in commitment. They were too God-intoxicated to be "astronomically intimidated." By their effort and example they brought an end to such ancient evils as infanticide and gladiatorial contests.

Things are different now. So often the contemporary church is a weak, ineffectual voice with an uncertain sound. So often it is an archdefender of the status quo. Far from being disturbed by the presence of the church, the power structure of the average community is consoled by the church's silent—and often even vocal—sanction of things as they are.

But the judgment of God is upon the church as never before. If today's church does not recapture the sacrificial spirit of the early church, it will lose its authenticity, forfeit the loyalty of millions, and be dismissed as an irrelevant social club with no meaning for the twentieth century. Every day I meet young people whose disappointment with the church has turned into outright disgust.

Perhaps I have once again been too optimistic. Is organized religion too inextricably bound to the status quo to save our nation and the world? Perhaps I must turn my faith to the inner spiritual church, the church

If the inexpressible cruelties of slavery could not stop us, the opposition we now face will surely fail.

within the church, as the true *ekklesia* and the hope of the world. But again I am thankful to God that some noble souls from the ranks of organized religion have broken loose from the paralyzing chains of conformity and joined us as active partners in the struggle for freedom. They have left their secure congregations and walked the streets of Albany, Georgia, with us. They have gone down the highways of the South on torturous rides for freedom. Yes, they have gone to jail with us. Some have been dismissed from their churches, have lost the support of their bishops and fellow ministers. But they have acted in the faith that right defeated is stronger than evil triumphant. Their witness has been the spiritual salt that has preserved the true meaning of the gospel in these troubled times. They have carved a tunnel of hope through the dark mountain of disappointment.

I hope the church as a whole will meet the challenge of this decisive hour. But even if the church does not come to the aid of justice, I have no despair about the future. I have no fear about the outcome of our struggle in Birmingham, even if our motives are at present misunderstood. We will reach the goal of freedom in Birmingham and all over the nation, because the goal of America is freedom. Abused and scorned though we may be, our destiny is tied up with America's destiny. Before the pilgrims landed at Plymouth, we were here. Before the pen of Jefferson etched the majestic words of the Declaration of Independence across the pages of history, we were here. For more than two centuries our forebears labored in this country without wages: they made cotton king; they built the homes of their masters while suffering gross injustice and shameful humiliation—and yet out of a bottomless vitality they continued to thrive and develop. If the inexpressible cruelties of slavery could not stop us, the opposition we now face will surely fail. We will win our freedom because the sacred heritage of our nation and the eternal will of God are embodied in our echoing demands.

Before closing I feel impelled to mention one other point in your statement that has troubled me profoundly. You warmly commended the Birmingham police force for keeping "order" and "preventing violence." I doubt that you would have so warmly commended the police force if you had seen its dogs sinking their teeth into unarmed, nonviolent Negroes. I doubt that you would so quickly commend the policemen if you were to observe their ugly and inhumane treatment of Negroes here in the city jail; if you were to watch them push and curse old Negro women and young Negro girls; if you were to see them slap and kick old Negro men and young boys; if you were to observe them, as they did on two occasions, refuse to give us food because we wanted to sing our grace together. I cannot join you in your praise of the Birmingham police department.

It is true that the police have exercised a degree of discipline in handling the demonstrators. In this sense they have conducted themselves rather "nonviolently" in public. But for what purpose? To preserve the evil system of segregation. Over the past few years I have consistently preached that nonviolence demands that the means we use must be as pure as the ends we seek. I have tried to make clear that it is wrong to use immoral means to attain moral ends. But now I must affirm that it is just as wrong, or perhaps even more so, to use moral means to preserve immoral ends. Perhaps Mr. Connor and his policemen have been rather nonviolent in public, as was Chief Pritchett in Albany, Georgia, but they have used the moral means of nonviolence to maintain the immoral end of racial injustice. As T. S. Eliot has said, "The last temptation is the greatest treason: To do the right deed for the wrong reason."

I wish you had commended the Negro sit-inners and demonstrators of Birmingham for their sublime courage, their willingness to suffer, and their amazing discipline in the midst of great provocation. One day the South will recognize its real heroes. They will be the James Merediths, with the noble sense of purpose that enables them to face jeering and hostile mobs, and with the agonizing loneliness that characterizes the life of the pioneer. They will be old, oppressed, battered Negro women, symbolized in a seventy-two-year-old woman in Montgomery, Alabama, who rose up with a sense of dignity and with her people decided not to ride segregated buses, and who responded with ungrammatical profundity to one who inquired about her weariness: "My feets is tired, but my soul is at rest." They will be the young high school and college students, the young ministers of the gospel and a host of their elders, courageously and nonviolently sitting in at lunch counters and willingly going to jail for conscience sake. One day the South will know that when these disinherited children of God sat down at lunch counters, they were in reality standing up for what is best in the American dream and for the most sacred values in our Judaeo-Christian heritage, thereby bringing our nation back to those great wells of democracy which were dug deep by the founding fathers in their formulation of the Constitution and the Declaration of Independence.

Never before have I written so long a letter. I'm afraid it is much too long to take your precious time. I can assure you that it would have been much shorter if I had been writing from a comfortable desk, but what else can one do when he is alone in a narrow jail cell, other than write long letters, think long thoughts, and pray long prayers?

If I have said anything in this letter that overstates the truth and indicates an unreasonable impatience, I beg you to forgive me. If I have said anything that understates the truth and indicates my having a patience that allows me to settle for anything less than brotherhood, I beg God to forgive me.

I hope this letter finds you strong in the faith. I also hope that circumstances will soon make it possible for me to meet each of you, not as an integrationist or a civil-rights leader but as a fellow clergyman and a Christian brother. Let us all hope that the dark clouds of racial prejudice will soon pass away and the deep fog of misunderstanding will be lifted from our fear-drenched communities, and in some not too distant tomorrow the radiant stars of love and brotherhood will shine over our great nation with all their scintillating beauty.

Yours for the cause of Peace and Brotherhood,
Martin Luther King, Jr.

Journal and Discussion Questions

1 Outline "Letter from Birmingham Jail." What is the thesis of Martin Luther King's overall argument? What is the central idea of each section of his letter? How does each section help explain King's thesis and attempt to persuade King's readers to this idea?

2 Summarize King's philosophy of nonviolent political resistance. What justifications does he argue to defend the civil rights movement's acts of civil disobedience, their decisions to disobey the law in specific situations? How does he describe and respond to readers' possible objections to civil disobedience as a political action? Why does King object to the language and actions advocated by Elijah Muhammad and the Black Muslim movement in their fight against racism?

3 What arguments in the clergymen's letter does King respond to? Does King represent the clergymen's argument fairly and accurately? What are his opposing arguments against these positions? Which of King's counterarguments are most persuasive, and why?

4 Why does King make a point of describing the four-step process for conducting "any nonviolent campaign"? Why is it important for his readers to know the process that the civil rights demonstrators in Birmingham went through before taking "direct action"?

5 King often discusses the definitions and possible meanings of words such as *tension*, *law*, and *extremism*. Why does he make these three terms key words in his argument? What different meanings of *tension*, *law*, and *extremism* does King discuss? How does King finally define the meanings of *tension*, *just and unjust law*, and *extremism*? How does he persuade his readers to accept these definitions?

6 King uses many comparisons in his argument, to Jesus, St. Paul, Thomas Jefferson, Socrates, Hitler and Nazi Germany, the unsuccessful 1956 Hungarian rebellion against the Soviet Union. What points is he making with these comparisons? Why did he choose these subjects for his arguments?

7 What kind of person does King represent himself as in "Letter to Birmingham Jail," in both the facts that he mentions about himself and in the impression about himself that he creates in his letter? How does his representation of himself in his argument (his *ethos*) contribute to the persuasiveness of his letter? How and why does he argue against the clergymen's representation of him as an "outsider"?

Topics for Writing

1 Analyze the arguments in Martin Luther King, Jr.'s "Letter from Birmingham Jail" that, under some circumstances, it is moral to disobey the law—or that it is immoral to obey some laws. Your essay should consider King's discussion of objections to civil disobedience and King's arguments for deciding whether or not civil disobedience is justified or necessary.

2 Write a research paper comparing the protest movement of Martin Luther King, Jr., and other civil rights leaders who practiced nonviolent resistance to civil rights leaders who advocated and practiced different methods of protest, such as Elijah Muhammad or Malcolm X. Your essay should take a position about these methods and consider the moral, political, and practical arguments that leaders made to justify their practices.

3 Write a research paper comparing King's ideas and practices for bringing about social change to the ideas and practices of another social movement, such as Mahatma Gandhi's opposition to British colonization of India, opposition to apartheid in South Africa, or recent protest movements such as the opposition to the war in Iraq or the pro-life or pro-choice movements. With recent movements, you might discuss the influence that King has had—or should have—on today's protesters.

LETTER FROM THE GAZA STRIP

BY RACHEL CORRIE

As an undergraduate at Evergreen State College, Rachel Corrie (1979–2003) was a prolific poet, writer, and artist who spent much of her time working for environmental causes and against hunger and homelessness. After she graduated in 2002, she went to Israel and the Gaza Strip to work as a peace activist and human rights observer for the International Solidarity Movement (ISM). Corrie supported the Palestinian cause in the Second Intifada, a continuing revolt against Israel's occupation of Palestinian lands that began in September 2000, and, on March 16, 2003, a month after she wrote this letter to her mother, she was crushed to death by an Israeli military bulldozer when she and other members of the ISM tried to prevent the bulldozer from destroying the home of a Palestinian family in the Gaza city of Rafah. Her death touched off an international controversy that examined whether or not Corrie's death was an accident and questioned her activism with the ISM. Her life, however, is celebrated in a number of songs and other artistic tributes, including a play, *My Name Is Rachel Corrie*, that Alan Rickman and Katharine Viner composed from Corrie's writings. This letter appears in *Let Me Stand Alone: The Journals of Rachel Corrie*, a 2008 collection of her poetry, letters, drawings, journal entries, and other writings edited by her family. In it, Corrie describes what it felt like to live in a war-torn country and analyzes the violent and nonviolent resistance of Palestinians in the Second Intifada. Further information about Corrie and more of her writings can be found at www.rachelcorrie.org/.

February 27, 2003

MAMA,

Love you. Really miss you. I have bad nightmares about tanks and bulldozers outside our house and you and me inside. Sometimes the adrenaline acts as an anesthetic for weeks—and then in the evening or at night it just hits me again—a little bit of the reality of the situation. I am really scared for the people here. Yesterday I watched a father lead his two tiny children, holding his hands, out into the sight of tanks and a sniper tower and bulldozers and jeeps because he thought his house was going to be exploded. Jenny and I stayed in the house with several women and two small babies. It was our mistake in translation that caused him to think it was his house that was being exploded—although it abuts the settler road immediately next to the Gush Katif settlement, so I think it is only a matter of time. In fact, the Israeli Army was in the process of detonating an explosive in the ground nearby. One that appears to have been planted by Palestinian resistance. This is in the area where Sunday about 150 men were rounded up and contained outside the settlement with gunfire over their heads and around them, while tanks and bulldozers destroyed twenty-five greenhouses—the livelihoods of three hundred people. The explosive was right in front of the greenhouses—right in the point of entry for tanks that might come back again. I was terrified to think that this man felt it was less of a risk to walk out in view of the tanks with his kids than to stay in his house. I was really scared that they were all going to be shot, and I tried to stand between them and the tank. This happens every day, but this father walking out with his two little kids just looking very sad happened to get my attention more at this particular moment, probably because I felt like it was our translation that made him leave.

I thought a lot about what you said on the phone about Palestinian violence not helping the situation. Sixty thousand workers from Rafah worked in Israel two years ago. Now only six hundred can go to Israel for jobs. Of these six hundred, many have moved because the three checkpoints between here and Ashkelon (the closest city in Israel) make what used to be a forty-minute drive, now a twelve-hour or impassable journey.

In addition, what Rafah identified in 1999 as sources of economic growth are all completely destroyed—the Gaza international airport (runways demolished, totally closed); the border for trade with Egypt (now with a giant Israeli sniper tower in the middle of the crossing); access to the ocean (completely cut off in the last two years by a checkpoint and the Gush Katif settlement); Mawassi village, closed for entry and exit for people between the ages of about fourteen and thirty-five. The wells in the settlement are deeper than the wells here; and the settlements in the Gaza Strip are located in the west, above the fresh-water aquifers. And then the IDF destroyed the two wells I told you about before.

The count of homes destroyed since the beginning of this Intifada is up around six hundred, by and large people with no connection to the resistance but who happen to live along the border. Most of these are refugee homes, people who landed here in 1948 when their homes in Israel/historic Palestine became unlivable. Rafah was three large families and about six hundred total people in 1948. Many of these families have already been relocated since their arrival in Rafah—most notably in the Canada and Brazil camps, which were moved back into the Gaza Strip when Israel withdrew from the Sinai. This in addition to the killings every several days. I think it is maybe official now that Rafah is the poorest place in the world.

There used to be a middle class here—recently. I imagine you're reading about that in the Amira Hass book. We also get reports that, in the past, Gazan flower shipments to Europe were delayed for two weeks at the Erez crossing for security inspections. You can imagine the value of two-week-old cut flowers in the European market, so that market dried up. And then the bulldozers come and take out people's vegetable farms and gardens. What is left for people? Tell me if you can think of anything. I can't.

So when someone says that any act of Palestinian violence justifies Israel's actions—not only do I question that logic in light of international law, which recognizes the right of people to legitimate armed struggle in defense of their land and their families; not only do I question that logic in light of the Fourth Geneva Convention, which prohibits collective punishment, prohibits the transfer of an occupying country's population into an occupied area, prohibits the expropriation of water resources and the destruction of civilian infrastructure such as farms; not only do I question that logic in light of the sheer ridiculousness of the notion that fifty-year-old Russian guns and homemade explosives can have any impact on the activities of one of the world's largest militaries backed by the world's only superpower, I also question that logic on the basis of common sense.

If any of us had our lives and welfare completely strangled, lived with children in a shrinking place where we knew (because of previous experience) that soldiers and tanks and bulldozers could come for us at any moment (which would perhaps be a somewhat less cruel death than starvation, chronic malnutrition, and nitrite poisoning caused from increasing reliance on wells located at a distance from settlements, eastward, where the water quality is poor), with no means of economic survival and our houses destroyed; if they came and destroyed all the greenhouses that we'd been cultivating for the last however long, and did this while some of us were beaten and held captive with 149 other people for several hours, do you think we might try to use somewhat violent means to protect the edge of the greenhouses, to protect whatever fragments remained? A bomb buried in the ground, after all, can't be detonated unless a large piece of machinery rolls over the top of it. I think about this especially when I see orchards and greenhouses and fruit trees destroyed—just years of care and cultivation. I think about you and how long it takes to make things grow and what a labor of love it is. I really think, in a similar situation, most people would defend themselves as best they could. I think Uncle Craig would. I think probably Grandma would. I think I would.

I really don't think it was the farmers who placed the explosive, so please don't interpret this that way. They report no previous resistance activity in their area. We interviewed them Monday, and it was clear from their faces that they were absolutely in shock. Most of them just kept repeating over and over again that they had no idea why their livelihoods were destroyed. I have no idea who planted the thing. For all I know, it was the Israeli army just messing around; but from its location, it seemed like common sense why it would be there.

You asked me about nonviolent resistance, and I mentioned the first Intifada. Much of the leadership of more moderate resistance during the first Intifada has been assassinated, deported, or held indefinitely. Settlement activity, in fact, increased in the years following

>
> **We help you because we think maybe you will go and tell people in your country that you lived with Muslims. We think they will know that we are good people. We are quiet people. We just want peace.**

Oslo. As I said before, in the early 1990s Israel and the United States did not prevent the development of Hamas. I think it was seen as less a threat to the power balance than secular resistance. But anyway, yes, there was Gandhian nonviolent resistance during the first Intifada. And, of course, there still is staunch nonviolent resistance. The vast majority of Palestinians right now, as far as I can tell, are engaging in Gandhian nonviolent resistance. Who do you think I'm staying with, in houses that are going to be demolished amid gunfire, which often happens with absolutely no response whatsoever from Kalashnikovs—resistance weapons—ringing all around? Who do you think are staffing the human rights centers? Who do you think are still trying to maintain their farms every day directly in sight of sniper towers? Who do you think engage in protest with us? What do you think this Palestinian-led movement is that I joined—that engages in nonviolent direct action? Who do you think continues to walk down Salah el-Din Street where children are shot? Who do you think these families are that I tell you about, who won't take any money from us even though they are very, very poor—and who say to us, "We are not a hotel. We help you because we think maybe you will go and tell people in your country that you lived with Muslims. We think they will know that we are good people. We are quiet people. We just want peace"? Do you think I'm hanging out with Hamas fighters? These people are being shot at every day—that, on top of the complete strangulation I described above—and they continue to go about their business as best they can in the sights of machine guns and rocket launchers. Isn't that basically the epitome of nonviolent resistance—doing what you need to do even though you are shot at?

When that explosive detonated yesterday it broke all the windows in the family's house. I was in the process of being served tea and playing with the two small babies. I'm having a hard time right now. Just feel sick to my stomach a lot from being doted on all the time, very sweetly, by people who are facing doom. I know that from the United States it all sounds like hyperbole. Honestly, a lot of the time the sheer kindness of the people here, coupled with the overwhelming evidence of the willful destruction of their lives, makes it seem unreal to me. I really can't believe that something like this can happen in the world without a bigger outcry about it. It hurts me, again, like it has hurt me in the past, to witness how awful we can allow the world to be. I felt after talking to you that maybe you didn't completely believe me. I think it's actually good if you don't, because I do believe pretty much above all else in the importance of independent critical thinking. And I also realize that with you I'm much less careful than usual about trying to source every assertion that I make. A lot of the reason for that is I know that you actually do go and do your own research. But it makes me worry about the job I'm doing. All of the situation that I tried to enumerate above—and a lot of other things—constitutes a somewhat gradual—often hidden, but nevertheless massive—removal and destruction of the ability of a particular group of people to survive. This is what I am seeing here. The assassinations, rocket attacks, and shooting of children are atrocities—but in focusing on them, I'm terrified of missing their context. The vast majority of people here—even if they had the economic means to escape, even if they actually wanted to give up resisting on their land and just leave (which appears to be maybe the less nefarious of Sharon's possible goals), can't leave. Because they can't even get into Israel to apply for visas, and because their destination countries won't let them in (both our country and Arab countries). So I think when all means of survival is cut off in a pen (Gaza) which people can't get out of—I think that qualifies as genocide. Even if they could get out I think it would still qualify as genocide. Maybe you could look up the definition of genocide according to international law. I don't remember it right now. I'm going to get better at illustrating this, hopefully. I don't like to use those charged words. I think you know this about me. I really value words. I really try to illustrate and let people draw their own conclusions. I'm just thinking about that. If I'm really honest I won't talk about the power imbalance when people ask about Palestinian violence. I will talk about resisting genocide.

Speaking of words—I absolutely abhor the use of polarities like "good" and "evil"—especially when applied to human beings. I think these words are the enemy of critical thinking. They are an escape from finding solutions and are an incitement to further violence. For a long time I've been operating from a certain core assumption which only recently I started to articulate as such. Just the belief that we are all essentially the same inside, and that our differences are by and large situational. That goes for everybody—Bush, bin Laden, me, you, Sarah, Chris, Dad, Gram, Palestinians, everybody of any particular religion, Uncle Craig, Tony Blair. I know there is a good chance that this assumption actually is false. But it's convenient, because it always leads to questions, and it usually leads to analysis of power dynamics—and the way privilege shelters people from the consequences of their actions. It's also convenient because it leads to some level of forgiveness, whether justified or not. And it leads to pretty immediate rejection of analysis that rests on ethnocentric explanations for everybody's behavior.

I question this assumption sometimes. Reagan, I think, very possibly didn't really understand what he was doing to people all over Latin America. Kennedy, possibly, didn't understand what he was doing to people in Southeast Asia. I think there's a good chance that Bush doesn't quite understand—but that's dwindling.

It's with people like Kissinger, Cheney, and Ariel Sharon that I start to wonder.

And isolated here, I start to wonder, how many people out there know? I will say that I think the vast majority of us who are in some way passively supporting this genocide are unaware of what it is. I don't think that is any excuse, but sometimes at night I quibble over it. I don't think it matters much. It certainly doesn't matter for the Palestinians. It is my own selfishness and will to optimism that wants to believe that even people with a great deal of privilege don't just idly sit by and watch. What we are paying for here is truly evil. The largest evil I have witnessed directly. Maybe the general growing class imbalance in the world and consequent devastation of working people's lives is a bigger evil. Being here should make me more aware of what it might mean to be a farmer in Colombia right now, for example.

Anyway, I'm rambling. Just want to write to my mom and tell her that I'm witnessing this chronic, insidious genocide, and I'm really scared, and questioning my fundamental belief in the goodness of human nature. This has to stop. I think it is a good idea for us all to drop everything and devote our lives to making this stop. I don't think it's an extremist thing to do anymore. I still really want to dance around to Pat Benatar and have boyfriends and make comics for my coworkers. But I also want this to stop. Disbelief and horror is what I feel. Disappointment. I am disappointed that this is the base reality of our world and that we, in fact, participate in it. This is not at all what I asked for when I came into this world. This is not at all what the people here asked for when they came into this world. This is not what they are asking for now. This is not the world you and Dad wanted me to come into when you decided to have me. This is not what I meant when I was two and looked at Capitol Lake and said, "This is the wide world and I'm coming to it." I did not mean that I was coming into a world where I could live a comfortable life and possibly, with no effort at all, exist in complete unawareness of my participation in

genocide. More big explosions somewhere in the distance outside.

I probably sound a little crazy, reminiscent maybe of going to Russia years ago, although that situation was not like this one. I know you wondered if going to Russia was a bad thing, because it sort of seemed to ruin me. I think the reason I went crazy was not because Russia was bad for me, but because of the initial disappointment in discovering that my government really did lie to me about the Russians, and in the massive absence of justice in the world, and again (through observing U.S. companies' investment in natural resource extraction in newly "democratized" Russia and the devastation of the Russian economy in the wake of the arms race) in discovering my participation in the subjugation of other people. When I come back from Palestine, I probably will have nightmares and constantly feel guilty for not being here, but I can channel that into more work. Coming here is one of the better things I've ever done. So when I sound crazy, or if the Israeli military should break with their racist tendency not to injure white people, please pin the reason squarely on the fact that I am in the midst of a genocide which I am also indirectly supporting, and for which my government is largely responsible.

I love you and Dad. Sorry for the diatribe.

Okay, some strange men next to me just gave me some peas, so I need to eat and thank them.

Rachel

Attachment:

P.S. Both Al-Haq and Al-Mezan are organizations that we work with some—mostly by giving them reports about what we witness. They have also offered some assistance in trying to go through Israeli courts to stop the demolition of houses that seem to be particularly targeted as acts of collective punishment—as opposed to the vast majority of houses here which are targeted because the Israeli military wants the land they stand on. You could do a web search. I think both have web sites.

Journal and Discussion Questions

1 Letters, of course, usually do not have a thesis or a title. Does Rachel Corrie's letter to her mother have a thesis? If so, what is it? If not, what are the main ideas that Corrie is arguing, and how are these ideas connected? What title would you give to this letter?

2 Outline Corrie's letter to her mother. Does Corrie "ramble" in her letter, as she says on this page? How does the story of her dream set up the rest of her letter? How does Corrie use the story of the explosion and the greenhouses to illustrate and tie together her larger arguments about the Israeli–Palestinian conflict?

3 Considering Corrie's work for a nonviolent peace organization, why does she defend some Palestinians' use of violence against Israeli military and civilians? What reasons does she give to justify violent resistance? Why do you think Corrie's mother objected to these violent acts? Is Corrie justifying terrorist acts? Why or why not?

4 Considering Corrie's analysis of why some Palestinians resort to violence, why do many Palestinians engage in "staunch nonviolent resistance" (page 456)? Why does Corrie engage in nonviolent protest? Why, on page 456, does she develop her argument about nonviolent resistance with a series of questions?

5 Corrie refers to her process of writing several times in her letter, especially regarding her use of sources and her choice of language. Why is it important for her to discuss how she writes? How does her use of language and sources reflect her "critical thinking"? How does she expect critical readers like her mother to read her writing? Compare Corrie's idea of critical thinking to ideas about critical thinking in the first three chapters of this textbook.

6 How does Corrie use sources and evidence to build her arguments? How does she use expressions of emotion to persuade her mother? Do you find her arguments persuasive? Why or why not?

7 How might Corrie have used the material in her letter to write a magazine article about life in the Gaza Strip? How might she have used this material in a newspaper editorial? What ideas in the letter might Corrie have omitted if she had written an article or an editorial? Why? What might she have added? Why?

Topics for Writing

1 Analyze Rachel Corrie's letter to her mother, focusing especially on her ideas and arguments about violent and nonviolent resistance.

2 Write a research paper about Rachel Corrie, either about why she became a figure of controversy or why she is regarded as a hero by many antiwar activists.

3 Write a research paper arguing about whether the actions taken by the Israeli government and military and/or by Palestinian opponents to Israel are justified or not.

WHERE HAVE ALL THE PROTESTS GONE? ONLINE.

BY JENNIFER EARL

Jennifer Earl is an associate professor of sociology at the University of California at Santa Barbara and director of the university's Center for Information Technology and Society. She has published many articles on social movements' exploitation of the Internet and information technology in academic journals such as the *American Sociological Review*, the *Annual Review of Sociology*, and *Social Science Computer Review*, and she is currently running a five-year research project entitled "The Internet, Activism, and Social Movements," which studies uses of the Internet to promote twenty different social causes. Earl wrote this news analysis for the *Washington Post* on February 4, 2007.

"I HAVEN'T SPOKEN AT AN ANTIWAR rally in 34 years," Jane Fonda acknowledged to her fellow Iraq war protesters on the Mall last weekend. According to accounts of the day, many of the participants in this latest rally were of Fonda's generation, caravanning to Washington once more, with grayer hair, pressing their cause.

The march, organized by the antiwar group United for Peace and Justice, attracted throngs of people, including members of Congress, actors, veterans and families of U.S. troops. Some came to the Mall to call for the impeachment of President Bush, others wanted greater support for returning veterans, but all came to call for an end to the war in Iraq. But even if their convictions seemed to echo those of the Vietnam War era, the way they got here this time was different—and a perfect example of how antiwar is waged in the Internet age.

On the UFPJ Web site, activists could download and print out an "Act Now to End the War!" flier in English, Spanish, Persian or Arabic. They could post a button about the march on their Facebook or MySpace pages. And they could review maps, travel information and other helpful hints (for example: "pots, pans, and plastic tubs all make great percussion instruments").

> **" Online activism dramatically reduces the time and money it takes to organize and participate in events. "**

These changes aren't radical, they're practical. As an organizing tool, the Internet allows protest planners to dramatically amplify their outreach efforts to mobilize a wider audience more quickly and more cheaply. All of this leads to broader and faster activism, though not necessarily to fundamental changes in how protests work.

However, the Internet hasn't become a venue just for facilitating the logistical details of old-fashioned protests, the place to find ride-sharing schedules and parking tips for the big day. Increasingly, the Internet has become the venue for protest—the new Mall, so to speak—where online-only activists deploy new technologies to challenge governments and corporations and promote causes mundane and sublime. I've done research, funded by the National Science Foundation, about the Internet and protests, and I've found that these efforts are transforming the way everyday citizens connect with and participate in activism and social movements.

Finding ways to participate on the Internet isn't hard. You don't even need to turn to an established activist group to create on online campaign. Web sites such as PetitionOnline.com allow anyone to create and manage a petition on the Web for free, and as their success stories suggest, only grass-roots politics can persuade powerful players to change their tune. Launched in 1999,

the site has housed tens of thousands of petitions and collected more than 47 million signatures.

When new technologies lower the barriers to participating in activism—"five-minute activists" can add their names to the bottom of a petition and then continue to surf the Web—they also allow new causes and issues to flood the protest marketplace. Some of them, such as campaigns to save canceled television shows or to fix problems in popular online games such as World of Warcraft, may seem frivolous to longtime activists, but they reflect the range of issues that can energize and mobilize younger generations.

Indeed, as my research with colleagues Alan Schussman and Katrina Kimport found, petitions surrounding youth culture and pop culture are common online. One petition called for the Backstreet Boys to give a concert in Asia "besides China & Japan" because "The Backstreet Boys have numerous fans in Asia" who want to see their show, according to the petitioners' statement. Others have tried to rouse support for free downloads of Disney Channel programming so kids who are still in school during their favorite shows don't have to miss them. And sports fans have called for EA Sports to add NCAA conferences to MVP NCAA Baseball 06 or NCAA Baseball 07.

While some rallying cries don't reach the ears or computer screens of the powerful, those on the receiving end can take online petitions seriously. When fewer than 1,000 subscribers of the now-defunct WebTV signed such a petition complaining about customer service, a company official responded on the site, offering his "support and agreement" as well as his "sincere assurances that we are heading in the right direction."

But online activism is not just for cranky customers, rabid gamers or television fans. Sometimes, it can reach the highest levels of political action. In 2000, and again in 2004, so-called vote trading or "vote pairing" Web sites popped up nationwide. These sites helped voters from different states coordinate their votes to undercut what many regarded as the undemocratic effects of the electoral college on presidential elections.

These sites helped transform voting—the icon of individualized and conventional political participation—into a collective and highly contentious political act. These vote-swappers took on one part of the Constitution (the electoral college), while relying on another (the First Amendment). Without the Internet, it is unlikely that this movement could have emerged, or that voters could have been matched so efficiently.

Online activism dramatically reduces the time and money it takes to organize and participate in events. Consider how hard it is to organize a physical petition—printing expenses, hiring petition gatherers to find good locations where there might be enough foot traffic to attract signers—vs. posting a text on PetitionOnline.com and advertising the link.

As some types of online activism allow people to take part quickly and easily, it opens the door for broader changes, shifting how regularly people take part in political actions. Such streamlined activism may lead to more frequent, and more committed, political engagement on the part of everyday citizens. And politicians seeking donations, votes and other kinds of support may look to tap into this new generation of self-selected, point-and-click activists. Much like the Web, these online petitions are an end in themselves as well as a gateway to new kinds of action.

Just last week, I informally polled students in a seminar I teach about these types of petitions. About 40 percent of them had participated in such online protest on pop culture topics, and many others were aware of these Web-based campaigns. To dismiss their actions as silly—

just because their objectives sometimes seem so—is to overlook the critical point: The next generation of citizens is learning how to organize around issues they care about, and they're doing so in their own way.

Sure, they may not be issues that many adults care about; after all, I would be more likely to sign a petition about a problem with a Microsoft Office product than one about a glitch in an online game. But as these students and their younger siblings grow older, these early experiences with online engagement may propel them into more politically oriented activism. Indeed, many of the debates over youth culture are closely tied to fights over intellectual property, fights that can quickly turn political. Activist groups such as Downhill Battle engage in online protests in their push to open up the recording industry. What would these scuffles look like, and how much could they grow, if tens of thousands of Napster alums joined them—or began online movements of their own?

"Silence is no longer an option," Fonda said last week. But standing on the Mall in Washington on a blustery January day is no longer the only option for making your voice heard.

Journal and Discussion Questions

1 What is the central claim that Jennifer Earl is arguing in "Where Have All the Protests Gone? Online."? How are activists using the Internet to promote their causes? What uses does Earl find most important? Why?

2 Outline "Where Have All the Protests Gone? Online." How does Earl use the introduction to make connections to different sections of her argument?

3 How does Earl compare the protest movements of Jane Fonda's generation 34 years ago to the activism of youths today? How does she compare how the two generations use the Internet in their activism? What is important about these differences?

4 How does Earl broaden people's normal definition of activism in "Where Have All the Protests Gone? Online."? How does this new definition serve her argument? Do you agree with this definition? Why or why not?

5 What benefits does Earl see in how people use the Internet for activist purposes? What problems does she see? Why does she think the benefits outweigh the problems? Do you agree? Why or why not?

6 What research did Earl use in her argument? How does she use this research to develop her ideas?

7 What effects does Earl predict will result from youth's online activism about matters such as online games, rock concerts, and television shows? Why? Do you agree? Why or why not?

Topics for Writing

1 Look up one of Earl's articles about Internet activism in a sociology journal and compare how she discusses this subject for a general audience, like readers of the *Washington Post*, and for an expert audience.

2 Write a research paper analyzing how people are using the Internet to promote social causes. Your essay might focus on one particular cause or one particular use of the Internet, such as online petitions.

3 Interview or survey students on your campus about their participation in online petitions and protests and write an essay agreeing or disagreeing with Earl's claim that the Internet is preparing students for more important activism later in their lives.

A LEADER IS MORE THAN A MESSENGER

BY TONI SMITH

Toni Smith was a senior and a member of the basketball team at Manhattanville College in Purchase, New York, when Congress voted to give President George W. Bush the authority to invade Iraq in 2003. Smith decided to protest invading Iraq by turning silently away from the American flag when the National Anthem was played before the start of each basketball game. Although attendance at Manhattanville College women's basketball games was small, Smith's protest received national attention, and her method of protest was the subject of heated debate for several weeks, especially on sports pages and sports channels. Many argued that Smith was wrong to use the American flag and the National Anthem in a political protest, and many also claimed that a sports event was an inappropriate place for a political protest. Smith wrote an argument that addressed her actions in the March 17, 2003, issue of *The Sporting News*, a prominent weekly sports newspaper. But rather than write an argument that defended her actions directly, she took the opportunity to write an opinion column to argue that sports events in the U.S. are a venue of almost constant attempts to persuade spectators. Although Smith mentions her protest only briefly near the end of her editorial, "A Leader Is More Than a Messenger" is an indirect defense of her protest as well as an argument about the roles of athletes in society.

SPORTS IN AMERICA HAVE BECOME MORE than just athletic events. Nowadays, sporting events are conducted as extravaganzas.

Every human emotion is triggered by the wide array of attractions, which collectively create a sense of euphoria. Before the actual event, there are pregame interviews and shows. During halftime, there is always entertainment, and then, for television viewers, there are postgame reports.

Throughout these events, advertisements are plastered on every possible space in the arenas, always vividly eye-catching. The television viewers are not exempt from these enticements, either; they have their 30 minutes of commercials to absorb. Let's also remember the cheerleaders and the alcohol. After all, what would sports be without them? There is room for all of these elements during athletic events: sex, alcohol, violence, religion (how many players thank God after a good game?) and any other aspect of life that

advertisements include. Yet, suddenly, we have no room for politics in sports? This is sadly naive.

Sports are filled with political messages, both implicit and explicit. If you are unaware that politics are embedded into every part of American life, I strongly encourage you to read between the lines. The fact "The Star-Spangled Banner" is played before every sporting event is political in itself. Regardless of what the American flag means to each individual, it is a political symbol that represents power and conquest. It has no relation to sports, so to ask everyone to salute it before a game is more of an imposition than to not play the anthem at all. Why is the national anthem even played before athletic events and not before movies, plays, graduations, holiday observances, etc.?

Based on the results of surveys conducted about my not facing the flag before games, it is apparent that a good percentage of people simply do not believe athletes should make their own political statements. This

Manhattanville's Toni Smith turns her back on the U.S. flag during the playing of the national anthem before a game against Mount St. Mary in Newburgh. (Dave Kennedy)

is also true for celebrities. The NBA required Mahmoud Abdul-Rauf to stand for the anthem, and there was debate over whether it was appropriate for Sheryl Crow to wear an antiwar T-shirt when she performed. Isn't this a little ironic? Athletes and celebrities are the people who have enough social influence to make their opinions heard. Wouldn't it be a waste if their only jobs as national figures were to look good and reiterate popular opinions? It might not be their obligation to be political leaders, but as role models, they have the opportunity to be influential in a way that most people don't have.

It is a blessing to have had the opportunity to touch so many lives through my actions, however unexpected. Contrary to what Mike Piazza and some others believe, my protest was not done for attention. That is a gross misunderstanding of my actions. It is obvious to anyone who has attended or played in Division III athletics that few people pay attention to the games or the players. In one way, I agree with Mets pitcher Al Leiter that people shouldn't care what I do. However, it is not because I am just some Division III nobody but because everyone is entitled to her/his own opinions, just as Piazza is free to openly support the upcoming war. Besides, America is composed of little nobodies, some of whom are Division III athletes and many of whom are the reason Leiter is the national figure he is. Furthermore, isn't it hypocritical that Piazza feels free to support the war and at the same time say it's wrong for me to mix sports and politics?

Athletes are encouraged to endorse everything from telephone plans to fast food chains. They also use their celebrity status to support certain organizations. So why are limitations all of a sudden invoked when an athlete expresses an unpopular opinion? If athletes promote only popular opinions, then their positions as role models and leaders should be revoked and replaced with "messengers."

Journal and Discussion Questions

1   What is the central position of Smith's argument, and what reasons does she give to support this position? Which reasons do you find most persuasive? Which reasons are weaker in your mind? Why?

2   Outline Smith's argument. Why does she wait until the third paragraph to mention her protest and until the fourth paragraph to discuss her protest in any detail? How does she relate her other points to her protest? Why does Smith barely mention the reason for her protest—her opposition to the impending war in Iraq?

3   Why does Smith mention criticism of her actions by professional baseball players Mike Piazza and Al Leiter, and how does she respond to their criticism? Is her refutation of their criticism persuasive? Why or why not?

4   In her lead and in her conclusion, Smith contrasts messengers to leaders and role models. What point is she making with this contrast? Is this contrast an effective frame for her argument? Why or why not?

5   Smith compares her attempt to persuade people about going to war with Iraq to other persuasive acts in sports—advertising, product endorsements by athletes, the performance of "The Star-Spangled Banner." What point is she making with these comparisons? Do you agree with her on this point? Why or why not?

6   "Regardless of what the American flag means to each individual, it is a political symbol that represents power and conquest," Smith writes in her second paragraph. What does she mean, and why is this idea important for her form of protest? How would you answer her question, "Why is the national anthem even played before athletic events and not before movies, plays, graduations, holiday observances, etc.?" What reasons do you think Smith would give?

7   Describe the photograph of Smith protesting. What argument is implied with her gesture and silence? Whether or not you agree with her position about the war in Iraq, what do you think of Smith's method of protest? Smith was often criticized for "turning her back on the flag." Does that phrase describe the photograph accurately? Why do you think people chose that phrase to describe Smith's protest?

Topics for Writing

1   Respond to Toni Smith's argument in "A Leader Is More Than a Messenger." You may write a direct argument about whether she should have opposed the invasion of Iraq in the way that she did. Or you may write a response to her analysis about sports and politics. You might look up some of the arguments about Smith's protest on the Internet.

2   Study the photograph of Smith's protest and her incorporation of the American flag, the National Anthem, and sports into her protest. Write an analysis explaining why her form of protest was such a lightning rod for attention, despite the fact that Manhattanville College basketball games normally receive little national attention. Was Smith's form of protest effective?

3   Write a research paper about the use of the American flag in political arguments and commercial advertising.

4   Argue whether athletes and celebrities should avoid involvement in political causes or whether they should use their fame to promote important causes.

Connecting the Readings

Compare what Rachel Corrie's letter from the Gaza Strip, Jennifer Earl's "Where Have All the Protests Gone? Online." and Toni Smith's "A Leader Is More Than a Messenger" suggest about why some college students become activists and what they can achieve.

Suggestions for Essays on WAR, TERRORISM, AND PROTEST

1 Analyze why people go to war, drawing on the arguments made by Eisenhower, Scott-Singley, Brison, and Zumwalt.

2 Describe the effects that war has on the people who fight the war and the civilians who live in a war zone, considering the selections by Eisenhower, Scott-Singley, Ut, Picasso, and Corrie.

3 Comparing the paintings and photographs by Delacroix, Picasso, Rosenthal, and Ut and the photograph of Smith's protest, explain and assess how visual art and displays are used to influence people's positions about war and political violence.

4 Write an argument about what means of persuasion are and are not justified in support of important political or moral causes. Incorporate the arguments of King, Corrie, Earl, and Smith in your argument.

5 Compare terrorism and civil disobedience as tactics that challenge government policies and practices drawing on some of the ideas of Brison, King, Corrie, and Earl.

6 Discuss whether the nature and threat of international terrorism calls for changes in how the United States conducts war, drawing on Scott-Singley, Roth, Zumwalt, and Brison.

Winter 1999/2000. Used by permission of the author.; **pp. 251, 253:** Bar graphs, "The Declining Use of the Word "Nigger" in News Stories in *The New York Times*" and "The Declining Use of the Word "Nigger" in the World's Major Newspapers" are reprinted with permission from *The Journal of Blacks in Higher Education*. ; **p. 257:** From HUNGER OF MEMORY: THE EDUCATION OF RICHARD RODRIGUEZ by Richard Rodriguez. Reprinted by permission of David R. Godine, Publisher, Inc. Copyright © 1982 by Richard Rodriguez.; **p. 261:** Copyright © 2006 by Lisa Delpit. This essay originally appeared in OTHER PEOPLE'S CHILDREN: CULTURAL CONFLICTS IN THE CLASSROOM by Lisa Delpit (The New Press, 2006) entitled "Education in a Multicultural Society: Our Future's Greatest Challenge" by Lisa Delpit. Reprinted by permission of The New Press. www.thenewpress.com.; **p. 271:** "A Stand Against Wikipedia" by Scott Jaschik, from *Inside Higher Ed*, January 26, 2007. Reprinted with permission of *Inside Higher Ed.*; **p. 273:** "Taking Women Students Seriously" from ON LIES, SECRETS, AND SILENCE: SELECTED PROSE 1966–1978 by Adrienne Rich. Copyright © 1979 by W.W. Norton & Company, Inc. Used by permission of the author and W.W. Norton & Company, Inc.; **p. 278:** "Freshmen Pay, Mentally and Physically, as They Adjust to Life in College" by Thomas Bartlett from *The Chronicle of Higher Education*, Feb. 2, 2002. Reprinted by permission of *The Chronicle of Higher Education.*; **p. 281:** "College and Allowance" by Lauren Silverman, posted on youthradio.org, 2005. Used by permission of Youth Radio.; **p. 290:** "Work, Labor, and Play" from A CERTAIN WORLD: A COMMONPLACE BOOK by W.H. Auden, Copyright © 1970 by W.H. Auden. Reprinted by permission of Curtis Brown, Ltd.; **p. 292:** "Working Life" by Nisha Ramachandran, published in *U.S. News and World Report*, April 17, 2006. Copyright 2006 *U.S. News & World Report*, L.P. Reprinted with permission.; **p. 294:** "Slouching and Digressing" by Heather Hunsaker, published in the "Tutor's Column" from *Writing Lab Newsletter* 30.6, Feb. 2006. Reprinted by permission of the RiCH Company.; **p. 297:** "Serving in Florida" from the book NICKEL AND DIMED: ON (NOT) GETTING BY IN AMERICA by Barbara Ehrenreich. Copyright © 2001 by Barbara Ehrenreich. Reprinted by permission of Henry Holt and Company, LLC.; **p. 302:** "A Week in the Life of a Part-Time Teacher" by Diana Claitor, originally published in GHOSTS IN THE CLASSROOM: STORIES OF COLLEGE ADJUNCT FACULTY—AND THE PRICE WE ALL PAY, edited by Michael Dubson. Reprinted by permission of the author.; **p. 305:** "I Want a Wife" by Judy Brady. Used by permission of the author.; **p. 310:** "High-Tech Jobs Are Going Abroad! But That's Okay" by Robert Reich, published in *The Washington Post*, Nov. 2, 2003. Reprinted by permission of the author.; **p. 313:** "Why the New Jobs Go to Immigrants" by David R. Francis. Reproduced with permission from the March 10, 2005 issue of *The Christian Science Monitor* (www.csmonitor.com). © 2005 The Christian Science Monitor. All rights reserved.; **p. 315:** "Cost of Illegal Immigration May Be Less Than Meets the Eye" by Eduardo Porter, from *The New York Times*, April 16, 2006. © 2006 The New York Times Company. Reprinted with permission.; **p. 318:** From BY THE LAKE OF SLEEPING CHILDREN: THE SECRET LIFE OF THE MEXICAN BORDER by Luis Urrea, copyright © 1996 by Luis Urrea. Used by permission of Doubleday, a division of Random House, Inc.; **p. 329:** "Ownership Society: Responsibility, Liberty, Prosperity" by David Boaz, posted at www.cato.org/special/ownership_society/boaz.html, 2004. Reprinted with permission of Cato Institute.; **p. 332:** "Disowned by the Ownership Society" by Naomi Klein, originally published in *The Nation*, Feb. 18, 2008. Reprinted by permission of Klein Lewis Productions.; **p. 337:** "Debt Smothers Young Americans" by Christina Dugas, from *USA Today*, February 13, 2001. Reprinted with permission.; **p. 348:** "Some Like It Hot—Wired Magazine article," adapted from FREE CULTURE by Lawrence Lessig, copyright © 2004 by Lawrence Lessig. Used by permission of The Penguin Press, a division of Penguin Group (USA) Inc.; **p. 352:** "Plagiarism a Problem for WSU Students" by Brandi Trapp, published in *The South End News*, Wayne State University, Dec. 12, 2006. Reprinted by permission of the author.; **p. 354:** "The Copycat Syndrome" by Meghan O'Rourke, from *Slate*, January 11, 2007. Reprinted by permission of United Media for Slate.com and Washingtonpost.Newsweek Interactive. All rights reserved.; **p. 360:** "Folklore and Music" by Zora Neale Hurston, originally written for *The Florida Negro*, 1938. Used with the permission of the Estate of Zora Neale Hurston.; **p. 368:** "Some Accounts of Witch-Riding" by Patricia K. Rickels, from *Louisiana Folklore Miscellany 2*, No. 1, August 1961. Reprinted by permission of Louisiana Folklore Miscellany.; **p. 375:** "Everyday Use" from IN LOVE & TROUBLE: STORIES OF BLACK WOMEN, copyright © 1973 by Alice Walker, reprinted by permission of Houghton Mifflin Harcourt Publishing Company.; **p. 380:** From AMERICAN QUILTS by Doris M. Bowman, copyright © 1991 Smithsonian Institution. Reprinted by permission of Smithsonian Institution Scholarly Press.; **p. 385:** "Let the Good Times Roll" by Chris Rose, from *The Times-Picayune*, Dec. 13, 2005. © 2005 The Times-Picayune Publishing Co. All rights reserved. Used with permission of *The Times-Picayune.*; **p. 387:** "Santa Claus" from THE COLLECTED POEMS OF HOWARD NEMEROV by Howard Nemerov. Used by permission of Margaret Nemerov.; **p. 389:** "Assaults on TV Misdirected" by Michael Medved, published in *USA Today*, May 23, 2005. Reprinted by permission of Inkwell Management.; **p. 393:** "A Drop in the Ocean" by John Powers, originally published in the *L.A. Weekly*, January 6, 2005. Reprinted by permission of the author.; **p. 396:** "Gangsters—Real and Unreal," from HIP HOP AMERICA by Nelson George, copyright © 1998 by Nelson George. Used by permission of Viking Penguin, a division of Penguin Group (USA) Inc.; **p. 404:** "Rhyme and Resist: Organizing the Hip-Hop Generation" by Angela Ards. Reprinted with permission from the July 26, 1999 issue of *The Nation.*; **p. 416:** "Movie Review: Junebug" by Andrea Kretchmer, published in *The Student Life*, Pomona College, Feb. 10, 2006. Reprinted by permission of the author.; **p. 425:** "Memories of Death," April 29, 2005 entry from Misoldierthoughts.blogspot.com. Used by permission of the author.; **p. 434:** "The Law of War in the War on Terror" by Kenneth Roth. Reprinted by permission of FOREIGN AFFAIRS (Vol. 83, No. 1, Jan/Feb 2004). Copyright 2004 by the Council of Foreign Relations, Inc. www.ForeignAffairs.org.; **p. 439:** "Laws of War Need to Change to Defeat 'Uncivilized' Enemy" by James Zumwalt, from *Army Times*, Dec. 2005. Reprinted by permission of the Army Times Publishing Company.; **p. 441:** "Gender, Terrorism, and War" by Susan J. Brison, from *Signs: Journal of Women in Culture and Society*, Autumn 2002, vol. 28, no.1, published by The University of Chicago Press. © 2002 by The University of Chicago Press. Used with permission.; **p. 444:** "Letter from Birmingham Jail" by Martin Luther King, Jr. Reprinted by arrangement with The Heirs to the Estate of Martin Luther King Jr., c/o Writers House as agent for the proprietor, New York, NY. Copyright 1963 Martin Luther King, Jr., copyright renewed 1991 Coretta Scott King.; **p. 453:** From LET ME STAND ALONE: THE JOURNALS OF RACHEL CORRIE by Rachel Corrie, edited by The Corrie Family. Copyright © 2008 by Craig and Cindy Corrie. Used by permission of W.W. Norton & Company, Inc.; **p. 458:** "Where Have All the Protests Gone? Online." by Jennifer Earl, originally published in *The Washington Post*, February 4, 2007. Reprinted by permission of the author.; **p. 460:** "My Turn" by Toni Smith, published in *The Sporting News*, March 17, 2003. Reprinted by permission.

Photos Page 69: Courtesy Dove Self-Esteem Fund; **p. 70:** Courtesy myrichuncle.com; **p. 78:** Bill Watterson, *Calvin and Hobbes*/Universal Press Syndicate; **p. 99:** Norman Rockwell Family Agency/*Saturday Evening Post*/Curtis Publishing; **p. 100:** Brian Lanker/*Topeka Capital-Journal*; **p. 104:** Robert Cochran, *A Photographer of Note: Arkansas Artist Geleve Grice* (Fayetteville: University of Arkansas Press, 2003), p. 110; **p. 131:** Office of National Drug Control Policy; **p. 177:** Photo by Paige DeShong. *Keeping Death: A Collaborative Exhibit of Poetry and Photography*, ed. Paige DeShong and Gilberto Lucero (El Paso: Blue Guitar P, 1998); **p. 196:** Wiley Miller, *Non Sequitur*/Universal Press Syndicate; **p. 205:** Dave Martin/AP Images; **p. 206:** Chris Graythen/AFP/Getty; **p. 269:** Aaron McGruder, *The Boondocks: Because I Know You Don't Read the Newspaper*/Universal Press Syndicate; **p. 284:** Courtesy The University of Alabama; **p. 285:** Courtesy University of Richmond; **p. 286:** Courtesy Grinnell College; **p. 307:** Scott Adams, *Dilbert*, "Engineers in the Mist"/United Media; **p. 308:** The United States Army; **p. 322:** From *Stolen Dreams* by David Parker/Lerner Publications Company, 1997; **p. 324:** Chien-Min Chung/Getty Images; **p. 325:** Lewis Hine/Library of Congress. ARC #523526; **p. 335 top:** Steve Breen, *The San Diego Union-Tribune*/Copley News Service; **p. 335 bottom:** Rob Rogers, *Pittsburgh Post-Gazette*/United Features Syndicate; **p. 340:** The Advertising Archives; **p. 341:** Courtesy, John Deere; **p. 342:** The Advertising Archives; **p. 351:** Garry Trudeau, *Doonesbury*/Universal Press Syndicate; **p. 381:** Harriet Powers/Alfred Harrell/American Folk Art Museum; **p. 382:** Polly Calistro/*Quilts and Quiltmaking in America, 1978–1996*. American Folklife Center, Library of Congress; **p. 383:** The AIDS Memorial Quilt, © 2008 The NAMES Project Foundation; **p. 391:** Joel Gordon; **p. 415:** Clay Jones/creators.com; **p. 427:** Louvre, Paris, France/Erich Lessing/Art Resource, NY; **p. 429:** Museo Nacional Centro de Arte Reina Sofia, Madrid, Spain/Art Resource, NY; **p. 431:** Joe Rosenthal/AP Images; **p. 433:** Nick Ut/AP Images; **p. 461:** Stuart Ramson/AP Images.

THE READER